Military Service Records:

A Select Catalog

of

National Archives

Microfilm Publications

Military Service Records:

A Select Catalog

of

National Archives

Microfilm Publications

National Archives Trust Fund Board
National Archives and Service Administration
Washington, DC
1985

Library of Congress Cataloging-in-Publication Data

National Archives Trust Fund Board.
　Military service records.

　Includes index.
　1. United States—Armed Forces—Records and
correspondence—Bibliography—Catalogs. 2. United
States—Armed Forces—Archives—Catalogs. 3. United
States—History, Military—Sources—Bibliograhy—
Catalogs. 4. United States. National Archives—
Catalogs. I. Title.
CD3033 1985 016.3556'0973 85-25925

ISBN 0-911333-07-X

Foreword

The National Archives and Records Administration is responsible for administering the permanently valuable noncurrent records of the Federal Government. The holdings of the National Archives now amount to more than 1.3 million cubic feet. They date from the First Continental Congress and consist of the basic records of the legislative, judicial, and executive branches of Government. The Presidential libraries of Herbert Hoover, Franklin D. Roosevelt, Harry S. Truman, Dwight D. Eisenhower, John F. Kennedy, Lyndon B. Johnson, and Gerald R. Ford contain the papers of those Presidents and many of their associates in office. These research resources document significant events in our Nation's history, but most of them are preserved for continuing practical use in the ordinary processes of Government; for the protection of individual rights; and for the research use of scholars, students, and other individual researchers.

The National Archives Microfilm Publication Program

Since 1940, the National Archives has been microfilming selected groups of Federal records that have high research value. Under this program, negative microfilm is retained by the National Archives and positive prints are made from these master negatives and sold at moderate prices. The chief purposes of the program are to make archival sources more easily accessible to libraries, research centers, and individuals and to insure against loss of valuable information should the original records be destroyed. In this way, microfilm publications are a partial answer to the researcher's need for more extensive publication of archival materials, because they provide a relatively inexpensive method by which he or she can obtain facsimile reproductions of entire series of documents.

Although the microfilm publication program is one of the oldest continuing programs of the National Archives, it was not firmly established financially until 1948, when a grant of $20,000 from the Rockefeller Foundation provided for accelerated production of microfilm and insured the continuation of the program through the establishment of a revolving fund. By 1982, more than 175,000 rolls of master negative microfilm had been produced.

National Archives microfilm publications now provide basic documentation for research in the fields of American, European, Far Eastern, African, and Latin American history as well as in local history and genealogy. They are also valuable for work in other fields, such as economics, public administration, political science, law, and ethnology. As the program has developed, more emphasis has been placed on microfilming groups of records that are directly related to one another, as in the case of records relating to the same general subject or to a specific geographic area. In this way researchers can obtain reasonably complete documentation in many fields of interest. For example, a number of microfilm publications document diplomatic, consular, and naval relations between the United States and the Far Eastern countries of China, Japan, and Korea from the late 18th century. Similarly, almost complete coverage of relations between the United States and other countries throughout the world is provided. Microfilm publications have also been produced concerning the administration of affairs in individual territories of the United States.

Types of Microfilm Publications

National Archives microfilm publications are divided into two series, identified by "M" numbers and "T" numbers. In general, records selected for filming as "M" publications have high research value for a variety of studies, and the ratio of research value to volume is high. Usually each publication reproduces an entire series of records. Most "M" publications include explanatory material prepared by archivists to help researchers glean information from the filmed records more easily. "M" publications usually have an introduction that describes the origin, content, and arrangement of the filmed records and lists related records. Some introductions also include special aids, such as indexes and registers.

Descriptive pamphlets (DPs) are available for many "M" publications. Each pamphlet contains the publication's introduction (including special lists or indexes prepared to simplify the use of the microfilm publication) and a table of contents that identifies the material contained on each roll. "M" publications that have descriptive pamphlets are indicated in this catalog by the symbol DP at the end of a publication title. The pamphlets are made available on request to prospective purchasers so they can evaluate more thoroughly the value of the publication's contents for their research.

"T" publications, unlike "M" publications, do not usually reproduce a complete series of records; that is, they may contain only segments, by date or subject, of a larger series. In many cases, "T" publications were produced in response to specific reference requests. Also, over the years the National Archives has accessioned as record material microfilm produced by other Federal agencies. Some of this film, when it is not defense classified and is deemed of sufficient research value, is reproduced and made available for sale as "T" publications. These publications are reproduced and sold exactly as they were filmed; they contain no introductions, nor are descriptive pamphlets available for them. All of the Immigration and Naturalization Service (INS) records described in this catalog are "T" publications that were filmed by and accessioned from the INS.

Catalogs of Microfilm Publications

This catalog is one in a series describing National Archives microfilm publications related to subjects of high research interest. Each catalog is being compiled through an extensive review of all microfilmed records to locate publications relevant to each topic. The catalogs contain both detailed descriptions of the records and roll-by-roll listings for each publication.

The initial six catalogs in the series cover the following topics:

American Indians
Black Studies
Diplomatic Records
Genealogical and Biographical Research
Immigrant and Passenger Arrivals
Military Service Records

These catalogs are part of a larger effort undertaken by the National Archives Trust Fund to increase public awareness of the availability of the records in the National Archives and to improve access to them. If you have suggestions of new catalog topics, new types of products based on the holdings, or new ways in which the Trust Fund can help you with your research, please contact the National Archives Trust Fund Board (NJ), National Archives, Washington, DC 20408.

Microfilm Pricing Policy

The price of each roll of microfilm in this catalog is $20. Prices are subject to change without advance public notice. Film can be bought as either individual rolls or a complete publication.

The microfilm price includes the cost of film stock, chemicals, boxes and reels, postage, and salaries. A fixed price per roll has been established because most of the costs of reproducing and selling microfilm are the same for all rolls of film, regardless of length. The establishment of such a price permits a substantial savings in order processing costs.

The National Archives microfilm publications program is financed from a trust fund established by the National Archives Trust Fund Board Act (44 U.S.C. 2307). Revenue received through the sale of microfilm publications is returned to the Trust Fund for use in financing additional publications and other products designed both to facilitate access to Federal records held by the National Archives and to make them more widely available to a larger portion of the public.

Microfilm Specifications

All microfilm sold through the National Archives Microfilm Publications program is silver-halide positive microfilm. Unless otherwise specified, it is 35mm reel microfilm, with plastic reels. Reduction ratios used range from 12:1 to 20:1. The number of frames on each reel varies.

In some instances, it is possible to obtain either microfilm in a different form (e.g., duplicate negative rather than positive) or paper copies. If you desire such services, please contact the Publications Services Branch (NEPS), National Archives, Washington, DC 20408 (phone: 202-523-3181), for a price quotation.

Contents

Records Relating to Service in the Regular U.S. Military

Veterans' Claims

Miscellaneous Records Relating to Military Service

Introduction

The National Archives and Records Administration (NARA) is the official repository for records of military personnel who have been discharged from the U.S. Air Force, Army, Marine Corps, and Navy. Those records available for public examination at the National Archives are a valuable source of information about an individual's military service, family, and medical history. These records can also be used to study military and social history.

Because of their research value, NARA has microfilmed many of these records, primarily those created before 1900. This catalog is organized by type of record; similar types of records are arranged chronologically. Brief descriptions of the records are followed by roll-by-roll listings of the contents. The catalog does not reproduce the records, however.

The first section explains *compiled military service records* of volunteer soldiers who fought for the United States in various wars and conflicts from the Revolutionary War through the Philippine Insurrection—1775 to 1902. During the 1890's, the War Department abstracted these records from such original records as muster rolls, returns, and medical and prison registers. The records usually show a soldier's presence or absence on certain dates, his rank and military organization, and the term of service. Sometimes they also show age, place of enlistment, and place of birth. These records are of value for proving military service, but generally don't have other genealogical information.

The second section of the catalog describes *records relating to service in the regular U.S. Army or Navy*. The War Department began to maintain personnel files for Regular Army officers in 1863 and for enlisted men in 1912. Records relating to service before those dates are scattered among many different series of War Department records—registers of enlistments, post and regimental returns, and correspondence. Similarly, records for naval officers and enlisted men were not compiled until after 1885 (after 1903 for enlisted men). Sources for earlier service consist of indexes to rendezvous reports, Marine Corps muster rolls, abstracts of service of naval officers, indexes to officers' records, and records of general courts-martial.

The third section treats records of veterans' *claims for bounty land and pensions*. Between 1776 and 1855, the Federal Government granted bounty land warrants entitling veterans to free land in specific areas of the public domain as an induce-

ment to enter military service. Applications for these bounty land warrants and pension files may contain a great deal of personal information about a veteran and his family. The files may show the veteran's name, age, and residence at the date of the application; the names of his wife and children; and dates of births, marriages, and deaths within the family. Pension records also document the veteran's military service by indicating his unit and the dates of his service.

The final section of the catalog describes *miscellaneous records that relate to military service:* additional records relating to Revolutionary War pay, settlement of accounts, and pensions; records relating to Confederates; records relating to the U.S. Military Academy cadets and U.S. Naval Academy midshipmen; and selected records relating to black servicemen.

Records relating to the following groups of military personnel are at the *National Personnel Records Center* in St. Louis, MO:

- U.S. Army officers and enlisted personnel completely separated after 1956. Personnel jackets of officers separated between 30 June 1917 and 1956 were destroyed by fire in 1972, as were jackets of enlisted men separated between 30 October 1912 and 1956.

- U.S. Air Force officers and enlisted men completely separated after 1956. Earlier jackets of the Army Air Corps and the U.S. Air Force were destroyed by fire in 1972.

- U.S. Navy officers completely separated after 1902 and enlisted men completely separated after 1885.

- U.S. Coast Guard officers completely separated after 1928 and enlisted personnel completely separated after 1914.

Requests for information about veterans should be submitted to the National Personnel Records Center (MPR), 9700 Page Blvd., St. Louis, MO 63132, using Standard Form 180, Request Pertaining to Military Records. This form is available from the St. Louis Center, the Government Printing Office, Federal Information Centers, local Veterans Administration offices, veterans service organizations, and the Reference Services Branch (NNIR), National Archives and Records Administration, Washington, DC 20408.

For additional information you may wish to refer to other NARA publications: *Military Service Rec-*

ords in the National Archives of the United States (General Information Leaflet 7); *Genealogical Research in the National Archives* (General Information Leaflet 5); and *Guide to Genealogical Research in the National Archives.*

Other related catalogs of microfilm publications of interest are: *Immigrant and Passenger Arrivals, Genealogical and Biographical Research, American Indians, Black Studies,* and *1790–1890 Federal Population Censuses.* These catalogs of microfilm publications do not reproduce the records, but briefly describe the records and tell what records are available on microfilm.

The records listed in this catalog are from the following record groups:

Record Group	Title
15	Records of the Veterans Administration
18	Records of the Army Air Forces
24	Records of the Bureau of Naval Personnel
29	Records of the Bureau of the Census
39	Records of the Bureau of Accounts (Treasury)
45	Naval Records Collection of the Office of Naval Records and Library
49	Records of the Bureau of Land Management
53	Records of the Bureau of the Public Debt

Record Group	Title
92	Records of the Office of the Quartermaster General
94	Records of the Adjutant General's Office, 1780s–1917
107	Records of the Office of the Secretary of War
109	War Department Collection of Confederate Records
125	Records of the Judge Advocate General (Navy)
127	Records of the United States Marine Corps
153	Records of the Judge Advocate General (Army)
217	Records of the United States General Accounting Office
391	Records of the United States Regular Army Mobile Units, 1821–1942
393	Records of the United States Army Continental Commands, 1821–1920
395	Records of the United States Army Overseas Operations and Commands, 1898–1942
405	Records of the United States Naval Academy
407	Records of the Adjutant General's Office, 1971–

This catalog was compiled by Cynthia G. Fox and Contance Potter with the assistance of Beverly Bagge and Mary Ryan. Jan Danis edited the final manuscript.

COMPILED MILITARY SERVICE RECORDS

Abstracts of the active military service of volunteer soldiers are called compiled military service records. Those held by the National Archives cover service during the Revolutionary War period, 1775–83; the Post-Revolutionary War period, 1784–1811; the War of 1812, 1812–15; the Indian wars, 1816–1860; the Mexican War, 1846–48; the Civil War, 1861–65; the Spanish-American War, 1898; and the Philippine Insurrection, 1898–1903. Volunteers also served during Indian disturbances, civil disorders, and disputes with Canada and Mexico. Microfilmed compiled service records for naval personnel are available only for the Revolutionary War.

The military service records of volunteer soldiers were abstracted onto cards from muster and pay-rolls, rank rolls, returns, hospital and prison records, accounts for subsistence, ration and ordnance records, receipts for pay and bounties, clothing returns, and other records. The abstracts for each soldier were placed in a jacket envelope bearing the soldier's name, rank, and military unit. In some instances, the envelope also includes one or more original documents relating specifically to that soldier.

A typical record gives the soldier's name, rank, military unit, and dates of entry into the service and separation by discharge, desertion, or death. It may also show the soldier's age, place of birth, and residence at the time of enlistment.

A compiled military service record is as complete as the records of an individual soldier or his unit. Some Civil War records also show facts about a soldier's imprisonment. If he was captured, his record may show the date of his release and parole, or if he died in prison, the date of his death. The National Archives also has some compiled military service records of Confederate officers, noncommissioned officers, and enlisted men, which are similar to the records of volunteer Union soldiers.

The service records were compiled under a War Department program begun some years after the Civil War to permit more rapid and efficient checking of military and medical records in connection with claims for pensions and other veterans' benefits. The abstracts were so carefully prepared that it is rarely necessary to consult the original records from which they were made. Although the War Department made every effort to assemble available official information, many compiled service records are not complete. Full records of the participation of a given unit may not have been available. A soldier may have served in a State militia unit that was never called into service by the Continental, Federal, or Confederate government. Records of such service, if available, are most likely in State archives or in the custody of the State adjutant general.

The compiled military service records are arranged by war, thereunder by State, thereunder by regiment or other military unit, and thereunder alphabetically by surname. To consult the records for a particular soldier, the researcher must know, or determine from an appropriate index, in which regiment he served. Not all of the indexes or compiled military service records have been microfilmed. The catalog notes when companion records are not available on microfilm.

Records of Revolutionary War Soldiers (Record Group 93)

Compiled military service records for men who fought in the Revolutionary War, 1775–83, were abstracted from records in the War Department Collection of Revolutionary War Records (Record Group 93). This record group resulted from the War Department's attempts to find substitutes for records destroyed by fire in 1800 and 1814.

Secretary of War William Belknap in 1873 made the first of several purchases of Revolutionary War records for the Department. In 1892 and 1894 Congress directed the other executive departments of the Federal Government to transfer military records of the Revolutionary War in their possession to the War Department. The last major addition to the collection occurred in 1914–15 when the War Department made photographic copies of Revolutionary War records in the possession of individuals and institutions in several States to supplement its holdings.

Indexes to Compiled Service Records

General Index to Compiled Military Service Records of Revolutionary War Soldiers. M860. 58 rolls. DP.

This microfilm publication reproduces the most comprehensive name index to American soldiers who served during the Revolution. The index also contains entries for several small series of Revolutionary War compiled military service records of sailors, members of army staff departments, and civilian employees—teamsters, laundresses, carpenters, and cooks—contracted to the American Army and Navy.

Each card of the index gives the name and unit of a soldier or civilian and sometimes his rank, profession, or office. The index may refer to more than one jacket envelope if a soldier served in more than one unit.

The compiled service records to which this index refers are microfilmed on M881.

Roll	Description
1	A–Ange
2	Angi–Ballan
3	Ballar–Bearne
4	Bearnh–Biso
5	Biss–Box
6	Boy–Brown, Joh
7	Brown, Jon–Bur
8	Bus–Cartel
9	Carter–Chp
10	Chr–Cold
11	Cole–Corm
12	Corn–Cul
13	Cum–Cy
14	D–Delone
15	Deloney–Dougg
16	Dough–Eccles
17	Ecclest–Fagei
18	Fager–Fond
19	Fonda–Fyk
20	Fyl–Glascoe
21	Glascow–Grego
22	Gregr–Hamle
23	Hamli–Hawkin
24	Hawkis–Hilk
25	Hill–Hop
26	Hor–Hur
27	Hus–Johnson, N.
28	Johnson, O.–Jw
29	K–Kinler
30	Kinley–Langden
31	Langdon–Lillie
32	Lillin–Lyon
33	Lyone–Matthews
34	Matthewson–McGinta
35	McGinte–Merrill
36	Merrills–Moore
37	Mooree–Nc
38	Ne–Olk
39	Oll–Pato
40	Patr–Ph
41	Pi–Pri
42	Pro–Q
43	R–Richard
44	Richards–Rolend
45	Rolens–Sanders
46	Sanderso–Shanna
47	Shanne–Sits
48	Sitsl–Souse
49	Sousl–Steward
50	Stewart–Swil
51	Swim–Thorn
52	Thoro–Tur
53	Tus–Voe
54	Vog–Wats
55	Watt–White, F.
56	White, G.–Willsi
57	Willso–Wright, J.
58	Wright, L.–Z

Index to Compiled Service Records of Revolutionary War Soldiers Who Served With the American Army in Connecticut Military Organizations. M920. 25 rolls. DP.

At the end of the Connecticut records is a series of service records labeled merely "Connecticut." The names in this miscellaneous series were taken generally from records that did not identify the name with a particular military organization.

Roll	Description
1	A
2	B–Ba
3	Be–Bl
4	Bn–Br
5	Bu–Ce
6	Ch–Cl
7	Co–Cy
8	D
9	E–Fo
10	Fr–Gl
11	Go–Gu
12	H–Hi
13	Ho–Hy
14	I–Ky
15	L
16	Ma–Mi
17	Mo–Oz
18	Pa–Pi
19	Pl–Ri
20	Ro–Sc
21	Se–Sm
22	Sn–Sy
23	T–V
24	W–We
25	Wh–Z

Index to Compiled Service Records of Revolutionary War Soldiers Who Served With the American Army in Georgia Military Organizations. M1051. 1 roll. DP.

Index to Compiled Service Records of Volunteer Soldiers Who Served During the Revolutionary War in Organizations from the State of North Carolina. M257. 2 rolls. 16mm. DP.

Roll	Description
1	A–G
2	R–Z

Revolutionary War Rolls

Revolutionary War Rolls, 1775–1783. M246. 138 rolls. DP.

This microfilm publication reproduces muster rolls, payrolls, strength returns, and other miscellaneous personnel, pay, and supply records of American Army units, 1775–83. A manuscript register of the series is filmed on roll 1.

American forces during the Revolutionary War included many types of military organizations created by the Continental Congress, States, towns, and counties. Regular units authorized by Congress formed the Continental Army, but this Army was frequently supplemented by units of militia and volunteers from the States, towns, and counties. The Revolutionary War rolls reproduced in this microfilm include those of units of the Continental Army and of units of militia, volunteers, and others who served with them. The larger entity is identified in this publication as the "American Army." Numbers in parentheses are "jacket" or folder numbers of the records for that organization on that roll.

Roll	Description
1	Register ("Catalogue of Records")
Connecticut	
2	1st Regiment, 1777–80 (1–6)
3	" (7–10)
4	" (11)
	1st Regiment, 1781–83 (12–21)
5	2d Regiment, 1777–80 (22–25)
6	" (26–29)
7	" (30–32)
	2d Regiment, 1781–83 (33–39)
8	" (40–42)
	3d Regiment, 1777–80 (43–44)
9	" (45–50)
10	" (51–52)
	3d Regiment, 1781–83 (53–62)
11	4th Regiment, 1777–80 (63–66)
12	" (67–72)
13	" (73–75)
	4th Regiment, 1781–82 (76–85)
	5th Regiment, 1777–80 (86–90)
14	" (91–93)
15	" (94–96)
	5th Regiment, 1781–82 (97–98)
16	" (99–107)
	6th Regiment, 1777–80 (108–109)
17	" (110–113)
18	" (114–117)
19	7th Regiment, 1777–80 (118–120)
20	" (121–124)
21	" (125–127)
	8th Regiment, 1777–80 (128)
22	" (129–131)
23	" (132–134)
24	" (135–137)
	9th Regiment, 1777–80 (138)
25	" (139–147)
	Connecticut Regiment, 1783 (148–154)
26	" (155–157)
	5th Regiment of Light Horse, 1776–79 (158)
	Backus' Regiment of Light Horse, 1776 (159)
	Skinner's Regiment of Light Horse, 1776 (160)
	Starr's Regiment of Light Horse, 1779 (161)
	Seymour's Regiment of Light Dragoons (162)

Roll	Description
	1st Regiment Forces, 1775 (163)
	1st Battalion State Regiment, 1776–77 (164)
	1st Regiment of Militia, 1778–79 (165)
	2d Regiment of Militia, 1776 (166)
	3d Regiment of Foot, 1775 (167)
	3d Regiment of Militia, 1776 (168)
	4th Regiment of Militia, 1775 (169)
	4th Regiment of Foot, 1776 (170)
	5th Regiment, 1775 (171)
	5th Regiment of Militia, 1776 (172)
	7th Regiment of Militia, 1776 (173)
	7th Regiment, 1775 (174)
	8th Regiment, 1775 (175)
	8th Regiment of Militia, 1776 (176)
	8th Regiment of Militia, 1780 (177)
	9th Regiment of Militia, 1776–81 (178)
	10th Regiment of Militia, 1776–77 (179)
	12th Regiment of Foot, 1776 (180)
	13th Regiment of Militia, 1776 (181)
	16th Regiment of Militia, 1776 (182)
	18th Regiment of Militia, 1776 (183)
27	20th Regiment of Militia, 1779–81 (184)
	21st Regiment of Militia, 1778–81 (185)
	22d Regiment of Militia, 1776 (186)
	25th Regiment of Militia, 1778 (187)
	25th Regiment, 1776 (188)
	33d Regiment of Foot, 1775 (189)
	[Averill's] Company, 1782 (190)
	[Bigelow's] Company of Artillery, 1776 (191)
	Belding's Regiment, 1777 (192)
	[Bennett's] Company of Militia, 1781 (193)
	[Bixby's] Company of Militia, 1776 (194)
	Bradley's Regiment, 1776–77 (195)
	[Bradley's] Company of Matrosses and Artillery, 1779–81 (196)
	[Bristol's] Company of Militia, 1779 (197)
	Burrell's Regiment, 1776–77 (198)
	Canfield's Regiment of Militia, 1781 (199)
	Chapman's Regiment of Militia, 1778 (200)
	Chester's Regiment of Militia, 1776–77 (201)
	Cook's Regiment of Militia, 1777 (202)
	Douglas' Regiment of Levies, 1776 (203)
	Douglas' Regiment, 1776 (204)
	Durkee's Company of Matrosses, 1782–84 (205)
	Elmore's Battalion, 1776–77 (206)
	Ely's Brigade of Teamsters, 1781 (207)
	Ely's Regiment, 1777 (208)
	Enos' Regiment, 1776–77 (209)
	Fitch's Independent Company, 1783 (210)
	Gallup's Company, 1776 (211)
	Gallup's Regiment, 1779 (212)
	Gay's Regiment, 1776 (213)
	Hand's Company of Militia, 1776 (214)
	Hooker's Regiment of Militia, 1777 (215)
	Johnson's Regiment of Militia, 1778 (216)
28	Latimer's Regiment of Militia, 1777–78 (217)
	Lee's Company of Guards, 1780 (218)
	Leffingwell's Company, 1777 (219)
	Lewis' Regiment, 1776 (220)
	Lockwood's Company of Coast Guards, 1780–81 (221)
	Lockwood's Company of Coast Guards, 1781–82 (222)
	Markham's Company of Militia, 1781 (223)
	Mason's Company of Militia, 1776 (224)
	Mason's Regiment of Militia, 1778 (225)
	Mather's Independent Company, 1776 (226)
	Matross Company at Norwalk, 1781 (227)
	McClallen's Regiment, 1782 (228)
	McClellan's Regiment, 1777 (229)
	McClellan's Regiment, 1778 (230)

Roll	Description
	McClellan's Regiment, 1781–82 (231)
	Mead's Regiment of Militia, 1779 (232)
	Miles' Brigade of Ox Teams, 1781–82 (233)
	Moseley's Detachment of Militia, 1778 (234)
	Mott's Regiment, 1776 (235)
	Mott's Company of Militia, 1776 (236)
	Newberry's Regiment, 1777 (237)
	Parker's Company of Teamsters, 1778 (238)
	Parson's Regiment, 1775 (239)
	Parson's Regiment of Militia, 1777 (240)
	Patrick's Brigade of Teamsters (241)
	Porter's Regiment, 1781 (242)
	Reed's Company of Militia, (243)
	Robinson's Company, 1777 (244)
	Sage's Regiment, 1776–77 (245)
	Corps of Sappers and Miners, 1779–81 (246)
	Shelden's Company, 1779 (247)
	Silliman's Regiment, 1776 (248)
	Talcott's Regiment, 1776 (249)
	Thompson's Company (250)
	Thomson's Regiment, 1777 (251)
	Tyler's Regiment, 1777 (252)
	Vaill's Company of Guards, 1781–82 (253)
	Van Deursen's Company of State Guards Artillery, 1781 (254)
	Wadworth's Company of Teamsters, 1777–80 (255)
	Ward's Regiment, 1777 (256)
	Waterbury's Regiment, 1776–77 (257)
	Whiting's Regiment, 1777 (258)
	Wells' Regiment of Militia, 1779 (259)
	Wells' Regiment, 1780–81 (260)
	Wolcott's Regiment, 1776 (261)
	Wolcott's Company of Militia, 1776 (262)
	Connecticut Line, Field, Staff, and Company Officers (263)
	Various Organizations (264)

Delaware:

Roll	Description
29	1st Battalion, New Castle County, 1777 (1)
	2d Regiment, New Castle County, 1778–81 (2)
	2d Battalion of Militia, 1776 (3)
	2d Regiment of Militia, 1780 (4)
	7th Regiment of Militia, 1782 (5)
	Flying Camp Battalion, 1776 (6)
	Delaware Regiment, 1777–80 (7–9 pt.)
30	" (9 pt.–11 pt.)
31	Delaware Regiment, 1777–83 (11 pt.)
	Delaware Regiment, 1776 (12)
	Latimer's Independent Company, 1776 (13)
	Various Organizations (14)

Georgia:

Roll	Description
32	1st Battalion, 1779–80 (1)
	2d Battalion, 1779–80 (2)
	3d Battalion, 1779–80 (3)
	4th Battalion, 1779 (4)
	Georgia Battalion, 1782–83 (5)
	Emanuel's Regiment of Militia, 1781–82 (6)
	Various Organizations (7)

Maryland:

Roll	Description
33	Gale's Independent Company of Artillery, 1779–80 (1)
	Smith's Artillery, 2d and 3d Companies, 1783 (2)
	1st Regiment, 1776 (3)
	1st Regiment, 1778–80 (4)
	1st Regiment, 1783 (5)
	1st Regiment Flying Camp, 1776 (6)
	2d Regiment, 1777–80 (7–15)
	2d Regiment, 1781 (16)
	3d Regiment, 1778–81 (17)

Roll	Description
34	3d Regiment, 1778 (18–19)
	4th Regiment, 1776–78 (20)
	4th Regiment, 1777–81 (21)
	5th Regiment, 1778–79 (22)
	5th Regiment, 1781 (23)
	6th Regiment, 1777–79 (24)
	7th Regiment, 1777–78 (25)
	34th Battalion of Militia, 1776 (26)
	37th Battalion of Militia, 1777 (27)
	Extraordinary Regiment, 1780 (28)
	Flying Camp Regiment (Ewing's), 1776 (29)
	Flying Camp Regiment (Griffith's), 1776 (30)
	Flying Camp Regiment (Richardson's), 1776 (31)
	Lansdale's Detachment, 1783 (32)
	Marbury's Detachment, 1784 (33)
	Washington County Militia Company, 1777 (34)
	Various Organizations (35)

Massachusetts:

Roll	Description
35	1st Regiment, 1777–81 (1–2)
	2d Regiment, 1777–81 (3)
36	3d Regiment, 1777–82 (4)
	3d Regiment, 1783 (5)
	4th Regiment, 1781–83 (6)
	5th Regiment, 1778–81 (7)
	5th Regiment, 1783 (8)
37	6th Regiment, 1777–80 (9)
	7th Regiment, 1777–81 (10)
	8th Regiment, 1778–80 (11)
	9th Regiment, 1778–81 (12)
38	10th Regiment, 1778–80 (13–14)
	12th Regiment, 1777–79 (15–17)
	13th Regiment, 1777 (18)
	15th Regiment, 1777–80 (19)
39	15th Regiment, 1777–79 (20)
	16th Regiment, 1777–80 (21–26)
40	(27–34)
	1st Regiment of Militia, 1776 (35)
	1st Regiment of Militia, Lincoln County, 1776 (36)
	1st Regiment of Guards, 1778 (37)
	3d Regiment of Militia, 1779 (38)
	4th Regiment of Militia, 1777 (39)
	4th Regiment of Militia, 1778–80 (40)
	18th Regiment, 1775 (41)
	25th Regiment of Foot, 1775 (42)
	32d Regiment of Militia, 1775 (43)
	Bailey's Regiment of Militia (44)
	Brewer's Regiment, 1776 (45)
	Brooks' Regiment of Militia, 1778 (46)
	Bullards' Regiment of Militia, 1776 (47)
	Burt's Company of Militia, 1776–77 (48)
	Cady's Detachment (or Regiment), 1776 (49)
	Carpenter's Company of Militia, 1779 (50)
	Carpenter's Regiment of Militia, 1776–78 (51)
	Cary's Regiment of Militia, 1780 (52)
	Cary's Regiment, 1776 (53)
	Cogswell's Regiment of Militia, 1778 (54)
41	Cowell's Company of Militia, 1776 (55)
	Crandon's Company, 1779 (56)
	Cushing's Regiment of Militia, 1777 (57)
	Denny's Regiment of Militia (58)
	Durfee's Company, 1778 (59)
	Fellows' Regiment, 1775 (60)
	French's Regiment, 1777 (61)
	Frye's Regiment, 1775 (62)
	Gerrish's Regiment, 1778 (63)
	Goodrich's Command, 1780 (64)
	Holman's Regiment of Foot, 1776 (65)
	Jacob's Regiment, 1778–79 (66)
	Hyde's Detachment of Militia, 1777 (67)
	Keyes' Regiment, 1777 (68)

Roll	Description
	Elmendorph's Company of Militia, 1777 (97)
	Field's Regiment of Militia, 1777–80 (98)
	Fish's Regiment of Militia, 1777 (99)
74	Fisher's Regiment of Militia, 1775–81 (100)
	Fondey's Party of Militia, 1780 (101)
	Freer's Regiment of Militia, 1777–79 (102)
	Gettman's Company of Rangers, 1776 (103)
	Golden's Company of Militia, 1776 (104)
	Graham's Company of State Troops (Ulster County), 1776 (105)
	Graham's Regiment of Militia, 1777–79 (106)
	Guards, Militia, 1777–78 (107)
	Hamman's Regiment of Militia, 1777–82 (108)
	Hardenburgh's Company of State Troops, 1776 (109)
	Hardenburgh's Regiment of Militia, 1776 (110) (111)
	Harper's Regiment of Militia, 1779 (112)
	Hasbrouck's Regiment of Militia, 1777 (113)
	Hathorn's Regiment of Militia, 1777–81 (114)
	Hay's Regiment of Militia, 1778–80 (115)
	Hopkins' Regiment of Militia, 1779 (116)
75	Horton's Company of Guards (Westchester County), 1777–78 (117)
	Humphrey's Regiment of Militia, 1776 (118)
	Humphrey's Regiment of Militia, 1777 (119)
	Jansen's Regiment of Militia, 1779–82 (120)
	Klock's Regiment of Militia, 1779–83 (121)
	Lamb's Company of Artillery, 1775–76 (122)
	Lansing's Detachment of Militia, 1777 (123)
	Livingston's Regiment of Militia, 1777–81 (124)
	Ludington's Regiment of Militia, 1777–80 (125)
	McClaughrey's Regiment of (Ulster County) Militia, 1776–81 (126)
	McCrea's Regiment of Levies, 1779 (127)
	Mills' Detachment of Horse, 1777 (128)
	Mills' Company of Guards, 1777–78 (129)
	Myrick's Company of Rangers, 1776–77 (130)
	Nicholson's Regiment, 1776 (131)
	Nicoll's Regiment of Levies, 1776 (132)
	Palmer's Regiment of Militia, 1776 (133)
	Pawling's Regiment of Levies and Militia, 1779–81 (134)
	Pawling's Regiment of Militia, 1776–77 (135)
76	Platt's Regiment of Associated Exempts, 1779 (136)
	Quackenbos' Regiment of Militia, 1779–80 (137)
	Reiley's Company of Rangers, 1778 (138)
	Rudd's Detachment of Militia, 1776 (139)
	Sacket's Company or Regiment of Various Westchester County Regiments (140)
	Schuyler's Regiment of Militia, 1781–82 (141)
	Schuyler's Regiment of Albany County Militia, 1777 (142)
	Snyder's Regiment of Militia, 1778–82 (143)
	Stevenson's Company of Guards (Westchester County), 1777 (144)
	Strait's Detachment of Militia, 1776 (145)
	Swartwout's Regiment of Militia, 1776 (146)
	Swartwout's Regiment of Associated Exempts, 1777 (147)
	Thomas' Battalion or Regiment of Militia, 1776–79 (148)
	Van Alstyne's Regiment of Militia, 1777–81 (149)
	Van Bergen's Regiment of Albany County Militia, 1777–80 (150)
	Van Brunt's Regiment of Militia, 1776 (151)
	Van Cortlandt's Regiment of Militia, 1777 (152)
	Vandenbergh's Regiment of Militia, 1777 (153)
	Vandenbergh's Regiment of Militia, 1779 (154)
	Van Denburgh's Regiment of Militia, 1778 (155)

Roll	Description
	Van Gaasbeck's Company of Albany County Militia, 1776 (156)
	Van Ness' Regiment of (Dutchess County) Minute Men, 1776 (157)
	Van Ness' Regiment Albany Co. of Militia (158)
	Van Rensselaer's Regiment, 1780–81 (159)
77	Van Rensselaer's Regiment of Militia (160)
	Van Rensselaer's Regiment of Militia (4th Regiment), 1776–81 (161)
	Van Rensselaer's Regiment of Militia, 1779 (162)
	Van Schaick's Battalion, 1776 (163)
	Van Schoonhoven's Regiment of Militia, 1778–82 (164)
	Van Veghten's Regiment of Militia (165)
	Van Woert's Regiment of Militia, 1779–80 (166)
	Vrooman's Regiment of Militia, 1779–83 (167)
	Webster's Regiment of Militia, 1780–82 (168)
	Weissenfels' Regiment of Levies, 1781–82 (169)
	Wemple's Regiment of Militia, 1780 (170)
	Wheelock's Command, 1777 (171)
	Whiting's Regiment of Militia, 1777–81 (172)
78	Willett's Regiment of Levies, 1781–83 (173)
	Williams' Regiment of Militia, 1778–81 (174)
	Winn's Company of Rangers, 1776 (175)
	Woodhull's Regiment, 1776 (176)
	Wood's Company of Exempts (Orange County), 1778–79 (177)
	Wood's Hired Guards, 1779 (178)
	Wynkoop's Regiment, 1776 (179)
	Yate's Regiment of Militia, 1779–80 (180)
	Various Organizations (181)

North Carolina:

Roll	Description
79	1st Regiment, 1775–83 (1)
	1st Regiment of Militia, 1780 (2)
	2d Regiment, 1778 (3)
	2d Regiment of Militia, 1780 (4)
	3d Regiment, 1777 (5)
	3d Battalion or Regiment, 1779 (6)
	6th Regiment, 1778 (7)
	7th Regiment, 1777 (8)
	8th Regiment, 1777 (9)
	10th Regiment, 1782 (10)
	North Carolina Regiment, 1782 (11)
	Line Regiments, 1777-83 (12)
	Troops of Light Dragoons, 1777–78 (13)
	Bynum's Company of Militia, 1781 (14)
	Collier's Regiment of Militia, 1780 (15)
	Graham's Tryon County Regiment, 1776 (16)
	Kingsbury's Company of Artillery, 1778 (17)
	Lytle's Regiment of Levies (Caswell County), 1778 (18)
	Porter's Company, Tryon County, 1777 (19)
	Seawell's Regiment of Militia, Pitt County, 1780 (20)
	Sharpe's Company of Light Horse, 1781 (21)
	Vernon's Company of Light Horse Militia, 1781 (22)
	Various Organizations (23)

Pennsylvania:

Roll	Description
80	1st Regiment, 1775 (1)
	1st Battalion, 1775 (2)
	1st Regiment Continental, 1776 (3)
	1st Regiment, 1777–80 (4)
	2d Regiment, 1777–79 (5–14)
81	" (15–16)
	3d Regiment, 1776 (17)
	3d Regiment (Line), 1776 (18)
	4th Regiment, 1776–77 (19)
	4th Regiment (Line), 1777 (20)
	5th Regiment, 1776 (21)

Roll	Description
	5th Regiment, 1776–80 (22–23)
82	" (24–31)
	6th Regiment, 1776 (32)
	6th Regiment, 1776–78 (33)
83	7th Regiment, 1777 (34)
	8th Regiment, 1778 (35)
	9th Regiment, 1777–78 (36)
84	10th Regiment (37)
	11th Regiment, 1777–78 (38)
	11th Regiment, 1779–80 (39)
	12th Regiment, 1776–78 (40)
	13th Regiment, 1777 (41)
	1st Regiment Flying Camp, 1776 (42)
	1st Battalion (or Regiment) Flying Camp, 1776 (43)
	1st Battalion of Bedford County Militia, 1777 (44)
	1st Battalion of Chester County Militia, 1776–77 (45)
	1st Battalion of Cumberland County Militia, 1776–77 (46)
	1st Regiment Flying Camp of Lancaster County, 1776 (47)
	1st Battalion of Philadelphia County Militia, 1776 (48)
	1st Battalion of Riflemen, Philadelphia County Militia, 1776 (49)
	1st Battalion of Westmoreland County Militia, 1777 (50)
	2d Regiment Flying Camp, 1776 (51)
	2d Battalion of Cumberland County Militia, 1776 (52)
	2d Battalion of Cumberland County Militia, 1777 (53)
	2d Battalion of Riflemen, Lancaster County, 1776–77 (54)
	2d Battalion of Westmoreland County Militia, 1777 (55)
	3d Battalion of Chester County Militia, 1776–77 (56)
	3d Battalion of Cumberland County Militia, 1776 (57)
	3d Battalion of Lancaster County Militia, 1776 (58)
	3d Battalion of Northumberland County Militia, 1779 (59)
	4th Battalion of Chester County Militia, 1776 (60)
	4th Battalion of Philadelphia County Militia, 1776 (61)
	5th Battalion of Chester County Militia, 1776 (62)
	5th Battalion of Cumberland County Militia, 1776 (63)
	5th Battalion of Philadelphia County Militia, 1776 (64)
	5th Battalion of York County Militia, 1777 (65)
	Andrews' Battalion of York County Militia, 1777–78 (66)
	Atlee's Musket Battalion, 1777 (67)
	Baxter's Battalion Flying Camp, 1776 (68)
	Barr's Detachment of Westmoreland County Militia, 1778 (69)
	Clugage's Battalion, 1778 (70)
	Burd's Battalion, 1776 (71)
	Clotz' Battalion Flying Camp, Lancaster County, 1776 (72)
	Duncan's Company of Volunteers (Pittsburgh), 1778 (73)
	Enslow's Company of Bedford County Militia, 1782–83 (74)

Roll	Description
	Ferreis' Battalion of Militia (Lancaster County), 1776 (75)
	Graff's Company, 1776 (76)
	Hall's Company, 1781 (77)
	Haller's Battalion Flying Camp, 1776 (78)
	Hart's Battalion of Bucks County Militia, 1776 (79)
	Matlock's Rifle Battalion, 1777 (80)
	Miles' Rifle Regiment, 1776 (81)
	Lochny's Battalion (81–1)*
	Moorhead's Independent Company, 1777–79 (82)
	Ott's Company of Washington County Militia (83)
	Philadelphia Light Horse Troop, 1780 (84)
	Rankin's Regiment (or Battalion) of York County Militia, 1777 (85)
	Reed's Volunteers, 1780–81 (86)
	Schott's Corps (Independent), 1778 (87)
	Shaver's Company of Volunteers, 1777 (88)
	Steel's Independent Company, 1777 (89)
	Swope's Regiment Flying Camp, 1776–80 (90)
	Van Etten's Company of Northhampton County, 1780–81 (91)
	Watt's Regiment Flying Camp, 1776 (92)
	Various Organizations (93)

Rhode Island:

Roll	Description
85	1st Regiment, 1777–80 (1–11)
	2d Regiment, 1777–80 (12)
86	" (13–20)
87	" (21–22)
	Rhode Island Regiment, 1781–83 (23–32)
	Rhode Island Detachment, June to December 1783 (33)
	2d Battalion Providence County Militia, 1781 (34)
	15th Regiment Militia, 1775 (35)
	Allen's Company of Militia, 1780–81 (36)
	Arnold's Regiment of Pawtuxet Rangers, 1776–82 (37)
	Babcock's Regiment of Militia, 1776–77 (38)
	Barrington Guards, 1778 (39)
	Barton's Light Corps, 1779 (40)
	Bowen's Regiment of Militia, 1778 (41)
	Burlingame's Company of Militia, 1778–79 (42)
	Cook's Regiment of Militia, 1777 (43)
	Cook's Regiment (44)
88	Crary's Regiment, 1777–79 (45)
	Elliott's Regiment of Artillery, 1776–78 (46)
	Kimball's Regiment of Militia, 1781 (47)
	Lippitt's Regiment, 1776 (48)
	Mathewson's Regiment, 1778 (49)
	Miller's Regiment of Militia, 1778 (50)
	Noyes' Regiment of Militia, 1777–78 (51)
	Onley's Regiment of Militia, 1781 (52)
	Peck's Regiment, 1780–81 (53)
	Potter's Regiment of Militia, 1781 (54)
	Sprague's 3d Company of Militia (Smithfield), 1778 (55)
	Thurston's 2d Company of Militia (Hopkinton) (56)
	Tillinghast's Regiment, 1781 (57)
	Topham's Regiment and Battalion, 1778–80 (58)
	Trusk's Company of Smithfield, 1778–79 (59)
	Warren Guards, 1778 (60)
	Waterman's Company, 1775–76 (61)
	Waterman's Regiment, 1776–77 (62)
	Whipple's Company of Cumberland Militia (63)
	Wilbur's Company, 1777 (64)
	Williams' 2d Company (Cranston), 1780 (65)
	Various Organizations (66)

Roll	Description
South Carolina:	
89	1st Regiment, 1779–80 (1)
	2d Regiment, 1779 (2)
	3d Regiment, 1777–81 (3)
	6th Regiment (Continental), 1779–80 (4)
	Hampton's Regiment of Light Dragoons, 1781–82 (5)
	Continental Regiment of Artillery, 1779–81 (6–7)
	Companies of Continental Troops, 1783 (8)
	Butler's Company of Militia, 1781–82 (9)
	Casey's Regiment, 1782 (10)
	Richardson's Command, 1775 (11)
	Various Organizations (12)

Roll	Description
Vermont:	
90	6th Regiment of Militia, 1780–81 (1)
	7th Regiment of Militia, 1782 (2)
	Abbott's Regiment of Militia, 1781 (3)
	Alger's Company, 1777 (4)
	Allen's Detachment, 1779–81 (5)
	Allen's Regiment, 1780–81 (6)
	Allen's Regiment, 1778–83 (7)
	Allen's Company of Volunteers, 1780 (8)
	Andrews' Company, 1782 (9)
	Bailley's Company, 1782 (10)
	Bates' Alarm Company, 1781 (11)
	Bentley's Command, 1778 (12)
	Blanchard's Company, 1781 (13)
	Bradley's Regiment, 1782–84 (14)
	Bramble's Company, 1781 (15)
	Briggs' Company of Militia, 1778 (16)
	Briggs' Company of Militia, 1782 (17)
	Brownson's Company, 1776 (18)
	Brownson's Detachment, 1776 (19)
	Brownson's Battalion, 1782 (20)
	Burke's and Gilson's Companies, 1781 (21)
	Calkins' Company of Militia, 1781 (22)
	Chittenden's Life Guards, 1781 (23)
	Clark's Company of Militia, 1778–80 (24)
	Coffeen's Company, 1781 (25)
	Colbe's Company, 1777–81 (26)
	Cottle's Company, 1780–81 (27)
	Cushman's Company, 1780–81 (28)
	Day's Command, 1780 (29)
	Dimmick's Company, 1779 (30)
	Douty's Regiment, 1781 (31)
	Durkee's Company of Militia, 1780–81 (32)
	Enos' Brigade, 1781 (33)
	Everest's Company of Rangers, 1780 (34)
	Fassett's Independent Company, 1776–77 (35)
	Fletcher's Regiment, 1779–81 (36)
	Gilbert's Company, 1780 (37)
	Green's Company of Rangers, 1781–82 (38)
	Guards, 1778 (39)
	Guards (Lt. Joseph Wickwire), 1781 (40)
	Guards (Sgt. Matthew Scott), 1781 (41)
	Guards, 1782 (42)
	Hall's Corps of Rangers, 1780 (43)
	Hawkins' Company of Minute Men, 1780 (44)
	Herrick's Regiment, 1778–81 (45)
	Hickok's Company, 1776 (46)
	Hoar's Company of Militia, 1780 (47)
	Hodge's Company, 1780 (48)
	Hoisington's Command of Rangers, 1776 (49)
	Holmes' Company, 1780–81 (50)
	Hunkins' Command of Militia, 1781 (51)
	Hutchins' Independent Company, 1781 (52)
	Lee's Regiment, 1781–82 (53)
	Lyon's Company, 1777 (54)
	Lyons' Regiment, 1781 (55)
	MacClure's Company, 1781 (56)
	Marsh's Party, 1777 (57)

Roll	Description
	Marsh's Regiment, 1778–81 (58)
	Marsh's Regiment, 1777 (59)
	Marston's Company, 1780–81 (60)
	Mattison's Company, 1781 (61)
	Mattison's Company of Militia, 1782 (62)
	Mead's Regiment of Militia, 1777 (63)
	Mirrick's Company, 1782 (64)
	Moseley's Company, 1781 (65)
	Nelson's Company, 1781 (66)
91	Olcott's Regiment, 1777–81 (67)
	Parkhurst's Company, 1781 (68)
	Parkhurst's Company, 1780 (69)
	Partridge's Command, 1781 (70)
	Post's Company, 1780 (71)
	Robinson's Company of Militia, 1780–81 (72)
	Robinson's Regiment of Militia, 1776–77 (73)
	Rubach's Garrison at Fort Ranger, 1778–79 (74)
	Safford's Company, 1778 (75)
	Salsbury's Company, 1777–81 (76)
	Sampson's Company, 1780 (77)
	Sawyer's Company, 1780 (78)
	Sergeant's Regiment (7th), 1782 (79)
	Scouts (Capt. Steel Smith), 1778 (80)
	Scouts (Lt. Asahel Smith), 1780 (81)
	Scouts (Lt. Hezekiah Silavay), 1780 (82)
	Scouts (Capt. Jacob Hall), 1781 (83)
	Scouts (Lt. Nathan Howland), 1780 (84)
	Scouts (Capt. John Sloan), 1777 (85)
	Scouts, Detachment of (Lt. Elijah Beenam), 1781 (86)
	Scouts (Capt. Phineas Williams), 1777 (87)
	Scouts (Maj. John Barron, Capt. Ebenezer Martin), 1776–81 (88)
	Scouts, 1777 (89)
	Smith's Command or Company, 1777–78 (90)
	Smith's Company, 1780–81 (91)
	Soper's Company, 1778 (92)
	Spooner's Company, 1781 (93)
	Sprague's Company, 1781 (94)
	Starr's Company, 1780 (95)
	Tyler's Company, 1780 (96)
	Upham's Company, 1780 (97)
	Wait's Battalion, 1780–81 (98)
	Walbridge's Regiment, 1780–82 (99)
	Wallace's Detachment, 1780 (100)
	Wallis' Company, 1782 (101)
	Warner's Regiment (102)
	Weld's Company of Militia, 1780 (103)
	White's Company of Militia, 1781 (104)
	Williams' Regiment, 1777 (105)
	Wolcott's Company, 1780 (106)
	Wood's Regiment, 1780–81 (107)
	Worrin's Regiment, 1778–82 (108)
	Various Organizations (Revolutionary War) (109)
	Brownson's Company, 1782 (110)
	Chaffee's Company, 1782 (111)
	Gaige's Company, 1779 (112)
	How's Company, 1782 (113)
	Moss' Party, 1779 (114)
	Party to Assist Sheriff, 1782 (115)
	Roberts' Party, 1779 (116)
	Smith's Party, 1779 (117)
	Wallis' Party, 1779 (118)
	Various Organizations to Assist Sheriff (119)
Virginia:	
92	1st Regiment, 1777–79 (1–14)
93	" (15–18)
	1st State Regiment, 1777–80 (19–22)
94	" (23–30)

Roll	Description
	7th Regiment, 1776 (83)
	8th Regiment, 1776 (84)
	9th Regiment, 1776 (85)
	10th Regiment, 1776 (86)
	11th Regiment, 1776 (87)
	12th Regiment, 1776 (88)
	13th Regiment, 1776 (89)
	14th Regiment, 1776 (90)
	15th Regiment, 1776 (91)
	16th Regiment, 1776 (92)
	17th Regiment, 1776 (93)
	18th Regiment, 1776 (94)
	19th Regiment, 1776 (95)
	20th Regiment, 1776 (96)
	21st Regiment, 1776 (97)
	22d Regiment, 1776 (98)
	23d Regiment, 1776 (99)
123	24th Regiment, 1776 (100)
	25th Regiment, 1776 (101)
	26th Regiment, 1776 (102)
	27th Regiment, 1776 (103)
	Forman's Regiment, 1777–79 (104–108)
	Gist's Regiment, 1777–79 (109–118)
124	Grayson's Regiment, 1777–79 (119–125)
125	" (126–128)
	Hartley's Regiment, 1777 (129)
	Henley's Regiment, 1778 (130)
	Lee's Regiment, 1777–79 (131)
	Malcolm's Regiment, 1777–79 (132–138)
126	" (139–144)
	Patton's Regiment, 1777–79 (145–152)
	Rawling's Regiment, 1776–79 (153)
127	Sherburne's Regiment, 1777–79 (154–160)
	Spencer's Regiment, 1777–80 (161)
128	" (162–170)
129	" (171–178)
	Thruston's Regiment, 1778 (179)
	Brown's Detachment of New Hampshire, Massachusetts, and Vermont Militia, 1775–76 (180)
	Canadian Volunteers, 1775 (181)
	Commander in Chief's Guard, 1777–83 (182)
	Delaware Indians, 1780–81 (183)
130	German Regiment (or Battalion), 1777–80 (184–190)
131	" (191–193)
	Hazen's Regiment, 1778–79 (194–207)
132	" (208–213)
	Invalid Corps, 1780–81 (214)
	Lee's Independent Company, 1776 (215)
	Livingston's Regiment, 1777–80 (216–218)
133	" (219–225)
	Morgan's Rifle Regiment, 1777–79 (226)
	Perry's Independent Company, 1776 (227)
	Steele's Detachment, Virginia and North Carolina, 1778 (228)
	Sullivan's Life Guard, 1779 (229)
134	Warner's Battalion or Regiment, 1777–79 (230)
	Various Organizations (231)

Miscellaneous:

Roll	Description
135	General and Staff; Field and Staff and Line Officers, 1775–83 (1)
	Guard Reports, 1776–80 (2)
	Hospital Department (3)
	Prisoners of War (4)
	Quartermaster General's Department, 1779–82 (5)
136	Returns of the French Army Under Count Rochambeau, 1781–82 (6)
	Returns of Brigades, Divisions, Armies, &c. (7–9)

Roll	Description
	Returns of Various Organizations, Signed by the Adjutants General of the Army (10)
137	Returns of the Army Under General Washington, July 19, 1775–Dec. 1782 (11–18)
138	Returns of the Army Under General Washington, Jan.–Aug. 1783 (19–20)

Compiled Service Records of Soldiers Who Served in the American Army During the Revolutionary War. M881. 1,096 rolls. DP.

This microfilm publication reproduces the compiled service records of soldiers who served in the American Army during the Revolutionary War. The American forces included many types of military organizations: some created by the Continental Congresses; others by the States, towns, and counties. Regular units, authorized by the Continental Congress, formed the Continental Army, but this Army frequently was supplemented by units of militia and volunteers from the States, towns, and counties. The compiled service records reproduced here contain records for the soldiers of the Continental Army and for the militia, volunteers, and others who served with them. The larger entity is referred to in these records as the "American Army."

A typical infantry regiment in the Continental Army, generally referred to as a regiment or battalion without the designation "infantry," might contain field officers, such as a colonel, lieutenant colonel, and major; a regimental staff including an adjutant, quartermaster, surgeon, surgeon's mate, paymaster, and chaplain; and 8 to 10 companies.

Cavalry and artillery regiments were organized in a similar way, although cavalry companies were frequently called troops. Artillery companies included specialized soldiers, such as bombardiers, gunners, and matrosses (gunner's mates who helped load, fire, and sponge the guns). The soldiers in artillery units often functioned individually, or in small groups, rather than as regiments.

Artificers were civilian or military mechanics and artisans employed by the Army to provide necessary services. Artificer companies included carpenters, blacksmiths, wheelwrights, harness makers, coopers, nailers, and farriers (blacksmiths who shoed horses).

Compiled service records for soldiers whose names are incomplete due to the mutilation or deterioration of the original records are arranged at the end of the other compiled service records for their units. Records for soldiers and employees listed by first name only in the original records are filed under that name. There are cross-references for names that appear in the records under more than one spelling.

Roll	Description
Continental troops:	
1	1st Regiment, Artillery
	A–Bo
2	Br–Cl
3	Co–D
4	E–G
5	H–J
6	K–Mc
7	Me–Q
8	R–Sp
9	St–Y

Roll	Description	Roll	Description
10	1st Regiment		21st Regiment
	A–E		22d Regiment
11	F–K	57	23d Regiment
12	L–Q		A–F
13	R–Z	58	G–P
14	1st Regiment, Light Dragoons	59	R–Y
	A–D.		24th Regiment
15	E–J	60	25th Regiment
16	K–R		26th Regiment
17	S–Z		A–J
18	2d Regiment, Artillery	61	K–W
	A–Ba		27th Regiment
19	Be–By	62	Armand's Independent Corps, Light Dragoons
20	C	63	Baldwin's Regiment, Artificers
21	D–E		A–J
22	F–G	64	K–Y
23	H	65	Forman's Regiment
24	J–K		A–R
25	L	66	S–W
26	Ma–Mc		Gist's Regiment
27	Me–N		A–B
28	O–Q	67	C–G
29	R	68	H–K
30	Sa–Sq	69	L–M
31	St–T	70	N–R
32	U–We	71	S
33	Wh–Y	72	T–Y
	2d Regiment	73	Grayson's Regiment
34	2d Regiment, Light Dragoons		A–F
	A–E	74	G–L
35	F–O	75	M–R
36	P–Y	76	S–Y
37	3d Regiment, Artillery	77	Gridley's and Knox's Regiment, Artillery
	A–B		Hartley's Regiment
38	C–D	78	Hazen's Regiment
39	E–Hi		A–Bi
40	Ho–L	79	Bl–By
41	M–P	80	C
42	Q–S	81	D
43	T–Y	82	E–F
	3d Regiment	83	G
	3d Regiment, Light Dragoons	84	H
44	4th Regiment, Artillery	85	I–K
	A–J	86	L
45	K–Y	87	Ma–Mc
46	4th Regiment	88	Me–O
	4th Regiment, Light Dragoons	89	P–R
	A–E	90	S
47	F–M	91	T–Z
48	N–Z	92	Henley's Regiment
49	5th Regiment	93	Lee's Legion
	6th Regiment	94	Lee's Regiment
	7th Regiment		Livingston's Battalion
50	8th Regiment		A–B
	9th Regiment	95	C–F
	10th Regiment	96	G–L
51	11th Regiment	97	M–R
	12th Regiment	98	S–Z
52	13th Regiment	99	Malcom's Regiment
	14th Regiment		A–H
53	15th Regiment	100	I–Y
54	16th Regiment	101	Morgan's Rifle Regiment
	17th Regiment		A–F
	18th Regiment	102	G–Mc
55	19th Regiment	103	Me–Y
56	20th Regiment	104	Patton's Regiment

Roll	Description
	A–E
105	F–N
106	O–Y
107	Count Pulaski's Legion
	A–M
108	N–Z
	Rawlings' Regiment
109	Sherburne's Regiment
	A–B
110	C–D
111	E–G
112	H–Mc
113	Me–Se
114	Sh–W
115	Spencer's Regiment
	A–Bo
116	Br–Cl
117	Co–D
118	E–G
119	H
120	J–L
121	Ma–Mc
122	Me–N
123	O–Ri
124	Ro–Sm
125	Sn–U
126	V–Y
127	Steven's Corps, Artillery
	A–K
128	L–Z
129	Thruston's Regiment
	Warner's Regiment
	A–H
130	J–Y
131	Corps of Artificers
	Corps of Engineers
132	Corps of Invalids
	Corps of Sappers and Miners
133	German Battalion
	A–Ba
134	Be–By
135	C–D
136	E–F
137	G–Ha
138	He–J
139	K
140	L–Ma
141	Mc–My
142	N–R
143	Sa–Sm
144	Sn–V
145	W–Z
146	Clark's Company, Artillery
	Jones' Company, Artillery
	Lee's Independent Company
	Captain Menard's Company, Canadian Volunteers
	Captain Montour's Company of Delaware Indians
147	Patten's Company, Artillery Artificers
	Randall's Company, Artillery
	Von Heer's Independent Troop
148	Independent Companies of Artificers, Carpenters, and Bakers

Roll	Description
	Artificers and Others Employed by Brig. Gen. James Clinton at Forts Constitution and Montgomery on Hudson River, Aug. 1–Dec. 1, 1776
	Artillery
149	Bateaumen
	Commander In Chief's Guard
150	A–D
151	E–J
152	K–R
153	S–Y
	Major General Sullivan's Life Guard
	Men Mustered by Colonel Ellis for New Hampshire Regiments, Continental Troops
154	Miscellaneous
	A–C
155	D–H
156	I–P
157	Q–Z
Connecticut:	
158	1st Regiment
	Ab–Am
159	An–Ba
160	Be–Bi
161	Bl–Bu
162	Ca–Ci
163	Cl–Con
164	Coo–Cu
165	Da–Di
166	Do–Dy
167	E–Fe
168	Fi–Fu
169	Ga–Go
170	Gr–Har
171	Har–He
172	Hi–Hy
173	I–La
174	Le–Ly
175	Ma–Me
176	Mi–My
177	Na–Pa
178	Pe–Pl
179	Po–Q
180	Ra–Ri
181	Ro–Ry
182	Sa–Sl
183	Sm–Sq
184	St–To
185	Tr–Wa
186	We–Wi
187	Wo–Y
	1st Regiment, Forces
188	2d Regiment
	Aa–Al
189	Am–Ba
190	Be–Bo
191	Br–By
192	Ca–Cl
193	Co–De
194	Di–E
195	F
196	G
197	Ha–He
198	Hi–Hy
199	I–K
200	L–Mc

Roll	Description
201	Me–N
202	O–Pe
203	Ph–Q
204	R
205	Sa–So
206	Sp–Sy
207	T–V
208	Wa–We
209	Wh–Y
210	2d Regiment (1776), Militia
	2d (Wyllys') Regiment
211	3d Regiment
	Ab–Ac
212	Ad–Av
213	Ba–Be
214	Bi–Br
215	Bu
216	Ca–Ch
217	Cl–Com
218	Con–Cu
219	D
220	E–Fe
221	Fi–Fu
222	Ga–Go
223	Gr–Han
224	Har–He
225	Hi–Hy
226	I–J
227	K–Li
228	Lo–Mc
229	Me–My
230	N–Pa
231	Pe–Pu
232	Ra–Ri
233	Ro–Ry
234	Sa–Sl
235	Sm–Sy
236	T–U
237	V–We
238	Wh–Wo
239	Wr–Z
	3d (Ely's) Regiment, Militia
	3d (Putnam's) Regiment
	3d (Starr's) Regiment, Light Horse
240	4th Regiment
	A
241	Ba–Bo
242	Br–Ch
243	Ci–Cy
244	D–E
245	F
246	G–Ha
247	He–I
248	J–L
249	M–O
250	P–Q
251	R–Se
252	Sh–Sy
253	T–Wa
254	We–Z
	4th (Backus') Regiment, Light Horse
	4th (Hinman's) Regiment
255	5th Regiment
	Ab–Af
256	Al–Ba

Roll	Description
257	Be–Bo
258	Br–By
259	Ca–Cl
260	Co–Cr
261	Cu–Dy
262	E–Fo
263	Fr–Go
264	Gr–Ha
265	He–Ho
266	Hu–Ji
267	Jo–K
268	L
269	Ma–Me
270	Mi–N
271	O–Pa
272	Pe–Pu
273	Ra–Ri
274	Ro–Ry
275	Sa–Sk
276	Sl–Sq
277	St–Ta
278	Te–Ty
279	U–Wa
280	We–Wh
281	Wi
282	Wo–Z
	5th Regiment (1775)
	5th Regiment (1776)
	5th Regiment, Light Horse
	5th Regiment, Militia
283	6th Regiment
	A
284	Ba
285	Be–Bo
286	Br–By
287	Ca–Cl
288	Co–Cy
289	D–E
290	F
291	G
292	Ha–Hi
293	Ho–Ji
294	Jo–Le
295	Li–Ma
296	Mc–Me
297	Mi–My
298	N–O
299	Pa–Po
300	Pr–R
301	Sa–So
302	Sp–Sw
303	Ta–Ty
304	V–Wh
305	Wi–Z
	Parson's (6th) Regiment
306	7th Regiment
	Aa–Am
307	An–Ban
308	Bar–Baw
309	Be–Bi
310	Bl–Bu
311	Ca–Cl
312	Co–Cu
313	D
314	E–F

Roll	Description	Roll	Description
315	G	363	Bradley's Regiment
316	Ha		Bull's Regiment, Light Dragoons, Militia
317	He–Ho		Burrall's Regiment
318	Hu–K	364	Canfield's Regiment, Militia
319	L–Me		Chapman's Regiment of Foot, Militia
320	Mi–O		Chester's Regiment
321	P		Cook's Regiment, Militia
322	R–Se	365	John Douglas' Regiment
323	Sh–Sq		William Douglas' Regiment
324	St–Sy	366	Elmore's Battalion
325	Ta–Tr		Ely's Regiment
326	Tu–Wh	367	Enos' Regiment, State Troops
327	Wi–Y	368	Enos' Regiment (1776-77)
	7th Regiment (1775)		Enos' Regiment (1777)
	7th Regiment (1776)		Gallup's Regiment
328	8th Regiment		Gay's Regiment
	A	369	Hooker's Regiment
329	Ba–Be		Johnson's Regiment
330	Bi–By	370	Latimer's Regiment, Militia
331	Ca–Cl		Lewis' Regiment, Militia
332	Co–Di	371	Mason's Regiment, Militia
333	Do–E		McClellan's Regiment
334	F		McClellan's Regiment (1777)
335	G		McClellan's Regiment, State Troops
336	Ha–Hi		Mead's Regiment, Militia
337	Ho–Hy		Moseley's Detachment, Militia
338	I–K		Mott's Regiment, Militia
339	L	372	Newberry's Regiment, Militia
340	Ma–Me		Parson's Regiment, Militia
341	Mi–O		Porter's Regiment, Militia
342	Pa–Po		Sage's Regiment
343	Pr–R		Selden's Regiment
344	Sa–Si	373	Seymour's Regiment, Militia, Light Dragoons
345	Sk–Sw		Silliman's Regiment
346	T–V		Skinner's Regiment of Light Horse, Militia
347	Wa–Wh		Swift's Regiment
348	Wi–Y		A–G
	8th Regiment (1775)	374	H–Y
	8th Regiment, Militia	375	Tallcott's Regiment
349	9th Regiment		Thomson's Regiment
	A–Ba		Tyler's Regiment
350	Be–Bu		Ward's Regiment
351	Ca–Di		Waterbury's Regiment
352	Do–G	376	J. Wells' Regiment, Militia
353	Ha–K		Levi Wells' Regiment
354	L–M		Whiting's Regiment, Militia
355	N–Ri		Wolcott's Regiment
356	Ro–S	377	Averill's Company
357	T–Wh		Begelow's Company of Artillery
358	Wi–Wy		Bennett's Company
	9th Regiment, Militia		Bixby's Company
	A–F		Bradley's Company of Matrosses
359	G–O		Bristol's Company, Militia
360	P–Y		Sergeant James Davidson's Guard
361	10th Regiment, Militia		Durkee's Company of Matrosses
	12th Regiment, Militia		Fitch's Independent Company, Volunteers
	13th Regiment, Militia		Gallup's Company
	16th Regiment, Militia		Hand's Company, Militia
	18th Regiment, Militia		Capt. Thomas Lawson's Company, Militia
362	20th Regiment, Militia		Lee's Company
	21st Regiment, Militia		Leffingwell's Company
	22d Regiment, Militia (Chapman's Regiment)		Capt. Elip't Lockwood's Company of Coast Guards
	25th Regiment (1776)		Isaac Lockwood's Company of Sea Coast Guards
	25th Regiment, Militia	378	Markham's Company, Militia
	Beebe's Regiment, State Troops		Mason's Company
	Belding's Regiment, Militia		Mather's Company
			Mott's Company
			Reed's Company, Militia

Roll	Description
	Robinson's Company
	Capt. Israel Seymour's Company
	Sheldon's Company
	Shipman's Company
	Capt. Richard Smith's Company
	Thomson's Company
379	Vaill's Company of Guards
	Van Deursen's Company of State Guards
	Wolcott's Company
	Field, Commissioned and Staff Officers of the Connecticut Line
	Company of Matrosses
	Corps of Sappers and Miners
	Teamsters
	Connecticut

Delaware:

Roll	Description
380	1st Battalion (New Castle County)
	2d Battalion, Militia
	2d Regiment, Militia
	2d Regiment (New Castle County), Militia
	A–G
381	H–W
	7th Battalion, Militia
	Hall's Regiment
382	A–Br
383	Bu–C
384	D–E
385	F–G
386	Ha–Hi
387	Ho–K
388	L–Ma
389	Mc–Mi
390	Mo–O
391	P–R
392	S–T
393	V–Y
394	Haslet's Regiment
	Battalion Flying Camp
395	Captain Latimer's Independent Company
	Captain William Peery's Independent Company
	Delaware

Georgia:

Roll	Description
396	1st Battalion
	2d Battalion
	3d Battalion
	4th Battalion
	Georgia Battalion
	Bickham's Company, Georgia Militia
	Captain Samuel Scott's Company

Maryland:

Roll	Description
397	1st Regiment
	A–L
398	M–Y
	1st Regiment, Flying Camp
399	2d Regiment
	A–G
400	H–R
401	S–Y
	3d Regiment
	A–B
402	C–K
403	L–Y
404	4th Regiment
405	5th Regiment
406	6th Regiment
407	7th Regiment
408	34th Battalion, Militia

Roll	Description
	37th Battalion, Militia
	Ewing's Regiment, Flying Camp
	Griffith's Regiment, Flying Camp
	Lansdale's Detachment
	Marbury's Detachment
	Rawling's Regiment
	Richardson's Regiment, Flying Camp
	German Regiment
	Regiment Extraordinary
	2d and 3d Companies, Artillery
	Gale's Company, Artillery
	Ott's Company, Militia
	Sarer's Company (Washington County), Militia
409	Maryland
	A–K
410	L–Y

Massachusetts:

Roll	Description
411	1st Regiment
	A–C
412	D–G
413	H–L
414	M–Q
415	R–T
416	U–Y
	1st Regiment, Guards
	1st Regiment, Militia
	1st Regiment (Lincoln County), Militia
417	2d Regiment
	A–C
418	D–J
419	K–R
420	S–Y
421	3d Regiment
	A–Cl
422	Co–G
423	H–M
424	N–S
425	T–W
	3d Regiment, Militia
426	4th Regiment
	A–M
427	N–Y
	4th Regiment, Militia
	4th Regiment (1777), Militia
428	5th Regiment
	A–E
429	F–O
430	P–Y
	5th Regiment (1783)
431	6th Regiment
	A–D
432	E–K
433	L–R
434	S–Y
435	7th Regiment
	A–G
436	H–R
437	S–Y
	8th Regiment
	A–C
438	D–L
439	M–Y
440	9th Regiment
	A–L
441	M–Z
442	10th Regiment
	A–L

Roll	Description
443	M–Z
	11th Regiment
444	12th Regiment
	A–C
445	D–G
446	H–M
447	N–R
448	S–Y
449	13th Regiment
	A–K
450	L–W
451	15th Regiment
	A–B
452	C–E
453	F–Hi
454	Ho–L
455	M–P
456	Q–S
457	T–Y
458	16th Regiment
	A–B
459	C–D
460	E–G
461	H–J
462	K–Mc
463	Me–P
464	R–S
465	T–Z
466	18th Regiment
	28th (Sargent's) Regiment
	31st (Phinney's) Regiment
	Bailey's Regiment
	Brewer's Regiment Artificers
	David Brewer's Regiment
	Jonathan Brewer's Regiment
	Bridges' Regiment
	Brooks' Regiment
	Bullard's Regiment
467	Major Cady's Detachment
	Carpenter's Regiment, Militia
	Cary's Regiment
	Simeon Cary's Regiment
	Cogswell's Regiment
468	Conver's Regiment
	Cotton's Regiment
	Cushing's Regiment
	Davis' Regiment, Militia
	Denny's Command, Militia
	Dike's Regiment
	Doolittle's Regiment
	Fellows' Regiment
	French's Regiment
	Frye's Regiment
469	Gardiner's Regiment
	Jacob Gerrish's Regiment
	Samuel Gerrish's Regiment
	Glover's Regiment
	Goodrich's Command, Militia
470	Hathaway's Regiment
	Heath's Regiment
	Holman's Regiment
	Hyde's Detachment, Militia
	Jacob's Regiment
	Keyes' Regiment
	Learned's Regiment
	Leonard's Regiment, Militia
	Little's Regiment
471	Mansfield's Regiment

Roll	Description
	Murray's Regiment
	Nixon's Regiment
	Paterson's Regiment
	Perce's Regiment
	Phinney's (31st) Regiment
	Poor's Regiment
472	Pope's Regiment
	Porter's Regiment
	Prescott's Regiment
	Prime's Regiment
	Putnam's Regiment
	Rand's Regiment
	Read's Regiment, Militia
	Reed's Regiment
	Robinson's Regiment
473	Scammon's Regiment
	Simonds' Detachment, Militia
	Smith's Regiment
	Sparhawk's Regiment, Militia
	Stearns' Regiment
	Thomas' Regiment
	Titcomb's Regiment
	Turner's Regiment
	Wade's Regiment
	Walker's Regiment
	Artemas Ward's Regiment, Militia
	Whitcomb's Regiment
	Whitney's Regiment
	George Williams' Regiment
	Samuel Williams' Regiment
474	Wood's Regiment, Militia
475	Woodbridge's Regiment
	Burt's Company, Guards, Militia
	Carpenter's Company
	Cowell's Company
	Crandon's Company
	Captain Elijah Demming's Company
	Durfee's Company
	Captain Pelatiah Eddy's Company
	Captain Moses French's Company
	Captain Ebenezer Gore's Company
	Captain Abraham Gould's Company
476	Captain James Leach's Company, Matrosses
	Captain Simeon Leach's Company
	Molten's Company
	Perry's Company, Minute Men
	Captain Jonathan Poor's Company, Militia
	Richardson's Company, Militia
	Captain Robinson's Company, Militia
	Captain Nathan Smith's Company
	Captain Phinehas Stearns' Company
	Captain Lemuel Stewart's Company
	Captain Wood's Company
	Massachusetts
	A–C
477	D–L
478	M–Z

New Hampshire:

Roll	Description
479	1st Battalion
	A–K
480	L–Y
481	1st Regiment
	A
482	Ba–Br
483	Bu–Ci
484	Cl–Cu
485	D
486	E–F
487	G

Roll	Description
488	Ha–Hi
489	Ho–J
490	K–L
491	Ma–Mc
492	Me–O
493	P–Q
494	R
495	Sa–Sl
496	Sm–Sy
497	T–We
498	Wh–Y
499	1st Regiment, Militia
	1st (Stark's) Regiment
	A–J
500	K–Y
501	2d Regiment
	A
502	Ba–Bo
503	Br–Bu
504	Ca–Cl
505	Co–Cu
506	D
507	E–F
508	G
509	Ha–He
510	Hi–I
511	J–K
512	L
513	Ma–Me
514	Mi–N
515	O–Q
516	R
517	Sa–Sh
518	Si–Sw
519	T–Wa
520	We–Z
521	2d (Poor's) Regiment
	A–L
522	M–Y
523	2d (Tash's) Regiment
524	3d Regiment
	A–B
525	C
526	D–F
527	G–H
528	I–M
529	N–Q
530	R–S
531	T–Y
	7th Regiment, Militia
	10th Regiment, Militia
	12th Regiment
	13th Regiment
532	Ashley's Regiment, Militia
533	Baldwin's Regiment
534	Bartlet's Regiment
535	Bedel's Regiment
	A–K
536	L–Y
537	Bell's Regiment
	Bellows, Jr.'s Regiment, Militia
	Major John Brown's Detachment of Militia, New Hampshire, Vermont, and Massachusetts
538	Chase's Regiment, Militia
539	Dame's Regiment
	Drake's Regiment, Militia

Roll	Description
	Evan's Regiment
	A–D
540	E–Z
541	Gale's Regiment
	Gerrish's Regiment, Volunteers
	Gilman's Regiment, Militia
	A–F
542	G–Y
543	Hale's Regiment, Militia
544	Hobart's Regiment, Militia
545	Kelley's Regiment
546	Lovewell's Regiment
	McClary's Regiment, Militia
	Mooney's Regiment
547	Moore's Regiment
	Morey's Regiment, Militia
	Moulton's Regiment, Militia
	Nichols' Regiment, Militia
	A–B
548	C–L
549	M–Y
550	Peabody's Regiment, State Troops
551	Reed's Regiment
552	Reynold's Regiment, Militia
	Scott's Battalion
	Senter's Regiment
	A–D
553	E–Y
	Stickney's Regiment, Militia
554	A–G
555	H–Y
556	Waldron's Regiment
	Webster's Regiment
	Welch's Regiment
	Wingate's Regiment
	A–K
557	L–Y
	Wingate's Regiment, Volunteers
	Wyman's Regiment
	A–C
558	D–Y
559	Atkinson's Company
	Baker's Company, Volunteers
	Berry's Company
	Lieutenant Bowers' Command
	Lieutenant Bragdon's Party
	Captain Butler's Company
	Captain Calef's Company
	Captain Chesley's Company
	Captain Cilley's Company
	Captain Clark's Company
	Captain Clifford's Company
	Captain Coffin's Company
	Collins' Company, Volunteers
	Captain William Cooper's Independent Company
	Captain Copps' Company
	Captain Robert Crawford's Company
560	Captain Daniels' Company
	Captain Ebenezer Dearing's Command
	Captain William Dearing's Carpenters
	Captain Dow's Company
	Lieutenant Dow's Command
	Eames' Company of Rangers
	Captain Elkins' Company
	Captain Emerson's Company
	Finlay's Company, Volunteers
	Captain Follett's Artillerymen
	Captain Ford's Company

Roll	Description
	Lieutenant French's Command
	Captain French's Company
561	Captain Gage's Company
	Giles' Company, Volunteers
	Haven's Company
	Hayes' Company
	Heald's Company
	Heath's Scouting Party
	Captain James Hill's Company
	Captain John Hill's Company
	Captain Hobbs' Company
	Captain Caleb Hodgdon's Company
	Captain Stephen Hodgdon's Company
	Lieutenant Houston's Command, Militia
	Hutchins' Company, Militia
	Hutchins' Company, Volunteers
	Hezekiah Hutchins' Company
	Sergeant Ladd's Command
	Captain Langdon's Company
	Captain Littlefield's Company
	Captain McGlaughlan's Command
	Captain McIntyre's Company
	Captain Mellin's Company
562	Captain Osborne's Company
	Captain Parker's Company
	Lieutenant Parr's Company
	Captain Parsons' Company
	Peabody's Company, Militia
	Captain Perkins' Command (Train of Artillery)
	Captain Philbrick's Company, Militia
	Lieutenant Samuel Piper's Company
	Captain Place's Company
	Captain Rawlings' Company
	Russell's Company, Rangers
	Captain Salter's Company, Artillery
	Captain Sias' Company
	Simpson's Ranging Company
	Captain Sloan's Company
	Smith's Company, Militia
	Smith's Company, Rangers
	Captain Jacob Smith's Company
	Lieutenant Stearns' Company
563	Thornton's Company
	Townes' Company
	Waldron's Company
	David Webster's Company (1776)
	David Webster's Company (1777)
	Jacob Webster's Company
	Webster's Company, Rangers
	Wiggins' Company
	Woodward's Company, Rangers
	Yeaton's Company
	Field Artillery Company
	Guard
564	Independent Rangers
	Scouts
	General Whipple and Staff
	New Hampshire
	A–B
565	C–F
566	G
567	H–L
568	M–Q
569	R–S
570	T–Y

New Jersey:

Roll	Description
571	1st Battalion (Somerset County)
	1st Regiment
	A
572	Ba–Bl

Roll	Description
573	Bo–By
574	Ca–Cl
575	Co–Cy
576	D
577	E–F
578	G
579	Ha
580	He–Hy
581	I–K
582	L
583	Ma–Mc
584	Me–My
585	N–O
586	P–Q
587	R
588	Sa–Sn
589	So–Sy
590	T
591	U–Wh
592	Wi–Z
593	1st Regiment (Bergen County)
	1st Regiment (Essex Militia)
	1st Regiment (Monmouth Militia)
594	2d Battalion
	2d Battalion (Hunterdon Militia)
595	2d Battalion (Middlesex)
	2d Battalion (Somerset)
596	2d Regiment
	A–B
597	Be–Br
598	Bu–Ch
599	Cl–Cy
600	D
601	E–Fe
602	Fi–Fu
603	G
604	H
605	I–K
606	L
607	Ma–Mc
608	Me–N
609	O–Pe
610	Pf–R
611	Sa–So
612	Sp–T
613	U–We
614	Wh–Z
615	3d Battalion (Gloucester Militia)
	3d Battalion (Middlesex Militia)
	3d Regiment
	A–Ba
616	Be–Bo
617	Br–Bu
618	Ca–Cu
619	D–E
620	F–G
621	H
622	I–K
623	L–Mc
624	Me–O
625	P–R
626	S
627	T–Z
628	4th Regiment
	A–B

Roll	Description
629	C
630	D–E
631	F–G
632	H
633	I–L
634	M
635	N–Q
636	R–Sc
637	Se–Sw
638	T–Y
639	Cumming's Battalion
	Dayton's Battalion
	A–K
640	L–Y
	David Forman's Regiment, Militia
	Samuel Forman's Regiment, Militia
641	Frelinghuysen's Battalion, Militia
	Hankinson's Regiment, Militia
	Holme's Battalion, Militia
	Martin's Regiment, Militia
	Newcomb's Regiment
642	Ogden's Regiment
643	Phillips' Regiment
	Phillips' Regiment, Militia
	Shreve's Battalion (Burlington Militia)
	Seely's Regiment
	Summers' Battalion
	Thomas' Battalion
	Van Cortlandt's Battalion, Militia
	Van Cortlandt's Regiment (1776)
	Eastern Battalion (Morris County)
644	Bonnel's Company
	Crane's Troop of Horse
	Huddy's Company, State Troops
	Lindsly's Company of Artificers
	Nixon's Company of Horse
	Outwater's Company, State Troops
	Asher F. Randolph's Company
	Squier's Company
	Walton's Company
	Wolverton's Company
	Light Horse Company (Elizabethtown)
645	New Jersey
	A–J
646	K–Y
New York:	
647	1st Battalion, Independent Companies
	1st Regiment
	A
648	Ba–Bl
649	Bo–By
650	Ca–Cl
651	Co–Cy
652	D
653	E–F
654	G
655	Ha–Hi
656	Ho–J
657	K–Le
658	Li–Ma
659	Mc
660	Me–My
661	N–O
662	P–Q
663	R
664	Sa–Sl
665	Sm–Sy

Roll	Description
666	T–U
667	V
668	Wa–Wh
669	Wi–Z
670	1st Regiment, New York Levies (1780)
671	2d Battalion (Col. Wempell), Militia
	A–O
672	P–Y
673	2d Regiment
	A
674	Ba–Bl
675	Bo–By
676	Ca–Cn
677	Co
678	Cr–Da
679	De–Dy
680	E–F
681	G
682	Ha–Hi
683	Ho–I
684	Ja–K
685	L
686	Ma–Mc
687	Me–My
688	N–O
689	P
690	Q–R
691	Sa–Si
692	Sk–Sq
693	St–To
694	Tr–V
695	Wa–Wh
696	Wi–Z
	2d Regiment (November 1776)
	2d Regiment, New York Levies (1776)
697	3d Regiment
	A–Br
698	Bu–D
699	E–G
700	Ha–K
701	L–M
702	N–Sh
703	Si–V
704	W–Z
705	3d Regiment (1776)
	3d Regiment, New York Levies
706	4th Regiment
	A–B
707	C
708	D–F
709	G–H
710	I–L
711	M
712	N–R
713	S
714	T–V
715	W–Z
716	4th Regiment (1776–81), Militia
	Humphrey's (4th) Regiment, Militia
717	5th Regiment
	A–B
718	C
719	D–F
720	G–H
721	I–L

Roll	Description
722	M–O
723	P–R
724	S
725	T–V
726	W–Y
727	Allison's Regiment, Militia
	Bellinger's Regiment, Militia
728	Benedict's Regiment of Associated Exempts, Militia
	Brinckerhoff's Regiment, Militia
	A–L
729	M–Z
	Budd's Regiment
730	Campbell's Battalion, Militia
	Cantine's Regiment, Militia
731	Church's Regiment
	Clyde's Regiment
732	Cooper's Regiment, Militia
733	Crane's Regiment, Militia
	Cuyler's Regiment, Militia
734	Joseph Drake's Regiment, Militia
	Samuel Drake's Regiment
735	DuBoy's Regiment, New York Levies
	Field's Regiment (Dutchess County), Militia
	Fish's Regiment, Militia
	Fisher's Regiment, Militia
	A–D
736	E–Y
	Freer's Regiment, Militia
737	Graham's Regiment, Militia
	A–P
738	Q–Y
	Hamman's Regiment, Militia
739	Hardenbergh's Regiment, Militia
	Harper's Regiment
740	Hasbrouch's Regiment, Militia
	A–L
741	M–Y
742	Hathorn's Regiment, Militia
743	Hay's Regiment, Militia
744	Hopkin's Regiment, Militia
	Humfrey's Regiment, Militia
745	Janson's Regiment, Militia
	A–Mc
746	Me–Y
747	Klock's Regiment, Militia
	A–K
748	L–Z
749	Lansing, Jr.'s Regiment, Militia
	Livingston's Regiment, Militia
750	Ludington's Regiment, Militia
751	McClaughry's Regiment, Militia
752	McCrea's Regiment, New York Levies
	Sergeant Mills' Detachment
	Nicholl's Regiment, New York Levies
	Nicholson's Regiment
	Palmer's Regiment, Militia
	Albert Pawling's Regiment, Militia
	A–J
753	K–Y
754	Levi Pawling's Regiment
755	Platt's Regiment of Associated Exempts
	Quackenbos' Regiment (Albany County), Militia
	Rudd's Detachment
	Philip Schuyler's Regiment, Militia
756	Stephen Schuyler's Regiment, Militia
	Snyder's Regiment (Ulster County Militia)
	A–E

Roll	Description
757	F–Y
	Captain Strait's Detachment, Militia
758	Jacobus Swartwout's Regiment (1776)
	Jacobus Swartwout's Regiment (1777)
759	Thomas' Regiment, Militia
760	Van Alstine's Regiment (Albany County Militia)
	Van Bergen's Regiment (Albany County Militia)
	Van Brunt's Regiment, Militia
	Van Cortlandt's Regiment, Militia
761	G. Vanden Bergh's Regiment (Albany Militia)
	Vanderburgh's Regiment, Militia
	Van Ness' Regiment
762	Van Rensselaer's Regiment
	A–R
763	S–Y
	Henry K. Van Rensselaer's Regiment (Albany County), Militia
	A–K
764	L–Z
	Robert Van Rensselaer's Regiment, Militia
765	Van Schaick's Battalion
766	Van Schoonhoven's Regiment (Albany County), Militia
767	Van Veghten's Regiment, Militia
768	Van Woert's Regiment, Militia
769	Vrooman's Regiment (Albany County), Militia
770	Webster's Regiment, Militia
771	Weissenfels' Regiment, New York Levies
	A–K
772	L–Y
773	Whiting's Regiment, Militia
	Willett's Regiment
	A–I
774	J–Z
775	Williams' Regiment, Militia
	Woodhull's Regiment
	Wynkoop's Regiment
	Yates' Regiment, Militia
	A–F
776	G–Y
777	Captain Baldwin's Company, Rangers
	Lieutenant Bowers' Company
	Bradt's Company, Rangers
	Captain James Cannon's Recruits
	Clark's Company, State Troops
	Captain Cooper's Company, Rangers
	Elmandorph's Company
	Fondey's Party, Militia
	Getman's Company, Rangers (2d Company, Tryon County)
	Captain Golden's Company, Militia
	Graham's Company, State Troops
	Hardenbergh's Company, State Troops
	Horton's Company, Guards
	Lamb's Company, Artillery
778	Captain Mills' Company, Guards
	Captain Myrick's Company, Rangers
	Reilay's Company, Rangers
	Stevenson's Company, Guards
	Van Gaasbeck's Company
	Wheelock's Command
	Winn's Company, Rangers
	Wood's Company of Exempt Militia
	Lieutenant Wood's Hired Guard
	Guards, Militia
	Men Received from Westchester County, New York, by Captain Richard Sackett
	New York
	A–C

Roll	Description
779	D–M
780	N–Z

North Carolina:

Roll	Description
781	1st Regiment
782	1st Regiment, Militia
	2d Regiment
	A–O
783	P–Y
	2d Regiment, Militia
	3d Regiment
	4th Regiment
	5th Regiment
784	6th Regiment
	7th Regiment
	8th Regiment
	9th Regiment
	10th Regiment
785	Collier's Regiment, Militia
	Graham's Regiment (Tryon County)
	Seawell's Regiment, Militia
	4th Company, North Carolina Regiment
	Bynum's Company, Militia
	Captain James Houston's Company, Rangers
	Kingsbury's Company, Artillery
	Colonel Francis Lock's Command
	Lieutenant Colonel Lytle's Command (Caswell County)
	Captain Charles Polk's Company, Militia
	Porter's Company
	Vernon's Company
	Light Dragoons
786	North Carolina

Pennsylvania:

Roll	Description
787	1st Battalion
	1st Battalion (Bedford County)
	1st Battalion (Chester County Militia)
	1st Battalion (Cumberland County Militia)
	1st Battalion (Philadelphia County)
	1st Battalion (Philadelphia County Militia)
	1st Battalion, Riflemen (Philadelphia County Militia)
	1st Battalion (Westmoreland County Militia)
	1st Battalion Flying Camp (Colonel Moor)
	1st Regiment
	A–G
788	H–N
789	O–Z
	1st Regiment (1775)
	1st Regiment Flying Camp (Lancaster County)
	1st Regiment Flying Camp (Colonel William Montgomery)
790	2d Battalion (Cumberland County Militia)
	2d (Davis') Battalion (Cumberland County Militia)
	2d Battalion, Riflemen (Lancaster County)
	2d Battalion (Northumberland County)
	2d Battalion (Philadelphia County)
	2d Battalion (Westmoreland County)
	2d Regiment
	A–B
791	C–E
792	F–H
793	I–L
794	M
795	N–R
796	S
797	T–Y
	2d Regiment Flying Camp
798	3d Battalion (Chester County Militia)

Roll	Description
	3d Battalion (Cumberland County Militia)
	3d Battalion (Lancaster County Militia)
	3d Battalion (Northumberland County Militia)
799	3d Regiment (1776)
800	3d Regiment
	A–C
801	D–G
802	H–L
803	M
804	N–R
805	S–Z
806	4th Battalion (Chester County Militia)
	4th Battalion (Philadelphia County Militia)
	4th Regiment
	A–G
807	H–Z
808	5th Battalion
	5th Battalion (Chester County Militia)
	5th Battalion (Cumberland County Militia)
	5th Battalion (Philadelphia County Militia)
	5th Battalion (York County Militia)
	5th Regiment
	A
809	B
810	C
811	D–E
812	F–G
813	H–I
814	J–K
815	L–Ma
816	McA–McG
817	McH–O
818	P–S
819	T–Z
820	6th Battalion (1776)
	6th Regiment
	A–K
821	L–Z
822	7th Battalion (Cumberland County Militia)
	7th Regiment
	A–F
823	G–L
824	M–P
825	Q–Y
826	8th Battalion (Chester County Militia)
	8th Regiment
827	9th Regiment
	A–E
828	F–L
829	M–P
830	R–Z
831	10th Regiment
	A–K
832	L–Y
833	11th Regiment
	A–M
834	N–Z
	11th Regiment (1779–80)
835	12th Regiment
836	13th Regiment
837	Andrew's Battalion, York Militia
	Atley's Regiment (Musket Battalion)
	Barr's Detachment (Westmoreland Militia)
	Baxter's Battalion (Northampton County)
	Burd's Battalion
	Clottz' Battalion Flying Camp (Lancaster County)

Roll	Description
	Ferreis' Battalion (Lancaster County Militia)
	Gardiner's Battalion
	Gardiner's Regiment, Militia
	Haller's Battalion Flying Camp
	Hart's Battalion (Bucks County)
	Lochry's Battalion
	Matlock's Rifle Battalion
	Peirce's Regiment
838	Schott's Corps
	Colonel Smith's Regiment
	Swope's Regiment Flying Camp
	Watts' Regiment Flying Camp
	German Regiment
	Colonel Samuel Miles' Rifle Regiment
	Black's Company (York County Militia)
	Captain John Boyd's Company of Rangers
	Major Robert Clugage's Command, Volunteers
	Captain Duncan's Company, Volunteers
	Captain George Enslow's Company (Bedford County Militia)
	Captain Andrew Graff's Company
	Hall's Company
	Moorhead's Independent Company
	His Excellency Joseph Reed's Command
	Captain Shaver's Company, Militia
	Captain Spaulding's Company
	Steel's Pennsylvania Independent Company
	Van Etten's Company (Northampton County), Volunteers
839	Troop of Philadelphia Light Horse
	Pennsylvania
	A–H
840	I–Z

Rhode Island:

Roll	Description
841	1st Regiment
	A–B
842	C
843	D–G
844	H–L
845	M–Q
846	R–S
847	T–W
848	2d Battalion (County of Providence), Militia
	2d Regiment
	A
849	B
850	C
851	D–E
852	F–G
853	H
854	I–L
855	M–N
856	O–Q
857	R–Se
858	Sh–Sw
859	T–V
860	W–Y
861	1st and 2d Regiments, Consolidated
	A–C
862	D–H
863	I–Q
864	R–T
865	U–Y
	12th Regiment
	14th Regiment
	15th Regiment, Militia
866	Allen's Detachment (June–December 1783)
	Babcock's Regiment, Militia

Roll	Description
	Colonel Barton's Light Corps
	Brown's Regiment
	Cook's Regiment, Militia
867	Crary's Regiment, State Troops
	A–H
868	I–Y
869	Elliott's Regiment, Artillery
870	Holden's Regiment
	Kimball's Regiment, Militia
	Lippitt's Regiment
	A–B
871	C–Z
872	Mathewson's Regiment
	Miller's Regiment, Militia
	Noyes' Regiment
	Olney's Regiment, Militia
	Peck's Regiment
	Potter's Regiment
873	Talman's Regiment
	Tillinghast's Regiment
	Topham's Regiment, State Troops
	A–B
874	C–H
875	I–Q
876	R–Z
877	Waterman's Regiment
	West's Regiment
	1st Company (Town of Cranston), Militia
	2d Company (Town of Cranston)
	2d Company (Hopkinton)
	3d Company (Town of Smithfield)
	Allen's Company, Militia
	Colonel Jabez Bowen's Command, Militia
	Burllinggame's Company
	Captain Christopher Champlin's Company
	Lieutenant Nathaniel Gould's Company
	Captain Samuel May's Company
	Captain Thayer's Company
	Trask's Company (Town of Smithfield)
878	Waterman's Company
	Whipple's Company (Cumberland Militia)
	Wilbur's Company, Militia
	Captain Timothy Wilmarth's Company
	Barrington Guards
	Pawtuxet Rangers
	Warren Guard
	Rhode Island

South Carolina:

Roll	Description
879	1st Regiment
	A–I
880	J–Y
881	2d Regiment
882	3d Regiment
	A–G
883	H–M
884	N–Y
	4th Regiment, Artillery
885	5th Regiment
886	6th Regiment
887	Casey's Regiment
	Hampton's Regiment, Light Dragoons
	Marshell's Regiment
	Thomson's Regiment
	1st Company
	2d Company
	3d Company
	Butler's Company, Militia
	Captain John Irwin's Company
	Singleton's Troop of Light Horse

Roll	Description
	Captain Michael Watson's Company, Volunteers South Carolina

Vermont:

Roll	Description
888	1st (Bradley's) Regiment, Militia
	3d (Wood's) Regiment, Militia
	6th Regiment, Militia
	7th (Sergeants') Regiment, Militia
	12th (Douty's) Regiment
889	15th (Warren's) Regiment, Militia
890	Abbot's Regiment, Militia
	Ebenezer Allen's Detachment, Militia
891	Ebenezer Allen's Regiment, Militia
	Ira Allen's Regiment, Militia
	A–C
892	D–Y
	Bronson's Detachment, Militia
	Enos' Brigade, Militia
893	Fletcher's Regiment
894	Lieutenant Hall's Corps of Rangers, Militia
	Herrick's Regiment, Militia
895	Lee's Regiment, Militia
	Lyon's Regiment, Militia
	Joel Marsh's Regiment, Militia
	Joseph Marsh's Regiment, Militia
	Mead's Regiment, Militia
896	Olcott's Regiment, Militia
	Robinson's Regiment, Militia
897	Wait's Battalion, Militia
898	Walbridge's Regiment, Militia
	A–P
899	R–Y
900	Captain Wallace's Detachment, Militia
	Warner's Regiment, Militia
	Williams' Regiment, Militia
901	Captain Alger's Company, Militia
	Captain Allen's Company, Militia
	Lieutenant Bailey's Company, Militia
	Captain Bates' Command, Militia
	Captain Bentley's Command, Militia
	Ensign Blanchard's Company, Militia
	Captain Bramble's Company, Militia
	Captain Briggs' Company, Militia
	Captain Brownson's Command
	Captain Burk's and Captain Gilson's Companies, Militia
	Captain Chaffe's Company
	Captain Clark's Company, Militia
	Captain Coffeen's Company, Militia
	Captain Colbe's Company, Militia
	Captain Cottle's Company, Militia
	Ensign Cushman's Command, Militia
	Major Day's Command, Militia
	Captain Dimmick's Company
	Durkee's Company, Militia
	Lieutenant Everest's Company, Rangers, Militia
	Captain Fasset, Jr.'s Independent Company
	Captain Gaige's Command
	Captain Gilbert's Company, Militia
	Captain Green's Company, Militia
	Captain Hawkins' Company of Minute Men, Militia
	Captain Hickok's Company, Militia
	Ensign Hoar's Company, Militia
	Captain Hodges' Company, Militia
	Hoisington's Command
	Lieutenant Holmes' Company, Militia
	Captain Howe's Company of Horse
	Captain Hunkins' Command, Militia
	Captain Hutchins' Independent Company, Militia

Roll	Description
902	Captain Macclure's Company, Militia
	Captain Marsh's Employees
	Captain Marston's Company, Militia
	Captain Mattison's Company, Militia
	Captain Mirrick's Company, Militia
	Captain Moseley's Company, Militia
	Lieutenant Moss' Command
	Captain Nelson's Company, Militia
	Captain Ebenezer Parkhurst's Company, Militia
	Captain Joseph Parkhurst's Company, Militia
	Ensign Partridge's Command, Militia
	Lieutenant Colonel Pearl's Command
	Lieutenant Post's Company, Militia
	Lieutenant Roberts' Command
	Captain Robinson's Company, Militia
903	Captain Safford's Company, Militia
	Captain Salsbury's Company, Militia
	Lieutenant Samson's Company, Militia
	Captain Sawyer's Company, Militia
	Major Smith's Command
	Captain Nathan Smith's Command (1777–78), Militia
	Major Nathan Smith's Command (1779)
	Lieutenant Asahel Smith's Company, Militia
	Captain Samuel Smith's Company, Militia
	Lieutenant Soper's Company, Militia
	Lieutenant Spooner's Company, Militia
	Captain Sprague's Company, Militia
	Captain Starr's Company, Militia
	Captain Tyler's Company, Militia
	Captain Upham's Company, Militia
	Captain Wallis' Command
	Captain Wallis' Company, Militia
	Captain Weld's Company, Militia
	Lieutenant White's Company, Militia
	Captain Wolcott's Company, Militia
	Governor Chittenden's Life Guard, Militia
	Scouts, Militia
904	Vermont

Virginia:

Roll	Description
905	1st Regiment
	A–D
906	E–O
907	P–Y
908	1st State Regiment
	A–Ba
909	Be–Bu
910	Ca–Cr
911	D–F
912	G–He
913	Hi–J
914	K–Ma
915	Mc–O
916	P–R
917	S
918	T–Y
919	1st and 10th Regiment
	A–Be
920	Bi–By
921	C
922	D–E
923	F–G
924	H
925	I–K
926	L
927	M
928	N–P
929	Q–Sh

Roll	Description
930	Si–Sy
931	T–V
932	W–Y
933	2d Brigade
	A–B
934	C–Fe
935	Fi–J
936	K–M
937	N–R
938	S–W
939	2d Regiment
	A–B
940	C
941	D–G
942	H–K
943	L–O
944	P–R
945	S–Y
946	2d State Regiment
	A–C
947	D–G
948	H–K
949	L–Q
950	R–W
951	3d Brigade
	3d Regiment (1776)
	3d Regiment
	A–Be
952	Bi–C
953	D–G
954	H–L
955	M–Sc
956	Se–Y
957	3d and 4th Regiment
	A
958	B
959	C
960	D–E
961	F–G
962	H–I
963	J–K
964	L–Ma
965	Mc–Mu
966	N–Q
967	R
968	Sa–St
969	Su–V
970	W–Y
971	3d and 7th Regiment
972	4th Regiment
	A–B
973	C–F
974	G–J
975	K–O
976	P–S
977	T–Y
	4th, 8th, and 12th Regiment
	A–D
978	E–Y
979	5th Regiment
	A–B
980	C–E
981	F–J
982	K–O
983	P–Sp
984	St–Y

Roll	Description
985	5th and 9th Regiment
986	5th and 11th Regiment
	A–Be
987	Bi–By
988	Ca–Co
989	Cr–E
990	F–G
991	H–I
992	J–La
993	Le–Ma
994	Mc–Mu
995	N–P
996	Q–R
997	S
998	T–Wa
999	We–Y
1000	6th Regiment
	A
1001	Ba–Bi
1002	Bl–By
1003	Ca–Cl
1004	Co–Cu
1005	D
1006	E–F
1007	G
1008	Ha–Ho
1009	Hu–J
1010	K–Ma
1011	Mc–My
1012	N–Pe
1013	Ph–R
1014	Sa–Sl
1015	Sm–Sy
1016	T
1017	V–Wh
1018	Wi–Y
1019	7th Regiment
	A
1020	Ba–Bo
1021	Br–By
1022	Ca–Cl
1023	Co–Cu
1024	D
1025	E–F
1026	G
1027	Ha–He
1028	Hi–J
1029	K–L
1030	Ma–Mc
1031	Me–N
1032	O–Q
1033	R
1034	Sa–Sm
1035	So–Sw
1036	T–Wa
1037	We–Y
1038	8th Regiment
	A
1039	Ba–Bo
1040	Br–Ca
1041	Ce–Cy
1042	D
1043	E–F
1044	G
1045	H

Roll	Description
1046	I–K
1047	L–Ma
1048	Mc
1049	Md–Mu
1050	N–P
1051	Q–R
1052	Sa–Sm
1053	Sp–V
1054	W–Y
1055	9th Regiment
	A–B
1056	C–D
1057	E–G
1058	H–K
1059	L–M
1060	N–R
1061	S–T
1062	V–Y
	10th Regiment
	A
1063	B–C
1064	D–H
1065	I–M
1066	N–R
1067	S–Y
1068	11th Regiment
	A–C
1069	D–I
1070	J–O
1071	P–Y
1072	11th and 15th Regiment
	A–J
1073	K–Y
1074	12th Regiment
	A–C
1075	D–K
1076	L–Q
1077	R–Z
1078	13th Regiment
	A–K
1079	L–Z
1080	14th Regiment
	A–D
1081	E–Mc
1082	Me–Y
1083	15th Regiment
	A–F
1084	G–O
1085	P–W
1086	Clark's Illinois Regiment, Virginia State Troops
1087	General Nelson's Corps, Light Dragoons
	Pendleton's Regiment, Militia
	Captain Rogers' Detachment, Militia
	Skilron's Detachment, Militia
	Taylor's Regiment
	Western Battalion, State Troops
	Detachment of the 5th Virginia and Some Other Regiments
	Detachment of Virginians
	Detachment of Virginia and North Carolina Troops
1088	Virginia Battalion
1089	Captain Robert Barnet's Company, Militia
	Captain Thomas Buck's Company, Dunmore County, Militia
	Captain Adam Clement's Company, Militia
	Ensign Colvin's Command, Militia

Roll	Description
	Captain Joshua Conkey's Company, Rangers
	Edmonds' Command, Artillery
	Captain Ford's Company, Militia
	Gaddis' Command (Monongalia Militia)
	Captain Thomas Gaddis' Company, Militia
	Captain Jonathan Hamby's Company, Militia
	Captain Benjamin Harrison's Company, Volunteers
	Captain Heth's Independent Company
	Captain Morgan's Company
	Captain William Nelson's Company, Militia
	Niscwange's Company, Frederick County, Militia
	Captain O'Hara's Independent Company
	Captain Parson's Company, Militia
	Captain Rader's Company, Militia
	Captain John Robert's Company
	Captain Scott's Company
	Captain Scott's Company, Militia
	Lieutenant Smith's Company
	Captain Watkins' Troop of Dragoons
	Frederick County, Militia
1090	Virginia
	A–B
1091	C–E
1092	F–H
1093	I–Mc
1094	Me–P
1095	Q–S
1096	T–Z

Records of Naval Personnel During the Revolutionary War (Record Group 93)

The naval and marine service records of the Revolutionary War are fragmentary. The information on the cards for the compiled military service records was carefully transcribed from lists of American sailors and vessels, payrolls, portage bills, and assignments of pay relating to ships of the Continental Navy and State navies, the frigate *Alliance*, the brigantines *Dartmouth* and *Polly*, the sloops *Independence* and *Montgomery*, the schooner *Putnam*, and the ship *Raleigh*; lists of American prisoners taken by the British ships *Gibralter*, *Hunter*, and *Felicity*; lists of vessels arriving and departing from Tribel's Landing in October 1781; and entries in volume 175 of the numbered record books in the Revolutionary War Manuscript Collection of the War Department Collection of Revolutionary War Records (RG 93), which includes the names of many sailors from New York and Virginia.

Indexes to Compiled Service Records

Index to Compiled Service Records of American Naval Personnel Who Served During the Revolutionary War. M879. 1 roll. DP.

This microfilm publication reproduces a name index to the compiled service records of American naval personnel who served during the Revolutionary War. Each of the approximately 1,000 cards in the index gives the name of a sailor or civilian employee. Sometimes his rank or profession is given, typically as seaman, surgeon, lieutenant, pilot, quartermaster, carpenter, or midshipman. There are cross-references for names that appear in the records under more than one spelling.

The names reproduced in this microfilm publication are duplicated in M860, the general index for Revolutionary War soldiers.

Compiled Service Records

Compiled Service Records of American Naval Personnel and Members of the Departments of the Quartermaster General and the Commissary General of Military Stores Who Served During the Revolutionary War. M880. 4 rolls. DP.

This microfilm publication reproduces the compiled service records of American naval personnel and members of the Departments of the Quartermaster General and Commissary General of Military Stores who served during the Revolutionary War.

The 17 unbound records abstracted for the compiled military service records filed under "Commissary General of Military Stores Department" consist of muster rolls, payrolls, and lists pertaining to Colonel Flower's regiment of artillery artificers. This regiment was composed primarily of civilian and military mechanics who were organized into companies of artificers and stationed at the various posts, forts, and laboratories within the jurisdiction of the Department.

There are cross-references for names that appear in the records under more than one spelling.

Roll	Description
1	Quartermaster General's Department
	Commissary General of Military Stores
	Department
	A–E
2	F–Y
3	Naval Personnel
	A–J
4	K–Y

Records of Volunteer Soldiers Who Served From 1784 Until 1811 (Record Group 94)

The U.S. Army between the end of the Revolutionary War and the beginning of the War of 1812 consisted of a small Regular Army supplemented, when necessary, with State and Territorial militia units called into national service. Volunteers, raised by individual States, Territories, or the National Government to meet specific emergencies, also constituted a part of the military establishment.

Record Group 94 contains the military service records of soldiers who served in the various Indian campaigns, insurrections, and disturbances of the post-Revolutionary period.

Indexes to Compiled Service Records

Index to Compiled Service Records of Volunteer Soldiers Who Served From 1784 to 1811. M694. 9 rolls. 16mm. DP.

This microfilm publication reproduces an alphabetical card index to the compiled service records of volunteer soldiers who served from 1784 to 1811. There are cross-references for names that appear in the records under more than one spelling and for service in more than one unit or organization. The service records are microfilmed on M905.

Roll	Description
1	A–B
2	C
3	D–F
4	G–Hi
5	Ho–L
6	M
7	N–R
8	S–Th
9	Ti–Z

Compiled Service Records

Compiled Service Records of Volunteer Soldiers Who Served From 1784 to 1811. M905. 32 rolls. DP.

This microfilm publication reproduces the compiled service records of volunteer soldiers who served from 1784 to 1811. The records were compiled from original records maintained by the Office of the Adjutant General. They are grouped by category: U.S. organizations, State organizations, or Territorial organizations. Thereunder they are arranged by unit, and thereunder alphabetically by surname. The recoreds are indexed on M694.

Roll	Description
U.S. organizations:	
1	Forerunners of the Regular Army of the United States
	1st American Regiment, 1784
	1st U.S. Regiment (Harmar), 1785–90
	A–L
2	M–Z
	Battalion of Artillery
	Captain Burbeck's Co.
	Captain Savage's Co.
3	U.S. Levies
	1st Regiment (Darke)
	A–L
4	M–Y
5	2d Regiment
	A–L
6	M–Y
	Miscellaneous Units

Roll	Description
	Allison's Regiment, 1790
	Captain Johnston's Corps of Artillery, 1785
	Shorey's Corps of Cherokee Scouts, 1800

State organizations:

Roll	Description
7	Georgia
	1st Regiment, Cavalry, Militia (Washington County)
	1st Regiment, Militia (Greene County)
	1st (Tripletts') Regiment, Militia
	2d (Lamar's) Regiment, Militia
	2d Regiment, 1st Brigade, 3d Division, Militia
	3d Regiment, Militia (Wilkes County)
	4th Regiment, Militia (Wilkes County)
	Camden County Regiment, Militia
8	Georgia Militia
9	Melton's Regiment, Militia
	Stewart's Command, Militia
	Watt's Command, Militia
	Scouts and Spies, Militia
	Kentucky
	6th Regiment, Militia
	9th (Trotter's) Regiment, Militia
	24th (Ramsay's) Regiment, Militia
	Adair's Regiment, Cavalry, Volunteers
10	Captain Baker's Co., Volunteers
	David Caldwell's Battalion, Cavalry, Volunteers
	John Caldwell's Battalion, Mounted Volunteers
11	Conn's Battalion, Mounted Volunteers
	Captain Dyal's Co., Volunteers
	Captain Geiger's Co., Mounted Riflemen
	Captain Gray's Co., Militia
12	Hall's Regiment, Cavalry, Volunteers
	Captain Holmes' Co., Militia
	Captain Hughes' Co., Militia
	Huston's Battalion, Mounted Volunteers
	Kentucky Volunteers (Various Organizations)
	Sergeant McAffry's Guard, Volunteers
	Lieutenant Modrel's Co., Militia
13	Captain Patterson's Co., Militia
	Price's Battalion, Mounted Volunteers
	Russell's Regiment, Cavalry, Volunteers
14	Russell's Battalion, Mounted Volunteers
	Captain Taylor's Co., Militia
	Major Wells' Corps, Mounted Riflemen
	Whitaker's Battalion, Mounted Volunteers
15	Generals and Staffs, Volunteer Militia
	Scouts and Spies
16	New Hampshire
	Captain Bell's Co.
	Captain Salter's Co., Matrosses
	New Jersey
	Captain Shaver's Troop, Light Dragoons, Volunteers
	Ohio
	Buell's Corps, Militia
	Pennsylvania
	Captain Crawford's Co., Rangers, Militia
	Captain Donahe's Detachment, Militia
	McCully's Corps, Riflemen, Militia
	Captain Van Horn's Co., Militia
	Scouts and Spies
17	Virginia
	7th Regiment (2d Battalion), Militia
	19th Regiment (1st Battalion), Militia
	20th Regiment, Militia
	33d (Mayo's) Regiment, Militia
	52d Regiment, Militia
	54th (Sharp's) Regiment, Militia

Roll	Description
18	113th Regiment, Militia
	115th Regiment, Militia
	Captain Armistead's Co., Militia
	Benn's Battalion (Campbell's Regiment), Militia
	Captain Bohannan's Co., Militia
19	Captain Bowden's Troop, Cavalry, Militia
	Captain Butt's Co., Militia
	Captain Coke's Troop, Cavalry, Militia
	Captain Day's Co., Militia
	Captain Dicks' Troop, Cavalry, Militia
	Capt. William Jones' Co., Militia
	Captain Jordan's Co., Militia
	Captain Kelsick's Co., Militia
	Captain Lee's Co., Militia
	Major Lewis' Command
	Captain Maurice's Co., Militia
	Captain Murdaugh's Troop, Cavalry, Militia
	Captain Pollard's Artillery Co., Militia
	Captain Sheppard's Troop, Cavalry, Militia
20	Capt. James Taylor's Co., Militia
	Capt. R. B. Taylor's Troop, Cavalry, Militia
	Capt. R. L. Taylor's Co., Militia
	Captain Veal's Co., Militia
	Virginia Militia (Various Organizations)
	Lieutenant Walter's Co., Militia
	Captain West's Co., Militia
	Lieutenant Woodroof's Co., Militia
	Scouts and Spies

Territorial organizations:

Roll	Description
21	Indian Territory
	1st (Jordan's) Regiment, Militia
	2d (Bartholomew's) Regiment, Militia
	4th (Decker's) Regiment, Militia
22	Lieutenant Berry's Detachment, Mounted Riflemen, Militia
	Captain DuBois' Co., Spies and Guides, Militia
	Indiana Territory Militia (Various Organizations)
	Parke's Squadron, Light Dragoons, Militia
	Captain Robb's Co., Mounted Riflemen, Militia
	Major Robb's Detachment, Militia
	Captain Spencer's Co., Mounted Riflemen, Militia
	General Staff, Militia
23	Illinois Territory
	Captain Alexander's Co., Militia
	Captain Ford's Co., Militia
	Ensign Judy's Detachment, Mounted Infantry, Militia
	Captain Whiteside's Co., Mounted Infantry, Militia
	Ensign Whiteside's Detachment, Mounted Infantry, Militia
	Louisiana Territory
	Captain Buis' Co., Dragoons, Militia
	Captain Ellis' Co., Dragoons, Militia
	Captain Journey's Co., Riflemen, Militia
	Louisiana Territory Militia (Various Organizations)
	Captain Pratte's Co., Militia
	Captain Shrader's Co., Dragoons, Militia
	Lieutenant Valois' Detachment, Dragoons, Militia
	Captain Wherry's Co., Dragoons, Militia
24	Mississippi Territory
	1st (Claiborne's) Regiment, Militia
	2d (Fitzpatrick's) Regiment, Militia
	5th Regiment, Militia

Roll	Description
25	Captain Davidson's Troops, Dragoons, Militia
	Lieutenant Hinds' Troop, Dragoons, Volunteers
	Orleans Territory
	8th Regiment, Militia
	10th Regiment, Militia
	DuBourg's Battalion, Militia
	Territory Northwest of the Ohio River
	Gano's Command, Militia
26	Territory South of the Ohio River
	2d (Scott's) Regiment, Militia (1793)
	Beard's Battalion, Militia
	Captain Beard's Co., Guards
	Ensign Blair's Detachment
	Ensign Brooks' Detachment
	Carter's Regiment, Militia
27	Christian's Regiment, Militia
	Cornet Davidson's Detachment
	Davidson County Rangers
	Doherty's Regiment, Militia
28	Donaldson's Regiment, Militia
	Ford's Regiment, Militia
	Sergeant Gibbon's Detachment
	Corporal Hazlett's Detachment, Mounted Militia
	Corporal Horton's Detachment, Mounted Infantry
	Johnson's Detachment, Mounted Militia
	Kennedy's Regiment, Militia
29	Knox County Regiment, Hamilton District Militia
	Ac–Ew
30	Fa–Ma
31	Mc–Yo
32	Sergeant Lowry's Detachment, Mounted Infantry
	Ore's Regiment, Militia
	Isaac Roberts' Regiment, Militia
	James Robert's Regiment, Militia
	Scott's Regiment, Militia (1794)
	Sumner County Militia
	Lieutenant Walker's Co., Rangers
	Lieutenant Williams, Detachment

Unfiled papers:

Aaron Adams
William Aggie
Thomas Anderson
Henry Anslee
Robert Barr
Stephen Cleaver
Charles Connor
Ebenezer Cummings
Sam R. Davidson
Timothy Demumbroe
John Dohathy
James Dougan
James Graham
Richard H. Greater
James Grimes
Thomas Hickman
Jonas Ingham
Josiah Ingham
Thomas James
Michael Kerrel
Baptiste Latulipe
G. A. Martin
Walter Maxey
James McCoy
Britton McDonald
Florence McGiggen

Roll	Description
	Charles McLean
	William O'Neal
	Francis Oumy
	Hanray Pickel
	John Nelson
	Samuel Philips
	John H. Robinson
	Frederick Simpf
	John Smiley
	Richard Taylor
	Nathaniel Teel
	John Twiggs
	Luke Vories
	James White
	Caleb Worley

Records of Volunteer Soldiers Who Served in the War of 1812 (Record Groups 94 and 407)

When the United States declared war against Great Britain in 1812, Congress authorized the President to increase the size of the Regular Military Establishment, to accept and organize volunteers, to raise units of Rangers and Sea Fencibles, and to create a Flotilla Service. The Ranger units were raised for the protection of the frontier along the Mississippi River and the adjacent States. The Sea Fencibles was the first organization of the U.S. Army charged exclusively with coastal defense. With the Flotilla Service, the Sea Fencibles protected ports, harbors, and the coast.

Some confusion arose as to whether service in some units had been rendered in the Regular Establishment or in the volunteers. The War Department, while abstracting and compiling these military service records, decided that the units of Rangers, Sea Fencibles, Flotillas, and some volunteer units that include the name "United States" or the initials "U.S." as part of their official designation were volunteer units and not units of the Regular Establishment. As a result of the confusion, records about members of these organizations are found in the records of the Regular Army (and Navy and Marine Corps for the Sea Fencibles and Flotilla Service) as well as in compiled military service records.

Regulars, volunteers, and militia units were also fighting Indians during the war years, 1812–15. Records of service in the Florida and Seminole War of 1812, the Peoria (Illinois) Indian War of 1813, and the Creek Indian War of 1813–14 are found in the War of 1812 segment of the compiled military records in Record Group 94.

Many of the War of 1812 volunteer units were mustered into service for short periods (30, 60, 90, and 120 days; 6, 9, and 12 months). Consequently, many people served more than one enlistment. There may be two or more compilations relating to the service of the same soldier. Generally, no cross-references refer to such service in other units or to earlier or later service in the same unit.

Members of volunteer units in the War of 1812 may also have served before or after that war, either as a volunteer or in the Regular Army or Navy. Some veterans whose records are in this segment served in the Revolutionary War and the War of 1812, and a few served in the Civil War as well as the War of 1812. Most War of 1812 soldiers, however, performed additional service in the 1784-1811 period or in the Indian wars after 1815.

Most of the compiled military service records for the War of 1812 are arranged by State or Territory and thereunder by unit; the others are for units whose complements were not limited to a single State or Territory, or whose designation did not include the name of a State, such as the U.S. Volunteers; U.S. Rangers; Sea Fencibles; Cherokee, Chickasaw, Choctaw, and Creek Indian regiments; 1st Battalion U.S. Volunteers (Louisiana); 2d Regiment Artillery (New York); and Captain Booker's Company, U.S. Volunteers (Virginia). Under the name of each unit, the compiled military service records are arranged alphabetically by surname of soldier.

Indexes to Compiled Service Records

Index to Compiled Service Records of Volunteer Soldiers Who Served During the War of 1812. M602. 234 rolls. 16mm. DP.

This microfilm publication reproduces an alphabetical card index to the compiled service records of volunteer soldiers who served during the War of 1812. Each index card gives the name of a soldier, his rank, and the unit or units in which he served. There are cross-references for names that appear in the records under more than one spelling.

The compiled service records to which the index applies are not on microfilm except for records of the Territory of Mississippi, M678.

Roll	Description
1	A–Ada
2	Adc–Ale
3	Alf–All
4	Alm–Ando
5	Andr–Arl
6	Arm–As
7	At–Az
8	B–Bai
9	Bak–Bal
10	Bam–Barm
11	Barn–Barr
12	Bars–Bat
13	Bau–Bean
14	Bear–Bek
15	Bel–Benn
16	Beno–Bez

Roll	Description
17	Bh–Bis
18	Bit–Blan
19	Blar–Boh
20	Boi–Boo
21	Bop–Bowe
22	Bowg–Boz
23	Br–Bran
24	Brar–Brid
25	Brie–Bron
26	Broo–Brown, I.
27	Brown, J.–Brox
28	Broy–Buc
29	Bud–Burf
30	Burg–Burr
31	Burs–By
32	C–Camo
33	Camp–Cap
34	Car–Carq
35	Carr–Carz
36	Cas–Caz
37	Cc–Chao
38	Chap–Che
39	Chi–Clap
40	Clar
41	Clas–Cly
42	Co–Colb
43	Colc–Coll
44	Colm–Conn
45	Cono–Coon
46	Coop–Cor
47	Cos–Cow
48	Cox–Crav
49	Craw–Cror
50	Cros–Cul
51	Cum–Cur
52	Cus–Dan
53	Dao–Davis, E.
54	Davis, F.–Davy
55	Daw–Ded
56	Dee–Denn
57	Deno–Dib
58	Dic–Diz
59	Dl–Dos
60	Dot–Dra
61	Dre–Dum
62	Dun–Duq
63	Dur–Ear
64	Eas–Edv
65	Edw–Elk
66	Ell–Em
67	En–Eu
68	Ev–Ez
69	F–Fat
70	Fau–Fh
71	Fi–Fis
72	Fit–Fl
73	Fo–For
74	Fos–Foz
75	Fr–Fre
76	Fri–Fuq
77	Fur–Gap
78	Gar–Gas
79	Gat–Ges
80	Get–Gilk

Roll	Description	Roll	Description
81	Gill–Gla	145	Miller, N.–Mis
82	Gle–Gooc	146	Mit–Mon
83	Good–Got	147	Moo
84	Gou–Graw	148	Mop–Morris, O.
85	Gray–Gree	149	Morris, P.–Mot
86	Gref–Gri	150	Mou–Muro
87	Gro–Gy	151	Murp–My
88	H–Halk	152	N–Nel
89	Hall–Hame	153	Nem–Nich
90	Hami–Hanf	154	Nick–Nors
91	Hang–Hark	155	Nort–Oc
92	Harl–Harris, V.	156	Od–Ord
93	Harris, W.–Harv	157	Ore–Owe
94	Harw–Hav	158	Owi–Pan
95	Haw–Haz	159	Pap–Parq
96	Hd–Hem	160	Parr–Pat
97	Hen–Herl	161	Pau–Ped
98	Herm–Hic	162	Pee–Perl
99	Hid–Hil	163	Perm–Pf
100	Him–Hod	164	Ph–Pic
101	Hoe–Holl	165	Pid–Pix
102	Holm–Hopi	166	Pl–Poq
103	Hopk–Hou	167	Por–Poz
104	Hov–Hub	168	Pr–Prim
105	Huc–Huk	169	Prin–Py
106	Hul–Hun	170	Q–Ranc
107	Huo–Hy	171	Rand–Raz
108	I	172	Re–Reed
109	J–Jan	173	Reef–Rez
110	Jaq–Je	174	Rh–Rich
111	Jh–Johnson, P.	175	Rick–Ris
112	Johnson, R.–Jond	176	Rit–Roberts, V.
113	Jone	177	Roberts, W.–Roby
114	Jonh–Kea	178	Roc–Rol
115	Keb–Kel	179	Rom–Rou
116	Kem–Ker	180	Rov–Rusp
117	Kes–Kim	181	Russ–Sai
118	Kin–Kir	182	Sak–San
119	Kis–Ko	183	Sap–Sce
120	Kr–Lamd	184	Sch–Scy
121	Lame–Lan	185	Se–Ses
122	Lao–Lav	186	Set–Shav
123	Law–Lec	187	Shaw–Shep
124	Led–Len	188	Sher–Shop
125	Leo–Lez	189	Shor–Sil
126	L'H–Lis	190	Sim–Siz
127	Lit–Lom	191	Sk–Sme
128	Lon–Lov	192	Smi–Smith, I.
129	Low–Lun	193	Smith, J.–Smith, R.
130	Lup–Mad	194	Smith, S.–Sni
131	Mae–Mann	195	Sno–Spal
132	Mano–Mars	196	Span–Spr
133	Mart–Masp	197	Sps–Star
134	Mass–Mau	198	Stas–Step
135	Mav–McB	199	Ster–Stez
136	McC–McCl	200	St. G–Ston
137	McCo–McCy	201	Stoo–Stro
138	McD–McF	202	Stru–Suts
139	McG–McKa	203	Sutt–Sy
140	McKe–McLm	204	T–Tav
141	McLo–McW	205	Taw–Ted
142	Me–Mep	206	Tee–Thol
143	Mer–Mic	207	Thom–Thompson, K.
144	Mid–Miller, M.	208	Thompson, L.–Thy

Roll	Description
209	Ti–Tod
210	Toe–Toz
211	Tr
212	Ts–Tur
213	Tus–U
214	V–Vang
215	Vanh–Vaz
216	Vd–Vy
217	W–Walk
218	Wall–Warc
219	Ward–Was
220	Wat–Waz
221	We–Welc
222	Weld–Wes
223	Wet–Whitc
224	White
225	Whitf–Wig
226	Wih–Wilk
227	Will–Williams, M.
228	Williams, N.–Willy
229	Wilm–Wilz
230	Wim–Wiz
231	Wl–Woodn
232	Woodr–Woy
233	Wr–Ya
234	Yb–Z

Index to Compiled Service Records of Volunteer Soldiers Who Served During the War of 1812 in Organizations From the State of Louisiana. M229. 3 rolls. 16mm. DP.

Roll	Description
1	A–D
2	E–Me
3	Mi–Z

Index to Compiled Service Records of Volunteer Soldiers Who Served During the War of 1812 in Organizations From the State of North Carolina. M250. 5 rolls. 16mm. DP.

Roll	Description
1	A–C
2	D–Hi
3	Ho–Mi
4	Mo–Sl
5	Sm–Z

Index to Compiled Service Records of Volunteer Soldiers Who Served During the War of 1812 in Organizations From the State of South Carolina. M652. 7 rolls. 16mm. DP.

Roll	Description
1	A–B
2	C–D
3	E–Ha
4	He–L
5	M–O
6	P–Sr
7	St–Z

Compiled Service Records

Compiled Service Records of Volunteer Soldiers Who Served During the War of 1812 in Organizations From the Territory of Mississippi. M678. 22 rolls. 16mm. DP.

This microfilm publication reproduces the compiled service records of volunteer soldiers who served in the War of 1812 in units from the Territory of Mississippi. The records are arranged according to an organizational breakdown and thereunder alphabetically by surname of soldier. There are cross-references of names that appear in the records under more than one spelling.

The compiled service records reproduced in this microfilm publication are indexed on M602.

Roll	Description
1	6th Regiment (1814–15)
	Battalion 7th Regiment (Perkins')
	A–B
2	C–G
3	H–L
4	M–Q
5	R–Y
6	13th Regiment (Nixon's)
	A–Q
7	R–Y
	14th Regiment (McBoy's)
	15th Regiment (Johnson's)
8	16th Regiment (Burrus')
9	18th Regiment (1814–15)
	Carson's Regiment
10	Claiborne's Regiment
	A–F
11	G–L
12	M–S
13	T–Z
	Dale's Battalion
	Hinds' Battalion, Cavalry
	A–C
14	D–I
15	J–Y
16	Neilson's Detachment
17	Nixon's Regiment
	A–D
18	E–L
19	M–R
20	S–Y
21	Smoot's Battalion
	Swayze's Detachment
	Drury M. Allen's Co., Mounted Gunmen
	John A. Allen's Co.
	Boyle's Co., Mounted Spies
	Bradberry's Co., Mounted Spies
	Calvit's Co., Mounted Infantry
	Cassity's Co., Mounted Spies
	Foster's Co., Mounted Infantry
22	Green's Co.
	Wilkin's Rifle Co.

Records of Volunteer Soldiers Who Served During Indian Wars and Disturbances (Record Groups 94 and 407)

In the decades following the War of 1812, volunteer units often served during Indian hostilities either assisting units of the Regular Army or acting independently. The compiled military service records, 1815–58, reflect volunteer service in the Seminole or Florida Wars, 1817–18, 1835–42, and 1855–58; Winnebago War, 1827; Sac and Fox War, 1831; Black Hawk War, 1832; Creek War, 1836–37; Indian Wars in Texas, 1849–51; the Indian (Creek) Removal, 1835–41; and various other disturbances.

The War Department did not recognize some Indian campaigns as wars, although the Treasury Department under various legislative acts reimbursed the States and Territories for the services of volunteer units. Following the Osage War, 1832; Heatherly War, 1836; Patriot and Aroostock War, 1838–39; and Cayuse War, 1848, volunteers or their heirs received bounty land and sometimes pensions.

Although most of the people who served during the period were free citizens of the United States, Indians also served in the U.S. interest at various times, especially the Choctaw, Creek and Friendly Creek (Apalachicola), Menominee, Potawatomi, Delaware, Shawnee, and Winnebago. Records for Indian units are generally separate.

The designations of volunteer units generally include the name of the State or Territory from which they served, but researchers should note that boundaries have changed. Service records of units of the militia mustered in from Green Bay in the Black Hawk war, for example, are found under Michigan Territory, not under Wisconsin.

Most of the compiled service records of volunteer soldiers who served during the Indian wars and disturbances are arranged alphabetically by State or Territory and by war or disturbance. The remaining units—Indian regiments and U.S. volunteers who served in the Utah Expedition, 1857–58—were not limited to any one State or Territory.

The records are further arranged according to an organizational breakdown ending with the regiment or independent battalion or company. Under each unit the service records are arranged alphabetically by surname of soldiers. The name of the unit in which a soldier served must be known to locate his compiled service records; using an index can give a researcher this information. The following table shows publication numbers for indexes currently available on microfilm.

Compiled service records for the Indian wars period are available on microfilm only for Florida, M1086.

Table 1: Microfilmed Indexes to Compiled Military Service Records of Volunteers During the Indian Wars

State	Disturbance	Date	Microfilm Publication Number
Alabama	Creek War	1836–37	M244
	Cherokee Removal	1838	M243
	Florida War	1836–38	M245
Florida	Florida War	1835–58	M1086
Georgia	Cherokee Disturbances and Removal	1836–38	M907
Louisiana	Florida War	1836	M239
	War of 1837–38	1837–38	M241
Michigan	Patriot War	1838–39	M630
New York	Patriot War	1838	M631
North Carolina	Cherokee Disturbances and Removal	1837–38	M256
Tennessee	Cherokee Disturbances and Removal, and Field and Staff of the Army of the Cherokee Nation	1836–39	M908

Index to Compiled Service Records of Volunteer Soldiers Who Served During Indian Wars and Disturbances, 1815–1858. M629. 42 rolls. 16mm. DP.

This microfilm publication reproduces an alphabetical card index to the compiled service records of volunteer soldiers who served in the various Indian wars or participated in the quelling of Indian disturbances or problems, 1815–58.

Along with the soldier's name, rank, and unit, each index card also includes the name of the war or disturbance. There are cross-references for names that appear in the records under more than one spelling.

Roll	Description
1	A–Ar
2	As–Ba
3	Be–Bl
4	Bo–Bri
5	Bro–By
6	C–Ce
7	Ch–Cl
8	Co–Cot
9	Cou–Dan
10	Dar–Do
11	Dr–E
12	F–Fo
13	Fr–Gh
14	Gi–Gra
15	Gre–Ham
16	Han–Haz
17	He–Hof
18	Hog–Hul
19	Hum–Joe
20	Joh–Ka
21	Ke–Ky
22	L–Le
23	Li–Map

Roll	Description
24	Mar–McC
25	McD–Mel
26	Mem–Moon
27	Moor–Na
28	Ne–Or
29	Os–Pel
30	Pem–Po
31	Pr–Re
32	Rg–Ro
33	Ru–Se
34	Sh–Smil
35	Smit–Sr
36	St–Sy
37	T–Th
38	Ti–Tz
39	U–Wap
40	War–Whid
41	Whig–Will
42	Wilm–Z

Records of Volunteer Soldiers Who Served During Cherokee Disturbances and Removal

The New Echota Treaty of May 1836 fixed the time after which Cherokee Indians who refused to voluntarily leave their land in Alabama and Georgia would be removed by force. In 1838 the War Department issued orders for Gen. Winfield Scott to remove immediately the remaining 2,000 Cherokees to Indian Territory (Oklahoma). The Army forced the Indians into stockade camps before starting out on the 1,800 mile march west. They arrived in Indian Territory in the spring of 1839.

Scott was ordered to take command of troops already in Cherokee country, including infantry, cavalry, and artillery. He also had the authority to call on the governors of the adjoining States for as many as 4,000 militia and volunteers.

These microfilm publications reproduce alphabetical card indexes to the compiled service records of volunteer soldiers who served in various organizations during the Cherokee disturbances and removal, 1836–39. In the service records and their related indexes, these operations are generally called the Cherokee War. The compiled military service records to which the indexes refer are not on microfilm.

Indexes to Compiled Service Records

Index to Compiled Service Records of Volunteer Soldiers Who Served During the Cherokee Disturbances and Removal in Organizations From the State of Alabama. M243. 1 roll. 16mm. DP.

Index to Compiled Service Records of Volunteer Soldiers Who Served During the Cherokee Disturbances and Removal in Organizations From the State of Georgia. M907. 1 roll. 16mm. DP.

Index to Compiled Service Records of Volunteer Soldiers Who Served During the Cherokee Disturbances and Removal in Organizations From the State of North Carolina. M256. 1 roll. 16mm. DP.

Index to Compiled Service Records of Volunteer Soldiers Who Served During the Cherokee Disturbances and Removal in Organizations From the State of Tennessee and the Field and Staff of the Army of the Cherokee Nation. M908. 2 rolls. 16mm. DP.

Roll	Description
1	Tennessee organizations A–K
2	L–Y Volunteer field and staff, Army of the Cherokee Nation, A–V

Compiled Service Records

There are no microfilmed compiled service records for volunteer soldiers who served during the Cherokee disturbances and removal.

Records of Volunteer Soldiers Who Served During the Creek War

In 1832, a Creek delegation signed a treaty that ceded all their tribal lands east of the Mississippi to the U.S. Government. The Creek were to leave Alabama as soon as they were ready to emigrate. The Government agreed to pay all of their expenses for removal and subsistence for one year after they had arrived in the West.

Provisions in the treaty, however, allowed some members of the tribe to remain behind. Hostilities resulted. The Federal Government was unable to prevent whites from attacking tribal members and the Creeks retaliated. In early 1836, Gen. Winfield Scott, in command of several thousand U.S. troops, State volunteers, and small bands of Indians, fought against the Creeks. After the Creeks' defeat, the Army forceably removed them to Indian Territory. In the spring of 1837, they arrived at Fort Gibson.

Only one index to these records is available on microfilm, M244, for Alabama soldiers. The compiled military service records to which the index refers are not on microfilm.

Index to Compiled Service Records

Index to Compiled Service Records of Volunteer Soldiers Who Served During the Creek War in Organizations from the State of Alabama. M244. 2 rolls. 16mm. DP.

Roll	Description
1	A–J
2	K–Z

Compiled Service Records

Roll 1 on M1086 lists the soldiers who served with the 5th Regiment (Mounted), Florida Militia, during the Creek War.

Records of Volunteer Soldiers Who Served During the Florida Wars

The Second Seminole War, 1836–43, resulted from the efforts of the United States to remove the Seminole Indians from Florida. The 1832 treaty of Payne's Landing had provided for a delegation of Indians to journey to the West and decide on the acceptability of the land set apart for them. The Seminoles agreed to leave Florida for the West within three years of giving their approval.

Disputes arose, however, when the Government insisted that the agreement to emigrate was fulfilled when the delegation approved the new lands, and the Seminoles asserted that the treaty would not take effect until they expressed satisfaction with their delegates' report.

The Federal Government ordered the Seminole Indians to gather on January 8, 1836, for removal—resistance would be met with force. The ensuing clash plunged both sides into seven years of hardship. Both free blacks and slaves fought with the Seminoles. The U.S. Army enlisted volunteers and mercenaries from other tribes. By 1843 the Army had forced all but a few hundred of the Indians to emigrate, in small groups, west of the Mississippi.

Indexes to Compiled Service Records

Only two State indexes are available on microfilm: M245 and M239 reproduce alphabetical card indexes to the compiled service records of volunteer soldiers who served in units from Alabama and Louisiana during the Florida Wars.

The compiled service records of soldiers who served in organizations from the State of Florida are also available.

Index to Compiled Service Records of Volunteers Soldiers Who Served During the Florida War in Organizations From the State of Alabama. M245. 1 roll. 16mm. DP.

Index to Compiled Service Records of Volunteer Soldiers Who Served During the Florida War in Organizations From the State of Louisiana. M239. 1 roll. 16mm. DP.

Compiled Service Records

Compiled Service Records of Volunteer Soldiers Who Served in Organizations From the State of Florida During the Florida Indian Wars, 1835–1858. M1086. 63 rolls. DP.

This microfilm publication reproduces the compiled service records of volunteer soldiers who served in Florida organizations during the Seminole Wars.

The records are arranged chronologically by war, thereunder by unit, and thereunder alphabetically by surname of soldier. The units are generally arranged as follows: numbered regiments, named battalions, named companies or detachments, brigades, and staff officers. The numbered units are arranged numerically; the named units alphabetically.

The records are indexed in M629. There is no separate State index on microfilm.

Roll	Description
Creek War:	
1	5th Regiment (Mounted), Florida Militia
Florida War:	
	1st Florida Mounted Militia (Bailey's), 3 months, 1840
	A–G
2	H–P
3	Q–Z
4	1st West Florida Militia (Brown's)
	A–R
5	S–W
	1st Florida Mounted Militia, 3 months, 1840–41
	A–E
6	F–L
7	M–V
8	W–Z
	1st Regiment (Warren's), Florida Militia, 1836
	A–S
9	T–Y
	1st (Warren's) Florida Mounted Militia, 1836–37
	A–H
10	I–Z
11	1st (Warren's) Florida Militia, 1837
	A–G
12	H–R
13	S–Z
14	1st (Warren's) Florida Mounted Volunteers, 6 months, 1837–38
	A–L
15	M–Y
16	1st (Warren's) Florida Mounted Militia, 1839–40
	A–I
17	J–S
18	T–Y
	2d East Florida Mounted Volunteers
	A–D

Roll	Description
	Weedon's Company (B), Florida Militia, 3 months, 1836–37
	Weedon's Company (B), Florida Militia, 3 months, 1837
	Whitner's Detachment, Florida Militia
	Capt. William Wyatt's Company, 3d Regiment, Florida Volunteers
	A–L
49	M–W
	1st Brigade, Florida Militia, 1836–37
	1st Brigade, Florida Militia, 6 months, 1837–38
	2d Brigade, Florida Militia, 1835–36
	2d Brigade, Florida Militia, 1837
	Call's Brigade, Florida Volunteers
	Read's Brigade, Florida Militia, 3 months, 1840; 3 months, 1840–41; and 3 months, 1841
	General Call and Staff, Florida Militia
	Quartermaster's Department, Florida Militia

Third Seminole War:

Roll	Description
50	1st Florida Mounted Volunteers
	A–H
51	I–S
52	T–Z
	Special Battalion (Smith's), Florida
	A–K
53	L–Y
	Addison's Company, Florida Mounted Militia
	Bradley's Independent Company, Florida (Foot) Volunteers
	A–J
54	K–Z
	Bullock's Company, Florida Mounted Volunteers, 6 months, 1856–57
	Bullock's Company, Florida Mounted Volunteers, 6 months, 1857
	Bullock's Company, Florida Mounted Volunteers, 6 months, 1857–58
	Carter's Company, Florida Mounted Volunteers
	A–G
55	H–W
	Durrance's Company, Florida Mounted Volunteers
56	Hart's Independent Company, Florida Mounted Volunteers
	Hooker's Independent Company, Florida Mounted Volunteers
	Jernigan's Independent Company, Florida Mounted Volunteers
57	Johnston's Company, Florida Mounted Volunteers
	Johnston's Independent Company, Florida Mounted Volunteers
58	E. T. Kendrick's Independent Company, Florida Mounted Volunteers
	William H. Kendrick's Independent Company, Florida Mounted Volunteers
	A–G
59	H–W
	Lesley's Company, Florida Mounted Volunteers
	A–H
60	J–Y
	McNeill's Company, Florida Mounted Volunteers
	A–L
61	M–Y
	Mickler's Company, Florida Mounted Volunteers
	Moseley's Independent Company, Florida Mounted Volunteers
62	Parker's Company, Florida Mounted Volunteers
	Pickett's Company, Florida Mounted Volunteers
	Snell's Company, Florida Mounted Volunteers

Roll	Description
	Sparkman's Independent Company, Florida Mounted Volunteers
	A–F
63	G–Z
	Turner's Detachment, Florida (Foot) Volunteers
	Captain Wright's Detachment, Florida
	Acting Assistant Surgeons, Florida
	Staff Officers, Florida

Records of Volunteer Soldiers Who Served During the War of 1837–1838

Index to Compiled Service Records

Index to Compiled Service Records of Volunteer Soldiers Who Served During the War of 1837–1838 in Organizations From the State of Louisiana. M241. 1 roll. 16mm. DP.

This microfilm publication reproduces an alphabetical card index to the compiled service records of volunteer soldiers of units from the State of Louisiana who served in the second Florida campaign, called the War of 1837–38 in these records. Troops under the command of Gen. Thomas Jesup fought against the Seminoles in the fall and winter of 1837–38.

Compiled Service Records

There are no microfilmed compiled service records for volunteer soldiers who served during the War of 1837–1838.

Records of Volunteer Soldiers Who Served During the Patriot War, 1838–1839 (Record Group 94)

The Patriot War involved Canadian rebels and their American supporters who hoped to free Canada from British domination. The "Patriots" were mostly American farmers and unemployed artisans. They made three different extensive plans in 1838 for widespread simultaneous attacks along the Canadian border, hoping eventually to join forces and establish a republic in Canada. When the plans failed, the movement came under the domination of a secret society, the Hunters and Chasers of the Eastern Frontier.

Congress passed a stronger neutrality act in March 1838. Federal troops were sent to the frontier and, in the border States, the militia was called out to suppress the plotters.

Only two alphabetical indexes are available on microfilm. The compiled military service records to which these indexes refer are not microfilmed.

Indexes to Compiled Service Records

Index to Compiled Service Records of Volunteer Soldiers Who Served From the State of Michigan During the Patriot War, 1838–1839. M630. 1 roll. 16mm. DP.

This microfilm publication reproduces an alphabetical card index to the compiled military service records of volunteers who served in Capt. Isaac S. Rowland's Independent Company, Brady Guards, Michigan Militia. This company is the only organization of volunteer soldiers from Michigan for which the National Archives has separate compiled service records for the Patriot War. Each index card gives the name of a soldier and his rank.

There are cross-references for names that appear in the records with more than one spelling.

Index to Compiled Service Records of Volunteer Soldiers Who Served From the State of New York During the Patriot War, 1838. M631. 1 roll. 16mm. DP.

Compiled Service Records

There are no microfilmed compiled service records for volunteer soldiers who served during the Patriot War.

Records of Volunteer Soldiers Who Served During the Mexican War (Record Group 94)

War with Mexico was declared on May 13, 1846, less than 6 months after Texas had been admitted to the Union. The act specified the service of the Regular Military and Naval Establishment and the use of volunteers and the militia. Militia service was limited to no more than 6 months of continuous service, while the volunteers could be mustered for 12 months or until the end of the war.

Some of the volunteers who served in the Mexican War had also served in the earlier Indian wars or would later serve in the Civil War. Some of the Texas volunteers were retained in service after the war to protect the frontier areas of Texas from Indian attack.

For an alphabetical list of volunteer officers in the Mexican War, showing rank and organization, see *Historical Register and Dictionary of the United States Army,* by Francis B. Heitman (Washington, 1903), 2:43–73.

Index to Compiled Service Records

Index to Compiled Service Records of Volunteer Soldiers Who Served During the Mexican War. M616. 41 rolls. 16mm. DP.

This microfilm publication reproduces an alphabetical card index to the compiled service records of volunteer soldiers who served during the Mexican War. Each index card gives the name of a soldier, his rank, and the unit or units in which he served. There are cross-references for names that appear in the records under more than one spelling.

Roll	Description
1	A–As
2	At–Ba
3	Bd–Bl
4	Bo–Bron
5	Brow–By
6	C–Cha
7	Che–Con
8	Coo–Cy
9	D–Dh
10	Di–Dy
11	E–Fa
12	Fe–Fo
13	Fr–Gh
14	Gi–Gre
15	Gri–Hap
16	Har–Hel
17	Hem–Hol
18	Hom–I
19	J
20	K–Kn
21	Ko–Len
22	Leo–Ly
23	M–Ma
24	Mc–McJ
25	McK–Me
26	Mi–Mop
27	Mor–Ne
28	Ni–O
29	P–Ph
30	Pi–Q
31	R–Rie
32	Rif–Ry
33	S–Se
34	Sh–Sme
35	Smi–St. D
36	Ste–Sz
37	T–Ti
38	To–V
39	W–We
40	Wh–Wil
41	Wim–Z

Compiled Service Records

These microfilm publications reproduce the compiled service records of volunteer soldiers who served during the Mexican War. They are arranged alphabetically by State or Territory, followed by the records of soldiers who served in Mormon organizations. The records are further arranged according to an organizational breakdown ending with the regiment or the independent battalion or company. Under each unit the service records are arranged alphabetically by surname of soldier.

Compiled Service Records of Volunteer Soldiers Who Served During the Mexican War in Organizations From the State of Mississippi. M863. 9 rolls. DP.

Roll	Description
	1st Infantry
1	A–G
2	H–O
3	P–Z
	2d Infantry
4	A–E
5	F–K
6	L–Q
7	R–Y
	Anderson's Rifles
8	A–L
9	M–Y

Compiled Service Records of Volunteer Soldiers Who Served During the Mexican War in Organizations From the State of Pennsylvania. M1028. 13 rolls. DP.

Roll	Description
	1st Infantry
1	A–Co
2	Cr–G
3	H–L
4	M–Q
5	R–S
6	T–Z
	2d Infantry
7	A–Ca
8	Ce–Fi
9	Fl–Hi
10	Ho–Li
11	Lo–M
12	N–Sl
13	Sm–Z

Compiled Service Records of Volunteer Soldiers Who Served During the Mexican War in Organizations From the State of Tennessee. M638. 15 rolls. 16mm. DP.

Roll	Description
	1st Infantry
1	A–F
2	G–O
3	P–Z
	1st Mounted Infantry
4	A–J
5	K–Y
6	2d Infantry
7	3d Infantry
	A–F
8	G–N
9	O–Z
10	4th Infantry
	A–G
11	H–O
12	P–Y
13	5th Infantry
	A–K

Roll	Description
14	L–Z
15	Wheat's Co., Mounted Volunteers

Compiled Service Records of Volunteer Soldiers Who Served During the Mexican War in Organizations From the State of Texas. M278. 19 rolls. 16mm. DP.

Roll	Description
1	1st Texas Mounted Rifles
	A–S
2	T–Y
	1st Texas Mounted Volunteers
	A–G
3	H–R
4	S–Y
	1st Texas Mounted Volunteers, 6 months, 1847
	A–C
5	D–Y
6	1st Texas Foot Riflemen
	A–R
7	S–Z
	2d Texas Mounted Volunteers
	A–G
8	H–Z
9	3d Texas Mounted Volunteers
10	Bell's Regiment, Texas Mounted Volunteers
	A–E
11	F–Me
12	Mi–S
13	T–Z
	Cady's Co., Texas Mounted Rangers
14	Chevallie's Battalion, Texas Mounted Volunteers
	A–L
15	M–Y
16	Beaver's Spy Co., Indians, Texas Mounted Volunteers
	Bell's Co., Texas Mounted Volunteers
	Conner's Co., Texas Mounted Volunteers
	Gillespie's Co., Texas Mounted Rangers
	Gray's Co., Texas Mounted Volunteers
17	Grumble's Co., Texas Mounted Volunteers
	Hill's Co., Texas Mounted Volunteers
	Lamar's Co., Texas Mounted Volunteers
	Price's Co., Texas Mounted Volunteers
	Robert's Co., Texas Mounted Volunteers
	Ross' Co., Texas Mounted Volunteers
18	McCulloch's Co., First Regiment, Texas Mounted Volunteers
	Seefeld's Co., Texas Volunteers
	Shivor's Co., Texas Volunteers
19	Smith's Co., Texas Mounted Volunteers
	Stopp's Co., Texas Mounted Volunteers
	Sutton's Co., Texas Mounted Volunteers
	Walker's Co., Texas Mounted Rangers
	Wyman's Co., Smith's Battalion, Texas Mounted Volunteers

Compiled Service Records of Volunteer Soldiers Who Served During the Mexican War in Mormon Organizations. M351. 3 rolls. 16mm. DP.

This microfilm publication reproduces the compiled service records of volunteer soldiers in two Mormon organizations that served in the Mexican War. The first of these organizations, the Mormon Battalion, Volunteers, was organized at Council Bluffs, Iowa, on July 16, 1846. This battalion consisted of five companies of Mormon emigrants, then en route to California, who enlisted for 1 year. At the end of this term of enlistment, an attempt was made to reenroll all the members, but only one company was organized at Los Angeles, Calif., on July 20, 1847. This second Mormon organization, designated as Capt. Davis' Company A, Mormon Volunteers, served for 6 months.

Roll	Military Unit
1	Mormon Battalion, Volunteers
	A–G
2	H–R
3	S–Z
	Capt. Davis' Company A, Mormon Volunteers

Records of Volunteer Union Soldiers Who Served During the Civil War (Record Group 94)

President Lincoln's proclamation in April 1861 called for 75,000 militiamen from the loyal States and Territories to suppress the rebellion in the Southern States. Subsequent proclamations and acts of Congress provided for additional increases in the size of the regular army and navy and called for additional volunteers and militiamen. The States and Territories met the requirements through activating the militia, voluntary enlistments, and the draft.

During the first 2 years of the war, many units were mustered for short periods (30, 60, and 90 days and 6, 9, and 12 months), but normal enlistments were for 1 to 3 years. Most soldiers served from units formed within their neighborhoods or States or Territories of residence.

A reenlisting soldier was not necessarily assigned to the same unit in which he had previously served, or even to the same branch of service, or arm of service. Disabled soldiers still capable of performing a service were assigned to the Veteran Reserve Corps (VRC).

Many units upon organization adopted or used a unique name, generally the name by which the unit had been known as a militia unit. When a unit was mustered into the Union army, the name was changed to conform with regulations of the Union Army. A unit designation usually consisted of a number, the State or Territory name, and the arm of service: for example, 1st Iowa Cavalry. Some unit designations included the name of the officer who formed the company, or its commanding officer. Some units had two or more successive designations: for example, 1st Pennsylvania Cavalry and 44th Pennsylvania Volunteers. State and Territory names were not used for units composed of soldiers from several States or Territories or for special units. Records are generally filed under the final designation for a particular unit.

There are compiled military service records for nearly all soldiers who were accepted for service in the Union army as militiamen or volunteers, 1861–65, whether or not they actually served. Records relating to soldiers who participated in actions that occurred between 1861 and 1865 are included in the records of the Civil War, even if the actions, such as Indian warfare, were unrelated to the war. The compiled military service records for Civil War soldiers are similar to those for other periods of service.

Records of enlisted men sometimes include information about age, residence at the time of enlistment, occupations at the time of enlistment, and physical description. Personal papers occasionally give additional information about residence, family, or business of officers and enlisted men. Information about heirs is sometimes found in records of hospitalization or death in service. The records generally refer to Federal service in other units during, before, and after the Civil War.

No general comprehensive name index to the compiled service records for Union army volunteer soldiers exists. Separate indexes are available for each State and Territory except South Carolina, which furnished no white troops to the Union army.

To locate the record of service of a particular soldier, the researcher may need to consult several indexes. A soldier may have enlisted in or been assigned to a unit from a different State or Territory from the one the researcher expects, or to a special unit composed of persons from several different areas. For example, a soldier from Tennessee might be in a unit from Kentucky.

Requests for Records

Inquiries about compiled military service records should be submitted on NATF Form 80, "Order for Copies of Veterans Records." Instructions for its use and an explanation of how orders are processed are printed on the form. When a military service file is found, documents that normally contain the basic information about the veteran will be selected and photocopied. Photocopies of the reproducible papers in the file can be furnished for a moderate cost per page.

Table 2: Microfilmed Indexes and Compiled Service Records for Union Army Volunteers

State	Index	Compiled Military Service Records
Alabama	M263	M276
Arizona	M532	
Arkansas	M383	M399
California	M533	
Colorado Territory	M534	
Connecticut	M535	

State	Index	Compiled Military Service Records
Dakota Territory	M536	
Delaware	M537	
District of Columbia	M538	
Florida	M264	M400
Georgia	M385	M403
Idaho Territory (see Washington Territory)		
Illinois	M539	
Indiana	M540	
Iowa	M541	
Kansas	M542	
Kentucky	M386	M397
Louisiana	M387	M396
Maine	M543	
Maryland	M388	M384
Massachusetts	M544	
Michigan	M545	
Minnesota	M546	
Mississippi	M389	M404
Missouri	M390	M405
Montana (see Washington Territory)		
Nebraska Territory	M547	
Nevada	M548	
New Hampshire	M549	
New Jersey	M550	
New Mexico Territory	M242	M427
New York	M551	
North Carolina	M391	M401
Ohio	M552	
Oregon	M553	
Pennsylvania	M554	
Rhode Island	M555	
South Carolina	None	
Tennessee	M392	M395
Texas	M393	M402
Utah Territory	M556	M692
Vermont	M557	
Virginia	M394	M398
Washington Territory	M558	
West Virginia	M507	M508
Wisconsin	M559	
Wyoming (see Washington Territory)		
U.S. Colored Troops	M589	
U.S. Volunteers, 1st–6th Regiments		M1017
Veterans Reserve Corps	M636	

Indexes to Compiled Service Records

Index to Compiled Service Records of Volunteer Union Soldiers Who Served in Organizations From the State of Alabama. M263. 1 roll. 16mm. DP.

The compiled service records to which this index applies are reproduced in M276.

Index to Compiled Service Records of Volunteer Union Soldiers Who Served in Organizations From the Territory of Arizona. M532. 1 roll. 16mm. DP.

This microfilm publication reproduces the index to the compiled service records of volunteer Union soldiers belonging to the 1st Regiment of Arizona Infantry. This regiment is the only organization of Union troops from the Territory of Arizona for which the National Archives and Records Administration has separate compiled service records.

Index to Compiled Service Records of Volunteer Union Soldiers Who Served in Organizations From the State of Arkansas. M383. 4 rolls. 16mm. DP.

The compiled service records to which this index applies are reproduced in M399.

Roll	Description
1	A–F
2	G–Mc
3	Me–S
4	T–Z

Index to Compiled Service Records of Volunteer Union Soldiers Who Served in Organizations From the State of California. M533. 7 rolls. 16mm. DP.

Roll	Description
1	A–Cl
2	Co–Fos
3	Fot–I
4	J–McD
5	McE–P
6	Q–St
7	Su–Z

Index to Compiled Service Records of Volunteer Union Soldiers Who Served in Organizations From the Territory of Colorado. M534. 3 rolls. 16mm. DP.

Roll	Description
1	A–Hap
2	Har–O
3	P–Z

Index to Compiled Service Records of Volunteer Union Soldiers Who Served in Organizations From the State of Connecticut. M535. 17 rolls. 16mm. DP.

Roll	Description
1	A–Bem
2	Ben–Buf
3	Bug–Coa
4	Cob–Den
5	Deo–Fin
6	Fir–Gra
7	Gre–Hi
8	Ho–Kee
9	Kef–Li
10	Ll–McK
11	McL–Neg
12	Neh–Pi
13	Pl–Ro
14	Rr–Sme
15	Smi–Tag
16	Tah–Wa
17	We–Z

Index to Compiled Service Records of Volunteer Union Soldiers Who Served in Organizations From the Territory of Dakota. M536. 1 roll. 16mm. DP.

This microfilm publication reproduces an alphabetical card index to the compiled service records of volunteer

Union soldiers belonging to the 1st Battalion of Dakota Cavalry. This battalion is the only organization of Union troops from the Territory of Dakota for which the National Archives and Records Administration has separate compiled service records.

Index to Compiled Service Records of Volunteer Union Soldiers Who Served in Organizations From the State of Delaware. M537. 4 rolls. 16mm. DP.

Roll	Description
1	A–D
2	E–La
3	Le–Ri
4	Ro–Z

Index to Compiled Military Service Records of Volunteer Union Soldiers who Served in Organizations from the District of Columbia. M538. 3 rolls. 16mm. DP.

Roll	Description
1	A–G
2	H–P
3	Q–Z

Index to Compiled Military Service Records of Volunteer Union Soldiers who Served in Organizations from the State of Florida. M264. 1 roll. 16mm. DP.

The compiled service records to which this index applies are reproduced on M400.

Index to Compiled Military Service Records of Volunteer Union Soldiers who Served in Organizations from the State of Georgia. M385. 1 roll. 16mm. DP.

The compiled service records to which this index applies are reproduced on M403.

Index to Compiled Military Service Records of Volunteer Union Soldiers who Served in Organizations from the State of Illinois. M539. 101 rolls. 16mm. DP.

Roll	Description
1	A–Alle
2	Allf–Aro
3	Arp–Bai
4	Bak–Baro
5	Barr–Beb
6	Bec–Beq
7	Ber–Blai
8	Blak–Bor
9	Bos–Bras
10	Brat–Brou
11	Brow–Buc
12	Bud–Bus
13	But–Can
14	Cap–Cat
15	Cau–Ch
16	Ci–Cl
17	Co–Com
18	Con–Cor
19	Cos–Crm
20	Cro–Cz
21	D–Dav
22	Daw–Des
23	Det–Dom
24	Don–Dud

Roll	Description
25	Due–Ea
26	Eb–El
27	Em–Ez
28	F–Fim
29	Fin–Fop
30	For–Frg
31	Fri–Gaq
32	Gar–Gik
33	Gil–Gon
34	Goo–Gred
35	Gree–Gs
36	Gu–Hall
37	Halm–Harl
38	Harm–Hav
39	Haw–Hem
40	Hen–Hic
41	Hid–Hof
42	Hog–Hot
43	Hou–Hul
44	Hum–I
45	J–Johnq
46	Johns–Jonk
47	Jons–Kek
48	Kel–Ker
49	Kes–Kj
50	Kl–Lac
51	Lad–Lau
52	Lav–Let
53	Leu–Ll
54	Lo–Lum
55	Lun–Mam
56	Man–Mas
57	Mat–McCi
58	McCl–McD
59	McE–McK
60	McL–Meh
61	Mei–Milk
62	Mill–Mll
63	Mo–Morf
64	Morg–Mum
65	Mun–Ned
66	Nee–Ni
67	No–Oh
68	Oi–Oz
69	P–Pax
70	Pay–Pe
71	Pf–Poh
72	Poi–Pt
73	Pu–Rav
74	Raw–Rem
75	Ren–Rik
76	Ril–Roc
77	Rod–Roz
78	Rr–San
79	Sap–Schr
80	Schs–Sew
81	Sex–She
82	Shf–Sil
83	Sim–Smith, C.
84	Smith, D.–Smy
85	Sn–Ss
86	Sta–Steu
87	Stev–Stra
88	Stre–Swa

Roll	Description
89	Swe–Ter
90	Tes–Til
91	Tim–Ts
92	Tu–Vang
93	Vanh–Waf
94	Wag–Ward
95	Ware–Weh
96	Wei–Whed
97	Whee–Wif
98	Wig–Willo
99	Willr–Wiz
100	Wn–Wr
101	Wu–Z

Index to Compiled Military Service Records of Volunteer Union Soldiers Who Served in Organizations From the State of Indiana. M540. 86 rolls. 16mm. DP.

Roll	Description
1	A–Al
2	Am–At
3	Au–Ban
4	Baq–Bc
5	Be–Ben
6	Beo–Bla
7	Ble–Bowh
8	Bowi–Brim
9	Brin–Brx
10	Bry–Bur
11	Bus–Cap
12	Car–Ce
13	Ch–Cla
14	Cle–Col
15	Com–Cor
16	Cos–Cri
17	Cro–Dap
18	Dar–Dek
19	Del–Doa
20	Dob–Dum
21	Dun–Ek
22	El–Ev
23	Ew–Fir
24	Fis–Fos
25	Fou–Fy
26	G–Gf
27	Gh–Gon
28	Goo–Gree
29	Gref–Haf
30	Hag–Hanm
31	Hann–Hart
32	Harv–Heh
33	Hei–Hia
34	Hib–Hok
35	Hol–Hot
36	Hou–Hum
37	Hun–Jack
38	Jaco–Johnso
39	Johnss–Ked
40	Kee–Ker
41	Kes–Kl
42	Kn–Land
43	Lane–Lee
44	Lef–Li
45	Ll–Lw

Roll	Description
46	Ly–Marr
47	Mars–Maz
48	Mc–McCr
49	McCu–McKi
50	McKl–Merh
51	Meri–Millf
52	Millg–Mon
53	Moo–Mor
54	Mos–Mu
55	My–Ne
56	Ni–O'B
57	Oc–Oz
58	P–Pat
59	Pau–Phf
60	Phi–Pop
61	Por–Q
62	R–Reec
63	Reed–Rice
64	Rich–Robb
65	Robe–Rose
66	Rosh–Sal
67	Sam–Scos
68	Scot–Shar
69	Shas–Shoo
70	Shop–Sk
71	Sl–Smith. V.
72	Smith, W.–Spi
73	Spl–Step
74	Ster–Sto
75	Str–Swan
76	Swap–Te
77	Th–Tin
78	Tip–Tur
79	Tus–Ve
80	Vi–Wam
81	Wan–Weh
82	Wei–White
83	Whitf–Willia
84	Willib–Wis
85	Wit–Wo
86	Wr–Z

Index to Compiled Military Service Records of Volunteer Union Soldiers Who Served in Organizations From the State of Iowa. M541. 29 rolls. 16mm. DP.

Roll	Description
1	A–Bam
2	Ban–Bi
3	Bl–Bro
4	Bru–Cas
5	Cat–Conn
6	Cono–Dap
7	Dar–Doy
8	Dr–Far
9	Fas–Gam
10	Gan–Grif
11	Grig–Hax
12	Hay–Hol
13	Hom–Ja
14	Je–Kh
15	Ki–Lel
16	Lem–Map
17	Mar–McF

Roll	Description
18	McG–Mil
19	Mim–Nei
20	Nel–Pat
21	Pau–Rak
22	Ral–Rod
23	Roe–Sem
24	Sen–Sm
25	Sn–Str
26	Stu–To
27	Tr–Ward
28	Ware–Wilh
29	Wili–Z

Index to Compiled Military Service Records of Volunteer Union Soldiers Who Served in Organizations From the State of Kansas. M542. 10 rolls. 16mm. DP.

Roll	Description
1	A–Br
2	Bu–C
3	D–F
4	G–Hom
5	Hon–Le
6	Lg–Mi
7	Mo–Ral
8	Ram–Sk
9	Sl–U
10	V–Z

Index to Compiled Military Service Records of Volunteer Union Soldiers Who Served in Organizations From the State of Kentucky. M386. 30 rolls. 16mm. DP.

The compiled service records to which this index applies are reproduced on M397.

Roll	Description
1	A
2	B–Bh
3	Bi–Bri
4	Bro–Cam
5	Can–Cok
6	Col–Cs
7	Cu–Dl
8	Do–Eu
9	Ev–Fr
10	Fu–Go
11	Gr–Hap
12	Har–He
13	Hi–Hup
14	Hur–J
15	K
16	L–Lo
17	Lu–McC
18	McD–Mik
19	Mil–My
20	N–O
21	P–Po
22	Pr–Rh
23	Ri–Ry
24	S–Sh
25	Si–Stam
26	Stan–Sy
27	T
28	U–Wa

Roll	Description
29	We–Wil
30	Wim–Z

Index to Compiled Military Service Records of Volunteer Union Soldiers Who Served in Organizations From the State of Louisiana. M387. 4 rolls. 16mm. DP.

The compiled service records to which this index applies are reproduced on M396.

Roll	Description
1	A–E
2	F–La
3	Le–R
4	S–Z

Index to Compiled Military Service Records of Volunteer Union Soldiers Who Served in Organizations From the State of Maine. M543. 23 rolls. 16mm. DP.

Roll	Description
1	A–Ba
2	Be–Brd
3	Bre–Car
4	Cas–Con
5	Coo–Dem
6	Den–Elm
7	Elr–Fri
8	Fro–Gra
9	Gre–Has
10	Hat–Hun
11	Hur–Ken
12	Ker–Lib
13	Lic–McB
14	McC–Mi
15	Mo–Of
16	O'G–Pil
17	Pin–Ric
18	Rid–Sc
19	Se–So
20	Sp–Sy
21	T–U
22	V–Whitc
23	White–Z

Index to Compiled Military Service Records of Volunteer Union Soldiers Who Served in Organizations From the State of Maryland. M388. 13 rolls. 16mm. DP.

The compiled service records to which this index applies are reproduced on M384.

Roll	Description
1	A–Bo
2	Br–Com
3	Con–D
4	E–Gh
5	Gi–He
6	Hi–Ka
7	Ke–L
8	M–Mi
9	Mo–Pi
10	Pl–Sa
11	Sc–Sr
12	St–V

Roll	Description
13	W–Z

Index to Compiled Service Records of Volunteer Union Soldiers Who Served in Organizations From the State of Massachusetts. M544. 44 rolls. 16mm. DP.

Roll	Description
1	A
2	Ba
3	Be–Bl
4	Boa–Broo
5	Brop–Bus
6	But–Ca
7	Ce–Cla
8	Cle–Con
9	Coo–Cun
10	Cur–Def
11	Deg–Dowl
12	Down–El
13	Em–Fis
14	Fit–Fuk
15	Ful–Gle
16	Gli–Gr
17	Gu–Hars
18	Hart–Her
19	Hes–Hos
20	Hot–Ja
21	Je–Kei
22	Kel–Kl
23	Kn–Lei
24	Lej–Lym
25	Lyn–Mat
26	Mau–McKa
27	McKe–Mis
28	Mit–Mun
29	Mur–N
30	O–Paq
31	Par–Ph
32	Pi–Q
33	R–Ric
34	Rid–Rr
35	Ru–Sc
36	Se–Si
37	Sk–Spa
38	Spe–Stor
39	Stot–Ten
40	Teo–Tr
41	Ts–Wal
42	Wan–Whe
43	Whi–Will
44	Wilm–Z

Index to Compiled Service Records of Volunteer Union Soldiers Who Served in Organizations From the State of Michigan. M545. 48 rolls. 16mm. DP.

Roll	Description
1	A–Aur
2	Aus–Bar
3	Bas–Bg
4	Bi–Bov
5	Bow–Bro
6	Bru–Cal
7	Cam–Cha
8	Che–Col
9	Com–Cra
10	Cre–Dav
11	Daw–Dom
12	Don–Ec
13	Ed–Fem
14	Fen–Fra
15	Frd–Gilk
16	Gill–Gri
17	Gro–Harp
18	Harr–Hen
19	Heo–Hon
20	Hoo–Hz
21	I–J
22	K–Kin
23	Kip–Lar
24	Las–Lol
25	Lom–Map
26	Mar–McC
27	McD–McW
28	Me–Mi
29	Mo–Mu
30	My–No
31	Nu–Paq
32	Par–Pf
33	Ph–Pr
34	Pu–Re
35	Rh–Rog
36	Roh–Sa
37	Sc–Sha
38	She–Sk
39	Sl–So
40	Sp–Sth
41	Sti–Sy
42	T–Ti
43	Tl–U
44	V
45	W–Wee
46	Weg–Wig
47	Wih–Wiz
48	Wo–Z

Index to Compiled Service Records of Volunteer Union Soldiers Who Served in Organizations From the State of Minnesota. M546. 10 rolls. 16mm. DP.

Roll	Description
1	A–Br
2	Bu–Da
3	De–F
4	G–Ho
5	Hu–Le
6	L'H–M
7	N–Re
8	Rh–Sl
9	Sm–U
10	V–Z

Index to Compiled Service Records of Volunteer Union Soldiers Who Served in Organizations From the State of Mississippi. M389. 1 roll. 16mm. DP.

The compiled service records to which the index applies are reproduced on M404.

Index to Compiled Service Records of Volunteer Union Soldiers Who Served in Organizations From the State of Missouri. M390. 54 rolls. 16mm. DP.

The compiled service records to which this index applies are reproduced on M405.

Roll	Description
1	A–Ar
2	As–Bar
3	Bas–Ber
4	Bes–Bon
5	Boo–Bre
6	Bri–Bry
7	Bu–By
8	C–Ch
9	Ci–Coo
10	Cop–Cz
11	D–Dh
12	Di–Duf
13	Dug–Em
14	En–Fir
15	Fis–Fr
16	Fu–Gig
17	Gil–Go
18	Gr–Gy
19	H–Hap
20	Har–Haz
21	He
22	Hh–Hoo
23	Hop–Hy
24	I–Jol
25	Jom–Kem
26	Ken–Kn
27	Ko–Ky
28	L–Leu
29	Lev–Ly
30	M–Mau
31	Mav–McJ
32	McK–Mex
33	Mey–Mi
34	Mo–Muk
35	Mul–Ni
36	No–O
37	P–Ph
38	Pi–Q
39	R–Re
40	Rh–Rod
41	Roe–Ry
42	S–Schm
43	Schn–Se
44	Sh–Sk
45	Sl–Sp
46	Sq–St.K
47	Sto–Sz
48	T–Tl
49	To–Vd
50	Ve–Wan
51	War–We
52	Wh–Will
53	Wilm–Wy
54	X–Z

Index to Compiled Service Records of Volunteer Union Soldiers Who Served in Organizations From the Territory of Nebraska. M547. 2 rolls. 16mm. DP.

(continued on next column)

Roll	Description
1	A–La
2	Le–Z

Index to Compiled Service Records of Volunteer Union Soldiers Who Served in Organizations From the State of Nevada. M548. 1 roll. 16mm. DP.

Index to Compiled Service Records of Volunteer Union Soldiers Who Served in Organizations From the State of New Hampshire. M549. 13 rolls. 16mm. DP.

Roll	Description
1	A–Bo
2	Br–Ci
3	Cl–Di
4	Do–Fo
5	Fr–Han
6	Hao–Ji
7	Jo–Lea
8	Leb–Me
9	Mi–Pe
10	Ph–R
11	S–St. D
12	Ste–V
13	W–Z

Index to Compiled Service Records of Volunteer Union Soldiers Who Served in Organizations from the State of New Jersey. M550. 26 rolls. 16mm. DP.

Roll	Description
1	A–Bar
2	Bas–Bo
3	Br–Cal
4	Cam–Com
5	Con–Dau
6	Dav–Dr
7	Du–Fh
8	Fi–Ga
9	Ge–Hal
10	Ham–He
11	Hi–Hy
12	I–Kem
13	Ken–La
14	Le–Mal
15	Mam–McG
16	McH–Moo
17	Mor–O'C
18	Od–Pl
19	Po–Ri
20	Ro–Scho
21	Schr–Sk
22	Sl–Ste
23	St.G–Ti
24	To–V
25	W–Wh
26	Wi–Z

Index to Compiled Service Records of Volunteer Union Soldiers Who Served in Organizations From the Territory of New Mexico. M242. 4 rolls. 16mm. DP.

The compiled service records to which this index applies are reproduced on M427.

Roll	Description
1	A–D

Roll	Description
2	E–L
3	M–Ri
4	Ro–Z

**Index to Compiled Service Records of Volunteer
Union Soldiers Who Served in Organizations From the
State of New York. M551. 157 rolls. 16mm. DP.**

Roll	Description	Roll	Description
1	A–Alc	57	Gun–Halk
2	Ald–Anc	58	Hall–Ham
3	And–Ar	59	Han–Harq
4	As–Bag	60	Harr–Harz
5	Bah–Bam	61	Has–Hay
6	Ban–Barq	62	Haz–Hem
7	Barr–Baw	63	Hen–Her
8	Bax–Bek	64	Hes–Hil
9	Bel–Beq	65	Him–Hog
10	Ber–Bim	66	Hoh–Horn
11	Bin–Bll	67	Horo–Hoz
12	Blo–Boq	68	Hu–Huns
13	Bor–Boz	69	Hunt–In
14	Bra–Brem	70	Io–Jem
15	Bren–Bron	71	Jen–Johnson, S.
16	Broo–Brown, J.	72	Johnson, T.–Jor
17	Brown, K.–Buc	73	Jos–Kb
18	Bud–Burm	74	Ke–Kellu
19	Burn–Bus	75	Kelly–Ken
20	But–Cal	76	Keo–Kinf
21	Cam–Carm	77	King–Kli
22	Carn–Cary	78	Klo–Kra
23	Cas–Chao	79	Kre–Lal
24	Chap–Clap	80	Lam–Las
25	Clar–Cle	81	Lat–Led
26	Cli–Cole	82	Lee–Leu
27	Colf–Conl	83	Lev–Lit
28	Comm–Cool	84	Liu–Lou
29	Coom–Cot	85	Lov–Lyn
30	Cou–Cra	86	Lyo–Mai
31	Cre–Cul	87	Maj–Marq
32	Cum–Dali	88	Marr–Matf
33	Dall–Davis, G.	89	Math–McA
34	Davis, H.–Dee	90	McB–McCl
35	Def–Derm	91	McCo–McDon
36	Dern–Dil	92	McDoo–McGr
37	Dim–Donl	93	McGu–McK
38	Donn–Dov	94	McL–McO
39	Dow–Due	95	McR–Mep
40	Duf–Dus	96	Mer–Milk
41	Dut–Edl	97	Mill
42	Edm–Ell	98	Milm–Mon
43	Elm–Eva	99	Moo–Morp
44	Eve–Far	100	Morr–Mq
45	Fas–Fik	101	Mu–Muro
46	Fil–Fit	102	Murp–Muz
47	Fiv–Foo	103	My–Neu
48	Fop–Frang	104	Nev–Nop
49	Frank–Fry	105	Nor–O'B
50	Fu–Gap	106	O'C–O'M
51	Gar–Gem	107	O'N–Ov
52	Gen–Gillh	108	Ow–Parq
53	Gilli–Gooc	109	Parr–Pek
54	Good–Gram	110	Pel–Pf
55	Gran–Greg	111	Ph–Pi
56	Greh–Gum	112	Pl–Pov
		113	Pow–Pup
		114	Pur–Ram
		115	Ran–Red
		116	Ree–Reo
		117	Rep–Rich
		118	Rici–Roa
		119	Rob–Roe
		120	Rof–Ros

Roll	Description
121	Rot–Ru
122	Rx–San
123	Sap–Schf
124	Schi–Scho
125	Schp–Sco
126	Scr–Sg
127	Sh–Sheo
128	Shep–Shy
129	Si–Sk
130	Sl–Smith, F.
131	Smith, G.–Smith, M.
132	Smith, N.–Soh
133	Soi–Sr
134	St–Sten
135	Steo–Stoc
136	Stod–Stu
137	Stv–Swi
138	Swo–Tc
139	Te–Thomm
140	Thomp–Til
141	Tim–To
142	Tr–Tul
143	Tum–Vam
144	Van F–Van S
145	Vant–Vo
146	Vr–Wall
147	Walm–War
148	Was–Wee
149	Weg–Wer
150	Wes–Whis
151	Whit–Why
152	Wi–Willg
153	Willi–Wilq
154	Wils–Wis
155	Wit–Woo
156	Wor–Yh
157	Yi–Z

Index to Compiled Service Records of Volunteer Union Soldiers Who Served in Organizations From the State of North Carolina. M391. 2 rolls. 16mm. DP.

The compiled service records to which this index applies are reproduced on M401.

Roll	Description
1	A–La
2	Le–Z

Index to Compiled Service Records of Volunteer Union Soldiers Who Served in Organizations From the State of Ohio. M552. 122 rolls. 16mm. DP.

Roll	Description
1	A–Alk
2	All–Ao
3	Ap–Az
4	B–Bam
5	Ban–Bar
6	Bas–Beb
7	Bec–Beno
8	Benr–Bir
9	Bis–Boh
10	Boi–Bowl
11	Bowm–Bra
12	Brc–Brou
13	Brow–Bru

Roll	Description
14	Bry–Burk
15	Burl–By
16	C–Carm
17	Carn–Caz
18	Ce–Clap
19	Clar–Cly
20	Co–Com
21	Con–Coq
22	Cor–Cral
23	Cram–Cry
24	Cu–Daq
25	Dar–Day
26	De–Der
27	Des–Dl
28	Do
29	Dr–Dus
30	Dut–Eh
31	Ei–En
32	Eo–Fao
33	Far–Fig
34	Fik–Fli
35	Flo–Fo
36	Fr
37	Fu–Garo
38	Garr–Gif
39	Gig–Gon
40	Goo–Grb
41	Gre–Gri
42	Gro–Hah
43	Hai–Ham
44	Han–Harp
45	Harr–Hat
46	Hau–Heh
47	Hei–Herp
48	Herr–Hilk
49	Hill–Hoc
50	Hod–Hon
51	Hoo–How
52	Hoy–Hum
53	Hun–Ip
54	Ir–Je
55	Jh–Jond
56	Jone–Kan
57	Kao–Kell
58	Kelm–Kil
59	Kim–Kis
60	Kit–Ko
61	Kr–Lam
62	Lan–Laz
63	Le–Lev
64	Lew–Ll
65	Lo
66	Lu–Mak
67	Mal–Mars
68	Mart–Max
69	May–McCl
70	McCo–McD
71	McE–McKe
72	McKi–McQ
73	McR–Met
74	Meu–Miller, Q.
75	Miller, R.–Mom
76	Mon–Mori
77	Mork–Mul

Roll	Description
78	Mum–My
79	N–Nich
80	Nick–Ob
81	O'C–Ou
82	Ov–Pas
83	Pat–Perl
84	Perm–Pin
85	Pip–Po
86	Pr–Q
87	R–Rec
88	Red–Ren
89	Reo–Ric
90	Rid–Robe
91	Robi–Rol
92	Rom–Rub
93	Ruc–Sam
94	San–Schl
95	Schm–Scot
96	Scou–Shae
97	Shaf–Sheo
98	Shep–Sho
99	Shp–Sim
100	Sin–Smith, Harry
101	Smith, Harvey–Sno
102	Snu–Sper
103	Spes–Star
104	Stas–Stev
105	Stew–Stou
106	Stov–Sum
107	Sun–Tax
108	Tay–Thomo
109	Thomp–Tol
110	Tom–Tup
111	Tur–Vane
112	Van F.–Vy
113	W–Wal
114	Wam–Wea
115	Web–Weo
116	Wep–White, V.
117	White, W.–Wilk
118	Will
119	Wilm–Wis
120	Wit–Wop
121	Wor–Yi
122	Yo–Z

Index to Compiled Service Records of Volunteer Union Soldiers Who Served in Organizations From the State of Oregon. M553. 1 roll. 16mm. DP.

Index to Compiled Service Records of Volunteer Union Soldiers Who Served in Organizations From the State of Pennsylvania. M554. 136 rolls. 16mm. DP.

Roll	Description
1	A–Alld
2	Alle–Ans
3	Ant–Az
4	B–Bam
5	Ban–Bars
6	Bart–Beat
7	Beau–Benn
8	Benn–Bh
9	Bi–Blak
10	Blam–Bon

Roll	Description
11	Boo–Box
12	Boy–Brea
13	Breb–Brn
14	Bro–Brr
15	Bru–Burj
16	Bruk–By
17	C–Cap
18	Car–Casp
19	Cass–Chr
20	Chu–Clo
21	Clu–Com
22	Con–Coo
23	Cop–Cral
24	Cram–Cro
25	Crs–Dam
26	Dan–Dav
27	Daw–Dem
28	Den–Did
29	Die–Dom
30	Don–Dov
31	Dow–Dunk
32	Dunl–Ec
33	Ed–El
34	Em–Eu
35	Ev–Fau
36	Fav–Fim
37	Fin–Fla
38	Fle–For
39	Fos–Frem
40	Fren–Fy
41	G–Gar
42	Gas–Gh
43	Gi
44	Gl–Got
45	Gou–Gref
46	Greg–Gry
47	Gu–Hai
48	Hak–Hank
49	Hanl–Harp
50	Harr–Has
51	Hat–Hec
52	Hed–Henm
53	Henn–Hh
54	Hi–Hip
55	Hir–Holl
56	Holm–Hot
57	Hou–Hug
58	Huh–Hy
59	I–Jem
60	Jen–Jom
61	Jon–Kar
62	Kas–Kek
63	Kel–Kene
64	Keng–Kh
65	Ki–Kis
66	Kit–Kon
67	Koo–Ky
68	L–Lat
69	Lau–Leh
70	Lei–Lez
71	Lh–Ln
72	Lo–Lov
73	Low–Ly
74	M–Manm

Roll	Description
75	Mann–Mart
76	Maru–Maz
77	Mc–McCh
78	McCi–McCo
79	McCr–McE
80	McF–McH
81	McI–McLd
82	McLe–McV
83	McW–Mes
84	Met–Miller, H.
85	Miller, I.–Mily
86	Min–Mon
87	Moo–Morq
88	Morr–Mt
89	Mu–Mur
90	Mus–Neh
91	Nei–Nn
92	No–Oe
93	O'F–Ow
94	Ox–Pat
95	Pau–Pe
96	Pf–Pom
97	Pon–Pr
98	Pu–Rat
99	Rau–Reg
100	Reh–Rez
101	Rh–Rie
102	Rif–Robb
103	Robe–Rok
104	Rol–Roz
105	Ru–Sal
106	Sam–Sche
107	Schi–Schu
108	Schw–Sel
109	Sem–Shap
110	Shar–Sher
111	Shes–Shr
112	Shu–Si
113	Sk–Smith, G.
114	Smith, H.–Smy
115	Sn–Spa
116	Spe–Star
117	Stas–Steu
118	Stev–Stom
119	Ston–Stt
120	Stu–Swef
121	Sweg–Te
122	Th–Tir
123	Tis–Trr
124	Tru–Vanc
125	Van D–Vw
126	W–Wals
127	Walt–Wath
128	Watk–Weil
129	Weim–Wer
130	Wes–White
131	Whitf–Willh
132	Willi–Wilson, F.
133	Wilson, G.–Witf
134	With–Woo
135	Wor–Yom
136	Yon–Z

Index to Compiled Service Records of Volunteer Union Soldiers Who Served in Organizations From the State of Rhode Island. M555. 7 rolls. 16mm. DP.

Roll	Description
1	A–B
2	C–D
3	E–Hi
4	Ho–Ma
5	Mc–Pa
6	Pe–Sm
7	Sn–Z

Index to Compiled Service Records of Volunteer Union Soldiers Who Served in Organizations From the State of Tennessee. M392. 16 rolls. 16mm. DP.

The compiled service records to which this index applies are reproduced on M395.

Roll	Description
1	A–Bl
2	Bo–By
3	C–Co
4	Cr–D
5	E–Gh
6	Gi–Hd
7	He–I
8	J–La
9	Le–Ma
10	Mc–Mi
11	Mo–O
12	P–Ra
13	Re–Se
14	Sh–Sy
15	T–Wa
16	We–Z

Index to Compiled Service Records of Volunteer Union Soldiers Who Served in Organizations From the State of Texas. M393. 2 rolls. 16mm. DP.

The compiled service records to which this index applies are reproduced on M402.

Roll	Description
1	A–Ma
2	Mc–Z

Index to Compiled Service Records of Volunteer Union Soldiers Who Served in Organizations From the Territory of Utah. M556. 1 roll. 16mm. DP.

This microfilm publication reproduces the alphabetical card index to the compiled service records of volunteer Union soldiers who served in Capt. Lot (Lott) Smith's Company, Utah Cavalry. This company is the only organization of Union troops from the Territory of Utah for which the National Archives and Records Administration has separate compiled service records.

The compiled service records to which this index applies are available on M692.

Index to Compiled Service Records of Volunteer Union Soldiers Who Served in Organizations From the State of Vermont. M557. 14 rolls. 16mm. DP.

Roll	Description
1	A–Be
2	Bh–Cal

Roll	Description
3	Cam–Cor
4	Cos–D
5	E–Ge
6	Gh–Ha
7	He–J
8	K–Lp
9	Lu–Mon
10	Moo–Peq
11	Per–Roo
12	Rop–So
13	Sp–Va
14	Ve–Z

Index to Compiled Service Records of Volunteer Union Soldiers Who Served in Organizations From the State of Virginia. M394. 1 roll. 16mm. DP.

The compiled service records to which this index applies are reproduced on M398.

Index to Compiled Service Records of Volunteer Union Soldiers Who Served in Organizations From the Territory of Washington. M558. 1 roll. 16mm. DP.

Index to Compiled Service Records of Volunteer Union Soldiers Who Served in Organizations From the State of West Virginia. M507. 13 rolls. 16mm. DP.

The compiled service records to which the index applies are reproduced on M508.

Roll	Description
1	A–Bon
2	Boo–Ch
3	Ci–De
4	Di–F
5	G–Ha
6	He–J
7	K–L
8	M–Me
9	Mg–Pa
10	Pe–Ro
11	Ru–Spe
12	Sph–V
13	W–Z

Index to Compiled Service Records of Volunteer Union Soldiers Who Served in Organizations From the State of Wisconsin. M559. 33 rolls. 16mm. DP.

Roll	Description
1	A–Bak
2	Bal–Be
3	Bh–Bre
4	Bri–Cah
5	Cai–Cli
6	Clo–Cro
7	Crs–Dh
8	Di–Ek
9	El–Fj
10	Fl–Ga
11	Ge–Gr
12	Gs–Har
13	Has–Hi
14	Ho–Hy
15	I–Ka
16	Ke–Ko

Roll	Description
17	Kr–Len
18	Leo–Mal
19	Man–McI
20	McJ–Mj
21	Mo–Ne
22	Ni–O
23	P–Pj
24	Pl–Reh
25	Rei–Ros
26	Rot–Schu
27	Schw–Sj
28	Sk–Sta
29	St. C–Ta
30	Tc–Ty
31	U–Wa
32	We–Wilk
33	Will–Z

Index to Compiled Service Records of Volunteer Union Soldiers Who Served with United States Colored Troops. M589. 98 rolls. 16mm. DP.

In May 1863 the War Department authorized the formation of the United States Colored Troops (U.S.C.T.). Most of the soldiers served in the infantry, but some served in the cavalry, engineer units, and in light and heavy artillery batteries. The Corps d'Afrique and other State organizations were redesignated when they became part of the U.S.C.T., with the exception of a few units raised in Massachusetts, Connecticut, and Louisiana.

Nearly all of the U.S.C.T. officers were white. Although the War Department imposed a stringent examination of all applicants, it discouraged blacks from applying. Only 75 to 100 black officers were appointed, and three-quarters of those served in Gen. Benjamin Butler's Department of Louisiana.

The soldiers of the U.S.C.T. met with varying reactions and treatment. In the trans-Mississippi West, the troops saw combat, while in the Department of Tennessee and in the South they were assigned fatigue work. In the East, they drew both combat and fatigue duty. In addition, they received unequal pay, poor equipment, and inadequate medical attention. In July 1864, Congress acted to remedy the pay inequality by authorizing equal pay, retroactive to January 1, 1864, for all who had been free as of April 19, 1861.

This microfilm publication reproduces an alphabetical card index to the compiled service records of volunteer Union soldiers who served with the U.S. Colored Troops. Each index card gives the name of a soldier, his rank, and the unit in which he served. There are cross-references for names that appear in the records under more than one spelling and for service in more than one unit or organization.

The compiled military service records to which this index refers are not microfilmed.

Roll	Description
1	A–Alk
2	All–Ande
3	Andl–Az
4	B–Baq
5	Bar–Bat
6	Bau–Ben
7	Beo–Blai

Roll	Description
8	Blak–Bor
9	Bos–Brag
10	Brah–Broo
11	Bros–Brown, J.
12	Brown, K.–Buf
13	Bug–Bus
14	But–Cam
15	Can–Car
16	Cas–Che
17	Chi–Cl
18	Co–Com
19	Con–Cot
20	Cou–Cr
21	Cs–Dau
22	Dav–Daz
23	De–Dic
24	Did–Dov
25	Dow–Dy
26	E–El
27	Em–Fa
28	Fe–Fl
29	Fo–Fran
30	Frap–Gak
31	Gal–Gh
32	Gi–Gn
33	Go–Graw
34	Gray–Gref
35	Greg–Gy
36	H–Ham
37	Han–Harris, K.
38	Harris, L.–Haw
39	Hax–Heno
40	Henr–Hik
41	Hil–Holl
42	Holm–Hoz
43	Hu–Hy
44	I–Jackson, I.
45	Jackson, J.–Jay
46	Je–Johnson, C.
47	Johnson, D.–Johnson, M.
48	Johnson, N.–Jom
49	Jon–Jont
50	Joo–Ke
51	Kh–Lah
52	Lai–Laz
53	Le–Lev
54	Lew–Loc
55	Lod–Ly
56	M–Marr
57	Mars–Mat
58	Mau–McD
59	McE–Mel
60	Mem–Mil
61	Mim–Moon
62	Moor–Morr
63	Mors–My
64	N–Ni
65	No–O
66	P–Pas
67	Pat–Pes
68	Pet–Pi
69	Pl–Pre
70	Pri–Ram
71	Ran–Ree

Roll	Description
72	Ref–Ric
73	Rid–Robe
74	Robi–Rok
75	Rol–Ry
76	S–Scl
77	Sco–Se
78	Sh
79	Si–Sme
80	Smi–Smith, J.
81	Smith, K.–So
82	Sp–Steu
83	Stev–Sty
84	Su–Tax
85	Tay–Thol
86	Thom–Thomp
87	Thoms–To
88	Tr–Ty
89	U–V
90	W–Ward
91	Ware–Wash
92	Wass–Wem
93	Wen–White
94	Whitf–Williams, E.
95	Williams, F.–Williams, T.
96	Williams, V.–Wils
97	Wilt–Wo
98	Wr–Z

Index to Compiled Service Records of Volunteer Union Soldiers Who Served in the Veteran Reserve Corps. M636. 44 rolls. 16mm. DP.

This microfilm publication reproduces an alphabetical card index to the compiled service records of volunteer Union soldiers who served in the Veteran Reserve Corps. The compiled military service records to which this index refers are not microfilmed.

The Veteran Reserve Corps was composed of deserving officers and enlisted men who were unfit for active field service because of wounds or disease contracted in the line of duty, but who were still capable of performing garrison duty. The Corps also included officers and enlisted men borne on the Army rolls who were absent from duty and in hospitals, in convalescent camps, or otherwise under the control of medical officers, but who were capable of serving as cooks, nurses, clerks, or orderlies at hospitals and as guards for hospitals or other public buildings. When the Corps was first authorized on April 28, 1863, it was known as the "Invalid Corps." Its name was changed to the Veteran Reserve Corps on March 18, 1864.

Roll	Description
1	A
2	Ba
3	Be–Bla
4	Ble–Bri
5	Bro–Bur
6	Bus–Ca
7	Ce–Cok
8	Col–Coz
9	Cr–Dau
10	Dav–Dom
11	Don–Dy
12	E
13	F–Fl

Roll	Description
14	Fo–Gal
15	Gam–Go
16	Gr–Gy
17	H–Har
18	Has–He
19	Hi–Hos
20	Hot–I
21	J–Ka
22	Ke–Ki
23	Kl–La
24	Le–Lo
25	Lu–Mat
26	Mau–McI
27	McK–Me
28	Mi–Mor
29	Mos–Ni
30	No–Pap
31	Par–Pi
32	Pl–Ra
33	Re–Ri
34	Ro–Ry
35	S–Sc
36	Se–Sh
37	Si–Sn
38	So–Sti
39	St.J–Sz
40	T–To
41	Tr–V
42	W–Wel
43	Wem–Wil
44	Wim–Z

Compiled Service Records

Compiled Service Records of Volunteer Union Soldiers Who Served in Organizations From the State of Alabama. M276. 10 rolls. 16mm. DP.

The compiled service records reproduced in this microfilm publication are indexed on M263.

Roll	Description
1	1st Cavalry
	A–Br
2	Bu–C
3	D–Go
4	Gr–H
5	I–L
6	M–Ne
7	Ni–Rh
8	Ri–Sp
9	St–V
10	W–Z
	Miscellaneous Card Abstracts Personal Papers

Compiled Service Records of Volunteer Union Soldiers Who Served in Organizations From the State of Arkansas. M399. 60 rolls. 16mm. DP.

The compiled service records reproduced in this microfilm publication are indexed on M383.

Roll	Description
1	1st Cavalry
	A–Bod
2	Bog–Cl
3	Co–D

Roll	Description
4	E–Gl
5	Go–Hi
6	Ho–Joh
7	Jon–Le
8	Li–McC
9	McD–N
10	O–Re
11	Rh–Sl
12	Sm–Ta
13	Te–We
14	Wh–Z
15	2d Cavalry
	A–Bo
16	Br–Cr
17	Cu–F
18	G–Ho
19	Hu–Mas
20	Mat–My
21	N–Ram
22	Ran–So
23	Sp–Wa
24	We–Y
	3d Cavalry
	A–Ba
25	Be–Ch
26	Cl–Fe
27	Fi–Ham
28	Han–Ji
29	Jo–Mat
30	Mau–Pas
31	Pat–Sa
32	Sc–U
33	V–Y
	4th Cavalry
	A–An
34	Ar–Br
35	Bu–Da
36	De–G
37	Ha–Je
38	Jo–Me
39	Mi–Poi
40	Pol–So
41	Sp–Wa
42	We–Y
	1st Battery, Light Artillery
	A–He
43	Hi–Y
	1st Infantry
	A–Al
44	An–B
45	C–Do
46	Dr–He
47	Hi–Le
48	Li–M
49	N–Ro
50	Ru–Sti
51	Sto–Wh
52	Wi–Y
	1st Battalion, Infantry
	A–K
53	L–Y
	2d Infantry
	A–Bo
54	Br–Da
55	De–I
56	J–Mc

Roll	Description
57	Me–Sc
58	Se–Z
59	4th Infantry
	Miscellaneous Card Abstracts of Cavalry, Light Artillery, and Infantry Records
	1st–4th Cavalry
	1st Battery, Light Artillery
	1st Infantry
	1st Infantry, 6 months, 1862
	2d Infantry
	4th Infantry
	Other Miscellaneous Card Abstracts
60	Personal Papers

Compiled Service Records of Volunteer Union Soldiers Who Served in Organizations From the State of Florida. M400. 11 rolls. 16mm. DP.

The compiled service records reproduced in this microfilm publication are indexed on M264.

Roll	Description
1	1st Cavalry
	A–C
2	D–Hi
3	Ho–K
4	L–Pi
5	Po–S
6	T–Y
	1st East Florida Cavalry
7	2d Cavalry
	A–Do
8	Dr–J
9	K–P
10	R–Wa
11	We–Y
	Unassigned Volunteers
	Miscellaneous Card Abstracts
	1st Cavalry
	2d Cavalry
	Personal Papers

Compiled Service Records of Volunteer Union Soldiers Who Served in Organizations From the State of Georgia. M403. 1 roll. 16mm. DP.

The compiled service records reproduced in this microfilm publication are indexed on M385.

Compiled Service Records of Volunteer Union Soldiers Who Served in Organizations From the State of Kentucky. M397. 515 rolls. 16mm. DP.

The compiled service records reproduced in this microfilm publication are indexed on M386.

Compiled Service Records of Volunteer Union Soldiers Who Served in Organizations From the State of Louisiana. M396. 50 rolls. 16mm. DP.

The compiled service records reproduced in this microfilm publication are indexed on M387.

Roll	Description
1	1st Cavalry
	A–Bl
2	Bo–Cl
3	Co–E
4	F–Ha
5	He–K

Roll	Description
6	L–Mc
7	Me–P
8	Q–Sl
9	Sm–U
10	V–Z
11	1st Battalion, Cavalry Scouts
12	2d Cavalry
	A–Gh
13	Gi–N
14	O–Z
15	1st Infantry
	A–Br
16	Bu–Dr
17	Du–Gi
18	Gl–H
19	I–K
20	L–Ma
21	Mc–Pa
22	Pe–Sa
23	Sc–Su
24	Sw–Z
25	1st New Orleans Infantry
	A–B
26	C–Do
27	Dr–Gl
28	Go–I
29	J–La
30	Le–Mc
31	Me–O
32	P–R
33	S–Te
34	Th–Z
35	2d Infantry
	A–B
36	C–E
37	F–Ha
38	He–K
39	L–Mi
40	Mo–Q
41	R–Sp
42	St–Z
43	2d New Orleans Infantry
44	5th Infantry, 60 days, 1863
45	Headquarters Troops, Department of the Gulf
	A–L
46	M–Z
47	Miscellaneous Card Abstracts of Records
	1st Cavalry
	2d Cavalry
	1st Infantry
48	1st New Orleans Infantry
	2d New Orleans Infantry
49	2d Infantry
	Headquarters Troops, Department of the Gulf
	Other Miscellaneous Card Abstracts
50	Personal Papers

Compiled Service Records of Volunteer Union Soldiers Who Served in Organizations From the State of Maryland. M384. 238 rolls. 16mm. DP.

The compiled service records reproduced in this microfilm publication are indexed on M388.

Roll	Description
1	1st Cavalry
	A–Bel

Roll	Description	Roll	Description
2	Ben–Buc	52	Bas–Bri
3	Bue–Co	53	Bro–Ci
4	Cr–D	54	Cl–Di
5	E–F	55	Do–Fa
6	G–Han	56	Fc–Gn
7	Har–Ho	57	Go–Hen
8	Hu–Ke	58	Her–Joh
9	Ki–Lo	59	Joi–Lai
10	Lu–Mid	60	Lam–Mar
11	Mil–N	61	Mas–Moore, F.
12	O–Ree	62	Moore, G.–Pf
13	Reg–Schi	63	Ph–Rowa
14	Schl–Smith, J.	64	Rowe–Smith, F.
15	Smith, M.–Thoma	65	Smith, G.–Ta
16	Thomp–Wa	66	Te–Wa
17	We–Z	67	We–Z
	1st Potomac Home Brigade, Cavalry		**1st Eastern Shore Infantry**
18	A–Bo	68	A–Bren
19	Br–Co	69	Brer–Dav
20	Cr–D	70	Day–Har
21	E–Gibb	71	Hay–La
22	Gibs–Hi	72	Le–M
23	Ho–Ki	73	N–R
24	Kl–McCo	74	S–Tr
25	McCr–Mo	75	Tu–Z
26	Mu–Pr		**2d Infantry**
27	Pu–Sh		A–Ad
28	Si–Te	76	Af–Bl
29	Th–Wh	77	Bn–Ca
30	Wi–Z	78	Ce–De
	2d Cavalry	79	Di–Fo
	A–Hi	80	Fr–Hane
31	Ho–Z	81	Hank–I
	Independent Co. M, 2d Cavalry	82	J–Lam
32	**3d Cavalry**	83	Lan–McD
	A–Br	84	McE–Na
33	Bu–D	85	Ne–Re
34	E–Ho	86	Rh–Shri
35	Hu–Ma	87	Shro–Ti
36	Mc–Pa	88	To–Wi
37	Pe–Sp	89	Wo–Z
38	St–W		**2d Eastern Shore Infantry**
39	Y		A–B
	Purnell Legion, Cavalry	90	C–D
	A–Do	91	E–H
40	Dr–Mc	92	I–Mi
41	Me–Tra	93	Mo–Sc
42	Tro–Y	94	Se–V
	Baltimore Battery, Light Artillery	95	W–Z
	A–Ga		**2d Potomac Home Brigade, Infantry**
43	Ge–Z		A–Ad
	Smith's Independent Co., Cavalry	96	Al–Br
44	A–S	97	Bu–Cr
45	T–W	98	Cu–Fo
	Battery A, Junior Light Artillery	99	Fr–Hen
	Battery B, Light Artillery	100	Her–Kep
	Battery B, 1st Light Artillery	101	Ker–McI
	A–Bo	102	McK–Pi
46	Br–Do	103	Pl–Se
47	Dr–Hi	104	Sh–Sy
48	Ho–McE	105	T–Whita
49	McF–Sc	106	White–Z
50	Se–Wh		**3d Infantry**
51	Wi–Z		A–Ban
	1st Heavy Artillery		
	1st Infantry		

Roll	Description
107	Bar–Br
108	Bu–C
109	D–Fl
110	Fo–Ha
111	He–Ke
112	Ki–Ma
113	Mc–Mu
114	My–Ri
115	Ro–Sh
116	Si–To
117	Tr–Wi
118	Wo–Z
	3d Potomac Home Brigade, Infantry
	A–Bo
119	Br–C
120	D–Fo
121	Fr–Har
122	Hat–J
123	K–L
124	M–Mille
125	Mills–Re
126	Rh–Sl
127	Sm–U
128	V–Z
129	4th Infantry, Old Organization
	4th Infantry, New Organization
	A–Bir
130	Bis–Don
131	Dop–Hen
132	Her–Mart
133	Marv–Ra
134	Re–Sp
135	St–Z
136	4th Potomac Home Brigade, Infantry
	5th Infantry
	A–Bis
137	Bit–Ca
138	Ce–Dop
139	Dor–Fr
140	Fu–Ha
141	He–Ka
142	Ke–Ll
143	Lo–Mel
144	Mem–N
145	O–Ri
146	Ro–Sha
147	She–Sy
148	T–Wei
149	Wel–Z
	6th Infantry
	A–Al
150	An–Car
151	Cas–E
152	F–Han
153	Har–La
154	Le–Moo
155	Mor–Rh
156	Ri–Sp
157	St–Wil
158	Win–Z
	7th Infantry
	A–Bl
159	Bo–Co
160	Cr–Fo
161	Fr–Hi

Roll	Description
162	Ho–Lig
163	Lil–M
164	N–Sc
165	Se–Wea
166	Web–Z
	8th Infantry
	A–Ben
167	Ber–Co
168	Cr–Fo
169	Fr–H
170	I–Ma
171	Mc–Pl
172	Po–Smith, E.
173	Smith, F.–Wh
174	Wi–Z
	9th Infantry
	A–F
175	G–R
176	S–Z
	10th Infantry
	A–Cha
177	Che–Ma
178	Mc–Z
179	11th Infantry
	A–G
180	H–Rie
181	Rig–Z
	11th Infantry, 100 days, 1864
	A–B
182	C–L
183	M–Z
184	12th Infantry, 100 days, 1864
	A–Th
185	Ti–Z
	13th Infantry
	A–Bel
186	Ben–Br
187	Bu–C
188	D–E
189	F–Go
190	Gr–He
191	Hi–Kn
192	Ko–Ma
193	Mc–My
194	N–Ra
195	Re–She
196	Shi–Stev
197	Stew–Wa
198	We–Z
	Baltimore Light Infantry, Volunteers
	McGowan's Independent Co., Patapsco Guards, Infantry
	A–F
200	G–Y
	Purnell's Legion, Infantry
	A
201	B–Ch
202	Cl–Ga
203	Ge–Je
204	Jo–Mc
205	Me–Ri
206	Ro–To
207	Tr–Z
	Unassigned Volunteers
208	Miscellaneous Card Abstracts of Records
	1st Cavalry

Roll	Description
	1st Potomac Home Brigade, Cavalry
	2d Cavalry
	3d Cavalry
	1st Light Artillery
	Battery A, Junior Artillery
	Battery B, Light Artillery
209	Baltimore Battery, Light Artillery, A–B
	1st Infantry
	A–Q
210	R–Z
	1st Eastern Shore Infantry
	2d Infantry,
	A–Co
211	Cr–Z
212	2d Eastern Shore Infantry
	2d Potomac Home Brigade, Infantry
	3d Infantry
	A–De
213	Di–Z
	3d Potomac Home Brigade, Infantry
	A–G
214	H–Z
	4th Infantry
215	5th Infantry
216	6th Infantry
	7th Infantry
	A–G
217	H–Z
	8th Infantry
	A–O
218	P–Z
	9th Infantry
	10th Infantry
	11th Infantry, 100 days
	12th Infantry, 100 days
219	13th Infantry
	Purnell's Legion, Infantry
	A–L
220	M–Z
	McGowan's Independent Co., Patapsco Guards, Infantry
	Other Miscellaneous Card Abstracts
221	Personal Papers, 1st Series
	A–Bo
222	Br–Ci
223	Cl–Divel
224	Dives–Ga
225	Ge–Hi
226	Ho–Ke
227	Ki–Ma
228	Mc–Mu
229	My–Ri
230	Ro–Si
231	Sk–Th
232	Ti–We
233	Wh–Z
234	Personal Papers, 2d Series
	B–E
235	F–K
236	L–O
237	P–S
238	T–Z

Compiled Service Records of Volunteer Union Soldiers Who Served in Organizations From the State of Mississippi. M404. 4 rolls. 16mm. DP.

The compiled service records reproduced in this microfilm publication are indexed on M389.

Roll	Description
1	1st Battalion, Mounted Rifles
	A–F
2	G–Mc
3	Me–Si
4	Sm–Y
	Miscellaneous Card Abstracts
	Personal Papers

Compiled Service Records of Volunteer Union Soldiers Who Served in Organizations From the State of Missouri. M405. 854 rolls. 16mm. DP.

The compiled service records reproduced in this microfilm publication are indexed on M390.

Roll	Description
1	1st Cavalry
	A–Ba
2	Be–Br
3	Bu–Cl
4	Co–De
5	Di–Fe
6	Fi–Go
7	Gr–He
8	Hi–Jon
9	Jor–La
10	Le–Ma
11	Mc–Moo
12	Mor–Pa
13	Pe–Rh
14	Ri–Sc
15	Se–Sp
16	Sr–To
17	Tr–Wh
18	Wi–Z
	1st State Militia, Cavalry
	A–As
19	At–B
20	C
21	D–E
22	F–Han
23	Har–Joh
24	Jon–Lo
25	Lu–Mil
26	Min–Pa
27	Pe–R
28	S–St
29	Su–Wh
30	Wi–Z
	1st Battalion, State Militia, Cavalry
	A–J
31	K–Z
	1st Battalion, U.S. Reserve Corps, Cavalry
	A–Gl
32	Go–Z
33	2d Cavalry (Merrill's Horse)
	A–Barl
34	Barn–Bri
35	Bro–Ch
36	Ci–Cy
37	D
38	E–Fo

Roll	Description
39	Fr–Ham
40	Han–Hok
41	Hol–Jo
42	Ju–La
43	Le–McCa
44	McCi–Moo
45	Mor–Pa
46	Pe–Re
47	Rh–Sc
48	Se–Sp
49	St–Th
50	Ti–Wel
51	Wer–Z
52	2d State Militia, Cavalry
	A–Bra
53	Bre–Co
54	Cr–E
55	F–Hal
56	Ham–Je
57	Jo–L
58	M–Moo
59	Mor–P
60	Q–Sc
61	Se–Su
62	Sw–Wh
63	Wi–Z
	2d Battalion, State Militia, Cavalry
	A–D
64	E–Mi
65	Mo–Y
66	3d Cavalry
	A–Be
67	Bi–By
68	C–Cr
69	Cu–Fi
70	Fl–Gr
71	Gu–H
72	I–La
73	Le–Mc
74	Me–O
75	P–Ri
76	Ro–So
77	Sp–V
78	W–Y
79	3d State Militia, Cavalry (1st Organization)
	A–F
80	G–Me
81	Mi–T
82	U–Z
	3d State Militia, Cavalry (2d Organization)
	A–Ba
83	Be–Ca
84	Ce–Dr
85	Du–G
86	H
87	I–Mar
88	Mas–Mu
89	My–Rh
90	Ri–Sl
91	Sm–U
92	V–Z
93	4th Cavalry
	A–Be
94	Bi–C
95	D–Fo

Roll	Description
96	Fr–Ham
97	Han–Hoy
98	Hu–Ko
99	Kr–Ma
100	Mc–Ne
101	Ni–Rh
102	Ri–Scho
103	Schr–Sto
104	Str–Wan
105	War–Z
106	4th State Militia, Cavalry
	A–Bo
107	Br–Cob
108	Cof–De
109	Di–Gl
110	Go–Hi
111	Ho–K
112	L–Me
113	Mi–Pa
114	Pe–Sc
115	Se–Ta
116	Th–Z
117	5th Cavalry
	A–E
118	F–Ki
119	Kl–P
120	R–V
121	W–Z
	5th State Militia, Cavalry
	A–Ca
122	Ch–Li
123	Lo–R
124	S–Z
125	5th State Militia, Cavalry (2d Organization)
	A–Bo
126	Br–Ca
127	Ch–D
128	E–Ga
129	Ge–He
130	Hi–Ke
131	Ki–Ma
132	Mc–My
133	N–Q
134	R–Sa
135	Sc–Ste
136	Sti–V
137	W–Z
138	6th Cavalry
	A–Bl
139	Bo–Cl
140	Co–De
141	Di–F
142	G–Ha
143	He–Ka
144	Ke–Ma
145	Mc–Mo
146	Mu–Ra
147	Re–Sh
148	Si–Sw
149	T–Wh
150	Wi–Z
151	6th State Militia, Cavalry
	A–Bo
152	Br–Cl
153	Co–Ei

Roll	Description
154	El–Han
155	Har–Hy
156	I–Ll
157	Lo–Mi
158	Mo–Ph
159	Pi–R
160	S–Sta
161	Ste–V
162	W–Z
163	7th Cavalry A–Be
164	Bi–Car
165	Cas–Cu
166	D–Ew
167	F–G
168	H–Ho
169	Hu–K
170	L–McCol
171	McCon–N
172	O–Rob
173	Roc–Sm
174	Sn–V
175	W–Z
176	7th State Militia, Cavalry A–Bel
177	Ben–Col
178	Com–El
179	Em–Gra
180	Gre–Hol
181	Hoo–K
182	L–Mc
183	Me–Pe
184	Ph–Sc
185	Se–Th
186	Ti–Y
187	8th Cavalry A–Bl
188	Bo–Cl
189	Co–El
190	Em–G
191	H–I
192	J–Li
193	Lo–Moo
194	Mor–Ra
195	Re–Sh
196	Si–V
197	W–Z
198	8th State Militia, Cavalry A–Bl
199	Bo–Ca
200	Ch–De
201	Di–Fo
202	Fr–Ha
203	He–Jo
204	Ju–Lu
205	Ly–Moo
206	Mor–Po
207	Pr–Sc
208	Se–Th
209	Ti–Z
210	9th Cavalry A–Fl
211	Fo–Ni
212	No–Z
213	9th State Militia, Cavalry

Roll	Description
	A–Bo
214	Br–Co
215	Cr–Fa
216	Fe–Han
217	Har–Hu
218	I–Lo
219	Lu–N
220	O–Ri
221	Ro–Sm
222	Sn–Wa
223	We–Z
	10th Cavalry A
224	B–Br
225	Bu–Cr
226	Cu–Fl
227	Fo–He
228	Hi–K
229	L–Mc
230	Me–O
231	P–Rog
232	Rom–Sr
233	St–U
234	V–Z
235	11th Cavalry A–Bo
236	Br–Col
237	Con–Em
238	En–Hal
239	Ham–I
240	J–L
241	M–Mo
242	Mu–Pr
243	Pu–Sh
244	Si–To
245	Tr–Y
246	11th State Militia, Cavalry A–F
247	G–Mi
248	Mo–S
249	T–Z
	12th Cavalry A–Bai
250	Bak–Bri
251	Bro–Cl
252	Co–Dr
253	Du–Gl
254	Go–Hof
255	Hol–Ken
256	Keo–Mar
257	Mas–Mi
258	Mo–Pr
259	Pu–Se
260	Sh–St
261	Su–Wa
262	We–Z
263	12th State Militia, Cavalry A–Ha
264	He–N
265	O–Z
266	13th Cavalry A–B
267	C–D
268	E–Ha
269	He–Ke

Roll	Description
270	Ki–Mc
271	Me–Q
272	R–Sl
273	Sm–Wal
274	Wam–Z
	14th Cavalry
	A–Bo
275	Br–D
276	E–Ji
277	Jo–Mc
278	Me–R
279	S–Y
280	14th State Militia, Cavalry
	A–G
281	H–Pl
282	Po–Y
283	15th Cavalry
	A–Do
284	Dr–La
285	Le–Sh
286	Si–Y
	16th Cavalry
	A–Bo
287	Br–Gl
288	Go–Ma
289	Mc–Sm
290	Sn–Y
291	Berry's Battalion, Cavalry
	Cass County Home Guard, Cavalry
	A–D
292	E–Z
293	Fremont's Body Guard, Cavalry
	Graham's Co., Cavalry
294	Smallwood's Co., Scouts and Guides, Cavalry, 3 months, 1861
	Sobolaski's Lancers, Cavalry
	Stewart's Battalion, Cavalry
295	1st Light Artillery
	A–Bao
296	Bar–Bod
297	Boe–Bur
298	Bus–Con
299	Coo–De
300	Di–Ei
301	El–Fl
302	Fo–Gl
303	Go–Hap
304	Har–Hig
305	Hil–I
306	J–Ki
307	Kl–Li
308	Lo–Ma
309	Mc–Me
310	Mi–My
311	N–Pe
312	Pf–Rh
313	Ri–Ry
314	S–Se
315	Sh–Ste
316	Sti–Ti
317	To–War
318	Was–Wig
319	Wil–Z
320	2d Light Artillery
	A–Bak
321	Bal–Be

Roll	Description
322	Bi–Bre
323	Bri–Ca
324	Ce–Da
325	De–Eh
326	Ei–Fl
327	Fo–Gh
328	Gi–Hal
329	Ham–Her
330	Hes–Hy
331	I–Ken
332	Ker–Kra
333	Kre–Li
334	Ll–Ma
335	Mc–Mil
336	Min–Ne
337	Ni–Pf
338	Ph–Reg
339	Reh–Ro
340	Ru–Schm
341	Schn–Se
342	Sh–Sta
343	Ste–The
344	Thi–V
345	W–We
346	Wh–Z
347	Backof's Battalion, Artillery, 3 months, 1861
	1st Flying Battery, Light Artillery
	A–K
348	L–Z
	Buell's Battery, Light Artillery
	Bullis' Battery, Light Artillery
	Kowald's Battery, Light Artillery
	Mann's Battery, Light Artillery
349	Sheldon's Battery, Light Artillery
	Wachman's Battery, Light Artillery
	Welfley's Battery, Light Artillery
350	1st Engineers
	A–B
351	C–D
352	E–Ha
353	He–Ll
354	Lo–O
355	P–Sl
356	Sm–V
357	W–Z
	Engineer Regiment of the West, Volunteers
	A–Ba
358	Be–Ca
359	Ch–E
360	F–He
361	Hi–L
362	M–Og
363	Oh–Sh
364	Si–U
365	V–Z
366	1st U.S. Reserve Corps, Infantry
	A–F
367	G–K
368	L–Sa
369	Sc–Z
370	1st U.S. Reserve Corps, Infantry, 3 months, 1861
	A–K
371	L–Z
372	1st Infantry, 3 months, 1861
373	1st State Militia, Infantry
	A–Bl

Roll	Description
374	Bo–C
375	D–E
376	F–Go
377	Gr–He
378	Hi–Ki
379	Kl–L
380	M–N
381	O–Ri
382	Ro–Se
383	Sh–T
384	U–Z
385	1st Regiment, Enrolled Militia, Missouri National Guard, Infantry
	2d U.S. Reserve Corps, Infantry
	A–F
386	G–M
387	N–Z
388	2d U.S. Reserve Corps, Infantry, 3 months, 1861
389	2d Infantry
	A–Br
390	Bu–Fo
391	Fr–Ha
392	He–Ki
393	Kl–La
394	Le–N
395	O–R
396	S–Sl
397	Sm–U
398	V–Z
399	2d Infantry, 3 months, 1861
	A–L
400	M–Z
401	3d U.S. Reserve Corps, Infantry
402	3d U.S. Reserve Corps, Infantry, 3 months, 1861
403	3d Infantry
	A–B
404	C–Fl
405	Fo–He
406	Hi–K
407	L–Mun
408	Mur–R
409	S–Sp
410	St–V
411	W–Z
412	3d Infantry, 3 months, 1861
	A–Ki
413	Kl–Z
414	4th U.S. Reserve Corps, Infantry
415	4th U.S. Reserve Corps, Infantry, 3 months, 1861
	A–Mc
416	Me–Z
417	4th Infantry
	A–J
418	K–Sp
419	St–Z
	4th Infantry, 3 months, 1861
	A–F
420	G–Z
421	5th U.S. Reserve Corps, Infantry, 3 months, 1861
	A–N
422	O–Z
	5th Infantry, 3 months, 1861
	A–F
423	G–Z

Roll	Description
424	5th Infantry
	A–F
425	G–L
426	M–Sc
427	Se–Z
428	6th Infantry
	A–Bl
429	Bo–Cl
430	Co–Do
431	Dr–F
432	G–Hi
433	Ho–K
434	L–Mc
435	Me–O
436	P–Sc
437	Se–Tr
438	Tu–Z
439	7th Infantry
	A–B
440	C
441	D–Fi
442	Fl–Hi
443	Ho–L
444	M
445	N–Re
446	Rh–St
447	Su–Y
448	8th Infantry
	A–Bl
449	Bo–Cl
450	Co–D
451	E–G
452	H–Ka
453	Ke–Ma
454	Mc–My
455	N–Ri
456	Ro–Sn
457	So–T
458	U–Z
459	10th Infantry
	A–Br
460	Bu–Da
461	De–F
462	G–H
463	I–L
464	M
465	N–Ri
466	Ro–Sh
467	Si–T
468	U–Z
469	11th Infantry
	A
470	B–Bl
471	Bo–By
472	C–Co
473	Cr–D
474	E–F
475	G
476	H–Hi
477	Ho–Ke
478	Ki–L
479	M–Mc
480	Me–N
481	O–Q
482	R

Roll	Description		Roll	Description
483	S–Sn		541	L–Ma
484	So–To		542	Mc–Mi
485	Tr–We		543	Mo–O
486	Wh–Z		544	P–Q
487	12th Infantry		545	R–Ry
	A–Bo		546	S–Sl
488	Br–E		547	Sm–Sw
489	F–Ha		548	T–Wa
490	He–Ka		549	We–Y
491	Ke–L		550	22d Infantry
492	M–Re		551	23d Infantry
493	Ri–Sc			A–Ba
494	Se–T		552	Be–Br
495	U–Z		553	Bu–Cl
496	13th Infantry		554	Co–Cu
497	15th Infantry		555	D–E
	A–Bl		556	F–G
498	Bo–C		557	H–Hi
499	D–E		558	Ho–J
500	F–Go		559	K–L
501	Gr–Hi		560	M–Mi
502	Ho–Kn		561	Mo–O
503	Ko–L		562	P–Ri
504	M–Ne		563	Ro–Sh
505	Ni–Ri		564	Si–Sw
506	Ro–Sc		565	T–Wa
507	Se–T		566	We–Z
508	U–Z		567	24th Infantry
509	16th Infantry			A–B
	17th Infantry		568	C–Di
	A–B		569	Do–G
510	C–G		570	H–I
511	H–J		571	J–L
512	K–L		572	M
513	M–P		573	N–P
514	R–Sc		574	R–Sm
515	Se–Z		575	So–V
516	18th Infantry		576	W–Z
	A–Bi		577	25th Infantry
517	Bl–By			A–B
518	Ca–Co		578	C–D
519	Cr–D		579	E–G
520	E–Ge		580	H–K
521	Gi–Ha		581	L–M
522	He–I		582	N–Sh
523	J–K		583	Si–Z
524	L–Ma		584	26th Infantry
525	Mc–My			A–Bo
526	N–Q		585	Br–C
527	R–Se		586	D–Fi
528	Sh–Sw		587	Fl–Ho
529	T–V		588	Hu–K
530	W–Wi		589	L–Ma
531	Wo–Z		590	Mc–O
	19th Infantry		591	P–R
532	21st Infantry		592	S–T
	A–Ba		593	U–Z
533	Be–Br		594	27th Infantry
534	Bu–Cl			A–B
535	Co–Da		595	C–G
536	De–E		596	H–L
537	F–Gl		597	M–R
538	Go–Ha		598	S–Z
539	He–I		599	27th Mounted Infantry
540	J–K		600	29th Infantry

Roll	Description
	A–Cl
601	Co–G
602	H–L
603	M–P
604	Q–Sn
605	So–Z
606	30th Infantry
	A–B
607	C–E
608	F–Ha
609	He–L
610	M–O
611	P–Sl
612	Sm–Z
613	31st Infantry
	A–Ca
614	Ce–F
615	G–I
616	J–Mc
617	Me–R
618	S
619	T–Z
620	32d Infantry
	A–C
621	D–H
622	I–M
623	N–Se
624	Sh–Z
625	32d Infantry (New Organization)
	A–H
626	I–S
627	T–Z
	33d Infantry
	A
628	B–Br
629	Bu–C
630	D–F
631	G–H
632	I–Ma
633	Mc–O
634	P–R
635	S
636	T–Z
	34th Infantry
637	35th Infantry
	A–Bo
638	Br–Co
639	Cr–E
640	F–Ha
641	He–K
642	L–Me
643	Mi–Re
644	Ri–S
645	T–Z
646	36th–38th Infantry
	39th Infantry
	A–D
647	E–Ll
648	Lo–Sc
649	Se–Z
650	40th Infantry
	A–B
651	C–F
652	G–J
653	K–Ma
654	Mc–Q

Roll	Description
655	R–St
656	Su–Z
657	41st Infantry
	A–B
658	D–Ha
659	He–K
660	L–M
661	N–R
662	S–T
663	V–Z
664	42d Infantry
	A–C
665	D–I
666	J–Q
667	R–Y
668	43d Infantry
	A–E
669	F–L
670	M–Sa
671	Sc–Y
672	44th Infantry
	A–D
673	E–Ma
674	Mc–Sc
675	Se–Z
676	45th Infantry
	A–G
677	H–P
678	R–Z
679	46th Infantry
	A–K
680	L–Y
681	47th Infantry
	A–G
682	H–P
683	R–Z
684	48th Infantry
	A–D
685	E–K
686	L–Ra
687	Re–Z
688	49th Infantry
	A–C
689	D–H
690	I–Mi
691	Mo–Sh
692	Si–Z
693	50th Infantry
	A–C
694	D–I
695	J–Mi
696	Mo–Sn
697	So–Z
698	51st Infantry
	A–C
699	D–G
699a	H–K
700	L–O
700a	P–Sl
701	Sm–Z
701a	52d Infantry
	54th Infantry
	55th Infantry
	63d Regiment, Enrolled Militia, Infantry, 60 days, 1864
702	Benton Cadets, Infantry

Roll	Description
	Gasconade County Battalion, U.S. Reserve Corps, Infantry
	Krekel's Battalion, U.S. Reserve Corps, Infantry
703	Phelps' Regiment, Infantry, 6 months, 1861
	A–R
704	S–Y
	1st Battalion Rifles, Infantry, 3 months, 1861, Bayles' Company (A)
	Sappers and Miners, Volunteers, Company A, 3 months, 1861
704a	Telegraph Corps, Volunteers
	Van Horn's Battalion, U.S. Reserve Corps, Infantry (Attached to Colonel Peabody's 13th Infantry)
705	Balz's Company, Sappers and Miners
	Dietrich's Company, U.S. Reserve Corps, Infantry
	King's Company (A), Railroad Patrol Guard, U.S. Reserve Corps, Infantry
	Ordnance Department, St. Louis, Mo.
	3d Marine Corps, Volunteers
	Unassigned Volunteers
	Missouri Home Guards
	A
706	B–Bo
707	Br–Ch
708	Ci–Da
709	De–E
710	F–Go
711	Gr–Ha
712	He–I
713	J–Kr
714	Ku–Ma
715	Mc–My
716	N–Pi
717	Pl–Ri
718	Ro–Sc
719	Se–Sr
720	St–Ti
721	To–We
722	Wh–Z
723	Miscellaneous Card Abstracts
	1st Cavalry
	A–K
724	L–Z
725	1st State Militia, Cavalry
	A–L
726	M–Z
	1st Battalion, State Militia, Cavalry
	1st Battalion, U.S. Reserve Corps, Cavalry
727	2d Cavalry
	A–J
728	K–T
729	U–Z
	2d State Militia, Cavalry
	A–L
730	M–Z
	2d Battalion, State Militia, Cavalry
731	3d Cavalry
	A–N
732	O–Y
	3d State Militia, Cavalry
	3d State Militia, Cavalry (2d Organization)
	A–D
733	E–Z
734	4th Cavalry
	A–M
735	N–Z

Roll	Description
	4th State Militia, Cavalry
	A–F
736	G–Z
737	5th Cavalry
	5th State Militia, Cavalry
	5th State Militia, Cavalry (2d Organization)
	A–F
738	G–Z
739	6th Cavalry
	A–R
740	S–Z
	6th State Militia, Cavalry
	A–Mc
741	Me–Z
	7th Cavalry
	A–F
742	G–Z
743	7th State Militia, Cavalry
744	8th Cavalry
	A–M
745	N–Z
	8th State Militia, Cavalry
	A–G
746	H–Y
747	9th Cavalry
	9th State Militia, Cavalry
	A–R
748	S–Z
	10th Cavalry
	A–J
749	K–Z
750	11th Cavalry
	A–L
751	M–Y
	11th State Militia, Cavalry
752	12th Cavalry
	A–L
753	M–Z
	12th State Militia, Cavalry
754	13th Cavalry
	A–S
755	T–Z
	14th Cavalry
	14th State Militia, Cavalry
756	15th Cavalry
757	16th Cavalry
	Berry's Battalion, Cavalry
	Cass County Home Guards, Cavalry
	Stewart's Battalion, Cavalry
	Van Horn's Battalion, Cavalry
758	1st Light Artillery
	A–G
759	H–Q
760	R–Z
761	2d Light Artillery
	A–F
762	G–L
763	M–R
764	S–Z
	Other Light Artillery
765	1st Engineers
	Engineer Regiment of the West
	A–G
766	H–Y
	1st Infantry, 3 months, 1861
	1st State Militia, Infantry
	A–D
767	E–Z

Roll	Description
768	1st U.S. Reserve Corps, Infantry
	1st U.S. Reserve Corps, Infantry, 3 months, 1861
	1st Northeast Missouri Infantry
	2d Infantry
769	2d U.S. Reserve Corps, Infantry
	2d U.S. Reserve Corps, Infantry, 3 months, 1861
	2d Northeast Missouri Infantry
	2d Infantry, 3 months, 1861
	3d Infantry
770	4th Infantry
	4th Infantry, 3 months, 1861
	4th U.S. Reserve Corps, Infantry, 3 months, 1861
	5th Infantry
	A–J
771	K–Z
	5th Infantry, 3 months, 1861
	5th U.S. Reserve Corps, Infantry, 3 months, 1861
	6th Infantry
	A–D
772	E–Z
773	7th Infantry
	8th Infantry
	A–D
774	E–Z
775	10th Infantry
776	11th Infantry
	A–J
777	K–Z
778	12th Infantry
	15th Infantry
	A–D
779	E–Z
780	17th Infantry
	18th Infantry
	A–E
781	F–Z
782	19th Infantry
	21st Infantry
	A–L
783	M–Y
	22d Infantry
784	23d Infantry
	A–R
785	S–Z
	24th Infantry
786	25th Infantry
	A–S
787	T–Z
	26th Infantry
788	27th Mounted Infantry
	27th Infantry
789	29th Infantry
790	30th Infantry
791	31st Infantry
792	32d Infantry (old)
793	32d Infantry (new)
	33d Infantry
	A–P
794	R–Z
	34th Infantry
	35th Infantry
795	39th Infantry
796	40th Infantry
797	41st Infantry

Roll	Description
798	42d Infantry
	43d Infantry
	A–N
799	O–Y
	44th Infantry
800	45th Infantry
	45th Militia
	46th Infantry
	A–L
801	M–Y
	47th Infantry
802	48th Infantry
803	49th Infantry
804	50th Infantry
805	51st Infantry
	Krekel's Battalion, U.S. Reserve Corps, Infantry
	Phelps' Infantry
	Staff Officers
	Other Miscellaneous Card Abstracts
	A–C
806	D–Z
807	Personal Papers
	A–Bl
808	Bo–Bra
809	Bre–Bry
810	Bu–By
811	C–Ci
812	Cl–Con
813	Coo–Cu
814	D–Di
815	Do–Dy
816	E–Fe
817	Fi–Fu
818	G–Go
819	Gr–Hal
820	Ham–Haz
821	He–Hi
822	Ho
823	Hu–Ji
824	Jo–Ka
825	Ke–Ko
826	Kr–La
827	Le–Lo
828	Lu–Mas
829	Mat–McG
830	McH–Me
831	Mi–Mor
832	Mos–Ne
833	Ni–O
834	P–Pi
835	Pl–Ra
836	Re–Ri
837	Ro–Ru
838	Ry–Sc
839	Se–Sh
840	Si–Sm
841	Sn–Sto
842	Str–Te
843	Th–Tr
844	Tu–Wal
845	Wam–Whe
846	Whi–Wil
847	Wim–Y
848	Z
	Personal Papers of Rejected Men

Roll	Description
	Personal Papers of Enrolled Militia
	A–J
849	K–S
850	T–Z
	Miscellaneous Papers Pertaining to Organizations

Compiled Service Records of Volunteer Union Soldiers Who Served in Organizations From the Territory of New Mexico. M427. 46 rolls. 16mm. DP.

The compiled service records reproduced in this microfilm publication are indexed on M242.

Roll	Description
1	1st Calvary
	A–Aq
2	Ar–Ba
3	Be–Br
4	Bu–Ca
5	Ce–Cu
6	Da–Dw
7	E–F
8	G–Go
9	Gr–Hi
10	Ho–K
11	L–Lo
12	Lu–Man
13	Mar–May
14	Mc–Mi
15	Mo–N
16	O–Pa
17	Pe–Re
18	Rh–Ry
19	Sa
20	Sc–Sp
21	St–To
22	Tr–Z
23	1st Infantry (Old Organization)
	A–Ga
24	Gi–Mi
25	Mo–Z
26	1st Infantry (New Organization)
	A–Ba
27	Be–Di
28	Do–Go
29	Gr–Lo
30	Lu–Mi
31	Mo–Pa
32	Pe–R
33	S
34	T–Z
35	1st Militia Infantry, 3 months, 1861–62
36	2d Infantry
	A–L
37	M–Z
38	3d Mounted Infantry, 6 months, 1861–62
	A–L
39	M–Z
40	4th Infantry
	5th Infantry
41	Perea's Battalion, Militia Infantry, 12 months, 1861–62
	Battalion Volunteers (1866–67)
	A–L
42	M–W

Roll	Description
	Alarid's Co. *See* Ortiz y Alarid's Independent Co.
	Duran's Co., Militia
	Gonzales' Independent Co., Militia, 3 months, 1861
	Graydon's Independent Co., Mounted Volunteers, 3 months, 1861–62
	Hubbell's Independent Co., Mounted Volunteers, 3 months, 1861
	Martinez' Independent Co., Mora County, Militia, 3 months, 1861–62
	Mink's Independent Co., Mounted Volunteers, 3 months, 1861
43	Ortiz y Alarid's Independent Co., 3 months, 1861–62
	Perea's Independent Co., Volunteers, 60 days, 1862
	Romero's Independent Co. (A), Militia Infantry, 3 months, 1861–62
	Sena's Co., A, 1st Militia, 2 months, 1862
	Simpson's Independent Co., Mounted Spies and Guides
	Tafolla's Independent Co., Militia, 3 months, 1861–62
	Vigil's Independent Co., Mounted Volunteers
44	Miscellaneous Card Abstracts
	1st Cavalry
	1st Infantry (Old)
	1st Infantry (New)
	A–H
45	1st Infantry
	I–Z
	1st Militia Infantry, 3 months
	2d Infantry
	3d Mounted Infantry, 6 months, 1861–62
46	4th Infantry
	5th Infantry
	Battalion Infantry
	Perea's Battalion, 3 months, 1861–62
	Miscellaneous Card Abstracts of Name Companies
	Other Miscellaneous Card Abstracts
	Personal Papers

Compiled Service Records of Volunteer Union Soldiers Who Served in Organizations From the State of North Carolina. M401. 25 rolls. 16mm. DP.

The compiled service records reproduced in this microfilm publication are indexed on M391.

Roll	Description
1	1st Infantry
	A–Bl
2	Bo–Cl
3	Co–Fe
4	Fi–Hi
5	Ho–La
6	Le–Mi
7	Mo–Pr
8	Pu–Sp
9	Sq–We
10	Wh–Z
	2d Infantry
	A–B
11	C–Je
12	Jo–Sc
13	Se–Y
	2d Mounted Infantry
	A–Bo

Roll	Description
14	Br–El
15	En–Ji
16	Jo–O
17	P–Sh
18	Si–Y
19	3d Mounted Infantry A–Cl
20	Co–G
21	H–La
22	Le–P
23	Q–St
24	Su–Y
25	Miscellaneous Card Abstracts 1st Infantry 2d Infantry 2d Mounted Infantry 3d Mounted Infantry Other Miscellaneous Card Abstracts Personal Papers

Compiled Service Records of Volunteer Union Soldiers Who Served in Organizations From the State of Tennessee. M395. 220 rolls. 16mm. DP.

The compiled service records reproduced in this microfilm publication are indexed on M392.

Roll	Description
1	1st Cavalry A–Bo
2	Br–Co
3	Cr–F
4	G–Hi
5	Ho–L
6	M–N
7	O–R
8	S–T
9	U–Y
10	1st Independent Vidette Cavalry A–G
11	H–P
12	R–W
	1st West Tennessee Cavalry
13	2d Cavalry A–B
14	C–E
15	F–Ha
16	He–J
17	K–Ma
18	Mc–O
19	P–Sc
20	Se–T
21	U–Z
22	3d Cavalry A–B
23	C–D
24	E–G
25	H–I
26	J–L
27	M–Pe
28	Ph–Sl
29	Sm–Y
30	4th Cavalry A–Bo
31	Br–C
32	D–F
33	G–Hl

Roll	Description
34	Ho–K
35	L–Mi
36	Mo–Q
37	R–S
38	T–Z
39	5th Cavalry A–Bo
40	Br–Co
41	Cr–E
42	F–G
43	H–I
44	J–L
45	M
46	N–Q
47	R–Sk
48	Sm–T
49	U–Y
50	6th Cavalry A–Bi
51	Bl–Ch
52	Cl–D
53	E–Go
54	Gr–Hi
55	Ho–K
56	L–Ma
57	Mc–N
58	O–Q
59	R
60	S
61	T–Wa
62	We–Z
63	7th Cavalry A–Br
64	Bu–D
65	E–Hi
66	Ho–Ma
67	Mc–Pi
68	Po–Sn
69	Sp–W
70	8th Cavalry A–Br
71	Bu–Co
72	Cr–F
73	G–Hi
74	Ho–La
75	Le–Mo
76	Mu–R
77	S–T
78	V–Y
79	9th Cavalry A–Ce
80	Ch–F
81	G–J
82	K–Ne
83	Ni–Sl
84	Sm–Y
85	10th Cavalry A–Cl
86	Co–G
87	H–L
88	M–P
89	Q–S
90	T–Y
91	11th Cavalry A–E

Roll	Description
92	F–K
93	L–R
94	S–Y
95	12th Cavalry
	A–Bo
96	Br–Co
97	Cr–G
98	H–K
99	L–Mi
100	Mo–Q
101	R–S
102	T–Z
103	13th Cavalry
	A–Cl
104	Co–Go
105	Gr–K
106	L–O
107	P–Sn
108	So–Y
109	Bradford's Battalion, 13th Cavalry
	14th Cavalry
110	1st Battalion, Light Artillery
	A–B
111	C–Fl
112	Fo–I
113	J–Ma
114	Mc–Re
115	Rh–S
116	T–Y
	Hurlbut's Battery, Light Artillery
117	1st Tennessee Infantry
	A–Br
118	Bu–C
119	D–F
120	G–Ho
121	Hu–L
122	M
123	N–Ri
124	Ro–Th
125	Ti–Y
126	1st Mounted Infantry
	A–F
127	G–M
128	N–Z
129	2d Infantry
	A–Ce
130	Ch–E
131	F–Ho
132	Hu–Ma
133	Mc–Q
134	R–S
135	T–Y
136	2d Mounted Infantry
	A–G
137	H–O
138	P–Y
139	3d Infantry
	A–D
140	E–K
141	L–P
142	R–Z
143	3d Mounted Infantry
144	4th Infantry
	A–B
145	C–F
146	G–J

Roll	Description
147	K–O
148	P–Sm
149	So–Y
150	4th Mounted Infantry
	A–G
151	H–Mc
152	Me–Sn
153	So–Y
154	5th Infantry
	A–Ch
155	Cl–E
156	F–Ha
157	He–L
158	M–O
159	P–Ri
160	Ro–S
161	T–Z
162	5th Mounted Infantry
	A–F
163	G–L
164	M–R
165	S–Y
166	6th Infantry
	A–B
167	C–E
168	F–Hi
169	Ho–Ma
170	Mc–Q
171	R–Sp
172	St–Y
173	6th Mounted Infantry
	A–K
174	L–Y
175	7th Infantry
176	7th Mounted Infantry
	A–F
177	G–O
178	P–Y
179	8th Infantry
	A–Cl
180	Co–F
181	G–H
182	I–Me
183	Mi–Ri
184	Ro–T
185	U–Y
186	8th Mounted Infantry
	A–K
187	L–Y
	9th Mounted Infantry
188	10th Infantry
	A–Br
189	Bu–Co
190	Cr–Fi
191	Fl–G
192	H–I
193	J–Lu
194	Ly–Mc
195	Me–N
196	O–Ra
197	Re–Sn
198	So–Wa
199	We–Z
	National Guard, East Tennessee
	Beaty's Co., Independent Scouts
200	Miscellaneous Card Abstracts

Roll	Description
	1st–10th Cavalry
201	11th Cavalry
	12th Cavalry
202	13th Cavalry
	Bradford's Battalion, 13th Cavalry
203	1st Battalion, Light Artillery
204	1st Infantry
	1st Mounted Infantry
	2d Infantry
	A–H
205	I–Y
	2d Mounted Infantry
	3d Infantry
	3d Mounted Infantry
	4th Infantry
206	4th Mounted Infantry
	5th Infantry
	5th Mounted Infantry
207	6th Infantry
	6th Mounted Infantry
208	7th Infantry
	7th Mounted Infantry
	8th Infantry
	8th Mounted Infantry
209	10th Infantry
	Other Miscellaneous Card Abstracts of Cavalry, Light Artillery, and Infantry Records
210	Personal Papers
	A–Br
211	Bu–Da
212	De–Ga
213	Ge–He
214	Hi–J
215	K–Ma
216	Mc–My
217	N–Q
218	R–Sl
219	Sm–T
220	U–Z

Compiled Service Records of Volunteer Union Soldiers Who Served in Organizations From The State of Texas. M402. 13 rolls. 16mm. DP.

The compiled service records reproduced in this microfilm publication are indexed on M393.

Roll	Description
1	1st Cavalry
	A–Bo
2	Br–D
3	E–G
4	H–J
5	K–Mc
6	Me–Q
7	R–Se
8	Sh–T
9	U–Z
10	2d Cavalry
	A–J
11	L–Z
12	2d Cavalry, 1 year, 1865
13	Independent Partisan Rangers, Texas Cavalry
	Hamilton's Body Guard, Texas Cavalry
	Miscellaneous Card Abstracts
	1st Cavalry
	2d Cavalry
	Independent Partisan Rangers, Texas Cavalry
	Hamilton's Body Guard, Texas Cavalry

Roll	Description
	Personal Papers

Compiled Service Records of Volunteer Union Soldiers Who Served in Organizations From the Territory of Utah. M692. 1 roll. 16mm. DP.

This microfilm publication reproduces the compiled service records of volunteer soldiers who served in Capt. Lot (Lott) Smith's Company, Utah Cavalry. This company is the only organization of Union volunteer soldiers from the Territory of Utah for which the National Archives and Records Administration has separate compiled service records.

The compiled service records reproduced in this microfilm publication are indexed on M556.

Compiled Service Records of Volunteer Union Soldiers Who Served in Organizations From the State of Virginia. M398. 7 rolls. 16mm. DP.

The compiled service records reproduced in this microfilm publication are indexed on M394.

Roll	Description
1	1st Infantry 3 months, 1861
	A–Re
2	Ri–Z
	16th Infantry
	A–F
3	G–M
4	N–Z
5	Loudoun County Rangers
	A–Mi
6	Mo–Z
	Loyal Eastern Virginia Volunteers
	A–O
7	P–Y
	Damron's Independent Co., Volunteers
	Miscellaneous Card Abstracts
	16th Infantry
	Loudoun County Rangers
	Loyal Eastern Virginia Volunteers
	Other Miscellaneous Card Abstracts
	Personal Papers

Compiled Service Records of Volunteer Union Soldiers Who Served in Organizations From the State of West Virginia. M508. 261 rolls. 16mm. DP.

The compiled service records reproduced in this microfilm publication are indexed on M507.

Roll	Description
1	1st Cavalry
	A–Bi
2	Bl–By
3	C–Cr
4	Cu–D
5	E–Gi
6	Gl–Ha
7	He–I
8	J–La
9	Le–Ma
10	Mc–Me
11	Mi–N
12	O–Q
13	R–Sa
14	Sc–Sm
15	Sn–Sy

Roll	Description
16	T–We
17	Wh–Z
18	2d Cavalry
	A–Bi
19	Bl–By
20	C–Co
21	Cr–D
22	E–G
23	H–Ho
24	Hu–La
25	Le–McE
26	McG–Mi
27	Mo–O
28	P–Ri
29	Ro–Sl
30	Sm–Th
31	Ti–Z
32	3d Cavalry
	A–B
33	C
34	D–Go
35	Gr–J
36	K–McF
37	McG–Pi
38	Pl–Sh
39	Si–Te
40	Th–Z
41	4th Cavalry
	A–G
42	H–Pi
43	Pl–Z
44	5th Cavalry
	A–B
45	C–Do
46	Dr–Hi
47	Ho–L
48	M
49	N–Sc
50	Se–T
51	U–Z
52	6th Cavalry
	A–Bl
53	Bo–Ca
54	Ch–Da
55	De–Fl
56	Fo–G
57	H–Ho
58	Hu–K
59	L–Ma
60	Mc–Mi
61	Mo–Pe
62	Ph–Ri
63	Ro–Sh
64	Si–Sq
65	St–Tu
66	Tw–We
67	Wh–Z
68	7th Cavalry
	A
69	B–Bo
70	Br–Ch
71	Cl–Cu
72	D–Er
73	Es–Go
74	Gr–Ha

Roll	Description
75	He–Je
76	Jo–Ll
77	Lo–Mc
78	Me–O
79	P
80	Q–Se
81	Sh–Sp
82	St–To
83	Tr–Wh
84	Wi–Z
85	1st Light Artillery
	A–Bi
86	Bl–By
87	C–Da
88	De–Fi
89	Fl–G
90	H–Ho
91	Hu–K
92	L–Ma
93	Mc–Mo
94	Mu–Q
95	R
96	S–Sn
97	So–Va
98	Ve–Z
99	1st Infantry
	A–Bo
100	Br–Co
101	Cr–F
102	G–He
103	Hi–K
104	L–Mc
105	Me–O
106	P–R
107	S–T
108	U–Z
109	1st Veteran Infantry
	A–J
110	K–Z
111	2d Veteran Infantry
	A–G
112	H–Sl
113	Sm–Z
	4th Infantry
	A–Bl
114	Bo–Cl
115	Co–Di
116	Do–Gl
117	Go–H
118	I–L
119	M–N
120	O–Ro
121	Ru–S
122	T–Z
123	5th Infantry
	A–B
124	C–Da
125	De–F
126	G–Je
127	Jo–L
128	M
129	N–R
130	S–Th
131	Ti–Z
132	6th Infantry

Roll	Description
	A–Ba
133	Be–Br
134	Bu–Cl
135	Co–Da
136	De–El
137	Em–F
138	G
139	H–He
140	Hi–Ji
141	Jo–K
142	L
143	M–Mc
144	Me–My
145	N–Pl
146	Po–Ri
147	Ro–Sh
148	Si–Sp
149	St–Sy
150	T–V
151	W–Wh
152	Wi–Z
153	7th Infantry
	A–Bi
154	Bl–Cl
155	Co–D
156	E–Gi
157	Gl–Hi
158	Ho–K
159	L–Mc
160	Me–My
161	N–R
162	S–St
163	Su–Z
164	9th Infantry
	A–Bl
165	Bo–Cl
166	Co–D
167	E–Ha
168	He–K
169	L–Me
170	Mi–P
171	R–Sh
172	Si–T
173	U–Y
174	10th Infantry
	A–Bo
175	Br–Co
176	Cr–F
177	G–Hi
178	Ho–Li
179	Lo–Me
180	Mi–O
181	P–R
182	S–Sq
183	St–Wa
184	We–Z
185	11th Infantry
	A–Bl
186	Bo–Cl
187	Co–D
188	E–Ha
189	He–J
190	K–L
191	M–Mi
192	Mo–Po

Roll	Description
193	Pr–R
194	S
195	T–Z
196	12th Infantry
	A–Bo
197	Br–C
198	D–Gi
199	Gl–H
200	I–Ma
201	Mc–Pa
202	Pe–Sm
203	Sn–Z
204	13th Infantry
	A–Ci
205	Cl–F
206	G–Ho
207	Hu–Ma
208	Mc–Rh
209	Ri–St
210	Su–W
211	Y–Z
	14th Infantry
	A–B
212	C–E
213	F–Hi
214	Ho–La
215	Le–M
216	N–R
217	S
218	T–Z
219	15th Infantry
	A–Ca
220	Ch–Fi
221	Fl–He
222	Hi–K
223	L–Me
224	Mg–Ri
225	Ro–S
226	T–Z
227	17th Infantry
	A–F
228	G–Ma
229	Mc–R
230	S–Z
231	Independent Company A, Infantry
	Independent Company B, Infantry
	Unassigned Men, M–S
232	Miscellaneous Card Abstracts
	1st Cavalry
	2d Cavalry
	3d Cavalry
	4th Cavalry
	5th Cavalry
	6th Cavalry
	7th Cavalry
	1st Light Artillery
	1st Infantry
	1st Veteran Infantry
	A–C
233	D–Z
234	2d Veteran Infantry
	A–N
235	O–Y
	4th Infantry
236	5th Infantry
	6th Infantry
	A–B

Roll	Description
237	C–M
238	N–Z
239	7th Infantry
	A–O
240	P–Z
	9th Infantry
241	10th Infantry
	A–L
242	M–Z
243	11th Infantry
244	12th Infantry
245	13th Infantry
246	14th Infantry
	A–M
247	N–Z
	15th Infantry
	A–F
248	G–Z
249	17th Infantry
	Independent Company A, Infantry
	Independent Company B, Infantry
	Other Miscellaneous Card Abstracts
250	Personal Papers
	A–Ce
251	Ch–E
252	F–H
253	I–Ma
254	Mc–Pf
255	Ph–Sq
256	Sr–Z
257	Personal Papers Arranged by Organization
	1st Light Artillery
	1st Infantry
	1st Veteran Infantry
	2d Veteran Infantry
	4th Veteran Infantry
	5th Infantry
	6th Infantry
	A–H
258	I–Z
	7th Infantry
	A–H
259	I–Y
	9th Infantry
	10th Infantry
	12th Infantry
260	13th Infantry
	14th Infantry
	15th Infantry
	16th Infantry
	17th Infantry
	A–C
261	D–Z
	Independent Companies
	First Loyal Eastern Virginia Volunteers
	J–W

Compiled Service Records of Former Confederate Soldiers Who Served in the 1st Through 6th U.S. Volunteer Infantry Regiments, 1864–1866. M1017. 65 rolls. DP.

This microfilm publication reproduces the compiled service records of former Confederate soldiers who served in the 1st–6th regiments of the U.S. Volunteer Infantry, 1864–66. The soldiers of the 1st–6th Volunteer Infantry regiments were Confederate prisoners of war who gained their release from prison by enlisting in the Union Army.

The first so-called Galvanized Yankees were enlisted between January and April 1864 and designated the 1st U.S. Volunteer Infantry. Because General Grant and others did not believe that ex-Confederate troops should be assigned to areas where they might have to fight their former comrades, the 1st U.S. Volunteer Infantry was ordered to the Northwestern Frontier to help quell the uprisings of the Plains Indians in August 1864.

Between September 1864 and May 1865, five more regiments were raised from among the prisoners incarcerated at Rock Island, Alton, Camp Douglas, and Camp Morton in Illinois; at Columbus, Ohio; and at Point Lookout, Maryland. All six regiments served in the West, where they protected settlers from Indians, restored stage and mail service, guarded survey parties for the Union Pacific Railroad, escorted supply trains, and rebuilt telegraph lines. The last Galvanized Yankees were mustered out of service in November 1866.

Roll	Description
1st U.S. Volunteers:	
1	A–Be
2	Bi–Car
3	Cas–Cy
4	D–Fa
5	Fe–G
6	H–Hou
7	How–K
8	L–Mc
9	Me–My
10	N–Pl
11	Po–R
12	S–So
13	Sp–V
14	W–Y
2d U.S. Volunteers:	
15	A–Bo
16	Br–Col
17	Com–D
18	E–G
19	H
20	J–L
21	M–Mo
22	Mu–Q
23	R–Sl
24	Sm–Y
3d U.S. Volunteers:	
25	A–Br
26	Bu–Do
27	Dr–G
28	H–Ji
29	Jo–Mc
30	Me–Po
31	Pr–Sp
32	St–Wa
33	We–Z
4th U.S. Volunteers:	
34	A–C
35	D–Gl
36	Go–J
37	K–M
38	N–Sp
39	St–Y
5th U.S. Volunteers:	
40	A–Bo

Roll	Description
41	Br–Cod
42	Cok–Di
43	Do–Gi
44	Gl–Hol
45	Hoo–Ki
46	Kl–L
47	M–Mi
48	Mo–Pa
49	Pe–Rod
50	Rol–Sp
51	St–T
52	V–Z

6th U.S. Volunteers:

53	A–Bo
54	Br–Coo
55	Cop–E
56	F–G
57	H
58	I–L
59	M–Mi
60	Mo–Q
61	R–Se
62	Sh–St
63	Su–Wh
64	Wi–Y

Personal papers:

65	A–Z

Records of Movements and Activities of Volunteer Union Organizations (Record Groups 94 and 407)

Beginning in 1890, the War Department compiled histories of the volunteer military organizations that served during the Civil War. The compiled records for each organization are in jacket-envelopes bearing the title "Record of Events" and giving the name of the unit. Many of the envelopes contain abstracts of the information found in the record-of-events section of the original muster rolls and returns. Also included are some cards showing the exact captions of the muster-in and muster-out rolls and the certifications by the mustering officers verifying the accuracy of the rolls. The jacket-envelopes for a few units contain no documents but only references to other units with which these units were merged.

Compiled service histories contain no information about individual soldiers. The abstracts instead relate to the stations, movements, or activities of each unit or part of it. Frequently there is information about the unit's organization or composition, strength and losses, and disbandment. Sometimes the cards also show the names of commanding officers, the dates the unit was called into service and mustered out, the terms of service, and similar information.

Compiled Records Showing Service of Military Units in Volunteer Union Organizations. M594. 225 rolls. DP.

This microfilm publication reproduces the compiled records that give histories of military units in volunteer Union organizations. Most of the records are arranged alphabetically by State or Territory, thereunder by type of unit (cavalry, artillery, or infantry), followed by militia, reserve, sharpshooter, and other organizations. Whenever possible, the units are arranged numerically within each type, for example, the 1st Cavalry, 1st Veteran Cavalry, 1st Mounted Rifles, and 2d Cavalry of New York.

The records for units from States and Territories are followed by the records of units that were not limited to any one State or Territory, such as the U.S. Colored Troops, U.S. Volunteers, and U.S. Veteran Reserve Corps.

Roll	Description
Alabama:	
1	1st Cavalry
Arizona:	
	1st Infantry
Arkansas:	
	1st–4th Cavalry
	1st Battalion, Light Artillery
	1st Battalion, Infantry, 3 months, 1862
	1st Infantry
	2d Infantry
	4th Infantry
California:	
2	1st Cavalry
	1st Battalion, Native Cavalry
	2d Cavalry
	1st Infantry
	1st Battalion, Mountaineers, Infantry
	2d Infantry
3	3d–8th Infantry
	Mounted Detachment, Infantry, 3 months, 1861
Colorado:	
4	1st Cavalry
	2d Cavalry
	McLain's Independent Battery, Light Artillery
	2d Infantry
	3d Infantry
	Denver City Home Guards, 6 months, 1861–62
Connecticut:	
5	1st Cavalry
	1st Heavy Artillery
	2d Heavy Artillery
	1st–3d Independent Battery, Light Artillery
	1st Infantry, 3 months, 1861–3d Infantry
	5th Infantry
	6th Infantry
6	7th–11th Infantry
7	12th–17th Infantry
8	18th Infantry
	20th–28th Infantry
	Garrison Guard, Infantry
Dakota Territory:	
9	1st Battalion, Cavalry
Delaware:	
	1st Battalion, Cavalry
	Capt. Milligan's Independent Cavalry
	Capt. Ahl's Independent Battery, Heavy Artillery
	Capt. Nields' Independent Battery, Light Artillery
	1st–9th Infantry

Roll	Description
	District of Columbia:
10	1st Cavalry
	Capt. Owens' Co., Militia, 3 months, 1861
	1st Infantry
	1st Battalion, Militia Infantry, 3 months, 1861
	2d Infantry
	2d–8th Battalion, Militia Infantry, 3 months, 1861
	Florida:
	1st Cavalry
	1st East Cavalry
	2d Cavalry
	Georgia:
	1st Battalion, Infantry
	Illinois:
11	1st–6th Cavalry
12	7th–12th Cavalry
13	13th–17th Cavalry
	Capt. Evans' Independent Co., Cavalry
	McClellan Dragoons, Cavalry
	1st Light Artillery
14	2d Light Artillery
	Capt. Bridges' Battery, Light Artillery
	Capt. Cogswell's Independent Battery, Light Artillery
	Chicago Board of Trade Battery, Light Artillery
	Chicago Mercantile Battery, Light Artillery
	Elgin Battery (5th Independent), Light Artillery
	Capt. Henshaw's Independent Battery, Light Artillery
	Capt. Smith's Battery A, Chicago Light Artillery
	Capt. Vaughn's Independent Battery, Light Artillery
	7th–9th Infantry, 3 months, 1861
15	10th–14th Infantry
16	15th Infantry
	14th and 15th Veteran Battalion, Infantry
	16th–20th Infantry
17	21st–26th Infantry
18	27th–32d Infantry
19	33d–37th Infantry
20	38th–42d Infantry
21	43d–47th Infantry
22	48th–53d Infantry
23	54th–58th Infantry
24	59th–64th Infantry
25	65th–75th Infantry
26	76th–82d Infantry
27	83d–90th Infantry
28	91st–97th Infantry
29	98th–105th Infantry
30	106th–114th Infantry
31	115th–123d Infantry
32	124th–135th Infantry, 100 days, 1864
33	136th–156th Infantry, 100 days, 1864
	1st Battalion, State Militia, Volunteers, 15 days, 1862
	Alton Battalion, Infantry, 100 days, 1864
	Capt. Kowald's Independent Co., Volunteers, Infantry, 3 months, 1861
	Capt. Perce's Co., State Militia Volunteers, Infantry, 30 days, 1862
	Capt. Walker's Independent Co., Infantry, 3 months, 1861
	Indiana:
34	1st–7th Cavalry
35	8th–13th Cavalry

Roll	Description
	Capt. Lamb's Independent Co., Mounted Scouts, Volunteer, Cavalry
	4th Battery, Light Artillery
36	5th–25th Battery, Light Artillery
	Wilder Battery, Light Artillery
	6th–8th Infantry, 3 months, 1861
37	9th–13th Infantry
38	14th–19th Infantry
39	20th–25th Infantry
40	26th–32d Infantry
41	33d–38th Infantry
	40th Infantry
42	42d–48th Infantry
43	49th–55th Infantry, 3 months, 1862
44	57th–66th Infantry
45	67th–70th Infantry
	72d–75th Infantry
46	76th Infantry, 30 days, 1862
	78th–86th Infantry
47	87th–89th Infantry
	91st–93d Infantry
	97th Infantry
	99th Infantry
	100th Infantry
48	101st Infantry
	115th–118th Infantry, 6 months, 1863–64
	120th Infantry
	123d Infantry
	124th Infantry
	128th–130th Infantry
	132d–134th Infantry, 100 days, 1864
49	135th Infantry, 100 days, 1864
	140th Infantry
	142d–156th Infantry
	Capt. Keasby's Independent Co., Infantry, 30 days, 1862
	Capt. Monroe's Independent Co., Legion, Infantry, 30 days, 1862
	Capt. Patton's Independent Co., Infantry, 30 days, 1862
	Iowa:
50	1st–4th Cavalry
51	5th–9th Cavalry
	Millard's Co., Sioux City, Cavalry
	1st–4th Independent Battery, Light Artillery
	1st Infantry, 3 months, 1861
52	2d–7th Infantry
53	8th–12th Infantry
54	13th–18th Infantry
55	19th–25th Infantry
56	26th–32d Infantry
57	33d–41st Infantry
	44th–48th Infantry, 100 days, 1864
	Kansas:
58	2d Cavalry
	5th–7th Cavalry
	9th Cavalry
	11th Cavalry
59	14th–16th Cavalry
	18th Battalion, Cavalry
	19th Cavalry
	1st Independent Battery, Light Artillery
	2d Independent Battery, Light Artillery
	Hopkins Battery, Light Artillery
	3d Battery, Light Artillery
	Fort Leavenworth Post, Light Artillery
	1st Infantry
	4th Infantry

Roll	Description
	6th Infantry
	8th Infantry
	10th Infantry
	12th Infantry
	13th Infantry
	17th Infantry, 100 days, 1864
	Capt. Abernathy's Home Guard, 30 days, 1861
	Capt. Kelly's Co., 10th Infantry
	Lt. Robinson's Co., 10th Infantry

Kentucky:

Roll	Description
60	1st–7th Cavalry
61	8th–17th Cavalry
	Ward's Independent Co., Capt. Twyman's Independent Co.
	1st Battery A–1st Battery C, Light Artillery
	1st Battery E, Light Artillery
	Capt. Simmond's Independent Battery, Light Artillery
	1st Infantry
	2d Infantry
62	3d–9th Infantry
63	10th–16th Infantry
64	17th–22d Infantry
	22d Infantry (Enrolled Militia)
65	23d–28th Infantry
	13th Infantry
	32d Infantry
66	33d–35th Infantry
	37th Infantry
	39th Infantry
	40th Infantry
	45th Infantry
	47th–49th Infantry
	52d–55th Infantry
	68th Infantry (Enrolled Militia)
	1st Battalion, Louisville Provost Guard
	Patterson's Independent Co., Infantry

Louisiana:

Roll	Description
67	1st Cavalry
	2d Cavalry (1st Battalion, Cavalry Scouts)
	2d Cavalry
	1st Infantry
	1st New Orleans Infantry
	2d Infantry
	2d New Orleans Infantry

Maine:

Roll	Description
68	1st Cavalry
	2d Cavalry
	1st Heavy Artillery
	1st Battalion, Light Artillery
	Garrison Artillery
	1st Battalion, Sharp Shooters, Infantry
	1st Regiment, Veteran Volunteers, Infantry
	1st Battalion, Infantry
	1st–3d Infantry, 3 months, 1861
69	4th–10th Infantry
70	11th–17th Infantry
71	19th–32d Infantry
	Coast Guard Infantry
	Capt. Cobb, Jr.'s Co., State Guards, Militia, 60 days, 1864
	State Guards, Militia, 60 days, 1864
	7th Unassigned Infantry
	9th Unassigned Infantry
	19th Unassigned Volunteer Infantry
	29th Unassigned Infantry
	30th Unassigned Infantry

Maryland:

Roll	Description
72	1st Cavalry

Roll	Description
	1st Potomac Home Brigade, Cavalry
	2d Cavalry, 6 months, 1863–64
	3d Cavalry
	Purnell Legion, Cavalry
	Capt. Smith's Independent Co., Cavalry
	1st Light Artillery
	Battery A, Junior Light Artillery, 6 months, 1863–64
	Battery B, Light Artillery, 6 months, 1863–64
	Baltimore Battery, Light Artillery
	1st Infantry
	1st Eastern Shore Infantry
73	2d Infantry
	2d Eastern Shore Infantry
	2d Potomac Home Brigade, Infantry
	3d Infantry
	3d Potomac Home Brigade, Infantry
	4th Infantry
	4th Potomac Home Brigade, Infantry
74	5th–13th Infantry
	Baltimore Light Infantry, Volunteers
	Purnell Legion, Infantry
	Capt. McGowan's Independent Co., Patapsco Guards, Volunteers

Massachusetts:

Roll	Description
75	1st–4th Cavalry
	1st Heavy Artillery
	1st Battalion, Heavy Artillery
	2d Heavy Artillery
76	3d Heavy Artillery
	4th Heavy Artillery
	29th Co., Unattached, Heavy Artillery
	30th Co., Unattached, Heavy Artillery
	1st Independent Battery–16th Battery, Light Artillery
	Maj. Cook's Co., Light Artillery
	1st Sharp Shooters, Volunteers
	2d Sharp Shooters, Volunteers
	1st Infantry
	2d Infantry
77	3d Infantry
	3d Infantry, 3 months, 1861
	3d Battalion, Riflemen, Militia
	4th Infantry
	4th Infantry, 3 months, 1861
	4th Battalion, Militia, Infantry
	5th Infantry
	5th Infantry, 3 months, 1861
	5th Battalion, Militia, Infantry, 100 days, 1864
	6th Infantry
	6th Militia, Infantry, 3 months, 1861
	6th Infantry, 100 days, 1864
	7th Infantry
	8th Infantry
	8th Infantry, 3 months, 1861
	8th Militia, Infantry
	9th–11th Infantry
78	12th Infantry
	13th Infantry
	15th–19th Infantry
79	20th–25th Infantry
80	26th–31st Infantry
81	32d–39th Infantry
82	40th Infantry
	42d Infantry
	42d Infantry, 100 days, 1864
	43d–53d Militia, Infantry
	56th–62d Infantry
	1st–13th Unattached Co., Militia Infantry, 90 days, 1864

Roll	Description
	15th Unattached Co., 100 days, 1864–27th Unattached Co., Militia Infantry, 1 year, 1864–65
	Boston Cadet Co., Militia, Infantry
	Salem Cadets, Militia, Infantry
	Capt. Staten's Co., Volunteers, Infantry, 6 months, 1862

Michigan:

Roll	Description
83	1st–5th Cavalry
84	6th–11th Cavalry
	1st U.S. Lancers, Cavalry
	Chandler Horse Guards, Cavalry
	6th Heavy Artillery
	1st Light Artillery
	13th Battery, Independent, Light Artillery
	14th Battery, Independent, Light Artillery
85	1st Engineers and Mechanics
	Capt. Howland's Independent Co., Engineers and Mechanics
	Hall's Independent Battalion, Sharp Shooters
	1st Sharp Shooters
	1st–3d (2d Organization) Infantry
86	4th (1st Organization)–10th Infantry
87	11th (1st Organization)–15th Infantry
88	16th–22d Infantry
89	23d–30th Infantry
	Provost Guards, Infantry
	Capt. Chadwick's Engineer Recruits, Volunteers

Minnesota:

Roll	Description
90	1st Cavalry (Mounted Rangers)
	2d Cavalry
	Col. Brackett's Battalion, Cavalry
	Hatch's Independent Battalion, Cavalry
	1st Heavy Artillery
	1st–3d Independent Battery, Light Artillery
	1st–3d Infantry
91	4th–11th Infantry

Mississippi:

Roll	Description
	First Battalion, Mounted Rifles

Missouri:

Roll	Description
92	1st Cavalry
	1st Battalion, State Militia, Cavalry
	1st Battalion, U.S. Reserve Corps, Cavalry
	1st State Militia, Cavalry
	2d Cavalry (Merrill's Horse)
	2d Battalion, State Militia, Cavalry
	2d State Militia, Cavalry
	3d Cavalry
93	3d State Militia, Cavalry (1st Organization)
	3d State Militia, Cavalry (2d Organization)
	4th Cavalry
	4th State Militia, Cavalry
	5th Cavalry
	5th State Militia, Cavalry (1st Organization)
	5th State Militia, Cavalry (2d Organization)
	6th Cavalry
	6th State Militia, Cavalry
94	7th Cavalry
	7th State Militia, Cavalry
	8th Cavalry
	8th State Militia, Cavalry
	9th Cavalry
	9th State Militia, Cavalry
95	10th Cavalry
	11th Cavalry
	11th State Militia, Cavalry
	12th Cavalry
	12th State Militia, Cavalry
	13th Cavalry

Roll	Description
	14th Cavalry
	14th State Militia
	15th Cavalry
	16th Cavalry
	Berry's Battalion, Cavalry
	Cass County Home Guards, Cavalry
	Gen. Fremont's Body Guard, Volunteers, Cavalry
	Capt. Smallwood's Guides and Scouts, Cavalry
	Capt. Sobolaski's Lancers, Cavalry
	Stewart's Battalion, Cavalry
	1st Light Artillery
96	2d Light Artillery
	Backof's Battalion, Light Artillery, 3 months, 1861
	Lt. Bulliss' Battery, Light Artillery
	Capt. Kowald's Battery, Light Artillery
	Landgraeber's Battery, Light Artillery (1st Flying Battery)
	Capt. Mann's Battery, Light Artillery
	Sheldon's Battery, Light Artillery
	Capt. Wachman's Battery, Light Artillery
	Capt. Welfley's Battery, Light Artillery
	1st Engineers
	Engineer Regiment of the West
	1st U.S. Reserve Corps, Infantry
	1st U.S. Reserve Corps, Infantry, 3 months, 1861
	1st Infantry
	1st State Militia, Infantry
	2d Infantry
	2d Infantry, 3 months, 1861
97	2d U.S. Reserve Corps, Infantry
	2d U.S. Reserve Corps, Infantry, 3 months, 1861
	3d Infantry
	3d Infantry, 3 months, 1861
	3d U.S. Reserve Corps, Infantry
	3d U.S. Reserve Corps, Infantry, 3 months, 1861
	4th Infantry
	4th U.S. Reserve Corps, Infantry
	4th U.S. Reserve Corps, Infantry, 3 months, 1861
	5th Infantry
	5th Infantry, 3 months, 1861
	5th U.S. Reserve Corps, 3 months, 1861
	6th Infantry
	7th Infantry
98	8th Infantry
	10th–13th Infantry
	15th–17th Infantry
99	18th Infantry
	19th Infantry
	21st–27th Infantry
	27th Mounted Infantry
	29th Infantry
100	30th–33d Infantry
	35th Infantry
	39th–51st Infantry
	Benton Cadets, Infantry
	Gasconade County Battalion, U.S. Reserve Corps
	Krekel's Battalion, U.S. Reserve Corps
	Phelps' Regiment, Infantry, 6 months, 1861
	1st Battalion Rifles, Infantry, 3 months, 1861
	Sappers and Miners, Volunteers, 3 months, 1861
	Van Horn's Battalion, U.S. Reserve Corps, Infantry
	Balz's Co., Sappers and Miners
	Capt. King's Co., Railroad Patrol Guard, U.S.R.C.

Nebraska:

Roll	Description
101	1st Cavalry

Roll	Description
	2d Battalion, Cavalry
	Omaha Scouts, Cavalry
	Pawnee Cavalry

Nevada:

Roll	Description
	1st Battalion, Cavalry
	1st Battalion, Infantry

New Hampshire:

Roll	Description
	1st Cavalry
	1st Heavy Artillery
	1st Infantry, 3 months, 1861
	2d Infantry
102	3d–8th Infantry
103	9th–18th Infantry
	Capt. Chandler's National Guards, State Militia, 60 days, 1864
	Capt. Haughton's Martin Guards, State Militia, 90 days, 1864
	Capt. Littlefield's Co., Strafford Guards, Militia 60 days, 1864

New Jersey:

Roll	Description
104	1st–3d Cavalry
	Van Reypen's Unattached Co., Cavalry
	Battery A–Battery E, Light Artillery
	1st Infantry
	1st Infantry, 3 months, 1861
	1st Battalion, Veteran Volunteers, Infantry
	2d Infantry
	2d Infantry, 3 months, 1861
	3d Infantry
	3d Infantry, 3 months, 1861
105	4th–10th Infantry
106	11th–15th Infantry
	21st–28th Infantry
107	29th–31st Infantry
	33d–35th Infantry
	37th–40th Infantry

New Mexico:

Roll	Description
	1st Cavalry
	1st Infantry (Old Organization)
	1st Infantry (New Organization)
	1st Militia, Infantry, 3 months, 1861–62
	2d Infantry
	3d Mounted Infantry, 6 months, 1861–62–5th Mounted Infantry
	Perea's Battalion, Militia, Infantry, 3 months, 1861–62
	Battalion Volunteers
	Capt. Alarid's Independent Co., Militia, Infantry, 3 months, 1861–62
	Capt. Duran's Co., Militia
	Capt. Gonzals' Independent Co., Militia, 3 months, 1861
	Graydon's Independent Co., Mounted Volunteers, 3 months, 1861–62
	Hubbell's Independent Co., Mounted Volunteers, 3 months, 1861
	Mink's Independent Co., Mounted Volunteers
	Capt. Sena's Co. A, First Militia, Infantry, 2 months, 1862
	Capt. Simpson's Independent Co., Mounted Spies and Guides
	Capt. Perea's Independent Co., Volunteers, 60 days, 1862
	Capt. Romero's Independent Co., Militia, Infantry, 3 months, 1861–62
	Capt. Tafolla's Independent Co., Militia, 3 months, 1861–62

New York:

Roll	Description
108	1st Cavalry

Roll	Description
	1st Veteran Cavalry
	1st Mounted Rifles, Cavalry
	2d Cavalry
	2d Veteran Cavalry
	2d Provisional Cavalry
	2d Mounted Rifles, Cavalry
	3d Cavalry
	3d State Militia, Cavalry
	3d Provisional Cavalry
109	4th–10th Cavalry
110	11th–23d Cavalry
111	24th–26th Cavalry
	Devin's Independent Co., State Militia, Cavalry, 3 months, 1861
	Oneida Independent Co., Cavalry
	2d–9th Heavy Artillery
112	10th Heavy Artillery
	13th–16th Heavy Artillery
	1st Marine Artillery
	1st Light Artillery
	1st Battalion, Light Artillery
	1st Battalion, Light Artillery, National Guard
	2d Battalion, Light Artillery
	3d Light Artillery
113	1st–34th Battery, Light Artillery
	1st Engineers
	2d Engineers
114	1st Battalion, Sharp Shooters
	1st–5th Infantry
	5th Veteran Infantry
	5th State Militia, Infantry, 3 months, 1861
	6th–8th Infantry
	8th State Militia, Infantry
	9th Infantry
115	10th–12th Infantry
	12th State Militia, Infantry, 3 months, 1861
	12th State Militia, Infantry, 3 months, 1862
	13th Infantry
	13th State Militia, Infantry, 3 months, 1861
	14th Infantry
	15th Engineers
	15th Engineers (New Organization)
	15th National Guard Infantry, 30 days, 1864
116	16th Infantry
	17th Infantry
	17th Veteran Infantry
	18th–20th Infantry
	20th State Militia, Infantry
	21st Infantry
	22d Infantry
	22d State Militia, Infantry, 3 months, 1862
	23d–25th Infantry
117	25th State Militia, Infantry, 3 months, 1861
	25th National Guard, Infantry
	26th–28th Infantry
	28th State Militia, Infantry, 3 months, 1861
	28th National Guard, Infantry, 100 days, 1864
	29th–34th Infantry
118	35th–37th Infantry
	37th State Militia, Infantry, 3 months, 1862
	37th National Guard, Infantry, 30 days, 1864
	38th–41st Infantry
119	42d–47th Infantry
	47th State Militia, Infantry, 3 months, 1862
120	48th–51st Infantry
121	52d–56th Infantry
	56th National Guard, Infantry, 100 days, 1864
	57th Infantry
122	58th Infantry
	58th National Guard, Infantry, 100 days, 1864

Roll	Description
	59th–61st Infantry
123	62d–67th Infantry
124	68th Infantry
	68th National Guard, Infantry, 30 days, 1863
	69th Infantry
	69th State Militia, Infantry, 3 months, 1861
	69th State Militia, Infantry, 3 months, 1862
	69th State Militia, Infantry, 3 months, 1864
	70th Infantry
	71st Infantry
	71st State Militia, Infantry, 3 months, 1861
	71st State Militia, Infantry, 3 months, 1862
	71st National Guard, Infantry
	72d Infantry
	73d Infantry
125	74th Infantry
	74th National Guard, Infantry, 30 days, 1863
	75th–77th Infantry
	77th National Guard, Infantry, 100 days, 1864
	78th Infantry
	79th Infantry
126	80th–83d Infantry
	84th National Guard, Infantry, 100 days, 1864
127	85th–90th Infantry
128	91st–93d Infantry
	93d National Guard, Infantry, 100 days, 1864
	94th Infantry
	95th Infantry
129	96th–98th Infantry
	98th National Guard, Infantry, 100 days, 1864
	99th Infantry
	99th National Guard, Infantry, 100 days, 1864
130	100th–102d Infantry
	102d National Guard, Infantry, 100 days, 1864
	103d–106th Infantry
131	107th–111th Infantry
132	112th Infantry
	114th–119th Infantry
133	120th–127th Infantry
134	128th Infantry
	131st–134th Infantry
	136th Infantry
	137th Infantry
	139th Infantry
135	140th–148th Infantry
136	149th–155th Infantry
137	156th–164th Infantry
138	165th Infantry
	168th–170th Infantry
	173d–177th Infantry
139	178th Infantry
	179th Infantry
	182d Infantry
	184th–193d Infantry
	Enfans Perdus, Independent Battalion, Infantry

North Carolina:

Roll	Description
	1st Infantry
	2d Infantry
	2d Mounted Infantry
	3d Mounted Infantry

Ohio:

Roll	Description
140	1st Cavalry
	2d Cavalry
	2d Battalion, Cavalry, 60 days, 1864
	3d Cavalry
	4th Cavalry
	4th Independent Battalion, Cavalry
	5th Cavalry

Roll	Description
	5th Independent Battalion, Cavalry, 6 months, 1863–64
141	6th–12th Cavalry
142	13th Cavalry
	3d Independent Co., Cavalry
	Capt. Bard's Independent Co., Cavalry
	Capt. Foster's 4th Independent Co., Cavalry
	Maj. McLaughlin's Squadron, Cavalry
	Capt. Bennett's Co., Union Light Guard, Cavalry
	Capt. Burdsall's Independent Co., Volunteers, Cavalry, 3 months, 1861
	1st Heavy Artillery
	2d Heavy Artillery
	1st Light Artillery
	1st Independent Battery, Light Artillery
	2d Light Artillery
	2d Independent Battery, Light Artillery, National Guard, 60 days, 1864
	3d–8th Independent Battery, Light Artillery
	8th Independent Battery, Light Artillery, National Guard, 60 days, 1864
	8th Independent Battery, Light Artillery, National Guard, 4 months, 1864–65
	10th–14th Independent Battery, Light Artillery
143	15th–22d Independent Battery, Light Artillery
	24th–26th Independent Battery, Light Artillery
	Capt. Cotter's Co., 1st Militia, Artillery
	Capt. Paulsen's Independent Battery, Militia, Light Artillery, 1 month, 1862
	Capt. W. R. Williams' Independent Co., Light Artillery
	Capt. W. S. Williams' Co., Light Artillery
	5th–8th Independent Co., Sharp Shooters
	1st Infantry
	2d Infantry
	2d Infantry, 3 months, 1861
	2d Militia, Infantry, 30 days, 1862
	3d Infantry
	3d Infantry, 3 months, 1861
	4th Infantry
	4th Battalion, Infantry
	4th Infantry, 3 months, 1861
144	5th Infantry–10th Infantry, 3 months, 1861
145	11th–16th Infantry
	16th Infantry, 3 months, 1861
146	17th Infantry–21st Infantry, 3 months, 1861
147	22d–27th Infantry
148	28th–33d Infantry
149	34th–40th Infantry
150	41st–43d Infantry
	45th–48th Infantry
151	49th–55th Infantry
152	56th–62d Infantry
153	63d–68th Infantry
154	69th–74th Infantry
155	75th–80th Infantry
156	81st–91st Infantry
157	92d–99th Infantry
158	100th–107th Infantry
159	108th–116th Infantry
	118th Infantry
160	120th–126th Infantry
	128th Infantry
	129th Infantry
161	130th–156th National Guard, Infantry
162	157th National Guard, Infantry
	159th–172d National Guard, Infantry
	173d–180th Infantry
163	181st–189th Infantry

Roll	Description
	191st–198th Infantry
	Lt. Col. Jones' Command, Volunteers
	Capt. Neff's Detachment, Cincinnati Rifles, Volunteers
	Independent Co., Dennison Guards, Infantry
	Independent Co., Trumbull Guards, Infantry
	Independent Co., Wallace Guards, Infantry

Oregon:

Roll	Description
	1st Cavalry
	Lt. Olney's Co., Cavalry
	1st Infantry

Pennsylvania:

Roll	Description
164	1st Battalion, Cavalry
	1st Reserve Cavalry
	1st Provisional Cavalry
	2d Cavalry
	2d Provisional Cavalry
	3d Cavalry
	3d Provisional Cavalry
	4th Cavalry
	5th Cavalry
165	6th–9th Cavalry
	11th Cavalry
	12th Cavalry
166	13th–19th Cavalry
167	20th Cavalry–22d Cavalry, 6 months, 1863–64
	Ringgold Battalion, Volunteers, Cavalry
	Capt. Hebble's Independent Cavalry, 100 days, 1864
	Capt. James' Independent Co., Philadelphia City Troop, Cavalry, 3 months, 1861
	Capt. Smith's Independent Co., Lafayette Cavalry, Volunteers
	Capt. Brown's Independent Co., Militia, Cavalry, Emergency, 1863
	Capt. Comly's Independent Co., Cavalry, Emergency, 1863
	Capt. Jones' Independent Co., Militia, Cavalry, Emergency, 1863
	Capt. Greenfield's Co., Washington Cavalry, Volunteers
	Capt. Lambert's Independent Co., Cavalry, 100 days, 1864
	Capt. McMullin's Independent Rangers, Cavalry, 3 months, 1861
	Lt. Mercereau's Unattached Co., Cavalry, 6 months, 1863–64
	Capt. Murray's Independent Co., Militia, Cavalry, Emergency, 1863
	Capt. Myers' Independent Co., Militia, Cavalry, Emergency, 1863
	Capt. Sanno's Independent Co., Cavalry, 100 days, 1864
	Capt. Stroud's Independent Co., Railroad Troop, Cavalry, 100 days, 1864
	Capt. Vandeve's Independent Co., Volunteers, Cavalry (Negley's Body Guard)
	Capt. Warren's Independent Co., Cavalry, 100 days, 1864
	Capt. Weaver's Independent Co., Mounted Volunteers, Cavalry, 1 year, 1864–65
	Capt. Palmer's Independent Co. (Anderson Troop), Cavalry
	2d Heavy Artillery
	2d Provisional Heavy Artillery
	3d Heavy Artillery
	5th Heavy Artillery
	6th Heavy Artillery
	Battery A, Independent Heavy Artillery
	Battery G, Independent Heavy Artillery

Roll	Description
	Capt. Montgomery's Co., Commonwealth Heavy Artillery, 3 months, 1861
168	1st Light Artillery
	1st Battalion, Light Artillery, 100 days, 1864
	Capt. Mueller's Independent Battery B, Light Artillery
	Capt. Thompson's Independent Battery C, Light Artillery
	Capt. Durell's Independent Battery D, Light Artillery
	Capt. Knap's Independent Battery E, Light Artillery
	Capt. Hampton's Independent Battery F, Light Artillery
	Capt. Nevin's Independent Battery H, Light Artillery
	Capt. Nevin's Independent Battery I, Light Artillery
	Independent Battery I, Light Artillery
	Capt. Hastings' Keystone Battery, Light Artillery, 1 year, 1862–63
	Capt. Hastings' Keystone Battery, 100 days, 1864
	Capt. Landis' Independent Battery, Light Artillery, Emergency, 1863
	Capt. Miller's Independent Battery, Light Artillery, Emergency, 1863
	Capt. Tyler's Independent Battery, Light Artillery, 6 months, 1863–64
	Capt. Ulman's Independent Battery, Light Artillery
	Capt. Woodward's Independent Battery, Light Artillery, 6 months, 1863
	1st Reserve Infantry
	1st Infantry, 3 months, 1861
	1st Battalion, Infantry, 3 months, 1863–64
	1st Battalion, Infantry, 100 days, 1864
	2d Reserve Infantry
	2d Infantry, 3 months, 1861
	2d Infantry, 6 months, 1863–64
	3d Reserve Infantry
169	3d Infantry, 3 months, 1861
	3d Infantry, 6 months, 1863–64
	4th Reserve Infantry
	4th Infantry, 3 months, 1861
	5th Reserve Infantry
	5th Infantry, 3 months, 1861
	6th Reserve Infantry
	6th Infantry, 3 months, 1861
	7th Reserve Infantry
	7th Infantry, 3 months, 1861
	8th Reserve Infantry
	8th Infantry, 3 months, 1861
	9th Reserve Infantry
	9th Infantry, 3 months, 1861
170	10th Reserve Infantry
	10th Infantry, 3 months, 1861
	11th Reserve Infantry
	11th Infantry
	11th Infantry, 3 months, 1861
	12th Reserve Infantry
	12th Infantry, 3 months, 1861
	13th Reserve Infantry
	13th–20th Infantry, 3 months, 1861
	20th Militia, Infantry, Emergency, 1863
171	21st Infantry, 3 months, 1861–28th Infantry
	28th Militia, Infantry, Emergency, 1863
	29th Infantry
	29th Militia, Infantry, Emergency, 1863
172	30th Infantry
	31st Infantry

Roll	Description
	33d Infantry
	45th–50th Infantry
173	51st–56th Infantry
174	57th Infantry
	58th Infantry
	61st–63d Infantry
	66th–68th Infantry
175	69th Infantry
	71st–76th Infantry
176	77th–79th Infantry
	81st–83d Infantry
177	84th Infantry
	85th Infantry
	87th Infantry
	88th Infantry
	90th Infantry
	91st Infantry
	93d Infantry
178	95th–100th Infantry
179	101st–107th Infantry
	109th Infantry
180	110th Infantry
	111th Infantry
	114th–116th Infantry
	118th Infantry
	119th Infantry
	121st Infantry
181	122d–139th Infantry
182	140th–149th Infantry
183	150th Infantry
	151st Infantry
	153d–158th Infantry
	165th–169th Infantry
	171st–174th Infantry
184	175th–179th Infantry
	183d Infantry
	184th Infantry
	186th Infantry
	187th Infantry
	188th Infantry
	190th–196th Infantry, 100 days, 1864
185	197th Infantry, 100 days, 1864–211th Infantry
	213th–215th Infantry
	Capt. Awl's Co., Militia, Infantry, 3 months, 1862
	Capt. Baldwin's Independent Co., Infantry, 9 months, 1862–63
	Lt. Col. Litzinger's Battalion, Infantry, Emergency, 1863
	Capt. Tanner's Independent Co., Infantry, 100 days, 1864
	Independent Co., Infantry, Acting Engineers
	Capt. Luther's Unassigned Co., Drafted Militia, Infantry, 9 months, 1863
	Independent Co. C, Infantry
	Capt. Spear's Independent Co., Militia, Infantry (City Police of Philadelphia)
	Capt. Mann's Independent Co., Militia, Infantry, Emergency, 1863
	Capt. Guthrie's Unattached Co., Drafted Militia, Infantry, 9 months, 1863
	Capt. Griffith's Independent Co., Drafted Militia, 6 months, 1863–64
	Capt. Hubbell's Co., Drafted Militia, 9 months, 1862–63
	Capt. Palmer's Independent Co., Infantry (Silver Greys)
	Capt. Jones' Independent Co., Infantry, 9 months, 1862–63

Roll	Description
	Capt. Rich's Independent Co., Infantry, 3 months, 1863
Rhode Island:	
186	1st–3d Cavalry
	7th Squadron, Cavalry, 3 months, 1862
	3d Heavy Artillery
	5th Heavy Artillery
	1st Light Artillery
	Capt. Tompkins' Battery, Light Artillery, 3 months, 1861
	1st Infantry, 3 months, 1861
187	2d Infantry
	4th Infantry
	7th Infantry
	9th–12th Infantry
	Independent Co. A, Hospital Guards, Infantry
Tennessee:	
188	1st–9th Cavalry
189	10th–13th Cavalry
	1st Battalion, Light Artillery
	1st Infantry
	1st Mounted Infantry
	2d Infantry
	2d Mounted Infantry
	3d Infantry
	3d Mounted Infantry
190	4th Infantry
	4th Mounted Infantry
	5th Infantry
	5th Mounted Infantry
	6th Infantry
	6th Mounted Infantry
	7th Infantry
	7th Mounted Infantry
	8th Infantry
	8th Mounted Infantry
	10th Infantry
	Co. A, East Tennessee National Guard
	Capt. Beaty's Independent Scouts (Mounted)
Texas:	
	1st Cavalry
	2d Cavalry
	2d Cavalry, 1 year, 1865
	Gen. Hamilton's Body Guard, Cavalry
	Vidal's Co., Independent Co., Partizan Rangers, Cavalry
Vermont:	
191	1st Cavalry
	1st Heavy Artillery
	1st Co., Heavy Artillery
	1st–3d Battery, Light Artillery
	1st Infantry, 3 months, 1861–3d Infantry
192	4th–8th Infantry
193	9th Infantry
	10th Infantry
	12th–17th Infantry
	1st Co., Drafted Men
	2d Co., Drafted Men
Virginia:	
	1st Infantry
	16th Infantry
	Loudon [Loudoun] County Independent Rangers
	1st Eastern Virginia Loyal Volunteers
	Capt. Damron's Independent Co., Volunteers
Washington Territory:	
	1st Infantry
West Virginia:	
194	1st–7th Cavalry

Roll	Description
195	1st Light Artillery
	1st Infantry
	1st Veteran Infantry
	2d Veteran Infantry
	4th–7th Infantry
196	9th–15th Infantry
	17th Infantry
	Co. A, Independent Exempts, Infantry
	Independent Co. B (Capt. West's), Infantry

Wisconsin:

Roll	Description
197	1st–4th Cavalry
	1st Heavy Artillery
	1st Independent Battery, Light Artillery
	2d Independent Battery, Light Artillery
198	3d–10th Independent Battery, Light Artillery
	12th Independent Battery, Light Artillery
	13th Independent Battery, Light Artillery
	1st–3d Infantry
	5th Infantry
199	6th–11th Infantry
200	12th–18th Infantry
201	19th–25th Infantry
202	26th–32d Infantry
203	33d–53d Infantry

U.S. Colored Troops:

Roll	Description
204	1st–5th Cavalry
	5th Massachusetts Cavalry
	6th Cavalry
	1st Heavy Artillery
	3d–5th Heavy Artillery
205	6th Heavy Artillery
	8th–14th Heavy Artillery
	1st Light Artillery
	2d Light Artillery
	Independent Battery, Light Artillery
	1st Infantry
	1st Infantry, 1 year, 1864
206	2d Infantry
	3d Infantry
	3d Tennessee Infantry
	4th–11th Infantry
207	12th–21st Infantry
208	22d–29th Infantry
	29th Connecticut Infantry
	30th–33d Infantry
209	34th–43d Infantry
210	44th–52d Infantry
211	53d–58th Infantry
212	59th–72d Infantry
213	73d–82d Infantry
214	83d–95th Infantry
215	96th–104th Infantry
	106th–108th Infantry
216	109th–118th Infantry
217	119th–125th Infantry
	127th Infantry
	128th Infantry
	135th–138th Infantry
	Capt. Powell's Regiment, Infantry
	Co. A, Unassigned, Infantry
	Co. A, Southord Infantry, Pa., 100 days, 1864
	Pioneer Corps, Cavalry Division, 16 Army Corps (A.D.)
	Pioneer Co., 1st Division, 16 Army Corps, Infantry (A. D.)
	Brigade Band, No. 1
	Brigade Band, No. 2
	Brigade Band, No. 1, Corps d'Afrique
	Brigade Band, No. 2, Corps d'Afrique

Roll	Description
	Quartermaster Detachment, Infantry

U.S. Volunteers:

Roll	Description
218	1st Sharp Shooters
	2d Sharp Shooters
	Signal Corps
	1st Veteran Volunteers, Engineers
	1st–9th Veteran Volunteers, Infantry (1 Army Corps)
219	1st–6th Volunteers
	1st Independent Co., Volunteers
	1st Co., Pontoniers, Volunteers
	Capt. Stufft's Independent Co., Indian Scouts, Volunteers (Indian Expedition to the Upper Missouri, 1864)

U.S. Veteran Reserve Corps:

Roll	Description
	1st–4th
220	5th–14th
221	15th–24th
222	1st Battalion
	2d Battalion
	1st–49th Co.
223	50th–107th Co.
224	108th–174th Co.
225	1st–7th Independent Co.
	Unassigned Detachments

Other U.S. organizations:

Brigade Bands
Departmental Corps, Department of the Monongahela
1st Indian Home Guards
2d Indian Home Guards
3d Indian Home Guards
4th & 5th Indian Home Guards
1st Battalion, Cavalry, Mississippi Marine Brigade
Light Battery, Mississippi Marine Brigade
1st Infantry, Mississippi Marine Brigade
Marine Regiment, U.S. Volunteers
General and Staff, Mississippi Marine Brigade
Signal Corps Detachment, Mississippi Marine Brigade
Ram Fleet, Mississippi Marine Brigade
Battalion, Pioneer Brigade (Army of the Cumberland)

Records of Confederate Soldiers Who Served During the Civil War (Record Group 109)

In April 1865, during the final days of the Civil War, as the Confederate Government evacuated Richmond, its archives were shipped south, burned, or abandoned. Some of the military records passed into the hands of Union Army officers and were sent to the War Department in Washington. There the Adjutant General in July 1865 established a bureau in his office for the "collection, safekeeping, and publication of Rebel Archives." In 1903 the Secretary of War persuaded the Governors of most Southern States to lend the War Department the

Confederate military personnel records in their possession for copying.

These captured and copied Confederate records, as well as Union prison and parole records, were abstracted by the War Department between 1903 and 1927 to compile military service records of Confederate officers, noncommissioned officers, and enlisted men. NARA, however, does not have any Confederate pension files, which are State, not Federal, records. For information on Confederate pensions, contact the Museum of the Confederacy, 1201 East Clay Street, Richmond, VA 23219.

The following microfilm publications reproduce indexes and compiled military service records of Confederate soldiers. Table 3 lists the corresponding publication numbers. The first publication described is a consolidated name index to all compiled service records of Confederate soldiers. Specific State and organizational indexes follow. Each index card gives the name of a soldier, his rank, the unit in which he served, and often a statement concerning the origin or background of that unit. There are cross-reference cards for names that appear in the records under more than one spelling.

Compiled service records for Confederate soldiers are arranged by State or Territory, and thereunder according to organizational breakdowns ending with either the regiment or independent battalion or company. Under each unit the service records are arranged alphabetically by surname.

Table 3: Microfilmed Indexes and Compiled Military Service Records for Confederate Army Volunteers

State	Index	Compiled Military Service Records
Consolidated	M253	–
Alabama	M374	M311
Arizona Territory	M375	M318
Arkansas	M376	M317
Florida	M225	M251
Georgia	M226	M266
Kentucky	M377	M319
Louisiana	M378	M320
Maryland	M379	M321
Mississippi	M232	M269
Missouri	M380	M322
North Carolina	M230	M270
South Carolina	M381	M267
Tennessee	M231	M268
Texas	M227	M323
Virginia	M382	M324
Organizations Raised Directly by the Confederate Government	M818	M258
General and Staff Officers	M818	M331
Unfiled Papers and Slips	–	M347

Indexes to Compiled Service Records

The following microfilm publication reproduces alphabetical indexes to the compiled service records of Confederate soldiers. The indexes to compiled service records of Confederate soldiers who served in organizations from States and Territories follow the consolidated index.

Consolidated Index to Compiled Service Records of Confederate Soldiers. M253. 535 rolls. 16mm. DP.

This microfilm publication reproduces an alphabetical card index to the compiled service records of Confederate soldiers. This consolidated, or master, index contains all the names of Confederate soldiers found in the records used in compiling the service records, regardless of whether the service was with a unit furnished by a particular State, with a unit raised directly by the Confederate Government, or as a staff officer.

Roll	Description
1	A–Adaholts
2	Adain–Adams, R.
3	Adams, S.–Agbert
4	Age–Alcutt
5	Ald–Alfont
6	Alford–Allen, James
7	Allen, Jason–Allguier
8	Allhams–Amay
9	Ambar–Anderson, I.
10	Anderson, J.–Andresse
11	Andreu–Applegate
12	Applehard–Armstrong, J.
13	Armstrong, K.–Aruvant
14	Arvea–Atkins, A.
15	Atkins, B.–Austin, J.
16	Austin, L.–Azu
17	B–Bailey, F.
18	Bailey, G.–Baker, A.
19	Baker, B.–Baldridge
20	Baldru–Balph
21	Balridge–Barbow
22	Barbr–Barlow, J.
23	Barlow, L.–Barnett, L.
24	Barnett, M.–Barrons
25	Barrontine–Basreaux
26	Bass–Battles
27	Battley–Bdnlefelt
28	Bea–Bearwood
29	Beary–Beckly
30	Beckman–Bell, G.
31	Bell, H.–Bendan
32	Bendec–Benson, J.
33	Benson, L.–Berry, L.
34	Berry, M.–Bibal
35	Bibb–Biochett
36	Biodd–Biyegas
37	Bize–Blackwell, F.
38	Blackwell, G.–Bland
39	Blandeau–Bloddo
40	Blodget–Boey
41	Bofard–Bolt
42	Bolta–Boojer
43	Book–Borzoni
44	Bos–Bourquine

Roll	Description
45	Bourre–Bowles
46	Bowley–Boyd, S.
47	Boyd, T.–Bradey
48	Bradfeild–Bradys
49	Braek–Bransem
50	Bransfield–Breatton
51	Breau–Brewyer
52	Brexson–Brily
53	Brim–Brocius
54	Brock–Brooks, Joel
55	Brooks, John–Brown, A.
56	Brown, B.–Brown, Jacob
57	Brown, Jacqueline–Brown, M.
58	Brown, N.–Brown, W.
59	Brown, Y.–Brusseaux
60	Brussel–Bryants
61	Bryar–Bueye
62	Bufalow–Bunford
63	Bungamar–Burgiss
64	Burgit–Burness
65	Burnet–Burrelson
66	Burrem–Bush, F.
67	Bush, G.–Butran
68	Butrell–Bzzle
69	C–Caldwell, G.
70	Caldwell, H.–Callow
71	Calloway–Campbell, D.
72	Campbell, E.–Cannafax
73	Cannahan–Capers
74	Capert–Carlsted
75	Carltain–Carpman
76	Carr–Carrolton
77	Carron–Carter, K.
78	Carter, L.–Caserto
79	Cases–Castons
80	Castor–Cavin
81	Cavinah–Chambers
82	Chambin–Chapman, H.
83	Chapman, I.–Cheeirs
84	Cheek–Childress, L.
85	Childress, M.–Christian
86	Christianburg–Clark, C.
87	Clark, D.–Clark, V.
88	Clark, W.–Clayton, O.
89	Clayton, P.–Clickley
90	Clide–Coans
91	Coap–Cockeran
92	Cockerel–Coirrier
93	Coissart–Coleman, I.
94	Coleman, J.–Collins, D.
95	Collins, E.–Colvert
96	Colville–Conkright
97	Conlan–Cononta
98	Conor–Cook, S.
99	Cook, T.–Cooper, L.
100	Cooper, M.–Cordeol
101	Corder–Costelbar
102	Costell–Cousey
103	Cousin–Cox, H.
104	Cox, I.–Craford
105	Craft–Cravy
106	Craw–Crely
107	Creman–Crocketts
108	Crockfield–Crouce
109	Crouch–Crump
110	Crumpacker–Cumly
111	Cumm–Curles
112	Curley–Czerney
113	D–Damzery
114	Dan–Dantagnan
115	Dante–Davenger
116	Davenpert–Davis, B.
117	Davis, C.–Davis, Jessey
118	Davis, Jetediah–Davis, R.
119	Davis, S.–Dawsey
120	Dawson–Dean, V.
121	Dean, W.–DeEspir
122	Deetche–Demory
123	Demos–Deqnire
124	Derabary–Dexton
125	Dey–Dickson, J.
126	Dickson, L.–Dinks
127	Dinmark–Dockey
128	Dockham–Donalds
129	Donaldson–Dorrity
130	Dorroch–Douglass, J.
131	Douglass, L.–Doyorn
132	Doyse–Druls
133	Drum–Dugane
134	Dugar–Duncan, G.
135	Duncan, H.–Dunn, J.
136	Dunn, L.–Durham, T.
137	Durham, W.–Dziuk
138	Eabank–Eastermond
139	Easternook–Ediker
140	Edilen–Edwards, Joel
141	Edwards, John–Elby
142	Elcaine–Elliott, K.
143	Elliott, L.–Elmondorf
144	Elmore–Englittle
145	Englond–Eshly
146	Eshman–Eubank
147	Eubankes–Evans, V.
148	Evans, W.–Ezzle
149	F–Fanver
150	Fanville–Farriott
151	Farris–Feezer
152	Feff–Fergusson
153	Ferhake–Fifsey
154	Fig–Fish
155	Fishach–Flago
156	Flaharty–Flether
157	Fletos–Flye
158	Flyin–Forcythe
159	Ford–Forrestier
160	Forreston–Foster, V.
161	Foster, W.–Foy
162	Foyard–Frazell
163	Frazer–Freezor
164	Fregan–Fry
165	Fryan–Fulton
166	Fults–Fyser
167	G–Gallawalk
168	Gallaway–Gantry
169	Gants–Garner, O.
170	Garner, P.–Garter
171	Gartey–Gaville
172	Gavin–Geordie

Roll	Description	Roll	Description
173	Geordon–Gibby	237	Hulbert–Hunny
174	Gibel–Gilbert, I.	238	Hunnycup–Hurdage
175	Gilbert, J.–Gillesia	239	Hurdel–Hutchins
176	Gillespe–Gilstrop	240	Hutchinson–Hyver
177	Gilter–Gleavy	241	Iaabell–Irvey
178	Gleber–Godfry	242	Irvin–Izzell
179	Godges–Gontin	243	Jabine–Jackson, O.
180	Gonto–Goodwich	244	Jackson, P.–James, J.
181	Goodwin–Gorely	245	James, K.–Jeanrett
182	Gorem–Graceson	246	Jeans–Jenninger
183	Gracey–Granger	247	Jennings–Jocy
184	Granget–Gray, I.	248	Jodie–Johnson, F.
185	Gray, J.–Green, F.	249	Johnson, G.–Johnson, John
186	Green, G.–Greene	250	Johnson, Johnathan–Johnson, V.
187	Greenebaum–Greshan	251	Johnson, W.–Johnston, N.
188	Gresher–Griffin, R.	252	Johnston, O.–Jones, Charles
189	Griffin, S.–Grimstone	253	Jones, Charley–Jones, James
190	Grin–Grubble	254	Jones, Jared–Jones, N.
191	Grubbs–Gunius	255	Jones, O.–Jones, William B.
192	Gunlach–Gywn	256	Jones, William C.–Jordon, C.
193	H–Haifry	257	Jordon, D.–Jyner
194	Haig–Haleton	258	Kaaf–Kearns
195	Haley–Hall, J.	259	Kearny–Keinle
196	Hall, K.–Halzie	260	Keinner–Kelloker
197	Ham–Hamilton	261	Kellom–Kemp, J.
198	Hamiltree–Hamrey	262	Kemp, K.–Kennedy, J.
199	Hamric–Hanky	263	Kennedy, K.–Kernop
200	Hanlan–Hardcustle	264	Kerns–Kibler
201	Harde–Hardy, K.	265	Kibley–Kimble
202	Hardy, L.–Harmann	266	Kimbler–King, G.
203	Harmans–Harreld	267	King, H.–King, Z.
204	Harrele–Harris, H.	268	Kingade–Kirkis
205	Harris, I.–Harris, Will	269	Kirklad–Kline
206	Harris, William–Harrold	270	Klineau–Koener
207	Harroldson–Harvew	271	Koenig–Kzeppa
208	Harvey–Hatch	272	Laack–Lajuste
209	Hatchar–Hawkins, E.	273	LaKaester–Lampton
210	Hawkins, F.–Hayes	274	Lams–Lane, J.
211	Hayett–Haywell	275	Lane, K.–Lanier, P.
212	Haywood–Heath	276	Lanier, R.–Lassetter
213	Heathcoat–Hellums	277	Lasseur–Lavystin
214	Hellundoll–Henderson, P.	278	Law–Laxton
215	Henderson, R.–Henlory	279	Lay–Lebist
216	Henly–Herage	280	Leblac–Lee, J.
217	Heral–Herrings	281	Lee, K.–Leigon
218	Herrington–Hibbots	282	Leihrs–Lequire
219	Hibbs–Higgerty	283	Ler–Lewinson
220	Higgeson–Hill, F.	284	Lewis–Lewis, V.
221	Hill, G.–Hillhouse	285	Lewis, W.–Limes
222	Hilliaid–Hinsor	286	Limet–Linticum
223	Hinston–Hockey	287	Lintinger–Liveless
224	Hockings–Hogam	288	Liveley–Lofits
225	Hogan–Holdeness	289	Loflan–Long, I.
226	Holder–Hollewman	290	Long, J.–Lores
227	Holley–Holmer	291	Loret–Loveless
228	Holmes–Holysinger	292	Lovelett–Lowrey
229	Holz–Hoovin	293	Lowrhead–Ludwick
230	Hoowie–Hornsdy	294	Ludwig–Lyells
231	Hornsey–Houseman	295	Lyen–Lyun
232	Housen–Howarde	296	M–Madison
233	Howardon–Hubban	297	Madix–Makay
234	Hubbard–Hudson, I.	298	Make–Manez
235	Hudson, J.–Huggleback	299	Manfield–Mantze
236	Hugh–Hulbard	300	Manual–Marquze

Roll	Description	Roll	Description
301	Marr–Martin, A.	365	P–Painter
302	Martin, B.–Martin, J.	366	Paintermuhl–Parish, L.
303	Martin, K.–Masner	367	Parish, M.–Parker, S.
304	Mason–Maswell	368	Parker, T.–Parrish, P.
305	Mata–Maton	369	Parrish, R.–Patnal
306	Matoney–Maxey	370	Pato–Pattman
307	Maxfield–Maynan	371	Patton–Paythress
308	Maynar–McAnliss	372	Payton–Peavyhouse
309	McAnn–McCalls	373	Peay–Penderhome
310	McCallum–McCaulay	374	Penders–Perkins, E.
311	McCauleff–McClittic	375	Perkins, F.–Perry
312	McClland–McCorde	376	Perryclear–Petty, I.
313	McCordel–McCrayer	377	Petty, J.–Phillippson
314	McCrayon–McDanie	378	Phillips–Philps
315	McDaniel–McDonald, J.	379	Philput–Pifling
316	McDonald, K.–McElry	380	Pig–Pitman, J.
317	McElsey–McGee, O.	381	Pitman, L.–Plylor
318	McGee, P.–McGrason	382	Plymail–Poogstardt
319	McGrat–McInturff	383	Pool–Porter, I.
320	McInturn–McKeown	384	Porter, J.–Pounders
321	McKer–McKyle	385	Pounds–Powers, H.
322	McLachlan–McLeny	386	Powers, I.–Prestorions
323	McLeod–McMillark	387	Prestrage–Price
324	McMillen–McNeigh	388	Pricer–Proctow
325	McNeil–McRea	389	Proddy–Pullamon
326	McReada–Meaes	390	Pullan–Pzburn
327	Meag–Meley	391	Qeugh–Qwimer
328	Melfi–Merphy	392	R–Raineu
329	Merr–Mhoon	393	Rainey–Rand
330	Miad–Milhan	394	Randal–Rathke
331	Milhare–Miller, Joh	395	Rathledge–Ray
332	Miller, Johann–Milliard	396	Rayal–Reconlley
333	Millicain–Mimus	397	Recor–Reed, J.
334	Min–Mitchell, F.	398	Reed, L.–Regestr
335	Mitchell, G.–Mizzles	399	Regg–Renfro
336	Moach–Monky	400	Renfrod–Reynolds, O.
337	Monlas–Moomaw	401	Reynolds, P.–Rice, H.
338	Moon–Moore, G.	402	Rice, I.–Richardson, J.
339	Moore, H.–Moore, Q.	403	Richardson, K.–Riddle
340	Moore, R.–Morary	404	Riddleback–Riley, J.
341	Moras–Morgan, M.	405	Riley, L.–Rives
342	Morgan, N.–Morris, I.	406	Rivet–Roberson, L.
343	Morris, J.–Morrison	407	Roberson, M.–Roberts, R.
344	Morriss–Moses	408	Roberts, S.–Robertson, V.
345	Mosesley–Moyze	409	Robertson, W.–Robinson, J.
346	Mozango–Muncell	410	Robinson, K.–Rodens
347	Muncey–Murphy, Joel	411	Roder–Rogers, E.
348	Murphy, John–Murtay	412	Rogers, F.–Roleson
349	Murtchin–Myzer	413	Roleter–Rose, V.
350	Naake–Navet	414	Rose, W.–Roundy
351	Navicy–Nehan	415	Roune–Royster
352	Nehar–Nelton	416	Royston–Rush, E.
353	Nelty–Newman, C.	417	Rush, F.–Russy
354	Newman, D.–Nicholas	418	Rust–Rzeppa
355	Nicholason–Nilch	419	S–Sams
356	Nile–Noleo	420	Samsan–Sanders
357	Noles–Norton, I.	421	Sandersalls–Satgee
358	Norton, J.–Nzon	422	Satham–Sawner
359	Oadel–Odeon	423	Sawrey–Scherrer
360	Oder–Oldhouse	424	Scherrick–Scotland
361	Olding–O'Neil	425	Scott–Scroble
362	O'Neill–Osborne	426	Scrock–Sebbitt
363	Osbornes–Owen, Joel	427	Sebel–Semzy
364	Owen, John–Ozuno	428	Sen–Shackford

Roll	Description
429	Shackle–Sharp
430	Sharpe–Sheery
431	Sheet–Shephard
432	Shephardson–Sheuburk
433	Sheudecker–Shoble
434	Shocase–Shulebranger
435	Shuler–Silmore
436	Siloff–Simon
437	Simonan–Sinckclear
438	Sinclair–Skelleton
439	Skelley–Slazy
440	Sleade–Smitchild
441	Smith–Smith, D.
442	Smith, E.–Smith, I.
443	Smith, J.–Smith, John
444	Smith, John A.–Smith, M. K.
445	Smith, M. L.–Smith, Thom
446	Smith, Thomas–Smith, W. J.
447	Smith, W. K.–Snidar
448	Snidel–Sonyley
449	Soo–Sparks, I.
450	Sparks, J.–Spencer, I.
451	Spencer, J.–Spratts
452	Sprauberry–Staley
453	Staliens–Stansen
454	Stanser–Steaton
455	Steavans–Stephens, I.
456	Stephens, J.–Stevens, G.
457	Stevens, H.–Stewart, I.
458	Stewart, J.–Stilts
459	Stilwell–Stone, F.
460	Stone, G.–Stovalt
461	Stovan–Strickland, J.
462	Strickland, K.–Stuart, I.
463	Stuart, J.–Sudduth
464	Sudellert–Summerhour
465	Summeril–Sutton, G.
466	Sutton, H.–Sweeney, J.
467	Sweeney, L.–Szymauski
468	T–Tannequin
469	Tanner–Tauzine
470	Tavall–Taylor, Joel
471	Taylor, John–Taylor, Z.
472	Taylors–Terrell, J.
473	Terrell, K.–Thibodeux
474	Thice–Thomas, J.
475	Thomas, K.–Thompson, B.
476	Thompson, C.–Thompson, L.
477	Thompson, M.–Thorntin
478	Thornton–Tidrow
479	Tidwal–Tinnie
480	Tinnille–Tolly
481	Tolman–Toury
482	Tous–Traylor
483	Trayman–Trouty
484	Trouzler–Tucker, V.
485	Tucker, W.–Turner, G.
486	Turner, H.–Turnly
487	Turnman–Tzson
488	U–Uzzle
489	Vaas–VanVoores
490	Van Vorice–Vaune
491	Vaunghn–Vickney
492	Vicknoir–Vyse

Roll	Description
493	W–Wagnut
494	Wagol–Walker, C.
495	Walker, D.–Walker, S.
496	Walker, T.–Wallace, R.
497	Wallace, S.–Walters, D.
498	Walters, E.–Ward, I.
499	Ward, J.–Warn
500	Warnac–Wasoon
501	Wass–Watson, G.
502	Watson, H.–Wauhope
503	Waukin–Webb, H.
504	Webb, I.–Weeks
505	Weelch–Wellox
506	Wells–West, B.
507	West, C.–Wethers
508	Wethersbee–Whidby
509	Whidden–White, I.
510	White, J.–White, V.
511	White, W.–Whitler
512	Whitley–Whitworth
513	Whity–Wilcot
514	Wilcox–Wilkierson
515	Wilkin–Williamoner
516	Williams–Williams, G.
517	Williams, H.–Williams, John
518	Williams, Johnney–Williams, T.
519	Williams, U.–Willifor
520	Williford–Wilmouth
521	Wilmut–Wilson, Joel
522	Wilson, John–Wilson, Willie
523	Wilson, Willis–Winkurn
524	Winlen–Witcover
525	Wite–Womun
526	Won–Wood
527	Woodail–Woods
528	Woodsell–Word
529	Wordall–Wright, D.
530	Wright, E.–Wright, William
531	Wright, William A.–Wyzzell
532	Xandry–Yearwood
533	Yeary–Young, I.
534	Young, J.–Yzanaga
535	Zaa–Zysmann

Index to Compiled Service Records of Confederate Soldiers Who Served in Organizations From the State of Alabama. M374. 49 rolls. 16mm. DP.

The compiled service records to which this index applies are reproduced on M311.

Roll	Description
1	A–Al
2	Am–Ay
3	B–Ba
4	Be–Bn
5	Bo–Bre
6	Bri–Buo
7	Bur–Cam
8	Can–Che
9	Chi–Com
10	Con–Cre
11	Cri–Dav
12	Daw–Do
13	Dr–Em
14	En–Fl

Roll	Description
15	Fo–Gar
16	Gas–Go
17	Gr–Gy
18	H–Harp
19	Harr–Haz
20	He–Hi
21	Ho–Hr
22	Hu–Ja
23	Je–Jop
24	Jor–Ki
25	Kl–La
26	Le–Ll
27	Lo–Mars
28	Mart–Maz
29	McA–McF
30	McG–Md
31	Me–Mi
32	Mo–Mt
33	Mu–N
34	O–Pas
35	Pat–Pis
36	Pit–Pz
37	Q–Rh
38	Ri–Roq
39	Ror–Sc
40	Se–Sim
41	Sin–Sm
42	Sn–Ste
43	Sti–Sy
44	T–Th
45	Ti–U
46	V–War
47	Was–Whi
48	Who–Wi
49	Wo–Z

Index to Compiled Service Records of Confederate Soldiers Who Served in Organizations From the Territory of Arizona. M375. 1 roll. 16mm. DP.

The compiled service records to which this index applies are reproduced on M318.

Index to Compiled Service Records of Confederate Soldiers Who Served in Organizations From the State of Arkansas. M376. 26 rolls. 16mm. DP.

The compiled service records to which this index applies are reproduced on M317.

Roll	Description
1	A
2	B–Bi
3	Bl–Bro
4	Bru–Ca
5	Ce–Cov
6	Cow–De
7	Di–E
8	F–Ga
9	Ge–Gy
10	H–Ha
11	He–Ho
12	Hu–Jol
13	Jom–Lar
14	Las–Ly
15	M–McC
16	McD–Mi

Roll	Description
17	Mo–N
18	O–Pl
19	Po–Rh
20	Ri–Sa
21	Sc–Sm
22	Sn–Sy
23	T
24	U–We
25	Wh–Wi
26	Wo–Z

Index to Compiled Service Records of Confederate Soldiers Who Served in Organizations From the State of Florida. M225. 9 rolls. 16mm. DP.

The compiled service records to which this index applies are reproduced on M251.

Roll	Description
1	A–Bru
2	Bry–Da
3	De–Gol
4	Gom–H
5	I–Mar
6	Mas–O
7	P–Sas
8	Sat–Til
9	Tim–Z

Index to Compiled Service Records of Confederate Soldiers Who Served in Organizations From the State of Georgia. M226. 67 rolls. 16mm. DP.

The compiled service records to which this index applies are reproduced on M266.

Roll	Description
1	A–All
2	Alm–At
3	Au–Barm
4	Barn–Bee
5	Beg–Blal
6	Blan–Bo
7	Br–Bron
8	Broo–Brya
9	Bryc–By
10	C–Carr
11	Cars–Cha
12	Che–Coc
13	Cod–Cook
14	Cool–Cri
15	Cro–Dave
16	Davi–Denk
17	Denm–Dot
18	Dou–Dy
19	E–Es
20	Et–Fin
21	Fip–Fra
22	Fre–Gas
23	Gat–Gon
24	Goo–Grie
25	Grif–Hall
26	Halm–Harp
27	Harr–Hays
28	Hayt–Hic
29	Hid–Holl
30	Holm–Hugg

Roll	Description
31	Hugh–Jac
32	Jae–Joh
33	Joi–Keke
34	Kel–King
35	Kinh–Lark
36	Larm–Ligg
37	Ligh–Ly
38	M–Maso
39	Mass–McCl
40	McCo–McGo
41	McGr–Mea
42	Meb–Min
43	Mip–Morm
44	Morn–My
45	N
46	O–Pari
47	Park–Pep
48	Per–Poll
49	Pols–Py
50	Q–Reic
51	Reid–Robb
52	Robe–Rot
53	Rou–Sa
54	Sc–Shep
55	Sher–Smis
56	Smit–Smo
57	Smy–Steo
58	Step–Stub
59	Stuc–Tel
60	Tem–Toc
61	Tod–U
62	V–Wall
63	Walm–Welk
64	Well–Wigi
65	Wigl–Will
66	Wilm–Worr
67	Wors–Z

Index to Compiled Service Records of Confederate Soldiers Who Served in Organizations From the State of Kentucky. M377. 14 rolls. 16mm. DP.

The compiled service records to which this index applies are reproduced on M319.

Roll	Description
1	A–Bi
2	Bl–Car
3	Cas–Cy
4	D–Fi
5	Fl–G
6	H–Hov
7	How–K
8	L–McC
9	McD–My
10	N–Q
11	R–Sc
12	Se–St. M
13	Sto–V
14	W–Z

Index to Compiled Service Records of Confederate Soldiers Who Served in Organizations From the State of Louisiana. M378. 31 rolls. 16mm. DP.

The compiled service records to which this index applies are reproduced on M320.

Roll	Description
1	A
2	B–Bers
3	Bert–Bram
4	Bran–By
5	C–Ci
6	Cl–Co
7	Cr–Dem
8	Den–Duo
9	Dup–Fh
10	Fi–Fu
11	G–Go
12	Gr–Hap
13	Har–Hg
14	Hi–I
15	J–Kep
16	Ker–Lat
17	Lau–Ll
18	Lo–Mar
19	Mas–McLa
20	McLe–Mi
21	Mo–My
22	N–O
23	P–Pl
24	Po–Re
25	Rh–Ry
26	S–Se
27	Sh–Sn
28	So–Taw
29	Tay–Va
30	Ve–We
31	Wh–Z

Index to Compiled Service Records of Confederate Soldiers Who Served in Organizations From the State of Maryland. M379. 2 rolls. 16mm. DP.

The compiled service records to which this index applies are reproduced on M321.

Roll	Description
1	A–K
2	L–Z

Index to Compiled Service Records of Confederate Soldiers Who Served in Organizations From the State of Mississippi. M232. 45 rolls. 16mm. DP.

The compiled service records to which this index applies are reproduced on M269.

Roll	Description
1	A–Ar
2	As–Bas
3	Bat–Bla
4	Ble–Bra
5	Bre–Bul
6	Bum–Carm
7	Carn–Clap
8	Clar–Cook
9	Cool–Cun
10	Cup–De
11	Dh–Dy
12	E
13	F–Fos
14	Fou–Gen
15	Geo–Grav
16	Gray–Hal

Roll	Description
17	Ham–Har
18	Has–Hig
19	Hil–Hov
20	How–Jac
21	Jad–Jone
22	Joni–K
23	L–Le
24	Li–Ly
25	Ma
26	McA–McGh
27	McGi–McW
28	Me–Moon
29	Moor–My
30	N–Or
31	Os–Peq
32	Per–Pre
33	Pri–Ree
34	Ref–Rob
35	Roc–Sat
36	Sau–Sh
37	Si–Smi
38	Smo–St. J
39	Sto–Tau
40	Tay–Tou
41	Tow–V
42	Wa
43	We–Wh
44	Wi–Wim
45	Win–Z

Index to Compiled Service Records of Confederate Soldiers Who Served in Organizations From the State of Missouri. M380. 16 rolls. 16mm. DP.

The compiled service records to which this index applies are reproduced on M322.

Roll	Description
1	A–Bi
2	Bl–By
3	C–Co
4	Cr–Dy
5	E–F
6	G–Haq
7	Har–Ho
8	Hu–Kl
9	Kn–Ma
10	Mc–Mt
11	Mu–Pi
12	Pl–Ry
13	S–Sr
14	St–T
15	U–Wh
16	Wi–Z

Index to Compiled Service Records of Confederate Soldiers Who Served in Organizations From the State of North Carolina. M230. 43 rolls. 16mm. DP.

The compiled service records to which this index applies are reproduced on M270.

Roll	Description
1	A–At
2	Au–Bas
3	Bat–Blam
4	Blan–Bre

Roll	Description
5	Bri–Bum
6	Bun–Carr
7	Cars–Clin
8	Clip–Corn
9	Coro–Cy
10	Da–Dev
11	Dew–Dy
12	E
13	Fa–Fran
14	Fras–Gilk
15	Gill–Gri
16	Gro–Harp
17	Harr–Henn
18	Heno–Hols
19	Holt–Hy
20	I–Jol
21	Jom–Ke
22	Kh–Las
23	Lat–Li
24	Ll–Maro
25	Marr–McC
26	McD–Mea
27	Meb–Moon
28	Moor–My
29	N–O
30	Pa–Pep
31	Per–Po
32	Pr–Reed
33	Reek–Robi
34	Robl–Sa
35	Sc–Sil
36	Sim–So
37	Sp–Stri
38	Stro–Thi
39	Tho–Ty
40	U–Was
41	Wat–Whi
42	Who–Win
43	Wio–Z

Index to Compiled Service Records of Confederate Soldiers Who Served in Organizations From the State of South Carolina. M381. 35 rolls. 16mm. DP.

The compiled service records to which this index applies are reproduced on M267.

Roll	Description
1	A
2	B–Bel
3	Ben–Box
4	Boy–Br
5	Bu–Carm
6	Carn–Cl
7	Co–Crat
8	Crau–Dee
9	Def–Dy
10	E–Fen
11	Fer–Fy
12	G–Gn
13	Go–Gy
14	H–Hat
15	Hau–Holc
16	Hold–Hy
17	I–Jon
18	Joo–K

Roll	Description
19	L–Lod
20	Lof–Mas
21	Mat–McJ
22	McK–Mir
23	Mis–My
24	N–O
25	P–Pl
26	Po–Ra
27	Re–Roc
28	Rod–Sch
29	Sci–Sl
30	Sm–Steu
31	Stev–Te
32	Th–U
33	V–Wei
34	Wel–Will
35	Wilm–Z

Index to Compiled Service Records of Confederate Soldiers Who Served in Organizations From the State of Tennessee. M231. 48 rolls. 16mm. DP.

The compiled service records to which this index applies are reproduced on M268.

Roll	Description
1	A–An
2	Ap–Barl
3	Barn–Ber
4	Bes–Bowe
5	Bowi–Brov
6	Brow–Bur
7	Bus–Cars
8	Cart–Cla
9	Cle–Coo
10	Cop–Cul
11	Cum–Ded
12	Dee–Dr
13	Du–El
14	Em–Fi
15	Fl–Fy
16	G–Gn
17	Go–Gri
18	Gro–Han
19	Hap–Hays
20	Hayt–Hi
21	Ho–Hud
22	Hue–Jen
23	Jep–Jy
24	K–Kl
25	Kn–Len
26	Leo–Ly
27	M–Math
28	Mati–McC
29	McD–McR
30	McS–Moon
31	Moor–My
32	N–Of
33	Og–Patt
34	Paty–Pl
35	Po–Ram
36	Ran–Ric
37	Rid–Roso
38	Ross–Sco
39	Scr–Simr
40	Sims–Sm

Roll	Description
41	Sn–Stif
42	Stig–Tax
43	Tay–Tom
44	Ton–V
45	W–Weat
46	Weav–Wilk
47	Will–Won
48	Wood–Z

Index to Compiled Service Records of Confederate Soldiers Who Served in Organizations From the State of Texas. M227. 41 rolls. 16mm. DP.

The compiled service records to which this index applies are reproduced on M323.

Roll	Description
1	A–As
2	At–Bd
3	Bea–Boc
4	Bod–Brou
5	Brow–Bz
6	C–Cha
7	Che–Con
8	Coo–Cy
9	D–Dez
10	Dh–Dz
11	E–Fem
12	Fen–Fug
13	Ful–Gl
14	Go–Gw
15	H–Harp
16	Harr–Hen
17	Heo–Hol
18	Hom–I
19	J
20	K
21	L–Lig
22	Lih–Mal
23	Man–McCl
24	McCo–McM
25	McN–Mol
26	Mom–My
27	N–Or
28	Os–Pet
29	Peu–Py
30	Q–Rie
31	Rif–Rum
32	Run–Sei
33	Sel–Sl
34	Sm–Stas
35	Stat–Sz
36	T–Ti
37	Tn–V
38	W–Wer
39	Wes–Will
40	Wilm–Wy
41	X–Z

Index to Compiled Service Records of Confederate Soldiers Who Served in Organizations From the State of Virginia. M382. 62 rolls. 16mm. DP.

The compiled service records to which this index applies are reproduced on M324.

(continued on next page)

Roll	Description
1	A–Am
2	An–Ay
3	B–Bar
4	Bas–Bh
5	Bi–Bop
6	Bor–Bre
7	Bri–Bry
8	Bu–Bz
9	C–Cars
10	Cart–Ci
11	Cl–Coli
12	Coll–Cow
13	Cox–Cr
14	Cu–Dav
15	Daw–D'J
16	Do–Dun
17	Dup–Eo
18	Ep–Fe
19	Fi–Fot
20	Fou–Gap
21	Gar–Gi
22	Gl–Gra
23	Gre–Hak
24	Hal–Harl
25	Harm–Haz
26	He–Hine
27	Hing–Ho
28	Hu–Hy
29	I–Joe
30	Joh–Ju
31	K–Kim
32	Kin–Lam
33	Lan–Lev
34	Lew–L'P
35	Lu–Mars
36	Mart–McCl
37	McCo–McW
38	Me–Mis
39	Mit–Mor
40	Mos–Nev
41	New–Orm
42	Orn–Pat
43	Pau–Ph
44	Pi–Pre
45	Pri–Ra
46	Re–Rim
47	Rin–Ros
48	Rot–Sa
49	Sc–Sha
50	She–Sim
51	Sin–Sm
52	Sn–Stee
53	Stef–Sus
54	Sut–Ta
55	Te–Tl
56	To–Tz
57	U–Walk
58	Wall–Welln
59	Wello–Wik
60	Wil–Wils
61	Wilt–Worn
62	Worr–Z

Index to Compiled Service Records of Confederate Soldiers Who Served in Organizations Raised Directly by the Confederate Government and of Confederate General and Staff Officers and Non-Regimental Enlisted Men. M818. 26 rolls. 16mm. DP.

This microfilm publication reproduces an alphabetical card index to the compiled service records of Confederate soldiers who served (1) in military organizations raised directly or otherwise formed by the Confederate Government or (2) in some capacity that did not involve belonging to a unit at or below the regimental level. The compiled service records indexed in this publication are reproduced on M258 and M331.

Roll	Description
1	A
2	B–Beo
3	Ber–Bre
4	Bri–By
5	C–Cle
6	Cli–Cz
7	D
8	E–Foo
9	For–Gon
10	Goo–Hap
11	Har–Hi
12	Hl–I
13	J–Ke
14	Ki–Li
15	Ll–Ma
16	Mc–Mh
17	Mi–My
18	N–Pa
19	Pe–Q
20	R–Ro
21	Ru–Sil
22	Sim–Stc
23	Ste–Thl
24	Tho–Wak
25	Wal–Wik
26	Wil–Z

Compiled Service Records

Compiled Service Records of Confederate Soldiers Who Served in Organizations From the State of Alabama. M311. 508 rolls. 16mm. DP.

The compiled service records in this microfilm publication are indexed on M374.

Roll	Description
1	1st Cavalry A–G
2	H–N
3	O–Y
4	2d Cavalry A–Co
5	Cr–Ha
6	He–Ma
7	Mc–R
8	S–Y
9	3d Cavalry A–D
10	E–K
11	L–Q
12	R–Z

Roll	Description
13	4th Cavalry
14	4th (Roddey's) Cavalry
15	4th (Russell's) Cavalry
	A–D
16	E–L
17	M–T
18	U–Y
	4th (Love's) Battalion, Cavalry
19	5th Cavalry
	A–L
20	M–Y
21	6th Cavalry
	A–I
22	J–U
23	V–Y
	7th Cavalry
	A–C
24	D–J
25	K–P
26	R–Y
27	8th Cavalry
	8th (Hatch's) Cavalry
	A–K
28	L–Y
	8th (Livingston's) Cavalry
29	9th Cavalry
	9th (Malone's) Cavalry
	A–I
30	J–Y
31	10th Cavalry
	11th Cavalry
	A–C
32	D–Z
33	12th Cavalry
	A–M
34	N–Z
	15th Cavalry
	24th Cavalry
35	Capt. Arrington's Co. A, City Troop (Mobile)
	Barbiere's Battalion, Cavalry
	A–F
36	G–Y
	Capt. Barlow's Co., Cavalry
37	Capt. Bowie's Co., Cavalry
	Capt. Brooks' Co., Cavalry Reserves
	Capt. Callaway's Co., Cavalry
	Capt. Falkner's Co., Cavalry (Chambers Cavalry)
	Capt. Chisolm's Co.
	Forrest's Cavalry
	A–M
38	N–Y
	Gachet's Co., Cavalry
	Graves' Co., Cavalry
	Hardie's Battalion, Cavalry Reserves
39	Holloway's Co., Cavalry
	Capt. Lenoir's Independent Co., Cavalry
	B–D
40	E–Y
	Lewis' Battalion, Cavalry
	A–G
41	H–Y
42	Logan's Co., Mounted Reserves
	Mobile City Troop
	Moreland's Regiment, Cavalry
	A–G
43	H–Y
44	Capt. Morris' Co. (Mounted Men)

Roll	Description
	Capt. Moses' Squadron, Cavalry
	Murphy's Battalion, Cavalry
	A–De
45	Di–L
46	M–Z
47	Roddey's Escort, Cavalry
	Stuart's Battalion, Cavalry
	Young's Co., Cavalry (State Reserves)
	1st Battalion, Artillery
	A–Ap
48	Ar–B
49	C
50	D–F
51	G–Ho
52	Hu–Lo
53	Lu–M
54	N–R
55	S–T
56	U–Z
57	2d Battalion, Light Artillery
	A–B
58	C–D
59	E–G
60	H–J
61	K–Mi
62	Mo–R
63	S
64	T–Y
65	State Artillery
	A–G
66	H–N
67	O–Z
	Bay Batteries
68	20th Battalion, Light Artillery
	A–J
69	K–Y
70	Clanton's Battery, Light Artillery
	Eufaula Light Artillery
	A–D
71	E–Y
72	Gid Nelson Light Artillery
	A–P
73	Q–Y
	Goldthwaite's Battery, Light Artillery
	A–F
74	G–Z
75	Hurt's Battery, Light Artillery
	A–P
76	R–Z
	Jeff Davis Artillery
	A–G
77	H–Y
78	Kolb's Battery, Light Artillery
	A–S
79	T–Y
	Lee's Battery, Light Artillery
80	Phelan's Co., Light Artillery
81	Capt. Seawell's Battery (Mohawk Artillery)
	Tarrant's Battery, Light Artillery
	A–S
82	T–Y
	Capt. Ward's Battery, Light Artillery
83	1st Infantry
	A–Ba
84	Be–Co
85	Cr–E
86	F–G

Roll	Description	Roll	Description
87	H	142	Hi–Je
88	I–Ll	143	Jo–Le
89	Lo–Mi	144	Li–Mc
90	Mo–P	145	Me–Pa
91	Q–Sl	146	Pe–R
92	Sm–V	147	S
93	W–Z	148	T–Wa
94	1st Conscripts	149	We–Y
95	1st Mobile Volunteers	150	5th Battalion, Volunteers
	A–Ma		A–De
96	Mc–Z	151	Di–J
97	1st Battalion, Cadets	152	K–M
	1st (Loomis') Battalion, Infantry	153	N–Si
98	2d Volunteer Militia	154	Sl–Y
	2d Infantry		5th Battalion (Blount's), Volunteers
	A–Bl	155	6th Infantry
99	Bo–Hi		A–Bl
100	Ho–O	156	Bo–Ch
101	P–Y	157	Ci–Da
102	3d Volunteer Militia	158	De–F
	3d Infantry	159	G
	A–Ba	160	H–Hi
103	Be–Ca	161	Ho–J
104	Ce–Di	162	K–Li
105	Do–Fo	163	Ll–Me
106	Fr–Ha	164	Mi–Pa
107	He–Je	165	Pe–R
108	Jo–L	166	S–Sp
109	M–Mi	167	St–V
110	Mo–Pe	168	W–Y
111	Ph–Ri		6th (McClellan's) Battalion, Infantry
112	Ro–Se	169	7th Infantry
113	Sh–Sw		A–J
114	T–Wa	170	K–Y
115	We–Z	171	8th Infantry
116	3d Alabama Reserves		A–Br
	A–R	172	Bu–Co
117	S–Y	173	Cr–E
	3d Battalion Reserves	174	F–G
118	4th Infantry	175	H–I
	A–Bl	176	J–L
119	Bo–Ca	177	M–Mo
120	Ch–Cr	178	Mu–Ra
121	Cu–Fl	179	Re–Sl
122	Fo–G	180	Sm–T
123	H–Ho	181	U–Z
124	Hu–Ki	182	9th Infantry
125	Kn–Ma		A–B
126	Mc–My	183	C–Do
127	N–P	184	Dr–G
128	Q–Sa	185	H
129	Sc–Sp	186	I–L
130	St–Tr	187	M
131	Tu–We	188	N–R
132	Wh–Z	189	S–Ti
133	4th Volunteer Militia	190	To–Y
	A–K	191	10th Infantry
134	L–Z		A–Br
135	4th Reserves	192	Bu–C
136	5th Infantry	193	D–F
	A–Bi	194	G–Ha
137	Bl–By	195	He–K
138	C	196	L–Mc
139	D–E	197	Me–Pa
140	F–Go	198	Pe–Sl
141	Gr–He		

Roll	Description
199	Sm–V
200	W–Z
201	11th Infantry
	A–B
202	C–D
203	E–Ha
204	He–L
205	M–O
206	P–R
207	S–Th
208	Ti–Y
209	12th Infantry
	A–B
210	C–E
211	F–He
212	Hi–Le
213	Li–M
214	N–P
215	R–S
216	T–Z
217	13th Infantry
	A–Bl
218	Bo–Ca
219	Ce–D
220	E–Gl
221	Go–Hi
222	Ho–K
223	L–Ma
224	Mc–N
225	O–Ri
226	Ro–Sm
227	So–V
228	W–Y
229	13th Battalion, Partisan Rangers
	14th Infantry
	A
230	B–Br
231	Bu–C
232	D–F
233	G–Ha
234	He–K
235	L–M
236	N–P
237	R–Sm
238	Sn–V
239	W–Y
240	15th Infantry
	A–Bo
241	Br–Co
242	Cr–Fl
243	Fo–He
244	Hi–J
245	K–Ma
246	Mc–My
247	N–Q
248	R–Sm
249	Sn–V
250	W–Z
	15th (First) Battalion, Partisan Rangers
	A–C
251	D–W
252	16th Infantry
	A–G
253	H–Pr
254	Pu–Z

Roll	Description
255	17th Infantry
	A–B
256	C–E
257	F–Hi
258	Ho–L
259	M–N
260	O–R
261	S–T
262	U–Y
	17th Battalion, Sharp Shooters
263	18th Infantry
	A–B
264	C–E
265	F–H
266	I–Ma
267	Mc–Q
268	R–Sp
269	St–Wi
270	Wo–Z
	18th Battalion, Volunteers
	A–I
271	J–Y
272	19th Infantry
	A–C
273	D–Hi
274	Ho–M
275	N–S
276	T–Z
277	20th Infantry
	A–B
278	C–F
279	G–I
280	J–Ma
281	Mc–Pa
282	Pe–Sn
283	Sp–Y
284	21st Infantry
	A–B
285	C–Di
286	Do–Ha
287	He–Ma
288	Mc–Q
289	R–S
290	T–Z
291	22d Infantry
	A–F
292	G–K
293	L–O
294	P–S
295	T–Y
296	23d Infantry
	A–C
297	Co–G
298	H–K
299	L–O
300	P–S
301	T–Y
	23d Battalion, Sharp Shooters
	A–H
302	J–W
	24th Infantry
	A–B
303	C–F
304	G–K
305	L–O
306	P–Sm

Roll	Description
307	So–Y
308	25th Infantry
	A–C
309	D–Ha
310	He–Ma
311	Mc–R
312	S–Z
313	26th (O'Neal's) Infantry
	A–E
314	F–K
315	L–Ri
316	Ro–Y
317	27th Infantry
	A–F
318	G–O
319	P–Z
320	28th Infantry
	A–C
321	D–G
322	H–K
323	L–O
324	P–Sn
325	Sp–Z
326	29th Infantry
	A–Co
327	Cr–G
328	H–K
329	L–M
330	N–Sm
331	So–Z
332	30th Infantry
	A–C
333	D–I
334	J–M
335	N–Sl
336	Sm–Y
337	31st Infantry
	A–B
338	C–G
339	H–L
340	M–P
341	Q–V
342	W–Y
	32d Infantry
	A–Bl
343	Bo–C
344	D–Gl
345	Go–J
346	K–Me
347	Mi–Ri
348	Ro–Te
349	Th–Y
	32d and 58th (Consolidated) Infantry
350	33d Infantry
	A–B
351	C–E
352	F–Hi
353	Ho–Mc
354	Me–Pu
355	Q–S
356	T–Y
357	34th Infantry
	A–C
358	D–Ho
359	Hu–M
360	N–Sm

Roll	Description
361	Sn–Z
362	35th Infantry
	A–P
363	R–Y
	36th Infantry
	A–B
364	C–G
365	H–L
366	M–R
367	S–Z
368	37th Infantry
	A–C
369	D–G
370	H–L
371	M–Rh
372	Ri–Y
373	38th Infantry
	A–C
374	D–Ho
375	Hu–Mi
376	Mo–S
377	T–Y
	39th Infantry
	A–Ch
378	Cl–J
379	K–R
380	S–Z
381	40th Infantry
	A–Ca
382	Ce–D
383	E–Ha
384	He–L
385	M–Pe
386	Ph–S
387	T–Z
388	41st Infantry
	A–B
389	C–D
390	E–G
391	H
392	I–Ma
393	Mc–N
394	O–Ri
395	Ro–So
396	Sp–To
397	Tr–Z
398	42d Infantry
	A–D
399	E–K
400	L–P
401	R–Y
402	43d Infantry
	A–C
403	D–I
404	J–N
405	O–Sn
406	So–Y
407	44th Infantry
	A–Br
408	Bu–C
409	D–Fo
410	Fr–He
411	Hi–K
412	L–Mi
413	Mo–P
414	Q–S

Roll	Description
415	T–Y
416	45th Infantry
	A–G
417	H–Q
418	R–Z
419	46th Infantry
	A–D
420	E–L
421	M–Sp
422	St–Y
423	47th Infantry
	A–Br
424	Bu–C
425	D–Go
426	Gr–Ho
427	Hu–Le
428	Li–M
429	N–R
430	S–Te
431	Th–Z
432	48th Infantry
	A–Cl
433	Co–G
434	H–L
435	M–P
436	Q–S
437	T–Z
	48th Militia
438	49th Infantry
	A–G
439	H–V
440	W–Y
	50th Infantry
	A–Cl
441	Co–G
442	H–L
443	M–R
444	S–Y
445	51st Partisan Rangers
	A–F
446	G–M
447	N–Z
448	53d Partisan Rangers
	A–C
449	D–H
450	I–Mi
451	Mo–Sn
452	So–Z
453	54th Infantry
	A–N
454	O–Z
	55th Volunteers
	A–B
455	C–Ha
456	He–P
457	R–Y
458	56th Partisan Rangers
	A–Ha
459	He–Sp
460	St–Y
	57th Infantry
	A–C
461	D–M
462	N–Y
463	58th Infantry
	A–G

Roll	Description
464	H–O
465	P–Z
466	59th Infantry
	A–F
467	G–K
468	L–P
469	R–Y
470	60th Infantry
	A–H
471	J–R
472	S–Z
473	61st Infantry
	A–D
474	E–J
475	K–Q
476	R–Z
477	62d Infantry
	A–F
478	G–O
479	P–Y
480	63d Infantry
	A–E
481	F–Ma
482	Mc–S
483	T–Z
	89th Militia
	94th Militia
	95th Militia
484	Hilliard's Legion
	A–Bo
485	Br–C
486	D–F
487	G–Ha
488	He–Ji
489	Jo–Ll
490	Lo–Mi
491	Mo–P
492	Q–Sl
493	Sm–Th
494	Ti–Z
495	Leighton Rangers
	Fire Battalion of Mobile
	Montgomery Guards
	Camp of Instruction, Talladega, Alabama
	A–C
496	D–I
497	J–P
498	Q–Z
499	Calhoun County Reserves
	Coosa County Reserves
	Fayette County Reserves
	Randolph County Reserves
	Shelby County Reserves
	Talladega County Reserves
	A–C
500	D–Y
501	Allen's Co.
	Capt. Belser's Co., Reserves
	Capt. Bligh's Co., Militia
	Capt. Campbell's Co., Militia
	Capt. Crawford's Co.
	Capt. Darby's Co., Auburn Home Guards, Volunteers
	Lt. Echols' Co. of Conscripts
	Capt. Fagg's Co., Lowndes Rangers, Volunteers
502	Capt. Freeman's Co., Prison Guard
503	Capt. Goldsmith's Independent Co., Volunteers

Roll	Description
	Capt. Gorff's Co. (Mobile Pulaski Rifles)
	Capt. Gueringer's Co., Militia
	Capt. Hardy's Co. (Eufaula Minutemen)
	Capt. Hert's Co.
	Capt. Hunt's Co., Militia
	Capt. Lee, Jr's., Co., Volunteers
	Capt. Lockett's Co., City Guards
	Capt. Meador's Co., Volunteers
	Capt. John Oden's Co., Mounted Infantry
	Capt. Orr's Co., Morgan Defenders
504	Capt. Palmer's Co., State Reserves
	Capt. Rabby's Coast Guard Co. No. 1, Volunteers
	Capt. Rankin's Co., Reserves
	Ready's Battalion, Reserves
	Reed's Supporting Force, 2d Congressional District
	Capt. Rives' Supporting Force, 9th Congressional District
	Lt. Stewart's Detachment, Local Defense
	Capt. Toomer's Co., Local Defense and Special Service (Chunchula Guards)
	Capt. West's Co., Militia
	Capt. Young's Co., Nitre and Mining Corps
505	Alabama Conscripts
	Battalion of Conscripts and Reserves
	Alabama Rebels
	Alabama Recruits
	Miscellaneous, Alabama
	A–B
506	C–I
507	J–R
508	S–Y

Compiled Service Records of Confederate Soldiers Who Served in Organizations From the Territory of Arizona. M318. 1 roll. 16mm. DP.

The compiled service records reproduced in this microfilm publication are indexed on M375.

Compiled Service Records of Confederate Soldiers Who Served in Organizations From the State of Arkansas. M317. 256 rolls. 16mm. DP.

The compiled service records reproduced in this microfilm publication are indexed on M376.

Roll	Description
1	1st Cavalry
	1st (Crawford's) Cavalry
	A–C
2	D–Y
	1st (Dobbin's) Cavalry
	A–Cl
3	Co–Y
	1st (Monroe's) Cavalry
4	A–Le
5	Li–Y
6	1st Mounted Rifles
	A–Cl
7	Co–Ge
8	Gi–H
9	I–L
10	M–Pa
11	Pe–Sp
12	St–Z
13	1st (Stirman's) Battalion, Cavalry
	A–R
14	S–Y

Roll	Description
	1st State Cavalry
	2d Cavalry
	A–Co
15	Cr–Ma
16	Mc–Y
17	2d Mounted Rifles
	A–Ch
18	Cl–Ha
19	He–L
20	M–R
21	S–Z
22	3d Cavalry
	A–C
23	D–I
24	J–Q
25	R–Z
	6th Battalion, Cavalry
26	7th Cavalry
27	8th Cavalry
	A–I
28	J–Y
29	10th (Witt's) Cavalry
	15th (Buster's) Battalion, Cavalry
	45th Cavalry
	A–H
30	I–Y
	46th (Crabtree's) Cavalry
31	47th (Crandall's) Cavalry
	48th Cavalry
	Anderson's Unattached Battalion, Cavalry
	Carlton's Cavalry
32	Davies' Battalion, Cavalry
	Gipson's Battalion, Mounted Rifles
	Gordon's Cavalry
	A–B
33	C–J
34	K–Tra
35	Tre–Z
	Harrell's Battalion, Cavalry
	McGehee's Cavalry
	A–F
36	G–Y
	Nave's Battalion, Cavalry
	Poe's Battalion, Cavalry
	Witherspoon's Battalion, Cavalry
37	Wright's Cavalry
	Abraham's Co., Mounted Volunteers
	Baker's Co., Mounted Volunteers
	Hooker's Co., Mounted Volunteers
	Reeve's Co., Cavalry
38	1st Field Battery (McNally's Battery)
	5th Battery, Light Artillery
	Clarkson's Battery, Light Artillery (Helena Artillery)
	Etter's Battery, Light Artillery
39	Hart's Battery, Light Artillery
	Key's Battery, Light Artillery
40	Marshall's Battery, Light Artillery
	Owen's Battery, Light Artillery
41	Pine Bluff Artillery
	River's Battery, Light Artillery
42	Thrall's Battery, Light Artillery
	Wiggins' Battery, Light Artillery
	A–C
43	D–Y
	Zimmerman's Battery, Light Artillery
44	1st Volunteers
45	1st Infantry

Roll	Description
	1st (Consolidated) Infantry
	1st Battalion, Infantry
46	1st (Colquitt's) Infantry
	A–Cl
47	Co–Go
48	Gr–J
49	K–Me
50	Mi–P
51	Q–Ta
52	Te–Z
53	2d Volunteers
	2d Infantry
	A–Ba
54	Be–Co
55	Cr–Go
56	Gr–J
57	K–Me
58	Mi–Rh
59	Ri–Ti
60	To–Y
61	2d (Consolidated) Infantry
	2d Battalion, Infantry
	3d Infantry
	A–An
62	Ap–Ca
63	Ch–El
64	Em–Ha
65	He–Ke
66	Ki–Mi
67	Mo–Re
68	Rh–S
69	T–Wi
70	Wo–Y
	3d (Consolidated) Infantry
	3d State Infantry
	4th Infantry
	A–Ba
71	Be–Dl
72	Do–Ho
73	Hu–Me
74	Mi–So
75	Sp–Y
76	4th State Infantry
	4th Battalion, Infantry
	A–Me
77	Mi–W
78	5th Infantry
	A–Cl
79	Co–Fr
80	Fu–Ja
81	Je–L
82	M–Q
83	R–Th
84	Ti–Y
	5th Militia
	5th State Infantry
85	6th Infantry
	A–Co
86	Cr–Gi
87	Gl–Je
88	Ji–Mi
89	Mo–Ro
90	Ru–Ti
91	To–Z
92	7th Infantry
	A–Co

Roll	Description
93	Cr–G
94	H–L
95	M–Pa
96	Pe–Sp
97	St–Y
98	7th Militia
	8th Infantry
	A
99	B–Br
100	Bu–C
101	D–Ge
102	Gi–H
103	I–L
104	M
105	N–Q
106	R–S
107	T–Y
108	8th Battalion, Infantry
	9th Infantry
	A–Bi
109	Bl–C
110	D–G
111	H–L
112	M–N
113	O–S
114	T–Z
115	10th Infantry
	A–H
116	I–S
117	T–Y
	10th Militia
	A–N
118	O–Y
	11th Infantry
	A–C
119	D–L
120	M–R
121	S–W
	11th and 17th (Griffith's) Consolidated Infantry
	A–Ca
122	Ch–L
123	M–S
124	T–Y
	12th Infantry
	A–D
125	E–P
126	R–Z
127	12th Battalion, Sharp Shooters
128	13th Infantry
	A–E
129	F–L
130	M–R
131	S–Y
	13th Militia
132	14th (McCarver's) Infantry
	A–R
133	S–Y
	14th (Powers') Infantry
	A–C
134	D–L
135	M–T
136	V–Z
	15th Infantry
137	15th (Johnson's) Infantry
	A–K
138	L–Y

Roll	Description
139	15th (Josey's) Infantry
	A–C
140	D–J
141	K–O
142	P–T
143	U–Y
	15th (Northwest) Infantry
	A–B
144	C–F
145	G–H
146	I–M
147	N–S
148	T–Y
149	15th Militia
150	16th Infantry
	A–F
151	G–M
152	N–Y
153	17th (Griffith's) Infantry
	A–H
154	I–S
155	T–Y
	17th (Lemoyne's) Infantry
156	18th Infantry
	A–G
157	H–O
158	P–Y
159	18th (Marmaduke's) Infantry
	A–J
160	K–Z
161	19th Infantry
	19th (Dawson's) Infantry
	A–B
162	C–F
163	G–K
164	L–O
165	P–V
166	W–Z
	19th (Dockery's) Infantry
	A–C
167	D–L
168	M–T
169	U–W
	20th Infantry
	A–B
170	C–H
171	I–P
172	Q–Y
173	21st Infantry
	A–E
174	F–L
175	M–R
176	S–Z
177	21st Militia
	23d Infantry
	A–B
178	C–H
179	I–Q
180	R–Y
181	24th Infantry
	A–D
182	E–L
183	M–R
184	S–Y
185	25th Infantry
	A–E

Roll	Description
186	F–L
187	M–R
188	S–Y
189	26th Infantry
	A–D
190	E–L
191	M–Q
192	R–V
193	W–Z
	27th Infantry
	A–Be
194	Bi–D
195	E–H
196	I–M
197	N–R
198	S–Wa
199	We–Y
	13th Infantry
	A–B
200	C–G
201	H–L
202	M–R
203	S–Y
204	31st Infantry
	A–F
205	G–Me
206	Mi–V
207	W–Y
	32d Infantry
	A–Cl
208	Co–Hi
209	Ho–O
210	P–Y
211	33d Infantry
	A–C
212	D–H
213	I–N
214	O–V
215	W–Z
	34th Infantry
	A–Bo
216	Br–G
217	H–Mi
218	Mo–S
219	T–Y
	35th Infantry
	A–Be
220	Bi–C
221	D–Ha
222	He–L
223	M–Pa
224	Pe–S
225	T–Z
226	36th Infantry
	A–E
227	F–K
228	L–R
229	S–Y
230	37th Infantry
	A–C
231	D–H
232	I–Pa
233	Pe–S
234	T–Y
	38th Infantry
	A

Roll	Description
235	B–E
236	F–J
237	K–P
238	R–Wa
239	We–Y
	45th Militia
240	50th Militia
241	51st Militia
	58th Militia
242	62d Militia
	Adams' Infantry
	Borland's Infantry
	Cocke's Infantry
	A–Bl
243	Bo–C
244	D–G
245	H–K
246	L–O
247	P–S
248	T–Y
	Crawford's Battalion, Infantry
249	Desha County Battalion, Militia
250	Hardy's Infantry
	A–E
251	F–L
252	M–R
253	S–Z
	Williamson's Battalion, Infantry
254	Capt. Ballard's Co., Infantry
	Capt. Clayton's Co., Infantry
	Clear Lake Independent Guards, Infantry
	Ernest's Co., Infantry
	Hutchison's Co., Infantry
	Kuykendall's Co., Infantry
	Louis' Co., Militia
	Sparks' Co., Infantry
	Willett's Co., Infantry
255	Miscellaneous, Arkansas
	A–I
256	J–Y

Compiled Service Records of Confederate Soldiers Who Served in Organizations From the State of Florida. M251. 104 rolls. 16mm. DP.

The compiled service records in this microfilm publication are indexed on M225.

Roll	Description
1	1st Cavalry
	A–E
2	F–K
3	L–R
4	S–Y
5	1st Battalion, Special Cavalry
6	2d Cavalry
	A–B
7	C–Di
8	Do–G
9	H–K
10	L–M
11	N–R
12	S–Te
13	Th–Z
14	3d Battalion, Cavalry
	A–J
15	K–Y

Roll	Description
16	5th Battalion, Cavalry
	A–F
17	G–O
18	P–Y
19	Capt. Fernandez's Mounted Company
	A–W
	Capt. Pickett's Company
	B–W
	Capt. Smith's Cavalry Company
	A–Y
	Capt. Abell's Light Artillery Company
	A–Y
20	Capt. Dunham's Milton Light Artillery Company
	A–Y
21	Capt. Dyke's Light Artillery Company
	A–Y
22	J–W
23	Kilcrease Light Artillery
	A–W
24	Capt. Perry's Light Artillery Company
	A–Z
25	1st Infantry
	A–B
26	C–F
27	G–K
28	L–Mo
29	Mu–Sm
30	Sn–Z
31	1st (Reserves) Infantry
	A–G
32	H–N
33	O–W
34	2d Infantry
	A–Bo
35	Br–Cl
36	Co–E
37	F–Ha
38	He–K
39	L–M
40	N–Ri
41	Ro–Ti
42	To–Z
43	2d Battalion, Infantry
	A–F
44	G–N
45	O–Y
46	3d Infantry
	A–Ca
47	Ch–F
48	G–I
49	J–Me
50	Mi–Rh
51	Ri–Sp
52	St–Z
53	4th Infantry
	A–Ch
54	Cl–G
55	H–La
56	Le–O
57	P–Sk
58	Sl–Y
59	5th Infantry
	A–Bi
60	Bl–Cl
61	Co–E
62	F–G

Roll	Description
63	H–I
64	J–L
65	M–Pe
66	Ph–R
67	S–Ti
68	To–Z
69	6th Infantry
	A–Ca
70	Ch–F
71	G–H
72	I–Ma
73	Mc–P
74	R–Sp
75	St–Y
76	7th Infantry
	A–Co
77	Cr–H
78	I–M
79	N–Sp
80	St–Z
81	8th Infantry
	A–B
82	C–Gl
83	Go–K
84	L–O
85	P–St
86	Su–Y
87	9th Infantry
	A–Cl
88	Co–Gi
89	Gl–J
90	K–N
91	O–Sl
92	Sm–Z
93	10th Infantry
	A–Ca
94	Ch–F
95	G–J
96	K–O
97	P–Sp
98	St–Z
99	11th Infantry
	A–D
100	E–J
101	K–Q
102	R–Y
103	Conscripts
	A–Z
	Campbellton Boys
	A–Y
	Capt. Harrison's Company
	C–W
	Capt. McBride's Company
	B–Y
104	Capt. Parson's Company
	A–W
	Florida Miscellaneous
	A–Y

Compiled Service Records of Confederate Soldiers Who Served in Organizations From the State of Georgia. M266. 607 rolls. 16mm. DP.

The compiled service records reproduced in this microfilm publication are indexed on M226.

Roll	Description
1	1st Cavalry

Roll	Description
	A–Cl
2	Co–G
3	H–L
4	M–R
5	S–Z
6	1st Battalion, Cavalry
	A–L
7	M–Z
8	First Battalion, Reserve Cavalry
9	1st Gordon Squadron, Cavalry (State Guards)
	2d Georgia Cavalry
	A–C
10	D–J
11	K–R
12	S–Z
13	2d Georgia Cavalry (State Guards)
14	2d Battalion, Cavalry
	A–J
15	K–Z
16	3d Cavalry
	A–C
17	D–J
18	K–R
19	S–Z
20	3d Cavalry (State Guards)
21	4th (Clinch's) Cavalry
	A–Ch
22	Cl–Go
23	Gr–K
24	L–M
25	N–Sm
26	Sn–Z
27	4th Cavalry (State Guards)
28	5th Cavalry
	A–C
29	D–G
30	H–Mc
31	Me–Sl
32	Sm–Z
33	6th Cavalry
	A–F
34	G–O
35	P–Y
	6th Battalion, Cavalry (State Guards)
	A–L
36	M–W
	7th Cavalry
	A–E
37	F–L
38	M–Z
39	7th Battalion, Cavalry (State Guards)
40	8th Cavalry
	A–J
41	K–Z
42	8th Battalion, Cavalry (State Guards)
	9th Battalion, Cavalry (State Guards)
43	10th Cavalry
44	10th Cavalry (State Guards)
45	10th Battalion, Cavalry (State Guards)
46	11th Cavalry
	A–H
47	I–Y
48	11th Cavalry (State Guards)
49	12th Cavalry
	A–E
50	F–M

Roll	Description
51	N–Y
52	12th Battalion, Cavalry (State Guards)
	12th (Robinson's) Cavalry (State Guards)
53	12th (Wright's) Cavalry (State Guards)
	13th Cavalry
	A–C
54	D–M
55	N–Y
56	15th Battalion, Cavalry (State Guards)
	16th Battalion, Cavalry (State Guards)
57	19th Battalion, Cavalry
58	20th Battalion, Cavalry
	A–G
59	H–O
60	P–Z
61	21st Battalion, Cavalry
	A–H
62	I–Z
63	22d Battalion, Cavalry (State Guards)
	24th Battalion, Cavalry
	A–C
64	D–Y
65	29th Cavalry
	A–J
66	K–Y
67	62d Cavalry
	A–D
68	E–J
69	K–R
70	S–Z
71	Capt. Alexander's Co., Cavalry
	Capt. Allen's Co., Cavalry
	Capt. Arnold's Co., Cavalry
	Capt. Asher's Co. (Murray Cavalry)
	Capt. Boddie's Co. (Troup [County] Independent Cavalry)
	Capt. Bond's Co., Cavalry (State Guards)
	Camden County Militia (Mounted)
	Capt. Corbin's Co., Cavalry
	Dorough's Battalion, Cavalry
72	Capt. Floyd's Co., Cavalry
	Capt. Gartrell's Co., Cavalry
	Capt. Hall's Co., Cavalry
	Hardwick Mounted Rifles
73	Capt. Hendry's Co., Cavalry (Atlantic and Gulf Guards)
	Capt. Humphrey's Co., Independent Cavalry (Reserves)
	Capt. Logan's Co., Cavalry (White County Old Men's Home Guards)
	Capt. Mayer's Co. (Appling Cavalry)
	Capt. Nelson's Independent Co., Cavalry
74	Capt. Newbern's Co., Cavalry (Coffee Revengers)
	Capt. Pemberton's Co., Cavalry
	Ragland's Co., Cavalry
	Roswell Battalion, Cavalry
	Capt. Rumph's Co. (Wayne Cavalry Guards)
	Capt. Russell's Co., Cavalry
	Lt. Waring's Co., Cavalry
	Capt. Young's Co., Cavalry (Alleghany Troopers)
75	9th Battalion, Artillery
	A–G
76	H–O
77	P–Y
78	11th Battalion, Artillery (Sumter Artillery)
	A–Cl

Roll	Description
79	Co–F
80	G–K
81	L–Ri
82	Ro–Y
83	12th Battalion, Light Artillery
	A–C
84	D–Ha
85	He–L
86	M–R
87	S–Z
88	14th (Montgomery's) Battalion, Light Artillery
	A–I
89	J–Y
90	22d Battalion, Heavy Artillery
	A–C
91	D–Hi
92	Ho–Me
93	Mi–R
94	S–Z
95	28th Battalion, Siege Artillery
	A–G
96	H–O
97	P–Z
98	Capt. Anderson's Battalion, Light Artillery
	Capt. Baker's Co., Artillery
99	Capt. Barnwell's Battery, Light Artillery
	Capt. Brooks' Co. (Terrell Light Artillery)
	A–M
100	N–Y
	Capt. Campbell's Independent Co., Siege Artillery
101	Capt. Carlton's Co. (Troup County Artillery)
102	Capt. Clinch's Battery, Light Artillery
	Capt. Croft's Battery, Light Artillery (Columbus Artillery)
	A–L
103	M–Y
	Capt. Daniell's Battery, Light Artillery
104	Capt. Ferrell's Battery, Light Artillery
	Capt. Fraser's Battery, Light Artillery
105	Capt. Guerard's Battery, Light Artillery
	Capt. Hamilton's Co., Light Artillery
	Capt. Hanleiter's Co., Light Artillery (Jo Thompson Artillery)
	A–L
106	M–Y
	Capt. Havis' Battery, Light Artillery
107	Capt. Howell's Co., Light Artillery
	Capt. Hudson's Co., Light Artillery (Arsenal Battery)
108	Capt. King's Battery, Light Artillery
	Capt. Lumpkin's Co., Artillery
109	Capt. Massenburg's Battery, Light Artillery (Jackson Artillery)
	Capt. Maxwell's Battalion, Regular Light Artillery
110	Capt. Maxwell's Regular Light Battery, Artillery
111	Capt. Milledge's Co., Light Artillery
112	Capt. Moore's Battery, Artillery
	Capt. Pritchard's Co., Light Artillery (Washington Artillery)
	Pruden's Battery, Artillery (State Troops)
	Capt. Ritter's Co., Light Artillery
	A–G
113	H–Z
	Capt. Scogin's Battery, Light Artillery (Griffin Light Artillery)
	Siege Train (Major Buist) Artillery

Roll	Description
114	Capt. Slaten's Co., Artillery (Macon Light Artillery)
115	Capt. Tiller's Co. (Echols Light Artillery)
	Capt. Van Den Corput's Co., Light Artillery
	A–G
116	H–Y
	Capt. Wheaton's Co., Artillery (Chatham Artillery)
	A–H
117	J–Z
118	1st Infantry
	A–R
119	S–Z
	1st Regulars
	A–Bo
120	Br–D
121	E–H
122	I–Mo
123	Mu–Sl
124	Sm–Y
125	1st Light Duty Men
	1st (Consolidated) Infantry
	1st Local Troops, Infantry
	A–C
126	D–J
127	K–Q
128	R–Z
129	1st Infantry (State Guards)
	A–M
130	N–Z
	1st (Fannin's) Reserves
	A–Ch
131	Cl–L
132	M–Z
133	1st (Olmstead's) Infantry
	A–B
134	C
135	D–Fi
136	Fl–Ha
137	He–K
138	L–Mc
139	Me–O
140	P–Sc
141	Se–Ti
142	To–Z
143	1st (Ramsey's) Infantry
	A–F
144	G–M
145	N–Y
146	1st (Symons') Reserves
	A–K
147	L–Z
148	1st Confederate Battalion, Infantry
	1st Militia
	1st Battalion, Sharp Shooters
	A–C
149	D–Mc
150	Me–W
151	1st Battalion, Infantry (State Guards)
	1st City Battalion, Infantry (Columbus)
	1st Troops and Defences (Macon)
	1st State Line
152	2d Infantry
	A–Cl
153	Co–G
154	H–Ma
155	Mc–R

Roll	Description
156	S–Y
	2d Militia
157	2d Reserves
	A–H
158	I–Y
159	2d Battalion, Infantry
	A–E
160	F–L
161	M–R
162	S–Y
163	2d Battalion, Sharp Shooters
	A–J
164	K–Z
165	2d Battalion, Infantry (State Guards)
	2d Battalion Troops and Defences (Macon)
166	2d State Line, Including Stapleton's and Storey's 3d Infantry
	A–Bo
167	Br–D
168	E–He
169	Hi–L
170	M–Pe
171	Ph–Ta
172	Te–Z
173	3d Reserves
	A–J
174	K–Y
175	3d Battalion, Infantry
	A–G
176	H–N
177	O–Z
178	3d Battalion, Sharp Shooters
	A–R
179	S–Y
	3d Battalion (State Guards)
180	4th Infantry
	A–B
181	C
182	D–F
183	G–He
184	Hi–La
185	Le–Me
186	Mi–Q
187	R–Sm
188	Sn–V
189	W–Z
190	4th Reserves
	A–H
191	I–Z
192	4th Battalion, Infantry (State Guards)
	4th Battalion, Sharp Shooters
	A–C
193	D–Y
194	5th Infantry
	A–Ca
195	Ch–Gi
196	Gl–J
197	K–N
198	O–Sp
199	St–Z
200	5th Reserves
	A–G
201	H–O
202	P–Z
203	5th Infantry (State Guards)
	5th Battalion, Infantry (State Guards)

Roll	Description	Roll	Description
204	6th Infantry	253	St–Z
	A–Br	254	10th Militia
205	Bu–Da		10th Battalion, Infantry
206	De–G		A–B
207	H–I	255	C–F
208	J–Ma	256	G–J
209	Mc–O	257	K–R
210	P–R	258	S–Y
211	S–Ta	259	11th Infantry
212	Th–Y		A–Bo
213	6th Infantry (State Guards)	260	Br–C
	A–M	261	D–Go
214	N–S	262	Gr–I
	6th Militia	263	J–L
	6th Reserves	264	M–N
	6th State Line	265	O–Se
215	7th Infantry	266	Sh–Wa
	A–Bl	267	We–Z
216	Bo–Cl		11th (State Troops)
217	Co–E		11th Battalion, Infantry (State Guards)
218	F–Ha	268	12th Infantry
219	He–J		A–Br
220	K–Mc	269	Bu–D
221	Me–Q	270	E–Ha
222	R–S	271	He–L
223	T–Wh	272	M–Pa
224	Wi–Y	273	Pe–Si
	7th Infantry (State Guards)	274	Sk–Wh
	A–H	275	Wi–Z
225	I–Y		12th Militia
226	8th Infantry	276	13th Infantry
	A–B		A–B
227	C–D	277	C–E
228	E–G	278	F–H
229	H–K	279	I–Ma
230	L–M	280	Mc–P
231	N–Sp	281	Q–Th
232	St–Z	282	Ti–Y
233	8th Infantry (State Guards)		13th Battalion, Infantry (State Guards)
	A–R	283	14th Infantry
234	S–Z		A–C
	8th Battalion, Infantry	284	D–G
	A–B	285	H–K
235	C–I	286	L–O
236	J–O	287	P–Sl
237	P–Z	288	Sm–Y
238	9th Infantry	289	14th Battalion, Infantry (State Guards)
	A–B	290	15th Infantry
239	C–F		A–Br
240	G–J	291	Bu–C
241	K–M	292	D–G
242	N–Sm	293	H–K
243	Sn–Y	294	L–Ni
	9th Infantry (State Guards)	295	No–Sm
	A–Mc	296	Sn–Z
245	Me–Z	297	16th Infantry
	9th Battalion, Infantry		A–B
	A–C	298	C–F
246	D–Y	299	G–J
247	10th Infantry	300	K–N
	A–Ca	301	O–Sp
248	Ch–E	302	St–Z
249	F–Hi	303	17th Infantry
250	Ho–L		A–C
251	M–O	304	D–I
252	P–Sp	305	J–M

Roll	Description	Roll	Description
306	N–S	359	O–Sm
307	T–Z	360	Sn–Y
	17th Battalion, Infantry (State Guards)	361	25th Infantry
308	18th Infantry		A–Bra
	A–B	362	Bre–C
309	C–E	363	D–G
310	F–H	364	H–K
311	I–Mc	365	L–M
312	Me–Q	366	N–Sa
313	R–S	367	Sc–Th
314	T–Y	368	Ti–Z
315	18th Battalion, Infantry	369	25th Battalion, Infantry (Provost Guard)
	A–D		A–I
316	E–Ma	370	J–Z
317	Mc–R	371	26th Infantry
318	S–Y		A–Cl
319	18th Battalion, Infantry (State Guards)	372	Co–F
	19th Infantry	373	G–I
	A–B	374	J–Ma
320	C–F	375	Mc–Q
321	G–J	376	R–S
322	K–M	377	T–Z
323	N–Sl		26th Battalion, Infantry
324	Sm–Z	378	27th Infantry
325	19th Battalion, Infantry (State Guards)		A–B
	20th Infantry	379	C–D
	A–Ba	380	E–He
326	Be–C	381	Hi–Mc
327	D–G	382	Me–Se
328	H–K	383	Sh–Z
329	L–M	384	27th Battalion, Infantry
330	N–R		A–N
331	S–Ti	385	O–Z
332	To–Z		27th Battalion, Infantry (Non-Conscripts)
333	21st Infantry	386	28th Infantry
	A–B		A–Co
334	C–D	387	Cr–He
335	E–Ha	388	Hi–Mc
336	He–K	389	Me–Sm
337	L–O	390	Sn–Y
338	P–S	391	29th Infantry
339	T–Z		A–Ce
340	22d Infantry	392	Ch–G
	A–B	393	H–K
341	C–D	394	L–M
342	E–Ha	395	N–Sl
343	He–K	396	Sm–Z
344	L–M	397	30th Infantry
345	N–R		A–C
346	S–Ti	398	D–H
347	To–Z	399	I–O
348	23d Infantry	400	P–Z
	A–B	401	31st Infantry
349	C–D		A–Ch
350	E–Ha	402	Cl–Go
351	He–L	403	Gr–J
352	M–P	404	K–M
353	Q–Ta	405	N–R
354	Te–Y	406	S–Th
	23d Battalion, Infantry, Local Defense (Athens Battalion, Enfield Rifle Battalion)	407	Ti–Z
355	24th Infantry	408	32d Infantry
	A–Ch		A–C
356	Cl–F	409	D–H
357	G–J	410	I–O
358	K–N	411	P–Z
		412	34th Infantry

Roll	Description
	A–F
413	G–M
414	N–Y
415	35th Infantry
	A–B
416	C–D
417	E–He
418	Hi–J
419	K–Mc
420	Me–Pe
421	Ph–Sh
422	Si–T
423	U–Z
424	36th (Broyles') Infantry
	A–D
425	E–K
426	L–Re
427	Ri–Y
428	36th (Villepigue's) Infantry
	A–I
429	J–Sn
430	Sp–Y
	37th Infantry
	A–C
431	D–Mo
432	Mu–Z
433	38th Infantry
	A–Bo
434	Br–Cr
435	Cu–F
436	G–Hi
437	Ho–L
438	M
439	N–Q
440	R–T
441	V–Y
442	39th Infantry
	A–Co
443	Cr–He
444	Hi–Mc
445	Me–Sl
446	Sm–Y
447	40th Infantry
	A–C
448	D–K
449	L–Sl
450	Sm–Z
	40th Battalion, Infantry
451	41st Infantry
	A–E
452	F–L
453	M–R
454	S–Z
455	42d Infantry
	A–Cl
456	Co–Ha
457	He–Mc
458	Me–Sl
459	Sm–Y
460	43d Infantry
	A–Cl
461	Co–G
462	H–L
463	M–R
464	S–Y
465	44th Infantry

Roll	Description
	A–B
466	C–E
467	F–Je
468	Jo–Mo
469	Mu–Sm
470	Sn–Z
471	45th Infantry
	A–Cl
472	Co–G
473	H–K
474	L–O
475	P–Sm
476	Sn–Z
477	46th Infantry
	A–B
478	C–D
479	E–Hi
480	Ho–L
481	M–O
482	P–Sn
483	So–Z
484	47th Infantry
	A–C
485	D–H
486	I–N
487	O–Sm
488	So–Z
489	48th Infantry
	A–B
490	C–D
491	E–G
492	H–I
493	J–Mc
494	Me–Ph
495	Pi–Sa
496	Sc–Ti
497	To–Z
498	49th Infantry
	A–B
499	C–Fl
500	Fo–H
501	I–Mc
502	Me–Ri
503	Ro–T
504	U–Y
505	50th Infantry
	A–B
506	C–E
507	F–J
508	K–N
509	O–Sp
510	St–Z
511	51st Infantry
	A–C
512	D–H
513	I–Me
514	Mi–Se
515	Sh–Z
516	52d Infantry
	A–D
517	E–J
518	K–R
519	S–Y
520	53d Infantry
	A–Cl

Roll	Description
521	Co–Gi
522	Gl–K
523	L–Pe
524	Ph–Wa
525	We–Y
	54th Infantry
	A–Ca
526	Ch–K
527	L–Re
528	Rh–Z
529	**55th Infantry**
	A–C
530	D–Hi
531	Ho–Mi
532	Mo–Se
533	Sh–Y
534	**56th Infantry**
	A–F
535	G–O
536	P–Y
537	**57th Infantry**
	A–D
538	E–J
539	K–R
540	S–Z
541	**59th Infantry**
	A–B
542	C–F
543	G–I
544	J–M
545	N–Sp
546	St–Y
547	**60th Infantry**
	A–B
548	C–D
549	E–Ha
550	He–La
551	Le–M
552	N–P
553	R–S
554	T–Y
555	**61st Infantry**
	A–B
556	C–E
557	F–H
558	I–Ma
559	Mc–Pa
560	Pe–Sm
561	Sn–Y
562	**63d Infantry**
	A–B
563	C–E
564	F–H
565	I–Mc
566	Me–Se
567	Sh–Z
568	**64th Infantry**
	A–G
569	H–P
570	Q–Z
571	**65th Infantry**
	A–D
572	E–J
573	K–P
574	Q–Z
575	**66th Infantry**

Roll	Description
	A–J
576	K–Z
577	**Arsenal Battalion, Infantry (Columbus)**
	Augusta Battalion, Infantry
	City Battalion, Infantry (Columbus)
	Coast Guard Battalion, Militia
	Cook's Battalion, Infantry (Reserves)
	Rowland's Battalion, Conscripts
	Youngblood's Battalion, Infantry
	Cobb's Guards, Infantry
	A–C
578	D–Y
	Cherokee Legion (State Guards)
	A–F
579	G–Y
580	**Cobb's Legion**
	A–Bl
581	Bo–Ca
582	Ch–D
583	E–Go
584	Gr–I
585	J–L
586	M–N
587	O–Rh
588	Ri–Sm
589	Sn–Wa
590	We–Z
591	**Floyd Legion (State Guards)**
592	**Phillip's Legion**
	A–Br
593	Bu–De
594	Di–G
595	H–I
596	J–L
597	M–N
598	O–R
599	S–Th
600	Ti–Z
601	**Smith's Legion**
602	Capt. Alexander's Co., Infantry
	Capt. Anderson's Co., Infantry (Anderson Guards)
	Athens Reserved Corps, Infantry
	Capt. Atwater's Co., Infantry
	Capt. Bard's Co., Infantry
	Capt. Barney's Co., Infantry (Richmond Factory Guards)
	Capt. Brook's Co., Infantry (Mitchell Home Guards)
	Capt. Caraker's Co., Infantry (Milledgeville Guards)
	Capt. Chapman's Co., Infantry (Defenders)
	Capt. Clemons' Co., Infantry
	Capt. Collier's Co., Infantry
603	Capt. Collier's Co., Infantry (Collier Guards)
	Conscripts, Georgia
	Capt. Dozier's Co., Infantry
	Capt. Ezzard's Co., Infantry
	Capt. Fuller's Co., Infantry
604	Capt. Garrison's Co., Infantry (Ogeechee Minute Men)
	Capt. Green's Co., Infantry (State Armory Guards)
	Capt. Grubb's Co., Infantry
	Capt. Hamlet's Co., Infantry
	Capt. Hansell's Co., Infantry (State Guards)
	Capt. Harris' Independent Co., Infantry (Brunswick Rifles)

Roll	Description
	Capt. Hendry's Co., Mounted Infantry (Pierce Mounted Volunteers)
	Capt. Holmes' Co., Infantry (Wright Local Guards)
	Capt. Howard's Co., Infantry (Non-Conscripts)
	Capt. Hull's Co., Infantry
605	Capt. Jackson's Co., Infantry
	Capt. Jones' Co., Infantry (Jones Hussars)
	Capt. Kay's Co., Infantry (Franklin County Guards)
	Capt. Lane's Co., Infantry (Jasper and Butts County Guards)
	Capt. Matthews' Co., Infantry (East to West Point Guards)
	Capt. Medlin's Independent Co., Infantry (High Shoals Defenders)
	Capt. Milner's Co., Infantry (Madison County Home Guard)
	Capt. Moore's Co., Infantry (Baldwin Infantry)
	Capt. Moring's Co., Infantry (Emanuel Troops)
	Capt. Pool's Co., Infantry
	Capt. Porter's Co. (Georgia Railroad Guards)
	Capt. Preston's Co. (Railroad Guards)
606	Rigdon Guards
	Capt. Roberts' Co., Exempts
	Capt. Russell's Co. (Newton Factory Employees)
	Capt. Taylor's Co.
	Capt. Thornton's Co. (Muscogee Guards)
	Lt. Weem's Detachment, Camp Guard (Augusta)
	Capt. White's Co.
	Capt. Witt's Co. (Express Infantry)
	Capt. Wyly's Co. (Mell Scouts)
	Whiteside's Naval Battalion, Infantry (Local Defense)
	Miscellaneous, Georgia
	A–C
607	D–Y

Compiled Service Records of Confederate Soldiers Who Served in Organizations From the State of Kentucky. M319. 136 rolls. 16mm. DP.

The compiled service records reproduced in this microfilm publication are indexed on M377.

Roll	Description
1	1st (Butler's) Cavalry
	A–Ge
2	Gi–Pa
3	Pe–Y
4	1st (Helm's) Cavalry
	A–Sk
5	Sm–Y
	1st Battalion, Cavalry
6	1st Mounted Rifles
	A–Ha
7	He–Y
8	2d Cavalry
	A–Mi
9	Mo–Y
	2d (Duke's) Cavalry
	A
10	B–Cl
11	Co–Go
12	Gr–Ke
13	Ki–M
14	N–Sp
15	St–Wi
16	Wo–Y
	2d (Woodward's) Cavalry

Roll	Description
	A–Ed
17	El–Mc
18	Me–Y
19	2d (Capt. Dortch's) Battalion, Cavalry
20	2d Battalion, Mounted Rifles
	A–L
21	M–Y
	3d Cavalry
	A–B
22	C–M
23	N–Z
	3d & 7th (Consolidated) Cavalry
	3d Battalion, Mounted Rifles
	A–Cl
24	Co–Mo
25	Mu–Y
	4th Cavalry
	A–An
26	Ar–Ca
27	Ch–Eb
28	Ed–Hi
29	Ho–Mc
30	Me–Re
31	Rh–Te
32	Th–Y
	5th Cavalry
	A
33	B–Ha
34	He–Ri
35	Ro–Y
36	6th Cavalry
	A–E
37	F–M
38	N–Y
39	7th Cavalry
	A–Co
40	Cr–Ho
41	Hu–Mi
42	Mo–St
43	Su–Z
	8th Cavalry
	A–Bo
44	Br–G
45	H–Mi
46	Mo–Th
47	Ti–Y
	9th Cavalry
	A–B
48	C–Gi
49	Gl–L
50	M–R
51	S–Wh
52	Wi–Y
	10th Cavalry
	A–L
53	M–Y
	10th (Diamond's) Cavalry
	A–Ch
54	Cl–I
55	J–Y
	10th (Johnson's) Cavalry
	A–F
57	G–Ma
58	Mc–S
59	T–Y
	11th Cavalry
	A–C

Roll	Description
60	D–S
61	T–Y
	12th Cavalry
	A–Cl
62	Co–I
63	J–Pa
64	Pe–Y
	8th and 12th (Consolidated) Cavalry
65	13th Cavalry
	A–Cl
66	Co–Ha
67	He–Pa
68	Pe–Z
69	14th Cavalry
70	Capt. Corbin's Men
	Jessee's Battalion, Mounted Riflemen
71	Kirkpatrick's Battalion
	Morehead's Regiment (Partisan Rangers)
	Capt. Bolen's Independent Co., Cavalry
	Buckner Guards, Cavalry
	A–F
72	G–Y
	Capt. Dudley's Independent Cavalry
	Capt. Field's Co. (Partisan Rangers)
	Capt. Jenkins' Co., Cavalry
73	Morgan's Men
	Capt. Rowan's Co. (Partisan Rangers)
74	Capt. Thompson's Co., Cavalry
	Capt. Byrne's Co., Horse Artillery
	Capt. Cobb's Co., Light Artillery
	A–G
75	H–Y
	Capt. Corbett's Co., Artillery
	Green's Battery, Light Artillery
	Lt. McEnnis' Detachment, Artillery
76	1st Infantry
	A–D
77	E–K
78	L–Ri
79	Ro–Y
80	2d Mounted Infantry
	A–B
81	C–D
82	E–G
83	H–I
84	J–L
85	M–Mo
86	Mu–Re
87	Ri–Sp
88	St–Wa
89	We–Y
	3d Mounted Infantry
	A–Be
90	Bi–Co
91	Cr–Gl
92	Go–Le
93	Li–Pe
94	Ph–Sm
95	Sn–Y
96	4th Mounted Infantry
	A–Bo
97	Br–Cr
98	Cu–F
99	G–Hi
100	Ho–Lo
101	Lu–N
102	O–Ro

Roll	Description
103	Ru–Te
104	Th–Wh
105	Wi–Z
	5th Mounted Infantry
	A
106	B
107	C
108	D–Gl
109	Go–H
110	I–Ma
111	Mc–Pi
112	Pl–Sm
113	Sn–V
114	W–Z
	6th Mounted Infantry
	A–Bl
115	Bo–D
116	E–Je
117	Jo–N
118	O–Sm
119	Sn–Y
120	7th Mounted Infantry
	A–Cr
121	Cu–Hi
122	Ho–M
123	N–S
124	T–Z
	8th Mounted Infantry
	A–Bo
125	Br–G
126	H–P
127	Q–Y
128	9th Mounted Infantry
	A–B
129	C–D
130	E–Ha
131	He–K
132	L–Mi
133	Mo–Re
134	Rh–Ta
135	Te–Z
	Ficklin's Battalion, Infantry
136	Miscellaneous, Kentucky

Compiled Service Records of Confederate Soldiers Who Served in Organizations From the State of Louisiana. M320. 414 rolls. 16mm. DP.

The compiled service records reproduced in this microfilm publication are indexed on M378.

Roll	Description
1	1st Cavalry
	A–Cl
2	Co–Ga
3	Ge–J
4	K–Me
5	Mi–Ra
6	Re–Ta
7	Te–Z
	1st Battalion, Cavalry (State Guards)
8	2d Cavalry
	A–Br
9	Bu–E
10	F–J
11	K–Mi
12	Mo–R

Roll	Description
13	S–Z
	2d Battalion, Cavalry (State Guards)
14	3d Cavalry
	3d (Harrison's) Cavalry
	A–K
15	L–Z
16	3d (Wingfield's) Cavalry
	A–Di
17	Do–L
18	M–R
19	S–Y
20	4th Cavalry
21	5th Cavalry
22	6th Cavalry
	A–L
23	M–Z
24	7th Cavalry
	A–Re
25	Ri–Y
	8th Cavalry
	A–N
26	O–Z
	13th Battalion (Partisan Rangers)
	A–D
27	E–M
28	N–Y
	18th Battalion, Cavalry
29	Ogden's Cavalry
30	Cavalry Squadron (Independent Rangers of Iberville), Militia
	Squadron Guides d'Orleans, Militia
	Mounted Rangers of Plaquemines, Militia
	Capt. Benjamin's Co., Cavalry
31	Capt. Bond's Co., Mounted Partisan Rangers
	Capt. Borge's Co. (Garnet Rangers), Militia
	Capt. Cagnolatti's Co., Cavalry (Chasseurs of Jefferson), Militia
	Capt. Cole's Co., Cavalry
	Capt. Delery's Co. (St. Bernard Horse Rifles), Militia
	Capt. Dreux's Cavalry, Co. A
32	Dubecq's Co., Cavalry
	Capt. Greenleaf's Co. (Orleans Light Horse), Cavalry
33	Capt. Lott's Co. (Carroll Dragoons), Cavalry
	Capt. Millaudon's Co. (Jefferson Mounted Guards)
	Capt. Miller's Independent Co., Mounted Rifles
	Capt. Norwood's Co. (Jeff Davis Rangers), Cavalry
	Capt. Nutt's Co. (Red River Rangers), Cavalry
	Capt. Webb's Co., Cavalry
34	1st Heavy Artillery
	A–Be
35	Bi–Br
36	Bu–Co
37	Cr–E
38	F–Go
39	Gr–I
40	J–La
41	Le–Me
42	Mi–Pe
43	Ph–Sa
44	Sc–Te
45	Th–Z
46	2d Battalion, Heavy Artillery
	8th Battalion, Heavy Artillery
	A–K

Roll	Description
47	L–Y
	1st Field Battery, Artillery
48	2d Field Battery, Light Artillery
	3d Battery (Benton's), Light Artillery
49	5th Field Battery (Pelican Light Artillery), Light Artillery
	6th Field Battery (Grosse Tete Flying Artillery), Light Artillery
	Beauregard Battalion Battery, Artillery
	Bridge's Battery, Light Artillery
	Capt. Castellanos' Battery, Artillery
50	Capt. Fenner's Battery, Light Artillery
51	Capt. Green's Co. (Louisiana Guard Battery), Artillery
	A–R
52	S–W
	Capt. Guyol's Co. (Orleans Artillery), Artillery
	Capt. Holmes' Co., Light Artillery
	Capt. Hutton's Co. (Crescent Artillery, Co. A), Artillery
	A–H
53	I–Y
	Capt. Kean's Battery (Orleans Independent Artillery), Artillery
54	Capt. King's Battery, Artillery
	Lafayette Artillery, Militia
	Capt. Landry's Co. (Donaldsonville Artillery), Artillery
	A–K
55	L–W
	Capt. Le Gardeur, Jr.'s, Co. (Orleans Guard Battery), Light Artillery
	A–C
56	D–Z
	Capt. McPherson's Battery (Orleans Howitzers), Militia
57	Capt. Moody's Co. (Madison Light Artillery), Artillery
	A–K
58	L–Z
	Ordnance Detachment
	Pointe Coupee Artillery
	A–Bi
59	Bl–J
60	K–Y
61	Siege Train Battalion
	Watson's Battery, Artillery
62	Washington Battalion, Artillery
	A–Bo
63	Br–C
64	D–Fo
65	Fr–Hi
66	Ho–La
67	Le–Me
68	Mi–Pe
69	Pf–Sc
70	Se–U
71	V–Z
72	1st Infantry
	1st (Nelligan's) Infantry
	A–Ba
73	Be–Ci
74	Cl–Do
75	Dr–Gl
76	Go–J
77	K–L
78	M
79	N–Ri

Roll	Description	Roll	Description
80	Ro–S	128	3d Regiment, 2d Brigade, 1st Division, Militia
81	T–Z		3d Regiment, 3d Brigade, 1st Division, Militia
82	1st (Strawbridge's) Infantry	129	4th Infantry
	A–B		A–B
83	C–D	130	C–De
84	E–Ha	131	Di–G
85	He–K	132	H–J
86	L–Mi	133	K–L
87	Mo–Re	134	M–O
88	Ri–S	135	P–R
89	T–Z	136	S–T
90	1st Reserves	137	U–Z
	1st Regiment, 2d Brigade, 1st Division, Militia	138	4th Regiment, European Brigade, Militia
91	1st Regiment, 3d Brigade, 1st Division, Militia		A–L
	1st Regiment, European Brigade, Militia	139	M–Z
	1st Regiment, French Brigade, Militia		4th Regiment, French Brigade, Militia
	A–B		A–C
92	C–La	140	D–Z
93	Le–Z	141	4th Regiment, 1st Brigade, 1st Division, Militia
94	1st Native Guards, Militia		A–Q
	A–G	142	R–Z
95	H–Z		4th Regiment, 2d Brigade, 1st Division, Militia
96	1st Chasseurs a pied, Militia	143	4th Regiment, 3d Brigade, 1st Division, Militia
	1st Battalion Infantry (State Guards)		4th Battalion, Infantry
97	1st (Rightor's) Special Battalion, Infantry		A–Bo
	A–F	144	Br–F
98	G–M	145	G–L
99	N–Z	146	M–R
100	1st (Wheat's) Special Battalion, Infantry	147	S–Z
	A–H	148	5th Infantry
101	J–Y		A–Br
102	2d Infantry	149	Bu–Co
	A–Bo	150	Cr–E
103	Br–Co	151	F–Go
104	Cr–Fo	152	Gr–Hi
105	Fr–G	153	Ho–Ko
106	H–Ji	154	Ku–L
107	Jo–L	155	M–Mo
108	M	156	Mu–Q
109	N–Rh	157	R–Sh
110	Ri–Sn	158	Si–T
111	So–Wh	159	V–Z
112	Wi–Z	160	5th Regiment, European Brigade (Spanish Regiment), Militia
	2d Regiment, 2d Brigade, 1st Division, Militia		A–F
113	2d Regiment, 3d Brigade, 1st Division, Militia	161	G–Pa
114	2d Reserve Corps	162	Pe–Z
115	2d Regiment, French Brigade, Militia	163	6th Infantry
116	3d Infantry		A–B
	A–B	164	C
117	C–D	165	D–Fl
118	E–Ha	166	Fo–G
119	He–K	167	H–Ja
120	L–Mo	168	Je–Li
121	Mu–R	169	Lo–Me
122	S–T	170	Mi–O
123	U–Z	171	P–R
	3d Regiment, European Brigade (Garde Francaise), Militia	172	S–Th
	A–D	173	Ti–Z
124	E–Z	174	6th Regiment, European Brigade (Italian Guards Battalion), Militia
125	3d Regiment, French Brigade, Militia	175	7th Infantry
	A–O		A–Br
126	P–Z	176	Bu–Cr
	3d Regiment, 1st Brigade, 1st Division, Militia	177	Cu–Fi
	A–K	178	Fl–Ha
127	L–Z		

Roll	Description
179	He–Ke
180	Ki–Ma
181	Mc–Mo
182	Mu–Re
183	Rh–Sp
184	St–V
185	W–Z
186	7th Battalion, Infantry
187	8th Infantry
	A–Bo
188	Br–Ce
189	Ch–Da
190	De–Em
191	En–Go
192	Gr–He
193	Hi–Ke
194	Ki–L
195	M–Mi
196	Mo–Og
197	Ol–Re
198	Rh–Sl
199	Sm–Th
200	Ti–Z
201	9th Infantry
	A–Bi
202	Bl–By
203	C–Co
204	Cr–E
205	F–G
206	H–Ho
207	Hu–K
208	L
209	M–Mi
210	Mo–Pe
211	Ph–R
212	S–Sp
213	St–Va
214	Vi–Z
215	9th Battalion, Infantry
	A–K
216	L–Z
217	10th Infantry
	A–Ca
218	Ch–E
219	F–H
220	I–L
221	M
222	N–R
223	S–V
224	W–Z
	10th Battalion, Infantry
	A–C
225	D–Z
226	11th Infantry
	A–D
227	E–K
228	L–Q
229	R–Z
230	11th Battalion, Infantry
	A–E
231	F–La
232	Le–P
233	R–Z
234	12th Infantry
	A–Bo

Roll	Description
235	Br–Co
236	Cr–Fo
237	Fr–Ha
238	He–J
239	K–L
240	M–Mo
241	Mu–Ra
242	Re–Si
243	Sk–U
244	V–Z
245	13th Infantry
	A–Ce
246	Ch–Fa
247	Fe–Ho
248	Hu–L
249	M–Mo
250	Mu–R
251	S–Tr
252	Tu–Z
	13th and 20th Infantry
253	14th Infantry
	A–B
254	C–Cu
255	D–Fe
256	Fi–G
257	H–I
258	J–L
259	M–Me
260	Mi–N
261	O–Ri
262	Ro–Su
263	Sw–Z
264	14th (Austin's) Battalion, Sharp Shooters
	A–L
265	M–Y
266	15th Infantry
	A–Ch
267	Cl–Em
268	En–Ho
269	Hu–L
270	M–Ni
271	No–Sm
272	So–Z
	15th (Weatherly's) Battalion, Sharp Shooters
273	16th Infantry
	A–Ca
274	Ch–D
275	E–Ha
276	He–Ke
277	Ki–Mi
278	Mo–Re
279	Rh–S
280	T–Z
281	16th Battalion, Infantry
	A–L
282	M–W
283	17th Infantry
	A–Ch
284	Cl–F
285	G–Je
286	Jo–Me
287	Mi–Ri
288	Ro–St
289	Su–Z
290	18th Infantry

Roll	Description
	A–Bo
291	Br–C
292	D–F
293	G–I
294	J–L
295	M–Pi
296	Pl–Sh
297	Si–Z
298	Consolidated 18th Regiment and Yellow Jacket Battalion, Infantry
	A–C
299	D–L
300	M–Z
301	19th Infantry
	A–B
302	C–Fa
303	Fe–Ho
304	Hu–L
305	M–Pe
306	Ph–Sn
307	Sp–Z
308	20th Infantry
	A–B
309	C–D
310	E–Ha
311	He–La
312	Le–Mo
313	Mu–Ro
314	Ru–Te
315	Th–Z
316	21st (Kennedy's) Infantry
	A–R
317	S–Z
	21st (Patton's) Infantry
	A–De
318	Di–Je
319	Jo–Mu
320	My–Sc
321	Se–Z
322	22d Infantry
	A–Co
323	Cr–He
324	Hi–Me
325	Mi–Se
326	Sh–Y
	22d (Consolidated) Infantry
	A–B
327	C–J
328	K–Ra
329	Re–Z
330	25th Infantry
	A–Co
331	Cr–Ha
332	He–L
333	M–Q
334	R–Te
335	Th–Z
336	26th Infantry
	A–Ca
337	Ce–Gr
338	Gu–Me
339	Mh–Z
340	27th Infantry
	A–Ch
341	Cl–Fi
342	Fl–Ho

Roll	Description
343	Hu–L
344	M–O
345	P–So
346	Sp–Z
347	28th (Gray's) Infantry
	A–Cl
348	Co–G
349	H–L
350	M–P
351	Q–V
352	W–Z
	28th (Thomas') Infantry
	A–B
353	C–G
354	H–M
355	N–Y
356	30th Infantry
	A–B
357	C–Fa
358	Fe–J
359	K–M
360	N–Sa
361	Sc–Z
362	31st Infantry
	A–Co
363	Cr–G
364	H–L
365	M–P
366	R–Th
367	Ti–Y
368	Algiers Battalion, Militia
	Assumption Regiment, Militia
	Battalion British Fusileers, Militia
	Battalion French Volunteers, Militia
	Bonnabel Guards, Militia
	Beauregard Regiment, Militia
	Beauregard Battalion, Militia
369	Bragg's Battalion, Militia
	British Guard Battalion, Militia
	A–G
370	H–W
	Catahoula Battalion
	Cazadores Espanoles Regiment, Militia
	A–F
371	G–Z
	Chalmette Regiment, Militia
	A–B
372	C–L
373	M–Z
374	Claiborne Regiment, Militia
	Confederate Guards Regiment, Militia
	A–G
375	H–S
376	T–Y
	Consolidated Crescent Regiment, Infantry
	A–Ch
377	Ci–H
378	I–M
379	N–U
380	V–Z
	Continental Cadets, Militia
	Continental Regiment, Militia
381	Crescent Cadets, Militia
	Crescent Regiment, Infantry
	A–Ca
382	Ce–F
383	G–K

Roll	Description
384	L–Q
385	R–S
386	T–Z
387	Fire Battalion, Militia
	A–R
388	S–Z
	Irish Regiment, Militia
389	Jackson Rifle Battalion, Militia
	Jeff Davis Regiment, Infantry
	La Fourche Regiment, Militia
	A–C
390	D–W
391	Leeds' Guards Battalion, Militia
	Lewis Regiment
	Lewis Guards, Militia
392	Louisiana and Government Employees Regiment
	Maddox's Regiment, Reserve Corps
	Mechanics Guard, Militia
393	Miles' Legion
	A–Di
394	Do–La
395	Le–Re
396	Rh–Z
397	Orleans Fire Regiment, Militia
398	Orleans Guards Regiment, Militia
	A–E
399	F–Me
400	Mi–Z
401	Pelican Regiment, Infantry
	Pointe Coupee Regiment, Militia
	Provisional Regiment, Louisiana Legion
	Red River Sharp Shooters
	Reserve Corps
	A–Me
402	Mi–Y
	Sabine Reserves
	St. James Regiment, Militia
403	St. John the Baptist Reserve Guards, Militia
	St. Martin's Regiment, Militia
	Terrebonne Regiment, Militia
	Vermillion Regiment, Militia
	Watkins' Battalion, Reserve Corps
	Weatherly's Battalion, Infantry
404	C. S. Zouave Battalion, Volunteers
	A–Da
405	De–G
406	H–L
407	M–R
408	S–Z
409	Capt. Barr's Independent Co. (Blakesley Guards), Militia
	Capt. Bickham's Co. (Caddo Militia)
	Capt. Brenan's Co. (Co. A, Shamrock Guards), Militia
	Conscripts, Louisiana
	A–O
410	P–Z
	French Co. of St. James, Militia
	Capt. Herrick's Co. (Orleans Blues)
411	Capt. Knap's Co. (Fausse River Guards), Militia
	Capt. Lartigue's Co. (Bienville Guards), Militia

Compiled Service Records of Confederate Soldiers Who Served in Organizations From the State of Maryland. M321. 22 rolls. 16mm. DP.

The compiled service records reproduced in this microfilm publication are indexed on M379.

Roll	Description
1	1st Cavalry
	A–C
2	D–G
3	H–Ll
4	Lo–Q
5	R–St
6	Su–Z
7	2d Battalion, Cavalry
	A–La
8	Le–Z
9	1st Battery, Artillery
	A–O
10	P–Y
	2d Battery, Artillery
	A–J
11	K–W
	3d Battery, Artillery
	A–F
12	G–Z
13	4th Battery Artillery
14	1st Infantry
	A–D
15	E–L
16	M–R
17	S–Z
18	2d Battalion, Infantry
	A–D
19	E–Ka
20	Ke–Ph
21	Pi–Z
22	Weston's Battalion
	Capt. Walter's Co. (Zarvona Zouaves)
	Miscellaneous, Maryland

Compiled Service Records of Confederate Soldiers Who Served in Organizations From the State of Mississippi. M269. 427 rolls. 16mm. DP.

The compiled service records reproduced in this microfilm publication are indexed on M232.

Roll	Description
1	1st Cavalry
	A–D
2	E–J
3	K–R
4	S–Z
5	1st Cavalry Reserves
	A–Q
6	R–Z
	1st (McNair's) Battalion, Cavalry (State Troops)
7	1st (Miller's) Battalion, Cavalry
	1st (Montgomery's) Battalion, Cavalry (State Troops)
	1st Choctaw Battalion, Cavalry
8	2d Cavalry
	A–C
9	D–Hi
10	Ho–Mc
11	Me–S
12	T–Y
13	2d State Cavalry
	A–G
14	H–O
15	P–Y
16	2d Cavalry Reserves
	2d Partisans
	2d Partisan Rangers

Roll	Description
	A–B
17	C–K
18	L–Sk
19	Sl–Y
	2d (Harris') Battalion, State Cavalry
	A–M
20	N–W
	2d Battalion Cavalry Reserves
	3d Cavalry
	A–B
21	C–L
22	M–Z
	3d Cavalry Reserves
23	3d Cavalry (State Troops)
24	3d (Ashcraft's) Battalion, Cavalry
	3d (Cooper's) Battalion, State Cavalry
25	3d Battalion, Cavalry Reserves
	4th Cavalry
	A–C
26	D–M
27	N–Y
	4th Cavalry, Militia
28	4th Battalion, Cavalry
29	5th Cavalry
	A–J
30	K–Y
31	6th Cavalry
	A–K
32	L–Y
33	6th Battalion, Cavalry
	7th Cavalry
	A–F
34	G–L
35	M–R
36	S–Y
37	8th Cavalry
	A–J
38	K–Y
39	9th Cavalry
40	10th Cavalry
	A–G
41	H–M
42	N–Y
43	11th (Perrin's) Cavalry
	A–K
44	L–Y
45	11th (Ashcraft's) Cavalry
	11th (Consolidated) Cavalry
	12th Cavalry
	A–E
46	F–O
47	P–Y
48	17th Battalion, Cavalry
49	18th Cavalry
	A–G
50	H–M
51	N–Y
	24th Battalion, Cavalry
	A–B
52	C–Y
53	28th Cavalry
	A–B
54	C–E
55	F–He
56	Hi–K
57	L–Me
58	Mi–Q

Roll	Description
59	R–Sl
60	Sm–V
61	W–Y
62	38th Cavalry
	A–C
63	D–H
64	I–P
65	R–Z
66	Jeff Davis Legion, Cavalry
	A–Cl
67	Co–F
68	G–K
69	L–M
70	N–Sp
71	St–Z
72	Davenport's Battalion, Cavalry (State Troops)
	Capt. Abbott's Co., Cavalry
	Capt. Armistead's Co., Partisan Rangers
	Capt. Bowen's Co. (Chulahoma Cavalry)
	Capt. Brown's Co. (Foster Creek Rangers), Cavalry
	Capt. Buck's Co., Cavalry
	Butler's Co., Cavalry Reserves
73	Capt. Drane's Co. (Choctaw County Reserves), Cavalry
	Capt. Duncan's Co. (Tishomingo Rangers), Cavalry
	Capt. Dunn's Co. (Mississippi Rangers), Cavalry
	Capt. Foote's Co., Mounted Men
	Capt. Gamblin's Co., Cavalry (State Troops)
	Garland's Battalion, Cavalry
	Capt. Garley's Co. (Yazoo Rangers), Cavalry
	Capt. Gibson's Co., Cavalry
	Capt. Grace's Co., Cavalry (State Troops)
74	Capt. Grave's Co. (Copiah Horse Guards)
	Capt. Hamer's Co. (Salem Cavalry)
	Ham's Regiment, Cavalry
	A–G
75	H–S
76	T–Y
	Hughes' Battalion, Cavalry
77	Capt. Knox's Co. (Stonewall Rangers), Cavalry
	Capt. Maxey's Co., Mounted Infantry (State Troops)
	Capt. Maxwell's Co. (State Troops) (Peach Creek Rangers)
	Mitchell's Co., Cavalry Reserves
	Capt. Montgomery's Independent Company (State Troops) (Herndon Rangers)
	Capt. Montgomery's Co. of Scouts
	Capt. Morphis' Independent Co. of Scouts
	Capt. Nash's Co. (Leake Rangers)
	Perrin's Battalion, State Cavalry
	A–K
78	L–Y
	Capt. Polk's Independent Co. (Polk Rangers), Cavalry
	Power's Regiment, Cavalry
79	Capt. Rhodes' Co., Partisan Rangers, Cavalry
	Capt. Russell's Co., Cavalry
	Capt. Semple's Co., Cavalry
	Capt. Shelby's Co. (Bolivar Greys), Cavalry
	Capt. Smyth's Co., Partisan Rangers
	Capt. Stewart's Co. (Yalobusha Rangers)
	Stockdale's Battalion, Cavalry
80	Street's Battalion, Cavalry
	Stabb's Battalion, State Cavalry
	Terrell's Unattached Co., Cavalry
	Capt. Vivion's Co., Cavalry

Roll	Description
	William's Co., Cavalry
	Capt. Wilson's Independent Co., Mounted Men (Neshoba Rangers)
	Yerger's Regiment, Cavalry
81	1st Light Artillery
	A–Bl
82	Bo–Cl
83	Co–Do
84	Dr–Go
85	Gr–Hi
86	Ho–K
87	L–Mc
88	Me–Po
89	Pr–Si
90	Sk–Tw
91	Ty–Y
92	14th Battalion, Light Artillery
	A–P
93	R–Y
	Capt. Bradford's Co. (Confederate Guards Artillery)
	A–K
94	L–Y
	Byrne's Battery, Artillery
	Capt. Cook's Co., Horse Artillery
	Culbertson's Battery, Light Artillery
	Capt. Darden's Co., Light Artillery (Jefferson Artillery)
	A–L
95	M–W
	Capt. English's Co., Light Artillery
	Capt. Graves' Co., Light Artillery (Issaquena Artillery)
	Capt. Hoole's Co., Light Artillery (Hudson Battery)
	A–G
96	H–Y
	Capt. Hoskins' Battery, Light Artillery (Brookhaven Light Artillery)
	Capt. Kittrell's Co. (Wesson Artillery), Artillery
97	Capt. Lomax's Co., Light Artillery
	Capt. Merrin's Battery, Light Artillery
	Capt. Richards' Co., Light Artillery (Madison Light Artillery)
	A–M
98	N–Y
	Capt. Roberts' Co. (Seven Stars Artillery), Artillery
	Capt. Stanford's Co., Light Artillery
	A–C
99	D–W
	Capt. Swett's Co., Light Artillery (Warren Light Artillery)
	A–O
100	P–W
	Capt. Turner's Co., Light Artillery
	Capt. Yates' Battery, Light Artillery
101	1st (Foote's) Infantry (State Troops)
	1st (Johnston's) Infantry
	A–Go
102	Gr–M
103	N–Y
104	1st (King's) Infantry (State Troops)
	A–K
105	L–Y
106	1st (Patton's) Infantry (Army of 10,000)
107	1st (Percy's) Infantry (Army of 10,000)
	1st Battalion, Infantry (Army of 10,000)

Roll	Description
108	1st State Troops, Infantry, 1864
	1st Battalion, State Troops, Infantry, 12 months, 1862–63
	A–O
109	P–Y
	1st Battalion, State Troops, Infantry, 30 days, 1864
110	1st Battalion, Sharp Shooters
	A–O
111	P–Y
	1st Infantry
	2d Infantry
	A
112	Ba–Br
113	Bu–Con
114	Coo–E
115	F–G
116	Ha–Ho
117	Hu–La
118	Le–McG
119	McH–O
120	P–R
121	S–St
122	Su–We
123	Wh–Y
	2d Mississippi Infantry (Army of 10,000)
124	2d Battalion, Infantry
	A–P
125	R–Z
	2d (Davidson's) Infantry (Army of 10,000)
	A–O
126	P–Y
	2d (Quinn's) Infantry (State Troops)
	A–Q
127	R–Z
	2d Battalion, Infantry (State Troops)
128	2d State Troops, Infantry, 30 days, 1864
129	3d Infantry (State Troops)
	A–R
130	S–Y
	3d Infantry
	A–B
131	C–F
132	G–K
133	L–O
134	P–Sp
135	St–Z
	3d Infantry (Army of 10,000)
136	3d Battalion, Infantry
	A–E
137	F–K
138	L–Q
139	R–We
140	Wh–Y
	3d Battalion, Infantry (State Troops)
	A–Ha
141	He–Y
142	3d Battalion, Reserves
	4th Infantry
	A–Co
143	Cr–Hi
144	Ho–Mi
145	Mo–Sh
146	Sm–Y
147	4th Infantry (State Troops)
	5th Infantry
	A–C

Roll	Description	Roll	Description
148	D–Hi	201	12th Infantry
149	Ho–Mc		A–Bra
150	Me–R	202	Bre–C
151	S–Y	203	D–F
152	5th Battalion, Infantry	204	G–Ha
	5th Infantry (State Troops)	205	He–K
	A–D	206	L–Mc
153	E–M	207	Me–Pe
154	N–Y	208	Ph–Si
155	6th Infantry	209	Sl–V
	A–E	210	W–Z
156	F–Li		13th Infantry
157	Lo–Ri		A
158	Ro–We	211	B
159	Wh–Y	212	C
	7th Infantry	213	D–F
	A–B	214	G–He
160	C–E	215	Hi–K
161	F–I	216	L–Mc
162	J–Mi	217	Me–Pa
163	Mo–Sa	218	Pe–Se
164	Sc–Z	219	Sh–T
165	7th Battalion, Infantry	220	U–Z
	A–Go	221	14th Infantry
166	Gr–O		A–Ca
167	P–Y	222	Ch–E
168	8th Infantry	223	F–H
	A–Cl	224	I–Ma
169	Co–F	225	Mc–O
170	G–K	226	P–Sp
171	L–O	227	St–Wh
172	P–Sn	228	Wi–Z
173	So–Y		14th (Consolidated) Infantry
	8th Battalion, Infantry	229	15th Infantry
174	9th Infantry		A–B
	A–Br	230	C–D
175	Bu–Do	231	E–Ha
176	Dr–Ha	232	He–L
177	He–K	233	M–O
178	L–Mc	234	P–Se
179	Me–P	235	Sh–T
180	Q–Sp	236	U–Z
181	Sr–We		15th (Consolidated) Infantry
182	Wh–Z	237	15th Battalion, Sharp Shooters
	9th Battalion Sharp Shooters		16th Infantry
	A–G		A
183	H–Y	238	B–Bo
184	10th Infantry	239	Br–Con
	A–B	240	Coo–D
185	C–D	241	E–Gl
186	E–G	242	Go–Hi
187	H–Le	243	Ho–K
188	Li–O	244	L–Ma
189	P–Sti	245	Mc–My
190	Sto–Y	246	N–Ri
191	11th Infantry	247	Ro–Sn
	A–Br	248	So–V
192	Bu–D	249	W–Z
193	E–G	250	17th Infantry
194	H–I		A–Bl
195	J–L	251	Bo–Ch
196	M–Mi	252	Cl–De
197	Mo–Pe	253	Di–F
198	Ph–R	254	G–Ha
199	S–Te	255	He–J
200	Th–Z		

Roll	Description
256	K–L
257	M–Mi
258	Mo–Pa
259	Pe–R
260	S–St
261	Su–Wa
262	We–Y
263	18th Infantry A–Bl
264	Bo–By
265	Ca–Coo
266	Cop–D
267	E–Gl
268	Go–Ha
269	He–J
270	K–L
271	M
272	N–Q
273	R–Sl
274	Sm–Ti
275	To–Z
276	19th Infantry A–Bo
277	Br–Co
278	Cr–F
279	G–He
280	Hi–J
281	K–Ma
282	Mc–N
283	O–Ri
284	Ro–Sp
285	St–V
286	W–Z
287	20th Infantry A–B
288	C–E
289	F–H
290	I–Mo
291	Mu–Sh
292	Si–Z
293	21st Infantry A–Bo
294	Br–C
295	D–Gl
296	Go–Je
297	Jo–Ma
298	Mc–O
299	P–Sh
300	Si–Th
301	Ti–Y
302	22d Infantry A–Cl
303	Co–Ge
304	Gi–H
305	I–Mc
306	Me–R
307	S–We
308	Wh–Z
	23d Infantry A–C
309	D–I
310	J–M
311	N–Sh
312	Si–Y
313	24th Infantry

Roll	Description
	A–Co
314	Cr–G
315	H–Li
316	Lo–O
317	P–Sp
318	St–Y
319	25th Infantry
320	26th Infantry A–Cl
321	Co–G
322	H–L
323	M–Pl
324	Po–Sn
325	So–Y
326	27th Infantry A–Ca
327	Ch–G
328	H–L
329	M–Pe
330	Ph–Sm
331	Sn–Y
332	29th Infantry A–C
333	D–I
334	J–M
335	N–Sm
336	So–Y
337	30th Infantry A–D
338	E–Le
339	Li–Q
340	R–Y
341	31st Infantry A–Ch
342	Co–Ge
343	Gi–K
344	L–N
345	O–Sl
346	Sm–Y
347	32d Infantry A–D
348	E–K
349	L–Ri
350	Ro–Y
351	33d Infantry A–D
352	E–J
353	K–M
354	N–Sl
355	Sm–Y
356	34th Infantry A–Cl
357	Co–He
358	Hi–Mi
359	Mo–Sh
360	Si–Y
361	35th Infantry A–Cl
362	Co–Go
363	Gr–Ke
364	Ki–N
365	O–Sl
366	Sm–Y
367	36th Infantry A–C

Roll	Description
368	D–Ho
369	Hu–M
370	N–Sm
371	So–Z
372	37th Infantry
	A–Ch
373	Cl–G
374	H–La
375	Le–N
376	O–Sn
377	Sp–Y
378	39th Infantry
	A–G
379	H–M
380	N–U
381	V–Y
	40th Infantry
	A–Ch
382	Cl–Ha
383	He–Ma
384	Mc–Sa
385	Sc–Y
386	41st Infantry
	A–Ca
387	Ch–Go
388	Gr–J
389	K–M
390	N–Se
391	Sh–Z
392	42d Infantry
	A–Ca
393	Ch–E
394	F–H
395	I–Mc
396	Me–P
397	Q–S
398	T–Y
399	43d Infantry
	A–Ch
400	Cl–F
401	G–H
402	I–Mc
403	Me–Ra
404	Re–S
405	T–Y
406	44th Infantry
	A–Cl
407	Co–Ha
408	He–McI
409	McK–Sh
410	Si–Y
411	46th Infantry
	A–De
412	Di–K
413	L–R
414	S–Z
415	48th Infantry
	A–B
416	C–D
417	E–He
418	Hi–L
419	M
420	N–R
421	S
422	T–Z

Roll	Description
423	Capt. Adair's Co. (Lodi Co.)
	Capt. Adam's Co. (Holmes County Independent)
	Capt. Applewhite's Co. (Vaiden Guards)
	Capt. Barnes' Co. of Home Guards
	Capt. Barr's Co.
	Capt. Berry's Co., Infantry (Reserves)
	Blythe's Battalion (State Troops)
	Capt. Burt's Independent Co. (Dixie Guards)
	Camp Guard (Camp of Instruction for Conscripts)
424	Capt. Clayton's Co. (Jasper Defenders)
	Capt. Comfort's Co., Infantry
	Conscripts, Mississippi
	Capt. Condrey's Co. (Bull Mountain Invincibles)
	Capt. Cooper's Co., Infantry
	Capt. Drane's Co. (Choctaw Silver Greys)
	Capt. Fant's Co.
	Capt. Gage's Co.
	Capt. Gage's Co. (Wigfall Guards)
	Gillenland's Battalion (State Troops)
	Capt. Gordon's Co. (Local Guard of Wilkinson County)
425	Capt. Grace's Co. (State Troops)
	Capt. Griffin's Co. (Madison Guards)
	Capt. Hall's Co.
	Capt. Henley's Co. (Henley's Invincibles)
	Capt. Hightower's Co.
	Hinds County Militia
	Capt. Hudson's Co. (Noxubee Guards)
	Capt. Lewis' Co., Infantry
	Capt. McCord's Co. (Slate Springs Co.)
	Capt. McLelland's Co. (Noxubee Home Guards)
	Capt. T. P. Montgomery's Co.
	Capt. Moore's Co. (Palo Alto Guards)
426	Capt. Morgan's Co. (Morgan Riflemen)
	Moseley's Regiment
	Capt. Packer's Co. (Pope Guards)
	Capt. Page's Co. (Lexington Guards)
	Capt. Patton's Co. (State Troops)
	Capt. D. J. Red's Co., Infantry (Red Rebels)
	Capt. S. W. Red's Co. (State Troops)
	Capt. Roach's Co. (Tippah Scouts)
	Capt. Roger's Co.
	Capt. Shield's Co.
	Capt. Standefer's Co.
	Lt. Stricklin's Co. (State Troops)
	Capt. Taylor's Co. (Boomerangs)
	Capt. Terry's Co.
427	Capt. Walsh's Co. (Muckalusha Guards)
	Wilkinson County Minute Men
	Capt. Kershaw Williams' Co. (Gray Port Greys)
	Capt. Thomas William's Co.
	Capt. Wilson's Co. (Ponticola Guards)
	Capt. Withers' Co., Reserve Corps
	Capt. Yerger's Co. (State Troops)
	Miscellaneous, Mississippi

Compiled Service Records of Confederate Soldiers Who Served in Organizations From the State of Missouri. M322. 193 rolls. 16mm. DP.

The compiled service records reproduced in this microfilm publication are indexed on M380.

Roll	Description
1	1st Cavalry
	A–Bo
2	Br–C
3	D–Go
4	Gr–I
5	J–L

Roll	Description
6	M–N
7	O–Sm
8	Sn–U
9	V–Y
10	1st Northeast Cavalry
	A–B
11	C–F
12	G–K
13	L–N
14	O–S
15	T–Y
16	1st and 3d (Consolidated) Cavalry
17	2d Cavalry
	A–C
18	D–H
19	I–Me
20	Mi–S
21	T–Z
	2d Northeast Cavalry (Franklin's Regiment)
22	3d Cavalry
	A–C
23	D–Ha
24	He–Me
25	Mi–Sp
26	St–Y
27	3d Battalion, Cavalry
	A–D
28	E–I
29	J–N
30	O–Sn
31	So–Z
32	4th Cavalry
	A–C
33	D–H
34	I–O
35	P–S
36	T–Z
37	5th Cavalry
	A–C
38	D–H
39	I–Q
40	R–Y
41	6th Cavalry
	A–C
42	D–I
43	J–P
44	Q–Y
45	7th Cavalry
	A–D
46	E–K
47	L–R
48	S–Y
49	8th Cavalry
	A–C
50	D–Hi
51	Ho–Mi
52	Mo–Sn
53	So–Y
54	9th (Elliott's) Cavalry
	A–J
55	K–Z
56	10th Cavalry
	A–G
57	H–Pi
58	Po–Z
59	12th Cavalry

Roll	Description
	A–F
60	G–M
61	N–Y
62	15th Cavalry
	A–L
63	M–Y
64	Boone's Regiment, Mounted Infantry
	Clardy's Battalion, Cavalry
	Coffee's Regiment, Cavalry
	A–F
65	G–Y
	Coleman's Regiment, Cavalry
	A–L
66	M–Y
	Davies' Battalion, Cavalry
	Ford's Battalion, Cavalry
	A–L
67	M–W
	Freeman's Regiment, Cavalry
	A–C
68	D–M
69	N–Y
70	Fristoe's Regiment, Cavalry
	A–M
71	N–Z
	Hunter's Regiment, Cavalry
	Jackman's Regiment, Cavalry
	Lawther's Partisan Rangers
72	Lawther's Temporary Regiment, Dismounted Cavalry
	Poindexter's Regiment, Cavalry
	A–P
73	Q–Y
	Preston's Battalion, Cavalry
74	Schnabel's Battalion, Cavalry
	Shaw's Battalion, Cavalry
75	Slayback's Regiment, Cavalry
76	Snider's Battalion, Cavalry
77	Williams' Regiment, Cavalry
78	Wood's Regiment, Cavalry
	A–L
79	M–Y
80	Capt. Beck's Co., Cavalry
	Capt. Hick's Co., Cavalry
	Capt. Hobbs' Co., Cavalry
	Capt. Stallard's Co., Cavalry
	Capt. Woodson's Co., Cavalry
81	1st Battery, Light Artillery
82	3d Battery, Light Artillery
83	13th Battery, Light Artillery
	1st Field Battery, Light Artillery
	2d Field Battery, Light Artillery
84	3d Field Battery, Light Artillery
	4th (Harris') Field Battery, Light Artillery
85	Capt. Barret's Co., Light Artillery
86	Capt. H. M. Bledsoe's Co., Light Artillery
	Capt. Joseph Bledsoe's Co., Artillery
87	Capt. Farris' Battery, Light Artillery (Clark Artillery)
88	Lt. Hamilton's (Prairie Gun) Battery, Light Artillery
	Capt. Landis' Co., Light Artillery
	A–H
89	J–Y
	Capt. Lowe's Co., Artillery (Jackson Battery)
90	Capt. McDonald's Co., Light Artillery
	Capt. Parson's Co., Light Artillery
	Capt. von Phul's Co., Light Artillery

Roll	Description		Roll	Description
91	Capt. Walsh's Co., Light Artillery		144	8th Battalion, Infantry
92	1st Infantry			A–J
	A–C		145	K–Z
93	D–G		146	9th Infantry
94	H–L			A–F
95	M–Q		147	G–M
96	R–V		148	N–Z
97	W–Z		149	9th Battalion, Sharp Shooters
	1st Battalion, Infantry		150	10th Infantry
98	1st and 4th (Consolidated) Infantry			A–B
	A–B		151	C–F
99	C–E		152	G–J
100	F–I		153	K–Mi
101	J–M		154	Mo–Sn
102	N–R		155	So–Y
103	S–Z		156	11th Infantry
104	2d Infantry			A–Cl
	A–B		157	Co–Gi
105	C		158	Gl–K
106	D–F		159	L–O
107	G–Ho		160	P–Sm
108	Hu–L		161	Sn–Z
109	M–N		162	12th Infantry
110	O–Se			A–Di
111	Sh–T		163	Do–K
112	U–Z		164	L–Po
113	2d and 6th (Consolidated) Infantry		165	Pr–Z
	3d Infantry		166	16th Infantry
	A–Bi			A–Cl
114	Bl–Co		167	Co–F
115	Cr–Fu		168	G–I
116	G–I		169	J–M
117	J–Me		170	N–Sn
118	Mi–Rh		171	So–Y
119	Ri–Ta		172	Clark's Regiment, Infantry
120	Te–Z			A–G
121	3d Battalion, Infantry		173	H–R
	A–O		174	S–Y
122	P–Y			Dorsey's Regiment
	3d and 5th (Consolidated) Infantry			Douglas' Regiment
123	4th Infantry			Parsons' Regiment
	A–C		175	Perkins' Battalion, Infantry
124	D–H		176	Phelan's Regiment
125	I–N			Searcy's Battalion, Sharp Shooters
126	O–Y			A–P
127	5th Infantry		177	R–Z
	A–Ca			Thompson's Command
128	Ch–Go			Winston's Regiment, Infantry
129	Gr–J		178	State Guard
130	K–M			A–Bi
131	N–Sl		179	Bl–By
132	Sm–Y		180	C–Cr
133	6th Infantry		181	Cu–E
	A–Ca		182	F–G
134	Ce–F		183	H–Hi
135	Ga–J		184	Ho–J
136	K–M		185	K–L
137	N–R		186	M–Mi
138	S–Z		187	Mo–Pe
139	7th Infantry		188	Ph–Ri
	8th Infantry		189	Ro–Sm
	A–Ch		190	Sn–Th
140	Cl–G		191	Ti–Wa
141	H–Me		192	We–Z
142	Mi–Si		193	Quantrill's Co.
143	Sk–Z			Miscellaneous, Missouri

Compiled Service Records of Confederate Soldiers Who Served in Organizations From the State of North Carolina. M270. 580 rolls. 16mm. DP.

The compiled service records reproduced in this microfilm publication are indexed on M230.

Roll	Description
1	1st Cavalry (9th State Troops)
	A–Ba
	Be–Ch
3	Cl–D
4	E–Go
5	Gr–I
6	J–Ma
7	Mc–Pa
8	Pe–Se
9	Sh–T
10	U–Y
11	2d Cavalry (19th State Troops)
	A–Bo
12	Br–C
13	D–G
14	H–K
15	L–O
16	P–Rog
17	Ros–Th
18	Ti–Z
19	3d Cavalry (41st State Troops)
	A–B
20	C–F
21	G–H
22	I–Mi
23	Mo–Q
24	R–Ste
25	Sti–Y
26	4th Cavalry (59th State Troops)
	A–Br
27	Bu–Fe
28	Fi–H
29	I–M
30	N–Sl
31	Sm–Y
32	5th Cavalry (63d State Troops)
	A–Ch
33	Cl–F
34	G–H
35	I–Mc
36	Me–Q
37	R–S
38	T–Z
39	5th Battalion, Cavalry
40	6th Cavalry (65th State Troops)
	A–F
41	G–M
42	N–Z
43	7th Battalion, Cavalry
44	8th Battalion, Partisan Rangers
	A–S
45	T–Y
	12th Battalion, Cavalry
	14th Battalion, Cavalry
46	15th Battalion, Cavalry, State Service
	16th Battalion, Cavalry
	Capt. Howard's Co. (Local Defense), Cavalry
	McRae's Battalion, Cavalry
	Capt. Swindell's Co., Partisan Rangers
47	1st Battalion, Heavy Artillery
	A–K

Roll	Description
48	L–S
49	T–W
	1st Artillery (10th State Troops)
	A–Ba
50	Be–By
51	C
52	D–F
53	G–He
54	Hi–J
55	K–Ma
56	Mc–N
57	O–Q
58	R–Se
59	Sh–Th
60	Ti–Z
61	2d Artillery (36th State Troops)
	A–Br
62	Bu–D
63	E–Ha
64	He–L
65	M–O
66	P–R
67	S
68	T–Z
69	3d Artillery (40th State Troops)
	A–Br
70	Bu–C
71	D–Ga
72	Ge–H
73	I–Le
74	Li–Mi
75	Mo–P
76	Q–So
77	Sp–Wai
78	Wal–Z
79	3d Battalion, Light Artillery
	A–G
80	H–N
81	O–W
82	10th Battalion, Heavy Artillery
	A–F
83	G–L
84	M–U
85	V–Y
	13th Battalion, Light Artillery
	A–B
86	C–G
87	H–O
88	P–V
89	W–Y
	Capt. Moseley's Co. (Sampson Artillery)
90	1st Infantry
	A–Bo
91	Br–Cl
92	Co–E
93	F–Ha
94	He–J
95	K–Ma
96	Mc–Pa
97	Pe–Se
98	Sh–U
99	V–Z
100	1st Infantry, 6 months, 1861
	A–G
101	H–O
102	P–Z

Roll	Description	Roll	Description
103	1st Junior Reserves	150	Ho–J
	A–J	151	K–Ma
104	K–V	152	Mc–O
105	W–Y	153	P–Rh
	1st Detailed Men	154	Ri–Sl
	1st Battalion, Junior Reserves	155	Sm–T
	1st Regiment, Militia	156	U–Y
106	2d Infantry	157	5th Senior Reserves
	A–Bre		A–R
107	Bri–Co	158	S–Y
108	Cr–F		6th Infantry
109	G–Hi		A–Ba
110	Ho–K	159	Be–Ca
111	L–M	160	Ch–D
112	N–R	161	E–He
113	S–Te	162	Hi–K
114	Th–Y	163	L–Mc
115	2d Battalion, Infantry	164	Me–Pa
	A–C	165	Pe–R
116	D–I	166	S
117	J–O	167	T–Wa
118	P–T	168	We–Z
119	U–Z	169	6th Senior Reserves
	2d Detailed Men	170	7th Infantry
	2d Junior Reserves		A–Bl
	A–E	171	Bo–Co
120	F–S	172	Cr–Fl
121	T–Y	173	Fo–He
	2d Conscripts	174	Hi–K
	2d Battalion, Local Defense Troops	175	L–Mc
	A–G	176	Me–Pe
122	H–W	177	Ph–Sk
123	3d Infantry	178	Sm–U
	A–Bl	179	V–Y
124	Bo–Ce	180	7th Senior Reserves
125	Ch–D	181	7th Battalion, Junior Reserves
126	E–G		8th Infantry
127	H–I		A–Ba
128	J–L	182	Be–C
129	M	183	D–G
130	N–P	184	H–J
131	Q–Sh	185	K–M
132	Si–Ti	186	N–Sl
133	To–Y	187	Sm–Z
134	3d Junior Reserves	188	8th Senior Reserves
	A–M	189	8th Battalion, Junior Reserves
135	N–Y		9th (1st) Battalion, Sharp Shooters
	3d Battalion, Senior Reserves		A–G
136	4th Infantry	190	H–W
	A–Br	191	11th (Bethel Regiment) Infantry
137	Bu–E		A–Bo
138	F–H	192	Br–Cl
139	I–Ma	193	Co–E
140	Mc–P	194	F–Har
141	R–S	195	Has–Ke
142	T–Y	196	Ki–McL
143	4th Senior Reserves	197	McM–Pi
	A–S	198	Po–Sl
144	T–Y	199	Sm–V
	4th Battalion, Junior Reserves	200	W–Y
145	5th Infantry	201	12th Infantry
	A–Be		A–Bo
146	Bh–Ch	202	Br–Co
147	Cl–D	203	Cr–E
148	E–Gl	204	F–Ha
149	Go–Hi		

Roll	Description	Roll	Description
205	He–K	261	Co–F
206	L–M	262	G–Ho
207	N–Q	263	Hu–L
208	R–Sm	264	Ma–Mi
209	Sn–Wa	265	Mo–P
210	We–Y	266	Q–Sh
211	13th Infantry	267	Sm–T
	A–Bo	268	U–Y
212	Br–C	269	20th Infantry
213	D–F		A–Bo
214	G–Hi	270	Br–Co
215	Ho–K	271	Cr–F
216	L–Me	272	G–Hi
217	Mi–P	273	Ho–Le
218	R–Sm	274	Li–O
219	Sn–V	275	P–Si
220	W–Y	276	Sk–V
221	13th Battalion, Infantry	277	W–Y
	A–R	278	21st Infantry
222	S–Y		A–Bo
	14th Infantry	279	Br–E
	A–Bi	280	F–H
223	Bl–D	281	I–Mc
224	E–G	282	Me–P
225	H–I	283	R–St
226	J–L	284	Su–Z
227	M–O	285	22d Infantry
228	P–Sh		A–B
229	Si–V	286	C
230	W–Z	287	D–G
231	15th Infantry	288	H–K
	A–Bo	289	L–M
232	Br–C	290	N–R
233	D–Go	291	S–Te
234	Gr–Hi	292	Th–Z
235	Ho–La	293	23d Infantry
236	Le–Mi		A–B
237	Mo–Ph	294	C
238	Pi–Sm	295	D–F
239	So–V	296	G–Hi
240	W–Z	297	Ho–K
241	16th Infantry	298	L–Mi
	A–B	299	Mo–Q
242	C–D	300	R–Se
243	E–Ha	301	Sh–T
244	He–K	302	U–Y
245	L–Mi	303	24th Infantry
246	Mo–Ro		A–Be
247	Ru–Te	304	Bi–Cl
248	Th–Y	305	Co–El
249	17th Infantry (1st Organization)	306	Em–G
	A–H	307	H–I
250	J–Y	308	J–L
251	17th Infantry (2d Organization)	309	M–Mo
	A–B	310	Mu–Ri
252	C–E	311	Ro–T
253	F–Har	312	V–Z
254	Has–K	313	25th Infantry
255	L–M		A–Br
256	N–Ri	314	Bu–C
257	Ro–Ta	315	D–F
258	Te–Y	316	G–Hi
259	18th Infantry	317	Ho–Li
	A–Bo	318	Lo–Mi
260	Br–Cl	319	Mo–Pl

Roll	Description
320	Po–Se
321	Sh–V
322	W–Z
323	26th Infantry A–Bo
324	Br–Cl
325	Co–E
326	F–Hi
327	Ho–K
328	L–Mc
329	Me–P
330	R–Sm
331	Sn–T
332	U–Z
333	27th Infantry A–B
334	C–E
335	F–He
336	Hi–K
337	L–M
338	N–Q
339	R–Sp
340	St–Wa
341	We–Y
342	28th Infantry A–Bo
343	Br–Co
344	Cr–F
345	G–Hi
346	Ho–K
347	L–Ma
348	Mc–O
349	P–R
350	S
351	T–Y
352	29th Infantry A–G
353	H–Pa
354	Pe–Z
355	30th Infantry A–Bo
356	Br–C
357	D–Go
358	Gr–J
359	K–Mi
360	Mo–P
361	R–S
362	T–Y
363	31st Infantry A–E
364	F–Le
365	Li–P
366	R–Wh
367	Wi–Y
	32d Infantry A–Bi
368	Bl–Cl
369	Co–D
370	E–G
371	H–Je
372	Jo–L
373	M–O
374	P–R
375	S
376	T–Z

Roll	Description
377	33d Infantry A–Bo
378	Br–Co
379	Cr–F
380	G–He
381	Hi–Le
382	Li–M
383	N–Ri
384	Ro–S
385	T–Z
	33d Militia
386	34th Infantry A–Ce
387	Ch–F
388	G–I
389	J–Mc
390	Me–Rh
391	Ri–Ti
392	To–Z
393	35th Infantry A–Ca
394	Ch–F
395	G–I
396	J–Mc
397	Me–Sh
398	Si–Z
399	37th Infantry A–Bl
400	Bo–Co
401	Cr–F
402	G–Hi
403	Ho–L
404	M–O
405	P–R
406	S–Te
407	Th–Y
408	38th Infantry A–B
409	C–D
410	E–Hi
411	Ho–L
412	M
413	N–Se
414	Sh–We
415	Wh–Y
	39th Infantry A–Ca
416	Ce–Hi
417	Ho–P
418	Q–Z
419	42d Infantry A–B
420	C–D
421	E–G
422	H–J
423	K–Me
424	Mi–Ri
425	Ro–S
426	T–Y
427	43d Infantry A–Bo
428	Br–C
429	D–G
430	H–J
431	K–Mc

Roll	Description
432	Me–Ri
433	Ro–Th
434	Ti–Y
435	44th Infantry A–Ch
436	Cl–F
437	G–J
438	K–M
439	N–R
440	S
441	T–Y
442	45th Infantry A–B
443	C–D
444	E–Ha
445	He–J
446	K–Ma
447	Mc–Pe
448	Ph–Sl
449	Sm–Wal
450	Wam–Y
451	46th Infantry A–B
452	C–F
453	G–Ho
454	Hu–L
455	M
456	N–R
457	S–Te
458	Th–Y
459	47th Infantry A–B
460	C–E
461	F–Hi
462	Ho–L
463	M–Pe
464	Ph–Tha
465	Tho–Y
466	48th Infantry A–B
467	C–E
468	F–He
469	Hi–La
470	Le–M
471	N–Se
472	Sh–Wa
473	We–Y 49th Infantry A–Bi
474	Bl–C
475	D–F
476	G–I
477	J–McF
478	McG–P
479	Q–S
480	T–Y
481	50th Infantry A–B
482	C–G
483	H–L
484	M–Sp
485	St–Y
486	51st Infantry A–Br
487	Bu–E

Roll	Description
488	F–Hi
489	Ho–L
490	Ma–Me
491	Mi–Q
492	R–Sp
493	St–Wa
494	We–Z
	51st Militia 52d Infantry A–Bi
495	Bl–C
496	D–G
497	H–K
498	L–O
499	P–Si
500	Sm–Z
501	53d Infantry A–B
502	C–E
503	F–Hi
504	Ho–Le
505	Li–M
506	N–R
507	S–T
508	V–Z
	54th Infantry A–B
509	C–F
510	G–K
511	L–O
512	P–Sh
513	Si–Y
514	55th Infantry A–Cl
515	Co–G
516	H–M
517	N–S
518	T–Y
519	56th Infantry A–B
520	C–Fa
521	Fe–Hi
522	Ho–L
523	M–Pi
524	Po–S
525	T–Y
526	57th Infantry A–B
527	C–D
528	E–G
529	H–Ke
530	Ki–Mi
531	Mo–P
532	R–Sr
533	St–Z
534	58th Infantry A–Co
535	Cr–Ha
536	He–Mi
537	Mo–Sl
538	Sm–Y
539	60th Infantry A–D
540	E–K
541	L–Q
542	R–V

Roll	Description
543	W–Y
	61st Infantry
	A–Bi
544	Bl–C
545	D–Ha
546	He–La
547	Le–N
548	O–Si
549	Sk–Y
550	**62d Infantry**
	A–C
551	D–H
552	I–N
553	O–S
554	T–Z
	64th Infantry (11th Battalion, Allen's Regiment)
	A–B
555	C–G
556	H–Mc
557	Me–R
558	S–Y
559	**66th Infantry (8th Battalion, Partisan Rangers; 13th Battalion**
	A–C
560	D–I
561	J–O
562	P–S
563	T–Y
	Capt. J. W. Whitman's Co., 66th Battalion, Militia
564	**67th Infantry**
565	**68th Infantry**
	Clark's Special Battalion, Militia
566	Cumberland County Battalion, Detailed Men
	Hill's Battalion, Reserves
	Mallett's Battalion (Camp Guard)
	A–P
567	Q–Y
	McCorkle's Battalion, Senior Reserves
	McLean's Battalion, Light Duty Men
	Thomas' Legion
	A–Bl
568	Bo–C
569	D–Ha
570	He–L
571	M–O
572	P–Se
573	Sh–Ti
574	To–Z
575	Capt. Allen's Co. (Local Defense)
	Capt. Bank's Co. (Currituck Guard)
	Capt. Bass' Co.
	Capt. Brown's Co.
	Conscripts, Unassigned
576	Capt. Cox's Co., Local Defense (Provost Guard, Kingston)
	Capt. Croom's Co., Local Defense (Kingston Guards, Kingston Provost Guard)
	Capt. Doughton's Co. (Alleghany Grays)
	Capt. Galloway's Co., Coast Guards
	Capt. Gibb's Co. (Local Defense)
	Capt. Giddins Co. (Detailed and Petitioned Men)
577	Capt. Griswold's Co., Local Defense (Provost Guard, Goldsboro)
	Home Guards
	Capt. Hoskins' Co. (Local Defense)
	Capt. Howard's Co., Prison Guards

Roll	Description
578	Capt. Jones' Co. (Supporting Force)
	Capt. Lawrence's Co., Volunteers (Wilson Partisan Rangers)
	Capt. Lee's Co., Local Defense (Silver Greys)
	Capt. Mallett's Co.
	Capt. McDugald's Co.
	A–M
579	N–Y
	Capt. McMillan's Co.
	Capt. Nelson's Co. (Local Defense)
	Capt. Snead's Co. (Local Defense)
580	Capt. Townsend's Co. (State Troops)
	Capt. Wallace's Co. (Wilmington Railroad Guard)
	Miscellaneous

Compiled Service Records of Confederate Soldiers Who Served in Organizations From the State of South Carolina. M267. 392 rolls. 16mm. DP.

The compiled service records reproduced in this microfilm publication are indexed on M381.

Roll	Description
1	**1st Cavalry**
	A–B
2	C–E
3	F–Hi
4	Ho–L
5	M–N
6	O–Se
7	Sh–V
8	W–Z
	1st Mounted Militia
	A–C
9	D–Y
10	**2d Cavalry**
	A–C
11	D–H
12	I–M
13	N–S
14	T–Y
	2d Battalion, Cavalry Reserves
15	**3d Cavalry**
	A–B
16	C–Di
17	Do–G
18	H–I
19	J–K
20	L–M
21	N–R
22	S–To
23	Tr–Z
24	**4th Cavalry**
	A–B
25	C–D
26	E–G
27	H–L
28	M–O
29	P–Sm
30	Sn–Z
31	4th Battalion, Cavalry
	4th Regiment, Cavalry Militia
32	**5th Cavalry**
	A–Ca
33	Ch–E
34	F–He
35	Hi–Mc

Roll	Description
36	Me–R
37	S–To
38	Tu–Z
39	6th Cavalry
	A–B
40	C–F
41	G–H
42	I–Mc
43	Me–Se
44	Sh–Y
45	7th Cavalry
	A–D
46	E–L
47	M–Sl
48	Sm–Y
49	10th Battalion, Cavalry
50	12th Battalion, Cavalry (4th Squadron Cavalry)
51	14th Battalion, Cavalry
52	17th (6th) Battalion, Cavalry
53	19th Battalion, Cavalry
	A–L
54	M–Z
	Capt. A. W. Cordes' Co., Cavalry (North Santee Mounted Rifles)
	Capt. Theodore Cordes' Co., Cavalry Militia (German Hussars)
	De Saussure's Squadron of Cavalry
	Capt. A. C. Earle's Cavalry
	Capt. Kirk's Co., Partisan Rangers
	A–G
55	H–Y
	Capt. Rodgers' Co., Cavalry (State Troops)
	Capt. Rutledge's Co., Cavalry Militia (Charleston Light Dragoons)
	Capt. Simon's Co., Volunteers (Etiwan Rangers)
	Capt. Trenholm's Co., Militia (Rutledge Mounted Riflemen)
	Capt. Trenholm's Co., Rutledge Mounted Riflemen and Horse Artillery
	A–S
56	T–Y
	Capt. Tucker's Co., Cavalry
	Capt. Walpole's Co., Cavalry (Stono Scouts)
57	1st Artillery
	A–Br
58	Bu–Da
59	De–Ga
60	Ge–Ho
61	Hu–K
62	L–Me
63	Mi–P
64	Q–Sq
65	St–Y
66	1st Regiment Artillery, Militia
67	2d Artillery
	A–Bo
68	Br–C
69	D–G
70	H–J
71	K–Me
72	Mi–P
73	R–Se
74	Sh–T
75	U–Z
76	3d (Palmetto) Battalion, Light Artillery
	A–B
77	C–Di

Roll	Description
78	Do–G
79	H–Je
80	Jo–L
81	M–Pl
82	Po–S
83	T–Y
84	Manigault's Battalion, Artillery
	A–C
85	D–H
86	I–Me
87	Mi–Si
88	Sk–Z
89	15th (Lucas') Battalion, Heavy Artillery
	A–G
90	H–M
91	N–Y
92	Capt. Bachman's Co., Artillery (German Light Artillery)
	Capt. Beauregard's Co., Light Artillery (Ferguson's Co., Light Artillery)
	A–F
93	G–Y
	Capt. Child's Co., Artillery
94	Capt. Fickling's Co., Artillery (Brooks Light Artillery)
95	Capt. Gaillard's Co., Light Artillery (Santee Light Artillery)
96	Capt. Garden's Co., Light Artillery (Palmetto Light Battery)
97	Capt. Gilchrist's Co., Heavy Artillery (Gist Guard)
98	Capt. Gregg's Co., Artillery (McQueen Light Artillery)
	Capt. Hart's Co., Horse Artillery, Volunteers (Washington Artillery)
99	Capt. Jeter's Co., Light Artillery (Macbeth Light Artillery)
100	Capt. J. T. Kanapaux's Co., Light Artillery (Lafayette Artillery)
101	Capt. Kelly's Co., Light Artillery (Chesterfield Artillery)
102	Capt. Lee's Co., Artillery
	Capt. Mathewes' Co., Heavy Artillery
103	Capt. Melchers' Co., Artillery (Co. B, German Artillery)
	Capt. Parker's Co., Light Artillery (Marion Artillery)
	A–F
104	G–W
105	Capt. Stuart's Co., Artillery (Beaufort Volunteer Artillery)
106	Capt. Wagener's Co., Light Artillery (Co. A, German Artillery)
	Capt. Walter's Co., Light Artillery (Washington Artillery)
	A–B
107	C–W
108	Capt. Mayham Ward's Co., Artillery (Waccamaw Light Artillery)
	A–T
109	V–Y
	Capt. Zimmerman's Co., Artillery (Pee Dee Artillery)
110	1st (Butler's) Infantry
	A–Bo
111	Br–Co
112	Cr–F
113	G–Hi

Roll	Description	Roll	Description
114	Ho–K	167	S–Te
115	L–Mi	168	Th–Y
116	Mo–Ri	169	2d State Troops 6 months, 1863–64
117	Ro–Te		A–J
118	Th–Y	170	K–Z
119	1st (Hagood's) Infantry	171	2d Reserves, 90 days, 1862–63
	A–Br		2d Battalion, Sharpshooters
120	Bu–E	172	3d Infantry
121	F–Hi		A–Cl
122	Ho–L	173	Co–F
123	M–O	174	G–J
124	P–Sp	175	K–Mi
125	St–Z	176	Mo–R
126	1st (McCreary's) Infantry (1st Provisional Army)	177	S–Th
	A–Br	178	Ti–Z
127	Bu–C	179	3d (Lawren's and James') Battalion, Infantry
128	D–Go		A–F
129	Gr–I	180	G–M
130	J–Ma	181	N–Y
131	Mc–N	182	3d Reserves, 90 days, 1862–63
132	O–R	183	3d Battalion Reserves
133	S–Th		3d State Troops, 6 months, 1863–64
134	Ti–Z		A–G
135	1st (Orr's) Rifles	184	H–Y
	A–Bo		4th Infantry
136	Br–Cl		A–D
137	Co–Fo	185	E–Mc
138	Fr–Ha	186	Me–Y
139	He–Ke		4th State Troops, 6 months, 1863–64
140	Ki–Ma		A–H
141	Mc–My	188	I–S
142	N–Ri	189	T–Z
143	Ro–S		4th Battalion, Reserves
144	T–Z	190	5th Infantry
145	1st Infantry, 6 months, 1861		A–B
	A–P	191	C
146	R–Z	192	D–F
	1st Regiment, Militia (Charleston Reserves)	193	G–He
147	1st Regiment Charleston Guard	194	Hi–L
	1st State Troops, 6 months, 1863–64	195	M
	A–D	196	N–R
148	E–Y	197	S–T
149	1st (Charleston) Battalion, Infantry (Gaillard's Battalion)	198	V–Z
	A–G	199	5th State Troops, 6 months, 1863–64
150	H–O		A–I
151	P–Z	200	J–Z
152	1st Battalion, Sharp Shooters	201	5th Reserves, 90 days, 1862–63
153	1st Regiment Rifles, Militia (Branch's Rifle Regiment)		A–S
	2d Infantry (2d Palmetto Regiment)	202	T–Y
	A–B		5th (Brown's) Battalion, Reserves
154	C–Dr		5th Militia
155	Du–G	203	6th Infantry
156	H–K		A–Bo
157	L–Mi	204	Br–Cl
158	Mo–P	205	Co–D
159	R–S	206	E–G
160	T–Z	207	H–J
161	2d Rifles	208	K–Ma
	A–B	209	Mc–Mi
162	C–De	210	Mo–Ri
163	Do–G	211	Ro–S
164	H–J	212	T–Z
165	K–Mc	213	6th Reserves, 90 days, 1862–63
166	Me–R		6th (Byrd's) Battalion, Infantry
			6th (Merriwether's) Battalion, Reserves
		214	7th Infantry

Roll	Description		Roll	Description
	A–Bo		267	P–Sl
215	Br–Cl		268	Sm–Wh
216	Co–D		269	Wi–Z
217	E–G			13th Battalion, Infantry (4th and Mattison's)
218	H–K		270	14th Infantry
219	L–M			A–Bo
220	N–R		271	Br–C
221	S–Ti		272	D–G
222	To–Z		273	H–K
223	7th Reserves 90 days, 1862–63		274	L–N
224	7th (Ward's) Battalion, State Reserves		275	O–R
	7th (Nelson's) Battalion, Infantry (Enfield Rifles)		276	S–T
	A–C		277	U–Z
225	D–Hi		278	15th Infantry
226	Ho–Me			A–B
227	Mi–R		279	C–E
228	S–Y		280	F–H
229	8th Infantry		281	I–L
	A–C		282	M–P
230	D–Ha		283	R–S
231	He–L		284	T–Z
232	M–O		285	16th Infantry (Greenville Regiment)
233	P–T			A–B
234	W–Z		286	C–F
	8th Reserves		287	G–H
	8th (Stalling's) Battalion, Reserves		288	I–O
235	9th Infantry		289	P–T
	A–F		290	V–Y
236	G–O			16th Regiment, Militia
237	P–Z		291	17th Infantry
	9th Reserves, 90 days, 1862–63			A–Ch
	A–B		292	Cl–F
238	C–Y		293	G–L
239	9th Battalion, Infantry (Pee Dee Legion)		294	M–O
240	10th Infantry		295	P–S
	A–Cl		296	T–Z
241	Co–G			17th Regiment, Militia
242	H–K		297	18th Infantry
243	L–M			A–B
244	N–Sl		298	C–F
245	Sm–Y		299	G–I
246	11th Infantry (9th Volunteers)		300	J–Ma
	A–B		301	Mc–P
247	C–D		302	Q–T
248	E–G		303	V–Z
249	H–K			18th Regiment, Militia
250	L–N		304	19th Infantry
251	O–Si			A–Cl
252	Sk–Wh		305	Co–G
253	Wi–Z		306	H–Ma
	11th Reserves 90 days, 1862–63		307	Mc–R
254	12th Infantry		308	S–Z
	A–B		309	20th Infantry
255	C–D			A–B
256	E–He		310	C–D
257	Hi–L		311	E–G
258	M–N		312	H–I
259	O–R		313	J–L
260	S–Te		314	M–O
261	Th–Z		315	P–R
262	13th Infantry		316	S
	A–B		317	T–Z
263	C–De		318	21st Infantry
264	Di–Ha			A–B
265	He–K		319	C–E
266	L–O		320	F–Hi

Roll	Description
321	Ho–Ma
322	Mc–Pi
323	Pl–S
324	T–Z
325	22d Infantry
	A–B
326	C–E
327	F–H
328	I–O
329	P–Sp
330	St–Y
331	23d Infantry (Hatch's Regiment, Coast Rangers)
	A–Cl
332	Co–F
333	G–J
334	K–M
335	N–Sl
336	Sm–Y
337	24th Infantry
	A–Cl
338	Co–G
339	H–K
340	L–Pa
341	Pe–S
342	T–Z
	24th Militia
	16th and 24th (Consolidated) Infantry
343	25th Infantry (Eutaw Regiment)
	A–B
344	C–E
345	F–H
346	I–Ma
347	Mc–O
348	P–Si
349	Sm–Z
	25th Militia
350	26th Infantry
	A–C
351	D–G
352	H–K
353	L–O
354	P–Sp
355	St–Y
356	27th Infantry (Gaillard's Regiment)
	A–Ca
357	Ce–G
358	H–L
359	M–R
360	S–Z
361	Battalion State Cadets, Local Defense Troops Charleston
	Capt. Charbonnier's Co., Militia (Pickens Rifles)
	Charleston Arsenal Battalion
	Conscripts, South Carolina
	Capt. Estill's Co., Infantry, Local Defense (Arsenal Guard, Charleston)
	Capt. Hamilton's Co., Provost Guard
362	Hampton Legion
	A–Be
363	Bi–Ch
364	Cl–D
365	E–G
366	H–I
367	J–L
368	M–N
369	O–R

Roll	Description
370	S–Th
371	Ti–Z
372	Holcombe Legion
	A–Bo
373	Br–Co
374	Cr–F
375	G–I
376	J–Ma
377	Mc–Pa
378	Pe–Sh
379	Si–V
380	W–Z
381	Manigault's Battalion, Volunteers
382	Ordnance Guards (Capt. Dotterer)
	Palmetto (1st Palmetto) Sharp Shooters (Jenkins Regiment)
	A–Bo
383	Br–C
384	D–Ge
385	Go–H
386	I–L
387	M
388	N–Sa
389	Sc–T
390	V–Z
391	Capt. Rhett's Co. (Brooks Home Guards)
	Capt. Senn's Co., Post Guard
	Capt. Shiver's Co.
	Capt. Simon's Co.
	South Carolina (Walker's) Battalion, Infantry
	Capt. Symons' Co., Sea Fencibles
392	Miscellaneous, South Carolina

Compiled Service Records of Confederate Soldiers Who Served in Organizations From the State of Tennessee. M268. 359 rolls. 16mm. DP.

The compiled service records reproduced in this microfilm publication are indexed on M231.

Roll	Description
1	1st Cavalry
2	1st (Carter's) Cavalry
	A–J
3	K–T
4	U–W
	1st (McNairy's) Battalion, Cavalry
5	2d Cavalry
	2d (Ashby's) Cavalry
	A–B
6	C–G
7	H–L
8	M–R
9	S–Y
10	2d (Smith's) Cavalry
	2d (Biffle's) Battalion, Cavalry
11	3d (Forrest's) Cavalry
	A–D
12	E–K
13	L–R
14	S–Y
15	4th Cavalry
16	4th (McLemore's) Cavalry
	A–D
17	E–M
18	N–Y
19	4th (Murray's) Cavalry
20	4th (Branner's) Battalion, Cavalry

Roll	Description
	A–L
21	M–Y
	5th Cavalry
22	5th (McKenzie's) Cavalry
	A–Cl
23	Co–G
24	H–Ma
25	Mc–Si
26	Sl–Z
27	5th (McClellan's) Battalion, Cavalry
28	6th (Wheeler's) Cavalry
	A–G
29	H–R
30	S–Y
	7th Cavalry
31	7th (Duckworth's) Cavalry
	A–D
32	E–K
33	L–P
34	R–Z
35	7th (Bennett's) Battalion, Cavalry
	8th Cavalry
36	8th (Smith's) Cavalry
	A–F
37	G–M
38	N–Z
39	9th Cavalry
	9th (Ward's) Cavalry
	A–B
40	C–L
41	M–Y
42	9th (Gantt's) Battalion, Cavalry
	A–J
43	K–Z
	10th Cavalry
44	10th (De Moss') Cavalry
	A–H
45	I–Y
	10th and 11th (Consolidated) Cavalry
	A–M
46	N–Y
	11th Cavalry
	11th (Gordon's) Battalion, Cavalry
47	11th (Holman's) Cavalry
	A–G
48	H–P
49	Q–Z
	12th Cavalry
50	12th (Green's) Cavalry
	A–I
51	J–Z
52	12th (Day's) Battalion, Cavalry
	A–G
53	H–M
54	N–Y
	13th Cavalry
55	13th (Gore's) Cavalry
	A–H
56	I–Y
57	14th Cavalry
	14th (Neely's) Cavalry
	A–H
58	I–Y
59	15th Cavalry
	15th (Consolidated) Cavalry
	A–Q
60	R–Y

Roll	Description
	15th (Stewart's) Cavalry
61	16th Cavalry
	16th (Logwood's) Cavalry
62	16th (Neal's) Battalion, Cavalry
	A–K
63	L–Y
64	17th Cavalry
	17th (Sander's) Battalion, Cavalry
65	18th (Newsom's) Cavalry
	A–P
66	R–Y
	19th (Biffle's) Cavalry
	A–C
67	D–L
68	M–Y
69	19th and 20th (Consolidated) Cavalry
	A–Mc
70	Me–Y
	20th Cavalry
71	20th (Russell's) Cavalry
	A–P
72	R–Z
	21st Cavalry
	21st (Carter's) Cavalry
73	21st (Wilson's) Cavalry
	A–L
74	M–Z
75	21st and 22d (Consolidated) Cavalry
76	22d Cavalry
	22d (Barteau's) Cavalry
	A–C
77	D–K
78	L–R
79	S–Z
	22d (Nixon's) Cavalry
	28th Cavalry
80	Allison's Squadron, Cavalry
	Capt. Clark's Independent Co., Cavalry
	Cooper's Regiment, Cavalry
81	Cox's Battalion
	Douglass' Battalion, Partisan Rangers
	Greer's Regiment, Partisan Rangers
	Holman's Battalion, Partisan Rangers
82	Capt. Jackson's Co., Cavalry
	Napier's Battalion, Cavalry
83	Newsom's Regiment, Cavalry
84	Nixon's Regiment, Cavalry
	Capt. J. J. Parton's Co., Cavalry
	Shaw's Battalion, Cavalry (Hamilton's Battalion)
	A–I
85	J–Y
	Capt. Jeremiah Co. Stone's Co. A, Lyons Cavalry
	Welcker's Battalion, Cavalry
	Capt. William's Co., Cavalry
	Wilson's Regiment, Cavalry
	Capt. Woodward's Co., Cavalry
86	1st Heavy Artillery (Jackson's Regiment)
	A–G
87	H–M
88	N–Z
89	Capt. Barry's Co., Light Artillery (Lookout Artillery)
90	Capt. Baxter's Co., Light Artillery
	Capt. Bibb's Co., Artillery (Washington Artillery)
91	Capt. Browne's Co., Light Artillery

Roll	Description
	Capt. Burrough's Co., Light Artillery (Rhett Artillery)
	Caruther's Battery, Heavy Artillery
	Capt. Fisher's Co., Artillery (Nelson Artillery)
92	Capt. Huggins' Co., Light Artillery
	Capt. Johnston's Co., Heavy Artillery, 12 months, 1861–62 (Southern Guards Artillery)
	Capt. Kain's Co., Light Artillery (Mabry Light Artillery)
	A–K
93	L–Y
	Capt. Lynch's Co., Light Artillery
94	Capt. Marshall's Co., Artillery (Steuben Artillery)
95	McClung's Co., Light Artillery
	Capt. Morton's Co., Light Artillery
96	Capt. Palmer's Co., Light Artillery (Reneau Battery)
	Capt. Phillips' Co., Light Artillery (Johnson Light Artillery)
	Capt. Polk's Battery, Light Artillery
	Capt. Ramsey's Battery, Artillery
97	Capt. Rice's Battery, Light Artillery
	Capt. Scott's Co., Light Artillery
	A–M
98	N–W
	Capt. Sparkman's Co., Light Artillery (Maury Artillery)
	Capt. Sterling's Co., Heavy Artillery
	Capt. Stewart's Co., Artillery
	Capt. Tobin's Co., Light Artillery (Memphis Light Battery)
	A–G
99	H–Y
	Capt. Weller's Co., Light Artillery
	Capt. Winson's Co., Light Artillery (Belmont Battery)
	A–C
100	D–Y
	1st Zouaves
	1st Light Artillery (1st Battalion, Light Artillery)
	Artillery (McCown's) Corps
101	1st (Feild's) Infantry
	A–C
102	D–H
103	I–M
104	N–Sm
105	Sn–Z
106	1st (Turney's) Infantry
	A–B
107	C–E
108	F–H
109	I–M
110	N–Sm
111	Sn–Z
112	1st (Feild's) and 27th (Consolidated) Infantry
	1st Consolidated Regiment, Infantry
	1st (Colms') Battalion, Infantry
	A–F
113	G–Y
114	2d (Robison's) Infantry (Walker Legion)
	A–C
115	D–Hi
116	Ho–Mi
117	Mo–R
118	S–Z
119	2d (Walker's) Infantry
	A–L

Roll	Description
120	M–Y
	2d Consolidated Regiment, Infantry
121	3d (Clack's) Infantry
	A–D
122	E–J
123	K–Re
124	Rh–Y
125	3d (Lillard's) Mounted Infantry
	A–E
126	F–L
127	M–R
128	S–Y
	3d Consolidated Regiment, Infantry
129	3d (Memphis) Battalion, Infantry
	4th Infantry
	A–B
130	C–G
131	H–M
132	N–Sl
133	Sm–Z
134	4th Consolidated Regiment, Infantry
	5th Infantry
	A–B
135	C–G
136	H–Mc
137	Me–Sh
138	Si–Y
139	6th Infantry
	A–D
140	E–K
141	L–R
142	S–Y
143	7th Infantry
	A–B
144	C–Fl
145	Fo–He
146	Hi–L
147	M–P
148	Q–S
149	T–Y
150	8th Infantry
	A–D
151	E–Mi
152	Mo–Y
153	9th Infantry
	A–F
154	G–Mc
155	Me–Y
156	10th Infantry
	A–F
157	G–Mc
158	Me–Z
159	11th Infantry
	A–C
160	D–H
161	I–M
162	N–S
163	T–Z
164	12th Infantry
	A–H
165	I–Y
166	12th (Consolidated) Infantry
	A–F
167	G–N
168	O–Y
169	13th Infantry

Roll	Description
	A–D
170	E–L
171	M–R
172	S–Z
173	14th Infantry
	A–B
174	C–G
175	H–Ma
176	Mc–R
177	S–Y
178	15th Infantry
	A–F
179	G–M
180	N–Z
181	16th Infantry
	A–C
182	D–I
183	J–M
184	N–S
185	T–Y
186	17th Infantry
	A–Co
187	Cr–G
188	H–L
189	M–Ri
190	Ro–Y
191	18th Infantry
	A–C
192	D–Ha
193	He–Mc
194	Me–R
195	S–Y
196	19th Infantry
	A–D
197	E–I
198	J–Rh
199	Ri–Z
200	20th Infantry
	A–C
201	D–He
202	Hi–Mi
203	Mo–Sh
204	Si–Y
205	21st Infantry
206	22d Infantry (Freeman's Regiment)
	A–L
207	M–Y
	22d Battalion, Infantry
	A–C
208	D–Y
209	23d Infantry (Martin's Regiment)
	A–C
210	D–H
211	I–Mi
212	Mo–R
213	S–Z
214	23d (Newman's) Battalion, Infantry
	A–N
215	O–Y
	24th Infantry
	A
216	B–D
217	E–H
218	I–N
219	O–S
220	T–Y

Roll	Description
221	24th (Maney's) Battalion, Sharp Shooters
222	25th Infantry
	A–C
223	D–H
224	I–N
225	O–So
226	Sp–Y
227	26th Infantry (3d East Tennessee Volunteers)
	A–C
228	D–Hi
229	Ho–O
230	P–Z
231	27th Infantry
	A–F
232	G–O
233	P–Y
234	28th Infantry (2d Mountain Regiment, Volunteers)
	A–H
235	J–Y
236	28th (Consolidated) Infantry
	A–I
237	K–Y
238	29th Infantry
	A–D
239	E–J
240	K–Q
241	R–Z
242	30th Infantry
	A–F
243	G–M
244	N–Y
245	31st Infantry (Col. A. H. Bradford)
	A–G
246	H–P
247	R–Y
248	32d Infantry
	A–B
249	C–F
250	G–J
251	K–O
252	P–S
253	T–Y
254	33d Infantry
	A–G
255	H–O
256	P–Y
257	34th Infantry (4th Confederate Regiment, Infantry)
	A–C
258	D–H
259	I–Q
260	R–Y
261	35th Infantry (5th Regiment Provisional Army, Mountain Rifle Regiment)
	A–D
262	E–I
263	J–M
264	N–Sm
265	Sn–Y
266	36th Infantry
267	37th Infantry (7th Regiment Provisional Army, 1st East Tennessee Rifle Regiment)
	A–C
268	D–K
269	L–P

Roll	Description
270	Q–Y
271	38th Infantry (8th Infantry, Looney's Regiment) A–D
272	E–L
273	M–R
274	S–Y
275	39th Mounted Infantry (Col. W. M. Bradford's Regiment, Volunteers, 31st Infantry) A–D
276	E–K
277	L–Re
278	Ri–Z
279	40th Infantry (5th Confederate Infantry, Walker's Regiment, Volunteers) A–I
280	J–Y
281	41st Infantry A–C
282	D–H
283	I–M
284	N–Sn
285	So–Y
286	42d Infantry A–D
287	E–K
288	L–Q
289	R–Y
290	43d Infantry (5th East Tennessee Volunteers, Gillespie's Regiment) A–Cl
291	Co–G
292	H–Mc
293	Me–Sl
294	Sm–Z
295	44th Infantry
296	44th (Consolidated) Infantry A–Cl
297	Co–Gl
298	Go–K
299	L–O
300	P–Sm
301	Sn–Y
302	45th Infantry A–Co
303	Cr–H
304	I–M
305	N–Sl
306	Sm–Y
307	46th Infantry A–O
308	P–Y 47th Infantry A–B
309	C–H
310	I–Re
311	Rh–Y
312	48th (Nixon's) Infantry A–F
313	G–M
314	N–Y
315	48th (Voorheis') Infantry A–J
316	K–Y
317	49th Infantry A–K
318	L–Y

Roll	Description
319	50th Infantry A–E
320	F–K
321	L–R
322	S–Y
323	50th (Consolidated) Infantry 51st Infantry A–G
324	H–Y
325	51st (Consolidated) Infantry A–K
326	L–Y
327	52d Infantry 53d Infantry A–H
328	I–Y
329	54th Infantry
330	55th (Brown's) Infantry A–I
331	J–Y
332	55th (McKoin's) Infantry
333	59th Mounted Infantry (Cooke's Regiment, 1st (Eakin's) Battalion, Infantry) A–D
334	E–K
335	L–R
336	S–Y
337	60th Mounted Infantry (Crawford's Regiment, 79th Infantry) A–C
338	D–L
339	M–Z
340	61st Mounted Infantry (Pitts' Regiment, 81st Infantry) A–F
341	G–M
342	N–Z
343	62d Mounted Infantry (Rowan's Regiment, 80th Infantry) A–K
344	L–Y
345	63d Infantry (Fain's Regiment, 74th Infantry) A–B
346	C–E
347	F–Ho
348	Hu–Me
349	Mi–Sa
350	Sc–Y
351	84th Infantry 121st Regiment, Militia 154th Senior Regiment, Infantry (1st Volunteers) A–Ba
352	Be–D
353	E–K
354	L–Q
355	R–Y
356	Lt. Blair's Co. (Local Defense Troops) Conscripts, Tennessee
357	Crew's Battalion, Infantry Detailed Conscripts, Tennessee (Local Defense and Special Service Troops, Nitre and Mining Bureau) Engineers Corps, Tennessee Harman's Regiment, Infantry Capt. McLin's Co., Volunteers (Local Defense Troops) Capt. Miller's Co., (Local Defense Troops)

Roll	Description
	Nashville (Hawkins') Battalion, Infantry
358	Capt. Park's Co. (Local Defense Troops)
	Capt. Sowell's Detachment, Infantry
	Capt. Spencer's Co., Infantry
	Sullivan County Reserves (Local Defense Troops)
	Capt. Tackitt's Co., Infantry
359	Miscellaneous, Tennessee

Compiled Service Records of Confederate Soldiers Who Served in Organizations From the State of Texas. M323. 445 rolls. 16mm. DP.

The compiled service records reproduced in this microfilm publication are indexed on M227.

Roll	Description
1	1st Cavalry, State Troops, 6 months, 1863–64
2	1st (McCulloch's) Cavalry (1st Mounted Riflemen) A–F
3	G–O
4	P–Z
5	1st (Yager's) Cavalry (1st Mounted Rifles) A–G
6	H–N
7	O–Z
8	1st Battalion, Cavalry, State Troops, 6 months, 1863–64
	2d Cavalry (2d Mounted Rifles) A–Bl
9	Bo–C
10	D–G
11	H–J
12	K–Me
13	Mi–Ri
14	Ro–Th
15	Ti–Z
16	2d Cavalry, State Troops, 6 months, 1863–64 A–M
17	N–Z
	2d Battalion, Cavalry, State Troops, 6 months, 1863–64
18	3d Cavalry (South Kansas–Texas Mounted Volunteers) A–Cl
19	Co–G
20	H–L
21	M–P
22	R–Te
23	Th–Z
	3d Cavalry, State Troops, 6 months, 1863–64 A–H
24	I–Z
	3d Battalion, Cavalry, State Troops, 6 months, 1863–64
	3d (Yager's) Battalion, Cavalry (3d Battalion, Mounted Rifles; Yager's Battalion, Mounted Volunteers) A–D
25	E–R
26	S–Z
	4th Cavalry (4th Mounted Volunteers, 1st Regiment, Sibley's Brigade) A–B
27	C–G
28	H–L
29	M–Ri
30	Ro–Wh

Roll	Description
31	Wi–Z
	4th Cavalry, State Troops, 6 months, 1863–64
32	5th Cavalry (5th Mounted Volunteers, 2d Regiment, Sibley's Brigade) A–D
33	E–J
34	K–O
35	P–Sq
36	St–Z
37	6th Cavalry (Stone's Regiment, 2d Cavalry) A–Cl
38	Co–G
39	H–L
40	M–P
41	R–St
42	Su–Y
43	6th Battalion, Cavalry (Gould's Battalion; 3d Battalion, Cavalry) A–M
44	N–Y
45	7th Cavalry (7th Mounted Volunteers; 3d Regiment, Sibley's Brigade) A–E
46	F–K
47	L–Ri
48	Ro–Z
49	8th Cavalry (Terry's Regiment, 1st Rangers, 8th Rangers) A–Co
50	Cr–Hn
51	Ho–Me
52	Mi–R
53	S–Z
54	8th (Taylor's) Battalion, Cavalry (Taylor's Battalion, Mounted Rifles) A–L
55	M–Z
56	9th Cavalry (Sims' Regiment, 4th Cavalry) A–C
57	D–He
58	Hi–Me
59	Mi–Sh
60	Si–Y
61	10th Cavalry (Locke's Regiment) A–Co
62	Cr–G
63	H–L
64	M–Q
65	R–Sp
66	St–Z
67	11th Cavalry (Young's Regiment, 3d Cavalry) A–Di
68	Do–Jo
69	Ju–Ro
70	Ru–Z
71	12th Cavalry (Parson's Mounted Volunteers, 4th Dragoons) A–E
72	F–L
73	M–R
74	S–Z
75	13th Cavalry (Burnett's Regiment, 13th Mounted Volunteers) A–Ca
76	Ce–Ga
77	Ge–J

Roll	Description
78	K–O
79	P–Sta
80	Ste–Z
81	14th Cavalry (Johnson's Mounted Volunteers, 1st Regiment, Johnson's Brigade)
	A–F
82	G–K
83	L–Ro
84	Ru–Y
85	15th Cavalry (2d Regiment, Johnson's Brigade)
	A–C
86	D–Ha
87	He–Me
88	Mi–Si
89	Sl–Y
90	16th Cavalry (Fitzhugh's Regiment; 3d Regiment, Johnson's Brigade)
	A–G
91	H–P
92	Q–Z
93	17th Cavalry (Moore's Regiment)
	A–C
94	D–J
95	K–P
96	R–Y
97	17th (Consolidated) Dismounted Cavalry
	A–K
98	L–Y
99	18th Cavalry (Darnell's Regiment)
	A–Ch
100	Cl–F
101	G–L
102	M–Q
103	R–Y
104	19th Cavalry (Burford's Regiment)
	A–Gi
105	Gl–O
106	P–Y
107	20th Cavalry (Bass' Regiment)
	A–F
108	G–N
109	O–Y
110	21st Cavalry (1st Lancers; 1st Regiment, Carter's Brigade)
	A–G
111	H–O
112	P–Z
113	22d Cavalry
	A–E
114	F–M
115	N–Y
116	23d Cavalry (Gould's Regiment, 27th Cavalry)
	A–G
117	H–Q
118	R–Y
119	24th Cavalry (Wilkes' Regiment; 2d Lancers; 2d Regiment, Carter's Brigade)
	A–C
120	D–Hi
121	Ho–Me
122	Mi–R
123	S–Z
124	24th and 25th (Consolidated) Cavalry
	A–L
125	M–Z
126	25th Cavalry (Gillespie's Regiment; 3d Lancers; 3d Regiment, Carter's Brigade)
	A–Da
127	De–Ha
128	He–Me
129	Mi–Sh
130	Si–Z
131	26th Cavalry (Debray's Regiment, Davis' Mounted Battalion)
	A–Ch
132	Ci–G
133	H–La
134	Le–O
135	P–So
136	Sp–Z
137	27th Cavalry (Whitfield's Legion; 1st Legion)
	A–Ca
138	Ch–Ge
139	Gi–J
140	K–N
141	O–So
142	Sp–Z
143	28th Cavalry (Randal's Regiment, 1st Lancers)
	A–E
144	F–K
145	L–R
146	S–Y
147	29th Cavalry (De Morse's Regiment)
	A–E
148	F–M
149	N–Y
150	30th Cavalry (Gurley's Regiment, 1st Partisans)
	A–G
151	H–N
152	O–Y
153	31st Cavalry (Hawpe's Regiment)
	A–F
154	G–M
155	N–Y
156	32d Cavalry (15th Cavalry, Crump's Battalion, Mounted Volunteers)
	A–C
157	D–G
158	H–L
159	M–She
160	Shi–Y
161	33d Cavalry (Duff's Partisan Rangers, 14th Battalion, Cavalry)
	A–C
162	D–J
163	K–R
164	S–Z
165	34th Cavalry (Alexander's Regiment, 2d Partisan Rangers)
	A–H
166	I–Z
167	35th Cavalry (Brown's Regiment)
	A–Da
168	De–H
169	I–O
170	P–To
171	Tr–Z
	35th Cavalry (Likens' Regiment)
172	36th Cavalry (Woods' Regiment, 32d Cavalry)
	A–C
173	D–Hi

Roll	Description
174	Ho–Me
175	Mi–Se
176	Sh–Z
177	37th Cavalry (Terrell's Regiment, 34th Cavalry) A–G
178	H–O
179	P–Z
180	Baird's Cavalry (4th Regiment, Arizona Brigade; Showalter's Regiment) A–L
181	M–Y
182	Baylor's Cavalry (2d Regiment, Arizona Brigade) A–L
183	M–Y
184	Benavides' Cavalry A–J
185	K–Z
186	Border's Cavalry (Anderson's Regiment) A–G
187	H–R
188	S–Y
	Border's Battalion, Cavalry
189	Bourland's Cavalry (Bourlands "Border" Regiment) A–L
190	M–Y
191	Chisum's Cavalry (Dismounted), (2d Partisan Rangers; Stone's Regiment)
192	Crump's Cavalry (Lane's Cavalry, 1st Partisan Rangers)
	Frontier Battalion, Cavalry
	Gano's Squadron, Cavalry
193	Gidding's Battalion, Cavalry A–R
194	S–Z
	Good's Battalion, Cavalry
195	Granbury's Consolidated Brigade (1st Consolidated Regiment)
	Hardeman's Cavalry (1st Regiment, Arizona Brigade; 31st Cavalry) A–K
196	L–Z
197	Madison's Cavalry (3d Regiment, Arizona Brigade; Phillips' Regiment) A–K
198	L–Z
199	Mann's Cavalry (Bradford's Regiment) A–I
200	J–S
201	T–Z
	Mann's Battalion, Cavalry
202	Martin's Cavalry (5th Partisan Rangers) A–K
203	L–Z
204	McCord's Frontier Cavalry A–G
205	H–Pe
206	Ph–Z
207	Morgan's Cavalry A–E
208	F–N
209	O–Y
210	Ragsdale's Battalion, Cavalry A–G
211	H–Re
212	Rh–Z
213	Saufley's Scouting Battalion, Cavalry

Roll	Description
	Steele's Command, Cavalry
	Terry's Cavalry A–F
214	G–Y
215	Waller's Cavalry A–G
216	H–Q
217	R–Z
218	Wells' Cavalry A–O
219	P–Z
	Wells' Battalion, Cavalry
220	Capt. Bone's Co., Cavalry
	Capt. Coopwood's Spy Co., Cavalry
	Capt. Doughty's Co., Cavalry, State Troops ("Refugio Spies")
	Capt. Durant's Co., Cavalry (Local Defense)
	Lavaca County Minutemen
	Capt. Lilley's Co., Cavalry (Pardoned Deserters)
221	Capt. McDowell's Co., Cavalry (Lockhart Volunteers)
	Capt. Nolan's Mounted Co. (Local Defense)
	Capt. Pearson's Co., Partisan Rangers (Local Defense)
	Capt. Ragsdale's Co., Cavalry (Red River Dragoons)
	Capt. W. H. Randolph's Co., Cavalry
	Capt. Sutton's Co., Cavalry (Graham Rangers)
	Capt. Terry's Mounted Co. (State Troops)
	Capt. Thomas' Co., Partisan Rangers, 4 months, 1862–63
	Capt. L. Trevenio's Co., Cavalry
	Capt. Trevenio's Squad, Partisan Mounted Volunteers
	Capt. Upton's Co., Cavalry (Local Defense)
222	1st Heavy Artillery A–Br
223	Bu–De
224	Di–Go
225	Gr–Kel
226	Kem–McLa
227	McLe–O
228	P–Sa
229	Sc–U
230	V–Z
231	1st Field Battery (Edgar's Co., Light Artillery)
232	2d Field Battery
	4th Field Battery (Van Dorn Light Artillery) A–Kra
233	Kri–Z
234	4th (Shea's) Battalion, Artillery
235	5th Field Battery
236	6th Field Battery
237	7th Field Battery (Moseley's Co., Light Artillery)
238	8th Field Battery
239	9th Field Battery (Lamar Artillery)
240	10th Field Battery
	11th Field Battery (Capt. Howell's Co., Light Artillery)
	12th Field Battery
241	14th Field Battery
	15th Field Battery
242	16th Field Battery
	17th Field Battery
	Dege's Battalion, Light Artillery
243	Capt. Douglas' Co., Artillery
	Capt. Good's Co., State Troops, Artillery (Dallas Light Artillery)

Roll	Description	Roll	Description
	Capt. Greer's Rocket Battery		4th Infantry, State Troops, 6 months, 1863–64
244	Capt. Hughes' Co., Light Artillery		A–Ha
	Capt. Jones' Co., Light Artillery	294	He–Z
	A–K		4th (Oswald's) Battalion, Infantry (German
245	L–Y		Battalion), 6 months, 1861–62
	Lt. H. van Buren's Co., Light Artillery	295	5th Infantry
246	1st Infantry (2d Infantry)		A–Be
	A–Bl	296	Bi–Ca
247	Bo–Ch	297	Ch–Da
248	Cl–D	298	De–Fi
249	E–G	299	Fl–Han
250	H–Ja	300	Har–Hu
251	Je–L	301	I–L
252	M–Mi	302	M–Mo
253	Mo–Pe	303	Mu–Q
254	Ph–R	304	R–Se
255	S–Sp	305	Sh–St
256	St–V	306	Su–V
257	W–Z	307	W–Z
258	1st State Troops		5th Infantry, State Troops, 6 months, 1863–64
	1st State Troops, Infantry, 6 months, 1863–64	308	6th Infantry (3d Infantry)
	A–G		A–Ce
259	H–S	309	Ch–Fi
260	T–Z	310	Fl–H
	1st (Burnett's) Battalion, Sharp Shooters	311	I–Me
	A–H	312	Mi–Ri
261	I–Y	313	Ro–St
262	1st Battalion, State Troops, Infantry	314	Su–Z
263	2d Infantry (1st Infantry, Moore's Regiment;		6th and 15th (Consolidated) Volunteers, Cavalry
	Galveston Regiment; Van Dorn Regiment)		and Infantry
	A–Br	315	7th (Gregg's) Infantry
264	Bu–Da		A–Ca
265	De–Gh	316	Ch–Go
266	Gi–Ho	317	Gr–Li
267	Hu–Ll	318	Lo–Pl
268	Lo–M	319	Po–S
269	N–Ri	320	T–Z
270	Ro–Sp	321	8th (Hobby's) Infantry
271	St–Z		A–B
272	2d State Troops, Infantry, 6 months, 1863–64	322	C–E
273	3d Infantry (1st Infantry, Luckett's Regiment)	323	F–Gri
	A–B	324	Gro–L
274	C–F	325	M–Pa
275	G–I	326	Pe–Sk
276	J–L	327	Sm–Z
277	M–O	328	9th (Nichols') Infantry (5th Infantry), 6 months,
278	P–Sa		1861–62
279	Sc–T		A–F
280	U–Z	329	G–Me
281	3d State Troops, Infantry, 6 months, 1863–64	330	Mi–Sc
	3d (Kirby's) Battalion, Infantry and Cavalry, 6	331	Se–Z
	months, 1861–62	332	9th (Young's) Infantry (8th Infantry, Maxey's
	A–E		Regiment)
282	F–Y		A–C
283	4th Infantry	333	D–Ho
	A–Bl	334	Hu–M
284	Bo–Cl	335	N–Sl
285	Co–D	336	Sm–Y
286	E–G	337	10th (Nelson's) Infantry
287	H–Je		A–B
288	Jo–L	338	C–E
289	M–Mi	339	F–I
290	Mo–Ra	340	J–L
291	Re–Sm	341	M–Po
292	Sn–Wa	342	Pr–S
293	We–Y	343	T–Z

Roll	Description
344	11th Infantry (Roberts' Regiment)
	A–B
345	C–E
346	F–I
347	J–Me
348	Mi–Ri
349	Ro–Ta
350	Tb–Z
351	11th (Spaight's) Battalion (Cavalry, Artillery, and Infantry)
	A–E
352	F–J
353	K–O
354	P–Sp
355	St–Z
356	12th Infantry (8th Infantry, Young's Regiment)
	A–Co
357	Cr–G
358	H–L
359	M–Pa
360	Pe–St
361	Su–Z
362	13th Volunteers (Cavalry, Artillery, and Infantry)
	A–Bo
363	Br–Co
364	Cr–F
365	G–He
366	Hi–K
367	L–Mi
368	Mo–P
369	Q–Sl
370	Sm–V
371	W–Z
372	14th (Clark's) Infantry
	A–D
373	E–K
374	L–R
375	S–Y
376	15th Infantry
	A–D
377	E–J
378	K–O
379	P–Sm
380	Sn–Z
381	16th Infantry (7th Infantry; Flournoy's Infantry)
	A–C
382	D–Ha
383	He–Me
384	Mi–Sl
385	Sm–Z
386	17th Infantry (Allen's Regiment)
	A–Cl
387	Co–G
388	H–Me
389	Mi–R
390	S–Y
391	18th (Ochiltree's) Infantry
	A–E
392	F–L
393	M–Ro
394	Ru–Y
395	19th Infantry
	A–C
396	D–H
397	I–M

Roll	Description
398	N–Sh
399	Si–Z
400	20th Infantry (Elmore's Regiment)
	A–Br
401	Bu–De
402	Di–Ge
403	Gi–Ja
404	Jo–L
405	M–Mi
406	Mo–Ra
407	Re–St
408	Su–Wa
409	We–Z
	20th Battalion, State Troops
410	21st Infantry (Spaight's Regiment)
	A–G
411	H–O
412	P–Y
413	22d (Hubbard's) Infantry
	A–D
414	E–K
415	L–Ri
416	Ro–Y
417	24th Battalion, Infantry, State Troops
	Bean's Battalion, Reserve Corps
	Chambers' Battalion, Reserve Corps, Infantry
418	Griffin's Battalion, Infantry (Griffin's Regiment, Infantry; 21st Regiment or Battalion, Infantry)
	A–E
419	F–L
420	M–Sp
421	St–Z
	Houston Battalion, Infantry (Detailed Men)
422	Timmons' Infantry
	A–Ha
423	He–O
424	P–Z
425	Waul's Legion (Infantry, Cavalry, and Artillery)
	A–Bl
426	Bo–Cl
427	Co–E
428	F–G
429	H–I
430	J–Ll
431	Lo–Me
432	Mi–Pa
433	Pe–Sa
434	Sc–Sr
435	St–V
436	W–Z
437	Capt. Arnold's Co., Infantry Riflemen, Militia
	Capt. Atkins' Co., State Troops (The Galveston Coast Guards)
	Capt. Benton's Co., Volunteers
	Brazoria County Minutemen
	Capt. Watts Cameron's Co., Infantry
	Carter's Co., Infantry (Austin City Light Infantry)
438	Capt. Cotton's Co., Infantry (Sabine Volunteers)
	Capt. Cunningham's Co., Infantry (The Mustang Grays)
	Capt. Currie's Co., Infantry
	Capt. Duke's Co., Volunteers (Jefferson Guards)
439	Capt. Edgar's Co., State Troops (Alamo City Guards)
	Capt. Gould's Co., State Troops (Clarksville Light Infantry)

Roll	Description
	Capt. Graham's Co., Mounted Coast Guards, State Troops
	Capt. Hampton's Co., State Troops (Victoria Blues)
	Capt. Killough's Co., Home Guards (Wheelock Home Guards)
440	Capt. Maxey's Co., Light Infantry and Riflemen (Lamar Rifles, State Service)
	Capt. McMinn's Co.
	Capt. McNeel's Co., Local Defense Troops (McNeel Coast Guards)
	Capt. Merriman's Co., Local Defense Troops (Orange County Coast Guards)
	Capt. Perry's Co., Local Defense Troops (Fort Bend Scouts)
	Capt. Rainey's Co., Volunteers (Anderson County Invincibles)
	Capt. Rutherford's Co., Infantry (Unattached)
	Capt. Simms' Co., Home Guards
441	Capt. Teague's Co., Volunteers (Southern Rights Guards)
	Capt. Teel's Co., State Troops, 6 months, 1861
	Capt. Townsend's Co., Infantry (Robertson Five Shooters)
	Capt. Whaley's Co., Infantry
	Capt. Yarbrough's Co., Infantry (Smith County Light Infantry)
442	Miscellaneous, Texas
	A–K
443	L–Z
444	Conscripts, Texas
	A–H
445	I–Z

Compiled Service Records of Confederate Soldiers Who Served in Organizations From the State of Virginia. M324. 1,075 rolls. 16mm. DP.

The compiled service records reproduced in this microfilm publication are indexed on M382.

Roll	Description
1	1st Cavalry
	A–Bl
2	Bo–Ch
3	Ci–Do
4	Dr–Fo
5	Fr–G
6	H
7	I–Ke
8	Ki–L
9	M–Me
10	Mi–O
11	P–Ri
12	Ro–Sl
13	Sm–Tr
14	Tu–Z
15	1st Battalion, Cavalry
	2d Cavalry
	A–Bi
16	Bl–Ch
17	Cl–D
18	E–G
19	H–I
20	J–Ma
21	Mc–Pa
22	Pe–Sp
23	St–Wa
24	We–Z

Roll	Description
25	3d Cavalry (2d Virginia Cavalry)
	A–Bi
26	Bl–Ce
27	Ch–Cu
28	D–Fi
29	Fl–G
30	H
31	I–J
32	K–Mi
33	Mo–Po
34	Pr–Sl
35	Sm–To
36	Tr–Wa
37	We–Y
38	4th Cavalry
	A–Br
39	Bu–C
40	D–E
41	F–G
42	H–I
43	J–L
44	M
45	N–Q
46	R–Sp
47	St–V
48	W–Z
49	5th Cavalry
	A–Bo
50	Br–C
51	D–Fl
52	Fo–Hi
53	Ho–Le
54	Li–N
55	O–R
56	S–T
57	U–Z
58	5th Cavalry 12 months, 1861–62, (4th Virginia Cavalry, Mullins' Regiment)
	A–De
59	Di–H
60	I–R
61	S–Y
	5th (Consolidated) Cavalry
62	6th Cavalry
	A–Be
63	Bi–Ca
64	Ce–D
65	E–Go
66	Gr–Hi
67	Ho–K
68	L–Mi
69	Mo–Pe
70	Ph–R
71	S–Th
72	Ti–Z
73	7th (Ashby's) Cavalry
	A–Br
74	Bu–Do
75	Dr–Ha
76	He–Ko
77	Kr–Mi
78	Mo–P
79	R–Sn
80	So–Z
81	8th Cavalry

Roll	Description
	A–B
82	C–F
83	G–K
84	L–P
85	Q–S
86	T–Y
87	9th Cavalry (Johnson's Regiment)
	A–Ba
88	Be–Br
89	Bu–Cl
90	Co–Di
91	Do–F
92	G–Has
93	Hat–Je
94	Jo–Le
95	Li–M
96	N–Po
97	Pr–Sh
98	Si–Sy
99	T–V
100	W–Wo
101	Wr–Y
	10th Cavalry
	A–Bo
102	Br–Cl
103	Co–D
104	E–G
105	H–J
106	K–Me
107	Mi–Ri
108	Ro–S
109	T–Z
110	11th Cavalry
	A–C
111	D–Hi
112	Ho–Mi
113	Mo–Se
114	Sh–Z
115	12th Cavalry (10th Virginia Cavalry)
	A–B
116	C–E
117	F–Hi
118	Ho–L
119	M–O
120	P–Si
121	Sl–Z
122	13th Cavalry (16th Battalion, Cavalry; 5th Cavalry) 12 months, 1861–62
	A–Bo
123	Br–Co
124	Cr–F
125	G–Ha
126	He–L
127	M–Pa
128	Pe–Sa
129	Sc–V
130	W
131	14th Cavalry
	A–Ch
132	Cl–F
133	G–I
134	J–Ma
135	Mc–Pa
136	Pe–Sp
137	St–Z

Roll	Description
138	14th Battalion, Cavalry (Burroughs' Battalion)
	15th Cavalry
	A–Ba
139	Be–Co
140	Cr–F
141	G–J
142	K–O
143	P–Sk
144	Sl–Y
145	15th Battalion, Cavalry (Northern Neck Rangers; Critcher's Battalion, Virginia Cavalry)
146	16th Cavalry
	A–F
147	G–Mc
148	Me–Sp
149	Sr–Y
	17th Cavalry
	A
150	B–Co
151	Cr–Go
152	Gr–Mc
153	Me–Sh
154	Si–Y
155	18th Cavalry
	A–E
156	F–L
157	M–R
158	S–Z
159	19th Cavalry
	A–E
160	F–L
161	M–Si
162	Sl–Z
163	20th Cavalry
	A–F
164	G–N
165	O–Y
166	21st Cavalry (Peters' Regiment)
	A–E
167	F–L
168	M–Sl
169	Sm–Y
	22d Cavalry (Bowen's Regiment, Virginia Mounted Riflemen)
	A–Ba
170	Be–I
171	J–Y
172	23d Cavalry
	A–H
173	I–V
174	W–Z
	24th Cavalry
	A–Bo
175	Br–D
176	E–Hi
177	Ho–Me
178	Mi–Sh
179	Si–Y
180	24th Battalion, Partisan Rangers (Scott's Battalion)
	25th Cavalry
	A–B
181	C–E
182	F–I
183	J–Mi
184	Mo–Sm

Roll	Description
185	Sn–Z
186	26th Cavalry
	32d Battalion, Cavalry
	A–F
187	G–Y
188	34th Battalion, Cavalry (1st Battalion, Virginia Mounted Rifles; Witcher's Battalion, Virginia Mounted Rifles)
	A–Hi
189	Ho–Y
190	35th Battalion, Cavalry
	A–E
191	F–M
192	N–Z
193	36th Battalion, Cavalry
	A–K
194	L–T
195	V–Z
	37th Battalion, Cavalry (Dunn's Battalion, Partisan Rangers)
	A–F
196	G–S
197	T–Y
	39th Battalion, Cavalry (Richardson's Battalion of Scouts; Guides and Couriers; 13th Battalion, Cavalry)
	A–C
198	D–Mc
199	Me–Z
200	40th Battalion, Cavalry
	A–E
201	F–N
202	O–Y
203	41st (White's) Battalion, Cavalry
204	46th Battalion, Cavalry
205	47th Battalion, Cavalry
	Caldwell's Battalion, Cavalry
206	Ferguson's (Guyandotte) Battalion, Cavalry
	Hounshell's Battalion, Cavalry (Partisan Rangers)
	A–L
207	M–Y
	Mosby's Regiment, Cavalry (Partisan Rangers)
	A–D
208	E–M
209	N–Y
210	O'Ferrall's Battalion, Cavalry
	Swann's Battalion, Cavalry (Carpenter's Battalion)
	Capt. Balfour's Co. (Mounted Riflemen)
	Capt. Jourdan's Co. (Rockbridge Rangers)
	Capt. McFarlane's Co., Cavalry
211	Capt. McNeill's Co., Cavalry (Partisan Rangers)
	Capt. Moorman's Co., Cavalry (Greenbrier Cavalry)
	Mounted Guard, 4th Congressional District, Virginia
	Patrol Guard, 11th Congressional District (Mounted)
	Capt. St. Martin's Co., Mounted Riflemen
	Capt. Sale's Co., Mounted Reserves, Rappahannock District, Virginia
212	Capt. Thurmond's Co., Cavalry (Partisan Rangers)
	Capt. Young's Co., Cavalry (Howitzers, Marine Artillery)
213	1st Artillery (2d Virginia Artillery)
	A–Bo
214	Br–Cl
215	Co–D
216	E–G
217	H–I
218	J–Ma
219	Mc–O
220	P–Ri
221	Ro–Sn
222	So–V
223	W–Z
224	1st Light Artillery (Pendleton's Regiment)
	1st Battalion, Light Artillery (Hardaway's Battalion; Moseley's Battalion)
225	2d Artillery
	A–S
226	T–Y
	3d Light Artillery (Local Defense)
227	10th (Allen's) Battalion, Heavy Artillery
	A–B
228	C–F
229	G–J
230	K–Sl
231	Sm–Y
232	12th Battalion, Light Artillery
	A–L
233	M–Z
234	13th Battalion, Light Artillery
	A–D
235	E–Mc
236	Me–S
237	T–Z
	18th Battalion, Heavy Artillery
	A–Ba
238	Be–E
239	F–H
240	J–M
241	N–Sn
242	So–Y
243	19th (Atkinson's) Battalion, Heavy Artillery
	A–Ca
244	Ch–D
245	E–I
246	J–M
247	N–S
248	T–Z
249	20th Battalion, Heavy Artillery
	A–C
250	D–Ha
251	He–N
252	O–Si
253	Sl–Z
254	38th (Read's) Battalion, Light Artillery
	A–Cl
255	Co–G
256	H–Ma
257	Mc–Se
258	Sh–Y
259	Capt. Allen's Co., Heavy Artillery (Lunenburg Artillery)
	A–P
260	R–W
	Capt. E. J. Anderson's Co., Light Artillery
261	Capt. R. M. Anderson's Co., Light Artillery (1st Co., Richmond Howitzers)
	A–L
262	M–Y

Roll	Description
263	Capt. Ancell's Co., Light Artillery
	Capt. Armistead's Co., Light Artillery (Matthew's Light Artillery)
	A–B
264	C–W
265	Capt. Barr's Co., Light Artillery
	Capt. Binford's Co., Volunteers (4th Co., Richmond Howitzers)
	Capt. Bowyer's Co., Heavy Artillery (Botetourt Artillery)
	Capt. Brander's Co., Light Artillery (Letcher Artillery)
	A–F
266	G–Y
267	Capt. G. W. Brown's Co., Horse Artillery
	Capt. J. S. Brown's Co., Light Artillery (Wise Artillery)
268	Capt. Bryan's Co., Artillery (Bryan Artillery; Monroe Artillery)
269	Capt. Carpenter's Co., Light Artillery (Alleghany Rough Artillery)
	A–L
270	M–Y
271	Capt. Carrington's Co., Light Artillery (Charlottesville Artillery)
	A–G
272	H–Y
273	Capt. J. W. Carter's Co., Horse Artillery
274	Capt. W. P. Carter's Co., Light Artillery
	A–K
275	L–W
276	Capt. Cayce's Co., Light Artillery (Purcell Artillery)
	A–E
277	F–Mc
278	Me–Z
279	Capt. G. B. Chapman's Co., Light Artillery (Monroe Battery)
	Capt. W. H. Chapman's Co., Light Artillery (Capt. J. K. Booton's Co., Dixie Artillery)
280	Capt. Clutter's Co., Light Artillery
	A–O
281	P–Z
	Capt. Coffin's Co., Heavy Artillery
282	Capt. Coleman's Co., Heavy Artillery
	Capt. Cooper's Co., Light Artillery
	A–Ch
283	Co–Y
	Courtney Artillery (Henrico Artillery)
	A–Cl
284	Co–L
285	M–Y
286	Capt. Curtis' Co., Artillery (Fredericksburg Artillery)
	Capt. Cutshaw's Co., Light Artillery (Jackson Artillery)
	Capt. Dance's Co., Artillery (Powhatan Artillery)
	A–D
287	E–W
288	Capt. Donald's Co., Light Artillery
289	Capt. Douthat's Co., Light Artillery (Botetourt Artillery)
	A–N
290	O–Z
	Capt. J. W. Drewry's Co., Artillery (South Side Artillery)

Roll	Description
291	Capt. Ellett's Co., Light Artillery (Crenshaw Battery)
	A–H
292	J–Y
293	Capt. Epes' Co., Heavy Artillery (Johnston Artillery)
294	Capt. Fleet's Co., Artillery (Middlesex Artillery)
	Capt. Forrest's Co., Artillery (Chesapeake Artillery)
	Capt. French's Co., Light Artillery (McComas Battery, Light Artillery; Giles Light Artillery)
295	Capt. Fry's Co., Light Artillery (Orange Artillery)
	A–H
296	J–W
297	Capt. Garber's Co., Light Artillery (Staunton Artillery)
	A–H
298	I–W
299	Goochland Light Artillery
	A–K
300	L–W
301	Capt. Archibald Graham's Co., Light Artillery (Rockbridge Artillery)
	A–F
302	G–N
303	O–Y
304	Capt. Edward Graham's Co., Horse Artillery (Petersburg Artillery)
305	Capt. Grandy's Co., Light Artillery (Norfolk Light Artillery Blues)
	A–K
306	Capt. Griffin's Co., Light Artillery (Salem Flying Artillery)
	A–B
307	C–Z
308	Capt. Hankins' Co., Light Artillery (Surry Light Artillery)
309	Capt. Hardwicke's Co., Light Artillery (Lee Battery)
310	Capt. Huckstep's Co., Light Artillery (Fluvanna Artillery)
	Capt. Jackson's Co., Horse Artillery (2d Organization 1863–65)
	Capt. Jeffress' Co., Light Artillery (Nottoway Light Artillery)
	A–E
311	F–Y
312	Capt. J. R. Johnson's Co., Light Artillery
	Capt. C. F. Johnston's Co., Artillery (Albemarle Artillery; Everett Artillery)
	A–O
313	P–W
	Capt. A. J. Jones' Co., Heavy Artillery (Pamunkey Artillery)
	A–H
314	J–W
315	Capt. L. F. Jones' Co., Artillery (2d Co., Richmond Howitzers)
	Capt. King's Co., Light Artillery (Saltville Artillery)
	Capt. Kevill's Co., Artillery (United Artillery)
316	Capt. Kirkpatrick's Co., Light Artillery (Amherst Artillery)
	A–L
317	M–W
	Capt. Kyle's Co., Heavy Artillery
318	Capt. Lamkin's Co., Light Artillery

Roll	Description
	Capt. Lowry's Co., Light Artillery (Centreville Rifles)
	A–G
319	H–Y
	Capt. Lanier's Co., Artillery
	Capt. Leake's Co., Light Artillery (Turner Artillery)
	Capt. Lurty's Co., Horse Artillery
	Capt. McClanahan's Co., Horse Artillery
320	Capt. Montgomery's Co., Light Artillery
	A–L
321	M–Y
322	Capt. Moore's Co., Light Artillery
	A–J
323	K–W
324	Capt. Motley's Co., Light Artillery (Pittsylvania Artillery)
	Capt. Nelson's Co., Light Artillery
	Capt. Otey's Co., Light Artillery (Local Defense)
	Capt. Page's Co., Light Artillery (Magruder Light Artillery)
325	Capt. Paris' Co., Artillery (Staunton Hill Artillery)
	Capt. Parker's Co., Light Artillery
	A–F
32	G–W
	Capt. Patteson's Co., Heavy Artillery (Campbell Battery)
327	Capt. Pegram's Co., Light Artillery (Branch Field Artillery)
	A–P
328	Q–Y
	Capt. Penick's Co., Light Artillery
	A–E
329	F–Y
330	Capt. Pollock's Co., Light Artillery (Fredericksburg Artillery)
	A–H
331	J–Y
332	Capt. B. F. Price's Co., Light Artillery (Danville Artillery)
	A–N
333	O–Z
	Capt. W. H. Rice's Co., Light Artillery (8th Star Artillery; New Market Artillery)
334	Capt. Richardson's Co., Artillery (James City Artillery)
	Capt. Rives' Co., Light Artillery (Nelson Light Artillery)
	A–G
335	H–W
336	Capt. Rogers' Co., Light Artillery (Loudoun Artillery)
	Capt. Daniel Shank's Co., Horse Artillery
	A–L
337	M–Z
	Capt. Shoemaker's Co., Horse Artillery (Beauregard Rifles, Lynchburg Beauregards)
	A–H
338	I–Y
339	Capt. B. H. Smith's Co., Artillery (3d Co., Richmond Howitzers)
	Capt. J. D. Smith's Co., Light Artillery (Bedford Light Artillery)
	A–G
340	H–W
341	Capt. Snead's Co., Light Artillery (Fluvanna Artillery)
342	Capt. Sturdivant's Co., Light Artillery

Roll	Description
	Capt. Taylor's Co., Light Artillery
	A–E
343	F–Y
344	Capt. Thompson's Co., Light Artillery (Portsmouth Light Artillery)
	Capt. Thornton's Co., Light Artillery (Caroline Light Artillery)
	A–B
345	C–R
346	S–Y
347	Capt. Turner's Co., Light Artillery
	Capt. Utterback's Co., Light Artillery
	A–N
348	O–Y
	Capt. Waters' Co., Light Artillery
	Capt. Weisiger's Co., Light Artillery
	Capt. Wilkinson's Co., Heavy Artillery (Co. A, Marion Artillery; Co. A, Richmond Local Guards)
349	Wise Legion, Artillery
	Capt. Wimbish's Co., Light Artillery (Long Island Light Artillery)
	Capt. Woolfolk's Co., Light Artillery (Ashland Light Artillery)
	A–G
350	H–Z
351	Capt. Wright's Co., Heavy Artillery (Halifax Artillery)
	Capt. Young's Co., Artillery (Halifax Light Artillery)
352	1st Infantry (Williams Rifles)
	A–Bl
353	Bo–Cl
354	Co–E
355	F–Hi
356	Ho–K
357	L–Ma
358	Mc–N
359	O–R
360	S–Th
361	Ti–Z
362	1st (Farinholt's) Reserves
	A–O
363	P–Z
	1st Battalion, Reserves
364	1st State Reserves (2d Class Militia)
	A–L
365	M–Z
	1st Reserves
366	1st Battalion, Infantry (1st Battalion, Virginia Regulars; Irish Battalion)
	A–Co
367	Cr–G
368	H–L
369	M–Q
370	R–Y
371	1st Battalion, Infantry, Local Defense (Ordnance Battalion, Armory Battalion)
372	2d Infantry
	A–Bi
373	Bl–Co
374	Cr–F
375	G–Hi
376	Ho–Le
377	Li–M
378	N–Ri
379	Ro–Sm

Roll	Description
380	Sn–T
381	U–Z
	2d Infantry, Local Defense
	A–C
382	D–Z
383	2d State Reserves
	A–J
384	K–Z
385	2d Battalion, Infantry, Local Defense (Waller's Battalion, Quartermaster Battalion)
386	2d Battalion Reserves
	3d Infantry
	A–Ba
387	Be–Cl
388	Co–Ed
389	El–Go
390	Gr–I
391	J–L
392	M–O
393	P–Sn
394	So–V
395	W–Y
396	3d Kanawha Regiment, Infantry
	3d Infantry, Local Defense
	A–E
397	F–M
398	N–Y
399	3d Reserves (Booker's Regiment, Reserves)
	A–R
400	S–Z
	3d (Archer's) Battalion, Reserves
401	3d (Christman's) Battalion, Reserves
	3d Battalion, Valley Reserves (Augusta County Reserves)
402	4th Infantry
	A–Bl
403	Bo–Ca
404	Ce–Da
405	De–F
406	G–Ha
407	He–J
408	K–L
409	M–N
410	O–P
411	R–Si
412	Sl–Ti
413	To–Wh
414	Wi–Z
415	4th Reserves (Preston's Regiment; 5th Regiment, Reserves)
	A–R
416	S–Z
	4th Battalion, Reserves
	4th Battalion, Infantry, Local Defense (Naval Battalion; Navy Department Battalion)
	A–G
417	H–Z
418	5th Infantry
	A–Ba
419	Be–Br
420	Bu–Co
421	Cr–E
422	F–Go
423	Gr–He
424	Hi–J
425	K–L

Roll	Description
426	M–N
427	O–Ri
428	Ro–Sp
429	St–V
430	W–Z
431	5th Battalion, Infantry (Wilson's Battalion; Archer's Battalion)
	A–H
432	J–S
433	T–Y
	5th Battalion, Infantry, Local Defense (Arsenal Battalion)
	5th Battalion, Reserves (Henry's Reserves)
434	6th Infantry
	A–Ba
435	Be–Br
436	Bu–Coo
437	Cor–D
438	E–Fo
439	Fr–G
440	H
441	I–La
442	Le–Ma
443	Mc–N
444	O–Ri
445	Ro–Sk
446	Sl–Sy
447	T–V
448	W–Wh
449	Wi
450	Wo–Z
	6th Battalion, Reserves (13th Battalion, Reserves; Smith's Battalion, Reserves)
	A–F
451	G–Y
452	6th (Tredegar) Battalion, Infantry, Local Defense
	7th Infantry
	A
453	B–Br
454	Bu–Co
455	Cr–E
456	F–G
457	H
458	I–L
459	M–N
460	O–R
461	S
462	T–Wa
463	We–Y
464	7th (1st Nitre) Battalion, Infantry, Local Defense
	7th Battalion, Reserves (5th Battalion, Valley Reserves)
465	8th Infantry
	A–Ba
466	Be–Bo
467	Br–C
468	D–F
469	G–Ho
470	Hu–Li
471	Lo–O
472	P–Sl
473	Sm–V
474	W–Y
	8th Battalion, Reserves (1st Battalion, Valley Reserves)
475	9th Infantry

Roll	Description
	A–Bi
476	Bl–By
477	Ca–Co
478	Cr–D
479	E–Go
480	Gr–Ha
481	He–J
482	K–Mi
483	Mo–Ph
484	Pi–R
485	S–To
486	Tr–Wa
487	We–Z
488	9th Battalion, Reserves (2d Battalion, Valley Reserves)
	9th (Hansbrough's) Battalion, Infantry
	9th Militia
489	10th Infantry
	A–Bo
490	Br–Co
491	Cr–F
492	G–H
493	I–L
494	M–N
495	O–R
496	S
497	T–Y
498	10th Battalion, Reserves (4th Battalion, Valley Reserves)
	11th Infantry
	A
499	B
500	C
501	D–E
502	F–Go
503	Gr–Hi
504	Ho–Ja
505	Je–K
506	L–Ma
507	Mc–My
508	N–P
509	Q–Sc
510	Se–Sw
511	T–Wa
512	We–Z
513	11th Battalion, Reserves (4th Battalion, Reserves; Wallace's Battalion, Reserves)
514	12th Infantry
	A–Bal
515	Ban–Bl
516	Bo–Br
517	Bu–Ch
518	Cl–Cr
519	Cu–D
520	E–F
521	G
522	H–Hi
523	Ho–J
524	K–Le
525	Li–Ma
526	Mc–My
527	N–Pa
528	Pe–Q
529	R–Sc
530	Se–Sp

Roll	Description
531	St–Tr
532	Tu–Wa
533	We–Wi
534	Wo–Z
	13th Infantry
	A–Bi
535	Bl–By
536	C
537	D–G
538	H–I
539	J–Ma
540	Mc–Pa
541	Pe–R
542	S–Te
543	Th–Y
544	14th Infantry
	A–Bi
545	Bl–Ch
546	Cl–Cu
547	D–E
548	F–G
549	H–J
550	K–Mc
551	Me–O
552	P–Q
553	R–Se
554	Sh–Sy
555	T–Wa
556	We–Wi
557	Wo–Y
	14th Militia
558	15th Infantry
	A–Ba
559	Be–Bu
560	By–C
561	D–F
562	G
563	H–Ho
564	Hu–La
565	Le–Mi
566	Mo–P
567	R–Sp
568	St–T
569	V–Y
570	16th Infantry (Colston's Regiment, Infantry; 26th Regiment, Infantry)
	A–Bi
571	Bl–Bu
572	C
573	D–E
574	F–G
575	H–Hu
576	I–Li
577	Lo–N
578	O–Ri
579	Ro–S
580	T–We
581	Wh–Z
582	17th Infantry
	A–Ba
583	Be–Bu
584	C
585	D–E
586	F–Go
587	Gr–Ha

Roll	Description
588	He–I
589	J–K
590	L–Ma
591	Mc–N
592	O–Q
593	R–Sh
594	Si–St
595	Su–V
596	W–Z
597	18th Infantry
	A–Ba
598	Be–By
599	C–Cl
600	Co–Da
601	De–E
602	F
603	G–Gl
604	Go–Ha
605	He–I
606	J–K
607	L–Ma
608	Mc–Mo
609	Mu–Pa
610	Pe–R
611	S–So
612	Sp–T
613	V–Wa
614	We–Wir
615	Wit–Z
616	19th Infantry
	A–Bl
617	Bo–By
618	C–Cr
619	Cu–E
620	F–Gi
621	Go–Ha
622	He–I
623	J–La
624	Le–Ma
625	Mc–My
626	N–Po
627	Pr–Sa
628	Sc–Ta
629	Te–We
630	Wh–Z
631	20th Infantry
	A–D
632	E–N
633	O–Y
634	21st Infantry
	A–Ba
635	Be–Cl
636	Co–Di
637	Do–F
638	G–Ha
639	He–K
640	L–M
641	N–P
642	R–Sh
643	Si–T
644	V–Y
645	21st Militia
	21st Battalion, Infantry (Pound Gap Battalion, Thompson's Battalion, Special Service Battalion)

Roll	Description
	A–B
646	C–Z
647	22d Infantry (1st Kanawha Regiment)
	A–Bo
648	Br–C
649	D–F
650	G–I
651	J–L
652	M–O
653	P–R
654	S–T
655	U–Z
	22d Battalion, Infantry (2d Battalion Infantry)
	A
656	B–E
657	F–J
658	K–P
659	Q–To
660	Tr–Y
661	23d Infantry
	A–B
662	C
663	D–F
664	G–Ha
665	He–J
666	K–Mo
667	Mu–Rh
668	Ri–Se
669	Sh–Ta
670	Te–Wal
671	Wan–Y
672	23d Battalion, Infantry (1st Battalion, Infantry; Hounshell's Battalion, Infantry; Derrick's Battalion, Infantry)
	A–B
673	C–F
674	G–L
675	M–R
676	S–Y
677	24th Infantry
	A–Ba
678	Be–By
679	C
680	D–E
681	F–G
682	H–Hi
683	Ho–Ke
684	Ki–Ma
685	Mc–O
686	P–R
687	S–So
688	Sp–T
689	U–We
690	Wh–Z
691	25th Infantry (Heck's Regiment)
	A–B
692	C–F
693	G–H
694	I–Ma
695	Mc–P
696	Q–S
697	T–Y
698	25th Battalion, Infantry (Richmond Battalion, Infantry; City Battalion, Infantry)
	A–Bi
699	Bl–By

Roll	Description
700	C–E
701	F–G
702	H–J
703	K–Mi
704	Mo–P
705	Q–S
706	T–Z
707	25th Militia
	26th Infantry
	A–Bi
708	Bl–By
709	C–Co
710	Cr–D
711	E–F
712	G
713	H–Ho
714	Hu–K
715	L–Me
716	Mi–O
717	P
718	R
719	S–Sp
720	St–To
721	Tr–We
722	Wh–Y
723	26th (Edgar's) Battalion, Infantry
	A–E
724	F–L
725	M–R
726	S–Z
	27th Infantry (6th Infantry)
	A
727	B–Ch
728	Cl–E
729	F–Ha
730	He–Li
731	Lo–N
732	O–R
733	S
734	T–Z
	28th Infantry
	A–Be
736	Bi–By
737	C–Co
738	Cr–Di
739	Do–Fi
740	Fl–G
741	H–Ho
742	Hu–Ke
743	Ki–Ma
744	Mc–Mi
745	Mo–O
746	P–Rh
747	Ri–Se
748	Sh–Sw
749	T–Wa
750	We–Wi
751	Wo–Z
	28th (Tabb's) Battalion, Infantry
752	29th Infantry
	A–B
753	C–D
754	E–G
755	H–J
756	K–Mc

Roll	Description
757	Me–Pl
758	Po–S
759	T–W
760	30th Infantry
	A–Bi
761	Bl–Ca
762	Ch–Do
763	Du–G
764	Ha–I
765	J–L
766	M–Pi
767	Po–Sa
768	Sc–Ta
769	Te–Y
770	30th Battalion, Sharp Shooters (1st Battalion, Sharp Shooters; Clarke's Battalion, Sharp Shooters)
	A–C
771	D–K
772	L–R
773	S–Z
774	31st Infantry
	A–C
775	D–Ja
776	Jo–P
777	Q–T
778	V–Y
	31st Militia
	A–C
779	D–Z
780	32d Infantry
	A–B
781	C
782	D–G
783	H–Joh
784	Jon–Ma
785	Mc–O
786	P–R
787	S
788	T–Wh
789	Wi–Y
790	33d Infantry
	A–By
791	C–D
792	E–Ha
793	He–J
794	K–L
795	M–N
796	O–R
797	S
798	T–Z
799	34th Infantry
	A–Bag
800	Bai–Bo
801	Br–By
802	Ca–Co
803	Cr–D
804	E–F
805	G
806	H–Hi
807	Ho–Je
808	Jo–K
809	L
810	M–Me
811	Mi–My

Roll	Description
812	N–Pa
813	Pe–Po
814	Pr–Ro
815	Ru–Si
816	Sl–Sy
817	T–V
818	W–Wh
819	Wi–Wo
820	Wr–Z
	34th Militia
821	**36th Infantry (2d Kanawha Infantry)** A–B
822	C
823	D–Fi
824	Fl–Ha
825	He–J
826	K–Ma
827	Mc–N
828	O–R
829	S–Sp
830	St–U
831	V–Y
832	**37th Infantry** A–B
833	C–D
834	E–G
835	H–K
836	L–N
837	O–R
838	S–V
839	W–Y
	37th Militia
840	**38th Infantry (Pittsylvania Regiment)** A–Bo
841	Br–Cl
842	Co–E
843	F–G
844	H
845	I–Ma
846	Mc–O
847	P–R
848	S–To
849	Tr–Y
850	**39th Infantry** A–K
851	L–Z
	39th Militia
852	**40th Infantry** A–Bo
853	Br–Co
854	Cr–F
855	G–H
856	I–Mc
857	Me–Ri
858	Ro–Sy
859	T–Y
860	**41st Infantry** A–Bl
861	Bo–Cl
862	Co–D
863	E–G
864	H
865	I–L
866	M–N
867	O–Ri

Roll	Description
878	Ro–St
879	Su–We
880	Wh–Y
	41st Militia
871	**42d Infantry** A–Ch
872	Cl–F
873	G–I
874	J–N
875	O–Sh
876	Si–Y
	43d Militia
877	**44th Infantry** A–B
878	C–F
879	G–I
880	J–Mc
881	Me–R
882	S–We
883	Wh–Y
	44th Battalion, Infantry (Petersburg City Battalion)
884	**45th Infantry** A–B
885	C–D
886	E–Ha
887	He–L
888	M–P
889	Q–Te
890	Th–Z
891	**45th Battalion, Infantry**
892	**46th Infantry (1st Regiment, Infantry, Wise Legion; 2d Regiment, Wise Brigade)** A–Bo
893	Br–C
894	D
895	E–Gi
896	Gl–Ha
897	He–I
898	J–Li
899	Lo–Mi
900	Mo–Pi
901	Pl–R
902	S
903	T–Tr
904	Tu–Wh
905	Wi–Z
	46th Militia
906	**47th Infantry** A–Bu
907	C–E
908	F–J
909	K–P
910	Q–Te
911	Th–Y
	47th Militia
912	**48th Infantry** A–D
913	E–H
914	I–P
915	Q–W
916	**49th Infantry** A–Cl
917	Co–F
918	G–J
919	K–N

Roll	Description	Roll	Description
920	O–Sm	976	L–M
921	Sn–Y	977	N–R
922	50th Infantry	978	S–Ta
	A–C	979	Te–Y
923	D–J	980	57th Infantry
924	K–R		A–Bl
925	S–Z	981	Bo–By
926	51st Infantry	982	C–D
	A–B	983	E–G
927	C–F	984	H–Ho
928	G–I	985	Hu–L
929	J–N	986	M–Mi
930	O–Se	987	Mo–P
931	Sh–T	988	Q–Se
932	U–Y	989	Sh–Sw
933	51st Militia	990	T–V
934	52d Infantry	991	W–Z
	A–B	992	58th Infantry
935	C–D		A–B
936	E–Ha	993	C–E
937	He–La	994	F–H
938	Le–O	995	I–Mi
939	P–Sh	996	Mo–Q
940	Si–T	997	R–S
941	V–Z	998	T–Z
942	52d Militia	999	58th Militia
943	53d Infantry	1000	59th Infantry (2d Regiment, Infantry, Wise
	A–Bi		Legion)
944	Bl–Co		A–Bi
945	Cr–E	1001	Bl–Ch
946	F–Gr	1002	Cl–D
947	Gu–H	1003	E–G
948	I–L	1004	H–I
949	M	1005	J–Ma
950	N–Re	1006	Mc–N
951	Ri–S	1007	O–R
952	T–Wa	1008	S–Te
953	We–Y	1009	Th–We
	53d Militia	1010	Wh–Y
954	54th Infantry		59th Militia
	A–C	1011	60th Infantry (3d Regiment, Infantry, Wise
955	D–Ho		Legion)
956	Hu–O		A–Bo
957	P–S	1012	Br–Co
958	T–Z	1013	Cr–Fi
959	54th Battalion, Infantry	1014	Fl–Ha
	54th Militia	1015	He–J
960	55th Infantry	1016	K–Ma
	A–Bl	1017	Mc–O
961	Bo–Bw	1018	P–R
962	C	1019	S–Te
963	D	1020	Th–Z
964	E–Ga	1021	61st Infantry (Wilson's Regiment, Infantry; 7th
965	Ge–Ha		[Wilson's] Battalion, Infantry)
966	He–K		A–Br
967	L–M	1022	Bu–C
968	N–Ri	1023	D–E
969	Ro–Sl	1024	F–G
970	Sm–V	1025	H–Hi
971	W–Z	1026	Ho–J
972	56th Infantry	1027	K–Mi
	A–B	1028	Mo–O
973	C–D	1029	P–Sh
974	E–G	1030	Si–V
975	H–K	1031	W–Y

Roll	Description
	61st Militia (Matthew's Battalion)
	A–C
1032	D–W
1033	62d Mounted Infantry (1st Partisan Rangers, 62d Partisan Rangers, 62d Infantry, 62d Cavalry, Imboden's Partisan Rangers)
	A–D
1034	E–J
1035	K–P
1036	Q–Z
1037	63d Infantry (McMahon's Regiment)
	A–C
1038	D–Hi
1039	Ho–Ma
1040	Mc–R
1041	S–Y
1042	64th Mounted Infantry (64th Infantry; 64th Cavalry; Slemp's Regiment, Infantry)
	A–C
1043	D–G
1044	H–L
1045	M–P
1046	Q–S
1047	T–Z
	64th Militia
1048	67th Militia
	72d Militia (Russell County Militia)
1049	74th Militia
	77th Militia
	79th Militia
1050	82d Militia
	86th Militia
	87th Militia
1051	88th Militia
	89th Militia
	92d Militia
	94th Militia
1052	97th Militia (Col. Mann Spitler's Militia; 2d Regiment; 7th Brigade, Militia)
1053	108th Militia
	109th Militia
	110th Militia
1054	111th Militia
	114th Militia
1055	115th Militia
	122d Militia
1056	129th Militia
1057	135th Militia
1058	136th Militia (3d Regiment, 7th Brigade, Militia)
1059	146th Militia (1st Regiment, 7th Brigade, Militia)
1060	151st Militia
	157th Militia
	162d Militia
1061	166th Militia
	188th Militia
	189th Militia
	190th Militia
	198th Militia
1062	Averett's Battalion, Reserves
	Burks' Regiment, Local Defense
	Carroll County Militia
1063	Cohoon's Battalion, Infantry (6th Battalion, North Carolina Infantry)
	French's Battalion, Infantry
	Grayson County Militia
1064	Montague's Battalion, Infantry
	Rockbridge County Reserves
1065	Scott County Militia

Roll	Description
	Tomlin's Battalion, Infantry
	Tuttle's Battalion, Local Defense
1066	Virginia State Line
1067	Wade's Regiment, Local Defense
	Washington County Militia
	Wythe County Militia
1068	Capt. Avis' Co., Provost Guard
	Lt. Bosher's Co., Local Defense
1069	Capt. Chappell's Co., Local Defense (Pickett Guard)
	Capt. Clark's Co., Reserve Forces
	Capt. Cooper's Co., Local Defense
	Capt. Dulany's Co., Local Defense (Home Guards)
	Capt. Durrett's Co., Local Defense
	Capt. Earhart's Co., Local Defense (Blacklick Home Guards)
	Capt. Ezell's Co., Local Defense
	Capt. French's Co., Local Defense
	Capt. Gregory's Co., Infantry (High Hill Greys)
	Guards and Scouts, Rockingham County, Virginia
	Capt. Hamilton's Co., Local Defense
	Capt. Henderson's Co., Local Defense
	Capt. Hobson's Co., 2d Class Militia
1070	Hood's Battalion, Reserves
	Capt. Hutter's Co., Infantry (The Southern Guard)
	Capt. Jordan's Co., Local Defense
	Capt. Keyser's Co., Reserves
	Capt. Lyneman's Co., Infantry
1071	Capt. Mallory's Co., Local Defense (Provost Guard)
	Capt. Mileham's Co., Infantry
	Lt. Morehead's Co., Local Defense
	Capt. Murphy's Co.
	Capt. Neff's Co., Local Defense (Mount Airy Home Guard)
	Capt. Patterson's Co., Local Defense (Home Guard, 1st District, Bland County)
	Capt. Scott's Co., Local Defense (Co. A, Greensville County Home Guard)
1072	Capt. Stowers' Co., Militia
	Capt. Sutherland's Co., Local Defense
	Capt. Tayloe's Co., Local Defense
	Capt. Taylor's Co., Volunteers (Young Guards)
	Capt. Thurston's Co., Reserve Forces
	Westmoreland County, Reserves
	Wise's Battalion, Volunteers
	Capt. Wolff's Co., 2d Class Militia
	Capt. Wood's Co., Local Defense
	Virginia Military Institute
1073	Miscellaneous, Virginia
	A–R
1074	S–Z
	Conscripts, Camp Lee, Virginia
	A–E
1075	F–Y

Compiled Service Records

Compiled Service Records of Confederate Soldiers Who Served in Organizations Raised Directly by the Confederate Government. M258. 123 rolls. 16mm. DP.

This microfilm publication reproduces the compiled service records of Confederate soldiers who served in military organizations raised directly or otherwise formed by the Confederate Government and therefore not identified with any one State. Two or three of these organizations seem to have been originally considered units of the Confederate Regular Army. Several others were raised among residents of Indian Territory; one was made up of foreigners recruited among Union prisoners of war.

Preceding the jacket-envelopes for the individual soldiers in each organizational unit, there are usually empty envelopes on which the officers of the unit are listed. Jacket-envelopes contain cards showing the exact captions of muster-in and muster-out rolls that were copied and the certifications of the mustering officers verifying the accuracy of the rolls. Record-of-events cards indicate the activities in which any part of the unit had been engaged. Because of the irregular way in which most of these units were organized, there are relatively few caption cards. Record-of-events cards are more numerous, but they sometimes do not contain any account of happenings because no such notation was made in the original records.

The compiled service records reproduced in this microfilmed publication are indexed on M818.

Roll	*Description*
	Nelson's Battalion, Confederate Artillery (31st Battalion, Virginia Light Artillery; 3d Battalion Reserve, Light Artillery)
	Lt. W. B. Ochiltree's Detachment of Recruits (Detachment of Regulars)
	Maj. R. C. M. Page's Battalion, Confederate Artillery (Carter's Battalion of Artillery; Braxton's Battalion of Artillery)
	Palmer's Battalion, Confederate Artillery (Robertson's Battalion of Artillery)
	Poague's Battalion, Artillery
	Richardson's Battalion, Confederate Light Artillery (Battalion A. 1st Corps Artillery, Army of Northern Virginia)
50	Maj. F. W. Smith's Battalion, Confederate Heavy Artillery
	Stark's Battalion, Confederate Light Artillery (Battalion B. 1st Corps Artillery, Army of Northern Virginia)
51	Stuart's Horse Artillery
	Capt. White's Battery, Horse Artillery
52	1st Confederate Infantry (1st Confederate Regiment, Georgia Volunteers)
	A–B
53	C–E
54	F–Ha
55	He–K
56	L–M
57	N–Ri
58	Ro–S
59	T–Y
60	1st Battalion, Confederate Infantry (Forney's Regiment, Confederate Infantry)
	A–K
61	L–W
62	2d Confederate Infantry
	3d Confederate Infantry
	A–D
63	E–W
64	4th Confederate Infantry (1st Regiment, Alabama, Tennessee, and Mississippi Infantry)
	A–F
65	G–N
66	O–Y
67	8th Battalion, Confederate Infantry (2d Foreign Battalion, Infantry; 2d Foreign Legion, Infantry)
68	9th Confederate Infantry (5th Confederate Infantry; 5th Confederate Regiment, Tennessee Infantry)
	A–F
69	G–Mi
70	Mo–Y
71	Bailey's Consolidated Regiment of Infantry
	Bradford's Corps, Scouts and Guards (Bradford's Battalion)
72	Brooks' Battalion, Confederate Regular Infantry
	Brush Battalion, C.S.A.
	A–O
73	P–W
	Lt. Cunningham's Ordnance Detachment (Capt. Cuyler's Ordnance Detachment)
	Capt. Davis' Co. of Guides, C.S.A.
	Exchanged Battalion, C.S.A. (Trans-Mississippi Battalion; Western Battalion)
	A–N
74	O–Z
	Forrest's Scouts, C.S.A.

Roll	*Description*
75	Gillum's Regiment (Henry Gillum's Regiment; Gillum's Regiment, Mounted Infantry; Gillum's Regiment, Mounted Riflemen)
	Lt. Haskell's Co., Infantry
	Jackson's Co., C.S.A.
	Capt. McDaniel's Co., Secret Service
	Stirman's Regiment, Sharp Shooters
	Tucker's Regiment, Confederate Infantry
	A–D
76	E–Z
	Lt. Young's (5th) Co., Retributors
77	1st Cherokee Mounted Rifles (1st Arkansas Cherokee Mounted Rifles)
	A–L
78	M–Y
79	1st Cherokee Mounted Volunteers (Watie's Regiment, Cherokee Mounted Volunteers; 2d Regiment, Cherokee Mounted Rifles, Arkansas; 1st Regiment, Cherokee Mounted Rifles or Riflemen)
	A–K
	L–Y
	1st Squadron, Cherokee Mounted Volunteers (Holt's Squadron, Cherokee Mounted Volunteers)
81	1st Chickasaw Infantry (Hunter's Regiment, Indian Volunteers)
82	1st Choctaw Mounted Rifles
83	1st Choctaw and Chickasaw Mounted Rifles
	A–G
84	H–N
85	O–Y
86	1st Creek Mounted Volunteers (1st Regiment, Creek Mounted Rifles or Riflemen; Creek Regiment, Mounted Indian Volunteers; 2d Regiment, Arkansas Creeks)
	A–H
87	I–S
88	T–Z
	1st Osage Battalion, C.S.A.
	1st Seminole Mounted Volunteers
	A–C
89	D–Y
90	2d Cherokee Mounted Volunteers (2d Regiment Cherokee Mounted Rifles or Riflemen)
91	2d Creek Mounted Volunteers
	Cherokee Regiment (Special Service)
	Deneale's Regiment, Choctaw Warriors (Deneale's Confederate Volunteers)
	Shecoe's Chickasaw Battalion, Mounted Volunteers
	Washington's Squadron of Indians, C.S.A. (Reserve Squadron of Cavalry)
	Capt. Wilkins' Co., Choctaw Infantry
	Miscellaneous Indian Records
92	1st Confederate Engineer Troops
	A–C
93	D–F
94	G–L
95	M–R
96	S–Z
97	2d Confederate Engineer Troops
	A–J
98	K–Z
99	3d Confederate Engineer Troops
	A–F
100	G–O
101	P–Z
102	4th Confederate Engineer Troops

Roll	Description
	A–R
103	S–Z
	Engineers, C.S.A.
	A–B
104	C–Di
105	Do–F
106	G–Hi
107	Ho–L
108	M–Ri
109	Ro–S
110	T–Y
111	Nitre and Mining Bureau, War Department, C.S.A.,
	A–H
112	I–N
113	P–W
114	Sappers and Miners
	A–K
115	L–Y
116	Signal Corps, C.S.A.
	A–B
117	C–F
118	G–L
119	M–N
120	O–S
121	T–Z
122	Bands, C.S.A.
	Lt. Click's Co., Ordnance Scouts and Guards, C.S.A.
	Infantry School of Practice
123	Invalid Corps
	Officers Surnamed Morgan, C.S.A.
	President's Guard, C.S.A.
	Miscellaneous Records

Compiled Service Records of Confederate General and Staff Officers, and Non-Regimental Enlisted Men. M331. 275 rolls. 16mm. DP.

This microfilm publication reproduces the compiled service records of Confederate officers and enlisted men who did not belong to any particular regiment, separate company or comparable unit, or special corps. This class of military personnel included general officers; officers and enlisted men of the so-called staff departments; members of army corps, division, and brigade staffs; and various appointees with special status such as aides-de-camp, military judges, chaplains, agents, and drillmasters.

The so-called staff departments were those of the Adjutant and Inspector General, the Quartermaster General, the Commissary General, the Medical Department, and the Ordnance Department.

The compiled service records reproduced in this microfilm publication are indexed on M818.

Roll	Description
1	A–Adams, J.
2	Adams, L.–Ak
3	Al–Alg
4	All–Alle
5	Alli–Am
6	An–Anderson, P.
7	Anderson, R.–Andr
8	Ang–Ap
9	Ar–Arm
10	Arn–As
11	At–Ay

Roll	Description
12	B–Bai
13	Bak–Bald
14	Bale–Bap
15	Bar–Bark
16	Barl–Barn
17	Barr–Baru
18	Bas–Bay
19	Bea
20	Bec–Beld
21	Bell–Belv
22	Bem–Ben
23	Ber–Bi
24	Bl–Blai
25	Blak–Bly
26	Bo–Bom
27	Bon–Bor
28	Bos–Box
29	Boy–Boz
30	Br–Bram
31	Bran–Braz
32	Bre
33	Bri
34	Bro–Brok
35	Bron–Brown, H.
36	Brown, I.–Brown, P.
37	Brown, R.–Bru
38	Bry
39	Bu–Buc
40	Bud–Bun
41	Bur–Burs
42	Burt–Bus
43	But–Bux
44	By–Cak
45	Cal–Calv
46	Cam–Camr
47	Can–Carl
48	Carm–Carre
49	Carri
50	Carro–Cart
51	Caru–Chai
52	Chal–Cham
53	Chan–Che
54	Chi–Cho
55	Chr–Clai
56	Clam–Clark, R.
57	Clark, S.–Clo
58	Clu–Cog
59	Coh–Cole
60	Colg–Conn
61	Cono–Coon
62	Coop–Cor
63	Cos–Cow
64	Cox–Coxw
65	Coy–Cri
66	Cro
67	Cru–Cummings
68	Cummins–Cup
69	Cur–Cy
70	D–Dan
71	DaP–Dave
72	Davi–Davis, R.
73	Davis, S.–Day
74	De–Den
75	DeP–Dic

Roll	Description	Roll	Description
76	Dig–Dix	140	Je–Johns
77	D'L——DOU	141	Johnson
78	Dov–Doz	142	Johnston
79	Dr	143	Jol–Jones, H.
80	DuB–Dul	144	Jones, I.–Jones, W.
81	Dum–Dun	145	Joo–Kea
82	Dup–Dy	146	Kee–Kemp
83	E–Edn	147	Ken–Keo
84	Edw–Ek	148	Ker–Key
85	El–Ellio	149	Ki–King
86	Ellis–Eo	150	Kinl–Kn
87	Ep–Eu	151	Ko–Lam
88	Eva	152	Lan–LaR
89	Eve–Ez	153	Las–Lawr
90	F–Far	154	Laws–Lea
91	Fau–Fen	155	LeB–Lee
92	Fer–Fil	156	Lef–Lev
93	Fin–Fis	157	Lew–Lin
94	Fit–Fitz	158	Lip–Loc
95	Fl–Fol	159	Lod–Lov
96	Fon–For	160	Low–Ly
97	Fos–Foy	161	M–Mac
98	Fr–Fre	162	Mad–Mal
99	Fri–Fy	163	Man–Mars
100	G–Gai	164	Mart–Mary
101	Gal–Gan	165	Mas–Mast
102	Gar–Garl	166	Mat–Max
103	Garm–Gary	167	May–Maz
104	Gas–Gea	168	McA–McCa
105	Ged–Gibb	169	McCh–McCl
106	Gibs–Gin	170	McCo–McCu
107	Gir–Gl	171	McD–McG
108	Go–Goo	172	McH–McK
109	Gor–Goz	173	McL–McMa
110	Gra	174	McMe–McW
111	Gre	175	Me–Mel
112	Gri–Gry	176	Mem–Mh
113	Gu–Gy	177	Mi–Mili
114	H–Hall	178	Mill–Milt
115	Halla–Ham	179	Mim–Miz
116	Han–Hap	180	Mo–Mon
117	Har–Hardm	181	Moo–Moot
118	Hardw–Harrin	182	Mor–Morg
119	Harris	183	Mori–Mort
120	Harrison–Hart	184	Mos–Murp
121	Harv–Hav	185	Murr–My
122	Haw–Hays	186	N–Ne
123	Hayw–Hemp	187	Ni–Nol
124	Hen–Hep	188	Nor–Ny
125	Her–Hey	189	O–O'K
126	Hi–Hill, G.	190	Ol–O'N
127	Hill, H.–Hilt	191	Oo–Oz
128	Hin–Hit	192	P–Pai
129	Ho–Holi	193	Pal–Pas
130	Holl–Holm	194	Pat–Pay
131	Holr–Hop	195	Pe–Pem
132	Hor–Hou	196	Pen–Pet
133	How–Hoy	197	Pey–Pic
134	Hu–Hul	198	Pie–Pit
135	Hum–Humr	199	Pl–Pon
136	Hun–Hup	200	Poo–Pos
137	Hur–Hy	201	Pot–Pra
138	I	202	Pre–Pric
139	Ja	203	Prit–Priv

Roll	Description
204	Pro–Q
205	R–Ram
206	Ran–Rank
207	Rann–Ray
208	Re–Ree
209	Rei–Rey
210	Rh–Rice
211	Rich–Rico
212	Rid–Rip
213	Rit–Roberts
214	Robertson
215	Robi–Rop
216	Ros–Roy
217	Ru–Ry
218	S–San
219	Sap–Sca
220	Sch–Sco
221	Scr–Seld
222	Sell–Ser
223	Ses–Sha
224	She–Shi
225	Sho–Simo
226	Simp–Slau
227	Slay–Smith, A.
228	Smith, B.–Smith, F.
229	Smith, G.–Smith, J.
230	Smith, L.–Smith, O.
231	Smith, P.–Smith, T.
232	Smith, W.–Smy
233	Sn–So
234	Sp–Sq
235	Sta
236	Ste–Sth
237	Sti–Sto
238	Str–Sty
239	Su–Sw
240	Sy–Talc
241	Tali–Tan
242	Tap–Taylor, I.
243	Taylor, J.–Taylor, W.
244	Te–Tev
245	Th–Thomas, L.
246	Thomas, M.–Thompson, G.
247	Thompson, H.–Thon
248	Thor–Thw
249	Tic–Toy
250	Tr–Tro
251	Tru–Tup
252	Tur–Tw
253	Ty–Van
254	Var–Ve
255	Vi–Wad
256	Wag–Walke
257	Walker–Walku
258	Wall–Walw
259	Wam–Warn
260	Warr–Was
261	Wat–Way
262	We–Wei
263	Wel–Wey
264	Wh–Whitc
265	White
266	Whited–Whitw
267	Who–Wilk

Roll	Description
268	Will–Williams, S.
269	Williams, T.–Wilm
270	Wils–Wim
271	Win–Wir
272	Wis–Wom
273	Woo–Wor
274	Wr
275	Wu–Z

Unfiled Papers and Slips Belonging to Confederate Compiled Service Records. M347. 442 rolls. 16mm. DP.

This microfilm publication reproduces an extensive series of papers that the War Department accumulated to interfile with the regular series of compiled service records of Confederate soldiers, but never interfiled. The records are arranged alphabetically by surname and there are cross-references for names that appear in the records under more than one spelling. Often names that sound alike are grouped together. It may be necessary, therefore, to search for a name under the various ways in which it could have been entered.

Roll	Description
1	A–Ac
2	Ad
3	Ae–Ale
4	Alf–Allen, R.
5	Allen, S.–Am
6	An–Ander
7	Andes–Aq
8	Ar–Arn
9	Aro–As
10	At–Au
11	Av–Bah
12	Bai
13	Baj–Bak
14	Bal
15	Bam–Barb
16	Barc–Barm
17	Barn–Barne
18	Barnh–Barz
19	Bas–Bat
20	Bau–Beak
21	Beal–Beasd
22	Bease–Bed
23	Bee–Benl
24	Benm–Beq
25	Ber–Bet
26	Beu–Bin
27	Bio–Biz
28	Bl–Blad
29	Blae–Blaz
30	Ble–Bn
31	Bo–Bol
32	Bom–Boo
33	Bop–Bov
34	Bow
35	Boy–Boz
36	Br–Brad
37	Brae–Bran
38	Brap–Bret
39	Breu–Brid
40	Brie–Briz
41	Bro–Bron
42	Broo–Brov

Roll	Description	Roll	Description
43	Brow–Brown, I.	107	Di–Dic
44	Brown, J.–Brown, P.	108	Did–Dl
45	Brown, R.–Browv	109	Do–Dom
46	Brox–Bru	110	Don–Dor
47	Bry–Brz	111	Dos–Dow
48	Bu–Buf	112	Dox–Dr
49	Bug–Bun	113	Du–Dug
50	Buo–Buri	114	Duh–Dunc
51	Burk–Burm	115	Dund–Dup
52	Burn	116	DuQ–Dz
53	Buro–Burz	117	Ea
54	Bus–Butl	118	Eb–Edn
55	Butn–Cah	119	Edo–Ef
56	Cai–Calk	120	Eg–Elle
57	Call–Caly	121	Elli–Elly
58	Cam–Campbell, I.	122	Elm–Eq
59	Campbell, J.–Camy	123	Er–Et
60	Can–Cap	124	Eu–Ev
61	Car–Carn	125	Ew–Faq
62	Caro–Carr	126	Far
63	Carra–Carten	127	Fas–Feq
64	Carter	128	Fer–Fie
65	Carterl–Casp	129	Fif–Fis
66	Cass–Cau	130	Fit–Fles
67	Cav–Chal	131	Flet–Fly
68	Cham–Chapa	132	Fo–Fordh
69	Chape–Chat	133	Fordr–Fo
70	Che–Child	134	Fot–Foz
71	Chile–Chr	135	Fra
72	Chu–Clark, C.	136	Fre–Fri
73	Clark, D.–Clark, S.	137	Frl–Ful
74	Clark, T.–Clay	138	Fum–Gai
75	Cle–Cli	139	Gal–Gaq
76	Clo–Cob	140	Gar–Garp
77	Coc–Cof	141	Garr–Gas
78	Cog–Cold	142	Gat–Gel
79	Cole–Colk	143	Gem–Gh
80	Coll–Colli	144	Gi–Gib
81	Collm–Conl	145	Gic–Gillf
82	Conm–Coog	146	Gillh–Giz
83	Cook–Cooks	147	Gl
84	Cool–Cop	148	Gn–Gon
85	Cor	149	Goo–Goods
86	Cos–Cov	150	Goodu–Gor
87	Cow–Coz	151	Gore–Goz
88	Cra–Crav	152	Gra–Gram
89	Craw–Cre	153	Gran–Graw
90	Cri–Cror	154	Gray–Green, I.
91	Cros–Croz	155	Green, J.–Green, L.
92	Cru–Cul	156	Green, M.–Gret
93	Cum–Cup	157	Greg–Grie
94	Cur–Cy	158	Grif–Grig
95	D–Dam	159	Gril–Groz
96	Dan–Daq	160	Gru–Gul
97	Dar–Dau	161	Gun–Gy
98	Dav–Davis, A.	162	H–Hald
99	Davis, B.–Davis, I.	163	Hale–Hall, J.
100	Davis, J.–Davis, N.	164	Hall, K.–Halz
101	Davis, O.–Davy	165	Ham–Hami
102	Daw–Daz	166	Haml–Hamy
103	De–Def	167	Han–Hann
104	Deg–Dem	168	Hano–Hard
105	Den–Der	169	Hare–Haro
106	Des–Dh	170	Harp–Harrio

Roll	Description	Roll	Description
171	Harris–Harris, J.	235	Lewis, S.–Lil
172	Harris, K.–Harris, Z.	236	Lim–Lio
173	Harriso–Hars	237	Lip–Liz
174	Hart–Harv	238	Ll–Lof
175	Harw–Hav	239	Log–Lone
176	Haw–Hax	240	Long–Lor
177	Hay–Haym	241	Los–Lov
178	Hayn–Hd	242	Low–Luc
179	He–Hef	243	Lud–Lw
180	Heg–Hende	244	Ly
181	Hendi–Henr	245	M–Maf
182	Hens–Her	246	Mag–Mak
183	Hes–Hic	247	Mal–Manl
184	Hid–Hilk	248	Manm–Marks
185	Hill	249	Markw–Mars
186	Hilla–His	250	Mart–Martin, L.
187	Hit–Hod	251	Martin, M.–Marz
188	Hoe–Hok	252	Mas–Mass
189	Hol–Holl	253	Mast–Matth
190	Holm–Hols	254	Matti–Max
191	Holt–Hopc	255	May–Maz
192	Hope–Hor	256	McA–McCal
193	Hos–Hov	257	McCam–McCi
194	How–Howe	258	McCl–McCon
195	Howi–Hud	259	McCoo–McCoy
196	Hue–Hug	260	McCr–McCy
197	Huh–Huns	261	McD–McDon
198	Hunt–Hurs	262	McDow–McF
199	Hurt–Hy	263	McG–McGo
200	I	264	McGr–McH
201	J–Jackson, L.	265	McI–McKe
202	Jackson, M.–Jal	266	McKi–McKu
203	Jam–Jaq	267	McL
204	Jar–Jem	268	McM
205	Jen–Jn	269	McN–McQ
206	Jo–Johnson, G.	270	McR–Mea
207	Johnson, H.–Johnson, K.	271	Meb–Men
208	Johnson, L.–Johnson, Z.	272	Meo–Mh
209	Johnv–Jones, G.	273	Mi–Miller, B.
210	Jones, H.–Jones, J.	274	Miller, C.–Miller, L.
211	Jones, K.–Jones, V.	275	Miller, M.–Millr
212	Jones, W.–Jordan, I.	276	Mills–Mis
213	Jordan, J.–Jy	277	Mit
214	K–Kee	278	Miu–Mom
215	Kef–Kelly, J.	279	Mon
216	Kelly, K.–Kenl	280	Moo–Moore, G.
217	Kenm–Kep	281	Moore, H.–Moore, O.
218	Ker–Kh	282	Moore, P.–Mop
219	Ki–Kine	283	Mor–Morgan, R.
220	King–Kingw	284	Morgan, S.–Morris, L.
221	Kini–Kir	285	Morris, M.–Morry
222	Kis–Kni	286	Mors–Mos
223	Kno–Ky	287	Mot–Mul
224	L–Lal	288	Mum–Murp
225	Lam	289	Murr–Muz
226	Lan–Lane	290	My
227	Lanf–Laq	291	N–NcC
228	Lar–Lau	292	Ne–Nei
229	Lav–Laz	293	Nel–Nev
230	Le–Led	294	New–Nez
231	Lee	295	Nia–Nl
232	Leec–Len	296	No–Nors
233	Leo–Lev	297	Nort–Ny
234	Lew–Lewis, R.	298	O–O'D

Roll	Description	Roll	Description
299	Oe–Ol	363	Sims–Siz
300	Om–O'R	364	Sk–Sli
301	Os–Ov	365	Slo–Smis
302	Ow–Oz	366	Smith, A.–Smith, E.
303	P–Pak	367	Smith, F.–Smith, J.
304	Pal–Pari	368	Smith, J. B.–Smith, J. X.
305	Park–Parker, T.	369	Smith, K.–Smith, R.
306	Parker, V.–Pas	370	Smith, S.–Smith, W.
307	Pat	371	Smith, W. F.–Smythey
308	Pau–Paz	372	Sn
309	Pe–Pee	373	So–Spa
310	Pef–Pen	374	Spe–Sph
311	Peo–Perq	375	Spi–Sr
312	Perr–Pes	376	St–Stap
313	Pet–Pf	377	Star–Stef
314	Ph–Philips, V.	378	Steg–Steph
315	Philips, W.–Pie	379	Stepl–St. M
316	Pif–Pit	380	Sto–Stot
317	Piv–Pok	381	Stou–Stri
318	Pol–Poo	382	Stro–Stua
319	Pop–Por	383	Stub–Sul
320	Pos–Powell	384	Sum–Sv
321	Powen–Pre	385	Sw–Sz
322	Pria–Priv	386	T–Tar
323	Pro–Pug	387	Tas–Taylor, I.
324	Puh–Py	388	Taylor, J.–Taylor, T.
325	Q	389	Taylor, U.–Teq
326	R–Ral	390	Ter–Thl
327	Ram–Ras	391	Tho–Thomi
328	Rat–Raz	392	Thoml–Thomson, J.
329	Re–Red	393	Thomson, K.–Thow
330	Ree–Reer	394	Thr–Til
331	Rees–Rem	395	Tim–Toi
332	Ren–Rez	396	Tol–Toz
333	Rh–Rich	397	Tr–Tro
334	Richa–Rict	398	Tru–Tup
335	Rid–Ril	399	Tur–Turn
336	Rim–Roa	400	Turp–Tz
337	Rob–Roberts	401	U–Val
338	Robertson–Robertson, K.	402	Vam–Vat
339	Robertson, L.–Robey	403	Vau–Ve
340	Robi–Rode	404	Vi–Vy
341	Rodg–Rody	405	W–Wak
342	Roe–Ror	406	Wal–Walker, S.
343	Ros–Rot	407	Walker, T.–Wall
344	Rou–Rs	408	Walm–Wap
345	Ru–Rul	409	War–Warl
346	Rum–Rus	410	Warm–Was
347	Rut–Ry	411	Wat–Watr
348	S–Sam	412	Wats–Way
349	San–Sanders	413	We–Wed
350	Sanderson–Sau	414	Wee–Weli
351	Sav–Sce	415	Welk–Wer
352	Sch	416	Wes–Wey
353	Sci–Sco	417	Wh–Whis
354	Scr–Sea	418	Whit–White, J.
355	Seb–Set	419	White, K.–Whitew
356	Seu–Shan	420	Whitf–Why
357	Shap–Shay	421	Wi–Wile
358	She–Shep	422	Wilf–Williams, A.
359	Sher–Shn	423	Williams, B.–Williams, I.
360	Sho–Shy	424	Williams, J.–Williams, N.
361	Si–Sil	425	Williams, O.–Willias
362	Sim–Simr	426	Willib–Wilr

Roll	Description
427	Wils–Wilson, I.
428	Wilson, J.–Wilson, R.
429	Wilson, S.–Wim
430	Win–Winl
431	Winm–Wir
432	Wis–Wl
433	Wo–Wood, I.
434	Wood, J.–Wood, Z.
435	Wooda–Woody
436	Woof–Woy
437	Wr–Wright, I.
438	Wright, J.–Wright, V.
439	Wright, W.–Wz
440	Y–Yn
441	Yo–Young, O.
442	Young, P.–Z and Miscellaneous

Records of Confederate Movements and Activities (Record Group 109)

Beginning in 1903, the War Department compiled abstract histories of the movements and activities of Confederate military units. Original muster rolls and returns were the principal sources of information on the caption cards and the envelopes that list officers. Rosters, payrolls, hospital registers, casualty lists, Union prison registers and rolls, parole rolls, and inspection reports were also abstracted.

Compiled Records Showing Service of Military Units in Confederate Organizations. M861. 74 rolls. DP.

This microfilm publication reproduces the compiled records of Confederate military units. Because many Confederate Army records were lost or destroyed by the end of the war, the compiled military histories of most units are incomplete.

Most of the records are arranged alphabetically by State, thereunder by type of unit (cavalry, artillery, or infantry), followed by reserve, militia, local defense, conscript, prison guard, instruction, or other organizations. The arrangement of compiled records for units raised directly or otherwise by the Confederate Government is similar except that the latter units are not broken down by State. Numbered units are listed first, followed alphabetically by the named units.

There are no record-of-events cards for a small number of State units that were mustered into Confederate service or for militia units that were never mustered into service. Lists of officers were prepared for many State militia units that were not mustered into service and for other organizations for which no rolls were found. These lists, which are filed under "Miscellaneous," appear at the end of records of State units and at the end of records of units raised directly by the Confederate Government. With a few exceptions, no lists were prepared for units from North Carolina.

Roll	Description
Alabama:	
1	1st Cavalry–Capt. Ward's Battery, Light Artillery
2	1st–11th Infantry
3	12th–28th Infantry
4	29th Infantry–48th Militia
5	49th Infantry–Miscellaneous, Alabama
Arizona:	
	Herbert's Battalion, Cavalry
Arkansas:	
6	1st Cavalry (Crawford's)–2d Battalion, Infantry
7	3d–14th Infantry (McCarver's)
8	14th Infantry (Powers')–27th Infantry
9	30th Infantry–Miscellaneous, Arkansas
Florida:	
10	1st Cavalry–4th Infantry
11	5th Infantry–Capt. Parson's Co.
Georgia:	
12	1st–12th Cavalry
13	12th Battalion, State Guards, Cavalry–Capt. Wheaton's Co. (Chatham Artillery)
14	1st Regulars–4th Battalion, State Guards, Infantry
15	4th Battalion, Sharpshooters–10th Battalion, Infantry
16	11th Infantry–23d Battalion, Local Defense (Athens Battalion, Enfield Rifle Battalion), Infantry
17	24th–37th Infantry
18	38th–57th Infantry
19	59th Infantry–Miscellaneous, Georgia
Kentucky:	
20	1st Cavalry (Butler's)–Capt. Thompson's Co., Cavalry
21	Capt. Byrne's Co., Horse Artillery–Miscellaneous, Kentucky
Louisiana:	
22	1st Cavalry–1st Special Battalion (Wheat's), Infantry
23	2d Infantry–6th Regiment, European Brigade (Italian Guards Battalion), Militia
24	7th Infantry–14th Battalion (Austin's), Sharpshooters
25	15th–31st Infantry
26	Algiers Battalion, Militia–Officers, Miscellaneous Organizations
Maryland:	
	1st Cavalry–Miscellaneous, Maryland
Mississippi:	
27	1st Cavalry–24th Battalion, Cavalry
28	28th Cavalry–1st Battalion, Sharpshooters
29	2d Infantry–5th Infantry, State Troops
30	6th–12th Infantry
31	13th–21st Infantry
32	22d–37th Infantry
33	39th Infantry–Miscellaneous, Mississippi
Missouri:	
34	1st Cavalry–Capt. Walsh's Co., Light Artillery
35	1st Infantry–8th Battalion, Infantry
36	9th Infantry–Miscellaneous, Missouri
North Carolina:	
37	1st Cavalry (9th State Troops)–Capt. Moseley's Co. (Sampson's Artillery)
38	1st Infantry–7th Battalion, Junior Reserves
39	8th–18th Infantry

Roll	Description
40	20th–32d Infantry
41	33d–49th Infantry
42	50th Infantry–Miscellaneous, North Carolina

South Carolina:

43	1st Cavalry–Capt. Walpole's Co., Cavalry
44	1st Artillery–Capt. Zimmerman's Co. (Pee Dee Artillery)
45	1st Infantry (Butler's)–3d State Troops (6 months, 1863–64)
46	4th Infantry–9th Battalion (Pee Dee Legion), Infantry
47	10th–19th Infantry
48	20th Infantry–Miscellaneous, South Carolina

Tennessee:

49	1st Cavalry (Carter's)–15th Cavalry (Stewart's)
50	16th Cavalry (Logwood's)–Artillery Corps (McCown's)
51	1st Infantry (Field's)–7th Infantry
52	8th Infantry–22d Battalion, Infantry
53	23d Infantry (Martin's Regiment)–35th Infantry (5th Regiment Provisional Army, Mountain Rifle Regiment)
54	36th–50th Infantry (Consolidated)
55	51st Infantry–Miscellaneous, Tennessee

Texas:

56	1st Cavalry, State Troops, 6 months, 1863–64– 12th Cavalry (Parson's Mounted Volunteers, 4th Dragoons)
57	13th Cavalry (Burnett's Regiment, 13th Mounted Volunteers)–29th Cavalry (De Morse Regiment)
58	30th Cavalry (Gurley's Regiment, 1st Partisans)– Capt. Upton's Co., Local Defense, Cavalry
59	1st Heavy Artillery–7th Infantry (Gregg's)
60	8th Infantry (Hobby's)–17th Infantry (Allen's Regiment)
61	18th Infantry (Ochiltree's)–Conscripts, Texas

Virginia:

62	1st Cavalry–12th Cavalry (10th Virginia Cavalry)
63	13th Cavalry (16th Battalion; 5th Cavalry, 12 months, 1861–62)–Capt. Thurmond's Co. (Partisan Rangers), Cavalry
64	1st Artillery (2d Virginia Artillery)–Capt. Young's Co. (Halifax Light Artillery)
65	1st Infantry (Williams' Rifles)–5th Battalion (Henry's Reserves)
66	6th–13th Infantry
67	14th Infantry–22d Battalion (2d Battalion), Infantry
68	23d Infantry–31st Militia
69	32d Infantry–43d Militia
70	44th–57th Infantry
71	58th Infantry–64th Militia
72	67th Militia–Conscripts, Camp Lee, Virginia

Organizations raised directly by the Confederate Government:

73	1st Confederate Cavalry–Capt. White's Battery, Horse Artillery
74	1st Confederate Infantry (1st Confederate Regiment, Georgia Volunteers)–Miscellaneous Records

Records of Volunteer Soldiers Who Served During the War With Spain (Record Groups 94 and 407)

During the Spanish-American War in 1898, volunteer soldiers served in existing State militia units accepted into Federal service, in additional units raised in States and Territories, and in units raised directly by the Federal Government.

Indexes to Compiled Service Records

General Index to Compiled Service Records of Volunteer Soldiers Who Served During the War With Spain. M871. 126 rolls. DP.

This microfilm publication reproduces an alphabetical card index to the compiled service records of volunteer soldiers in the war with Spain. Each index card gives the name of a soldier, his rank, and the unit in which he served. Some cards also refer to miscellaneous personal papers. There are cross-references to names that appear in the records under more than one spelling.

Except for the Florida Infantry, the compiled service records to which this index applies are not on microfilm.

Roll	Description
1	A–Alk
2	All–And
3	Ane–Au
4	Av–Bal
5	Bam–Bar
6	Bas–Beg
7	Beh–Ber
8	Bes–Blal
9	Blam–Bon
10	Boo–Boz
11	Bra–Bre
12	Bri–Browm
13	Brown–Bru
14	Bry–Burk
15	Burl–Caf
16	Cag–Cark
17	Carl–Casr
18	Cass–Cher
19	Ches–Clarki
20	Clarks–Cold
21	Cole–Conn
22	Cono–Cors
23	Cort–Cra
24	Cre–Cun
25	Cup–Dar
26	Das–Dea
27	Deb–Dh
28	Di–Dona
29	Donb–Drep
30	Dres–Dw
31	Dy–Ei
32	Ek–Er
33	Es–Far
34	Fas–Fir
35	Fis–Fol

Roll	Description
36	Fom–Fran
37	Frar–Ful
38	Fun–Gas
39	Gat–Gih
40	Gil–Goe
41	Gof–Grah
42	Grai–Greg
43	Grei–Gut
44	Guv–Hall
45	Halm–Harc
46	Hard–Hars
47	Hart–Hax
48	Hay–Hem
49	Hen–Hex
50	Hey–Hn
51	Ho–Holl
52	Holm–Hov
53	How–Hul
54	Hum–Iso
55	Isr–Jer
56	Jes–John
57	Joho–Judi
58	Judk–Kei
59	Kel–Ken
60	Keo–Kirb
61	Kirc–Ko
62	Kr–Lal
63	Lam–Lat
64	Lau–Lef
65	Leg–Lik
66	Lil–Log
67	Loh–Lun
68	Lup–Mah
69	Mai–Marr
70	Mars–Mat
71	Mau–McCa
72	McCe–McCu
73	McD–McG
74	McH–McM
75	McN–Meo
76	Meq–Millen
77	Miller–Min
78	Mio–Moon
79	Moor–Morrin
80	Morris–Mul
81	Mum–My
82	N–Ne
83	Ni–Ny
84	O–Ol
85	Om–Pag
86	Pah–Pat
87	Pau–Pes
88	Pet–Pim
89	Pin–Pov
90	Pow–Pz
91	Q–Rb
92	Re–Rej
93	Rek–Rif
94	Rig–Robe
95	Robi–Ror
96	Ros–Rus
97	Rut–Sa
98	Sb–Schr
99	Schu–Sek

Roll	Description
100	Sel–Sha
101	She–Shin
102	Ship–Simo
103	Simp–Smis
104	Smit–Smith, L
105	Smith, M–Som
106	Son–Sq
107	Sr–Steu
108	Stev–Stp
109	Str–Su
110	Sv–Taw
111	Tay–Thi
112	Tho–Tik
113	Til–Tref
114	Treg–Tz
115	U–Va
116	Ve–Wak
117	Wal–Wap
118	War–Waz
119	Wea–Wer
120	Wes–Whitl
121	Whitm–Wilk
122	Will–Wilr
123	Wils–Woj
124	Wol–Woz
125	Wr–Yos
126	Yot–Z

Index to Compiled Service Records of Volunteer Soldiers Who Served During the War With Spain in Organizations From the State of Louisiana. M240. 1 roll. 16mm. DP.

Index to Compiled Service Records of Volunteer Soldiers Who Served During the War With Spain in Organizations From the State of North Carolina. M413. 2 rolls. 16mm. DP.

Roll	Description
1	A–K
2	L–Z

Compiled Service Records

Compiled Service Records of Volunteer Soldiers Who Served in the Florida Infantry During the War With Spain. M1087. 13 rolls. DP.

This microfilm publication reproduces the compiled service records of volunteer soldiers in the Florida Infantry who served during the war with Spain.

Some of the jacket-envelopes are used as cross-references for names of volunteers that appear in the records under more than one spelling. The records are arranged alphabetically by surname.

Roll	Description
1	Record of Events–Bo
2	Br–Cl
3	Co–Do
4	Dr–Gi
5	Gl–He
6	Hi–J
7	K–Ma
8	Mc–My

Roll	Description
9	N–Pi
10	Po–Sc
11	Se–Th
12	Ti–Wi
13	Wo–Personal Papers

Records of Volunteer Soldiers Who Served During the Philippine Insurrection (Record Group 94)

Following the Spanish-American War, Spain ceded the Philippine Islands to the United States. By 1899, except for Manila, which was held by the Americans, the Philippines were held by Filipino revolutionaries. In 1902 the revolutionary forces surrendered, but guerrillas continued to fight throughout the period of American rule.

The acts of Congress authorizing the raising of troops to fight in the Philippines allowed for the recruitment of volunteers from all the continental States and Territories and from the Philippines. Some units were composed of men from a single place, but many were made up of individuals from more than one place. Accordingly, units of volunteers accepted into Federal service did not include the name of the State or Territory as part of their official designation, as had been customary in previous wars. Designations, therefore, do not provide a clue as to the State or Territory of residence of people serving in the unit, even if the unit was formed in a single State.

Index to Compiled Service Records

Index to Compiled Service Records of Volunteer Soldiers Who Served During the Philippine Insurrection. M872. 24 rolls. DP.

This microfilm publication reproduces an alphabetical card index to the compiled service records of volunteer soldiers who participated in halting the Philippine Insurrection. Each index card gives the name of a soldier, his rank, and the unit or units in which he served. Some cards also refer to miscellaneous personal papers. There are cross-references to names that appear in the records under various spellings.

Roll	Description
1	A–Ba
2	Be–Bo
3	Br–By
4	C–Cl
5	Co–Cz
6	D–Dr
7	Du–Fl
8	Fo–Go
9	Gr–Har
10	Has–Ho
11	Hu–Ka
12	Ke–Ky
13	L
14	Ma–McF
15	McG–Mi
16	Mo–Ny
17	O–Pl
18	Po–Ri
19	Ro–Sc
20	Se–Sn
21	So–Sz
22	T–V
23	W–Wh
24	Wi–Z

Compiled Service Records

There are no microfilmed compiled service records for volunteer soldiers who served during the Philippine Insurrection.

Records Relating to Service in the Regular U.S. Military Establishment

Regular military forces are maintained both in war and in peace by the Federal Government. They are also referred to as Standing Military Forces.

Records Relating to Service in the U.S. Army (Record Groups 94, 391, and 407)

Registers of Enlistments

Registers of enlistments generally contain information relating to the enlistment and termination of service of enlisted personnel. Register entries may contain the individual's name, military organization, physical description, date and place of birth, enlistment information, and remarks. Complete service information is not given for every individual; in particular, the date or reason for termination of service may not be supplied. Naval enlistments are usually recorded in rendezvous reports or other enlistment returns.

Muster Rolls

A *muster roll* is a list of all troops present on parade or otherwise accounted for on the day of muster or review of troops under arms. They are useful for identifying individuals, officers, and enlisted men. Musters were held to count the number of soldiers assigned to the unit, to inspect their arms and accoutrements, and to examine their condition. The muster roll from which the names were called was also the voucher from which the paymaster issued pay.

Usually included with the muster rolls are descriptive rolls; muster-in rolls; the regular muster-for-pay rolls for individuals, detachments, companies, and regiments; and muster rolls for field, staff, and band. Muster-for-pay rolls, the largest series, include the names of personnel of the organization, with names of commissioned officers and noncommissioned officers coming first, followed by names of privates

in alphabetical order. Given are the date and place of enlistment, by whom the soldier was enrolled and for what period, the date of muster into service, the date and amount of the last pay and for what period; and remarks, which may include disposition of any absentees, notes of desertions, and deaths.

Regular Army troops usually mustered for pay on the last day of February, April, June, August, October, and December. Muster and descriptive rolls give additional information including place of birth, age at date of muster, previous occupation, color of hair and eyes, complexion, bounty paid and amount due, clothing accounts, and remarks. Special musters of troops were taken at various times, and such records may include all or most of the information contained on the muster-for-pay rolls.

Registers of Enlistments in the United States Army, 1798–1914. M233. 81 rolls.

This microfilm publication reproduces registers of names of enlisted men in the Regular Army. The information was compiled from enlistment papers, muster rolls of the Regular Army, and other records. Except for pension records, these registers may be the only source of information on enlisted personnel serving in the Regular Army during the 19th century.

Entries for each man may show: when, where, and by whom he was enlisted; period of enlistment; place of birth; age at time of enlistment; civilian occupation; physical description; unit or regiment to which he was assigned; and additional remarks.

The records are arranged chronologically and thereunder alphabetically by first letter of surname (i.e., Smith, Saunders, Sutherland, Samuels). The entries for individual soldiers are chronological by date of enlistment.

Roll	Description
1798–May 17, 1815:	
1	A–B
2	B
3	C
4	D–E, H
5	F–G
6	H
7	I–L
8	L–M
9	M–O
10	P–R

Roll	Description
11	M, P, R–S
12	S–W
13	W, Y–Z

May 17, 1815–June 30, 1821:

Roll	Description
14	A–D
15	D–H
16	I–M
17	N–Z

June 1821–1858:

Roll	Description
18	June 1821–Dec. 1827
19	Jan. 1828–35
20	1835–39
21	1840–June 1846
22	July 1846–Oct. 1850
23	Jan. 1847–June 1849 (Mexican War enlistments)
24	Oct. 1850–Dec. 1854
25	Jan. 1855–Sept. 1857
26	Oct. 1857–58

1859–70:

Roll	Description
27	1859–63
	A–K
28	L–Z
29	1864–65
	A–K
30	L–Z
31	1866
	A–O
32	P–Z
33	1867
	A–O
34	P–Z
35	1868
36	1869–70
	A–O
37	P–Z

1871–77:

Roll	Description
38	A–G
39	H–O
40	P–Z

1878–84:

Roll	Description
41	A–G
42	H–O
43	P–Z

1885–June 1909:

Roll	Description
44	1885–90
	A–K
45	L–Z
46	1891–92
	A–Z
47	1893–97
	A–K
48	L–Z
49	1898
	A–K
50	L–Z
51	1899
	A–K
52	L–Z
53	1900
	A–K
54	L–Z
55	1901–May 1902
	A–K
56	L–Z
57	June 1902–June 1904

Roll	Description
	A–K
58	L–Z
59	July 1904–Dec. 1905
	A–K
60	L–Z
61	1906–7
	A–K
62	L–Z
63	1908–June 1909
	A–K
64	L–Z

1909–13:

Roll	Description
65	A–D
66	E–K
67	L–Q
68	R–Z

Special and miscellaneous enlistment categories, 1816–1914:

Roll	Description
69	Miscellaneous Registers (including Mounted Ranger, 1832–33, and Porto Rico Provisional Infantry, 1901–14)
70	Indian Scouts, 1866–77
71	Indian Scouts, 1878–1914
72	Philippine Scouts, Oct. 1901–13
73	Ordnance, Commissary, and Post Quartermaster Sergeants, 1833–91, and Clerks and Messengers, 1816–72
74	Hospital Stewards, 1854–99
75	Duplicates, A–G, 1816–62
76	Duplicates, H–Z, 1859–62
77	Duplicates, 1862–63
78	Duplicates, 1863–64
79	Regiments of Artillery and Infantry, 1828–52, and Lists of Officers, 4th Regiment of Infantry
80	Record of Prisoners, 1872–1901
81	Miscellaneous Indexes, 1865–1914

Returns

Every commander of a post or regiment was required to furnish *returns,* or personnel reports, to the Adjutant General's Office (AGO) at specified intervals, usually monthly, on forms provided by the AGO. The commander reported the station of the troops, the strength of each unit, and the names of commissioned and enlisted personnel and their whereabouts. Separate series of returns are available for departments, divisions, districts, regiments, posts, and other military organizations; however, only those for posts and regiments are available on microfilm.

Post returns are reports, usually monthly, of many military posts, camps, and stations. Returns generally show the units that were stationed at a particular post and their strength, the names and duties of the officers, the number of officers present and absent, a list of official communications received, and a record of events. In the early 19th century the form used for post returns was usually the same as the one used for regimental or organizational returns. The forms were usually altered, however, when the return was used specifically for posts, and by 1829 a separate printed form had evolved for the post return. In general, the returns for a specific post cover the period of the official existence of that post.

Returns of regiments and companies reported unit strength in total number of men present, absent, sick, or on extra daily duty, and accounted for officers and enlisted men by name. The station of the unit and a record of events was often given. Additional information was required on returns from time to time.

This body of records, used in conjunction with the muster rolls, may serve as a valuable source for information about the military careers of Regular Army enlisted men and officers.

Although most of the records in these publications are the monthly returns from posts, regiments, and other military organizations, the AGO filed other records and returns with the monthly returns, which include:

Historical data files, compiled during the 1920s and 1930s, consist of correspondence mainly between the AGO and regimental commanders about records of events, numbers of killed and wounded, and troop movements. The files also contain rosters, histories, and lists of stations of companies.

A War Department Order of 1826 required *returns of field and company officers,* when absent from their regiment or company on detached service, as often as the nature of their detail was changed. Between 1846 and about 1861, again after 1898, and during periods of campaigns, there are many returns for battalions, companies, and detachments filed with the regimental monthly returns. There are, however, a few scattered returns for the period before 1846. For the most part the information contained on the returns of the independent units has been consolidated in the regular regimental monthly return.

Special field returns and field returns were submitted by regiments, companies, and detachments. An 1895 regulation required that whenever the strength of a separated command was temporarily or permanently increased or diminished by moving any organization, "the commanding officer will immediately inform the Adjutant General of the Army direct, designating the organization moved, number and names of officers, and strength of men, animals, and arms."

Army Regulations required that *annual returns of casualties,* by regiment, were to be transmitted at the close of every year. Although Army regulations carried this provision until the revision of 1881, it had been declared no longer necessary by the Adjutant General in 1870. Usually the annual return was a recapitulation of the totals appearing under "Alterations" (gains and losses) in the main section of the monthly regimental returns for the year. By 1884 this information was required on a quarterly basis. Over the years different information was required; however, all the forms had space for designating the posts and stations at which deaths, desertions, apprehensions, and surrenders occurred. On some of the 1864 forms there was a "Remarks" section for listing the name of each enlisted man with information such as date, place, and cause of alteration.

A General Order of 1862 required *returns of casualties.* After "every battle, skirmish, or other engagement" every regiment or detached part of a regiment was to forward to the AGO a return of those killed, wounded, and missing.

A few *trimonthly field returns* were filed with the regimental monthly returns. Because the information requested on this form was already submitted directly to the Surgeon General and the AGO did not need the information, the form was abolished in 1899.

Returns From United States Military Posts, 1800–1916. M617. 1,550 rolls. DP.

This microfilm publication reproduces returns from U.S. military posts from the early 1800s to 1916, with a few returns extending through 1917.

Most of the records are monthly post returns, but they also include morning reports, field returns, rosters of officers, and related papers that were added to the collection by the AGO either as supplementary information or as substitutes for missing post returns. Field returns, for example, generally show the movement of troops or detachments in the field from units stationed at the post. Among the related papers are some cards that contain information pertaining to wars and skirmishes with Indians. The records also include papers containing historical information about the post, lists of officers and commanders of the post, and data relating to the establishment and abandonment of the post. These related papers appear on the microfilm before the returns for the post to which they pertain. A few duplicate and corrected copies of returns are included. Corrected copies of specific returns are generally filed after the original return.

The AGO filed post returns alphabetically by the name of the post and thereunder in chronological order; however, there was no standard practice for dealing with names such as D. A. Russell or George G. Meade, which may be filed by the last name or by the first name or initial. There may be variations in spellings of names or locations of some posts, especially in the Philippine Islands.

When the name of a post was changed, the new name was generally the one under which the returns were consolidated. In some instances, however, the Adjutant General's Office kept the earlier returns under the original name and filed the later returns under the new name. Returns for some posts, such as the multiple installations at Manila, P.I., were filed under the name of the city.

In this publication, the filing scheme used by the Adjutant General's Office has been followed, except when returns for a post totaled less than 20. In such cases, returns were removed by the National Archives and filed in a second alphabetical sequence beginning on roll 1492. On rolls 1–1491, each roll contains returns for a single post, although returns for a specific post may be filmed on more than one roll. On rolls 1492–1550, where the number of returns is less than 20 (except for some posts in the Philippine Islands), returns for several posts are reproduced on each roll. The returns for posts in the Philippine Islands that are reproduced on rolls 1492–1550 were found after the filming of the first alphabetical sequence had been completed.

This publication contains returns for the Civil War period that were used by the Record and Pension Office of the War Department when it compiled the service records of persons who served in the Civil War. Returns from which information was abstracted were stamped with the word "carded." Returns that were examined but from which no information was taken were stamped "not carded."

For a list of cross-references for names of posts, consult the descriptive pamphlet.

Roll	Description
1	Abercrombie, Fort, N. Dak.
	Aug. 1858–Sept. 1877
2	Aberdeen, Miss.
	Mar. 1871–Apr. 1873
3	Adams, Fort, R.I.
	Jan. 1816–Dec. 1869
4	Jan. 1870–Dec. 1879
5	Jan. 1880–Dec. 1895
6	Jan. 1896–Dec. 1905
7	Jan. 1906–Dec. 1913
8	Adjuntas, P.R.
	Oct. 1898–July 1900
9	Aguadilla, P.R.
	Sept. 1898–July 1900
10	Aibonito, P.R.
	Jan. 1899–Oct. 1900
11	Aiken, S.C.
	Apr. 1866–Apr. 1877
12	Albiquin [Abiquiu], N. Mex.
	Apr. 1849–Oct. 1851
13	Albuquerque, N. Mex.
	Oct. 1846–July 1867
14	Alcatraz Island, Calif.
	Dec. 1859–Dec. 1879
15	Jan. 1880–Dec. 1891
16	Jan. 1892–Dec. 1902
17	Jan. 1903–Dec. 1916
18	Alexandria, La.
	June 1865–Jan. 1875
19	Alexandria, Va.
	Sept. 1861–Feb. 1869
20	Alger, Russell A., Camp, Va.
	May–Aug. 1898
21	Allegheny Arsenal, Pa.
	July 1833–Dec. 1879
22	Jan. 1880–Dec. 1895
23	Jan. 1896–Dec. 1905
24	Alton, Ill.

Roll	Description
	Feb. 1862–June 1865
25	American Lake, Wash.
	July 1904–July 1914
26	Anderson, Camp, Calif.
	Mar. 1862–July 1865
27	Anderson, S.C.
	May 1866–Dec. 1867
28	Andrews, Fort, Mass.
	Feb. 1902–Dec. 1913
29	Angel Island, Calif.
	Jan. 1864–Dec. 1877
30	Jan. 1878–Dec. 1890
31	Jan. 1891–Mar. 1900
32	Annapolis, Md.
	Feb. 1862–Jan. 1866
	Camp Parole, Md.
	Feb. 1863–July 1865
33	Apache, Fort, Ariz.
	May 1870–Dec. 1887
34	Jan. 1888–Dec. 1903
35	Jan. 1904–Dec. 1916
36	Apalachicola Arsenal, Fla.
	Oct. 1840–Aug. 1845
37	Aparri, Cagayan de Luzon, P.I.
	July 1902–May 1908
38	Arbuckle, Fort, Okla.
	Aug. 1850–June 1870
39	Armistead, Fort, Md.
	Apr. 1898–June 1914
40	Armistead, Camp, Tenn.
	July 1832–Jan. 1835
41	Armstrong, Fort, Ill.
	Aug. 1819–Apr. 1836
42	Assiniboine, Fort, Mont.
	May 1879–Dec. 1891
43	Jan. 1892–Dec. 1903
44	Jan. 1904–May 1911
45	Atascadero, Calif.
	Aug. 1904–Oct. 1910
46	Atimonan, Tayabas, P.I.
	Mar. 1903–Dec. 1910
47	Atkinson, Fort, Iowa
	June 1840–Jan. 1849
48	Atkinson, Fort, Kans.
	Aug. 1850–Sept. 1854
49	Atkinson, Fort, Nebr.
	July 1821–May 1827
50	Atlanta, Ga.
	Mar. 1866–Dec. 1881
51	Aubrey, Fort, Kans.
	Oct. 1865–Apr. 1866
52	Augur Barracks, P.I.
	May 1899–Dec. 1907
53	Jan. 1908–Dec. 1916
54	Augusta, Ga.
	May 1865–July 1868
55	Augusta Arsenal, Ga.
	Jan. 1822–July 1849
56	Oct. 1860–Dec. 1884

Roll	Description		Roll	Description
57	Jan. 1885–Dec. 1903		90	Jan. 1906–Dec. 1916
58	Jan. 1904–Dec. 1916		91	Bayamo, Cuba
59	Austin, Tex.			July 1899–Oct. 1901
	Nov. 1848–Aug. 1875		92	Beale's Springs, Camp, Ariz.
60	Avery, Camp, Corregidor, P.I.			Mar. 1871–Mar. 1874
	Feb. 1908–July 1914		93	Beaufort, S.C.
61	Babbitt, Camp, Calif.			Feb. 1862–Aug. 1868
	Oct. 1862–Mar. 1866		94	Bedloe's Island, N.Y.
62	Bacolod, Negros Occidental, P.I.			Jan.–June 1814
	July 1899–Dec. 1902		95	Belknap, Fort, Tex.
63	Bacon, J. M., Camp, Minn.			June 1851–Aug. 1867
	Oct. 1898–May 1900		96	Bellingham, Fort, Wash.
64	Bad Lands, Cantonment, N. Dak.			Aug. 1856–Apr. 1860
	Nov. 1879–Mar. 1883		97	Bellona Arsenal, Va.
65	Baker, Fort, Calif.			June 1821–Dec. 1833
	Mar. 1862–Dec. 1905		98	Benicia Arsenal, Calif.
66	Jan. 1906–Dec. 1913			Aug. 1851–Dec. 1870
67	Baker, Camp, Oreg.		99	Jan. 1871–Dec. 1883
	Aug. 1862–July 1863		100	Jan. 1884–Dec. 1897
68	Balabac, Palawan, P.I.		101	Jan. 1898–Dec. 1916
	May 1910–Sept. 1913		102	Benicia Barracks, Calif.
69	Balamban, Cebu, P.I.			Apr. 1849–Dec. 1870
	May 1902–Jan. 1910		103	Jan. 1871–Dec. 1885
70	Balayan, Bantangas, P.I.		104	Jan. 1886–Dec. 1896
	July 1902–Mar. 1908		105	Jan. 1897–Apr. 1908
71	Baliuao, Bulacan, P.I.		106	Bennett, Fort, S. Dak.
	June 1899–Feb. 1905			May 1870–Dec. 1880
72	Baltimore, Md.		107	Jan. 1881–Dec. 1891
	Sept. 1814–Mar. 1815;		108	Benton Barracks, Mo.
	Feb.–May 1866			Sept. 1861–Dec. 1865
73	Draft Rendezvous		109	Benton, Fort, Mont.
	May 1864–Apr. 1866			July 1867–May 1881
74	Banks, Fort, Mass.		110	Berthold, Fort, N. Dak.
	Mar. 1899–Dec. 1905			May 1865–June 1867
75	Jan. 1906–Dec. 1913		111	Bidwell, Camp, Chico Butte County, Calif.
76	Baracoa, Cuba			Aug. 1863–May 1865
	Mar. 1899–Aug. 1900		112	Bidwell, Fort, Surprise Valley, Calif.
77	Barrancas, Fort, Fla.			July 1865–Dec. 1879
	July 1821–Aug. 1887		113	Jan. 1880–Oct. 1893
78	May 1888–Dec. 1905		114	Binan, Laguna, P.I.
79	Jan. 1906–June 1914			Mar. 1900–Apr. 1906
80	Barry, Fort, Calif.		115	Binangonan, Rizal, P.I.
	Jan. 1908–Dec. 1913			May 1900–Mar. 1906
81	Bascom, Fort, N. Mex.		116	Bliss, Fort, Tex.
	Aug. 1863–Nov. 1870			Jan. 1854–Dec. 1871
82	Batesville, Ark.		117	Jan. 1872–Dec. 1885
	Sept. 1866–Mar. 1869		118	Jan. 1886–Dec. 1897
83	Baton Rouge Arsenal, La.		119	Jan. 1898–Dec. 1908
	Sept. 1865–May 1871		120	Jan. 1909–Dec. 1916
84	Baton Rouge Barracks, La.		121	Boac, Marinduque, Mindoro, P.I.
	June 1821–Dec. 1835			Sept. 1900–Nov. 1908
85	Apr. 1836–Dec. 1860		122	Boise Barracks, Idaho
86	July 1865–June 1879			June 1863–Dec. 1875
87	Bayard, Fort, N. Mex.		123	Jan. 1876–Dec. 1891
	Aug. 1866–Dec. 1879		124	Jan. 1892–Dec. 1903
88	Jan. 1880–Dec. 1894			
89	Jan. 1895–Dec. 1905			

Roll	Description
125	Jan. 1904–Aug. 1913
126	Bongao, Jolo, P.I. May 1900–June 1904
127	Borongan, Samar, P.I. Mar. 1901–June 1909
128	Boston Harbor, Mass. Aug. 1815–July 1821 Draft Rendezvous July 1863–Jan. 1864
129	Bowie, Fort, Ariz. July 1862–Dec. 1882
130	Jan. 1883–Oct. 1894
131	Bowling Green, Ky. Aug. 1866–Mar. 1869
132	Brady, Fort, Mich. June 1822–Dec. 1841
133	Jan. 1842–July 1857
134	May 1866–Dec. 1882
135	Jan. 1883–Dec. 1896
136	Jan. 1897–Dec. 1905
137	Jan. 1906–Dec. 1916
138	Bragg, Fort, Calif. June 1857–Sept. 1864
139	Brashear City, La. Aug. 1864–Dec. 1866
140	Brazos Island, Tex. June 1846–Aug. 1848
141	Brazos, Tex., Post on Clear Fork Sept. 1851–Mar. 1854
142	Brazos Santiago, Tex. Mar. 1864–July 1867
143	Breckinridge, Fort, N. Mex. July 1860–June 1861
144	Brenham, Tex. July 1865–May 1870
145	Bridgeport, Ala. Apr. 1864–June 1866
146	Bridger, Fort, Wyo. June 1858–Nov. 1890
147	Brooke, Fort, Fla. Jan. 1824–Dec. 1840
148	Jan. 1841–July 1858
149	Apr. 1866–Dec. 1882
150	Brook's Point, Palawan, P.I. Sept. 1910–Oct. 1913
151	Brown, Fort, Tex. May 1846–Feb. 1861
152	June 1866–Dec. 1886
153	Jan. 1887–Dec. 1902
154	Jan. 1903–Sept. 1915
155	Brownsville, Tex. May 1865–Jan. 1869; May 1914–Sept. 1915
156	Buchanan, Fort, N. Mex. Nov. 1856–May 1862
157	Buffalo Barracks, N.Y. Jan. 1838–Sept. 1845
158	Buford, Fort, N. Dak. June 1866–Dec. 1879
159	Jan. 1880–Sept. 1895
160	Bumpus, Camp, Tacloban, Leyte, P.I. July 1902–May 1913
161	Burgwin, Cantonment, N. Mex. Sept. 1852–May 1860
162	Butler, Camp, Ill. Feb. 1862–July 1866
163	Cabanatuan, Nueva Ecija, P.I. July 1902–Oct. 1905
164	Cady, Camp, Calif. Feb. 1865–Apr. 1871
165	Cagayan, Mindanao, P.I. Apr. 1900–May 1904
166	Caibarién, Barracks, Cuba Apr. 1899–Feb. 1909
167	Cairo, Ill. Sept. 1861–Apr. 1866
168	Calamba, Laguna, P.I. May 1900–Sept. 1906
169	Calapan, Mindoro, P.I. July 1902–Mar. 1911
170	Calexico, Camp, Calif. Jan. 1911–Dec. 1916
171	Caloocan, Rizal, P.I. Feb. 1899–Dec. 1904
172	Camagüey, Cuba Oct. 1906–Dec. 1908
173	Camden, Ark. June 1865–Mar. 1869
174	Cameron, Fort, Utah May 1872–Apr. 1883
175	Canby, Fort, Wash. Apr. 1864–Dec. 1880
176	Jan. 1881–Dec. 1897
177	Jan. 1898–Dec. 1913
178	Canton, Ohio Sept. 1901–Dec. 1909
179	Cap El, Camp, Calif. Feb. 1856–Mar. 1857
180	Cape Girardeau, Mo. Aug. 1861–July 1865
181	Capron, Fort, Fla. Apr. 1850–May 1858
182	Cárdenas and Cárdenas Barracks, Cuba Dec. 1898–Feb. 1909
183	Carlisle Barracks, Pa. May 1812–Dec. 1858
184	Jan. 1859–Dec. 1872
185	Jan. 1873–Oct. 1879 Depot for Drafted Men July 1863–May 1865
186	Carroll, Fort, Md. Apr. 1898–June 1914
187	Cascades, Fort, Wash. Sept. 1855–Oct. 1861
188	Casey, Fort, Wash. Sept. 1899–Dec. 1913
189	Casper, Fort, Wyo. Oct. 1865–July 1867

Roll	Description
190	Cass, Fort, Tenn.
	Apr. 1835–Nov. 1838
191	Castle Pinckney, S.C.
	Nov. 1850–Dec. 1866
192	Caswell, Fort, N.C.
	June 1865–Dec. 1903
193	Jan. 1904–Apr. 1914
194	Cebu, Cebu, P.I.
	July 1902–Feb. 1904
195	Chadbourne, Fort, Tex.
	Apr. 1849–Nov. 1867
196	Champlain Arsenal, Vt.
	June 1833–May 1872
197	Charleston Harbor, S.C.
	Dec. 1819–June 1852
198	Charleston, S.C.
	Apr. 1865–Dec. 1870
199	Jan. 1871–Apr. 1879
200	Charleston Arsenal, S.C.
	Mar. 1869–Aug. 1873
201	Charlotte, N.C.
	Mar. 1866–Aug. 1873
202	Chase, Camp, Ohio
	Apr. 1862–Jan. 1866
203	Chattanooga, Tenn.
	Nov. 1863–Apr. 1879
204	Chester, S.C.
	June 1866–Jan. 1873
205	Cheyenne Depot, Camp at, Wyo.
	June 1873–Aug. 1882
206	Cheyenne Ordnance Depot, Wyo.
	May 1879–Feb. 1890
207	Chickamauga, Ga.
	Sept. 1895–Aug. 1910
208	Churchill, Fort, Nev.
	July 1860–Sept. 1869
209	Ciego de Avila, Camagüey, Cuba
	Feb. 1899–Dec. 1907
210	Cienfuegos, Cuba
	Feb. 1899–Jan. 1909
211	Cincinnati, Ohio
	Oct. 1862–Oct. 1865
212	City Point, Va.
	Mar. 1865–May 1867
213	Clark, Fort, Tex.
	June 1852–Feb. 1861
214	Dec. 1866–Dec. 1881
215	Jan. 1882–Dec. 1892
216	Jan. 1893–Dec. 1905
217	Jan. 1906–Dec. 1916
218	Clarksville, Tenn.
	Jan. 1863–July 1865
219	Clinch, Fort, near Barrancas and Pensacola, Fla.
	July 1823–Sept. 1834
220	Clinch, Fort, on Withlacooche River, Fla.
	Oct. 1836–May 1842
221	Clinch, Fort, Amelia Island at Fernandina, Fla.
	Aug. 1864–Aug. 1898
222	Cobb, Fort, Okla.
	Oct. 1859–Apr. 1861
223	Coffee, Fort, Ark.
	June 1834–Sept. 1838

Roll	Description
224	Colfax, La.
	Apr. 1873–Jan. 1876
225	Collins, Fort, Colo.
	Jan. 1863–Aug. 1866
226	Colorado, Camp, Tex.
	Aug. 1856–Jan. 1861
227	Colorado River, Camp on the, Ariz.
	Nov. 1868–Mar. 1871
228	Columbia, S.C.
	Apr. 1866–Dec. 1877
229	Columbia Arsenal, Tenn.
	May 1889–June 1904
230	Columbia, Fort, Wash.
	July 1898–Dec. 1906
231	Jan. 1907–Dec. 1913
232	Columbus, Ky.
	Apr. 1862–Apr. 1869
233	Columbus, Miss.
	May 1867–Nov. 1876
234	Columbus, N. Mex.
	July 1914–Feb. 1916
235	Columbus Barracks, Ohio
	Jan. 1864–Dec. 1877
236	Jan. 1878–Dec. 1892
237	Jan. 1893–Dec. 1905
238	Jan. 1906–Dec. 1916
239	Draft Rendezvous
	Apr. 1863–July 1865
	Todd Barracks
	Jan.–July 1866
	11th Co. of Recruits
	Aug. 1906–Oct. 1912
240	Colville, Fort, Wash.
	June 1859–Sept. 1882
241	Concho, Fort, Tex.
	Dec. 1867–Dec. 1878
242	Jan. 1879–June 1889
243	Concord, N.H.
	Mar. 1862–Apr. 1866
244	Connell, Camp, Samar, P.I.
	Jan. 1903–Aug. 1914
245	Connor, Camp, Idaho
	May 1863–Mar. 1865
246	Conrad, Fort, N. Mex.
	Nov. 1851–Feb. 1854
247	Constancia, Cuba
	Nov. 1906–Dec. 1908
248	Constitution, Fort, N.H.
	June 1821–Oct. 1839
249	Aug. 1841–May 1868
250	May 1898–Dec. 1905
251	Jan. 1906–May 1914
252	Cooke, Camp, Mont.
	July 1866–Mar. 1870
253	Cooper, Camp, Tex.
	July 1851–Jan. 1861
254	Corinth, Miss.
	June 1862–June 1870
255	Corpus Christie, Tex.
	Sept. 1845–Nov. 1898

Roll	Description
256	Cotabato, Mindanao, P.I.
	Jan. 1900–Nov. 1913
257	Cottonwood, Nebr.
	Sept. 1863–Dec. 1865
258	Coushatta, Camp, La.
	Oct. 1874–Nov. 1876
259	Covington and Newport, Ky.
	Sept. 1862–Oct. 1865
260	Covington, Fort, Md.
	Nov. 1814–Apr. 1815
261	Craig, Fort, N. Mex.
	Mar. 1854–Dec. 1870
262	Jan. 1871–June 1885
263	Crawford, Fort, Colo.
	Oct. 1880–Aug. 1890
264	Crawford, Fort, Wis.
	Feb. 1817–Dec. 1834
265	Jan. 1835–June 1856
266	Crescent City, Calif.
	Jan. 1856–June 1858
267	Crittenden, Camp, Ariz.
	Apr. 1868–Dec. 1872
268	Crittenden, Fort, Utah
	July 1858–May 1861
269	Crockett, Fort, Tex.
	Mar. 1911–Sept. 1915
270	Croghan, Fort, Tex.
	Mar. 1849–Nov. 1853
271	Crook, Fort, Calif.
	June 1857–May 1866
272	Crook, Fort, Nebr.
	June 1896–Dec. 1905
273	Jan. 1906–Dec. 1916
274	Crow Creek Agency, S. Dak.
	Feb. 1864–Apr. 1871
275	Cummings, Fort, N. Mex.
	Oct. 1863–Sept. 1866
276	Curtis, Camp, Calif.
	Oct. 1862–May 1865
277	Custer, Fort, Mont.
	July 1877–Apr. 1898
278	Dade, Fort, Fla.
	Feb. 1900–Dec. 1916
279	Daet, Ambos Camarines, P.I.
	May 1900–Apr. 1907
280	Dahlonega, Ga.
	Jan. 1867–May 1869
281	Dakota, Fort, S. Dak.
	Jan. 1866–May 1869
282	Dakota City, Nebr.
	Nov. 1863–May 1865
283	Dalama, Mindanao, P.I.
	May 1910–Sept. 1913
284	Dallas, Fort, Fla.
	Feb. 1838–May 1858
285	Dalles, Fort, Oreg.
	May 1850–June 1867
286	Danao, Cebu, P.I.
	Oct. 1907–Nov. 1909
287	Danville, Ky.
	Feb. 1867–Mar. 1869
288	Dapitan, Mindanao, P.I.
	Apr. 1900–July 1912

Roll	Description
289	Darlington, S.C.
	Apr. 1866–July 1868
290	Date Creek, Camp, Ariz.
	July 1866–Aug. 1873
291	Datil Creek, Camp on, N. Mex.
	Oct. 1885–Sept. 1886
292	Davao, Mindanao, P.I.
	Feb. 1900–Feb. 1913
293	Davids Island, N.Y.
	July 1866–Sept. 1874
294	July 1878–June 1896
295	Davis, Fort, Alaska
	June 1900–Dec. 1907
296	Jan. 1908–Dec. 1916
297	Davis, Fort, Tex.
	Sept. 1854–Dec. 1878
298	Jan. 1879–June 1891
299	Dawa, Samar, P.I.
	July 1906–Nov. 1907
300	Dearborn, Fort, Ill.
	June 1816–May 1837
301	Defiance, Fort, N. Mex.
	Sept. 1851–Apr. 1861
302	Delaware, Fort, Del.
	Jan. 1825–Sept. 1870
303	Mar. 1898–Dec. 1913
304	Del Rio, Camp, Tex.
	Feb. 1884–Apr. 1916
305	Dennison, Camp, Ohio
	Feb. 1862–Aug. 1865
306	De Russy, Fort, Hawaii
	Nov. 1908–Dec. 1913
307	Des Moines, Iowa
	Sept. 1834–Feb. 1846
308	Oct. 1903–Dec. 1916
309	De Soto, Fort, Fla.
	Feb. 1902–Dec. 1908
310	Jan. 1909–Sept. 1914
311	Detroit, Mich.
	Aug. 1815–Dec. 1817
312	Jan. 1818–Sept. 1842
313	Detroit Arsenal, Mich.
	Mar. 1838–Aug. 1875
314	Detroit Barracks, Mich.
	Oct. 1842–May 1866
315	Deynaud, Fort, Fla.
	Feb. 1838–Apr. 1858
316	Dipolog, Mindanao, P.I.
	Apr. 1906–May 1912
317	Discharge, Camp, Pa.
	Oct. 1864–July 1865
318	Dodge, Fort, Iowa
	Sept. 1850–May 1853
319	Dodge, Fort, Kans.
	Jan. 1866–Oct. 1882
320	Doña Ana, N. Mex.
	June 1849–Sept. 1851
321	Donaldsonville, La.
	June 1864–Jan. 1871
322	Donelson, Fort, Tenn.
	Sept. 1862–Apr. 1867
323	Douglas, Ariz.
	Jan. 1911–Dec. 1916

Roll	Description
324	Douglas, Fort, Utah Oct. 1862–Dec. 1874
325	Jan. 1875–Dec. 1886
326	Jan. 1887–Dec. 1898
327	Jan. 1899–Dec. 1906
328	Jan. 1907–Dec. 1916
329	Dover, Ark. Oct. 1866–Mar. 1869
330	Downes, Camp, Ormoc, Leyte, P.I. July 1902–Dec. 1906
331	Jan. 1907–May 1913
332	Drum Barracks, Calif. Mar. 1862–Nov. 1871
333	Duchesne, Fort, Utah Aug. 1886–Dec. 1903
334	Jan. 1904–Jan. 1912
335	Duncan, Fort, Tex. Mar. 1849–Mar. 1861
336	Mar. 1868–Aug. 1883
337	Du Pont, Fort, Del. June 1898–Dec. 1905
338	Jan. 1906–Dec. 1913
339	Dyea, Alaska Feb. 1898–June 1899
340	Eagle Pass, Camp, Tex. Jan. 1892–Sept. 1916
341	Edwards, Fort, Ill. Mar. 1822–June 1824
342	Egbert, Fort, Alaska June 1899–Aug. 1911
343	Eldridge, Camp, Los Banos, Laguna, P.I. Nov. 1900–Dec. 1907
344	Jan. 1908–Dec. 1916
345	Elizabethtown, Ky. Mar. 1871–Feb. 1873
346	Elliott, Fort, Tex. Sept. 1874–Oct. 1890
347	Ellis, Fort, Mont. Aug. 1867–Dec. 1876
348	Jan. 1877–Nov. 1886
349	Ellis Island, N.Y. Jan.–July 1814
350	Elmira, N.Y. Draft Rendezvous July 1863–Mar. 1866
351	El Paso, Tex. Feb. 1848–Sept. 1916
352	Empire, Panama, C.Z. Nov. 1914–Dec. 1916
353	Ethan Allen, Fort, Vt. Sept. 1894–Dec. 1906
354	Jan. 1907–Dec. 1916
355	Evansville, Ind. Sept. 1863–Aug. 1865
356	Ewell, Fort, Tex. May 1852–Nov. 1855
357	Fairfield, Fort, Maine Sept. 1841–Aug. 1843
358	Fanning, Fort, Fla. Nov. 1838–Jan. 1843
359	Farmville, Va.

Roll	Description
	June 1867–Jan. 1870
360	Far West, Fort, Calif. Sept. 1849–Apr. 1852
361	Fayette, Mo. July 1863–Jan. 1864
362	Fayetteville, Ark. Jan. 1863–Mar. 1869
363	Federal Hill, Fort, Md. Nov. 1863–Aug. 1865
364	Fernandina, Fla. Jan. 1818–Sept. 1898
365	Fetterman, Fort, Wyo. July 1867–Apr. 1882
366	Fillmore, Fort, N. Mex. Sept. 1851–Sept. 1862
367	Fisher, Fort, N.C. Mar. 1865–Mar. 1867
368	Flagler, Fort, Wash. Sept. 1899–Dec. 1906
369	Jan. 1907–Dec. 1913
370	Foote, Fort, Md. June 1864–Nov. 1878
371	Foster, Fort, Maine Jan. 1905–May 1914
372	Frankfort, Ky. Mar. 1871–June 1876
373	Frankford Arsenal, Pa. June 1833–Dec. 1876
374	Jan. 1877–Dec. 1897
375	Jan. 1898–Dec. 1916
376	Franklin, Ky. Dec. 1866–Oct. 1867
377	Franklin, La. July–Oct. 1865
378	Franklin, Tex. Mar. 1863–Oct. 1865
379	Fred Steele, Fort, Wyo. May 1868–Dec. 1877
380	Jan. 1878–Nov. 1886
381	Fredericksburg, Va. Aug. 1865–Mar. 1869
382	Fremont, Fort, S.C. Apr. 1900–Dec. 1906
383	Jan. 1907–July 1913
384	Gadsden, Fort, Fla. May 1818–July 1821
385	Gailard, Camp, Culebra, C.Z. Mar. 1915–Dec. 1916
386	Gaines, Fort, Ala. Aug. 1865–Dec. 1914
387	Gainesville, Fla. Apr. 1866–Oct. 1868
388	Gallatin, Tenn. Jan. 1863–Apr. 1869
389	Gallipolis, Ohio June 1863–June 1865
390	Gallup's Island, Mass. Feb. 1864–Mar. 1866
391	Galveston, Tex. July 1865–May 1870

Roll	Description
392	Gamble, R., Fort, Fla.
	Aug. 1839–Jan. 1843
393	Gandara, Samar, P.I.
	Apr. 1905–Mar. 1911
394	Garland, Fort, Colo.
	Aug. 1858–Dec. 1872
395	Jan. 1873–Nov. 1883
396	Gaston, Fort, Calif.
	Jan. 1859–Dec. 1874
397	Jan. 1875–June 1892
398	Gates, Fort, Tex.
	Oct. 1849–Feb. 1852
399	George G. Meade, Camp, Pa.
	Aug. 1898–Aug. 1899
400	Georgetown, S.C.
	Apr. 1866–Oct. 1868
401	Getty, Fort, R.I.
	Apr. 1910–Dec. 1913
402	Gibbon, Fort, Alaska
	Aug. 1899–Dec. 1906
403	Jan. 1907–Dec. 1916
404	Gibson, Fort, Okla.
	Apr. 1824–Dec. 1844
405	Jan. 1845–Aug. 1871
406	July 1872–Oct. 1897
407	Giesboro Point, D.C.
	Aug. 1863–Sept. 1864
408	Gilmer, Fort, Ga.
	Sept. 1838–Feb. 1842
409	Goldsboro, N.C.
	Apr. 1866–Oct. 1869
410	Goodwin, Fort, Ariz.
	May 1864–Mar. 1871
411	Governors Island, N.Y.
	Jan. 1814–July 1815
412	Graham, Fort, Tex.
	Apr. 1849–Oct. 1853
413	Grand River Agency, S. Dak.
	May 1870–May 1875
414	Grant, Fort, Ariz.
	Oct. 1865–Dec. 1874
415	Jan. 1875–Dec. 1894
416	Jan. 1895–Oct. 1905
417	Grant, Camp, Calif.
	Oct. 1863–Nov. 1865
418	Gratiot, Fort, Mich.
	Aug. 1815–June 1821
419	Oct. 1828–June 1846
420	Nov. 1848–May 1879
421	Greble, Fort, R.I.
	May 1898–Dec. 1905
422	Jan. 1906–Dec. 1913
423	Greenville, La.
	Aug. 1864–Mar. 1869
424	Greenville, S.C.
	Mar. 1866–Sept. 1877
425	Greenville, Tex.
	Jan. 1869–May 1870
426	Gregg, Camp, Bayambang, P.I.
	Jan. 1903–Dec. 1908

Roll	Description
427	Jan. 1909–Jan. 1916
428	Grenada, Miss.
	July 1866–Aug. 1870
429	Griffin, Fort, Tex.
	July 1867–May 1881
430	Guanajay, Cuba
	Jan. 1899–Jan. 1909
431	Guantánamo, Cuba
	Mar. 1899–Mar. 1902
432	Guinayangan, Tayabas, P.I.
	Nov. 1901–Feb. 1906
433	Guthrie, Okla.
	Apr. 1889–June 1891
434	Guyandotte, W. Va.
	Oct. 1867–Mar. 1869
435	Hale, Fort, S. Dak.
	July 1870–July 1884
436	Hall, Fort, Idaho
	May 1870–May 1883
437	Halleck, Fort, N. Dak.
	Dec. 1864–July 1866
438	Halleck, Fort, Idaho
	July 1863–Nov. 1864
439	Halleck, Fort, Nev.
	June 1867–Dec. 1875
440	Jan. 1876–Dec. 1886
441	Hamilton Barracks, Mantanzas, Cuba
	Jan. 1900–Dec. 1908
442	Hamilton, Fort, N.Y.
	Oct. 1834–Dec. 1859
443	Jan. 1860–Dec. 1876
444	Jan. 1877–Dec. 1892
445	Jan. 1893–Dec. 1905
446	Jan. 1906–Dec. 1913
447	Hamilton, Camp, Va.
	June 1861–Feb. 1869
448	Hancock Barracks, Maine
	June 1828–Aug. 1845
449	Hancock, Fort, N.J.
	Feb. 1898–Dec. 1905
450	Jan. 1906–Dec. 1913
451	Hancock, Camp, N. Dak.
	Nov. 1872–Nov. 1877
452	Hancock, Fort, Tex.
	July 1884–Sept. 1895
453	Harker, Fort, Kans.
	Oct. 1864–Mar. 1873
454	Harney, Fort, Oreg.
	Aug. 1867–June 1880
455	Harpers Ferry, W. Va.
	Oct. 1859–Mar. 1866
456	Harrisburg, Pa.
	Aug. 1862–Mar. 1866
457	Harrison, Fort, Ind.
	Mar. 1816–Apr. 1818
458	Harrison, Benjamin, Fort, Ind.
	July 1906–Dec. 1916
459	Harrison, William Henry, Fort, Mont.
	Sept. 1895–Dec. 1905

Roll	Description
460	Jan. 1906–Sept. 1914
461	Hart's Island, N.Y.
	Mar. 1864–Mar. 1867
462	Hartshorne, Camp, Laoang, Samar, P.I.
	May 1900–June 1906
463	Hartsuff, Fort, Nebr.
	Nov. 1874–Apr. 1881
464	Hatch's Ranch, N. Mex.
	Nov. 1856–Feb. 1862
465	Hatteras, Fort, N.C.
	Sept. 1861–Jan. 1868
466	Havana, Cuba
	Havana Artillery
	Jan. 1899–Oct. 1903
	Cabaña Barracks
	Jan. 1899–Feb. 1904
467	Columbia Barracks
	Oct. 1898–Mar. 1909
468	Piratechnia Military
	Jan. 1899–Aug. 1901
	Santa Clara Battery
	Jan. 1899–Aug. 1901
	Various Locations
	Dec. 1898–July 1907
469	Hays, Fort, Kans.
	Nov. 1865–Dec. 1875
470	Jan. 1876–Oct. 1889
471	Hayt, Camp, Oras, Samar, P.I.
	July 1902–Nov. 1911
472	Heath, Fort, Mass.
	Jan. 1905–Dec. 1913
473	Heilman, Fort, Fla.
	May 1836–May 1841
474	Hempstead, Fort, Tex.
	July 1865–Mar. 1869
475	Henry Barracks, Cayey, P.R.
	Feb. 1899–Dec. 1906
476	Jan. 1907–Dec. 1916
477	Hilton Head, S.C.
	Dec. 1861–Jan. 1900
478	Holly Springs, Miss.
	May 1867–Sept. 1877
479	Holguín, Cuba
	Jan. 1899–Feb. 1909
480	Horse Springs, N. Mex.
	Oct. 1885–Aug. 1886
481	Hoskins, Fort, Oreg.
	July 1856–Apr. 1865
482	Hot Springs, Ark., U.S. Army and Navy
	General Hospital
	Mar. 1887–Dec. 1904
483	Jan. 1905–Dec. 1916
484	Houston, Tex.
	Dec. 1848–Apr. 1868
485	Howard, Camp, Idaho
	Aug. 1877–July 1881
486	Howard, Fort, Md.
	June 1899–Dec. 1906
487	Jan. 1907–June 1914
488	Howard, Fort, Wis.
	Jan. 1818–Dec. 1830
489	Jan. 1831–May 1852

Roll	Description
490	Huachuca, Fort, Ariz.
	Mar. 1877–Dec. 1888
491	Jan. 1889–Dec. 1898
492	Jan. 1899–Dec. 1906
493	Jan. 1907–Dec. 1916
494	Hualpai, Camp, Ariz.
	May 1869–Aug. 1873
495	Hudson, Fort, Tex.
	Sept. 1856–Mar. 1868
496	Humacao, P.R.
	Nov. 1898–Aug. 1900
497	Humboldt, Fort, Calif.
	Jan. 1853–Dec. 1866
498	Humboldt, Tenn.
	Jan. 1863–June 1876
499	Hunt, Fort, Va.
	Apr. 1899–Dec. 1907
500	Jan. 1908–Dec. 1913
501	Huntsville, Ala.
	Aug. 1864–Feb. 1899
	Camp Albert G. Forse
	Camp Wheeler
502	Iligan, Mindanao, P.I.
	Apr. 1900–Sept. 1903
503	Iloilo, Panay, P.I.
	Nov. 1902–Sept. 1910
504	Imus, Cavite, P.I.
	Sept. 1899–Apr. 1907
505	Indang, Cavite, P.I.
	May 1900–Dec. 1904
506	Independence, Camp, Calif.
	July 1862–July 1877
507	Independence, Fort, Mass.
	July 1816–Nov. 1833
508	Feb. 1836–Dec. 1868
509	Jan. 1869–Nov. 1879
510	Independence, Mo.
	Apr. 1862–Aug. 1864
511	Indianapolis, Ind.
	Apr. 1863–Apr. 1867
512	Indianapolis Arsenal, Ind.
	Jan. 1866–Dec. 1881
513	Jan. 1882–Apr. 1903
514	Indianapolis, Ind.
	Burnside Barracks and Camp Morton
	Jan.–Nov. 1865
	Draft Rendezvous
	Dec. 1863–July 1865
515	Indianola, Tex.
	Sept. 1866–July 1869
516	Infanta, Tayabas, P.I.
	June 1905–Oct. 1911
517	Inge, Fort, Tex.
	Mar. 1849–Jan. 1869
518	Ipil, Mindanao, P.I.
	July 1910–Aug. 1912
519	Ironton and Pilot Knob, Mo.
	Sept. 1861–Aug. 1865
520	Isabela de Basilan, Mindanao, P.I.
	Mar. 1909–Aug. 1913

Roll	Description
521	Jackson, Fort, La.
	Dec. 1830–Dec. 1866
522	Jan. 1867–June 1914
523	Jackson Barracks, La.
	Feb. 1837–Dec. 1869
524	Jan. 1870–Dec. 1884
525	Jan. 1885–Dec. 1900
526	Jan. 1901–Dec. 1906
527	Jan. 1907–June 1914
528	Jackson, Mich.
	Draft Rendezvous
	Mar. 1864–Dec. 1866
529	Jackson, Miss.
	May 1865–Aug. 1877
530	Jackson, Tenn.
	Sept. 1862–Mar. 1863
531	Jacksonville, Fla.
	Mar. 1862–Nov. 1898
532	James, Camp, Leyte, P.I.
	Sept. 1902–Mar. 1911
533	James, Fort, S. Dak.
	Jan.–Oct. 1866
534	Jaqua, Camp, Calif.
	Oct. 1863–Mar. 1866
535	Jay, Fort, N.Y.
	May 1821–Dec. 1839
536	Jan. 1840–Dec. 1859
537	Jan. 1860–Dec. 1873
538	Jan. 1874–Dec. 1885
539	Jan. 1886–Dec. 1897
540	Jan. 1898–Dec. 1905
541	Jan. 1906–Dec. 1916
542	Jefferson, Fort, Fla.
	Jan. 1861–Dec. 1868
543	Jan. 1869–July 1898
544	Jefferson, Fort, Tex.
	Dec. 1867–May 1871
545	Jefferson Barracks, Mo.
	July 1826–Dec. 1839
546	Jan. 1840–Dec. 1851
547	Jan. 1852–Dec. 1869
548	Jan. 1870–Dec. 1888
549	Jan. 1889–Dec. 1897
550	Jan. 1898–Dec. 1905
551	Jan. 1906–Dec. 1916
552	Jefferson City, Mo.
	Nov. 1861–Oct. 1863
553	Jeffersonville, Ind.
	Feb. 1866–Mar. 1877
554	Jessup, Fort, La.
	May 1822–Dec. 1831
555	Jan. 1832–Jan. 1846
556	John A. Rucker, Camp, Ariz.

Roll	Description
	Dec. 1878–Oct. 1880
557	John Hay, Camp, Benguet, P.I.
	Aug. 1907–Dec. 1916
558	Johnston, Fort, N.C.
	Feb. 1818–Dec. 1868
559	Jan. 1869–Feb. 1881
560	Jones, Fort, Calif.
	Oct. 1852–June 1858
561	Josiah Simpson General Hospital, Va.
	Sept. 1898–July 1900
562	Jossman, Camp, Guimaras, P.I.
	Oct. 1902–June 1912
563	Kansas City, Mo.
	Apr. 1862–July 1865
564	Kearny, Forts, Nebr.
	May 1846–Apr. 1848;
	June 1848–Dec. 1860
565	Jan. 1861–May 1871
566	Kearny, Fort, R.I.
	Apr. 1910–Dec. 1913
567	Keithley, Camp, Mindanao, P.I.
	Jan. 1905–Dec. 1916
568	Kennebec Arsenal, Maine
	Sept. 1833–Dec. 1871
569	Jan. 1872–Dec. 1888
570	Jan. 1889–Dec. 1903
571	Kent, Fort, Maine
	Sept. 1841–Aug. 1845
572	Keogh, Fort, Mont.
	Sept. 1876–Dec. 1886
573	Jan. 1887–Dec. 1897
574	Jan. 1898–July 1912
575	Key West and Key West Barracks, Fla.
	Jan. 1831–Dec. 1856
576	Jan. 1857–Dec. 1874
577	Jan. 1875–Dec. 1897
578	Jan. 1898–Dec. 1907
579	Jan. 1908–June 1915
	General Hospital at Key West
	Apr.–Aug. 1898
580	King, Camp, Fla.
	Mar. 1827–June 1829
581	King, Fort, Fla.
	July 1832–Feb. 1843
582	Klamath, Fort, Oreg.
	Aug. 1863–Dec. 1876
583	Jan. 1877–June 1890
584	Knox, Fort, Maine
	July 1863–July 1898
585	Kodiak, Fort, Alaska
	June 1868–Sept. 1870
586	Lafayette, Fort, N.Y.
	Apr. 1822–Apr. 1868

Roll	Description
587	Lampasas, Tex.
	May 1867–June 1870
588	Lancaster, Ky.
	Nov. 1870–June 1876
589	Lancaster, Fort, Tex.
	Aug. 1855–Mar. 1861
590	Lane, Fort, Oreg.
	Sept. 1853–Aug. 1856
591	Laoag, Ilocos Norte, P.I.
	Jan. 1900–Nov. 1902
592	La Popa Barracks, Cuba
	Mar. 1899–June 1900
593	Lapwai, Fort, Idaho
	Nov. 1862–Dec. 1873
594	Jan. 1874–Aug. 1884
595	Laramie, Fort, Wyo.
	June 1849–Dec. 1860
596	Jan. 1861–Dec. 1876
597	Laramie, Fort, Wyo.
	Jan. 1877–Mar. 1890
598	Lares, P.R.
	Nov. 1898–Mar. 1900
599	Larned, Fort, Kans.
	Nov. 1859–Dec. 1869
600	Jan. 1870–July 1878
601	Las Cruces, N. Mex.
	Mar. 1863–Aug. 1865
602	Las Vegas, N. Mex.
	Feb. 1848–June 1851
603	Latham, Camp, Calif.
	Sept. 1861–Aug. 1862
604	Lauderdale, Fort, Fla.
	Feb. 1839–Jan. 1842
605	Lauderdale, Miss.
	Apr. 1867–Dec. 1869
606	Laurensville, S.C.
	Dec. 1867–Oct. 1876
607	Lawrence, Kans.
	Dec. 1857–Oct. 1865
608	Lawton, Fort, Wash.
	July 1901–Dec. 1916
609	Lawtonville, S.C.
	Feb. 1866–Jan. 1867
610	Leavenworth, Kans.
	Aug. 1827–Dec. 1850
611	Jan. 1851–Dec. 1869
612	Jan. 1870–Dec. 1890
613	Jan. 1891–Dec. 1898
614	Jan. 1899–Dec. 1906
615	Jan. 1907–Dec. 1916
616	Leavenworth, Fort, Kans. Schools
	Apr. 1906–Dec. 1916
617	U.S. Disciplinary Barracks
	May 1875–Aug. 1895
618	Feb. 1906–Dec. 1916
	Leavenworth, Kans.
619	Arsenal
	Jan. 1863–May 1874
620	Ordnance Depot
	Nov. 1881–Mar. 1891

Roll	Description
	City Guard
	Jan.–Sept. 1865
621	Lebanon, Ky.
	Oct. 1863–Oct. 1876
622	Leon Springs, Tex.
	June 1908–Aug. 1910
623	Levett, Fort, Maine
	May 1903–Dec. 1913
624	Lewis, Fort, Colo.
	Oct. 1878–Aug. 1891
	Cantonment Rio de la Plata, Colo.
	Aug. 1880–Jan. 1881
625	Lexington, Ky.
	Apr. 1863–Dec. 1872
626	Lexington, Mo.
	Mar. 1862–June 1865
627	Lincoln, Camp, Calif.
	July 1862–May 1869
628	Lincoln, A., Fort, N. Dak.
	Dec. 1872–Dec. 1880
629	Jan. 1881–Dec. 1902
630	Jan. 1903–Aug. 1913
631	Ordnance Depot
	Mar. 1879–Oct. 1889
632	Lincoln, Fort, Tex.
	Jan. 1849–July 1852
633	Lipa, Batangas, P.I.
	June 1902–Jan. 1905
634	Liscum, Fort, Alaska
	Jan. 1900–Dec. 1907
635	Jan. 1908–Dec. 1916
636	Little Rock and Little Rock Barracks, Ark.
	Sept. 1863–Dec. 1876
637	Jan. 1877–Aug. 1890
638	Livingston, Ala.
	Oct. 1874–Nov. 1876
639	Livingston, Fort, La.
	Nov. 1864–Dec. 1866
640	Livingston, Tex.
	Oct. 1868–June 1870
641	Logan, Fort, Colo.
	Oct. 1887–Dec. 1899
642	Jan. 1900–Dec. 1908
643	Jan. 1909–Dec. 1916
644	Logan, Fort, Mont.
	June 1870–Oct. 1880
645	Logan, Camp, Oreg.
	Dec. 1866–Dec. 1868
646	Logan H. Roots, Fort, Ark.
	July 1896–Dec. 1906
647	Jan. 1907–Dec. 1916
648	Los Lunas, N. Mex.
	Jan. 1852–Aug. 1860
649	Los Pinos, N. Mex.
	Sept. 1862–Aug. 1866
650	Louisiana Purchase Exposition, St. Louis, Mo.
	Nov. 1903–Mar. 1905
651	Louisville, Ky.
	July 1862–June 1871

Roll	Description
652	Draft Rendezvous
	Feb. 1864–Apr. 1866
	Taylor Barracks
	Sept. 1866–June 1873
653	Lowell, Fort, Ariz.
	Jan. 1866–Dec. 1877
654	Jan. 1878–Mar. 1891
655	Lowell, Fort, N. Mex.
	Dec. 1867–July 1869
656	Lucban, P.I.
	Dec. 1899–Mar. 1902
657	Ludlow Barracks, Mindanao, P.I.
	May 1900–Dec. 1907
658	Jan. 1908–Dec. 1916
659	Lyon, Fort, Colo.
	Aug. 1860–Dec. 1869
660	Jan. 1870–Dec. 1880
661	Jan. 1881–Nov. 1889
662	Lyon, Camp, Idaho
	June 1865–Mar. 1869
663	Lyon, Fort, Maine
	Dec. 1907–Dec. 1913
664	Lyon, Fort, N. Mex.
	Aug. 1860–Nov. 1861
665	McClellan, Camp, Iowa
	Apr. 1863–Nov. 1865
666	McDermit, Fort, Nev.
	Aug. 1865–Dec. 1875
667	Jan. 1876–July 1889
668	McDowell, Fort, Ariz.
	Jan. 1866–Dec. 1874
669	Jan. 1875–Dec. 1890
670	McDowell, Fort, Calif.
	Sept. 1863–Dec. 1905
671	Jan. 1906–Dec. 1916
672	McGarry, Camp, Nev.
	Oct. 1865–Dec. 1868
673	McGrath, Camp, Batangas, P.I.
	Apr. 1902–Dec. 1916
674	McHenry, Fort, Md.
	Nov. 1814–Dec. 1834
675	Jan. 1835–Dec. 1859
676	Jan. 1860–Dec. 1874
677	Jan. 1875–Dec. 1886
678	Jan. 1887–Dec. 1897
679	Jan. 1898–Dec. 1905
680	Jan. 1906–July 1912
681	McIntosh, Fort, Tex.
	Mar. 1849–Dec. 1870
682	Jan. 1871–Dec. 1880
683	McIntosh, Fort, Tex.
	Jan. 1881–Dec. 1891
684	Jan. 1892–Dec. 1902
685	Jan. 1903–Dec. 1908

Roll	Description
686	Jan. 1909–Dec. 1916
687	McKavett, Fort, Tex.
	Mar. 1852–Dec. 1872
688	Jan. 1873–June 1883
689	MacKenzie, Camp, Cuba
	Apr. 1900–Jan. 1902
690	MacKenzie, Camp, Ga.
	Nov. 1898–Mar. 1899
691	MacKenzie, Fort, Wyo.
	June 1899–Dec. 1906
692	Jan. 1907–Dec. 1916
693	MacKinac, Fort, Mich.
	Feb. 1816–Dec. 1836
694	Jan. 1837–Sept. 1856
695	May 1857–Dec. 1874
696	Jan. 1875–Dec. 1888
697	Jan. 1889–Aug. 1895
698	McKinley, Camp, Hawaii
	Aug. 1898–June 1907
699	McKinley, Fort, Maine
	Dec. 1902–Dec. 1907
700	Jan. 1908–Dec. 1913
701	McKinley, William, Fort, Rizal, P.I.
	Apr. 1904–Dec. 1910
702	Jan. 1911–Dec. 1916
	School for Bakers and Cooks
	Dec. 1915–Aug. 1916
	Field Hospital No. 4
	Apr. 1916
	Hospital Corps Detachment
	Mar.–Dec. 1916
703	McKinney, Fort, Wyo.
	Oct. 1876–Dec. 1887
704	Jan. 1888–Nov. 1894
705	McPherson, Fort, Ga.
	Dec. 1870–Dec. 1891
706	Jan. 1892–Dec. 1906
707	Jan. 1907–Dec. 1916
	General Hospital
	May 1898–May 1899
708	McPherson, Fort, Nebr.
	Jan. 1866–Dec. 1872
709	Jan. 1873–May 1880
710	McRae, Fort, N. Mex.
	June 1863–Oct. 1876
711	McRee, Fort, Fla.
	Mar. 1901–Dec. 1907
712	Jan. 1908–June 1914
713	Mabry, Camp, Tex.
	July–Sept. 1906
714	Macabebe, Pampanga, P.I.
	June 1907–Dec. 1913
715	Macomb, Fort, Fla.
	Apr. 1839–Jan. 1843

Roll	Description
716	Macomb, Fort, La.
	Jan. 1828–Aug. 1866
717	Macon, Fort, Ga.
	Mar. 1866–Dec. 1898
718	Macon, Fort, N.C.
	Dec. 1834–Dec. 1867
719	Jan. 1868–May 1877
720	Madison, Ark.
	May 1867–Apr. 1869
721	Madison Barracks, N.Y.
	Jan. 1823–Dec. 1839
722	Jan. 1840–Dec. 1870
723	Jan. 1871–Dec. 1884
724	Jan. 1885–Dec. 1897
725	Jan. 1898–Dec. 1906
726	Jan. 1907–Dec. 1916
727	Maginnis, Fort, Mont.
	Aug. 1880–July 1890
728	Makar, Mindanao, P.I.
	Feb. 1902–Aug. 1911
729	Malahi (Malagi) Island Military Prison and Post, P.I.
	July 1902–Jan. 1906
730	Manati, P.R.
	Nov. 1898–Jan. 1904
731	Manila, P.I.
	1st Brigade and Post of Manila
	Aug. 1901–Apr. 1905
732	Manila Arsenal
	May 1899
	Manila Artillery Garrison
	July 1902–June 1903
	Bagumbayan
	Nov. 1913–Sept. 1914
	Block House No. 3
	Apr. 1899
	Cavalry Command
	Jan.–June 1899
733	Cuartel de Espana
	July 1902–Dec. 1909
734	Jan. 1910–Dec. 1916
735	Cuartel de Fortin
	Aug. 1898–Apr. 1899
	Cuartel de Infanteria
	Sept. 1898
	Cuartel de Malate
	Sept. 1898–Mar. 1905
	Cuartel de Meisic
	Aug. 1898–May 1906
736	Camp Dewey
	July–Aug. 1898
	Engineer Garrison
	Aug. 1901–Apr. 1903
	Exposition Grounds
	Aug. 1900–Feb. 1901
	Malate Barracks
	June 1902–Mar. 1905
	Hospital No. 3
	Dec. 1902–Jan. 1903
	Division Hospital
	July 1904–Dec. 1909
737	Jan. 1910–Dec. 1916

Roll	Description
738	La Loma Church
	Apr. 1899
	Luneta
	Feb. 1903–Dec. 1904
	Camp MacArthur
	Jan.–Aug. 1913
	Medical Supply Depot
	Dec. 1909–Dec. 1916
739	Ordnance Depot
	Apr. 1901–Dec. 1908
740	Jan. 1909–Dec. 1916
741	Camp Otis
	Jan.–Mar. 1910
	Pasay Cavalry Barracks
	June–Dec. 1901
	Pasay Garrison
	July 1902–June 1905
	Provost Guard
	Sept. 1898–July 1901
742	Santa Mesa
	July 1902–May 1906
	Miscellaneous Returns
	Aug. 1898–Feb. 1903
743	Mansfield, Fort, R.I.
	Feb. 1901–Dec. 1913
744	Manzanillo, Cuba
	Oct. 1898–Apr. 1902
745	Marcy, Fort, N. Mex.
	May 1849–Dec. 1865
746	Jan. 1866–Dec. 1882
747	Jan. 1883–Sept. 1894
748	Margosatubig, Mindanao, P.I.
	Oct. 1903–Sept. 1913
749	Marion, Va.
	May 1867–Feb. 1869
750	Mariquina, Rizal, P.I.
	July 1899–Jan. 1906
751	Mariveles, Bataan, P.I.
	Oct. 1902–Sept. 1907
752	Marshall, Fort, Md.
	Jan. 1863–July 1866
753	Maryland Heights, Md.
	Nov. 1864–Apr. 1865
754	Mason, Fort, Calif.
	Oct. 1863–Dec. 1874
755	Jan. 1875–Dec. 1888
756	Jan. 1889–Dec. 1902
757	Jan. 1903–Dec. 1908
758	Jan. 1909–Dec. 1916
759	Mason, Fort, Tex.
	July 1851–Dec. 1869
760	Massachusetts, Fort, Colo.
	June 1852–July 1858
761	Matanzas, Cuba
	Jan. 1899–Nov. 1908
762	Mayagüez, P.R.
	Aug. 1898–Mar. 1903
763	Meade, Fort, Fla.
	Dec. 1849–Aug. 1857
764	Meade, Fort, S. Dak.
	Aug. 1878–Dec. 1891

Roll	Description
765	Jan. 1892–Dec. 1903
766	Jan. 1904–Dec. 1916
767	Medicine Butte, Camp, Wyo.
	Sept. 1885–Apr. 1887
768	Mellon, Fort, Fla.
	Mar. 1837–Apr. 1842
769	Memphis, Tenn.
	Dec. 1864–Mar. 1869
770	Meridian, Miss.
	May 1866–Dec. 1872
771	Merrill, Fort, Tex.
	Mar. 1850–Nov. 1855
772	Merritt, Camp, Calif.
	May–Aug. 1898
773	Merritt, Camp, Mont.
	Jan. 1892–July 1898
774	Mexican Border
	Patrol Districts:
	Feb. 1915–Nov. 1916
	Arizona District
	May–July 1916
	Big Bend District
	May–July 1916
	Big Bend Cavalry Patrol District
	Mar.–May 1915
	Eagle Pass District
	May–July 1916
	El Paso District
	June–July 1916
	Fabens Cavalry Patrol District
	Feb.–May 1915
	Laredo District
	May–Nov. 1916
	Western Texas Cavalry Patrol District
	June 1915–Feb. 1916
775	Micanopy, Fort, Fla.
	June 1836–Jan. 1843
776	Michie, Fort, N.Y.
	June 1898–Dec. 1913
777	Mifflin, Fort, Pa.
	Jan. 1813–Apr. 1866
778	Miley, Fort, Calif.
	July 1902–Dec. 1913
779	Miller, Fort, Calif.
	May 1851–Sept. 1864
780	Mills, Fort, Corregidor, P.I.
	July 1908–Dec. 1916
781	Misamis, Mindanao, P.I.
	Apr. 1900–Feb. 1905
782	Missoula, Fort, Mont.
	June 1877–Dec. 1893
783	Jan. 1894–Dec. 1908
784	Jan. 1909–Dec. 1916
785	Mitchell, Fort, Ala.
	Aug. 1825–Apr. 1840
786	Mobile, Ala.
	Mar. 1866–June 1898
787	Mojave, Fort, Ariz.
	Apr. 1859–Dec. 1872
788	Jan. 1873–July 1890

Roll	Description
789	Momungan, Mindanao, P.I.
	June 1910–Dec. 1913
790	Moniac, Fort, Fla.
	Aug. 1838–Aug. 1842
791	Monroe, La.
	Aug. 1865–Apr. 1877
792	Monroe, Fort, Va.
	Oct. 1823–Dec. 1835
793	Jan. 1836–Dec. 1853
794	Jan. 1854–Dec. 1870
795	Jan. 1871–Dec. 1883
796	Jan. 1884–Dec. 1897
797	Jan. 1898–Dec. 1907
798	Jan. 1908–Dec. 1913
799	Arsenal
	Jan. 1863–Dec. 1877
800	Jan. 1878–Dec. 1895
801	Jan. 1896–Dec. 1901
802	Artillery School
	Apr. 1906–Dec. 1916
803	Montgomery, Ala.
	July 1865–July 1871
804	Monument, Kans.
	Dec. 1865–Aug. 1868
805	Morgan, Fort, Ala.
	June 1822–Dec. 1868
806	Mar. 1898–Dec. 1905
807	Jan. 1906–Dec. 1914
808	Morgan, Fort, Colo.
	June 1865–Apr. 1868
809	Morganton, N.C.
	Apr. 1867–Nov. 1877
810	Morris, Camp, Calif.
	June–Oct. 1863
811	Morrison, Camp, Ilocos Sur, P.I.
	Feb. 1903–Dec. 1904
812	Morton, Camp, and Burnside Barracks, Ind.
	Apr. 1863–Nov. 1865
813	Mott, Fort, N.J.
	Dec. 1897–Dec. 1905
814	Jan. 1906–Dec. 1913
815	Moultrie, Fort, S.C.
	Apr. 1824–Oct. 1860
816	June 1903–June 1914
817	Mount Gretna, Pa.
	Sept. 1899–July 1909
818	Mount Sterling, Ky.
	Apr. 1871–Dec. 1872
819	Mount Vernon Barracks, Ala.
	Jan. 1833–Dec. 1878
820	Jan. 1879–Dec. 1894
821	Munfordville, Ky.
	June 1863–June 1865
822	Myer, Fort, Va.
	Oct. 1864–Dec. 1876
823	Jan. 1877–Dec. 1890
824	Jan. 1891–Dec. 1904

Roll	Description
825	Jan. 1905–Dec. 1916
826	June 1899–Sept. 1905
	Signal Corps
827	Myers, Fort, Fla.
	Feb. 1850–Jan. 1865
828	Nacogdoches, Tex.
	July 1836–Feb. 1870
829	Naga, Cebu, P.I.
	July 1902–Sept. 1909
830	Naic, Cavite, P.I.
	Apr. 1900–Apr. 1908
831	Napoleonville, La.
	June 1864–Nov. 1865
832	Nashville, Tenn.
	Dec. 1862–Dec. 1873
833	Jan. 1874–Feb. 1877
	Garrison Artillery
	Sept. 1863–July 1865
834	Nasugbu, Batangas, P.I.
	Nov. 1905–Sept. 1909
835	Natchez, Miss.
	Dec. 1863–July 1870
836	Natchitoches, La.
	June 1821–Nov. 1876
837	New Bedford, Mass.
	June 1863–May 1865
838	New Bern, N.C.
	Jan. 1832–Dec. 1867
839	Newberry, S.C.
	May 1867–July 1875
840	New Haven, Conn.
	July 1863–Oct. 1865
	Draft Rendezvous
841	New Iberia, La.
	June 1865–Oct. 1868
842	New Madrid, Mo.
	June 1862–Apr. 1865
843	New Orleans, La.
	Oct. 1821–Mar. 1869
844	Dec. 1872–May 1898
	Camp of Distribution
	Sept. 1864–June 1866
845	Newport Barracks, Ky.
	Apr. 1839–Dec. 1857
846	Jan. 1858–Dec. 1871
847	Jan. 1872–Dec. 1882
848	Jan. 1883–Nov. 1894
849	Newport, R.I.
	Mar. 1813–Jan. 1822
850	Newport News, Va.
	Aug. 1861–Nov. 1906
851	New Smyrna, Fla.
	May 1837–Oct. 1853
852	New Utrecht, N.Y.
	May–Nov. 1814
853	New York Arsenal, N.Y.
	Jan. 1863–Dec. 1881
854	Jan. 1882–Dec. 1897

Roll	Description
855	Jan. 1898–Dec. 1916
856	New York Harbor, N.Y.
	Mar. 1813–June 1852
857	Niagara, Fort, N.Y.
	Aug. 1818–Sept. 1854
858	Dec. 1861–Dec. 1877
859	Jan. 1878–Dec. 1890
860	Jan. 1891–Dec. 1901
861	Jan. 1902–Dec. 1908
862	Jan. 1909–Dec. 1916
	Niagara Frontier
	Mar. 1813–Dec. 1839
863	Nichols, Camp, Rizal, P.I.
	Nov. 1913–Dec. 1916
864	Niobrara, Fort, Nebr.
	Apr. 1880–Dec. 1894
865	Jan. 1895–Sept. 1906
866	Nogales, Ariz.
	Apr. 1887–July 1916
867	Nome Lackee Reserve, Calif.
	Jan. 1855–Mar. 1858
868	Norfolk, Va.
	Jan. 1866–Jan. 1870
869	Norfolk Harbor, Va.
	Mar. 1817–Feb. 1824
870	North Fork of the Canadian River,
	Cantonment on, Okla.
	Mar. 1879–June 1882
871	North Platte, Nebr.
	Mar. 1875–Dec. 1877
872	Nueva Caceres, Cebu, P.I.
	June 1900–Feb. 1905
873	Nuevitas, Cuba
	Dec. 1898–Feb. 1900
874	Nye, Camp, Nev.
	Oct. 1864–Sept. 1865
875	Oglethorpe, Fort, Ga.
	Jan. 1905–Dec. 1910
876	Jan. 1911–Dec. 1916
877	Ojo Caliente, N. Mex.
	May 1879–Mar. 1882
878	Oklahoma, Camp, Okla.
	May 1889–July 1892
879	Omaha, Nebr.
	Aug. 1863–Dec. 1873
880	Jan. 1874–Dec. 1885
881	Jan. 1886–Sept. 1896
882	July 1905–Dec. 1910
883	Jan. 1911–Dec. 1916
	Camp Thayer
	Oct. 1909
	Ordnance Depot
	Apr. 1890–Feb. 1891
884	Ontario, Fort, N.Y.
	Nov. 1838–Dec. 1867
885	Jan. 1868–Dec. 1880

Roll	Description
886	Jan. 1881–Dec. 1900
887	Jan. 1901–Dec. 1908
888	Jan. 1909–Dec. 1916
889	Orford, Fort, Oreg. Oct. 1849–Sept. 1856
890	Oroquieta, Mindanao, P.I. July 1900–Feb. 1905
891	Otis, E.S., Camp, Panama Oct. 1911–Dec. 1916
892	Overton, Camp, Mindanao, P.I. Oct. 1903–Dec. 1910
893	Jan. 1911–Sept. 1917
894	Oxford, Miss. Jan. 1872–Feb. 1873
895	Paducah, Ky. Sept. 1861–Dec. 1872
896	Pantar, Mindanao, P.I. June 1910–Nov. 1913
897	Paola, Kans. Apr. 1864–Aug. 1865
898	Parapet, Camp, La. May 1862–Feb. 1866
899	Pembina, Fort, N. Dak. June 1870–Dec. 1881
900	Jan. 1882–July 1895
901	Pena Colorado, Camp, Tex. Mar. 1880–Feb. 1893
902	Pensacola, Fla. July 1821–Jan. 1857
903	May 1862–Dec. 1874
904	Feb. 1875–Apr. 1888
905	Petersburg, Va. Apr. 1865–Jan. 1870
906	Petite Coquille, La. July 1821–Nov. 1827
907	Pettit Barracks, Mindanao, P.I. Dec. 1899–Dec. 1908
908	Jan. 1909–Dec. 1916
909	Philadelphia, Pa. Apr. 1862–Mar. 1866 Draft Rendezvous Aug. 1863–June 1865 Recruiting District June 1812–Oct. 1813
910	Philip [Phil] Kearny, Fort, Wyo. July 1866–July 1868
911	Picatinny Arsenal, N.J. July 1885–Dec. 1899
912	Jan. 1900–Dec. 1916
913	Pickens, Fort, Fla. Apr. 1834–Mar. 1868
914	Mar. 1898–Dec. 1906
915	Jan. 1907–June 1914
916	Pickering, Fort, Mass. Jan. 1864–Sept. 1898
917	Pickering, Fort, Tenn. Nov. 1862–June 1865
918	Picolata, Fla. Mar. 1836–Oct. 1842

Roll	Description
919	Pierce, Fort, Fla. Jan. 1839–July 1842
920	Pierre, Fort, S. Dak. July 1855–May 1857
921	Pike, Fort, La. Jan. 1828–Apr. 1846
922	Nov. 1848–May 1871
923	Pikesville Arsenal, Md. June 1833–Dec. 1868
924	Jan. 1869–May 1880
925	Pikit, Fort, Mindanao, P.I. Oct. 1906–Sept. 1913
926	Pilot Butte, Camp, Wyo. Sept. 1885–Feb. 1899
927	Pinar del Rio, Cuba Dec. 1898–Feb. 1909
928	Pine Bluff, Ark. Nov. 1863–Mar. 1869
929	Pine Camp, N.Y. May 1908–Sept. 1910
930	Pineville, La. Feb. 1875–May 1877
931	Pittsburgh, Pa. Apr. 1864–Nov. 1865 Draft Rendezvous July 1863–Sept. 1865 Pittsburgh Arsenal Oct. 1821–Dec. 1828
932	Placetas, Cuba Feb. 1899–Feb. 1909
933	Plaquemine, La. Nov. 1863–Nov. 1865
934	Platte Bridge, Nebr. July 1855–Apr. 1859
935	Plattsburg Barracks, N.Y. Feb. 1813–Dec. 1841
936	Jan. 1842–Dec. 1870
937	Jan. 1871–Dec. 1882
938	Jan. 1883–Dec. 1897
939	Jan. 1898–Dec. 1905
940	Jan. 1906–Dec. 1916
941	Pleasant, Fort, Fla. Nov. 1838–Oct. 1842
942	Poinsett, Fort, Fla. Oct. 1839–Feb. 1843
943	Point, Fort, Calif. Feb. 1861–Dec. 1865
944	Jan. 1866–June 1898
945	Point Bonita, Calif. July 1903–June 1909
946	Poland, Camp, Tenn. Aug.–Dec. 1898
947	Polk, Fort, Tex. Mar. 1846–Jan. 1850
948	Polloc, Mindanao, P.I. May 1900–Dec. 1912
949	Ponce, P.R. Aug. 1898–Mar. 1903

Roll	Description
950	Popham, Fort, Maine Nov. 1864–July 1866
951	Poplar River, Camp, Mont. Oct. 1880–Oct. 1893
952	Porter, Fort, N.Y. June 1864–Dec. 1873
953	Jan. 1874–Dec. 1884
954	Jan. 1885–Dec. 1897
955	Jan. 1898–Dec. 1907
956	Jan. 1908–Dec. 1916
957	Port Hudson, La. July 1863–May 1866
958	Preble, Fort, Maine June 1820–Apr. 1836
959	Oct. 1840–Dec. 1867
960	Jan. 1868–Dec. 1880
961	Jan. 1881–Dec. 1894
962	Jan. 1895–Dec. 1905
963	Jan. 1906–Dec. 1913
964	Presidio of Monterey, Calif. Jan. 1847–July 1895
965	Sept. 1902–Dec. 1909
966	Jan. 1910–Dec. 1916
967	Presidio of San Francisco, Calif. Mar. 1847–Dec. 1859
968	Jan. 1860–Dec. 1871
969	Jan. 1872–Dec. 1885
970	Jan. 1886–Dec. 1897
971	Jan. 1898–Dec. 1907
972	Jan. 1908–Dec. 1916 Camp Schofield Sept.–Oct. 1863 Camp Sumner July–Aug. 1861 Depot of Recruit Instructions July 1902–July 1903
973	Letterman General Hospital Dec. 1898–Dec. 1900
974	Jan. 1901–Dec. 1903
975	Jan. 1904–Dec. 1906
976	Jan. 1907–Dec. 1911
977	Jan. 1912–Dec. 1916
978	Provost Guard Sept. 1864–July 1865 Miscellaneous Returns Apr. 1898–Feb. 1915
979	Puerto Princesa, Palawan, P.I. June 1901–Dec. 1906
980	Jan. 1907–Oct. 1913
981	Puerto Príncipe, Cuba Nov. 1898–Mar. 1900
982	Pulaski, Fort, Ga. Mar. 1862–Dec. 1865

Roll	Description
983	Jan. 1866–Oct. 1873
984	Quarry Heights, C.Z. Apr. 1915–Dec. 1916
985	Quitman, Fort, Tex. Sept. 1858–Jan. 1877
986	Raleigh, N.C. Mar. 1866–May 1877
987	Rancho del Chino, Calif. Sept. 1850–Aug. 1852
988	Randall, Fort, S. Dak. June 1856–Dec. 1866
989	Jan. 1867–Dec. 1879
990	Jan. 1880–Nov. 1892
991	Randall, Camp, Wis. Mar. 1863–June 1866
992	Ransom, Fort, N. Dak. June 1867–Apr. 1872
993	Reading, Camp, Calif. May 1852–June 1867
994	Regan Barracks, Albay, P.I. Jan. 1904–Dec. 1916
995	Reina Regente, Mindanao, P.I. Oct. 1906–Sept. 1913
996	Remount, Camp, Md. July 1864–May 1865
997	Reno, Camp, Ariz. Oct. 1867–Feb. 1870
998	Reno, Fort, Okla. Aug. 1874–Dec. 1884
999	Jan. 1885–Dec. 1896
1000	Jan. 1897–Apr. 1908
1001	Reno, Camp, Wis. Apr. 1864–Nov. 1865
1002	Reno, Fort, Wyo. Sept. 1865–Aug. 1868
1003	Revere, Fort, Mass. Jan. 1901–Dec. 1906
1004	Jan. 1907–Dec. 1913
1005	Reynolds, Fort, Colo. June 1867–May 1872
1006	Rice, Fort, N. Dak. July 1864–Dec. 1870
1007	Jan. 1871–Nov. 1878
1008	Richardson, Fort, Tex. June 1866–May 1878
1009	Richmond, Va. Apr. 1865–June 1870
1010	Ridgely, Fort, Minn. Apr. 1853–Apr. 1867
1011	Riley, Fort, Kans. May 1853–Dec. 1860
1012	Jan. 1861–Dec. 1871
1013	Jan. 1872–Dec. 1884

Roll	Description
1014	Jan. 1885–Dec. 1894
1015	Jan. 1895–Dec. 1902
1016	Jan. 1903–Dec. 1909
1017	Jan. 1910–Dec. 1916
1018	Maneuver Camps
	Sept. 1902–Aug. 1910
	School for Bakers and Cooks
	Sept. 1908–Oct. 1916
	Mounted Service School
	July 1909–Jan. 1917
1019	Ringgold, Fort, Tex.
	Oct. 1848–Apr. 1861
1020	July 1865–Dec. 1874
1021	Jan. 1875–Dec. 1884
1022	Jan. 1885–Dec. 1894
1023	Jan. 1895–Dec. 1904
1024	Jan. 1905–Sept. 1915
1025	Rio Mimbres, N. Mex.
	Aug. 1863–Aug. 1866
1026	Ripley, Fort, Minn.
	Apr. 1849–Dec. 1865
1027	Jan. 1866–July 1877
1028	Robinson, Fort, Nebr.
	Apr. 1874–Dec. 1884
1029	Jan. 1885–Dec. 1894
1030	Jan. 1895–Dec. 1906
1031	Jan. 1907–Dec. 1916
1032	Rochester, N.Y.
	Dec. 1838–May 1841
1033	Rock Island Arsenal, Ill.
	Jan. 1869–Dec. 1878
1034	Jan. 1879–Dec. 1896
1035	Jan. 1897–Dec. 1908
1036	Jan. 1909–Dec. 1916
1037	Rock Island Barracks, Ill.
	Nov. 1863–Aug. 1865
1038	Rodman, Fort, Mass.
	June 1898–Dec. 1907
1039	Jan. 1908–Dec. 1916
1040	Rolla, Mo.
	Sept. 1861–July 1865
1041	Romblon, Romblon, P.I.
	Dec. 1899–Mar. 1902
1042	Rome, Ga.
	June 1833–July 1868
1043	Rosecrans, Fort, Calif.
	Aug. 1903–Apr. 1914
1044	Rosecrans, Fort, Tenn.
	Aug. 1863–June 1865
1045	Rouses Point, N.Y.
	Sept. 1838–Sept. 1862
1046	Rowell Barracks, Cuba
	Jan. 1899–Oct. 1903

Roll	Description
1047	Ruby, Camp, Nev.
	Sept. 1862–Sept. 1869
1048	Ruger, Fort, Hawaii
	Aug. 1909–Dec. 1913
1049	Russell, Fort, Fla.
	Mar. 1839–July 1842
1050	Russell, D.A., Fort, Wyo.
	Sept. 1867–Dec. 1875
1051	Jan. 1876–Dec. 1886
1052	Jan. 1887–Dec. 1894
1053	Jan. 1895–Dec. 1904
1054	Jan. 1905–Dec. 1912
1055	Jan. 1913–Nov. 1916
	Maneuver Camps
	July 1906–Aug. 1910
1056	Sabine, Camp, La.
	Apr. 1836–Aug. 1838
1057	Saginaw, Mich.
	July 1822–Apr. 1824
1058	Sagua Barracks and Sagua la Grande, Cuba
	Apr. 1899–Feb. 1909
1059	St. Albans, Vt.
	Mar.–Sept. 1865
1060	St. Augustine, Fla.
	June 1821–Dec. 1837
1061	Jan. 1838–Dec. 1865
1062	Jan. 1866–Dec. 1880
1063	Jan. 1881–Dec. 1891
1064	Jan. 1892–Apr. 1909
1065	St. Charles, Ark.
	Jan.–June 1865
1066	St. Louis, Mo.
	Dec. 1861–Oct. 1865
1067	Arsenal
	Nov. 1833–Dec. 1874
1068	Jan. 1875–Dec. 1889
1069	Jan. 1890–Mar. 1904
1070	Barracks
	Jan. 1871–June 1878
1071	St. Martinsville, La.
	May 1873–May 1877
1072	St. Michael, Fort, Alaska
	Sept. 1897–Dec. 1906
1073	Jan. 1907–Dec. 1916
1074	St. Philip, Fort, La.
	May 1821–Aug. 1866
1075	Nov. 1890–Dec. 1905
1076	Jan. 1906–June 1914
1077	Salem, Mo.
	Sept. 1862–May 1864
1078	Salisbury, N.C.
	Apr. 1866–Nov. 1867

Roll	Description
1079	Sam Houston, Fort, Tex. Sept. 1890–Dec. 1900
1080	Jan. 1901–Dec. 1907
1081	Jan. 1908–Dec. 1911
1082	Jan. 1912–Dec. 1916 Coast Artillery Detachment May 1916 School for Bakers and Cooks May–Sept. 1916
1083	San Antonio, Tex. Oct. 1845–Dec. 1872
1084	Jan. 1873–Dec. 1882
1085	Jan. 1883–Aug. 1890
1086	Arsenal Aug. 1870–Dec. 1880
1087	Jan. 1881–Dec. 1895
1088	Jan. 1896–Dec. 1907
1089	Jan. 1908–Dec. 1916
1090	Barracks July 1857–Mar. 1861
1091	San Carlos, Ariz. Oct. 1882–Dec. 1890
1092	Jan. 1891–June 1900
1093	Sancti Spíritus, Cuba Nov. 1898–June 1900
1094	Sanders, Fort, Wyo. Sept. 1866–May 1882
1095	San Diego, Tex. Apr. 1878–Apr. 1882
1096	San Diego Barracks, Calif. Apr. 1849–Dec. 1860
1097	Jan. 1861–June 1871
1098	June 1873–Dec. 1886
1099	Jan. 1887–Dec. 1896
1100	Jan. 1897–Sept. 1903 School of Aviation Aug. 1913–Dec. 1916
1101	Sandusky and Johnson's Island, Ohio Jan. 1862–June 1865
1102	Sandy Hook Proving Grounds, N.J. Jan. 1814–July 1866
1103	Nov. 1890–Dec. 1903
1104	Jan. 1904–Dec. 1916
1105	San Elizario, Tex. Nov. 1849–Aug. 1851
1106	San Felipe, Tex. Sept. 1876–Jan. 1881
1107	San Isidro, Nueva Ecija, P.I. July 1902–Aug. 1908
1108	San Jacinto, Tex. Feb. 1899–June 1914
1109	San Juan, P.R. Oct. 1898–Dec. 1905
1110	Jan. 1906–Dec. 1911
1111	Jan. 1912–Dec. 1916 General Hospital

Roll	Description
	Oct. 1898–Dec. 1899
1112	San Juan Island, Wash. July 1859–June 1874
1113	San Luis, Cuba Sept. 1898–Nov. 1901
1114	San Luis Rey, Calif. Mar. 1849–June 1852
1115	San Mateo, Rizal, P.I. Apr. 1900–May 1908
1116	San Pedro, Iloilo, P.I. Oct. 1910–Oct. 1917
1117	Santa Barbara, Calif. Jan.–Dec. 1864
1118	Santa Catalina Island, Calif. Jan.–Sept. 1864
1119	Santa Clara, Cuba Feb. 1899–Apr. 1908
1120	Santiago, Cuba June 1898–Jan. 1904
1121	Oct. 1908–Feb. 1909
1122	Santo Tomas, Batangas, P.I. May 1900–June 1907
1123	Sara, Panay, P.I. Mar. 1900–Jan. 1902
1124	Sauk Centre, Minn. July 1864–Nov. 1865
1125	Savannah, Ga. Jan. 1824–Dec. 1850
1126	June 1865–Dec. 1874
1127	Jan. 1875–Mar. 1899 General Hospital Mar.–July 1899
1128	Schofield, Camp, Va. Jan. 1866–Jan. 1870
1129	Schofield Barracks, Hawaii Jan. 1909–Dec. 1916
1130	Schuyler, Fort, N.Y. Feb. 1861–Dec. 1879
1131	Jan. 1880–Dec. 1890
1132	Jan. 1891–Dec. 1901
1133	Jan. 1902–Dec. 1907
1134	Jan. 1908–June 1914
1135	Schuylkill Arsenal, Pa. Oct. 1848–Aug. 1866
1136	Scott, Fort, Ga. Nov. 1817–Sept. 1821
1137	Scott, Fort, Kans. Jan. 1861–Oct. 1865
1138	Scott, Fort, Mo. May 1842–Apr. 1853
1139	Scott, Martin, Fort, Tex. May 1849–Nov. 1853
1140	Screven, Fort, Ga. Mar. 1898–Dec. 1907
1141	Jan. 1908–Dec. 1916

Roll	Description
1142	Sea Girt, N.J. May 1903–Sept. 1908
1143	Sedalia, Mo. Jan. 1862–May 1865
1144	Sedgwick, Fort, Colo. Nov. 1864–May 1871
1145	Selden, Fort, N. Mex. May 1865–Dec. 1871
1146	Jan. 1872–Dec. 1882
1147	Jan. 1883–Jan. 1891
1148	Selma, Ala. July 1866–Mar. 1869
1149	Sengal, Basilan, P.I. June 1910–Aug. 1913
1150	Sequoia National Park, Calif. May 1891–Aug. 1913
1151	Severn, Fort, Md. Jan. 1815–Aug. 1845
1152	Sewall, Fort, Mass. Apr. 1816–Aug. 1898
1153	Seward, Fort, N. Dak. June 1872–Sept. 1877
1154	Shafter, Fort, Hawaii July 1907–Dec. 1916; Department Hospital Nov. 1912–July 1913; School for Bakers and Cooks Oct. 1915–Nov. 1916
1155	Shannon, Fort, Fla. Feb. 1839–July 1843
1156	Shaw, Fort, Mont. July 1867–Dec. 1875
1157	Jan. 1876–Dec. 1882
1158	Jan. 1883–Sept. 1891
1159	Sheridan, Fort, Ill. Nov. 1887–Dec. 1896
1160	Jan. 1897–Dec. 1904
1161	Jan. 1905–Dec. 1909
1162	Jan. 1910–Nov. 1916
1163	Sheridan, Camp, Nebr. Apr. 1874–Apr. 1881
1164	Sheridan Point, Va. Mar. 1898–Mar. 1899
1165	Sherman, Fort, Idaho Apr. 1878–Dec. 1888
1166	Jan. 1889–July 1900
1167	Ship Island, Miss. Jan. 1862–Apr. 1870
1168	Shipp, Camp, Ala. Sept. 1898–Jan. 1899
1169	Shreveport, La. June 1865–Oct. 1876
1170	Siasi, Siasi, P.I. Sept. 1899–Sept. 1913
1171	Sidney Barracks, Nebr. Oct. 1870–Dec. 1881
1172	Jan. 1882–June 1894
1173	Sill, Fort, Okla. Mar. 1869–Dec. 1875
1174	Jan. 1876–Dec. 1887
1175	Jan. 1888–Dec. 1900
1176	Jan. 1901–Dec. 1908
1177	Jan. 1909–Jan. 1917
1178	Simcoe, Fort, Wash. Aug. 1856–May 1859
1179	Sisseton, Fort, S. Dak. June 1864–Dec. 1872
1180	Jan. 1873–Dec. 1880
1181	Jan. 1881–June 1889
1182	Sitka, Alaska Sept. 1867–May 1877
1183	Skagway, Alaska Feb. 1898–Sept. 1904
1184	Slocum, Fort, N.Y. July 1896–Dec. 1905
1185	Jan. 1906–Dec. 1916
1186	Smallwood, Fort, Md. Jan. 1905–June 1914
1187	Smith, Fort, Ark. Aug. 1820–Dec. 1846
1188	Jan. 1847–Dec. 1865
1189	Jan. 1866–Aug. 1871
1190	Smith, C.F., Fort, Mont. Aug. 1866–July 1868
1191	Smith, C.F., Camp, Oreg. July 1866–Oct. 1869
1192	Snake River, Wyo. Jan. 1880–July 1883
1193	Snelling, Fort, Minn. Aug. 1822–Dec. 1836
1194	Jan. 1837–Dec. 1845
1195	Jan. 1846–May 1858
1196	Nov. 1861–Dec. 1873
1197	Jan. 1874–Dec. 1884
1198	Jan. 1885–Dec. 1896
1199	Jan. 1897–Dec. 1906
1200	Jan. 1907–Dec. 1916
1201	Draft Rendezvous Feb. 1864–Mar. 1866; Detachment of Hospital Corps June 1915–Dec. 1916; Ordnance Depot Nov. 1889–Oct. 1894
1202	Socorro, N. Mex. Nov. 1849–Aug. 1851
1203	Soledad, Cuba Nov. 1906–Jan. 1909
1204	Sonoma, Calif. Apr. 1847–Dec. 1851
1205	Sorsogon, P.I. Apr. 1900–July 1904

Roll	Description
1206	Southeastern Kansas, Post of Dec. 1869–Mar. 1873
1207	Spartanburg, S.C. Mar. 1871–Mar. 1877
1208	Spokane, Fort, Wash. Oct. 1880–Dec. 1890
1209	Jan. 1891–June 1899
1210	Springfield Armory, Mass. Apr. 1876–Dec. 1888
1211	Jan. 1889–Dec. 1901
1212	Jan. 1902–Dec. 1916
1213	Stambaugh, Camp, Wyo. Sept. 1870–May 1878
1214	Standish, Fort, Mass. Mar. 1902–Dec. 1913
1215	Stansbury, Fort, Fla. Mar. 1839–Mar. 1843
1216	Stanton, Fort, N. Mex. May 1855–Dec. 1867
1217	Jan. 1868–Dec. 1877
1218	Jan. 1878–Dec. 1887
1219	Jan. 1888–July 1896
1220	Stark, Fort, N.H. Nov. 1905–May 1914
1221	Steilacoom, Wash. Oct. 1849–Dec. 1859
1222	Jan. 1860–Mar. 1868
1223	Stevens, Fort, Oreg. Apr. 1865–Dec. 1874
1224	Jan. 1875–Dec. 1900
1225	Jan. 1901–Dec. 1906
1226	Jan. 1907–Dec. 1913
1227	Stevenson, Fort, N. Dak. July 1867–Dec. 1875
1228	Jan. 1876–Aug. 1883
1229	Stockton, Fort, Tex. Apr. 1859–Dec. 1874
1230	Jan. 1875–June 1886
1231	Stotsenburg, Camp, Pampanga, P.I. Aug. 1899–Dec. 1908
1232	Jan. 1909–Dec. 1916
1233	Strong, Fort, Mass. Mar. 1898–Dec. 1906
1234	Jan. 1907–Dec. 1914
1235	Sullivan, Fort, Maine June 1821–Dec. 1849
1236	Jan. 1850–Oct. 1873
1237	Sullivans Island, S.C. Oct. 1897–Jan. 1902
1238	Sully, Fort, S. Dak. June 1864–Dec. 1874
1239	Jan. 1875–Dec. 1884
1240	Jan. 1885–Oct. 1894
1241	Sumner, Fort, N. Mex. Dec. 1862–June 1869
1242	Sumter, Fort, S.C. Dec. 1860–June 1914

Roll	Description
1243	Supply, Fort, Okla. Nov. 1868–Dec. 1879
1244	Jan. 1880–Dec. 1894
1245	Surigao, Mindanao, P.I. Apr. 1900–Feb. 1904
1246	Taal, Batangas, P.I. May 1900–June 1903
1247	Tabaco, Albay, P.I. Apr. 1900–Dec. 1904
1248	Tagabiran, Samar, P.I. Apr. 1905–Oct. 1911
1249	Tallahassee, Fla. May 1865–June 1871
1250	Tampa, Fla. Apr.–Aug. 1898
1251	Tampanan, Mindanao, P.I. May 1910–Sept. 1913
1252	Tanauan, Leyte, P.I. May 1900–Mar. 1910
1253	Tanay, Rizal, P.I. June 1903–Feb. 1906
1254	Taos, N. Mex. Sept. 1848–Mar. 1861
1255	Taylor, Fort, Fla. Jan. 1861–Dec. 1863
1256	Taylor, Cantonment, La. Aug. 1821–May 1824
1257	Tejon, Fort, Calif. Aug. 1854–Sept. 1864
1258	Terrebonne, La. July 1864–Nov. 1865
1259	Terrett, Fort, Tex. Feb. 1852–Jan. 1854
1260	Terry, Fort, N.Y. May 1898–Dec. 1906
1261	Jan. 1907–Mar. 1915
1262	Ter-waw, Fort, Calif. Oct. 1857–May 1862
1263	Texas City, Tex. Jan. 1913–Sept. 1915
1264	Thibodaux, La. Oct. 1864–Nov. 1865
1265	Thomas, Camp, Ariz. Aug. 1876–Jan. 1891
1266	Thomas, Fort, Ky. Aug. 1890–Dec. 1900
1267	Jan. 1901–Dec. 1908
1268	Jan. 1909–Dec. 1916 General Hospital May 1898–Feb. 1899
1269	Thomas, Camp, Ohio Dec. 1861–Nov. 1865
1270	Thomas, George H., Camp, Ga. Apr. 1898–Dec. 1904
1271	Thorn, Fort, N. Mex. Jan. 1854–Feb. 1859
1272	Thornburgh, Fort, Utah Sept. 1881–Oct. 1883

Roll	Description
1273	Three Forks Owyhee, Camp, Idaho
	Apr. 1867–June 1871
1274	Tongass, Fort, Alaska
	Apr. 1868–Oct. 1870
1275	Torrey Barracks, Mindanao, P.I.
	Sept. 1900–Dec. 1907
1276	Jan. 1908–Jan. 1914
1277	Totten, Fort, N.Y.
	Apr. 1864–Dec. 1875
1278	Jan. 1876–Dec. 1887
1279	Jan. 1888–Dec. 1901
1280	Jan. 1902–Dec. 1907
1281	Jan. 1908–July 1914
1282	Totten, Fort, N. Dak.
	July 1867–Dec. 1877
1283	Jan. 1878–Dec. 1890
1284	Townsend, Fort, Wash.
	Oct. 1856–Dec. 1883
1285	Jan. 1884–Mar. 1895
1286	Towson, Fort, Okla.
	June 1824–Dec. 1840
1287	Jan. 1841–May 1854
1288	Travis, Fort, Tex.
	Aug. 1911–June 1914
1289	Treadwell, Camp, Pampanga, P.I.
	Sept. 1909–Aug. 1914
1290	Trenton, N.J.
	July 1863–Dec. 1865
	Draft Rendezvous
1291	Trumbull, Fort, Conn.
	Jan. 1816–Sept. 1837
1292	June 1842–Dec. 1866
1293	Jan. 1867–Dec. 1876
1294	Jan. 1877–Dec. 1889
1295	Jan. 1890–Dec. 1900
1296	Jan. 1901–Sept. 1910
1297	Tubac, Ariz.
	June 1864–Feb. 1868
1298	Tucson, Ariz.
	May 1862–Sept. 1866
1299	Tucuran, Mindanao, P.I.
	Oct. 1900–Dec. 1912
1300	Tulerosa, Fort, N. Mex.
	May 1872–Oct. 1874
1301	Tuscaloosa, Ala.
	May 1869–Dec. 1870
1302	Tyler, Tex.
	Mar. 1867–Apr. 1870
1303	Umpqua, Fort, Oreg.
	July 1856–July 1862
1304	Union, Camp, Calif.
	Sept. 1861–May 1866
1305	Union, Fort, N. Mex.
	July 1851–Dec. 1865

Roll	Description
1306	Jan. 1866–Dec. 1874
1307	Jan. 1875–Dec. 1883
1308	Jan. 1884–Apr. 1891
1309	Arsenal
	Jan. 1863–Dec. 1876
1310	Jan. 1877–Feb. 1883
1311	Union, W. Va.
	Apr. 1867–Oct. 1869
1312	Union City, Tenn.
	Jan. 1863–June 1869
1313	Unionville, S.C.
	Apr. 1866–Oct. 1874
1314	Valdez, Alaska
	Sept. 1905–Dec. 1916
1315	Vancouver Barracks, Wash.
	Sept. 1849–Dec. 1859
1316	Jan. 1860–Dec. 1869
1317	Jan. 1870–Dec. 1881
1318	Jan. 1882–Dec. 1892
1319	Jan. 1893–Dec. 1901
1320	Jan. 1902–Dec. 1907
1321	Jan. 1908–Dec. 1916
1322	Vancouver Arsenal
	Jan 1859–Dec. 1870
1323	Jan. 1871–Dec. 1881
1324	Vancouver Barracks
	Jan. 1882–Sept. 1894
	Ordnance Depot
1325	Verde, Fort, Ariz.
	Jan. 1866–July 1881
1326	Apr. 1882–Apr. 1891
1327	Verde, Camp, Tex.
	July 1856–Mar. 1869
1328	Vicars, Camp, Mindanao, P.I.
	June 1902–Dec. 1907
1329	Jan. 1908–July 1913
1330	Vicksburg, Miss.
	July 1863–Oct. 1876
1331	Wacahoota, Fort, Fla.
	June 1840–Aug. 1842
1332	Wacasassa, Fort, Fla.
	Mar. 1839–Jan. 1843
1333	Waco, Tex.
	Aug. 1866–Sept. 1870
1334	Wadsworth, Fort, N.Y.
	Jan. 1814–Dec. 1872
1335	Jan. 1873–Dec. 1887
1336	Jan. 1888–Dec. 1897
1337	Jan. 1898–Dec. 1905
1338	Jan. 1906–Dec. 1913
1339	Wallace, Fort, Kans.
	Mar. 1866–Dec. 1873

Roll	Description
1340	Jan. 1874–May 1882
1341	Wallace, Camp, Luzon, P.I.
	Jan. 1903–Dec. 1907
1342	Jan. 1908–May 1912
1343	Walla Walla, Fort, Wash.
	Aug. 1856–May 1867
1344	Aug. 1873–Dec. 1885
1345	Jan. 1886–Dec. 1895
1346	Jan. 1896–Dec. 1904
1347	Jan. 1905–Sept. 1910
1348	Wallen, Camp, Ariz.
	May 1866–Oct. 1869
1349	Ward, Fort, Wash.
	Nov. 1903–Dec. 1907
1350	Jan. 1908–Dec. 1913
1351	Ward Cheney, Camp, Cavite, P.I.
	May 1907–Sept. 1914
1352	Warner, Camp, Oreg.
	Aug. 1865–Sept. 1874
1353	Warren, Fort, Mass.
	July 1816–Dec. 1872
1354	Jan. 1873–Dec. 1884
1355	Jan. 1885–Dec. 1895
1356	Jan. 1896–Dec. 1906
1357	Jan. 1907–Dec. 1913
1358	Warrensburg, Mo.
	July 1862–July 1865
1359	Warrenton, Ga.
	May 1869–Jan. 1871
1360	Warsaw, Ky.
	Oct. 1866–July 1868
1361	Warwick, Camp, and Warwick Barracks, Cebu, P.I.
	Mar. 1904–Dec. 1908
1362	Jan. 1909–Dec. 1916
1363	Washakie, Fort, Wyo.
	Aug. 1870–Dec. 1880
1364	Jan. 1881–Dec. 1892
1365	Jan. 1893–Dec. 1903
1366	Jan. 1904–Mar. 1909
1367	Washington, Ark.
	Nov. 1866–Mar. 1869
	Washington, D.C.
1368	Army Medical School
	July 1909–Dec. 1916
1369	Army War College
	Sept. 1907–Dec. 1916
1370	Arsenal
	June 1833–Dec. 1871
1371	Jan. 1872–May 1881
1372	Barracks
	Feb. 1881–Dec. 1891
1373	Jan. 1892–Dec. 1902
1374	Jan. 1903–Dec. 1907

Roll	Description
1375	Jan. 1908–Dec. 1916
1376	School for Bakers and Cooks
	Dec. 1908–Aug. 1916
	Barracks Engineer School
	Nov. 1910–Dec. 1916
	Engineer School
	July 1909–Dec. 1916
	Detachment
1377	Garrison
	Feb. 1861–June 1898
	Camp Baker
	Mar. and Apr. 1864
	Camp Barry
	Apr. 1862–June 1865
	Camp Buford
	Aug. and Sept. 1863
	Camp Cliffburne
	June 1865
1378	Camp Duncan
	Sept. 1861
	Camp East of the Capitol
	Oct. 1861–Mar. 1863
	Fort Greble
	Sept. and Oct. 1867
	Lincoln Barracks
	Nov. 1867–Mar. 1869
	Camp Marshall
	Sept.–Dec. 1863
	Mason's Island
	Nov. 1863–Mar. 1864
	Reynolds Barracks
	May 1866–June 1868
	Russell Barracks
	Apr. 1866–Oct. 1868
	Sedgwick Barracks
	May 1866–June 1870
	Todd Barracks
	May–Oct. 1866
1379	Walter Reed General Hospital
	Jan. 1900–Dec. 1908
1380	Jan. 1909–Dec. 1916
1381	Washington, La.
	June–Nov. 1865
1382	Washington, Fort, Md.
	Nov. 1814–Oct. 1839
1383	Oct. 1848–Dec. 1868
1384	Jan. 1869–Dec. 1900
1385	Jan. 1901–Dec. 1906
1386	Jan. 1907–Dec. 1913
1387	Washita, Fort, Okla.
	June 1834–Apr. 1861
1388	Watertown Arsenal, Mass.
	June 1833–Dec. 1871
1389	Jan. 1872–Dec. 1883
1390	Jan. 1884–Dec. 1896
1391	Jan. 1897–Dec. 1906

Roll	Description
1392	Jan. 1907–Dec. 1916
1393	Watervliet Arsenal, N.Y.
	Jan. 1822–Dec. 1868
1394	Jan. 1869–Dec. 1878
1395	Jan. 1879–Dec. 1895
1396	Jan. 1896–Dec. 1906
1397	Jan. 1907–Dec. 1916
1398	Watson, Camp, Oreg.
	June 1863–Apr. 1869
1399	Wayne, Fort, Ill.
	Oct. 1838–Apr. 1842
1400	Wayne, Fort, Ind.
	Mar. 1813–Mar. 1819
1401	Wayne, Fort, Mich.
	Dec. 1861–Dec. 1873
1402	Jan. 1874–Dec. 1885
1403	Jan. 1886–Dec. 1897
1404	Jan. 1898–Dec. 1907
1405	Jan. 1908–Dec. 1916
1406	Waynesville, Mo.
	Sept. 1862–July 1865
1407	Webster, Fort, N. Mex.
	Jan. 1852–Dec. 1860
1408	Weld, Camp, Colo.
	Dec. 1862–June 1864
1409	Weller, Fort, Calif.
	Jan.–Sept. 1859
1410	West, Fort, N. Mex.
	Feb. 1863–Jan. 1864
	West Point, N.Y.
1411	U.S. Military Academy
	Jan. 1819–Dec. 1828
1412	Jan. 1829–Dec. 1838
1413	Jan. 1839–Dec. 1852
1414	Jan. 1853–Dec. 1865
1415	Jan. 1866–Dec. 1872
1416	Jan. 1873–Dec. 1880
1417	Jan. 1881–Dec. 1890
1418	Jan. 1891–Dec. 1900
1419	Jan. 1901–Dec. 1907
1420	Jan. 1908–Dec. 1916
1421	Wetherill, Fort, R.I.
	Feb. 1901–Dec. 1906
1422	Jan. 1907–Dec. 1913
1423	Wheeling, W. Va.
	Nov. 1862–June 1865
1424	Whetstone Indian Agency, S. Dak.
	June 1870–Apr. 1872
1425	Whipple Barracks, Ariz.
	Dec. 1863–Dec. 1874
1426	Jan. 1875–Dec. 1886
1427	Jan. 1887–Dec. 1897

Roll	Description
1428	Jan. 1898–Dec. 1907
1429	Jan. 1908–Aug. 1913
1430	White, Fort, Fla.
	Mar. 1838–May 1842
1431	White River, Colo.
	Dec. 1879–Aug. 1883
1432	Whitman, Fort, Wash.
	May 1911–Dec. 1913
1433	Wikoff, Camp, N.Y.
	Aug.–Oct. 1898
1434	Wilhelm, Camp, Tayabas, P.I.
	Apr. 1901–Dec. 1906
1435	Jan. 1907–June 1912
1436	Wilkins, Fort, Mich.
	May 1844–Aug. 1870
1437	William H. Seward, Fort, Alaska
	Mar. 1898–Dec. 1908
1438	Jan. 1909–Dec. 1916
1439	William Penn, Camp, Pa.
	Oct. 1863–Aug. 1865
1440	Williams, Fort, Maine
	Nov. 1898–Dec. 1906
1441	Jan. 1907–Dec. 1913
1442	Willow Grove, Camp, Ariz.
	Aug. 1867–Sept. 1869
1443	Wilmington, Del.
	May 1863–Aug. 1864
1444	Wilimington, N.C.
	Aug. 1865–July 1868
1445	Winchester, Va.
	May 1866–Jan. 1870
1446	Winfield Scott, Fort, Calif.
	Dec. 1882–Dec. 1913
1447	Winfield Scott, Camp, Nev.
	Dec. 1866–Feb. 1871
1448	Wingate, Fort, N. Mex.
	Oct. 1862–Dec. 1871
1449	Jan. 1872–Dec. 1882
1450	Jan. 1883–Dec. 1893
1451	Jan. 1894–Dec. 1902
1452	Jan. 1903–Dec. 1907
1453	Jan. 1908–Oct. 1914
1454	Winnebago, Fort, Wis.
	Oct. 1828–Aug. 1845
1455	Wint, Fort, Grande Island, P.I.
	Sept. 1907–Aug. 1916
1456	Wolcott, Fort, R.I.
	Jan. 1816–Apr. 1837
1457	Wood, Fort, N.Y.
	June 1837–Dec. 1870
1458	Jan. 1871–Dec. 1888
1459	Jan. 1889–Dec. 1902

Roll	Description
1460	Jan. 1903–Dec. 1908
1461	Jan. 1909–Dec. 1916
1462	Worden, Fort, Wash.
	May 1902–Dec. 1906
1463	Jan. 1907–Dec. 1913
1464	World's Columbian Exposition, Chicago, Ill.,
	War Department Exhibit
	Jan. 1893–Feb. 1894
1465	Worth, Fort, Tex.
	June 1849–Aug. 1853
1466	Wrangell, Fort, Alaska
	May 1868–May 1900
1467	Wright, Camp, in Round Valley, Calif.
	Dec. 1862–Dec. 1869
1468	Jan. 1870–Nov. 1887
1469	Wright, Camp, near Warner's Ranch, Calif.
	Oct. 1861–Apr. 1862
1470	Wright, George, Fort, Wash.
	July 1899–Dec. 1907
1471	Jan. 1908–Dec. 1916
1472	Wright, H.G., Fort, N.Y.
	Feb. 1901–Dec. 1907
1473	Jan. 1908–Dec. 1913
1474	Yam Hill, Fort, Oreg.
	July 1856–June 1866
1475	Yates, Camp, Ill.
	Sept. 1863–Aug. 1865
1476	Yates, Fort, N. Dak.
	June 1875–Dec. 1884
1477	Jan. 1885–Dec. 1893
1478	Jan. 1894–Sept. 1903
1479	Yellowstone, Fort, Wyo.
	Aug. 1886–Dec. 1897
1480	Jan. 1898–Dec. 1907
1481	Jan. 1908–Oct. 1916
1482	Yerba Buena Island, Calif.
	Mar. 1868–July 1878
1483	Yorktown, Va.
	May 1862–Oct. 1881
1484	Yorkville, S.C.
	Mar. 1871–Dec. 1876
1485	Yosemite National Park, Calif.
	May 1891–Nov. 1903
1486	May 1904–Sept. 1913
1487	Yuma, Ariz.
	June 1885–July 1916
1488	Yuma, Fort, Calif.
	Oct. 1850–Dec. 1865
1489	Jan. 1866–Dec. 1876
1490	Jan. 1877–May 1885
1491	Zarah, Fort, Kans.
	Nov. 1864–Nov. 1869
1492	Abbeville, S.C.
	Oct. 1868
	Abo Pass, Camp near, N. Mex.
	Dec. 1861–Jan. 1862
	Abra de Ilog, Mindoro, P.I.
	Mar. 1902
	Abulug, Cagayan, P.I.
	Jan.–Apr. 1903
	Adams, Fla.
	Jan. and Feb. 1827

Roll	Description
	Adams, Fort, Fla.
	Dec. 1838
	Alafia, Camp, Fla.
	Aug. 1849–Oct. 1850
	Alaminos, Laguna, P.I.
	Mar. and Apr. 1905
	Alamo Hueco, Camp, N. Mex.
	Feb. and Mar. 1911
	Albany, N.Y.
	Feb. 1864–Mar. 1866
	Albuera, Leyte, P.I.
	Sept. 1907–Jan. 1908
	Alburgh Springs, Vt.
	Feb. 1839
	Alderson, Camp near, Ind. Terr.
	May 1894
	Alert, Camp, Calif.
	Oct. 1861–May 1862
	Alex Chambers, Camp, Mont.
	Aug. 1889
	Alfonso XIII, Paragua, P.I.
	Jan. 1902–Mar. 1903
	Alger, Camp, Ga.
	Sept. 1897
	Alkali, Nebr.
	Oct. 1864–Dec. 1865
	Allendale, S.C.
	Oct. 1876
	Alliance, Ohio
	June and July 1898
	Alva, Camp, Luzon, P.I.
	July–Sept. 1899
	Alvord, Camp, Oreg.
	Sept. 1865–May 1866
	Ambulong, Batangas, P.I.
	June 1903–Dec. 1904
	Amite, La.
	Feb. 1868–Feb. 1869
	Anderson's Grove, Dak. Terr.
	July 1867
	Andrews, Camp, Calif.
	May 1884
	Andrews, Fort, Fla.
	Mar. 1839–May 1840
1493	Ann, Fort, Fla.
	Dec. 1837–Mar. 1838
	Annie, Camp, Mo.
	Mar. 1863
	Annutteeliga, Fla.
	Nov. 1840–Apr. 1841
	Antipolo, Rizal, P.I.
	July–Oct. 1902
	Antique, Camp, Albay, P.I.
	June and July 1905
	Apalachicola, Fla.
	June 1865
	Apalit, Pampanga, P.I.
	June 1900
	Arayat, Pampanga, P.I.
	May 1900–Aug. 1903
	Arbuckle, Fort, Fla.
	Jan.–Apr. 1850
	Arbuckle, Camp, Ind. Terr.
	Apr. 1833–Oct. 1834

Roll	Description
	Arecibo, P.R.
	Dec. 1898–Mar. 1900
	Argao, Cebu, P.I.
	July 1902–Jan. 1903
	Armistead, Fort, Fla.
	Nov. 1840–Apr. 1841
	Armstrong, Fort, Fla.
	Jan. 1837
	Armstrong, Fort, Hawaii
	July–Dec. 1913
	Arroyo, P.R.
	Aug. 1898
	Artemisa, Cuba
	Nov. 1906–Apr. 1907
	Astoria, Oreg.
	May 1850–Sept. 1851
	Athens, Ga.
	Apr.–Aug. 1867
	Athens, Ohio
	Aug. 1904
	Atkinson, Fort, Fla.
	Aug.–Oct. 1825
	Jan.–June 1839
	Atkinson, Camp, La.
	June 1830–Dec. 1831
	Auburn, N.Y.
	Feb. and Mar. 1864
	Branch Depot for Drafted Men
	Augusta, Ga.
	Nov. 1911
	Signal Corps
	Aviation School
	Auscila [Aucilla], Fort, Fla.
	June 1839–Aug. 1840
	Austin Arsenal, Tex.
	Oct. 1845–Feb. 1846
	Avery, Camp, Samar, P.I.
	Mar.–Aug. 1905
1494	Bacon, Sorsogon, P.I.
	Dec. 1901–Sept. 1902
	Bacoor, Cavite, P.I.
	Apr.–Sept. 1900
	Badoc, Ilocos Norte, P.I.
	Dec. 1900
	Baganga, Mindanao, P.I.
	Jan. 1900–Oct. 1910
	Bagdad, Ky.
	Apr.–Aug. 1871
	Baker, Camp, Fla.
	Jan. 1840
	Balangiga, Samar, P.I.
	Sept.–Nov. 1907
	Baleman [Bateman], Camp, Kans.
	Feb. and Mar. 1858
	Baler, Principe, P.I.
	July–Nov. 1902
	Bamban, Tarlac, P.I.
	Aug. 1902–Apr. 1903
	Banan, Batangas, P.I.
	Apr. 1900–Apr. 1904
	Banate, Panay, P.I.
	Jan. and Feb. 1900
	Banes, Cuba
	May–Nov. 1899
	Bankhead, Fort, Fla.
	Apr. 1838
	Banning, Camp, Calif.
	Jan. and Feb. 1859
	Bantayan, Camp, Albay, P.I.
	Feb.–May 1905
	Barbour, Cantonment, Missouri River

Roll	Description
	Oct. 1825–Apr. 1826
	Barbour, Fort, Fla.
	May 1841–May 1842
	Barceloneta, P.R.
	Nov. 1898–Jan. 1899
	Bardstown, Ky.
	Mar. 1862
	Barker, Fort, Fla.
	Feb.–Aug. 1840
	Barnard, Fort, Va.
	Dec. 1864–Aug. 1865
	Barnard, Richardson, and Scott, Forts, Va.
	Sept.–Dec. 1862
	Barnett, Ga.
	Jan. 1870–Jan. 1871
	Barnwell, S.C.
	Mar. 1866; Sept. 1874
	Barrett, Fort, Ariz.
	May and June 1862
	Basey, Samar, P.I.
	Sept. 1901–Jan. 1903
	Bataan Survey Detachment, Balanga, P.I.
	Dec. 1915–Feb. 1916
	Batangas, P.I.
	Mar.–June 1903
	Batangas Province, Luzon, P.I.
	May and June 1900
	Baton Rouge, La.
	Feb.–Nov. 1826
	Battery Barracks, N.Y.
	June 1865–Mar. 1866
	Bauan, Batangas, P.I.
	May and June 1900
	Baxter Barracks, Vt.
	Sept. 1865
1495	Bay, Laguna, P.i.
	Sept. 1904–Feb. 1905
	Bayambang, Pangasinan, P.I.
	July–Dec. 1902
	Bayamon, P.R.
	Nov. 1898–Aug. 1899
	Baybay, Leyte, P.I.
	May and June 1901; July–Dec. 1902
	Bay of St. Louis, Mo.
	Aug. 1824–Oct. 1827
	Bayou Boeuf, La.
	May 1865
	Bayou Sara, La.
	Mar.–Oct. 1876
	Bayuyungan, Batangas, P.I.
	Sept. 1904–Feb. 1905
	Beach Street Barracks, Mass.
	Sept.–Nov. 1865
	Beardsley, Camp, Albay, P.I.
	Jan. 1905
	Beau [Bean], Camp, Samar, P.I.
	Mar. and Apr. 1907
	Beaufort, N.C.
	May 1832–Nov. 1834
	Beaumont, Tex.
	July 1865
	Beauvais Station, Nebr.
	Oct. 1864–May 1865
	Beaver Creek, Camp on, Mont.
	Sept. 1890
	Beaver Creek, Tex.
	May 1880
	Beecher, Camp, Kans.
	Nov. 1868–May 1869
	Bejucal, Cuba

Roll	Description
	Nov. 1906–May 1907
	Belfast Batteries, Maine
	Mar. and Apr. 1865
	Belle Fontaine, Mo.
	July 1821–June 1826
	Bellevue Rifle Range, Nebr.
	July 1887–Aug. 1892
	Belton, Tex.
	July 1868–Feb. 1869
	Berry, Camp, Maine
	Sept. 1863–Mar. 1864
	Berry, Fort, Va.
	Nov. 1864–Aug. 1865
	Bethel, Tenn.
	Nov. and Dec. 1862
	Bettens, Camp, Wyo.
	June–Oct. 1892
	Betulan [Butulan], Mindanao, P.I.
	June and July 1911
	Beverly, Va.
	Jan. 1863
	Biddle, Camp, Pa.
	Aug.–Dec. 1864
	Bienvenue, Fort, Fla.
	Apr. and May 1850
	Big Black, Miss.
	June 1867
	Big Blue, Camp on, Kans.
	Aug. 1857
	Big Sioux River, Camp on the, Mont.
	Apr.–July 1856
	Big Stone Lake, Camp on, Minn.
	June 1860; May 1867
	Big Witchita [Wichita], Camp on, Tex.
	Feb. 1855
1496	Binang, Laguna, P.I.
	Aug. 1905
	Binangonan de Lampon, Tayabas, P.I.
	Oct. 1904–May 1905
	Binatoc [Binatac], Samar, P.I.
	Aug. 1903
	Birds Point, Mo.
	Feb. 1862
	Birney, Camp, Md.
	Mar. 1864
	Black, Camp, N.Y.
	May–Sept. 1898
	Blackville, S.C.
	Aug.–Oct. 1876
	Bladensburg, Camp near, Md.
	Sept. 1861
	Blake, Camp, N. Mex.
	Aug. 1856
	Blake, Camp, Tex.
	Apr.–Sept. 1854
	Blakely, Camp, Ala.
	Jan.–June 1820
	Bloomfield, Mo.
	Mar.–July 1863
	Blue Springs, Mo.
	Apr. and May 1863
	Blunt, Fort, Cherokee Nation
	June–Nov. 1863
	Bogo, Cebu, P.I.
	Dec. 1901–Jan. 1903
	Bois d'Arc Creek, Camp on, I.T.
	Nov. 1886
	Bojelebung
	Nov. 1909–Mar. 1911
	[Bojelbung],
	Basilan, P.I.

Roll	Description
	Bolivar, Tenn.
	Oct. 1862–Apr. 1863
	Bolivar Heights, W. Va.
	July 1864
	Bonnet Carré, La.
	Dec. 1862–May 1865
	Boonville, Mo.
	Mar. 1862–June 1865
	Boston, Camp, Mindanao, P.I.
	Sept. 1910–Feb. 1911
	Boston, Tex.
	Feb.–June 1869
	Botany Bay Island, S.C.
	May 1863
1497	Bowie Station, Ariz.
	Jan.–June 1886
	Bowyer, Fort, Ala.
	July 1821
	Boyd, Camp, N. Mex.
	Jan.–July 1886
	Boynton Prairie, Camp at, Calif.
	Mar.–July 1864
	Braden, Fort, Fla.
	Jan. 1840–May 1842
	Bradford, Camp, Md.
	July 1864
	Brady, Camp, Mex.
	Oct. 1846
	Brattleboro Barracks, Vt.
	Aug. 1863–Mar. 1864
	Brattleboro, Vt.
	July 1863–June 1864
	Draft Rendezvous
	Brazos Agency, Camp at, Tex.
	Mar.–June 1859
	Brennan, Camp, Fla.
	Jan. 1842
	Brest, Mich.
	May 1908
	Bristol, Va.
	Jan.–May 1866
	Brooke, Camp, Nebr.
	Sept. 1888
	Brooke, Frank, Fort, Fla.
	Jan. 1839–May 1840
	Brookhaven, Miss.
	May 1867–Nov. 1868
	Brooklyn, N.Y.
	Nov. 1814
	Brown, Camp, Santa Rosa Island, Fla.
	July–Nov. 1861
	Brown, Camp, South of St. Mary's River, Fla.
	Mar.–Aug. 1842
	Brown, Fort, Fla.
	Feb.–Sept. 1840
	Brunswick, Ga.
	Apr.–Sept. 1870
	Bryan, Tex.
	Oct. 1868–Sept. 1869
	Buchanan, Camp, Tex.
	Nov. 1855
	Buffalo, Tex.
	Aug. 1849
	Buffalo Bayou, Tex.
	Oct. 1914
	Buffalo Springs, Colo.
	Apr. 1865
	Buffalo Springs, Tex.
	Apr.–Dec. 1867
	Bugason, Panay, P.I.
	Aug. 1900–Apr. 1901

Roll	Description
1498	Bulacan, Luzon, P.I.
	May and June 1900
	Bulalacao, Mindoro, P.I.
	Apr.–June 1908
	Bulan, Sorsogon, P.I.
	Apr. 1900–Sept. 1902
	Bulao, Samar, P.I.
	Oct. 1905–Apr. 1908
	Bullitt's Bayou, La.
	May 1865
	Buranen [Burauen], Leyte, P.I.
	July 1906–July 1907
	Burbank, Camp, Tex.
	Dec. 1854
	Burlington, Vt.
	July 1813; Apr. 1815
	Burnside, Camp, Ky.
	Jan.–Sept. 1864
	Burrowville, Ark.
	July–Oct. 1867
	Burwell, Camp, Tex.
	Nov. 1855
	Butler, Fort, Fla.
	Nov. 1838–Feb. 1839
	Butler, Mo.
	Apr.–June 1862
	Butler, Camp, Va.
	June 1861–Feb. 1862
	Butuan, Mindanao, P.I.
	Sept. 1901–Apr. 1902
	Byrne, Camp, Mo.
	Apr. 1862
1499	Cabancalan, Negros Occidental, P.I.
	July–Dec. 1902
	Cabuyao, Laguna, P.I.
	July 1902–Aug. 1903
	Cadwallader, Camp, Pa.
	July 1865–May 1866
	Cagpile, Samar, P.I.
	May–Sept. 1905
	Caguas, P.R.
	Jan. 1899
	Calais, Maine
	Apr. and May 1866
	Calanag Station, Tayabas, P.I.
	May–Nov. 1904
	Calarian Prison, Mindanao, P.I.
	July 1911–Sept. 1912
	Calasiao, Pangasinan, P.I.
	July–Dec. 1902
	Calbayog, Samar, P.I.
	Mar. 1900–Dec. 1902
	Caldwell, Kans.
	June 1880–July 1885
	Caldwell, Camp, N.C.
	Aug. 1871
	Calhoun, Mo.
	Nov. and Dec. 1862
	Calhoun, Fort, Va.
	Aug. 1861–Feb. 1862
	Calivo, Panay, P.I.
	Feb. 1900–Sept. 1902
	Call, Camp, Suwannee Old Town, Fla.
	July–Oct. 1836
	Call, Fort, Volusia, Fla.
	Dec. 1836–Feb. 1838
	Callahan's Ranch, Camp near, Calif.
	May 1855
	Calumpit, Bulacan, P.I.
	May 1900–Sept. 1903
	Calvert, Tex.

Roll	Description
	Oct. 1869–May 1870
1500	Camden, Camp, S.C.
	Oct. 1876
	Cameron, Camp, Ariz.
	Sept. 1866–Feb. 1867
	Cameron, Camp, N. Mex.
	Oct. and Nov. 1861
	Cameron, Tex.
	Jan.–May 1870
	Camiling, Luzon, P.I.
	Dec. 1899
	Camuy, P.R.
	Oct. 1898–Jan. 1899
	Canadian, Camp, Ind. Terr.
	June–Aug. 1834
	Canadian River, N. Mex.
	June and July 1873
	Canayan, Isabela, P.I.
	Jan.–Mar. 1903
	Canby, Fort, N. Mex.
	Sept. 1863–Oct. 1864
	Candaba, Luzon, P.I.
	May and June 1900
	Candelaria, Tayabas, P.I.
	Jan.–Mar. 1906
	Candon, Ilocos Sur, P.I.
	Apr. and May 1904
	Canto, Cuba
	July and Aug. 1899
	Canton, Tex.
	Nov. 1868–July 1869
	Canfield, Cantonment, Nebr.
	Nov. and Dec. 1855
	Capiz, Panay, P.I.
	Dec. 1899–June 1903
1501	Caraga, Mindanao, P.I.
	June–Dec. 1900
	Caranian, Samar, P.I.
	Feb.–July 1902
	Carigara, Leyte, P.I.
	July 1902–Mar. 1903
	Carleton, Camp, Calif.
	Nov. 1861–Mar. 1862
	Carlisle, Camp, W. Va.
	Jan.–Mar. 1862
	Carmona, Cavite, P.I.
	May–Aug. 1905
	Carolina, P.R.
	Oct. 1898–Jan. 1899
	Carondelet, Mo.
	Apr. 1865
	Carrington, Camp, Ind.
	Apr. 1863–Aug. 1864
	Carrizo, Tex.
	Jan.–June 1893
	Carrollton, Ala.
	Sept. 1874
	Carter, Camp, Corregidor, P.I.
	Jan. 1908
	Casa Colorado, Camp near, N. Mex.
	Dec. 1857
	Casey, Fort, Fla.
	Mar.–Nov. 1850
	Casey, Camp, Va.
	July 1864–Mar. 1865
	Casper, Wyo.
	Sept. 1904
	Cass, Camp, Calif.
	June–Aug. 1859
	Cass, Fort, Va.
	May 1865

Roll	Description
	Cassville, Mo.
	June 1861–Jan. 1864
	Cassville, W. Va.
	July–Oct. 1868
	Cantanauan, Tayabas, P.I.
	Nov. 1903–Jan. 1904
	Catarman, Samar, P.I.
	Jan. and Feb. 1902
	Catbalogan, Samar, P.I.
	July 1902–Aug. 1903
	Catubig, Samar, P.I.
	June and July 1905
	Cauayan, Isabela, P.I.
	Jan. and Mar. 1903
	Cavite, Luzon, P.I.
	Aug. 1898–June 1900
	Cavite, Viejo, Luzon, P.I.
	May–Aug. 1900
	Cayuse Station, Oreg.
	Camp of Instruction
	Sept. 1889
1502	**Cedar Keys, Fla.**
	July 1864–June 1865
	Cedar Point, Colo.
	July 1867–July 1868
	Center, Fort, Fla.
	Jan. 1856–Aug. 1857
	Centreville, Tex.
	Mar. 1867–Apr. 1868
	Ceredo, W. Va.
	Apr.–Sept. 1867
	Chacon, Camp on the, Tex.
	May–Aug. 1854
	Chalmette, La.
	Jan.–May 1865
	Chambers, Fort, near Hobucketoopa,(Ill.?)
	Jan.–July 1806
	Chambersburg, Pa.
	July 1865
	Charles' Ferry, Fla.
	June and July 1842
	Charleston, Miss.
	Nov. 1869
	Charleston, W. Va.
	Mar.–Oct. 1870
	Charlotte, Camp, Tex.
	June 1880
	Charlottesville, Va.
	Feb.–June 1866
	Chehalis, Fort, Wash.
	Feb. 1860–May 1861
	Chelan, Camp, Wash.
	Aug. 1879–Sept. 1880
	Cheraw, S.C.
	May 1871
	Cheyenne River, Camp on the, S. Dak. (1)
	Aug. 1867
	Cheyenne River, Camp on the, S. Dak. (2)
	Apr.–Dec. 1890
	Cheyenne and Arapaho Agency, Camp at, Ind. Terr.
	June 1870–Apr. 1871
1503	**Chicago, Ill.**
	Apr. 1865–June 1872
	Chicago, Ill.
	Oct.–Dec. 1916
	U.S. Aviation Station and Detachment of the Aviation Section, Signal Corps
	Chicaskie River, Camp on, Ind. Terr.
	July and Aug. 1884
	Chilocco Creek, Camp on, Ind. Terr.

Roll	Description
	Mar. and Apr. 1885
	Chipola, Fort, Fla.
	Nov. 1841–May 1842
	Chokonikla, Fort, Fla.
	Oct. 1849–June 1850
	Church Butte [Buttes] Station, Utah
	Oct. 1865
	Ciales, P.R.
	Nov. 1898–Feb. 1899
	Ciboletta [Cibolletta], N. Mex.
	Sept. 1850–Sept. 1851
	Circle City, Alaska
	Sept. 1898–July 1900
	Clarke, Fort, Fla.
	Feb. 1840
	Clarksburg, Va.
	Apr. 1862
	Clark's Mill, Mo.
	Sept.–Nov. 1862
	Clarksville, Tex.
	Oct. 1868–Feb. 1870
	Cleveland, Ohio
	Oct. 1839–Sept. 1841
	Cleveland, Camp, Ohio
	Sept. 1863–Dec. 1864
	Clinch (3), Fort, near Tampa Bay, Fla.
	Jan.–May 1850
	Clines Ranch, Colo.
	July and Aug. 1882
	Clinton, Ky.
	June 1863
	Clinton, La.
	July 1876–Apr. 1877
	Clinton, Mo.
	May 1862–Nov. 1863
	Coalsmouth, W. Va.
	May 1863
	Coamo, P.R.
	Aug. 1898–Apr. 1899
1504	**Coburn, Camp, Maine**
	Sept.–Nov. 1865
	Coffee, Camp, Ala. near Chickasaw Agency, Ind. Terr.
	Apr.–Nov. 1834
	Coffeyville, Kans.
	May–Sept. 1880
	Cogswell, Camp, N. Mex.
	Sept. 1860
	Coinjock Station, N.C.
	Mar. 1865
	College Park, Md.
	Nov. 1911; Apr. 1912
	Signal Corps
	Aviation School
	Colleton, S.C.
	May 1866
	Collins, G. H., Camp, Dak. Terr.
	Aug.–Oct. 1875
	Columbia, Mo.
	Feb. 1862–July 1865
	Columbia, Tenn.
	Feb. and Mar. 1865
	Columbus, Ga.
	Apr. 1867–July 1868
	Columbus, Nebr. T.
	Oct. 1864–Mar. 1865
	Columbus, Tex.
	Apr. 1869–May 1870
	Comanche Agency, Camp near, Tex.
	Mar.–May 1859
	Comargo [Camargo], Camp near, Mex.

Roll	Description
	Nov. 1846
	Compostela, Mindanao, P.I.
	Oct. 1910–Sept. 1911
	Comstock, Tex.
	June 1916
	Conception, Camp, Tex.
	Mar.–June 1846
	Conception [Concepcion], Camp, Panay, P.I.
	Mar.–Oct. 1902
	Concordia, Camp, Tex.
	Feb.–Dec. 1868
	Connelly, Camp, N. Mex.
	Dec. 1861
	Conness, Camp, Utah
	May–Sept. 1864
	Conrad, Camp, Ga.
	Dec. 1898–Feb. 1899
	Consolacion, Leyte, P.I.
	May–July 1901
	Consolacion del Sur, Cuba
	Nov. 1906–Apr. 1907
	Converse, Fort, Va.
	Jan.–Mar. 1865
	Cony, Camp, Maine
	Dec. 1865–Mar. 1866
	Coosawhatchie Subdistrict, Lawtonville, S.C.
	Jan. 1866
1505	Coron, Busuanga, P.I.
	Jan.–Aug. 1902
	Corozal, C.Z.
	Aug. 1915–Dec. 1916
	Corregidor Island, P.I.
	July 1899–Nov. 1902
	Corse, Camp, Iowa
	Sept. 1909
	Corsicana, Tex.
	Jan.–May 1870
	Cotton, Camp, Tex.
	Mar.–Oct. 1916
	Cotton Gin, Tex.
	Jan.–Mar. 1868
	Cottonville, Ala.
	Apr. 1864
	Cottonwood Creek, Camp on, Kans.
	July–Sept. 1868
	Couch, Camp, Pa.
	Aug. 1863–Jan. 1864
	Council City, Alaska
	July–Sept. 1900
	Council Grove, Kans.
	Sept. 1864
	Covington, Fort, N.Y.
	Sept. 1838–Apr. 1839
	Cow Creek, Kans.
	Sept. 1865
	Crab Orchard, Ky.
	Oct. 1871–Nov. 1872
	Craig, Fort, Va.
	Dec. 1864
	Crane, Camp, Calif.
	July 1852
	Crane, Fort, Fla.
	Jan.–Apr. 1837
	Crane Creek, Mo.
	Oct. and Nov. 1862
	Crawford, Camp, Samar, P.I.
	Dec. 1907–Apr. 1908
	Creedmoor, N.Y.
	Aug. 1879; July 1887
	Creek Nation, Ala.
	Oct. 1828–Sept. 1858

Roll	Description
1506	Crisfield, Kans.
	July 1885
	Cristo, Cuba
	Dec. 1898–Mar. 1900
	Croghan, Fort, Iowa
	June 1842–Sept. 1843
	Crook, Camp, Mont.
	Apr.–Nov. 1890
	Crook, Camp, S. Dak.
	June and July 1890
	Cross, Fort, Fla.
	Dec. 1838–May 1842
	Crossman, Camp, Utah
	Nov. and Dec. 1858
	Cubero, N. Mex.
	July–Oct. 1862
	Cudarangan, Mindanao, P.I.
	Oct. 1906–July 1908
	Culaman, Camp, Mindanao, P.I.
	Nov. 1910
	Culion, Coron, P.I.
	Feb. 1902
	Cumberland, Md.
	July–Oct. 1864
	Cumberland Gap, Ky.
	Apr. 1865
	Cummings, Fort, Fla.
	Mar. 1839–Feb. 1841
	Currey, Camp, Oreg.
	Sept. 1865–Apr. 1866
	Curtin, Camp, Pa.
	Mar.–July 1862
	Curtis, Fort, Ark.
	Jan.–Mar. 1865
	Curtis, Camp, Colo. Terr.
	Apr.–Dec. 1863
	Cuyler, Camp, Kans. Terr.
	July 1858
	Cuyo, Cuyos Islands, P.I.
	June 1901–Feb. 1902
1507	Dade (1), Fort, Fla. Old Fort Dade
	Jan. 1837–Oct. 1849
	Dagami, Leyte, P.I.
	Aug. 1906–Nov. 1907
	Dagupan, Pangasinan, P.I.
	Apr. 1902–Sept. 1903
	Dallas, Camp, Fla.
	Sept. and Oct. 1873
	Dallas, Tex.
	July–Oct. 1868; Oct. 1915
	Danbury, Conn.
	Aug. 1912
	Daniels, Camp, Fla.
	May–Nov. 1855
	Dan Smith's Ranch, Nebr. Terr.
	Oct.–Dec. 1864
	Danville, Mo.
	Feb.–Apr. 1862
	Danville, Va.
	May 1865–Apr. 1866
	Dasmarinas, Cavite, P.I.
	Apr. 1900–Oct. 1905
	Dauphin Island, Ala.
	Aug. 1864–Aug. 1865
	Davenport, Fort, Fla.
	Feb.–Oct. 1839
	David Hunter, Camp, S.C.
	Aug.–Oct. 1875
	Davidson, Camp, Kans.
	June–Sept. 1868
	Day, Camp, Oreg.

Roll	Description
	Aug. 1860
	Dayton, Camp at, Oreg.
	June 1866
	Decatur, Ala.
	June 1864–May 1865
	Dechard [Decherd], Tenn.
	Oct. 1868
	Delaware Recruiting District, Wilmington, Del.
	Apr.–July 1812
	Delphi, Ind.
	Sept. 1906
	Deming, Camp, N. Mex.
	July–Dec. 1916
	Demopolis, Ala.
	Oct. 1868
	Denver, Colo.
	Apr. 1865–June 1870
	De Peyster, Camp, S.C.
	Nov. and Dec. 1874
	Depot No. 1, Big Cypress Swamp, Fla.
	Apr. 1857
	Depot No. 1, Camp near, Fla.
	Mar. and Apr. 1856
	Depot No. 2, Big Cypress Swamp, Fla.
	May 1857
	De Valls Bluff, Ark.
	Nov. 1863–Nov. 1866
	Devin, Camp, Wyo.
	June and July 1878
	Dix, Fort, Md.
	Sept. 1864–Mar. 1865
	Dodge, Camp, Utah
	Dec. 1865–Feb. 1866
	Dolores, Samar, P.I.
	July–Sept. 1902
1508	Donsol, Sorsogon, P.I.
	May 1900–Mar. 1902
	Dorado, P.R.
	Oct. 1898–Jan. 1899
	Dos Caminos, Cuba
	July 1898
	Downers Station, Kans.
	May 1867–May 1868
	Downey, Camp, Alameda County, Calif.
	Aug. 1861
	Downey, Camp, Contra Costa County, Calif.
	Sept. 1861
	Downing, Fort, Fla.
	Feb.–May 1840
	Dragoon Bridge, Honey Lake Valley, Calif.
	Aug. 1860–May 1861
	Drane, Fort, Fla.
	Jan.–Dec. 1836
	Drayton, Fort, Otter Island, S.C.
	Feb.–Apr. 1862
	Dryden, Tex.
	June 1916
	Dry Wood Station, Mo.
	Oct. 1863
	Dulag, Leyte, P.I.
	July 1902–Mar. 1907
	Dulany, Fort, Fla.
	Nov. 1837–May 1858
	Dumaguete, Negros, P.I.
	July 1902–Aug. 1911
	Dumanjug, Cebu, P.I.
	July–Dec. 1902
	Dun Glen, Nev.
	Jan. and Feb. 1866
	Dutch Harbor, Alaska
	Aug. 1898

Roll	Description
	Duval, Fort, Fla.
	Nov. and Dec. 1826
1509	Eagle Rock Bridge, Idaho
	Sept. 1878
	Eastern Point Fort, Mass.
	Apr. 1864–June 1865
	Eastman, Camp, Utah
	Jan. and Feb. 1859
	Easton, Camp, N. Mex.
	July 1863
	Eastport, Miss.
	Apr. 1865
	Eatmans Ferry, Tex.
	Oct. 1914
	Eaton, Camp, Cherokee Nation
	June–Oct. 1830
	Econfinee, Fort, Fla.
	Mar.–May 1840
	Edgefield, S.C.
	Oct. 1868–Apr. 1877
	Edgefield, Tenn.
	Feb.–Aug. 1865
	Edinburg, Tex.
	May 1853–Dec. 1865
	Egmont Key, Fla.
	July 1899–Jan. 1900
	El Caney, Cuba
	June 1898–Aug. 1899
	El Cobie [Cobre], Cuba
	Sept. and Oct. 1899
	El Deposito, P.I.
	June 1900
	Eldorado, Camp, Ariz.
	Jan.–July 1867
	El Dorado, Ark.
	Sept. 1867
	Eleven; Number, Fort, Fla.
	Aug. 1839–June 1840
	Elkins, Camp, Wyo.
	June–Oct. 1892
	Ellsworth, Fort, Va.
	Sept. 1862–Sept. 1864
	El Reventon, Ariz. Terr.
	Aug. 1862–May 1864
	El Valle, Mex.
	Dec. 1916
	Emmet Crawford, Camp, Ind. Terr.
	June 1886
	Emory, Camp, Ga.
	Jan. 1869
	Erenas, Samar, P.I.
	Jan. 1902
	Erie, Pa.
	Apr. 1866–Mar. 1867
	Ethan Allen, Fort, Va.
	July–Oct. 1864
	Eufaula, Ala.
	Sept. and Oct. 1874
	Eutaw, Ala.
	Oct. 1870
	Everett Peabody, Camp, Mo.
	Sept. 1907–Oct. 1909
	Everglades, Fla.
	Feb. 1857
1510	Fabens, Tex.
	May and June 1916
	Fairmont, W. Va.
	Oct. and Nov. 1868
	Fairview, Camp, N. Mex.
	Mar.–June 1886
	Fajardo, P.R.

Roll	Description
	Nov. 1898–Feb. 1899
	Falls Church, Va.
	Apr. 1865
	Falmouth, Va.
	Feb.–May 1863
	Farm Island, Post near, Dak. Terr.
	Nov. 1863–May 1864
	Fauntleroy, Camp, Calif.
	Nov. 1856
	Fayetteville, N.C.
	Apr.–Dec. 1867
	Fayetteville, Tenn.
	Oct. 1868
	Fayetteville, W. Va.
	July 1864
	Fifteen; Number, Fort, Fla.
	Apr. 1839–June 1840
	Fillmore, Camp, Ark.
	June–Aug. 1851
	Fillmore, Camp, Colo.
	Apr.–Oct. 1865
	Fire Steel Creek, Post near, Dak. Terr.
	Sept.–Dec. 1865
	Fishers Island, N.Y.
	July 1888
	Fitzgerald, Camp, Calif.
	June–Sept. 1861
	Florence, S.C.
	Oct. 1868
	Floyd, Fort, Ga.
	Nov. 1838–Sept. 1839
	Floyd, Fort, Neb. Terr.
	July 1857
	Forsyth, Mo.
	May 1862
	Foster, Fort, Fla.
	Mar. 1837–Sept. 1849
	Four, Number, Fort, Fla.
	Apr. 1839–June 1841
	Frank, Camp, Okla.
	Sept. 1898
	Franklin, Mo.
	May 1863–July 1865
	Frazer, Fort, Fla.
	Dec. 1837–Apr. 1838
	Frederick, Md., U.S.A.
	General Hospital
	Sept.–Nov. 1862
	July 1863–Oct. 1864
	French Creek, N.Y.
	Dec. 1838–Mar. 1839
	Fudge, Camp, La.
	Dec. 1837
	Fulton, Fort, Fla.
	Feb.–June 1840
	Fulton, Mo.
	Mar. 1862–Mar. 1865
	Furlong, Camp, N, Mex.
	Mar.–July 1916
1511	Gaines, Fort, Ind. Terr.
	Apr. 1849
	Galisteo, N. Mex.
	Nov. 1851–Jan. 1852
	Galt, Camp, Fla.
	Jan. and Feb. 1857
	Gamble, Camp, Mo.
	June–Aug. 1862
	Gardenier, Camp, Tex.
	May–July 1854

Roll	Description
	Gardner, Camp, Mont. Terr.
	Apr. 1857
	Garesche, Battery, Va.
	Dec. 1864–May 1865
	Gaston, N.C.
	Nov. and Dec. 1865
	Gatlin, Fort, Fla.
	Nov. 1838–Oct. 1849
	Gatun, C.Z.
	Feb.–Dec. 1916
	Gauley Bridge, W. Va.
	Mar. 1863
	Gazan, Marinduque, P.I.
	June 1902
	Genoa, Camp, Tex.
	Apr. 1914
	George, Fort, Maine
	Aug. 1815–June 1816
	George, Camp, Utah Terr.
	Jan. 1866
	Gerona, Luzon, P.I.
	July 1902–Apr. 1903
	Getty, Fort, S.C.
	Feb. 1902–May 1903
	Gettysburg, Pa.
	May 1909–Aug. 1910
	Gibara, Cuba
	Nov. 1898–Dec. 1899
	Gibson, Fort, Camp near, Choctaw Nation, Ind. Terr.
	May and June 1833
	Gila River, Camp on the, Ariz. Terr.
	June–Nov. 1882
	Gila River, Summer Camp on the, Ariz. Terr.
	May 1873
	Gilbert, Camp, Ky.
	Feb. 1862
	Gilleland, Fort, Fla.
	July 1837–Mar. 1839
	Gilman, Camp, Ga.
	Nov. and Dec. 1898
	Gilman's Station, Nebr.
	Oct. 1864–May 1865
	Gingaron [Ginigaran], Negros, P.I.
	Dec. 1902–Jan. 1903
1512	Glan, Mindanao, P.I.
	Sept. 1910–Mar. 1911
	Glasgow, Ky.
	Dec. 1863
	Glasgow, Mo.
	Mar.–Aug. 1862
	Glover, Fort, Mass.
	Apr. and May 1865
	Goldfield, Nev.
	Dec. 1907–Feb. 1908
	Goliad, Tex.
	Aug. 1866–Mar. 1868
	Goodrich's Landing, La.
	Aug. 1864
	Governor's Palace, Iloilo, P.I.
	Feb.–Sept. 1899
	Graham, N.C.
	Oct. 1870
	Grand Ecore, La.
	May 1868–Feb. 1869
	Grand Island, Nebr. Terr.
	Mar. 1865
	Grand Rapids, Mich.
	Oct. 1863–Apr. 1864
	Draft Rendezvous
	Grande Ronde, Oreg. Terr.

Roll	Description
	Feb.–June 1856
	Grant, Fort, C.Z.
	Dec. 1913–Oct. 1916
	Grant, Camp, at Mount Pleasant, Mo.
	May 1862
	Grant, Camp, at Wellsville, Mo.
	Apr. 1862
	Grant, Camp, Riverside Park, N.Y., N.Y.
	Aug. 1885–May 1886
	Greble, Camp, Pa.
	Oct.–Dec. 1861
	Greenbush, Cantonment, N.Y.
	Aug. 1814–June 1821
	Greenfield, Mo.
	Dec. 1862
	Greensboro, Ala.
	Oct. and Nov. 1874
	Greensboro, Miss.
	Apr.–Dec. 1867
	Greensboro, N.C.
	May–Dec. 1867
	Greenville, Mo.
	Apr.–Oct. 1862
	Greenwood, Camp, Dak. Terr.
	July 1865
	Greenwood, La.
	May 1873–May 1874
1513	Grierson, Camp, Ariz. Terr.
	Sept. and Oct. 1889
	Grierson, Camp, Kans.
	Nov. 1867
	Griffin, Fort, Fla.
	Jan.–May 1840
	Griswold, Fort, Conn.
	May–Oct. 1898
	Guayama, P.R.
	Aug. 1898–Feb. 1899
	Guayanilla, P.R.
	July 1898
	Gubat, Luzon, P.I.
	June 1900–Sept. 1901
	Guenther, F. L., Camp, N.Y.
	May–Dec. 1901
	Guinan [Guiunan], Samar, P.I.
	Dec. 1900–Dec. 1902
	Guinay [Gumay], Samar, P.I.
	Apr.–Sept. 1905
	Guines, Cuba
	Apr. 1908–Jan. 1909
	Guinobatan, Albay, P.I.
	Sept. 1905–Jan. 1906
1514	Hachita, N. Mex.
	Dec. 1915–July 1916
	Hadley, Camp, Mo.
	July 1909
	Hainey, Camp, Tex.
	Feb.–July 1853
	Halleck, Fort, Nebr. Terr.
	Apr.–June 1863
	Halpine, Camp, Kans.
	Feb. 1862
	Hamburg, S.C.
	Oct. and Nov. 1874
	Hamburg, Tenn.
	Aug. and Sept. 1862
	Hamer, Fort, Fla.
	Dec. 1849–Oct. 1850
	Hamilton, Fort, Fla.
	Aug. 1841–Jan. 1843
	Hamilton, Camp, Ky.
	Aug.–Oct. 1898

Roll	Description
	Hamilton, Camp, Tenn.
	Oct. 1898
	Hamilton, Camp, Tex.
	Aug. 1853
	Hampstead, Camp, (?)
	Sept. 1814
	Hancock, Camp, Ga.
	July–Oct. 1886
	Hancock Creek, Fla.
	Nov. 1849
	Hannibal City, Mo.
	Dec. 1861
	Hanson, Fort, Fla.
	Mar. 1838–June 1840
	Harlee, Fort, Fla.
	Apr. 1837–Oct. 1838
	Harlingen, Tex.
	Aug. 1915–Apr. 1916
	Harriet, Fort, Fla.
	Mar.–Aug. 1840
	Harrison, Fort, Fla.
	Apr.–Sept. 1841
	Harrison's Landing, Va.
	Oct. 1864–Apr. 1865
	Harrisonville, Mo.
	June 1862–Nov. 1863
	Hartford, Conn.
	July 1863–Dec. 1865
	Hart's Mill, Tex.
	Aug. 1862–Mar. 1863
	Harvie, Fort, Fla.
	Nov. 1841–Feb. 1842
	Haskell, Camp, Ga.
	Nov. 1898
	Haven, Camp, Conn.
	June–Aug. 1898
	Heiman, Henry, and Donelson, Forts, Ky.
	May 1862–June 1863
	Helena, Ark.
	June 1859–Sept. 1869
	Helena, Mont.
	Nov. 1877–May 1894
	Helena, Tex.
	Mar. 1868–Apr. 1870
	Henderson, Fort, Ga.
	Nov. 1838–Mar. 1842
	Henderson, Ky.
	Oct. 1862
	Henly, Camp, N. Mex.
	Apr.–Aug. 1886
1515	Hermann, Mo.
	Nov. 1864–June 1865
	Hickman, Ky.
	Apr.–June 1862
	Hickmans Mill, Mo.
	May 1864
	Highbridge, Tex.
	Mar. 1911
	High Hill, Mo.
	Feb.–Apr. 1862
	Highwassee, (Tenn.?)
	May 1811
	Hill, Camp, Va.
	Dec. 1864
	Hillhurst, Wash.
	Aug. and Sept. 1910
	Hinks, Camp, Pa.
	Dec. 1865–Mar. 1866
	Hoffman, Camp, Kans.
	July–Nov. 1867
	Holbrook, Camp, Ariz.

Roll	Description
	July–Sept. 1882
	Hollenbush, Camp, Calif.
	June 1857
	Holmes, Fort, Fla.
	Feb. 1840–July 1841
	Holt, Cantonment, near Washington, D.C.
	Jan. and Feb. 1862
	Holt, Fort, Ky.
	Oct. 1861–Jan. 1862
	Holt, Joe, General Hospital, Ind.
	Sept. 1864–June 1865
	Hook, Fort, Fla.
	Feb. and Mar. 1839
	Hooker, Camp, Calif.
	Aug.–Oct. 1862
	Hope, Camp, Fla.
	Nov. 1822–Mar. 1823
	Hope, Idaho
	July 1894
	Hot Wells, Tex.
	July 1916
	Houston, Mo.
	July 1862–Apr. 1864
	Howard, Camp, Calif.
	June 1888
	Hudson, Mo.
	Feb.–May 1862
	Huguet Springs, Va.
	May–Aug. 1868
	Hulbert, Fort, Fla.
	Feb.–Apr. 1840
	Hunt, Camp, Tex.
	May 1902
	Hunter, Fort, Fla.
	Feb.–June 1840
	Huntington, Fort, N.C.
	Feb.–May 1836
	Huntsville, Ark.
	May 1867
	Huntsville, Mo. and Camp Hunt
	Feb.–July 1862
	Huntsville, Tex.
	Oct.–Dec. 1868
	Hut-ta-mi-nes Village, Camp at, Utah
	Sept. 1852
1516	Ilges, Camp, Ariz.
	Mar.–June 1867
	Ilogan, Isobela [Ilagan, Isabela], P.I.
	May–Nov. 1902
	Iloilo and Jaro, Panay, P.I.
	Feb.–Apr. 1899
	Indan, Ambos Camarines, P.I.
	Nov. 1905–Jan. 1906
	Indian Key, Fla.
	Aug. and Sept. 1869
	Indian Valley, Oreg.
	May 1877
	Isabela Sagunda, P.R.
	Oct. and Nov. 1898
	Island No. 10, Tenn.
	Jan. 1863–May 1864
	Ives, Camp, Tex.
	Oct. 1859–Dec. 1860
	Jackson, Fort, Fla.
	Dec. 1838–Aug. 1840
	Jackson, Camp, Ind. Terr.
	Feb. 1833
	Jackson, Cantonment, Tex.
	Oct. and Nov. 1854
	Jacksonport, Ark.
	Apr. 1866–Feb. 1867

Roll	Description
	Jackson's [Jackson] Hole, Wyo.
	July 1895
	Jacksonville, Ala.
	Mar.–June 1870
	Jacob A. Augur, Camp, Tex.
	Aug. 1909
	James Island, Fla.
	June–Aug. 1838
	Jamestown Exposition, Va.
	Apr.–Dec. 1907
	Janivay [Janiuay], Panay, P.I.
	May 1900
	Jasper, Fort, Dak. Terr.
	Jan. 1866
	Jefferson Davis, Camp, Miss.
	July–Oct. 1848
	Jiguani, Cuba
	June–Aug. 1899
	Jimenez, Mindanao, P.I.
	Feb. 1901–Apr. 1902
	John A.T. Hull, Camp, Iowa
	Sept. and Oct. 1910
	Johnson, Camp, Ariz.
	Oct. 1862
	Johnson, Camp, Tex.
	Sept. 1862
	Johnson's Island, Ohio
	Dec. 1864–May 1866
	Johnsonville, Tenn.
	Oct. and Nov. 1868
	Johnston, Camp, Tex.
	Mar.–Oct. 1852
	Jolo, Siasi, and Bongao, P.I.
	June and July 1902
	Julesburg, Colo.
	Sept. 1864–May 1865
	Julita, Leyte, P.I.
	Nov. and Dec. 1906
	Junction, Colo.
	May and June 1865
	Junction Station, Colo.
	Oct. and Nov. 1864
	Jupiter, Fort, Fla.
	Feb. 1855–Aug. 1857
1517	Kamehameha, Fort, Hawaii
	Jan.–Dec. 1913
	Kanapaha, Fort, Fla.
	July and Aug. 1838
	Kansas, Troops on the Border
	Aug. 1863–May 1864
	Kaufman, Tex.
	Oct. 1867–Feb. 1868
	Kaw Reservation, Camp on, Kans.
	June 1868
	Kearny, Camp, Iowa
	Dec. 1863–Feb. 1866
	Kenay, Fort, Alaska
	Apr. 1869–Aug. 1870
	Kenner, La.
	Cavalry Camp of Instruction
	Dec. 1864–Mar. 1865
	Kennerville, La.
	Feb. and Mar. 1864
	Kenton, Tenn.
	Dec. 1862
	Keokuk, Iowa
	July 1863–Sept. 1864
	Key Largo, Fla.
	Feb. 1857
	Kissimmee, Fort, Fla.
	Feb. 1850–Aug. 1857

Roll	Description
	Klamath Lake, Camp on, Oreg.
	Sept. 1860
	Klamath River, Camp on, Calif.
	Sept. 1857
	Klikitat [Klickitat] River, Wash.
	Apr. 1856
1518	La Feria, Tex.
	Sept. 1915
	La Grange, Tenn.
	Dec. 1862
	Laguan, Samar, P.I.
	May 1901–Feb. 1903
	Laguna, N. Mex.
	Oct. 1851–Jan. 1852
	Laguna Ranch, Camp at, Tex.
	Sept. 1907
	Lake Charles, La.
	May 1877–June 1878
	Lake City, Fla.
	Apr. 1867–Aug. 1868
	Lakeland, Fla.
	May–Aug. 1898
	Lake Providence, La.
	Jan.–Dec. 1868
	La Loma, Luzon, P.I.
	Sept. 1899
	La Mesilla, Ariz.
	Aug. 1862–Oct. 1863
	Lamine Cantonment, Mo.
	Feb. and Mar. 1862
	Lancaster, S.C.
	Sept. and Oct. 1876
	Landang, Sacol [Lanang, Saccol], P.I.
	July 1910–May 1911
	Lander, Camp, Ind. Terr.
	Oct. 1865–May 1866
	Lands End, S.C.
	June–Aug. 1898
	Lane, Fort, Fla.
	Dec. 1837–Feb. 1838
	Langaran, Mindanao, P.I.
	June–Oct. 1901
	Lang's Ranch, N. Mex.
	July–Nov. 1885
	La Paz, Camp, Ariz. Terr.
	Apr. 1874–Apr. 1875
	La Paz, Leyte, P.I.
	Aug. 1906–Oct. 1907
	La Pena, Camp, Tex.
	May–Sept. 1854
1519	Laramie, Fort, Idaho
	Aug. 1863
	Laramie, Fort, Camps near, Neb. Terr.
	May 1856–Sept. 1859
	Laramie River, Camps on the, Neb. Terr.
	July–Sept. 1858
	Laramie River, Camp on the, Wyom. Terr.
	May–Sept. 1873
	Laredo, Camp near, Tex.
	Jan. 1860
	Laredo, Tex.
	Mar. 1914–June 1916
	Larena, Negros Oriental, P.I.
	Aug.–Oct. 1911
	Las Animas, Tex.
	May–Oct. 1854
	Las Marias, P.R.
	Sept. 1898–May 1899
	Las Vegas, Camp near, N. Mex.
	Mar. 1858
	Las Vegas, Camp, Tex.

Roll	Description
	May–July 1854
	Laua, Camp, Davao, P.I.
	Aug. 1911
	Lavaca, Tex.
	Aug. 1866
	Lawrence J. Hearn, Camp, Calif.
	Sept.–Dec. 1916
	Lawson, Fort, Fla.
	May–Nov. 1839
	Lawson, Camp, Tex.
	Oct. 1859–Apr. 1860
	Lazelle, Camp, Tex.
	June and July 1890
	Lebak [Lebac], Mindanao, P.I.
	Feb. 1911–Aug. 1912
	Lebanon, Mo.
	May 1862–Sept. 1863
	Legaspi, Albay, P.I.
	Apr. 1900–Dec. 1903
	Leib Barracks, near Clarksburgh (W. Va.?)
	Nov. 1861
	Leon, Panay, P.I.
	Dec. 1899
	Leona, Tex.
	Aug.–Nov. 1866
	Lewisburg, Tenn.
	Oct. 1868
	Lewiston, Idaho
	Aug. 1877
	Lewiston, N.Y.
	Sept. 1908
	Libmanan, Camarines Sur, P.I.
	June–Nov. 1901
	Ligao, Albay, P.I.
	Apr. 1904–June 1905
	Ligton, Bulacan, P.I. Convict Camp
	Apr.–June 1906
1520	Lincoln, Camp, Santa Rosa Island, Fla.
	Dec. 1861–Apr. 1862
	Lincoln, Abraham, Camp, Maine
	Mar.–July 1863
	Lincoln, Camp, N. Mex.
	May–Aug. 1866
	Lincolnton, N.C.
	Mar–Sept. 1872
	Lingayen, Pangasinan, P.I.
	July–Dec. 1902
	Linn Creek, Mo.
	Mar. and Apr. 1862
	Lippitt, Calif.
	Jan. and Feb. 1862
	Liscum Barracks, China
	Oct. 1900–May 1901
	Lithia Springs, Ga.
	Aug. and Sept. 1898
	Little Arkansas, Kans.
	May and June 1865
	Little Blue River, Camp on the, Nebr. Terr.
	July and Aug. 1857
	Little Blue Station, Nebr. Terr.
	Oct.–Dec. 1864
	Little Folly Island, S.C.
	Apr. 1864
	Little Obion, Ky.
	Feb. 1863
	Live Oak Creek, Camp on, Tex.
	Apr–Sept. 1854
	Llano Grande, Tex.
	Aug. 1916
	Llorente, Camp, Samar, P.I.
	Jan.–Oct. 1905

Roll	Description
	Loboo, Batangas, P.I.
	Sept. 1900–Jan. 1902
	Lockhart, Tex.
	July–Oct. 1867
	Loder, Camp, Mont. Terr.
	July–Sept. 1879
	Lodge Pole Creek, Camp on, Mont. Terr.
	Aug. 1889
	Lolumboy [Lolomboy], P.I.
	Apr. 1900
	Loma, Camp, Colo. Terr.
	May 1873
	Long Island, N.Y.
	Sept. 1814
	Long Point Batteries, Mass.
	May 1864–May 1865
	Long Prairie, Minn.
	Nov. 1858–Oct. 1860
	Lookout, Fort, Nebr. Terr.
	July 1856–May 1857
	Lookout, Fort, Camp near, Nebr.
	May–July 1856
	Lopeno, Camp, Tex.
	Apr. 1856
	Lopez, Tayabas, P.I.
	Aug. 1902–June 1903
	Loquilocan [Loquilocon], Samar, P.I.
	Jan.–May 1905
	Loring, Cantonment, Oreg.
	Aug. 1849–Apr. 1850
1521	Los Angeles, Calif.
	Mar. 1847–Dec. 1863
	Los Banos, Laguna, P.I.
	Jan.–Aug. 1904
	Los Valles, N. Mex.
	Nov. 1863–May 1864
	Louisa, Ky.
	Nov. 1864–Apr. 1869
	Louisiana, District of
	Dec. 1809
	Low, Camp, Calif.
	Jan.–Mar. 1865
	Lowell, Camp, Tex.
	Sept.–Nov. 1866
	Lowell Barracks, D.C.
	May and June 1866
	Lower Levee Steam Press, La.
	Jan.–Apr. 1866
	Lower Sioux Agency, Minn.
	July 1859
	Luayan [Luayon], Mindanao, P.I.
	Jan. and Feb. 1911
	Lubungan, Mindanao, P.I.
	Jan–June 1911
	Luce, S. B., Camp, N.Y.
	July and Aug. 1889
	Luis Lopez, N. Mex.
	Aug. 1862
	Lumbang, Laguna, P.I.
	Dec. 1901
	Lumbatan [Lumbacan], Mindanao, P.I.
	July 1910–July 1911
	Lumberton, N.C.
	Nov. 1870–Apr. 1871
	Lyford, Tex.
	Oct. 1915–Apr. 1916
	Lynchburg, Camp near, Va.
	Jan.–June 1866
	Lyon, Fort, Calif.
	June–Aug. 1862
	Lyons Creek, Camp on, Kans.

Roll	Description
	Sept. 1868
	Lytle Barracks, Ohio
	Feb. 1864
1522	McAllen, Camp, Tex.
	July and Aug. 1916
	McClary, Fort, N.H.
	Aug. 1864
	McClure, Fort, Fla.
	Feb. and Mar. 1839
	McComb City, Miss.
	Jan. 1876–Apr. 1877
	McCrabb, Fort, Fla.
	Feb.–Aug. 1840
	McDowell, Camp, Calif.
	July–Oct. 1864
	McDowell Military Prison, (?)
	Jan. 1862
	McGregor, N.Y.
	July 1885
	McKeen, Fort, Dak. Terr.
	June–Nov. 1872
	McLane, Fort, N. Mex.
	Jan.–June 1861
	McLaurin, Camp, Miss.
	Sept. and Oct. 1898
	McLean, Fort, Ariz.
	Jan. and Feb. 1863
	McRay, Fort, Fla.
	Jan.–June 1857
	McRee, Fort, Fla.
	May 1842–Apr. 1845
	McRee, Station, N.C.
	Dec. 1830–Apr. 1831
	Maasin, Leyte, P.I.
	July–Nov. 1902
	Machiasport, Maine
	Feb.–May 1865
	Mackall, Camp, Calif.
	Apr. 1857
	Macon, Miss.
	Oct. 1876
	Macon, Mo.
	Oct. 1863–Aug. 1864
	Mactaon, Samar, P.I.
	July–Sept. 1905
	Madison, Ind.
	Sept. 1863; June 1864
	Madison, Wis.
	Mar.–June 1865
	Maggoffin, Camp, N. Mex.
	Apr. 1854
	Magruder, Fort, Va.
	Mar. 1864–Mar. 1865
	Magtaon, Samar, P.I.
	July 1905–Oct. 1906
	Majayjay, P.I.
	May 1900
1523	Malaig, Mindanao, P.I.
	June 1910–June 1911
	Malalog [Malalag], Mindanao, P.I.
	Sept. 1910–Aug. 1911
	Malaybalay, Mindanao, P.I.
	Feb.–Sept. 1912
	Malco Inlet, Camp at, Fla.
	Jan. 1857
	Malita, Camp, Mindanao, P.I.
	June 1910–Aug. 1911
	Malitbog, Leyte, P.I.
	Aug. 1901
	Malolas [Malolos], Luźon, P.I.
	Mar. 1899–May 1900

Roll	Description
	Maluhi [Malahi] Island, P.I.
	Mar. 1904
	Malusu [Maluso], Basilan, P.I.
	Sept.–Nov. 1910
	Manapla, P.I.
	Jan. 1902
	Manatu, Camp, Fla.
	Oct. and Nov. 1849
	Mangaldan, Luzon, P.I.
	July–Nov. 1902
	Mangarin, Mindoro, P.I.
	Oct. 1901–Mar. 1902
	Mankato, Minn.
	Dec. 1862–Mar. 1863
	Mankin's Woods, Md.
	July 1864
	Mansfield, Camp, La.
	Feb. 1863
	Mansfield, Camp, N. Mex.
	Aug. 1857
	Many, Fort, Fla.
	Aug. 1841–May 1842
	Marahui, Mindanao, P.I.
	Nov. 1903–Dec. 1904
	Marathon, Tex.
	Jan.–Mar. 1911
	Marcy, Fort, Va.
	July and Aug. 1864
	Marfa, Tex.
	Mar. 1911; May 1915
	Marianna, Fla.
	Feb. 1866–Feb. 1869
	Marias Crossing, Camp near, Mont.
	July–Oct. 1878
1524	Marion, N.C.
	Dec. 1874–July 1875
	Marion, S.C.
	Sept. 1874–Jan. 1877
	Marion, Camp, S.C.
	Nov. 1898–Feb. 1899
	Mariquina Road, P.I.
	July 1899
	Marshall, Mo.
	Aug. 1863; May 1865
	Marshall, Tex.
	Jan. 1866–Dec. 1868
	Marshfield, Mo.
	Sept. 1863
	Martin, Camp, Ind. Terr.
	Dec. 1886–Oct. 1887
	Martin Scott, Fort, Tex.
	Oct. and Nov. 1866
	Masbate, Masbate, P.I.
	Nov. 1901–Apr. 1902
	Mason, Fort, Ariz. Terr.
	Aug. 1865–Aug. 1866
	Massac, Fort, Ill. Terr.
	Mar. 1806–Mar. 1813
	Matagorda Island, Tex.
	Jan. 1864
	Matnog, Sorsogon, P.I.
	Feb. 1901
	Matti [Mati], Mindanao, P.I.
	June–Nov. 1900
	Mauban, Tayabas, P.I.
	Dec. 1901–May 1902
	Mayari and Mayari Barracks, Cuba
	Jan. 1899–Aug. 1900
	Mayer's Springs, Cantonment at, Tex.
	Sept. 1880–Jan. 1881
	Mayorga, Leyte, P.I.

Roll	Description
	Jan.–Apr. 1907
	Meacham's Ranch, Wash. Terr.
	July and Aug. 1878
	Medicine Lodge, Mont.
	July 1882
	Mellonville, Fla.
	May–July 1866
	Menicke, Camp, Samar, P.I.
	Jan.–May 1906
	Mercedes, Luzon, P.I.
	May 1907
	Merriam, Camp, Calif.
	Oct. 1898
	Mesilla, N. Mex.
	Oct. 1863–Feb. 1864
	Mexico, Mo.
	Mar. 1862–Apr. 1864
	Meycauayan and Polo, Luzon, P.I.
	May 1900
1525	Miami, Fla.
	June and July 1898
	Midway Station, Nebr. Terr.
	Feb.–June 1865
	Miembres Valley, Camp in, N. Mex.
	Aug. 1857
	Miller, Camp, (?)
	July 1826
	Miller, Fort, Mass.
	Mar.–June 1865
	Miller, Cantonment, N.T.
	Apr. and May 1856
	Millikens Bend, La.
	June 1863–Nov. 1865
	Mineola, N.Y., Aviation Station
	Nov. and Dec. 1916
	Minera, Tex.
	Mar. 1911
	Minalabac, P.I.
	Nov. 1900
	Mishler, Camp, N. Mex.
	Apr. and May 1862
	Mission, Tex.
	Sept. 1915
	Mississippi City, Miss.
	July–Oct. 1865
	Mitchell, Fort, Dak. Terr.
	Jan–Apr. 1866
	Mitchell, Fort, Fla.
	Mar. 1840
	Mitchell, Camp, Ga.
	June 1883–Oct. 1885
	Mojalobas, Mindanao, P.I.
	Aug. 1911
	Mompissin, Camp, Mindanao, P.I.
	Sept. and Oct. 1910
	Montalban, Rizal, P.I.
	June 1900–Feb. 1905
	Montevallo, Ala.
	Oct. 1865–Jan. 1866
	Montgomery, Camp, Md.
	June–Sept. 1828
	Monticello, Ark.
	May–Nov. 1867
	Monticello, Fla.
	Feb. 1866
	Montpelier, Cantonment, Ala.
	Aug.–Nov. 1820
	Morehead City, N.C.
	Dec. 1863–May 1866
	Morgan, Cantonment, Fla.
	Aug. 1841–Dec. 1842

Roll	Description
	Morgan, John T., Camp, Ala.
	July–Sept. 1915
	Morgan, Camp. Ga.
	Aug. 1825–Feb. 1826
	Morganzia, La.
	Mar.–May 1865
	Morong, Luzon, P.I.
	Apr.–June 1900
	Morris, Fort, Fla.
	Nov. 1849
	Morris Island, S.C.
	May 1864–Feb. 1865
1526	Moulder, Camp, Fla.
	Feb. 1857
	Mount Pleasant, Tex.
	June 1867–Mar. 1868
	Mount Vernon, Ky.
	Apr.–Sept. 1871
	Muckleshute, Wash. Terr.
	Mar. 1856–July 1857
	Mud Bridge, Va.
	May and June 1863
	Mullallus, Nebr.
	Oct.–Dec. 1864
	Mullan, Idaho
	Sept. 1899
	Muntinlupa, Luzon, P.I.
	May–Dec. 1900
	Murat, Fort, Fla.
	June–Aug. 1840
	Murfreesboro, Tenn.
	Sept. 1862–Mar. 1870
	Murray, Camp, Utah
	Aug. 1885
	Mutiong, Samar, P.I.
	Nov. 1906–Dec. 1907
	Myakka, Fort, Fla.
	Nov. 1849–Feb. 1850
1527	Naches River and Fort Naches, Wash.
	May–July 1856
	Naco, Ariz.
	Mar. 1911–Feb. 1915
	Nasisi, Camp, Albay, P.I.
	Aug. 1905
	Nebraska City, Nebr.
	Jan.–Apr. 1864
	Negaunee, Mich.
	Aug. 1865–July 1866
	Nelson, Camp, Ky.
	Nov. 1863–July 1865
	New Albany, Ind.
	Apr. 1865
	New Archangel, Alaska
	Oct. and Nov. 1867
	New Creek, W. Va.
	July 1864
	New Jersey Recruiting District
	June 1812
	New Kiowa, Kans.
	Aug. and Sept. 1885
	Newnan, Ga.
	Sept.–Nov. 1898
	Newnansville, Fla.
	Aug. 1836–June 1837
	Newport Barracks, N.C.
	Oct. 1863–May 1864
	Niantic, Conn.
	May 1898
	Nicholas, Camp, N. Mex.
	June–Sept. 1865
	Noel, Fort, Fla.

Roll	Description
	Mar. 1839–Jan. 1842
	Noria, N. Mex.
	Feb. and Mar. 1911
	North, Fort, Va.
	Mar. 1865
	North Carolina Arsenal, N.C.
	Aug. 1844–Mar. 1861
	North Fork of the Platte River, Camp on the (?)
	Aug. 1855
	Northwest Landing, Va.
	Feb. and Mar. 1864
	Noveleta, P.I.
	July–Sept. 1900
1528	Oak Creek, Camp on, Ariz. Terr.
	June 1881
	Oakland, Calif.
	July 1909
	Ocilla, Fort, Fla.
	Sept. 1841–June 1842
	Odelltown, Canada
	Mar. 1814
	O'Fallons Bluffs, Nebr.
	Oct. 1864–May 1865
	Ogdensburg, N.Y.
	Jan. 1839–Mar. 1840
	Okeefanokee [Okefenokee] Swamp, Ga.
	Feb.–Apr. 1839
	Olathe, Kans.
	June 1864–June 1865
	Old Fort Cedar, Camp near, Neb. Terr.
	Feb.–Apr. 1856
	Old Ponca Agency, Dak. Terr.
	June and July 1870
	Olmus, Camp, Tex.
	Dec. 1845–Feb. 1846
	Omaha Agency, Nebr.
	May 1904
	Opelika, Ala.
	Mar. 1872–Apr. 1875
	Opelousas, La.
	May–Sept. 1869
	Oquendo Nueva, Samar, P.I.
	Nov. 1901
	Orangeburgh, S.C.
	Mar. 1866
	Oras, Samar, P.I.
	Oct. 1902–Sept. 1905
	Ormoc, Leyte, P.I.
	July–Nov. 1902
	Oro Blanca, Camp near, Ariz. Terr.
	Oct. 1893
	Osceola, Mo.
	July 1862
	Ossabaw Island, Ga.
	Feb. and Mar. 1863
	Otis, Camp, Hawaii
	Sept. and Oct. 1898
	Overton, Camp, Ariz.
	June 1903
	Ozark, Mo.
	Aug.–Dec. 1862
1529	Pacific City, Mo.
	Nov. 1861–Jan. 1862
	Paete, Laguna, P.I.
	Mar. 1900–Mar. 1902
	Pagsanjan, Luzon, P.I.
	June 1900
	Paksabangan, Mindanao, P.I.
	Sept. 1910–June 1911
	Palapag, Samar, P.I.

Roll	Description
	July–Sept. 1905
	Palestine, Tex.
	Sept. 1868–Jan. 1869
	Palm Beach, Fla.
	Feb. and Mar. 1913
	Palma Soriano, Cuba
	May 1899–Mar. 1900
	Palmyra, Mo
	Mar. 1863
	Palo Blanco, Camp, Tex.
	Aug. 1855
	Paluan, Mindoro, P.I.
	Aug.–Nov. 1902
	Panama Coast Artillery District, C.Z.
	Sept.–Dec. 1916
	Paniqui, Tarlac, P.I.
	Apr. 1903
	Paracale, Camarines Norte, P.I.
	Dec. 1901–July 1902
	Paraje, N. Mex.
	June 1862
	Paranaque, Luzon, P.I.
	Nov. 1900
	Paranas, Samar, P.I.
	May and June 1906
1530	Parang, Mindanao, P.I.
	Feb. 1902–Dec. 1909
1531	Parole, Camp, Pa.
	Aug. and Sept. 1863
	Pasaiao [Pasacao] Camarines Sur, P.I.
	May 1901–May 1902
	Pasig, Luzon, P.I.
	Apr. 1900–Sept. 1902
	Pass Christian, Camp, Miss.
	June 1843–July 1845
	Pass Manchac and De Sair, La.
	Dec. 1864–May 1865
	Patterson, Mo.
	Sept. 1864–June 1865
	Pavillion Key, Fla.
	Mar.–May 1857
	Pawnee Agency, Nebr. Terr.
	Sept. 1863–Oct. 1865
	Pawnee Ranche, Nebr. Terr.
	Oct. and Nov. 1864
	Payne, Fort, Ala.
	July–Sept. 1838
	Payne, Camp, Nebr. Terr
	Aug. 1858
	Peach Springs, Camp, Ariz. Terr.
	July 1894
	Pecan, Camp, Tex.
	July 1856
	Pecos River, Camp on, Tex.
	Sept. 1857–Apr. 1858
	Pedigan, Luzon, P.I.
	Nov. and Dec. 1900
	Pelouse [Palouse] River, Wash. Terr.
	Sept. 1858
	Pendencia, Tex
	Oct. 1859
	Peralto, N. Mex.
	May–Sept. 1862
	Perry, Camp, Ohio
	Aug. 1907–July 1913
	Perryville, Camp near, Md.
	Dec. 1861–Jan. 1862
	Peyton, Fort, Fla.
	July 1837–June 1840
	Phantom Hill, Fort, Tex.
	Feb. 1857; Jan. 1872

Roll	Description
	Pharr, Tex.
	Sept. and Oct. 1915
	Phelps, Camp, Tex.
	Jan. and Feb. 1852
	Pike, Cantonment, Mo.
	July–Sept. 1827
	Pila, Laguna, P.I.
	Nov. 1900
	Pilar, Sorsogon, P.I.
	Jan. 1905–Mar. 1906
	Pilatka, Fla.
	Aug.–Dec. 1849
	Pilatka, Fort, Fla.
	June–Sept. 1838
	Pillow, Fort, Tenn.
	Jan. 1863–Feb. 1864
	Pilot Grove, Tex.
	July 1868–Feb. 1869
	Pimos Villages, Ariz. Terr.
	Apr. and June 1862
1532	Pinal, Camp, Ariz.
	Dec. 1870–June 1871
	Pinamalayan, Mindoro, P.I.
	Oct. 1901–Dec. 1902
	Pine Ridge Agency, S. Dak.
	Nov. 1890–June 1891
	Pio, Camp, Mindanao, P.I.
	June 1910–Feb. 1911
	Pittsburg Landing, Tenn.
	June 1862–Dec. 1867
	Pittsfield, Mass.
	Aug.–Nov. 1813
	Platte River, Camp on, Nebr. Terr.
	June 1859
	Platt Point, N.Y.
	May 1814
	Plum Creek, Nebr.
	Sept. 1864–Dec. 1865
	Plummer, Camp, N. Mex.
	Nov. 1866–Oct. 1867
	Plymouth, N.C.
	May–Dec. 1867
	Pocatello, Idaho
	May 1894
1533	Point, Fort, Tex.
	Mar. 1898–June 1900
	Point Isabel, Tex.
	Oct. 1867–Feb. 1869
	Point Loma, Camp, Calif.
	Mar. 1911
	Point Lookout, Md.
	May–July 1865
	Pola, Mindoro, P.I.
	Oct. 1901–Nov. 1903
	Polk, Camp, Oreg.
	Oct. 1865–Mar. 1866
	Polo, Bulacan, P.I.
	July 1903–Aug. 1906
	Polvo, Tex.
	Jan. and Feb. 1911
	Polvodera [Polvadera], N. Mex.
	Sept. 1862
	Ponca Agency, Ind. Terr.
	Mar.–Aug. 1885
	Poncas Island, Nebr.
	Jan. and Feb. 1856
	Pond Creek, Kans.
	Mar. and Apr. 1866
	Ponka, Fort, Dak. Terr.
	Jan.–Apr. 1866
	Port Eads, La.

Roll	Description
	May 1898
	Port Gibson, Miss.
	Feb.–Nov. 1876
	Porter, Camp, Mont.
	Nov. 1880–Nov. 1881
	Porter, Camp, Utah
	Jan. 1859
	Portland, Maine
	Draft Rendezvous
	Sept. 1863–Aug. 1865
	Portland, Oreg.
	Exposition Grounds
	May–Oct. 1905
1534	Prairie Dog Creek, Kans. Terr
	June–Aug. 1859
	Prentiss, Camp, Calif.
	May–Oct. 1859
	Presidio, Camp near, Tex.
	Sept. 1880–Feb. 1881
	Preston, Fort, Fla.
	Feb. 1840–Feb. 1842
	Price, Camp, Ariz.
	Apr.–Oct. 1882
	Price, Camp, Ind. Terr.
	Aug. 1889
	Progreso, Tex
	Oct. 1915
	Puerto Padre, Cuba
	Apr. 1899–Jan. 1900
	Punta Rassa, (?)
	Nov. 1837
	Punta Separacion, Paragua, P.I.
	Oct. 1902–Mar. 1903
	Purcell, Camp near, Ind. Terr.
	May–Aug. 1889
	Quapaw, Camp, and Quapaw Reserve, Ind. Terr.
	May 1880–July 1881
	Quincy, Ill.
	U.S. General Hospital
	Aug. 1864
1535	Ragay, Ambos Camarines, P.I.
	Jan.–Dec. 1904
	Rains, Camp, Dak. Terr.
	Aug.–Oct. 1878
	Rampart, Camp, Alaska
	Aug. 1899–Aug. 1901
	Rancho de Jurupa, Calif.
	Sept. 1852–Mar. 1854
	Ranchuelo, Cuba
	Nov. 1906–July 1907
	Rankin, Camp, Colo. Terr.
	Feb.–Sept. 1865
	Rawlins, Camp, Ariz.
	Apr.–Aug. 1870
	Rawling [Rawlins], Fort, Utah Terr.
	July 1870–June 1871
	Rayado, N. Mex.
	May 1850–Aug. 1854
	Red Cloud Agency, Dak. Terr.
	Nov. 1877–May 1879
	Red Fork, Ark. Terr.
	June–Oct. 1834
	Red Willow, Camp, Nebr.
	May–Nov. 1872
1536	Reed, Camp, Idaho Terr.
	July 1865–May 1866
	Reeve's Station, Mo.
	Mar.–July 1862
	Refugio, Tex.
	Sept. 1867–Feb. 1868

Roll	Description
	Reid, Fort, Fla.
	July 1840–Jan. 1841
	Reilly, Camp, Peking, China
	Oct. 1900–May 1901
	Reinosa, Mex.
	Dec. 1847
	Relief, Camp, Utah Terr.
	Apr. and May 1864
	Remedios, Cuba
	Mar. 1899
	Repose, Fort, Fla.
	Mar. 1842
	Rexford, Mich.
	May and June 1911
	Reynolds, Camp, Mont. Terr.
	June 1866
	Reynolds, Fort, Va.
	Dec. 1864–June 1865
	Reynolds Creek, Idaho
	June 1878
	Richardson, Fort, Va.
	June 1864–Aug. 1865
	Richmond, La.
	Feb.–Apr. 1868
	Richmond, N. Mex.
	May 1882–Sept. 1883
	Richmond, Tex.
	June–Oct. 1866
	Ricketts, Camp, Tex.
	Dec. 1851–Mar. 1852
	Riker's Island, N.Y.
	Draft Rendezvous
	July 1863–Feb. 1864
	Riley, Camp, Calif.
	Feb. 1849–Mar. 1850
	Riley, Camp, Tenn.
	Sept. and Oct. 1838
	Rio Gana, P.R.
	Aug. 1898
	Rio Grande, Camp at the Mouth of the, (Tex?)
	Dec. 1846
	Rio Pecos, Camp at the Mouth of the, Tex.
	Sept. 1880–Feb. 1881
	Rio Piedras, P.R.
	Sept. 1898–Mar. 1899
1537	Roanoke Island, N.C.
	Jan. 1865–Mar. 1866
	Robinson, Camp, Wis.
	May–Aug. 1915
	Rock Springs, Camp, Calif.
	Apr.–Dec. 1867
	Rockland, Maine
	Apr. and May 1865
	Rockport, Mo.
	Feb. 1864
	Rockwell, Camp, Ind. Terr.
	Sept. 1888
	Rocky Canon, Ariz. Terr.
	Sept. 1879
	Rocky Creek, Neb. Terr.
	July 1857
	Roger Jones, Fort, Fla.
	Mar.–May 1839
	Roma, Tex.
	Jan. 1852–Dec. 1865
	Rosa, Fort, Ga.
	Oct. 1841
	Rosario, Camp, Tex.
	June 1860
	Rosebury [Roseburg], Camp near, Oreg.
	June 1860

Roll	Description
	Ross' Landing, Tenn.
	June 1838
	Round Top, Tex.
	Apr.–Dec. 1867
	Round Valley, Calif.
	Mar. 1892
	Round Valley, Utah Terr.
	Aug. 1858
	Ruby Valley, Utah Terr.
	June and July 1860
	Rush Valley, Utah
	Apr. 1859–Apr. 1866
	Russell, Fort, at Key Biscayne, Fla.
	Feb.–Sept. 1839
	Russell, Camp, Ind. Terr.
	June 1884–Apr. 1885
	Russell, Camp, Oreg.
	Dec. 1864–Apr. 1865
	Russell's Landing, Fla.
	Dec. 1849–Mar. 1850
	Rutherfordton, N.C.
	June 1871–Oct. 1872
1538	Sabinal, Camp, Tex.
	July and Aug. 1856
	Sablayan, Mindoro, P.I.
	June–Aug. 1903
	Sacketts [Sackets] Harbor, N.Y.
	Nov. 1813; June 1815
	Sacramento, Calif.
	July 1894
	Sag Harbor, N.Y.
	Jan. and Feb. 1814
	Sagua de Tanamo, Cuba
	Oct. 1898–Oct. 1899
	Sagumbal, Tonquil [Tonguil], P.I.
	Sept.–Nov. 1910
	St. Andrews Bay, Fla.
	Jan.–Aug. 1839
	St. Asaphs, Va.
	Feb. 1909
	St. Charles, Mo.
	Feb.–Apr. 1862
	St. Helena Island, S.C.
	Dec. 1863–June 1864
	St. Joseph, La.
	Jan.–Apr. 1868
	St. Joseph, Mo.
	Aug. 1863–Nov. 1864
	St. Marks, Fort, Fla.
	May 1818–Oct. 1824
	St. Paul Island, Alaska
	May 1869–Sept. 1870
	St. Peter, Minn.
	Nov. 1862–June 1863
	St. Simons [Simon] Island, Ga.
	June 1863; Aug. 1898
	Salina, Kans.
	Sept. 1864–Aug. 1865
	Salinena, Camp, Tex.
	May 1854–Apr. 1856
	Salisbury Beach, Mass.
	Mar.–May 1865
	Salomague, Ilocos Sur, P.I.
	Sept. 1902–Jan. 1903
	Salt Fork River, Camp at, Ind. Terr.
	Mar. 1885
	Saltillo, Miss.
	Jan. and Feb. 1872
	Salt Lake, Camp at, Tex.
	May–Nov. 1854
	Salt Lake City, Utah

Roll	Description
	Dec. 1865–Mar. 1866
	Salubrity, Camp, La.
	May 1844–June 1845
1539	Samal, Bataan, P.I.
	Apr. 1905–June 1907
	Sam Fordyce, Tex.
	Mar. 1911;
	Sept. 1915
	San Antonio, Luzon, P.I.
	June 1900
	San Antonio Wells, Tex.
	May–Aug. 1854
	San Augustine, Tex.
	Oct. 1868–Mar. 1869
	San Benito, Tex.
	Sept. 1915–Mar. 1916
	San Bernardino, Calif.
	Feb. 1858–Sept. 1861
	Sanderson, Fort, Fla.
	July 1840–Jan. 1841
	San Diego, Camp, Calif.
	Mar. 1911
	San Diego de los Banos, Cuba
	May 1899
	Sand Springs, Mo.
	Aug.–Oct. 1862
	San Fabian, Pangasinan, P.I.
	July–Nov. 1902
	San Felipe, Cavite, P.I.
	Aug. 1898
	San Felipe Neri, P.I.
	June 1900–Nov. 1902
	San Fernando, P.I.
	Sept. 1899
	San Fernando, Pampanga, P.I.
	July 1902–May 1914
	San Fernando de Union, Luzon, P.I.
	Mar. 1900–Dec. 1902
	San Francisco, Calif. Provost Guard
	Sept. 1864–July 1865
	San Francisco de Malabon, Cavite, P.I.
	Apr. 1900–Nov. 1904
	San German, P.R.
	Dec. 1898–Oct. 1899
	San Ignacio, Tex.
	May–Oct. 1868
	San Isidoro, N. Mex.
	Nov. 1849–June 1850
	San Isidro, Luzon, P.I.
	May 1900
1540	San Joaquin, Panay, P.I.
	July 1902–Jan. 1903
	San Jose, Batangas, P.I.
	Nov. 1900–Sept. 1902
	San Jose, Calif.
	Apr.–June 1848
	San Jose de Buenavista, Panay, P.I.
	Jan. 1900–Jan. 1903
	San Jose de Saganoy [Laganoy], P.I.
	Jan. 1901–Jan. 1902
	San José River, Cuba
	June 1898
	San Juan de Bocboc, Batangas, P.I.
	Oct. 1900–Mar. 1903
	San Julian, Samar, P.I.
	June–Oct. 1905
	San Luis, Pampanga, P.I.
	May and June 1900
	San Miguel, Calif.
	June and July 1850
	San Pedro, Summer Camp near, Calif.

Roll	Description
	Aug. 1892
	San Pedro, Camp on the, Tex.
	July 1854
	San Pedro Tunisan [Tunasan], Laguna, P.I.
	Jan.–Sept. 1905
	San Rafael, Bulacan, P.I.
	May 1900
	San Ramon Farm, Mindanao, P.I.
	June 1911–Dec. 1912
1541	Santa Barbara, Panay, P.I.
	July–Sept. 1902
	Santa Cruz, Camp at, Calif.
	July 1887–Sept. 1889
	Santa Cruz, Cavite, P.I.
	July–Dec. 1902
	Santa Cruz, Marinduque, P.I.
	July 1900–June 1902
	Santa Fe, N. Mex.
	Dec. 1847–June 1860
	Santa Maria, Bulacan, P.I.
	July 1903
	Santa Rita, Samar, P.I.
	July 1901–June 1907
	Santa Rita Mines, Camp near, Ariz. Terr.
	Mar.–May 1867
	Santa Rosa, Laguna, P.I.
	Mar. 1903–Dec. 1904
	Santa Tomas, N. Mex.
	Dec. 1854–Jan. 1855
	Santurce, P.R.
	Oct. 1898–May 1899
	San Ysidro, Calif.
	June 1912–Jan. 1913
	Sargent, Camp, Nebr.
	Aug. and Sept. 1867
	Sariaya, Tayabas, P.I.
	May–Nov. 1904
	Sault De St. Maries, (?)
	June 1823
	Savannah, Mo.
	Oct. 1863–Apr. 1864
	Schofield, Camp, Mo.
	July 1862
	Schrader Barracks, Ky.
	Apr. 1869
	Scott, Fort, Va.
	Dec. 1864–Aug. 1865
	Scott, J. M., Camp, Tex.
	May–Dec. 1854
	Scott, Winfield, Cantonment, E. Fla.
	Aug. 1841–May 1842
	Searle, Fort, Fla.
	Jan. 1840–May 1841
1542	Seguin, Tex.
	Sept. 1867–Feb. 1868
	Selvies River, Camp on, (?)
	Nov. 1865
	Sevilla, Cuba
	June 1898
	Seward, Fort, Calif.
	Sept.–Dec. 1861
	Seward, Fort, S.C.
	Feb.–June 1862
	Seymour, Battery, Ga.
	May 1863
	Seymour, Camp, N.C.
	Sept. 1871
	Sheep Creek, Mont.
	Aug. 1889
	Shelbyville, Ky.
	Sept. 1871–Dec. 1872

Roll	Description
	Sherman, Fort, C.Z.
	June–Aug. 1914
	Sherman, Tex.
	Mar.–Aug. 1867
	Sherrard, Fort, Fla.
	Apr.–Dec. 1839
	Sherrod, Fort, Fla.
	Mar.–May 1842
	Shunk, Camp, Utah
	Dec. 1858
	Siboney, Cuba
	June–Aug. 1898
	Sigaboy, Camp, Mindanao, P.I.
	Oct. 1910–Aug. 1911
	Silang, Cavite, P.I.
	Apr. 1900–Nov. 1904
	Simmons, Fort, Fla.
	Nov. 1841–Feb. 1842
	Simmons, Fort, Camp opposite, Fla.
	Feb. 1857
	Simon Drum, Fort, Fla.
	Mar. 1855–Apr. 1856
	Sindangan, Mindanao, P.I.
	May 1910–Jan. 1911
	Sinitoan [Siniloan], Luzon, P.I.
	Apr.–Sept. 1900
	Sinoloan [Siniloan], Laguna, P.I.
	July 1901–Apr. 1902
	Sioux City, Iowa
	Feb. 1865–Apr. 1866
	Sioux Falls, Dak. Terr.
	July–Dec. 1865
1543	Siquijor, Negros Oriental, P.I.
	Aug.–Oct. 1911
	Sixteen, Number, Fort, Fla.
	Dec. 1839–June 1840
	Skull Valley, Ariz. Terr.
	Apr. 1866–May 1867
	Smead, Camp, Fla.
	Sept. 1856–May 1857
	Smith, Camp, Mich.
	Aug. 1889
	Smith, C. F., Camp, Ky.
	Feb. 1862
	Smithland, Ky.
	Nov. 1861–Oct. 1865
	Smithville, N.C.
	June 1865–May 1866
	Socorro, Cuba
	July 1899–Jan. 1900
	Solano, Bayombong, P.I.
	Feb. and Mar. 1900
	Soledad Pass, Calif.
	Aug. 1876
	Songo, Cuba
	July–Nov. 1898
	South Loop [Loup] Fork, Nebr. Terr.
	May and June 1865
	South Pass, Camp, Rocky Mts.
	June 1845
	Southern District, N. Mex.
	Apr. 1862
	Sparta, Wis.
	Aug. 1910
	Spirit Lake, Iowa
	Dec. 1864–June 1865
	Spokane Falls, Wash. Terr.
	Oct. 1877–Mar. 1878
	Spotted Tail Agency, Dak. Terr.
	Dec. 1877–July 1878
	Springfield, Ill.

Roll	Description
	Feb. 1864–Nov. 1865
	Springfield, Mo.
	Mar. 1862–Jan. 1864
	Springfield, Tenn.
	Apr. 1865
1544	Stage, Fort, Mass.
	June–Aug. 1898
	Stanford, Fort, Ariz.
	May 1862
	Stanford, Camp, Calif.
	July–Oct. 1863
	Stanislaus, Camp, Calif.
	Apr.–Nov. 1849
	Stanton, Camp, Md.
	Nov. 1863–Feb. 1864
	Starke, Fort, Fla.
	Nov. and Dec. 1840
	Staten Island, N.Y.
	Mar. 1814–May 1815
	Staunton, Camp, Mo.
	July 1849
	Steele, Camp, Calif.
	June 1852
	Stevenson, Ala.
	Feb.–June 1865
	Stiffinalgee Bluff, Fla.
	Nov. and Dec. 1838
	Stoddert, Fort, Ala.
	Nov. 1806–Nov. 1807
	Strong, E. B., Camp, Tex.
	Nov. and Dec. 1855
	Strong, Fort, Va.
	Mar. 1864
	Strowbridge, Camp, Calif.
	Apr. 1855
	Sturgeon, Mo.
	Feb.–May 1862
	Sturgis, J. G., Camp, Dak. Terr.
	July–Sept. 1878
	Suffolk, Va.
	May 1862–May 1863
	Sugar Creek, Camp, Kans.
	Dec. 1861–Jan. 1862
	Sulat, Samar, P.I.
	July–Sept. 1901
	Sullivan, Fort, Fla.
	Jan.–Oct. 1839
	Sulphur Springs, Dak. Terr.
	Sept. and Oct. 1865
	Sulphur Springs, Mo.
	June–Aug. 1862
	Sulphur Springs, Tex.
	Aug. 1868–Feb. 1869
	Summerville, Ga.
	Jan.–July 1870
	Summerville [Summersville], W. Va.
	Sept. 1861–Mar. 1862
	Swanton, Vt.
	Sept.–Dec. 1838
	Sykes, Camp, Dak. Terr.
	May–Aug. 1872
	Syracuse, Mo.
	Dec. 1861
1545	Taberville, Mo.
	May 1863
	Tacloban, Leyte, P.I.
	July–Dec. 1902
	Taft, Samar, P.I.
	Jan.–Sept. 1905
	Tagabiran, Samar, P.I.
	May 1907

Roll	Description
	Tagaloan [Tagoloan], Mindanao, P.I.
	Sept. 1901
	Taguig, Luzon, P.I.
	May–Dec. 1900
	Talagutan [Talagutun], Mindanao, P.I.
	June and July 1911
	Talavera, Nueva Ecija, P.I.
	July 1902–Feb. 1903
	Talisay, Batangas, P.I.
	Sept. 1902
	Talladega, Ala.
	May–Oct. 1865
	Taranguan [Tarangnan], Samar, P.I.
	Jan.–Oct. 1905
	Tarlac, Tarlac, P.I.
	May 1901–May 1903
	Taviran, Samar, P.I.
	Feb. 1906
	Taylor, Camp, Calif.
	Sept. 1859
	Taylor Barracks, Ky.
	July 1871
	Taylor, Fort, Wash. Terr.
	Aug. and Sept. 1858
	Tay Tay [Taytay], Luzon, P.I.
	May 1900
	Tayug, Pangasinan, P.I.
	Jan. 1901–Apr. 1902
	Tecate, Calif.
	Mar. 1911–Nov. 1914
	Tecumseh, Kans. Terr.
	Dec. 1856–Feb. 1857
	Ten, Number, Fort, Fla.
	Aug. 1839–June 1840
	Teton Pass, Idaho
	Aug. 1895
	Texas Indian Agency, Camp at, Ind. Terr.
	Sept. 1859
	Thirteen, Number, District, Fla.
	Apr. 1839
	Thomas, Fort, Tenn.
	Mar. 1863–Apr. 1864
	Thomasville, Ga.
	Oct. 1865–Jan. 1866
	Thompson, Fort, Dak. Terr.
	July 1866–May 1867
	Thompson, Fort, Fla.
	Feb. 1838–Dec. 1854
	Thompson, Camp, Kans.
	Apr. 1858
	Thornton, Camp, Tex.
	Mar. 1849
	Thoroughfare Gap, Camp at, Va.
	Aug. 1898
	Three, Number, Fort, Fla.
	Apr. 1839–June 1840
	Thunder Butte, Camp, S. Dak.
	Dec. 1907
	Tiaon [Tiaong], Tayabas, Luzon, P.I.
	June 1900–July 1902
1546	Tillinghast, Fort, Va.
	Apr. and May 1865
	Timpanogas, Camp, Utah
	Mar. 1859
	Tipton, Mo.
	Mar.–May 1862
	Toledo, Cebu, P.I.
	Dec. 1904–Mar. 1905
	Tollgate, Camp, Oreg.
	July and Aug. 1909
	Tolosa, Leyte, P.I.

Roll	Description
	Nov. 1906–Mar. 1909
	Toponish Creek, Wash. Terr.
	July 1856
	Torrijas [Torrijos], Marinduque, P.I.
	Oct. 1900–Sept. 1901
	Totten, Fort, N.C.
	Oct.–Dec. 1864
	Traders Hill, Ga.
	Oct. 1819–Nov. 1820
	Treadwell, Alaska
	May 1907
	Trenton, Tenn.
	Oct. 1862
	Trinidad, Camp, Tex.
	Mar. 1868–Feb. 1869
	Troy, Mo.
	Mar. and Apr. 1862
	Truckee, Calif.
	July 1894
	Tubigon, Bohol, P.I.
	July 1902–Jan. 1903
	Tugucgarao [Tuguegarao], Cagayan, P.I.
	July 1902–Aug. 1903
	Tulare, Camp, Calif.
	Apr.–July 1871
	Tumaium [Tumauini], Isabela, Luzon, P.I.
	Nov. 1902–June 1903
	Tunga, P.I.
	Dec. 1906–Jan. 1907
	Turkey Creek, Fla.
	Dec. 1856
	Turkey Creek, Camp on, Tex.
	Sept.–Nov. 1854
	Tuskegee, Ala.
	Oct. and Nov. 1870
	Twelve, Number, Fort, Fla.
	Apr. 1839–June 1840
	Twenty, Number, Fort, Fla.
	June–Oct. 1839
	Twiggs, Camp, Miss.
	July 1849–Sept. 1853
	Tybee Island, Ga.
	June 1823–Apr. 1862
	Tyler, Camp, Utah Terr.
	Feb. 1859
1547	Union, Fort, Mont. Terr.
	June and July 1865
	Union Point, Ga.
	Aug.–Nov. 1869
	Upper San Pedro, Ariz. Terr.
	Sept. 1866
	Upperville, Va.
	July–Sept. 1827
	Uptons Hill, Va.
	Oct. 1861
	Utuado, P.R.
	Oct. 1898–July 1899
	Valley, Fort, Ga.
	July 1870
	Val Verde, Camp, N. Mex.
	May 1862
	Van Buren, Ark.
	May 1864–Jan. 1865
	Van Dorn, Camp, Kans. Terr.
	July 1859
	Vasquey Canyon, Calif.
	Apr. and May 1894
	Victoria, Tex.
	Jan. 1866–Jan. 1867
	Vidalia, La.
	Aug. 1865–Oct. 1867

Roll	Description
	Vieques, P.R.
	Dec. 1898–May 1899
	Vigan, Luzon, P.I.
	Jan. 1900–Dec. 1902
	Vigilance, Camp, N. Mex.
	May–July 1852
	Villaba, Leyte, P.I.
	Sept. 1906
	Vincennes, (?)
	Mar.–May 1806
	Vinton, Fort, Fla.
	Apr. 1839–May 1850
	Virac, Catanduanes, P.I.
	Apr. 1900–Dec. 1904
	Virginia, Camp, Va.
	July–Sept. 1884
	Vogdes, Camp, S.C.
	Oct. 1876
	Vose, Fort, Fla.
	Nov. 1841–May 1842
1548	Wacissa, Fort, Fla.
	Feb.–July 1839
	Waco, Camp near, Ga.
	July and Aug. 1898
	Waco, Ga., U.S. Rifle Range
	Apr. and May 1910
	Wade, Camp, Okla.
	Oct. 1889–Dec. 1890
	Walbach, Camp, Fla.
	Dec. 1856
	Walbach, Camp, Neb. Terr.
	Sept. 1858–Apr. 1859
	Walhalla S.C.
	Apr. 1866
	Wallace, Camp, Idaho
	June–Sept. 1865
	Wallowa Valley, Oreg.
	Aug. 1875
	Walnut Creek, Camp on, Ariz. Terr.
	Oct. 1881
	Ward, Fort, Va.
	Sept. 1862–Aug. 1865
	Warren, Camp, Mo.
	Sept. 1862
	Warrenton, Mo.
	Jan. 1862–Feb. 1863
	Warrenton, Va.
	July 1868–Jan. 1869
	Washburn, Camp, Wis.
	Aug. 1863–Aug. 1865
	Washington, La.
	Aug.–Oct. 1865
	Washington, Camp, near Gaithersburg, Md.
	June 1882–Sept. 1883
	Washington, Camp, (N.J.?)
	June–Sept. 1839
	Washington, Fort, Pa.
	July 1863
	Wayne, Fort, Ga.
	Dec. 1821–May 1823
	Waynesboro, Tenn.
	Oct. and Nov. 1868
1549	Wea Reservation, Camp on, Kans. Terr.
	Apr.–Sept. 1860
	Weatherford, Tex.
	June 1867–Mar. 1868
	Webster, Camp, Ala.
	July and Aug. 1836
	Weil Farm, Camp, Ky.
	Sept. 1898
	Wellsville, Mo.

Roll	Description
	Feb. and Mar. 1862
	Wenham, Mass.
	Mar. 1864
	Westport, Mo.
	Aug. 1863–Jan. 1864
	Wetherill, Camp, at Greenville, S.C.
	Dec. 1898
	Wharton, Tex.
	Sept. 1868–Mar. 1869
	Wheelock, Fort, Fla.
	July 1840–Feb. 1842
	Whipple, Camp, Fla.
	Feb. 1857
	White River, New Post on, Wash. Terr.
	Apr. 1856
	Whitesboro, Tex.
	Dec. 1898
	Whittelsey, Camp, Dak. Terr.
	July–Sept. 1867
	Wickenburg, Ariz.
	Apr. 1866
	Wilcox, Camp, en route to Jefferson Barracks, (?)
	Feb. 1858
	Wilds, Fort, Ga.
	Aug.–Oct. 1838
	Willcox, Camp, Va.
	May–Sept. 1868
	Williams, Fort, Va.
	Dec. 1864–Aug. 1865
	Williamsburg, Va.
	June 1862–Mar. 1869
	Willow Creek, Colo. Terr.
	Sept. 1874
	Winchester, Miss.
	May–Oct. 1867
	Winfield Scott, Camp, Wash.
	June 1879
	Winnebago, Fort, M.T.
	Jan. 1831
	Winnebago Agency, Camp at, Nebr.
	May–Aug. 1889
	Winnsboro, La.
	Aug.–Nov. 1869
	Winthrop, Camp, Ind. Terr.
	Sept. 1865–Mar. 1867
	Winthrop, Fort, Mass.
	Dec. 1864–May 1865
	Winthrop, Mass., Mortar Battery
	May–Nov. 1898
1550	Wood, A. E., Camp, Calif.
	Apr. 1905
	Wood, Camp, Oreg.
	Sept. 1867
	Wood, Camp, Tex.
	Jan. 1860–Feb. 1861
	Wood, G. W. F., Camp, Tex.
	May–Sept. 1857
	Woodbury, Fort, Va.
	June 1864
	Woodland, Tex.
	Oct. 1868
	Woodville, Miss.
	Aug.–Nov. 1867
	Woodville, Tex.
	Apr. 1867–May 1868
	Wool, Camp, Calif.
	May–Sept. 1855
	Wool, Fort, Va.
	Mar.–July 1862
	Worth, Camp, La.

Roll	Description
	Dec. 1836
	Worth, Camp, Tex.
	Feb. 1854
	Worth, Fort, Va.
	Dec. 1864–Aug. 1865
	Wright, Samar, P.I.
	May–Nov. 1906
	Wyman, Fort, Mo.
	July 1863–Dec. 1864
	Yakima River, Wash. Terr.
	May–Aug. 1856
	Yanco [Yauco], P.R.
	Dec. 1898–May 1899
	Yankton Agency, Dak. Terr.
	Dec. 1865–Mar. 1866
	Yazoo City, Miss.
	July–Sept. 1867
	Ybor, Camp, Fla.
	May 1898
	Yellow Bluff, Fla.
	Mar. 1864–Mar. 1865
	Yellow Medicine, Minn.
	June 1857–Sept. 1860
	Young, S.B.M., Camp, Ga.
	Nov. 1898
	Young's Point, La.
	May 1867–Jan. 1868

Returns From Regular Army Infantry Regiments, June 1821–December 1916. M665. 300 rolls. DP.

This microfilm publication reproduces the monthly returns that the AGO received from Regular Army infantry regiments from June 1821 to December 1916. The returns are arranged by regiment and thereunder chronologically.

Roll	Description
1st Infantry:	
1	June 1821–Dec. 1832
2	Jan. 1833–Dec. 1843
3	Jan. 1844–Dec. 1848
4	Jan. 1849–Dec. 1855
5	Jan. 1856–Dec. 1864
6	Jan. 1865–Dec. 1873
7	Jan. 1874–Dec. 1881
8	Jan. 1882–Dec. 1889
9	Jan. 1890–Dec. 1897
10	Jan. 1898–Dec. 1900
11	Jan.–Dec. 1901
12	Jan. 1902–Dec. 1904
13	Jan. 1905–Dec. 1909
14	Jan. 1910–Dec. 1916
2d Infantry:	
15	June 1821–Dec. 1832
16	Jan. 1833–Dec. 1843
17	Jan. 1844–Dec. 1848
18	Jan. 1849–Dec. 1853
19	Jan. 1854–Dec. 1860
20	Jan. 1861–Dec. 1866
21	Jan. 1867–Dec. 1873
22	Jan. 1874–Dec. 1883
23	Jan. 1884–Dec. 1892
24	Jan. 1893–Dec. 1898
25	Jan. 1899–Dec. 1900
26	Jan. 1901–Dec. 1903
27	Jan. 1904–Dec. 1909
28	Jan. 1910–Dec. 1916

Roll	Description
3d Infantry:	
29	July 1821–Dec. 1832
30	Jan. 1833–Dec. 1842
31	Jan. 1843–Dec. 1849
32	Jan. 1850–Dec. 1859
33	Jan. 1860–Dec. 1866
34	Jan. 1867–Dec. 1875
35	Jan. 1876–Dec. 1885
36	Jan. 1886–Dec. 1894
37	Jan. 1895–Dec. 1899
38	Jan. 1900–Dec. 1905
39	Jan. 1906–Dec. 1910
40	Jan. 1911–Dec. 1916
4th Infantry:	
41	June 1821–Dec. 1831
42	Jan. 1832–Dec. 1842
43	Jan. 1843–Dec. 1850
44	Jan. 1851–Dec. 1859
45	Jan. 1860–Dec. 1866
46	Jan. 1867–Dec. 1875
47	Jan. 1876–Dec. 1885
48	Jan. 1886–Dec. 1895
49	Jan. 1896–Dec. 1900
50	Jan. 1901–Dec. 1905
51	Jan. 1906–Dec. 1910
52	Jan. 1911–Dec. 1916
5th Infantry:	
53	June 1821–Dec. 1831
54	Jan. 1832–Dec. 1842
55	Jan. 1843–Dec. 1851
56	Jan. 1852–Dec. 1861
57	Jan. 1862–Dec. 1869
58	Jan. 1870–Dec. 1879
59	Jan. 1880–Dec. 1889
60	Jan. 1890–Dec. 1898
61	Jan. 1899–Dec. 1903
62	Jan. 1904–Dec. 1909
63	Jan. 1910–Dec. 1916
6th Infantry:	
64	June 1821–Dec. 1832
65	Jan. 1833–Dec. 1843
66	Jan. 1844–Dec. 1848
67	Jan. 1849–Dec. 1854
68	Jan. 1855–Dec. 1861
69	Jan. 1862–Dec. 1868
70	Jan. 1869–Dec. 1878
71	Jan. 1879–Dec. 1888
72	Jan. 1889–Dec. 1897
73	Jan. 1898–Dec. 1900
74	Jan. 1901–Dec. 1904
75	Jan. 1905–Dec. 1909
76	Jan. 1910–Dec. 1916
7th Infantry:	
77	June 1821–Dec. 1831
78	Jan. 1832–Dec. 1842
79	Jan. 1843–Dec. 1850
80	Jan. 1851–Dec. 1859
81	Jan. 1860–Dec. 1866
82	Jan. 1867–Dec. 1873
83	Jan. 1874–Dec. 1884
84	Jan. 1885–Dec. 1895
85	Jan. 1896–Dec. 1899
86	Jan. 1900–Dec. 1901
87	Jan. 1902–Dec. 1905

Roll	Description
88	Jan. 1906–Dec. 1910
89	Jan. 1911–Dec. 1916
8th Infantry:	
90	July 1838–Dec. 1847
91	Jan. 1848–Dec. 1857
92	Jan. 1858–Dec. 1865
93	Jan. 1866–Dec. 1873
94	Jan. 1874–Dec. 1882
95	Jan. 1883–Dec. 1892
96	Jan. 1893–Dec. 1899
97	Jan. 1900–Dec. 1901
98	Jan. 1902–Dec. 1905
99	Jan. 1906–Dec. 1910
100	Jan. 1911–Dec. 1916
9th Infantry:	
101	May 1847–Aug. 1848
102	Mar. 1855–Dec. 1862
103	Jan. 1863–Dec. 1869
104	Jan. 1870–Dec. 1879
105	Jan. 1880–Dec. 1889
106	Jan. 1890–Dec. 1898
107	Jan. 1899–Dec. 1900
108	Jan. 1901–Dec. 1902
109	Jan. 1903–Dec. 1906
110	Jan. 1907–Dec. 1910
111	Jan. 1911–Dec. 1916
10th Infantry:	
112	May 1847–Aug. 1848
113	Mar. 1855–Dec. 1862
114	Jan. 1863–Dec. 1870
115	Jan. 1871–Dec. 1879
116	Jan. 1880–Dec. 1890
117	Jan. 1891–Dec. 1899
118	Jan. 1900–Dec. 1901
119	Jan.–Dec. 1902
120	Jan. 1903–Dec. 1906
121	Jan. 1907–Dec. 1910
122	Jan. 1911–Dec. 1916
11th Infantry:	
123	Apr. 1847–July 1848
124	Aug. 1861–Dec. 1865
125	Jan. 1866–Dec. 1872
126	Jan. 1873–Dec. 1882
127	Jan. 1883–Dec. 1892
128	Jan. 1893–Dec. 1899
129	Jan. 1900–Dec. 1902
130	Jan. 1903–Dec. 1906
131	Jan. 1907–Dec. 1910
132	Jan. 1911–Dec. 1916
12th Infantry:	
133	July 1847–July 1848
134	Aug. 1861–Dec. 1863
135	Jan. 1864–Dec. 1867
136	Jan. 1868–Dec. 1875
137	Jan. 1876–Dec. 1885
138	Jan. 1886–Dec. 1896
139	Jan. 1897–Dec. 1900
140	Jan. 1901–Dec. 1903
141	Jan. 1904–Dec. 1909
142	Jan. 1910–Dec. 1916
13th Infantry:	
143	June 1847–July 1848; Nov. 1861–Dec. 1863
144	Jan. 1864–Dec. 1867

Roll	Description
145	Jan. 1868–Dec. 1876
146	Jan. 1877–Dec. 1886
147	Jan. 1887–Dec. 1895
148	Jan. 1896–Dec. 1900
149	Jan. 1901–Dec. 1904
150	Jan. 1905–Dec. 1909
151	Jan. 1910–Dec. 1916

14th Infantry:

Roll	Description
152	July 1847–Apr. 1848
153	July 1861–Dec. 1865
154	Jan. 1866–Dec. 1872
155	Jan. 1873–Dec. 1882
156	Jan. 1883–Dec. 1892
157	Jan. 1893–Dec. 1898
158	Jan. 1899–Dec. 1900
159	Jan. 1901–Dec. 1903
160	Jan. 1904–Dec. 1906
161	Jan. 1907–Dec. 1910
162	Jan. 1911–Dec. 1916

15th Infantry:

Roll	Description
163	Apr. 1847–May 1848
164	Dec. 1861–Dec. 1865
165	Jan. 1866–Dec. 1872
166	Jan. 1873–Dec. 1880
167	Jan. 1881–Dec. 1889
168	Jan. 1890–Dec. 1897
169	Jan. 1898–Dec. 1900
170	Jan. 1901–Dec. 1903
171	Jan. 1904–Dec. 1909
172	Jan. 1910–Dec. 1916

16th Infantry:

Roll	Description
173	July 1861–Dec. 1864
174	Jan. 1865–Dec. 1869
175	Jan. 1870–Dec. 1879
176	Jan. 1880–Dec. 1889
177	Jan. 1890–Dec. 1897
178	Jan. 1898–Dec. 1901
179	Jan. 1902–Dec. 1904
180	Jan. 1905–Dec. 1909
181	Jan. 1910–Dec. 1916

17th Infantry:

Roll	Description
182	Aug. 1861–Dec. 1865
183	Jan. 1866–Dec. 1871
184	Jan. 1872–Dec. 1880
185	Jan. 1881–Dec. 1889
186	Jan. 1890–Dec. 1897
187	Jan. 1898–Dec. 1900
188	Jan. 1901–Dec. 1904
189	Jan. 1905–Dec. 1908
190	Jan. 1909–Dec. 1916

18th Infantry:

Roll	Description
191	Dec. 1861–Dec. 1862
192	Jan. 1863–Dec. 1864
193	Jan. 1865–Dec. 1870
194	Jan. 1871–Dec. 1880
195	Jan. 1881–Dec. 1889
196	Jan. 1890–Dec. 1897
197	Jan. 1898–Dec. 1900
198	Jan. 1901–Dec. 1902
199	Jan. 1903–Dec. 1905
200	Jan. 1906–Dec. 1909
201	Jan. 1910–Dec. 1916

19th Infantry:

Roll	Description
202	Aug. 1861–Dec. 1865
203	Jan. 1866–Dec. 1870
204	Jan. 1871–Dec. 1879
205	Jan. 1880–Dec. 1888
206	Jan. 1889–Dec. 1897
207	Jan. 1898–Dec. 1900
208	Jan. 1901–Dec. 1904
209	Jan. 1905–Dec. 1909
210	Jan. 1910–Dec. 1916

20th Infantry:

Roll	Description
211	Dec. 1866–Dec. 1873
212	Jan. 1874–Dec. 1881
213	Jan. 1882–Dec. 1889
214	Jan. 1890–Dec. 1897
215	Jan. 1898–Dec. 1900
216	Jan. 1901–Dec. 1904
217	Jan. 1905–Dec. 1909
218	Jan. 1910–Dec. 1916

21st Infantry:

Roll	Description
219	Dec. 1866–Dec. 1872
220	Jan. 1873–Dec. 1880
221	Jan. 1881–Dec. 1889
222	Jan. 1890–Dec. 1897
223	Jan. 1898–Dec. 1900
224	Jan. 1901–Dec. 1904
225	Jan. 1905–Dec. 1908
226	Jan. 1909–Dec. 1916

22d Infantry:

Roll	Description
227	Dec. 1866–Dec. 1873
228	Jan. 1874–Dec. 1881
229	Jan. 1882–Dec. 1889
230	Jan. 1890–Dec. 1897
231	Jan. 1898–Dec. 1900
232	Jan. 1901–Dec. 1903
233	Jan. 1904–Dec. 1906
234	Jan. 1907–Dec. 1910
235	Jan. 1911–Dec. 1916

23d Infantry:

Roll	Description
236	Nov. 1866–Dec. 1873
237	Jan. 1874–Dec. 1882
238	Jan. 1883–Dec. 1890
239	Jan. 1891–Dec. 1897
240	Jan. 1898–Dec. 1900
241	Jan. 1901–Dec. 1902
242	Jan. 1903–Dec. 1906
243	Jan. 1907–Dec. 1910
244	Jan. 1911–Dec. 1916

24th Infantry:

Roll	Description
245	Dec. 1866–Dec. 1872
246	Jan. 1873–Dec. 1880
247	Jan. 1881–Dec. 1889
248	Jan. 1890–Dec. 1897
249	Jan. 1898–Dec. 1899
250	Jan. 1900–Dec. 1901
251	Jan. 1902–Dec. 1905
252	Jan. 1906–Dec. 1909
253	Jan. 1910–Dec. 1916

25th Infantry:

Roll	Description
254	Jan. 1867–Dec. 1873
255	Jan. 1874–Dec. 1882
256	Jan. 1883–Dec. 1890
257	Jan. 1891–Dec. 1897
258	Jan. 1898–Dec. 1900
259	Jan. 1901–Dec. 1903

Roll	Description
260	Jan. 1904–Dec. 1908
261	Jan. 1909–Dec. 1916

26th Infantry:

Roll	Description
262	Dec. 1866–June 1869
263	Mar. 1901–Dec. 1902
264	Jan. 1903–Dec. 1905
265	Jan. 1906–Dec. 1910
266	Jan. 1911–Dec. 1916

27th Infantry:

Roll	Description
267	Dec. 1886–July 1869
268	Apr. 1901–Dec. 1903
269	Jan. 1904–Dec. 1906
270	Jan. 1907–Dec. 1910
271	Jan. 1911–Dec. 1916

28th Infantry:

Roll	Description
272	Oct. 1866–Apr. 1869
273	Mar. 1901–Dec. 1902
274	Jan. 1903–Dec. 1905
275	Jan. 1906–Dec. 1909
276	Jan. 1910–Dec. 1916

29th Infantry:

Roll	Description
277	Dec. 1866–Mar. 1869
278	Mar. 1901–Dec. 1904
279	Jan. 1905–Dec. 1909
280	Jan. 1910–Dec. 1916

30th Infantry:

Roll	Description
281	Dec. 1866–Apr. 1869
282	Aug. 1901–Dec. 1903
283	Jan. 1904–Dec. 1907
284	Jan. 1908–Dec. 1911
285	Jan. 1912–Dec. 1916

31st Infantry:

Roll	Description
286	Dec. 1866–Apr. 1869; Aug.–Dec. 1916

32d Infantry:

Roll	Description
287	Sept. 1866–May 1869; Aug.–Dec. 1916

33d Infantry:

Roll	Description
288	Dec. 1866–May 1869; July–Dec. 1916

34th Infantry:

Roll	Description
289	Dec. 1866–Mar. 1869; July–Dec. 1916

35th Infantry:

Roll	Description
290	Dec. 1866–Aug. 1869; July–Dec. 1916

36th Infantry:

Roll	Description
291	Dec. 1866–May 1869; July–Dec. 1916

37th Infantry:

Roll	Description
292	Nov. 1866–Dec. 1869; July–Dec. 1916

38th Infantry:

Roll	Description
293	Feb. 1867–Dec. 1869

39th Infantry:

Roll	Description
294	Oct. 1866–Apr. 1869

40th Infantry:

Roll	Description
295	Nov. 1866–Apr. 1869

41st Infantry:

Roll	Description
296	Dec. 1866–Dec. 1869

42d Infantry:

Roll	Description
297	Dec. 1866–Apr. 1869

43d Infantry:

Roll	Description
298	Jan. 1867–Mar. 1869

44th Infantry:

Roll	Description
299	Dec. 1866–May 1869

45th Infantry:

Roll	Description
300	Dec. 1866–June 1869

Returns From Regular Army Cavalry Regiments, 1833–1916. M744. 117 rolls. DP.

This microfilm publication reproduces the monthly returns received by the AGO from the Regular Army cavalry regiments, and the predecessor dragoon and rifle regiments, from August 1833 to December 1916.

The returns are arranged numerically by regiment number from 1st to 17th. For the first six regiments, the number is the one given by the redesignation of August 1861. Thus the returns of the 1st Cavalry begin in 1833 with those of the U.S. Regiment of Dragoons and continue through several name changes to that of the 1st Cavalry Regiment in August 1861. The returns of the 2d Cavalry through the 6th Cavalry regiments have been similarly filmed. The returns of the 3d Regiment of Dragoons (the Mexican War unit) have been filmed after those of the 2d Cavalry, which was initially known as the 2d Dragoons.

Historical data has been filmed before the monthly returns for each regiment. Any other returns filed by the AGO are filmed after the December returns for that year in the following order: annual and quarterly returns of alterations and casualties; monthly returns of battalions, companies, detachments, and squadrons; special field returns and field returns; returns of casualties; and tri-monthly field returns. There are two exceptions to this arrangement. The returns of the Regiment of Mounted Riflemen for 1854–60 and the returns of the 8th Cavalry Regiment of 1866–1904 have been filmed in the same order in which they are bound: company, field, and other miscellaneous returns for a specific month have been filed immediately after each pertinent monthly return.

Roll	Military Units	Inclusive Dates
1st Cavalry:		
1	U.S. Dragoons	Aug. 1833–May 1836
	1st Dragoons	June 1836–Mar. 1843
	U.S. Dragoons	Apr. 1843–Mar. 1844
	1st Dragoons	Apr.–Dec. 1844
2	"	1845–47
3	"	1848–50
4	"	1851–59
5	"	Jan. 1860–Aug. 1861
	1st Cavalry	Sept. 1861–Dec. 1866
6	"	1867–76
7	"	1877–86
8	"	1887–96
9	"	1897–1900
10	"	1901–2
11	"	1903–5
12	"	1906–10
13	"	1911–16
2d Cavalry:		
14	2d Dragoons	Dec. 1836–Feb. 1843
	U.S. Riflemen	Mar. 1843–Mar. 1844
	2d Dragoons	Apr. 1844–Dec. 1845
15	"	1846–48
16	"	1849–55

Roll	Military Units	Inclusive Dates
19	2d Dragoons	1872–79
17	"	Jan. 1856–July 1861
18	"	1864–71
20	"	1880–87
21	"	1888–95
22	"	1896–1900
23	"	1901–4
24	"	1905–8
25	"	Jan. 1909–Oct. 1913

3d Dragoons:

| 26 | | May 1847–July 1848 |

3d Cavalry:

27	Mounted Riflemen	Oct. 1846–Dec. 1850
29	"	Jan. 1859–July 1861
30	3d Cavalry	1868–75
31	"	1876–84
32	"	1885–93
33	"	1894–98
34	"	1899
35	"	1900
36	"	1901–2
37	"	1903–6
38	"	1907–10
39	"	1911–16

4th Cavalry:

40		Mar. 1855–Dec. 1963
	1st Cavalry	Mar. 1855–July 1861
41	4th Cavalry	1864–71
42	"	1872–76
43	"	1877–83
44	"	1884–89
45	"	1890–96
46	"	1897–99
47	"	1900–1
48	"	1902–5
49	"	1906–10
50	"	1911–16

5th Cavalry:

51		Mar. 1855–Dec. 1863
	2d Cavalry	Mar. 1855–July 1861
52	5th Cavalry	1864–71
53	"	1872–76
54	"	1877–85
55	"	1886–93
56	"	1894–98
57	"	1899–1901
58	"	1902–3
59	"	"
60	"	1910–16

6th Cavalry:

61		Aug. 1861–Dec. 1867
62		1868–74
63		1875–80
64		1881–85
65		1886–91
66		1892–98
67		1899–1902
68		1903–7
69		1908–11
70		1912–16

7th Cavalry:

71		Sept. 1866–Dec. 1873
72		1874–81
73		1882–88

Roll	Military Units	Inclusive Dates
74		1889–96
75		1897–1900
76		1901–5
77		1906–10
78		1911–16

8th Cavalry:

79		Sept. 1866–Dec. 1874
80		1875–82
81		1883–89
82		1890–97
83		1898–1904
84		1905–7
85		1908–11
86		1912–16

9th Cavalry:

87		Oct. 1866–Dec. 1872
88		1873–80
89		1881–87
90		1888–95
91		1896–1900
92		1901–4
93		1905–9
94		1910–16

10th Cavalry:

95		Sept. 1866–Dec. 1872
96		1873–80
97		1881–88
98		1889–96
99		1897–1900
100		1901–4
101		1905–9
102		1910–16

11th Cavalry:

103		Mar. 1901–Dec. 1903
104		1904–9
105		1910–16

12th Cavalry:

106		Mar. 1901–Dec. 1904
107		1905–9
108		1910–16

13th Cavalry:

109		May 1901–Dec. 1905
110		1906–10
111		1911–16

14th Cavalry:

112		Mar. 1901–Dec. 1904
113		1905–10
114		1911–16

15th Cavalry:

115		Mar. 1901–Dec. 1903
116		1904–9
117		1910–16

16th Cavalry:

| | | July–Dec. 1916 |

17th Cavalry:

| | | July–Dec. 1916 |

Returns From Regular Army Artillery Regiments, June 1821–January 1901. M727. 38 rolls. DP.

This microfilm publication reproduces the monthly returns received from Regular Army artillery regiments by the AGO from June 1821 to January 1901. The returns consist mainly of copies that were submitted directly to the AGO. Over the years, however, as that Office received field records for safekeeping, it tried to make its collection of regimental returns as complete as possible by using field copies to fill gaps.

The AGO filed regimental monthly returns numerically by regiment number, and they have been microfilmed in the same order. Historical data has been filmed before the monthly returns for each regiment. Following the December returns, any additional returns filed by the AGO for that year appear in the following order: annual or quarterly returns of alterations and casualties; monthly returns of battalions, companies, and detachments; special field returns and field returns; returns, of casualties; and trimonthly field returns.

Roll 38 contains the returns of the Astor Battery, an artillery detachment of the Regular Army, which was organized under the authority of the Secretary of War on May 26, 1898. John Jacob Astor presented the funds to the United States to support the Astor Battery. Three officers and a complement of men who enlisted in the Regular Army for 3 years were assigned to the battery. When the battery was mustered out in February 1899, men not entitled to discharge were transferred to artillery regiments.

Roll	Description
1st Regiment:	
1	June 1821–Dec. 1830
2	Jan. 1831–Dec. 1840
3	Jan. 1841–Dec. 1850
4	Jan. 1851–Dec. 1860
5	Jan. 1861–Dec. 1870
6	Jan. 1871–Dec. 1880
7	Jan. 1881–Dec. 1895
8	Jan. 1896–Jan. 1901
2d Regiment:	
9	June 1821–Dec. 1830
10	Jan. 1832–Dec. 1840
11	Jan. 1841–Dec. 1850
12	Jan. 1851–Dec. 1860
13	Jan. 1861–Dec. 1870
14	Jan. 1871–Dec. 1880
15	Jan. 1881–Dec. 1893
16	Jan. 1894–Jan. 1901
3d Regiment:	
17	June 1821–Dec. 1830
18	Jan. 1831–Dec. 1840
19	Jan. 1841–Dec. 1850
20	Jan. 1851–Dec. 1860
21	Jan. 1861–Dec. 1870
22	Jan. 1871–Dec. 1888
23	Jan. 1889–Dec. 1897
24	Jan. 1898–Jan. 1901
4th Regiment:	
25	Dec. 1821–Dec. 1830
26	Jan. 1831–Dec. 1840
27	Jan. 1841–Dec. 1850
28	Jan. 1851–Dec. 1860
29	Jan. 1861–Dec. 1870
30	Jan. 1871–Dec. 1877
31	Jan. 1878–Dec. 1892
32	Jan. 1893–Jan. 1901
5th Regiment:	
33	Aug. 1861–Dec. 1871
34	Jan. 1872–Dec. 1884

Roll	Description
35	Jan. 1885–Dec. 1897
36	Jan. 1898–Jan. 1901
Other units:	
37	6th Regiment:
	Mar. 1898–Jan. 1901
38	7th Regiment:
	Mar. 1898–Jan. 1901
	Astor Battery:
	June 1898–Jan. 1899

Returns From Regular Army Field Artillery Batteries and Regiments, February 1901–December 1916. M728. 14 rolls. DP.

This microfilm publication reproduces the monthly returns received from Regular Army field artillery batteries and regiments by the Adjutant General's Office from February 1901 to December 1916. It also includes related AGO forms and correspondence that were filed with these returns.

The field artillery unit from 1901 to May 1907 was the battery, but after May 1907 it was the regiment. Although the information required on the monthly return for either a battery or a regiment was essentially the same, the two forms differed. The regimental monthly return form provided for the regimental commander to consolidate the information that he had received from several batteries.

The monthly company or battery return consisted of five sections. The main section accounted for officers and men present, on special duty, sick, and so forth by aggregates. Another section listed absent enlisted men by name and stated the nature, commencement, termination, and place of absence.

The record of events section noted (1) actions in which the company, or any part of it, had been engaged, including scouting expeditions, marches, and changes of stations; (2) everything of interest relating to the discipline, efficiency, or service of the company, with such information as date, place, and distance marched; and (3) names and ranks of officers and soldiers killed, missing, or wounded in action, with dates and places.

The presence and absence of officers was accounted for. The reverse side of the form in 1901 included a section where all commissioned officers were named. The date on which the officer was assigned to, transferred to, joined or rejoined the company; the date that he assumed or was relieved from command of the company or from any special duty; and dates of all departures and returns were also included. Another list gave names of those who resigned or died or who were transferred from the company.

The final section—alterations—listed, by name, men gained or lost since the last return and gave the date of all transfers to and from the company.

Roll	Description	Dates
Batteries:		
1	1st–5th	Feb. 1901–May 1907
2	6th–10th	Feb. 1901–May 1907
3	11th–15th	Feb. 1901–May 1907
4	16th–20th	Feb. 1901–May 1907
5	21st–25th	Feb. 1901–May 1907
6	26th–30th	Feb. 1901–May 1907
Regiments:		
7	1st	June 1907–Dec. 1916

Roll	Description	Dates
8	2d	June 1907–Dec. 1911
9	2d	Jan. 1912–Dec. 1916
10	3d	June 1907–Dec. 1916
11	4th	June 1907–Dec. 1916
12	5th	June 1907–Dec. 1911
13	5th	Jan. 1912–Dec. 1916
14	6th	June 1907–Dec. 1916
	7th–9th	July–Dec. 1916

Returns From Regular Army Coast Artillery Corps Companies, February 1901–June 1916. M691. 81 rolls. DP.

This microfilm publication reproduces the monthly returns received from Regular Army Coast Artillery Corps companies, bands, mine planters, and provisional regiments by the Adjutant General's Office from February 1901 to June 1916. There are a few returns as late as January 1917. For a description of the five main sections of the return and the information provided, see M728.

Roll	Description
Company:	
	Feb. 1901–June 1916
1	1st and 2d
2	3d and 4th
3	5th and 6th
4	7th and 8th
5	9th and 10th
6	11th and 12th
7	13th and 14th
8	15th and 16th
9	17th and 18th
10	19th and 20th
	Feb. 1901–May 1916
11	21st
	Feb. 1901–June 1916
	22d
12	23d and 24th
13	25th and 26th
14	27th and 28th
15	29th and 30th
16	31st and 32d
17	33d and 34th
18	35th
	Apr. 1901–June 1916
	36th
	Feb. 1901–June 1916
19	37th and 38th
20	39th and 40th
21	41st
	Feb. 1901–Aug. 1916
	42d
	Feb. 1901–June 1916
22	43d and 44th
23	45th and 46th
24	47th and 48th
25	49th and 50th
26	51st and 52d
27	53d and 54th
28	55th and 56th
29	57th and 58th
30	59th and 60th
31	61st and 62d
32	63d and 64th
33	65th and 66th
	Apr. 1901–June 1916

Roll	Description
34	67th
	Feb. 1901–June 1916
	68th
35	69th
	Feb. 1901–May 1916
	70th
	Feb. 1901–June 1916
36	71st and 72d
37	73d and 74th
38	75th and 76th
39	77th and 78th
40	79th and 80th
41	81st and 82d
	Apr. 1901–June 1916
42	83d and 84th
43	85th and 86th
44	87th and 88th
45	89th and 90th
46	91st and 92d
47	93d
	Apr. 1901–May 1916
	94th
	June 1901–June 1916
48	95th and 96th
	July 1901–June 1916
49	97th
	Aug. 1901–June 1916
	98th
	Aug. 1901–Mar. 1914
50	99th
	Aug. 1901–June 1916
	100th
51	101st
	102d
52	103d
	104th
53	105th
	106th
54	107th
	108th
	Sept. 1901–June 1916
55	109th
	110th
	Aug. 1901–May 1916
56	111th
	Aug. 1901–June 1916
	112th
	Sept. 1901–June 1916
57	113th
	Aug. 1901–June 1916
	114th
58	115th
	116th
	Oct. 1901–June 1916
59	117th
	118th
60	119th
	120th
61	121st
	122d
62	123d
	124th
	Oct. 1901–May 1916
63	125th
	Oct. 1901–June 1916
	126th
	June 1907–June 1916
64	127th

Roll	Description
	128th
	Aug. 1907–June 1916
	129th
	130th
65	131st
	132d
	133d
	134th
66	135th
	136th
	137th
	Aug. 1907–May 1916
	138th
	Aug. 1907–June 1916
	139th
67	140th
	141st
	142d
	143d
	144th
68	145th
	146th
	147th
	148th
	149th
69	150th
	151st
	152d
	153d
	Aug. 1907–May 1916
	154th
	Aug. 1907–June 1916
70	155th
	156th
	157th
	Sept. 1907–June 1916
	158th
	159th
71	160th
	161st
	Nov. 1907–June 1916
	162d
	163d
	164th
72	165th
	166th
	167th
73	168th
	169th
	Jan. 1908–June 1916
	170th

Band:

Roll	Description
	Feb. 1901–Feb. 1916
74	1st and 2d
75	3d
	Feb. 1901–Dec. 1916
	4th
	Feb. 1901–Feb. 1916
76	5th and 6th
77	7th
	Apr. 1901–Feb. 1916
	8th
	June 1901–Jan. 1916
78	9th
	June 1901–Feb. 1916
	10th
	Mar. 1907–Feb. 1916
79	11th
	Apr. 1907–Feb. 1916
	12th

Roll	Description
	Mar. 1907–Feb. 1916
	13th and 14th

U.S. Army Mine Planter:

Roll	Description
	Jan. 1908–Dec. 1916
80	*Col. George Armistead*
	June 1909–May 1914
	Gen. Royal T. Frank
	Dec. 1907–Mar. 1909
	Gen. Henry J. Hunt
	Dec. 1907–Nov. 1908
	Gen. Henry Knox
	July 1909–Dec. 1916
81	*Gen. S. M. Mills*
	July 1909–Jan. 1917
	Gen. E. O. C. Ord
	Oct. 1907–June 1916
	Maj. Samuel Ringgold
	June 1909–Dec. 1916
	Gen. John M. Schofield

Other Units:

Roll	Description
	Mar. 1911
	1st Separate Brigade
	Provisional Regiments

Returns of the Corps of Engineers, April 1832–December 1916. M851. 22 rolls. DP.

This microfilm publication reproduces the monthly returns received by the Adjutant General's Office from the Corps of Engineers from April 1832 to December 1916. The monthly returns required of the Corps (bureau or staff department) varied little over the period although the forms were reprinted many times. The returns reported the strength of each staff department in total numbers of officers present and absent and gave a specific accounting of officers by name, rank, and assignment. The returns reproduced here are arranged chronologically.

Roll	Description
1	Apr. 1832–Dec. 1848
2	Jan. 1849–Dec. 1863
3	Jan. 1864–Dec. 1868
4	Jan. 1869–Dec. 1872
5	Jan. 1873–Dec. 1875
6	Jan. 1876–Dec. 1878
7	Jan. 1879–Dec. 1881
8	Jan. 1882–Dec. 1884
9	Jan. 1885–Dec. 1886
10	Jan. 1887–Dec. 1888
11	Jan. 1889–Dec. 1890
12	Jan. 1891–Dec. 1892
13	Jan. 1893–Dec. 1894
14	Jan. 1895–Dec. 1896
15	Jan. 1897–Dec. 1898
16	Jan. 1899–Dec. 1900
17	Jan. 1901–Dec. 1902
18	Jan. 1903–Dec. 1904
19	Jan. 1905–Dec. 1907
20	Jan. 1908–Dec. 1910
21	Jan. 1911–Dec. 1913
22	Jan. 1914–Dec. 1916

Returns From Regular Army Engineer Battalions, September 1846–June 1916. M690. 10 rolls. DP.

This microfilm publication reproduces the monthly returns received from Regular Army engineer battalions by the Adjutant General's Office from September 1846 to

June 1916. Because of changes in the forms over the years, the type and detail of information varies. The records are arranged by battalion.

Roll	Description
1st Battalion:	
1	Sept. 1846–June 1849
	Dec. 1861–Dec. 1874
2	Jan. 1875–Dec. 1889
3	Jan. 1890–Dec. 1898
4	Jan. 1899–Dec. 1907
5	Jan. 1908–June 1916
2d Battalion:	
6	Mar. 1901–Dec. 1907
7	Jan. 1908–July 1916
3d Battalion:	
8	Mar. 1901–Dec. 1907
9	Jan. 1908–July 1916
Band:	
10	Mar. 1901–Nov. 1916

Correspondence Relating to the Service of Regular Army Officers

The following microfilm publications contain references to individuals who served as officers in the Regular Army. The correspondence files for the Commission Branch are microfilmed only for 1863–70. An index is available on microfilm for 1871–94 for reference to officers who served during that period.

Letters Received by the Commission Branch of the Adjutant General's Office, 1863–1870. M1064. 527 rolls. DP.

This microfilm publication reproduces the letters and their enclosures received by the Commission Branch of the Adjutant General's Office, 1863–70.

The letters and enclosures were received from Regular and Volunteer officers, noncommissioned officers, and enlisted men; heads of War Department bureaus; Cabinet members; the President; Congressmen; State, Territorial, and local officials; and private citizens. The correspondence primarily concerns appointments, transfers, assignments, duties, examinations, promotions, discharges, courts-martial, resignations, and pay of individual officers, hospital stewards, ordnance sergeants, post and regimental sutlers, and superintendents of military cemeteries. It also covers applicants for all of these positions.

There also are a number of files that do not concern individuals. Among these are letters, orders, and opinions establishing policies and precedents affecting military personnel; communications from staff officers and from company and post commanders requesting personnel; letters from regimental and company commanders reporting on the service of their units during the Civil War or during engagements with Indians; and memorandums transmitting the names of newspapers in which the War Department was authorized to place advertisements. A few letters that primarily concern military operations or other subjects unrelated to personnel matters were filed in the Commission Branch by error or because they contained references to individual officers or noncommissioned officers. File S234 CB 1869, for example, is a report of Bvt. Maj. Gen. Eugene A. Carr's operation against Indians, June 30–July 20, 1869. Carr's report was filed among the Commission Branch letters received because he recommended brevet promotions for several individuals.

According to the recordkeeping practice of the time, letters received were entered in registers alphabetically in one of the following ways: by initial letter of writer's surname; by the office of the writer; or by the person whom the letter concerned and thereunder by date of receipt. The letters are arranged to correspond with entries in the registers and are numbered in a separate numerical sequence for each letter of the alphabet for each year. The entries in the registers are not strictly chronological because the letters were entered according to date received rather than date written. There often was a considerable lapse of time between the date a letter was written and the date it was received.

Letters received were endorsed on the back or on a separate cover sheet with the writer's name and title or the name of the person whom the letter concerned, the date and place the letter was written and a summary of its content, the date the letter was received in the Commission Branch, and the file number assigned to the letter in the register. The Commission Branch file designations consist of the initial letter of the surname of the writer or the person who is the subject of the letter, the file number, the letters "CB" for Commission Branch, and the year the letter was received: G251 CB 1866, for example.

Commission Branch clerks sometimes consolidated all the AGO documents relating to an individual under one file number. Preceding most of the consolidations is a memorandum that lists the file citations of all the documents included. At the bottom of these memorandums are references to other files concerning the same individual that were not included in the consolidations because they were forwarded to another office or because they concerned more than one person. Much of the information on the memorandums is duplicated at the back or on the cover sheet of the document under which the records are consolidated. A consolidation may contain correspondence dated as early as the 1820s or as late as the 1930s.

Within a consolidation, the letters are arranged chronologically by year; thereunder, all documents bearing a Commission Branch file citation are arranged alphabetically and then numerically. Documents with other file citations are filed by year after the Commission Branch files for the same year in the following order: ACP, AGO, Record and Pension Office, Military Secretary's Office, Volunteer Service Division, Enlisted Branch, Headquarters of the Army, and Army of the Potomac. Documents with no file citation are filed by year following all documents with file citations for that year. Documents with no file citation and no date are filed at the end of the consolidation.

The descriptive pamphlet that accompanies this microfilm publication includes a list of the names of some prominent individuals and the file citations under which their records were consolidated. A name and subject index to these files, 1863–70, is not yet available on microfilm, and references in the descriptive pamphlets to microfilm publication M1068 are premature.

Roll	Description	Roll	Description
1863:		64	W207–W414
1	A2–A194	65	W415–W557
2	A195–A338	66	W560–W723
3	A339–B115	67	W724–Z9
4	B116–B245	**1864:**	
5	B247–B311	68	A3–A346
6	B312–B588	69	A347–A614
7	B589–B808	70	B4–B390
8	B810–B1021	71	B393–B768
9	B1023–B1169	72	B769–B1154
10	B1171–B1445	73	B1158–B1323
11	C4–C198	74	B1327–B1533
12	C200–C511	75	B1534–B1720
13	C512–C733	76	B1722–B1838
14	C734–C950	77	B1839–B1958
15	C951–C1177	78	C1–C347
16	D2–D210	79	C348–C900
17	D213–D451	80	C904–C1099
18	D452–D670	81	C1100–C1364
19	E1–E263	82	C1365–C1465
20	F1–F309	83	C1466–D20
21	F311–F529	84	D21–D167
22	G2–G177	85	D168–D459
23	G181–G407	86	D462–D762
24	G409–G674	87	D767–E199
25	H1–H278	88	E202–E395
26	H279–H593	89	F1–F406
27	H596–H792	90	F407–F606
28	H793–H984	91	G3–G267
29	H985–H1149	92	G268–G572
30	H1150–I59	93	G576–G802
31	J1–J273	94	H1–H332
32	K1–K225	95	H333–H574
33	K226–K381	96	H579–H835
34	L2–L205	97	H836–H1117
35	L206–L380	98	H1118–H1255
36	L381–L530	99	H1256–H1504
37	M1–M101	100	H1505–J203
38	M103–M126	101	J205–K26
39	M127–M348	102	K29–K377
40	M349–M632	103	K378–L313
41	M633–M799	104	L314–L662
42	M800–M928	105	L663–M134
43	M929–M1072	106	M136–M576
44	M1073–M1303	107	M577–M936
45	N1–N222	108	M938–M1141
46	O1–P90	109	M1143–M1352
47	P91–P314	110	M1353–M1553
48	P316–P445	111	M1554–M1789
49	P449–P576	112	N1–O135
50	Q1–R248	113	O142–P128
51	R254–R433	114	P129–P503
52	R434–R576	115	P506–P722
53	S3–S269	116	P723–P1070
54	S271–S533	117	Q2–R206
55	S537–S686	118	R208–R502
56	S688–S991	119	R505½–R707
57	S992–S1171	120	R708–S241
58	S1172–S1396	121	S242–S581
59	S1397–S1566	122	S582–S1034
60	T2–T254	123	S1035–S1299
61	T255–T471	124	S1300–S1589
62	U2–V132	125	S1591–S1923
63	W2–W206	126	S1925–T116

Roll	Description		Roll	Description
127	T118–T452		190	M856–M1132
128	T453–T719		191	M1136–M1269
129	U2–V134		192	M1272–M1419
130	V135–V228		193	M1421–M1548
131	W3–W264		194	M1550–M1700
132	W266–W594		195	N1–N158
133	W596–W945		196	N159–N471
134	W947–W1165		197	O1–O262
135	W1166–Z8		198	P9–P149
			199	P150–P445
1865:			200	P449–P625
136	A4–A259		201	P626–P640
137	A260–A452		202	P645–P873
138	A455		203	P874–P947
139	A455		204	Q3–Q71
140	A455		205	Q72–Q313
141	A456–A713		206	R3–R179
142	B3–B197		207	R180–R311
143	B200–B376		208	R314–R424
144	B379–B684		209	R425–R528
145	B687–B1034		210	R533–R754
146	B1035–B1333		211	R755–R919
147	B1338–B1687		212	S1–S151
148	B1689–B1847		213	S152–S237
149	C2–C164		214	S239–S388
150	C166–C365		215	S389–S597
151	C366–C714		216	S600–S884
152	C715–C1109		217	S886–S1222
153	C1112–C1439		218	S1224–S1280
154	C1441–C1663		219	S1281–S1506
155	D7–D194		220	S1508–S1622
156	D196–D569		221	S1624–S1816
157	D570–D804		222	S1817–S2102
158	E2–E218		223	S2104–S2257
159	E219–E407		224	S2258–S2344
160	F2–F169		225	T4–T336
161	F170–F399		226	T338–T675
162	F400–F636		227	T676–V17
163	G1–G224		228	V18–V233
164	G226–G552		229	W7–W108
165	G553		230	W115–W270
166	G554–G702		231	W272–W500
167	G702		232	W503–W800
168	G704–G852		233	W804–W1033
169	H3–H140		234	W1035–W1246
170	H141		235	W1248–W1437
171	H144–H355		236	W1438–Z12
172	H356–H598			
173	H600–H798		*1866:*	
174	H800–H1127		237	A5–A176
175	H1129–H1410		238	A178–A368
176	H1413–H1559		239	A375–B199
177	I3–J21		240	B203–B299
178	J23–J124		241	B301–B617
179	J127–J334		242	B619–B960
180	K2–K232		243	B962–B1359
181	K234–K513		244	B1361–B1669
182	L2–L148		245	B1671–B1948
183	L151–L338		246	B1950–B2121
184	L341–L464		247	C10–C258
185	L465–L744		248	C263–C588
186	M1–M299		249	C591–C967
187	M302–M532		250	C968–C1353
188	M534–M604		251	C1356–C1580
189	M605–M854		252	D2–D182
			253	D184–D413

Roll	Description		Roll	Description
254	D415–D632		317	B1477–B1707
255	D633–D871		318	B1710–B2156
256	E5–E202		319	B2161–B2271
257	E205–E398		320	B2273–B2342
258	F5–F302		321	C2–C322
259	F303–F538		322	C324–C697
260	F539–G245		323	C698–C892
261	G249–G413		324	C893–C1098
262	G415–G592		325	C1099–C1120
263	G595–G866		326	C1123–C1349
264	H2–H447		327	D2–D295
265	H451–H713		328	D296–D448
266	H716–H998		329	D451–D528
267	H999–H1184		330	D529–D630
268	H1187–H1381		331	D631
269	H1383–H1570		332	D632–D697
270	I1–J190		333	E1–E290
271	J193–K217		334	F4–F435
272	K219–K528		335	G1–G190
273	L1–L192		336	G192–G526
274	L193–L456		337	G527–G796
275	L457–L686		338	H1–H398
276	L689–L760		339	H402–H624
277	M2–M37		340	H628–H857
278	M38–M369		341	H861–H1261
279	M371–M742		342	I1–J149
280	M744–M928		343	J150–J333
281	M930–M938		344	K2–K239
282	M949–M1381		345	K241–K438
283	M1382–M1626		346	L5–L298
284	M1627–M1709		347	L300–L478
285	N3–N306		348	L483–L559
286	O1–O219		349	L561–M52
287	P1–P274		350	M53–M146
288	P276–P526		351	M147–M293
289	P533–P813		352	M296–M563
290	P815–Q183		353	M564–M917
291	R5–R364		354	M918–M1022
292	R365–R683		355	M1023–M1376
293	R684–R800		356	M1378–M1464
294	S2–S358		357	N1–N123
295	S359–S714		358	N124–N309
296	S716–S1015		359	O3–O237
297	S1018–S1254		360	P1–P175
298	S1261–S1581		361	P177
299	S1583–S1755		362	P178–P403
300	S1756–S1911		363	P405–P620
301	T1–T310		364	P621–P760
302	T314–T571		365	Q9–R201
303	T578–T639		366	R205–R390
304	U3–W55		367	R391–R524
305	W57		368	R528–R755
306	W58–W283		369	S4–S272
307	W285–W519		370	S273–S292
308	W521–W832		371	S293–S383
309	W836–W1079		372	S386–S598
310	W1080–W1464		373	S604–S799
311	W1465–Z22		374	S801–S1139
1867:			375	S1140–S1275
312	A1–A309		376	S1279–S1670
313	A310–B255		377	T2–T280
314	B264–B677		378	T282–T584
315	B682–B1087		379	T585–W38
316	B1088–B1472		380	W40–W189

Roll	Description
381	W190–W305
382	W311–W529
383	W530–W759
384	W763–W863
385	W864–W884
386	W885–W1149
387	W1150–Z9

1868:

Roll	Description
388	A2–B151
389	B159–B571
390	B576–B590
391	B590–B591
392	C3–C179
393	C184–C255
394	C256–C431
395	C435–C484
396	C485–D64
397	D65–D247
398	E1–F89
399	F91–F181
400	G1–G127
401	G130–H111
402	H114–H348
403	H349–H402
404	I3–K137
405	L1–L175
406	M3–M253
407	M254–M443
408	M444–M486
409	M489–M528
410	N1–O72
411	P5–P258
412	P271–Q71
413	R12–R156
414	R157–R222
415	R228–R349
416	S4–S77
417	S78–S262
418	S265–S503
419	S504–S648
420	S650–T44
421	T46–W26
422	W27–Z1

1869:

Roll	Description
423	A2–A108
424	A111–B35
425	B37–B130
426	B132–B306
427	C2–C124
428	C130–C265
429	D1–D94
430	D100–E64
431	F1–G28
432	G31–G86
433	G87–H71
434	H73
435	H74–H262
436	I3–L53
437	L54–L126
438	M2–M143
439	M146–M151
440	M156–M272
441	N2–O45
442	P4–P130

Roll	Description
443	P132–P228
444	Q2–R57
445	R58–S38
446	S40–S131
447	S133–S184
448	S191–S235
449	S236–S318
450	T5–V43
451	W1–W80
452	W81–W167
453	W168–Z3

1870:

Roll	Description
454	A1–A429
455	A431–A542
456	B1–B129
457	B140–B174
458	B176
459	B177–B217
460	B222–B299
461	B300–B349
462	B353–B418
463	C1–C86
464	C94–C280
465	C284–C319
466	C320–C423
467	C426–D54
468	D56–D151
469	D154–D204
470	D205–F37
471	F39–F77
472	F82–G35
473	G38–G122
474	G124–G210
475	H1–H166
476	H167–H279
477	H281–H419
478	H421–J72
479	J75–J84
480	K4–K41
481	K48–K121
482	K131–K141
483	L1–L46
484	L49–L165
485	M7–M163
486	M164–M237
487	M240–M347
488	M350–M387
489	N4–N91
490	O2–P130
491	P133–P282
492	P283–P329
493	P331–P399
494	P400
495	P403–Q39
496	R1–R105
497	R107–R163
498	R175–R203
499	R205–R217
500	R221–R224
501	R225–R258
502	R260–R269
503	R272–R295
504	R297–R314
505	R318–R343

Roll	Description
506	R347–R357
507	R359–R383
508	R384–R402
509	R403–R443
510	R445–R494
511	R499–R515
512	S1–S107
513	S109–S168
514	S169–S213
515	S217–S288
516	S289–S369
517	S371–S410
518	S411–T37
519	T40–T82
520	T96–T159
521	T168–V44
522	V46–W83
523	W86–W208
524	W210–W265
525	W267
526	W274–W287
527	W290–Z6

Name and Subject Index to the Letters Received by the Appointment, Commission, and Personal Branch of the Adjutant General's Office, 1871–1894. M1125. 4 rolls. DP.

This microfilm publication reproduces an alphabetical card index to the letters received by the Appointment, Commission, and Personal Branch of the AGO, 1871–94. The index is principally to names, but it also includes a limited number of subject references. Staff members of the National Archives and Records Administration compiled the index to facilitate research in the AGO records.

The correspondence files to which this index refers are not currently available on microfilm. The index may prove useful, however, in searching for information relating to Regular Army officers.

Roll	Description
1	A–Do
2	Dr–Kl
3	Kn–Rh
4	Ri–Z

Records Relating to Service in the U.S. Navy and U.S. Marine Corps (Record Groups 24, 125, and 127)

Records relating to service in the American Navy in the Revolutionary War, 1775–83; in the U.S. Navy for officers, 1798–1902, and for enlisted men, 1789–1885; and in the U.S. Marine Corps, 1798–1895, are held by the National Archives. Naval service records of the Revolutionary War are fragmentary, showing only such information as the serviceman's name and rank, the name of the vessel on which he served, and the dates of his service or the dates he was paid.

Records relating to the service of commissioned officers in the Navy after the Revolutionary War but before 1846 give each officer's name, rank, State of birth, sometimes age or date of birth, date of residence, and dates of service. Records for 1846 and later contain the above information and occasionally give the date and place of an officer's death in service or the date of his retirement.

Records relating to a Navy enlisted man's service before 1846 usually give only his name and rating, the names of the vessels on which he served, and the dates of his service. Later records also give an enlisted man's age and place of birth and occasionally place of enlistment.

Records of commissioned officers in the Marine Corps usually show each officer's name and rank and the date of his appointment or acceptance of a commission. They may also give his age and residence. Service records for enlisted marines usually show the man's name and age, and the date, place, and term of enlistment.

The National Personnel Records Center in St. Louis holds the individual personnel records (jackets) of Navy commissioned officers separated after 1902, Navy enlisted personnel separated after 1885, and Marine Corps enlisted personnel separated after 1905.

Indexes to Rendezvous Reports

Indexes to Rendezvous Reports (Navy Enlistments) Through 1884

The following microfilm publications reproduce alphabetical name indexes to the U.S. Navy rendezvous reports (enlistments), 1846–84. The indexes were filmed by the U.S. Navy before transferring the records to the National Archives. The Navy filmed the cards for the Civil War, 1861–65, separately.

Each card shows the name of the individual; rendezvous (place of enlistment or vessel on which enlisted); date of enlistment or return (the roll on which the name first appeared); and a space for a "Record of Service." Although the amount of information varies, the entry under "Record of Service" may provide the date of reassignment or discharge, the names of vessels on which the individual served, or the date of death.

The records to which these indexes refer are not on microfilm, but they are open to researchers at the National Archives.

Index to Rendezvous Reports, Before and After the Civil War (1846–1861, 1865–1884). T1098. 32 rolls. 16mm.

Roll	Description
1	A, Bon–Bailey, Sam'l
2	Bailey, Sam'l–Benson, Benjamin
3	Benson, Bernard–Bronson, Harry
4	Bronson, William–Burns, M.E.
5	Burns, M.H.–Cervenka, Jos.
6	Cervenka, Jos.–Cooly, Patrick
7	Coomadt, Andrew–Darineil, Jno.
8	Davy, H.T.–Dow, Austin
9	Dow, Benjamin–Fenarty, Thos.
10	Fenderson, Jno.–Foley, John
11	Foley, John–Goddard, N.P.
12	Goddard, N.P.–Greif, William
13	Greig, John–Hawley, Chas.
14	Hawley, Chas. P.–Hook, Fred
15	Hook, Fred'k–Jones, Daniel
16	Jones, Daniel–Jyttropsen, R.D.
17	Kaack, Heinrich–Lavery, William
18	Lavery, William–Lundberg, Thomas
19	Lundburg, Adolph–McMillan, Angus
20	McMillan, Angus–Meanol, Adam
21	Meany, Francis A.–Mulholland, James
22	Mulholland, John–Obre, Edward
23	O'Brien, Edwards–Pettyjohn, James H.
24	Petukin, Chas. L.–Redding, M.
25	Redding, Martin–Rudinos, Santiago
26	Rupell, Charles–Sharpe, Charles
27	Sharpe, Frederick–Smith, Wm.
28	Smith, Wm.–Sturtevant, W.P.
29	Sturtevent, Wm. P.–Townsend, T.
30	Townsend, Treadwell–Washington, Corbin
31	Washington, Corbin–William, Thos.
32	William, Thos.–Zylinicke, Alfons

Index to Rendezvous Reports, Civil War, 1861–1865. T1099. 31 rolls. 16mm.

Roll	Description
1	Abaling, Louis–Barth, Theodore
2	Barthel, Eugene A.–Bowen, William
3	Bowen, William–Burns, Jno.
4	Burns–Champ, Samuel
5	Champion, Chris–Coveliers, Albert
6	Covell, Almeron–Day, Thos. P.
7	Day, Vandewater–Duskin, William
8	Duson, Albert–Fitzgerald, John
9	Fitzgerald, John–Girraty, John
10	Girraty, John–Hale, Sherman
11	Hale, Sherman–Hewit, Benjamin
12	Hewit, John–Ingersoll, Hiram
13	Ingersoll, Jas.–Justin, William H.
14	Kaab, William–Langen, Thomas
15	Langen, Thomas–Lowd, William
16	Lowden, Frances–McGarth, Christopher
17	McGarth, Christopher–McGuire, Peter
18	McGuire, Peter–Maney, Patrick
19	Maney, Richard–Moore, Charles W.
20	Moore, Cicero–Muller, Jno. Philip
21	Muller, Julius–O'Keefe, Patrick
22	O'Keefe, Robert–Peterson, Chas.
23	Peterson, Charles–Richards, Frank W.
24	Richards, Geo.–Ryan, Daniel
25	Ryan, Dan'l–Sloane, John

Roll	Description
26	Sloane, John M.–Stanton, Robert
27	Stanton, Robert–Thompson, Robert
28	Thompson, Robert–Wallace, John
29	Wallace, John–William, John
30	Williams, John–Yerry, Edward
31	Yerkes, Henry–Zwicker, Frank

Indexes to World War I and Later Rendezvous Reports

The following microfilm publications reproduce finding aids to records that are in the custody of the National Personnel Records Center. Requests for information about Navy officers separated since 1902, Navy enlisted men separated since 1885, Marine Corps officers separated after 1895, and Marine Corps enlisted men separated after 1905 should be made on Standard Form 180, "Request Pertaining to Military Records." Send these requests to Military Personnel Records, 9700 Page Boulevard, St. Louis, MO 63132.

Index to Rendezvous Reports, Armed Guard Personnel, 1917–1920. T1101. 3 rolls. 16mm.

The index card shows the name of the individual, the name of the vessel on which he served and dates of service, and the place where the records and accounts were held. The index sometimes indicates the individual's assigned job.

Roll	Description
1	Abbott, Henry J.–Luebke, Charles
2	Luke, Wilmer L.–Visnow, Norman S.
3	Visocky, William M.–Zwick, Walter

Index to Rendezvous Reports, Naval Auxiliary Service, 1917–1918. T1100. 1 roll. 16mm.

The index cards, arranged alphabetically, show the name, the date of enlistment, and the name of the vessel on which the individual served and the dates he was assigned and left the vessel.

Other Records

Muster Rolls of the U.S. Marine Corps, 1789–1892. T1118. 123 rolls.

This microfilm publication reproduces the U.S. Marine Corps muster rolls for 1789–1892. There is some duplication of roll numbers. Most volumes are indexed by the name of the vessel or the station. The roll list below is arranged by the inclusive dates, not by the roll number.

The muster rolls were filmed chronologically as they appeared in bound volumes. They are monthly, quarterly, or in some cases annual lists of individuals serving in the U.S. Marine Corps either at land stations or on board vessels. Entries on the lists are arranged by rank. While the amount of information varies, muster rolls generally show for an individual Marine name and rank, the name of the station or vessel on which he served, the date of enlistment, and term of enlistment. A separate column for remarks may provide information about reassignments, promotions, discharges, or desertions.

Roll	Description
1	Aug. 1798–Dec. 1806
2	Jan. 1807–Dec. 1809
3	Jan. 1810–Dec. 1812
4	Jan. 1813–June 1814
5	July 1814–Dec. 1815
1	Jan. 1816–Dec. 1818
2	Jan. 1819–Dec. 1821
3	Jan. 1822–Dec. 1823
4	Jan. 1824–Dec. 1825
5	Jan. 1826–Dec. 1827
6	Jan. 1828–Dec. 1829
7	Jan. 1830–Dec. 1831
8	Jan. 1832–Dec. 1833
9	Jan. 1834–Dec. 1835
25	Jan. 1836–July 1836
26	Aug. 1836–Dec. 1836
27	Jan. 1837–June 1837
28	July 1837–Dec. 1837
10	Jan. 1838–Dec. 1839
11	Jan. 1840–Dec. 1840
12	Jan. 1841–Dec. 1841
13	Jan. 1842–Dec. 1842
14	Jan. 1843–Dec. 1843
15	Jan. 1844–Dec. 1844
16	Jan. 1845–Dec. 1845
45	Jan. 1846–June 1846
46	July 1846–Dec. 1846
47	Jan. 1847–June 1847
48	July 1847–Dec. 1847
49	Jan. 1848–Apr. 1848
50	May 1848–July 1848
51	Aug. 1848–Dec. 1848
17	Jan. 1849–Dec. 1849
18	Jan. 1850–Dec. 1850
19	Jan. 1851–Dec. 1851
20	Jan. 1852–Dec. 1852
21	Jan. 1853–Dec. 1853
22	Jan. 1854–Dec. 1854
23	Jan. 1855–Dec. 1855
24	Jan. 1856–Dec. 1856
25	Jan. 1857–Dec. 1857
26	Jan. 1858–Dec. 1858
27	Jan. 1859–Dec. 1859
28	Jan. 1860–Dec. 1860
79	Jan. 1861–Apr. 1861
80	May 1861–July 1861
81	Aug. 1861–Oct. 1861
82	Nov. 1861–Dec. 1861
83	Jan. 1862–Mar. 1862
84	Apr. 1862–June 1862
85	July 1862–Sept. 1862
86	Oct. 1862–Dec. 1862
87	Jan. 1863–Mar. 1863
88	Apr. 1863–June 1863
89	July 1863–Aug. 1863
90	Sept. 1863–Oct. 1863
91	Nov. 1863–Dec. 1863
92	Jan. 1864–Feb. 1864
93	Mar. 1864–Apr. 1864
94	May 1864–June 1864
95	July 1864–Aug. 1864
96	Sept. 1864–Oct. 1864

Roll	Description
97	Nov. 1864–Dec. 1864
98	Jan. 1865–Feb. 1865
99	Mar. 1865–Apr. 1865
100	May 1865–June 1865
101	July 1865–Aug. 1865
102	Sept. 1865–Oct. 1865
103	Nov. 1865–Dec. 1865
29	Jan. 1866–June 1866
30	July 1866–Dec. 1866
31	Jan. 1867–June 1867
32	July 1867–Dec. 1867
33	Jan. 1868–June 1868
34	July 1868–Dec. 1868
35	Jan. 1869–June 1869
36	July 1869–Dec. 1869
37	Jan. 1870–June 1870
38	July 1870–Dec. 1870
39	Jan. 1871–June 1871
40	July 1871–Dec. 1871
41	Jan. 1872–June 1872
42	July 1872–Dec. 1872
43	Jan. 1873–June 1873
44	July 1873–Dec. 1873
45	Jan. 1874–June 1874
46	July 1874–Dec. 1874
47	Jan. 1875–June 1875
48	July 1875–Dec. 1875
49	Jan. 1876–June 1876
50	July 1876–Dec. 1876
51	Jan. 1877–June 1877
52	July 1877–Dec. 1877
53	Jan. 1878–June 1878
54	July 1878–Dec. 1878
55	Jan. 1879–June 1879
56	July 1879–Dec. 1879
57	Jan. 1880–June 1880
58	July 1880–Dec. 1880
59	Jan. 1881–June 1881
60	July 1881–Dec. 1881
61	Jan. 1882–June 1882
62	July 1882–Dec. 1882
63	Jan. 1883–June 1883
64	July 1883–Dec. 1883
65	Jan. 1884–June 1884
66	July 1884–Dec. 1884
67	Jan. 1885–June 1885
68	July 1885–Dec. 1885
69	Jan. 1886–June 1886
70	July 1886–Dec. 1886
71	Jan. 1887–June 1887
72	July 1887–Dec. 1887
73	Jan. 1888–June 1888
74	July 1888–Dec. 1888
75	Jan. 1889–June 1889
76	July 1889–Dec. 1889
77	Jan. 1890–June 1890
78	July 1890–Dec. 1890
79	Jan. 1891–Jun. 1891
80	July 1891–Dec. 1891
81	Jan. 1892–June 1892
82	July 1892–Dec. 1892

Abstracts of Service Records of Naval Officers ("Records of Officers"), 1798–1893. M330. 19 rolls.

This microfilm publication reproduces abstracts of records of service of naval officers for May 1798–December 1893. The records relate to most Navy and Marine Corps officers, volunteer officers of the Civil War, some noncommissioned officers, and a few professors and teachers at the U.S. Naval Academy. The abstracts refer to letters sent conveying appointments, to orders and letters accepting resignations, and to applications for appointment as midshipmen or cadets. Because the abstracts are bound chronologically in lettered volumes, information about a particular officer can be located only if the approximate date of his commission is known.

There are two parts to volumes J–O; each part is microfilmed separately. Part 1 relates to officers above the rank of master, and part 2 to officers of the rank of master or below. Some volumes are indexed; in others the entries are arranged alphabetically.

An entry shows the name of the officer, the date of his appointment, the date and nature of changes in his rank, and, where pertinent, the date and nature of the termination of his service.

Roll	Description	Dates
1	A–B	May 1798–Dec. 1803
2	C–D	Jan. 1804–Mar. 1813
3	E–F	Apr. 1813–Aug. 1825
4	G	Sept. 1825–Dec. 1831
5	H	Jan. 1832–June 1840
6	I	July 1840–Dec. 1845
7	J–1	Jan. 1846–Dec. 1858
8	J–2	Jan. 1846–Dec. 1858
9	K–1	Jan. 1859–Dec. 1863
10	K–2	Jan. 1859–Dec. 1863
11	L–1	Jan. 1864–Dec. 1871
12	L–2	Jan. 1864–Dec. 1871
13	M–1	Jan. 1872–Dec. 1878
14	M–2	Jan. 1872–Dec. 1878
15	N–1	Jan. 1879–Dec. 1888
16	N–2	Jan. 1879–Dec. 1888
17	O–1	Jan. 1889–Dec. 1893
18	O–2	Jan. 1889–Dec. 1893
19	Officers with the rank of Captain, Master, Commandant, Lieutenant, Surgeon, Surgeon's Mate, Purser, and Passed Midshipman, 1799–1829	

Index to Officers' Jackets, 1913–1925 ("Officers Directory"). T1102. 2 rolls.

This microfilm publication reproduces the Naval Bureau of Personnel's location registers for officer personnel files or jackets. The names are arranged by file number and are annotated with the physical location of the file as of March 1948 when the Navy filmed the registers. Because the registers are arranged by Navy file number, any search would be lengthy and difficult. The records would be useful only to locate a file number for an individual or to determine if a jacket was extant in 1948. A researcher might wish to consult these registers if the result of a search at the Military Personnel Records Center, where the records are held, is negative.

Roll	Description
1	500–55,999
2	60,000–89,999

Records of General Courts-Martial and Courts of Inquiry of the Navy Department, 1799–1867. M273. 198 rolls.

This microfilm publication reproduces court-martial and other personnel records from the Department of Navy, 1799–1867. The records include name indexes and registers and transcripts of proceedings of general courts-martial and courts of inquiry.

Information given in the records includes, when applicable: name of the sailor charged; his rating, ship or station, and other service information; the alleged offense; place and date of trial; and the sentence. Roll 2 is 16mm microfilm; all other rolls are 35mm.

Roll	Description	Dates
1	Alphabetical Index, Cases 1–3072	June 27, 1799–Mar. 20, 1861
2	Alphabetical Card Index	1861–67
3	Vol. 1, Cases 1–29	June 27, 1799–Aug. 15, 1805
4	Vol. 2, Cases 30–74	Aug. 16, 1805–Jan. 16, 1810
5	Vol. 3, Cases 75–119½	Feb. 16, 1810–Oct. 12, 1812
6	Vol. 4, Cases 120–159	Nov. 11, 1812–Feb. 19, 1814
7	Vol. 5, Cases 160–199	Apr. 11, 1814–Feb. 17, 1815
8	Vol. 6, Cases 200–229	Apr. 4, 1815–Jan. 25, 1816
9	Vol. 7, Cases 230–264	Jan. 26, 1816–June 5, 1817
10	Vol. 8, Cases 265–289	May 13, 1817–Feb. 10, 1818
11	Vol. 9, Cases 290–330	Feb. 3, 1818–Mar. 1, 1819
12	Vol. 10, Cases 331–355	Mar. 4, 1819–Mar. 1, 1820
13	Vol. 11, Cases 356–376	Apr. 3, 1820–Mar. 12, 1821
14	Vol. 12, Cases 377–395¼	May 10, 1821–Apr. 13, 1822
15	Vol 13, Cases 395½–403	Jan. 9, 1822–Apr. 19, 1823
16	Vol. 14, Cases 403½–413	June 10, 1823–Jan. 23, 1824
17	Vol. 15, Cases 414–424½	Jan. 28–Dec. 1, 1824
18	Vol. 16, Cases 425–430	Jan. 12–Aug. 16, 1825
19	Vol. 17, Cases 430¼–434	June 21–Sept. 5, 1825
20	Vol. 18, Cases 435–449	Aug. 18, 1825–Dec. 12, 1827
21	Vol. 19, Cases 450–465	Aug. 6, 1827–Sept. 20, 1828
22	Vol. 20, Cases 466–489	Apr. 10, 1828–Apr. 27, 1829
23	Vol. 21, Cases 490–509	Jan. 3, 1821–Oct. 9, 1830
24	Vol. 22, Cases 510–522	Aug. 9–Oct. 8, 1830
25	Vol. 23, Cases 523–531	Apr. 30, 1827–Dec. 8, 1830
26	Vol. 24, Cases 532–539	Jan. 3–Aug. 10, 1831

Roll	Description	Dates
27	Vol. 25, Cases 540–554	Sept. 30, 1831–Feb. 9, 1832
28	Vol. 26, Cases 555–579	May 7, 1832–Jan. 19, 1833
29	Vol. 27, Cases 580–593	Dec. 20, 1832–Dec. 17, 1833
30	Vol. 28, Cases 594–601	Apr. 3, 1804–Aug. 21, 1834
31	Vol. 29, Cases 602–618	Sept. 6, 1834–May 1, 1835
32	Vol. 30, Cases 619–629	Jan. 7–Dec. 7, 1835
33	Vol. 31, Cases 630–649	Mar. 18, 1835–July 11, 1837
34	Vol. 32, Cases 651–670	June 20, 1837–Jan. 9, 1839
35	Vol. 33, Cases 671–695	Oct. 13, 1838–Aug. 24, 1839
36	Vol. 34, Cases 696–713	Aug. 24, 1839–July 7, 1840
37	Vol. 35, Cases 714–728	Feb. 18, 1840–June 8, 1841
38	Vol. 36, Cases 729–747	Oct. 14, 1840–Oct. 23, 1841
39	Vol. 37, Case 748 (part)	Apr. 29, 1839–June 22, 1840
40	Vol. 38, Case 748 (part) Exhibits	
41	Vol. 39, Cases 749–768	Jan. 7, 1840–Mar. 30, 1841
42	Vol. 40 (part), Cases 769–771	June 8–July 14, 1841
43	Vol. 40 (part), Cases 772–776	July 9–Nov. 23, 1841
44	Vol. 41, Cases 777–789	Nov. 5, 1841–Mar. 10, 1842
45	Vol. 42, Cases 790–799	Mar. 7–June 29, 1842
46	Vol. 43, Cases 800–826	June 28–Aug. 13, 1842
47	Vol. 44, Cases 827–829	Aug. 17–Sept. 15, 1842
48	Vol. 45, Cases 830–843	Sept. 15–Dec. 12, 1842
49	Vol. 46, Case 844	Dec. 28, 1842–Mar. 28, 1843
50	Vol. 47, Case 844, Original Notes Taken at the Court Martial	
51	Vol. 48, Case 844, Original Notes Taken at the Court Martial	
52	Vol. 49 (part), Cases 845–851	Sept. 26, 1842–Apr. 25, 1843
53	Vol. 49 (part), Cases 852–864	May 17–June 27, 1843
54	Vol. 50, Cases 865–876	June 8, 1841–Oct. 28, 1843
55	Vol. 51, Cases 877–909	Dec. 18, 1843–June 17, 1844
56	Vol. 52 (part), Cases 910–915	May 26, 1842–Aug. 16, 1844
57	Vol. 52 (part), Cases 916–929	Oct. 14–Nov. 20, 1844
58	Vol. 53, Cases 930–968	July 14, 1842–May 7, 1845
59	Vol. 54 (part), Cases 969–970	June 2–July 14, 1845
60	Vol. 54 (part), Cases 971–989	July 5, 1845–Jan. 3, 1846

Roll	Description	Dates
61	Vol. 55, Cases 990–1025	Mar. 4, 1846–Feb. 6, 1847
62	Vol. 56, Cases 1026–1065	Jan. 25–Dec. 31, 1847
63	Vol. 57, Cases 1066–1114	Dec. 30, 1847–Jan. 17, 1849
64	Vol. 58 (part), Cases 1115–1147	Feb. 4, 1847–May 22, 1849
65	Vol. 58 (part), Cases 1148–1154	June 4–Sept. 12, 1849
66	Vol. 59, Cases 1155–1186	Sept. 19, 1849–Dec. 16, 1850
67	Vol. 60, Case 1187	Dec. 16, 1850–Feb. 1, 1851
68	Vol. 61, Cases 1188–1209	Dec. 24, 1850–Feb. 18, 1851
69	Vol. 62, Cases 1210–1238	Feb. 15, 1848–Apr. 29, 1850
70	Vol. 63, Cases 1239–1268	May 15, 1850–May 10, 1851
71	Vol. 64 (part), Case 1269 (part)	Nov. 20, 1850–Feb. 8, 1851
72	Vol. 64 (part), Case 1269 (part)	Feb. 10–Apr. 7, 1851
73	Vol. 65 (part), Cases 1270–1300	July 2–Sept. 24, 1851
74	Vol. 65 (part), Cases 1301–1304	June 14–Oct. 22, 1851
75	Vol. 66, Cases 1305–1369	Aug. 18, 1851–June 11, 1852
76	Vol. 67, Cases 1370–1401	Sept. 23, 1850–Sept. 15, 1852
77	Vol. 68, Cases 1402–1449	July 20, 1852–May 17, 1853
78	Vol. 69, Cases 1450–1499	Jan. 20, 1853–Mar. 23, 1854
79	Vol. 70, Cases 1500–1525	Dec. 22, 1853–Aug. 2, 1854
80	Vol. 71, Cases 1526–1574	Apr. 27, 1852–Mar. 6, 1855
81	Vol. 72, Cases 1575–1634	Dec. 15, 1854–Aug. 15, 1855
82	Vol. 73, Cases 1635–1717	June 26, 1855–Apr. 9, 1856
83	Vol. 74, Cases 1718–1834	July 25, 1855–July 30, 1856
84	Vol. 75, Cases 1835–1934	July 18, 1856–Jan. 6, 1857
85	Vol. 76, Cases 1935–2044	Dec. 9, 1856–May 28, 1857
86	Vol. 77, Cases 2045–2144	Jan. 21–Nov. 25, 1857
87	Vol. 78, Cases 2145–2224	Dec. 31, 1856–May 3, 1858
88	Vol. 79, Cases 2225–2329	Mar. 31, 1857–Sept. 21, 1858
89	Vol. 80, Cases 2330–2364	Dec. 14, 1857–Oct. 29, 1858
90	Vol. 81, Cases 2365–2439	Aug. 2, 1858–Jan. 6, 1859
91	Vol. 82, Cases 2440–2529	June 11, 1858–May 2, 1859
92	Vol. 83, Cases 2530–2655	Dec. 28, 1858–Dec. 2, 1859
93	Vol. 84, Cases 2656–2759	July 11, 1859–May 5, 1860

Roll	Description	Dates	Roll	Description	Dates
94	Vol. 85, Cases 2760–2799 Cases 3000–3014	Nov. 19, 1858–July 5, 1860	127	Vol. 118, Cases 3587–3605	July 15–Sept. 4, 1864
95	Vol. 86, Cases 3015–3029	Oct. 4, 1859–Mar. 15, 1860	128	Vol. 119, Case 3606	Aug. 5–Sept. 10, 1864
96	Vol. 87, Cases 3030–3049	Nov. 1, 1859–Aug. 8, 1860	129	Vol. 120, Cases 3608–3643	Apr. 30–Oct. 6, 1864
97	Vol. 88, Cases 3050–3081	Jan. 16, 1853–Aug. 17, 1861	130	Vol. 121, Cases 3644–3679	June 1–Nov. 1, 1864
98	Vol. 89, Cases 3082–3107	Aug. 22, 1861–June 8, 1863	131	Vol. 122, Cases 3680–3709	Oct. 3–Nov. 30, 1864
99	Vol. 90, Cases 3108–3129	Mar. 4–July 25, 1862	132	Vol. 123, Cases 3710–3731	Oct. 24, 1864–Jan. 3, 1865
100	Vol. 91, Cases 3130–3145	July 17–Oct. 22, 1862	133	Vol. 124, Cases 3732–3756	Nov. 1–Dec. 2, 1864
101	Vol. 92, Cases 3146–3167	Oct. 21, 1862–Jan. 1, 1863	134	Vol. 125, Cases 3757–3781	Oct. 11, 1864–Feb. 13, 1865
102	Vol. 93, Cases 3168–3179	Dec. 24, 1862–Feb. 16, 1863	135	Vol. 126, Cases 3782–3799	Dec. 31, 1863–Feb. 20, 1865
103	Vol. 94, Cases 3180–3199	Jan. 24–Mar. 20, 1863	136	Vol. 127, Cases 3800–3825	July 7, 1864–Mar. 8, 1865
104	Vol. 95, Cases 3200–3209	Mar. 5–Apr. 25, 1863	137	Vol. 128, Cases 3826–3832	Dec. 15, 1864–Feb. 27, 1865
105	Vol. 96, Cases 3210–3220	Apr. 24–May 13, 1863	138	Vol. 129, Cases 3833–3844	Jan. 18–Mar. 25, 1865
106	Vol. 97, Cases 3221–3240	May 12–July 17, 1863	139	Vol. 130, Cases 3845–3860	Nov. 28, 1864–Apr. 5, 1865
107	Vol. 98, Cases 3241–3253	May 30–Oct. 20, 1863	140	Vol. 131, Cases 3861–3879	Nov. 26, 1864–Mar. 31, 1865
108	Vol. 99, Cases 3254–3267	June 8–July 2, 1863	141	Vol. 132, Cases 3880–3899	Nov. 28, 1864–Apr. 22, 1865
109	Vol. 100, Cases 3268–3284	June 30–Aug. 3, 1863	142	Vol. 133, Cases 3900–3923	Feb. 10–June 16, 1865
110	Vol. 101, Cases 3285–3306	July 15–Aug. 15, 1863	143	Vol. 134, Cases 3924–3942	Oct. 3, 1864–July 11, 1865
111	Vol. 102, Cases 3307–3324	Aug. 17–Sept. 11, 1863	144	Vol. 135, Cases 3943–3967	Mar. 21–Aug. 15, 1865
112	Vol. 103, Cases 3325–3338	Sept. 11–Oct. 10, 1863	145	Vol. 136, Cases 3968–3988	Mar. 22–July 18, 1865
113	Vol. 104, Cases 3339–3363	Oct. 1–28, 1863	146	Vol. 137, Cases 3989–3990	Mar. 16–Apr. 4, 1865
114	Vol. 105, Cases 3364–3389	Oct. 19–Nov. 20, 1863	147	Vol. 138, Cases 3991–4012	Mar. 10–Apr. 28, 1865
115	Vol. 106, Cases 3390–3402	Nov. 6–Dec. 16, 1863	148	Vol. 139, Cases 4013–4032	May 5–27, 1865
116	Vol. 107, Cases 3403–3420	Nov. 19, 1863–Jan. 4, 1864	149	Vol. 140, Cases 4033–4048	Apr. 7–May 29, 1865
117	Vol. 108, Cases 3421–3442	Dec. 8, 1863–Jan. 2, 1864	150	Vol. 141, Cases 4049–4055	Apr. 19–June 8, 1865
118	Vol. 109, Cases 3443–3469	Dec. 16, 1863–Feb. 4, 1864	151	Vol. 142, Cases 4056–4070	May 2–Nov. 7, 1865
119	Vol. 110, Cases 3470–3489	Jan. 2–June 22, 1864	152	Vol. 143, Case 4071	Nov. 7–Dec. 1, 1865
120	Vol. 111, Cases 3490–3499	Jan. 30–Feb. 20, 1864	153	Vol. 144, Case 4072	May 3–19, 1864
121	Vol. 112, Cases 3500–3511	Feb. 1–Mar. 30, 1864	154	Vol. 145, Case 4072	May 20–June 20, 1864
122	Vol. 113, Cases 3512–3523	Dec. 19, 1863–Mar. 25, 1864	155	Vol. 146, Cases 4072½–4097	June 6–July 26, 1865
123	Vol. 114, Cases 3524–3532	Mar. 12–Apr. 30, 1864	156	Vol. 147, Cases 4098–4129	June 14–Aug. 31, 1865
124	Vol. 115, Cases 3533–3560	May 3–June 29, 1864	157	Vol. 148, Cases 4130–4149	Aug. 8–Oct. 26, 1865
125	Vol. 116, Cases 3561–3569	June 18–Oct. 4, 1864	158	Vol. 149, Cases 4150–4168	Sept. 1–Nov. 3, 1865
126	Vol. 117, Cases 3570–3586	May 31–July 29, 1864	159	Vol. 150, Cases 4169–4182	Oct. 6–Nov. 27, 1865
			160	Vol. 151, Cases 4183–4201	Nov. 6, 1865–Jan. 9, 1866
			161	Vol. 152, Cases 4204–4223	Dec. 4, 1865–Feb. 27, 1866
			162	Vol. 153, Cases 4224–4238	Jan. 24–Apr. 7, 1866

Roll	Description	Dates
163	Vol. 154, Cases 4239–4244	Jan. 17–Apr. 20, 1866
164	Vol. 155, Cases 4245–4260	Feb. 26–Apr. 21, 1866
165	Vol. 156, Cases 4261–4277	Feb. 26–May 17, 1866
166	Vol. 157, Cases 4278–4299	Dec. 19, 1865–June 11, 1866
167	Vol. 158, Cases 4300–4320	Apr. 4–Sept. 12, 1864
168	Vol. 159, Cases 4321–4332	Feb. 15, 1864–June 20, 1865
169	Vol. 160, Cases 4333–4348	Nov. 11, 1863–May 17, 1865
170	Vol. 161, Cases 4349–4358	June 7, 1860–Jan. 15, 1866
171	Vol. 162, Cases 4359–4365	Feb. 25, 1864–June 22, 1865
172	Vol. 163, Cases 4366–4372	Mar. 24, 1864–Mar. 28, 1865
173	Vol. 164, Cases 4373–4391	Feb. 16, 1864–Dec. 23, 1865
174	Vol. 165, Cases 4392–4397	Nov. 23, 1864–Feb. 3, 1866
175	Vol. 166, Cases 4398–4410	Aug. 4, 1862–July 7, 1866
176	Vol. 167, Cases 4411–4434	Feb. 9–June 18, 1866
177	Vol. 168, Cases 4435–4459	Apr. 23–Aug. 14, 1866
178	Vol. 169, Cases 4460–4469	Aug. 11, 1862–July 12, 1866
179	Vol. 170, Cases 4471–4497	July 16–Nov. 24, 1866
180	Vol. 171, Cases 4498–4509	Nov. 14–Dec. 15, 1866
181	Vol. 172, Cases 4510–4526	Sept. 23, 1861–Oct. 22, 1866
182	Vol. 173, Cases 4527–4549	Sept. 24, 1864–Jan. 15, 1867
183	Vol. 174, Cases 4550–4563	Jan. 16–Feb. 22, 1867
184	Vol. 175, Cases 4564–4577	Feb. 7–Mar. 6, 1867
185	"Miscellaneous" (cases)	Sept. 3, 1839–Nov. 1, 1870
186	Vol. 1, Trial of Commodore Charles Wilkes	Mar. 9–31, 1864
187	Vol. 2, Trial of Commodore Charles Wilkes	Mar. 31–Apr. 25, 1864
188	Vol. 3, Trial of Commodore Charles Wilkes, Exhibits	
189	Vol. 1, Trial of Franklin W. Smith	Sept. 15–Oct. 8, 1864
190	Vol. 2, Trial of Franklin W. Smith	Oct. 10–Nov. 4, 1864
191	Vol. 3, Trial of Franklin W. Smith	Nov. 5–Dec. 1, 1864
192	Vol. 4, Trial of Franklin W. Smith	Dec. 2, 1864–Jan. 13, 1865
193	Vol. 5, Trial of Benjamin G. Smith	Jan. 13–Feb. 2, 1865
193	Vol. 6, Trial of Benjamin G. Smith	Sept. 15–Oct. 8, 1864
195	Vol. 7, Trial of Benjamin G. Smith	Oct. 10–Nov. 4, 1864
196	Vol. 8, Trial of Benjamin G. Smith	Nov. 5–30, 1864
197	Vol. 9, Trial of Benjamin G. Smith	Nov. 30, 1864–Jan. 12, 1865
198	Vol. 10, Trial of Benjamin G. Smith	Jan. 16–31, 1865

VETERANS' CLAIMS

Military Bounty Land Warrants and Pensions (Record Groups 15, 49, and 217)

Bounty Land Warrants

Military *bounty land warrants* were certificates giving eligible veterans rights to free land in the public domain. Congress used bounty land warrants to encourage enlistments during the Revolutionary War. From 1781 until 1855 the Federal Government continued to issue bounty land warrants to veterans or their heirs as a reward for service. A succession of administrative units of the War Department processed the applications for warrants. In 1849 responsibility was transferred to the Department of the Interior.

The National Archives has bounty land warrant application files based on service in wartime between 1775 and 1855. The majority of the bounty land applications available on microfilm relate to service during the Revolutionary War.

For additional information on land records, see *Genealogical and Biographical Research: A Select Catalog of Microfilm Publications.*

Pension Records

The National Archives has *pension applications* and *records of pension payments* for veterans, their widows, and other heirs. They are based on service in the Armed Forces of the United States between 1775 and 1916 but not to duty in the service of the Confederate States of America, 1861–65. In a few cases, the Federal Government assumed responsibility for pensions based on service in State military organizations, and records of these pensions are also in the National Archives. Most pension records are found among the Records of the Veterans Administration (Record Group 15).

The Federal Government provided three principal types of pensions:

- Disability or invalid pensions were awarded to servicemen for physical disabilities incurred in the line of duty.

- Service pensions were awarded to women and children whose husbands or fathers had served in wartime for specified periods.

- Widows' pensions were awarded to women and children whose husbands or fathers had served for specified periods or had been killed in war.

Pension legislation during the Revolutionary War was designed to encourage enlistment and acceptance of commissions and to prevent desertion and resignation. After the war, pensions became a form of reward for services rendered. Both during and after the Revolution, the States, as well as the Federal Government, awarded pensions based on participation in the conflict. The records reproduced in these microfilm publications pertain only to pensions granted or paid pursuant to public and private acts of the U.S. Government. Public acts, under which the majority of such pensions were authorized, encompassed large classes of veterans or their dependents who met common eligibility requirements. Private acts concerned specific individuals whose special services or circumstances merited consideration, but who could not be awarded pensions under existing public acts.

The records contain both historical and genealogical information. Historical information pertaining to the organization of military units, movement of troops, details of battles and campaigns, and activities of individuals, may be obtained from application statements of veterans; from affidavits of witnesses; and from the muster roll, diary, order, or orderly books that were occasionally submitted as proof of service and were not sent by the Bureau of Pensions to another Government Department or Agency. Naval and privateer operations are documented by applications, affidavits, and orders in some files based on service at sea. A few files contain letters written to or by soldiers and sailors during the Revolutionary War, which give firsthand accounts of military, naval, and civil events and conditions. Furloughs, passes, pay receipts, enlistment papers, commissions, warrants, and other original records of the period 1775–83 are also in some of the files.

Generally, the records were not microfilmed unless they contain genealogical information.

The following information is typical of what may be found in applications for pensions or bounty land warrants based on a veteran's service at any period. *A veteran's application* typically shows the veteran's name, rank, military unit, period of service, residence at time of mustering-in, residence at time of application, birthplace, age or date of birth, and, when the claim was made on the basis of need, a list of property. *A widow's application* shows most of the same information about the veteran noted above as well as the widow's name, age, residence at time of application, maiden name, date and place of marriage, and date and place of her husband's death. *An application of a child or heir* shows the information about the veteran and widow noted above, the heir's name, heir's place and date of birth, residence at the time of application, and date of the mother's death.

In application files, there are often supporting documents such as discharge papers, affidavits and deposition of witnesses, narratives of events during service (to prove that the veteran had served at a particular time although he might not have documentary evidence), marriage certificates, birth records, death certificates, pages from family Bibles, and other papers.

Requests for Records

Inquiries about pension and bounty land claims should be submitted on NATF Form 80, "Order for Copies of Veterans Records." Instructions for its use and an explanation of how orders are processed are printed on the form. When a pension claim file is found, documents that normally contain the basic information of a personal nature about the veteran and his family will be selected and photocopied. The selected documents generally contain the basic information in the pension file; the remaining documents rarely contain any additional genealogical data. Photocopies of the reproducible papers in the claim file can be furnished for a moderate cost per page.

Revolutionary War Bounty Land Warrant Applications and Pensions

During the Revolutionary War, Congress used pension legislation and the promise of free land to encourage enlistment and the acceptance of commissions. After the war, such legislation constituted a reward for service already rendered. Pension and bounty land warrant applications are based on the participation of American military, naval, and marine officers, and enlisted personnel in the Revolutionary War.

A bounty land warrant application file contains documents relating to claims for bounty lands: an application by the veteran or his widow for a warrant, sometimes a discharge certificate submitted by the veteran or his heirs as evidence of service, and a jacket showing whether the claim was approved or disapproved.

The pension records are arranged in alphabetical order by surname of the veteran. When two or more veterans have the same surname and given name, the further arrangement of the files is generally alphabetical by the State or organization in which a veteran served, or by the words "Continental," "Navy," or some other designation. Within each file, the records are unarranged.

Several types of pension files exist: survivors, widows, rejected, and pre-1800 disability. A fire in the War Department in 1800 destroyed Revolutionary War pension applications and related papers submitted before that date. Consequently, if a veteran applied for a disability or invalid pension before 1800, his file will show his name, the State or organization in which he served, and a file symbol.

Selected Records From Revolutionary War Pension and Bounty Land Warrant Application Files, 1800–1900. M805. 898 rolls. DP.

This publication reproduces records of interest to genealogists selected from the 80,000 pension and bounty land warrant application files. The complete pensions are reproduced on M804.

For a copy of the DP that lists the microfilm available on M805, write Publications Sales Branch (NEPS), Room 505, National Archives, Washington, DC 20408.

Revolutionary War Pension and Bounty Land Warrant Application Files, 1800–1900. M804. 2,670 rolls. DP.

This microfilm publication reproduces in their entirety the 80,000 pension and bounty land warrant application files. The records are arranged in alphabetical order. The names of most of the servicemen for whom a pension or bounty land warrant application files is reproduced in this publication are listed in *Index of Revolutionary War Pension Applications*, by Max E. Hoyt *et. al.*, (Washington, D.C., 1966).

Roll	Description
1	Aaron, William–Abbot, Ezra
2	Abbot, George–Abbot, William
3	Abbott, Aaron–Abbott, Moses
4	Abbott, Nathaniel–Abell, Thomas
5	Aber, Israel–Abston, John
6	Acart, Frederick–Ackler, Leonard
7	Ackley, Abraham–Acres, George
8	Acron, Gabriel–Adams, Bryant
9	Adams, Daniel–Adams, Ezekiel
10	Adams, Francis–Adams, Issacher
11	Adams, Jacob–Adams, Joel
12	Adams, John
13	Adams, Jonas–Adams, Luke
14	Adams, Mark–Adams, Phinehas
15	Adams, Reuben–Adams, Shubael
16	Adams, Silas–Adams, Titus

Roll	Description	Roll	Description
17	Adams, Walter–Adamy, John	81	Asay, Samuel–Ashcroft, John
18	Adare, James–Aderton, John	82	Ashe, John–Ashley, Zenas
19	Adkin, Samuel–Adye, John	83	Ashlock, James–Ashton, Thomas
20	Aeisla, Coonrod–Ahl, John	84	Ashur, Gad–Aston, James
21	Aiken, Andrew–Aitchley, Abraham	85	Atayataghronghta, Lewis–Atkerson, John
22	Akaley, John–Akley, Samuel	86	Atkins, Alexander–Atkins, Robert
23	Alban, George–Albrecht, Martin	87	Atkinson, Amos–Atkison, Henry
24	Albright, Adam–Alday, Seth	88	Atset, Joseph–Atwill, Peter
25	Alden, Alpheus–Alder, Jeremiah	89	Atwood, Amos–Atwood, Zaccheus
26	Alderman, Daniel–Aldrich, Jesse	90	Aubony, Thomas–Ausburn, Robert
27	Aldrich, Joel–Aleshite, John	91	Ausley, Jesse–Austin, Ezekiel
28	Alexander, Abraham–Alexander, James	92	Austin, George–Austin, Joshua
29	Alexander, Jeremiah–Alexander, Susannah	93	Austin, Moses–Auxtier, Samuel
30	Alexander, Thomas–Alexander, William	94	Avary, Gardener–Averill, Wyman
31	Alfin, William–Algier, Nathaniel	95	Avery, Abel–Avery, John
32	Algood, John–Allembaugh, Peter	96	Avery, Jonathan–Avery, Williams
33	Allen, Abel–Allen, Azor	97	Avis, Robert–Ayers, Ebenezer
34	Allen, Barnabas–Allen, Daniel	98	Ayers, Elihu–Azelip, Richard
35	Allen, David–Allen, Elihu	99	Baars, John–Babbitt, Samuel
36	Allen, Elijah–Allen, Howard	100	Babbs, John–Babcock, Jesse
37	Allen, Ichabod–Allen, Jason	101	Babcock, Job–Babcock, William
38	Allen, Jedediah–Allen, John(pt.)	102	Baber, James–Backman, Jacob
39	Allen, John(pt.)–Allen, Jonathan	103	Backus, Abner–Bacon, Henry
40	Allen, Joseph–Allen, Moses	104	Bacon, Isaiah–Bacon, Norman
41	Allen, Nathan–Allen, Phinehes	105	Bacon, Oliver–Badel, Moody
42	Allen, Reuben–Allen, Samuel	106	Badgely, Joseph–Bagent, John
43	Allen, Seth–Allen, Vincent	107	Bagg, Oliver–Bailes, Robert
44	Allen, William–Allerton, Jonathan	108	Bailey, Aaron–Bailey, Ephraim
45	Alley, Abram–Alling, Stephen	109	Bailey, George–Bailey, Joel
46	Allis, Aron–Allison, Thomas	110	Bailey, John–Bailey, Josiah
47	Allman, Edward–Almond, William	111	Bailey, Loudon–Bailey, Samuel
48	Almy, John–Alverson, John	112	Bailey, Silas–Bailey, William
49	Alvey, John–Alworth, James	113	Bailis, Eldridge–Baird, Thomas
50	Amacker, John–Amerman, Powel	114	Baith, George–Baker, Bradford
51	Ames, Aaron–Ames, Jotham	115	Baker, Charles–Baker, Ezekiel
52	Ames, Levi–Amminet, John	116	Baker, George–Baker, Joel
53	Ammon, Christopher–Amyx, Matthew	117	Baker, John–Baker, Jonathan
54	Anders, James–Anderson, Denney	118	Baker, Joseph–Baker, Nicholas
55	Anderson, Edward–Anderson, Jacob	119	Baker, Pardon–Baker, Seth
56	Anderson, James	120	Baker, Silas–Baker, Waterman
57	Anderson, John–Anderson, Peter	121	Baker, William–Baldry, Isaac
58	Anderson, Richard–Anderson, Timothy	122	Baldwin, Aaron–Baldwin, Enoch
59	Anderson, William–Andrekin, Francis	123	Baldwin, Henry–Baldwin, John
60	Andress, David–Andrews, Benjamin	124	Baldwin, Jonathan–Baldwin, Reuben
61	Andrews, David–Andrews, Israel	125	Baldwin, Samuel–Baley, Henry
62	Andrews, James–Andrews, Josiah	126	Baley, John–Ball, David
63	Andrews, Lemuel–Andrews, Stephen	127	Ball, Ebenezer–Ball, Jonathan
64	Andrews, Thomas–Andros, Thomas	128	Ball, Joseph–Ballantine, Ebenezer
65	Andrus, Benjamin–Andruss, William	129	Ballard, Alexander–Ballard, Nathan
66	Angel, Abiather–Angling, John	130	Ballard, Philip–Ballou, Jesse
67	Angst, Nicholas–Ante, Philip	131	Ballou, Nathaniel–Bancraft, John
68	Anthony, Abraham–Antrim, John	132	Bancroft, Benjamin–Banghart, Barney
69	Aorson, Aaron–Appleby, William	133	Bangs, Adnah–Bankes, Andrew
70	Applegate, Andrew–Applegate, Zebulon	134	Banks, Benjamin–Banks, Nathan
71	Appleman, David–Arbuckle, William	135	Banks, Nehemiah–Banta, Samuel
72	Archabald, John–Arington, John	136	Bantham, John–Barber, George
73	Arman, Thomas–Armsted, William	137	Barber, Henry–Barber, Nathan
74	Armstrong, Abel–Armstrong, Isaac	138	Barber, Obadiah–Barber, Zachariah
75	Armstrong, Jabez–Armstrong, Joshua	139	Barbey, Elijah–Bardsley, William
76	Armstrong, Martin–Arney, Christian	140	Bardwell, Obadiah–Barker, Benjamin
77	Arno, John–Arnold, Israel	141	Barker, Charles–Barker, Isaac
78	Arnold, Jabez–Arnold, Owen	142	Barker, Jacob–Barker, Nathaniel
79	Arnold, Remington–Arnott, Samuel	143	Barker, Oliver–Barker, Zenas
80	Arraby, Jack–Arwood, John	144	Barkers, James–Barlow, David

Roll	Description	Roll	Description
145	Barlow, George–Barnard, Grove	209	Belman, Dewalt–Bemies, Henry
146	Barnard, John–Barner, John	210	Bemis, Amasa–Bemis, Thaddeus
147	Barnes, Aaron–Barnes, David	211	Bemiss, Edmond–Benedict, George
148	Barnes, Ebenezer–Barnes, Jonah	212	Benedict, Isaac–Benedict, William
149	Barnes, Jonathan–Barnes, William	213	Beneger, George–Benjamin, Daniel
150	Barnet, Benjamin–Barnett, Joel	214	Benjamin, Darius–Benner, Peter
151	Barnett, John–Barney, Prince	215	Bennet, Aaron–Bennet, Jeremiah
152	Barney, Samuel–Barnitz, Jacob	216	Bennet, Jesse–Bennet, William
153	Barns, Abraham–Barns, Lowell	217	Bennett, Aaron–Bennett, Daniel
154	Barns, Nehemiah–Barnum, Seth	218	Bennett, David–Bennett, Jeremiah
155	Barnum, Stephen–Barr, James	219	Bennett, Jesse–Bennett, Phineas
156	Barr, John–Barret, William	220	Bennett, Reuben–Bennett, Wolcott
157	Barrett, Abraham–Barrett, Miles	221	Benneville, Daniel–Benson, John
158	Barrett, Nathaniel–Barringer, Walter	222	Benson, Jonah–Bentheusen, William
159	Barrington, Joseph–Barron, William	223	Bently, Azel–Bently, Thomas
160	Barrons, Abraham–Barrows, William	224	Benton, Abijah–Benton, Zebulon
161	Barrup, Andrew–Barter, Pelatiah	225	Bentschoten, Ignus–Berringer, David
162	Barth, Nicholas–Bartle, John	226	Berry, Asahel–Berry, Jeremiah
163	Bartlet, Adonijah–Bartlett, Daniel	227	Berry, Joel–Berry, Robert
164	Bartlett, Ebenezer–Bartlett, Jonathan	228	Berry, Samuel–Berry, Zebulun
165	Bartlett, Joseph–Bartlett, Silas	229	Berryhill, Alexander–Best, Samuel
166	Bartlett, Solomon–Bartman, Joseph	230	Besterfield, Andrew–Betton, John
167	Barto, Morris–Barton, Nicholas	231	Betts, Aron–Betts, Zophar
168	Barton, Peter–Bason, Daniel	232	Bettsworth, Charles–Bezard, John
169	Bass, Edward–Bassett, Cornelius	233	Bias, James–Bickford, Eli
170	Bassett, David–Bassett, Nathaniel	234	Bickford, John–Bicknell, Thomas
171	Bassett, Peter–Batchelder, Josiah	235	Biddie, John–Bigelar, Nicholas
172	Batchelder, Mark–Bateman, Zadock	236	Bigelow, Abijah–Bigelow, William
173	Bates, Aaron–Bates, Doughty	237	Bigford, Samuel–Biles, Thomas
174	Bates, Eleazer–Bates, James	238	Bill, Abiel–Billing, Samuel
175	Bates, John–Bates, Phinehas	239	Billings, Abel–Billings, Stephen
176	Bates, Reuben–Bathrick, Stephen	240	Billingsley, John–Bing, John
177	Bathurst, Lawrence–Battin, John	241	Bingham, Aaron–Bingham, Thomas
178	Battis, John–Baum, John	242	Bingley, Lewis–Bird, Henry
179	Bauman, Charles–Baxter, Benjamin	243	Bird, Isaac–Birdwell, Benjamin
180	Baxter, Cornelius–Baxter, William	244	Birge, David–Bish, Frederick
181	Bay, Andrew–Bayley, John	245	Bishop, Abraham–Bishop, Jared
182	Bayley, Jonas–Bayliss, Sarah	246	Bishop, Jeremiah–Bishop, Paul
183	Baylor, George–Beach, Ashbel	247	Bishop, Richard–Bishop, Zepheniah
184	Beach, Dan–Beach, Obil	248	Bison, Charles–Bissell, Thomas
185	Beach, Reuben–Beakney, James	249	Bisson, Charles–Bivins, William
186	Beal, Azariah–Beale, William	250	Bixbe, Benjamin–Bizzel, Amy
187	Beall, Archibald–Beals, Uriah	251	Blachford, Uriah–Black, Joab
188	Beam, Anthony–Bean, Ebenezer	252	Black, John–Black, William
189	Bean, Henry–Beans, William	253	Blackard, Willyoube–Blackly, Thomas
190	Bear, Catharine–Beard, William	254	Blackman, Chloe–Blackman, Zachariah
191	Bearden, John–Bearmor, Lewis	255	Blackmar, Holland–Blackwelder, Isaac
192	Bears, Foard–Beatman, William	256	Blackwell, Abraham–Blaine, Ephraim
193	Beatty, Alexander–Beaty, William	257	Blair, Abraham–Blair, William
194	Beaulieu, Lewis–Bechtel, Philip	258	Blaisdell, Daniel–Blake, Isaac
195	Beck, Andrew–Becker, William	259	Blake, Jacob–Blake, Jonathan
196	Beckes, Benjamin–Becktel, George	260	Blake, Joseph–Blake, Willing
197	Beckwith, Abner–Beckwith, William	261	Blakely, Enos–Blaksley, Enos
198	Becraft, Abraham–Bedworth, William	262	Blalack, Charles–Blanchard, Ephraim
199	Beebe, Alexander–Beebe, Roderick	263	Blanchard, Francis–Blanchard, Nathaniel
200	Beebe, Roswell–Beedy, Rosiah	264	Blanchard, Peter–Blanchard, William
201	Beek, Thomas–Been, Henry	265	Blancher, Anthony–Blankenbaker, Nicholas
202	Beer, James–Beers, Zacheriah	266	Blankenship, Abel–Blasdell, William
203	Beerworth, John–Belcher, Supply	267	Blashfield, James–Blazeur, Lawrence
204	Belden, Azor–Belfield, John	268	Bleakley, George–Bleuford, William
205	Belknap, Abel–Bell, Henry	269	Blevens, Daniel–Blish, Ezra
206	Bell, Isaac–Bell, John	270	Bliss, Asa–Bliss, John
207	Bell, Jonathan–Bell, William	271	Bliss, Jonathan–Blizzard, Burton
208	Bellamy, Abner–Bellows, Timothy	272	Blockmon, Chloe–Bloggett, Benjamin

Roll	Description
273	Blood, Abel–Bloodgood, John
274	Bloom, Abraham–Bloxsom, Scarborough
275	Blue, Adrian–Blunk, Andrew
276	Blunt, Asher–Blythe, Mary
277	Boachus, George–Boardman, William
278	Boardwine, Backus–Bodfish, William
279	Bodine, Frederick–Bogge, John
280	Boggs, Alexander–Bohonon, Stephen
281	Boice, Abraham–Boley, Prestley
282	Bolick, Casper–Bolter, Lemuel
283	Bolton, Aaron–Bonar, Henry
284	Bond, Adonijah–Bondy, John
285	Bone, Archibald–Bonnell, Samuel
286	Bonner, John–Bonsall, Clement
287	Bonsted, Frederick–Boomer, Martin
288	Boon, Elisha–Booten, Travis
289	Booth, Beverly–Booth, William
290	Boothby, William–Borden, William
291	Borders, Christopher–Boskitt, John
292	Boss, Adam–Boston, Winthrop
293	Bostwick, Amos–Boswell, William
294	Bosworth, Allen–Bosworth, Zadock
295	Botan, Daniel–Boucher, Richard
296	Bouck, John–Bouncy, Joseph
297	Bourn, Ebenezer–Bouton, William
298	Bouttell, Joseph–Bowels, Samuel
299	Bowen, Aaron–Bowen, Jeremiah
300	Bowen, Joel–Bowen, Samuel
301	Bowen, Simeon–Bowerman, Peter
302	Bowers, Alpheus–Bowers, Josiah
303	Bowers, Lemuel–Bowland, Thomas
304	Bowles, Benjamin–Bowling, William
305	Bowman, Abiathar–Bowman, William
306	Bownd, Obadiah–Boyce, William
307	Boyd, Abraham–Boyd, John
308	Boyd, Joseph–Boyd, William
309	Boyden, Amos–Boyer, Valentine
310	Boyers, Asamus–Boyle, Thomas
311	Boyles, Charles–Boynton, Thomas
312	Boyt, Jacob–Bozzell, Reuben
313	Brabrook, Benjamin–Brackett, William
314	Brackin, William–Bradford, Ezekiel
315	Bradford, Gamaliel–Bradish, Daniel
316	Bradley, Aaron–Bradley, Francis
317	Bradley, Gee–Bradley, Moses
318	Bradley, Nathan–Bradley, William
319	Bradly, James–Bradwell, Nathaniel
320	Brady, Benjamin–Bragdon, William
321	Bragg, Benjamin–Brainerd, Timothy
322	Braithwaite, William–Branard, Ansel
323	Branch, Aholiab–Brandon, William
324	Brandow, Nicholas–Brant, Simeon
325	Branthifer, Adam–Braswell, Sampson
326	Bratcher, Charles–Bray, William
327	Braydon, Solomon–Breech, Thomas
328	Breed, Allen–Breeze, Stephen
329	Breidegan, John–Brevett, John
330	Brewer, Abraham–Brewer, Isaac
331	Brewer, James–Brewer, William
332	Brewington, Joshua–Brey, Christopher
333	Brian, Daniel–Bridges, John
334	Bridges, Joseph–Briges, Benjamin
335	Briggs, Aaron–Briggs, Delius
336	Briggs, Edmund–Briggs, Jesse
337	Briggs, Job–Briggs, Owen
338	Briggs, Paul–Briggs, Zephaniah
339	Brigham, Aaron–Brigham, Winslow
340	Bright, Francis–Brillifont, James
341	Brim, Henry–Brink, Peter
342	Brinker, Henry–Brister, John
343	Bristol, Austin–Britt, Richard
344	Brittain, James–Britton, John
345	Britton, Jonathan–Brizendine, William
346	Broach, Benoni–Brocaw, Isaac
347	Brock, Bezzant–Brockus, John
348	Brockway, Asa–Broile, Philip
349	Brokaw, Abraham–Bronson, Titus
350	Broocke, William–Brookover, John
351	Brooks, Ahira–Brooks, David
352	Brooks, Ebenezer–Brooks, Joel
353	Brooks, John–Brooks, Littleton
354	Brooks, Micajah–Brooks, Thaddeus
355	Brooks, Thomas–Brooks, Zachariah
356	Brookshier, John–Brougher, Christian
357	Broughton, Bartholomew–Brower, William
358	Brown, Aaron–Brown, Amos
359	Brown, Andrew–Brown, Benedict
360	Brown, Benjamin–Brown, Caleb
361	Brown, Charles–Brown, Cyrus
362	Brown, Daniel
363	Brown, David–Brown, Edward
364	Brown, Eleazer–Brown, Esek
365	Brown, Ezekiel–Brown, Humphrey
366	Brown, Ichabod–Brown, Jacob
367	Brown, James
368	Brown, Jebediah–Brown, Job
369	Brown, John (Conn.)–Brown, John (Mass.)
370	Brown, John (Navy)–Brown, John M.
371	Brown, Jonah–Brown, Jonathan
372	Brown, Joseph
373	Brown, Joshua–Brown, Moses
374	Brown, Nathan–Brown, Nicholas
375	Brown, Obadiah–Brown, Purchis
376	Brown, Reuben–Brown, Sampson
377	Brown, Samuel
378	Brown, Sanford–Brown, Thaddeus
379	Brown, Thomas–Brown, Waller
380	Brown, William (Armand's Corps)–Brown, William (N.Y.)
381	Brown, William (N.C.)–Browne, John
382	Brownell, Gardner–Browning, William
383	Brownlee, Alexander–Broyles, Michael
384	Bruce, Abijah–Bruce, William
385	Bruch, Lewis–Brumpton, Robert
386	Brundage, Israel–Brus, Edward
387	Brush, Alexander–Brutton, Arthur
388	Bryan, Asa–Bryan, John
389	Bryan, Joseph–Bryant, Billa
390	Bryant, Caleb–Bryant, Jesse
391	Bryant, John–Bryant, Stephen
392	Bryant, Thomas–Bryson, Samuel
393	Bube, Thaddeus–Buchter, Mathias
394	Buck, Aaron–Buck, Israel
395	Buck, Joel–Buck, Zebediah
396	Buckalaw, John–Bucklip, Charles
397	Buckman, Asa–Buckstaff, Peter
398	Budd, Bristol–Buel, Solomon
399	Buell, Daniel–Buffum, Samuel
400	Buford, Abraham–Buie, John

Roll	Description	Roll	Description
401	Buker, Israel–Bull, William	465	Canous, John–Capin, Thomas
402	Bullard, Aaron–Bullard, Thomas	466	Caple, Samuel–Carbury, Francis
403	Bullefant, James–Bullock, William	467	Card, Elisha–Cardwell, Wiltshire
404	Bully, Benjamin–Bumpus, William	468	Care, Tunis–Carhartt, John
405	Bumstead, Joseph–Bunn, Samuel	469	Carick, Adam–Carleton, Timothy
406	Bunnel, Amos–Burbage, Thomas	470	Carley, Albert–Carlow, Daniel
407	Burbank, Benjamin–Burbeck, Thomas	471	Carlton, Ambrose–Carmack, William
408	Burbridge, George–Burch, Zachariah	472	Carman, Abraham–Carnagey, William
409	Burcham, David–Burdge, Michael	473	Carnahan, Andrew–Carothers, Thomas
410	Burdick, Adam–Burdick, Walter	474	Carpanter, Philip–Carpenter, Elias
411	Burdin, John–Burges, William	475	Carpenter, Elijah–Carpenter, Joshua
412	Burgess, Anthony–Burgess, William	476	Carpenter, Lewis–Carpenter, William
413	Burget, Lambert–Burk, Jonathan	477	Carper, John–Carr, Jesse
414	Burk, Joseph–Burkdoff, John	478	Carr, John–Carr, Robert
415	Burke, Edmund–Burlew, Abraham	479	Carr, Samuel–Carregen, Gilbert
416	Burley, Ebenezer–Burlingame, William	480	Carrel, Aaron–Carrington, Timothy
417	Burlinggame, Christopher–Burnap, Naomi	481	Carris, Peter–Carshaw, Abraham
418	Burnell, Ephraim–Burnet, William	482	Carson, Alexander–Cart, William
419	Burnett, Andrew–Burney, Samuel	483	Carter, Aaron–Carter, Gideon
420	Burnham, Abner–Burnham, Jeremiah	484	Carter, Giles–Carter, James
421	Burnham, John–Burnham, Josiah	485	Carter, Jirah–Carter, John
422	Burnham, Moses–Burnley, James	486	Carter, Jonah–Carter, Rufus
423	Burns, Alexander–Burns, William	487	Carter, Samuel–Carter, William
424	Burnside, James–Burr, Joel	488	Carteret, John–Carty, Timothy
425	Burr, Jonathan–Burrance, Robert	489	Cartz, Thomas–Carwill, Zachariah
426	Burrel, Zachariah–Burriss, John	490	Cary, Aaron–Cary, William
427	Burritt, Andrew–Burrowes, Eden	491	Caryl, John–Case, Isaiah
428	Burrows, Aaron–Burrows, William	492	Case, James–Casewell, Simeon
429	Burrus, Jacob–Burtless, William	493	Casey, Archibald–Casey, William
430	Burton, Absalom–Burton, Lewis	494	Casgrove, Thomas–Casky, Joseph
431	Burton, Marshall–Busey, Josiah	495	Caslar, Richard–Cass, Theophilus
432	Bush, Abijah–Bush, Japhet	496	Cassada, John–Casterline, Loammi
433	Bush, John–Bush, Ziba	497	Castile, Samuel–Castor, William
434	Bushee, Consider–Bussard, Jacob	498	Caswell, Abraham–Caswell, Zebulon
435	Bussell, Daniel–Butland, Nathan	499	Catchum, Hugh–Catlett, Thomas
436	Butler, Allin–Butler, James	500	Catlin, Abel–Catterlin, Jonathan
437	Butler, Jethro–Butler, Josiah	501	Caughey, John–Cavett, Richard
438	Butler, Lawrence–Butler, Solomon	502	Cavilier, John–Cezar, Levy
439	Butler, Stephen–Butler, Zebulon	503	Chace, Aquila–Chadwell, William
440	Butman, Benjamin–Butterfield, William	504	Chadwick, Abijah–Chadwick, William
441	Butterfoss, Andrew–Butts, William	505	Chafe, Joel–Chaffy, Thomas
442	Buxton, Abijah–Buzzell, Solomon	506	Chalfant, Achsa–Chamberlain, Ephraim
443	Byam, Jesse–Byington, Zuba	507	Chamberlain, Freegift–Chamberlayne, Edward
444	Byland, Samuel–Byxbe, Ebenezer	508	Chamberlin, Aaron–Chamberlin, William
445	Caar, Thomas–Cadwell, Theodore	509	Chambers, Alexander–Chambers, William
446	Cady, Abijah–Cady, Zadok	510	Champ, William–Champlin, Newport
447	Caesar, Jesse–Cains, Richard	511	Champlin, Oliver–Chancler, Julius
448	Cairll, David–Caldwell, John	512	Chandler, Abiel–Chandler, Joel
449	Caldwell, Joseph–Caldwell, William	513	Chandler, John–Chandler, Mordecai
450	Caleb, Henry–Calkins, Nathaniel	514	Chandler, Moses–Chandler, Zebedee
451	Call, Alexander–Callaway, Samuel	515	Chandley, William–Chapelon, Peter
452	Callender, John–Cambell, Silvanus	516	Chapen, Abijah–Chapin, Luke
453	Cambray, Louis–Camp, Chauncy	517	Chapin, Nathan–Chapline, Abraham
454	Camp, Edward–Camp, William	518	Chapman, Abner–Chapman, Constant
455	Campbell, Abraham–Campbell, Christopher	519	Chapman, Dan–Chapman, Ezekiel
456	Campbell, Daniel–Campbell, Jacob	520	Chapman, Frederik–Chapman, John
457	Campbell, James–Campbell, Jesse	521	Chapman, Joseph–Chapman, Rufus
458	Campbell, John	522	Chapman, Salathiel–Chapman, Zachariah
459	Campbell, Joseph–Campbell, Robert	523	Chappel, Benjamin, Jr.–Chapple, John
460	Campbell, Samuel–Campbell, Walter	524	Chard, Barce–Chartier, Samuel
461	Campbell, William–Campbell, Winny	525	Chase, Aaron–Chase, Grindal
462	Campen, James–Candee, Samuel	526	Chase, Isaac–Chase, Moses
463	Candel, Absalom–Cann, William	527	Chase, Nathaniel–Chase, William
464	Cannaday, John–Cannon, William	528	Chasey, John–Cheard, Caleb

Roll	Description	Roll	Description
529	Cheatham, Benjamin–Chendweth, John	593	Coe, Abner–Coe, Zachariah
530	Cheney, Benjamin–Cheney, William	594	Coelman, David–Coffin, John
531	Chenoweth, John–Chesebrough, Perez	595	Coffin, Lemuel–Coggeshall, William
532	Cheshier, James–Cheston, John	596	Coggin, Robert–Cogswell, William
533	Cheuvront, Joseph–Chilcott, Thomas	597	Cohen, Abraham–Colbey, Christopher
534	Child, Abel–Child, Zachariah	598	Colborn, Robert–Colburn, Zeruiah
535	Childers, Abraham–Childrey, William	599	Colby, Aaron–Colby, Salem
536	Childs, Abel–Chilson, Joseph	600	Colby, Samuel–Coldwell, Robert
537	Chilton, Andrew–Chittam, John	601	Cole, Abel–Cole, Charles
538	Chittenden, Abraham–Chivvis, William	602	Cole, Daniel–Cole, Gideon
539	Choat, Benjamin–Christeyance, Isaac	603	Cole, Hamlin–Cole, Job
540	Christiaan, Charles–Christie, Thomas	604	Cole, John–Cole, Justin
541	Christler, David–Chun, Silvester	605	Cole, Landal–Cole, Sands
542	Church, Alexander–Church, Elihu	606	Cole, Seth–Cole, Zephaniah
543	Church, Fairbanks–Church, Joshua	607	Colebath, George–Coleman, Job
544	Church, Nathaniel–Church, Willard	608	Coleman, Joel–Coleman, Robert
545	Churchell, Caleb–Churchill, William	609	Coleman, Samuel–Coley, William
546	Chute, David–Claflin, Timothy	610	Colfax, Jonathan–Collester, John
547	Clagett, Horatio–Clapp, Dwelly	611	Collett, Isaac–Collier, William
548	Clapp, Earl–Claridge, Levin	612	Collin, Michael–Collins, Isaac
549	Clark, Aaron–Clark, Augustus	613	Collins, Jabez–Collins, John
550	Clark, Barnabas–Clark, Champion	614	Collins, Jonathan–Collins, Robert
551	Clark, Charles–Clark, Dennis	615	Collins, Samuel–Collins, William
552	Clark, Ebenezer–Clark, Eliphalet	616	Collinsworth, John–Coltman, Robert
553	Clark, Elisha–Clark, Francis	617	Colton, Alpheus–Colvin, Samuel
554	Clark, Gardner–Clark, Hezekiah	618	Colwell, Arthur–Combs, William
555	Clark, Ichabod–Clark, Jacob	619	Comee, Oliver–Commins, William
556	Clark, James	620	Como, Francis–Comstock, Caleb
557	Clark, Jeptha–Clark, John (Del.)	621	Comstock, Daniel–Conable, Samuel
558	Clark, John (Md.)–Clark, John (N.J.)	622	Conant, Able–Conant, William
559	Clark, John (N.Y.)–Clark, John S.	623	Conaway, Charles–Condy, Thomas
560	Clark, Jonas–Clark, Jonathan	624	Cone, Beriah–Cone, William
561	Clark, Joseph	625	Conery, Stephen–Conine, Philip
562	Clark, Joshua–Clark, Lyman	626	Conk, John–Conklin, Seth
563	Clark, Maltiah–Clark, Nathaniel	627	Conklin, Thomas–Conn, William
564	Clark, Nicholas–Clark, Robert	628	Connally, Michael–Connely, Nicholas
565	Clark, Rodman–Clark, Samuel	629	Conner, Andrew–Conner, Wright
566	Clark, Sarah–Clark, Wells	630	Connerly, William–Conrad, Rachel
567	Clark, William (Conn.)–Clark, William (Mass.)	631	Conrey, John–Converse, Thomas
568	Clark, William (N.H.)–Clark, Zelotes	632	Conway, Elizabeth–Conyne, Peter
569	Clarke, Abashaba–Clarke, Joshua	633	Cook, Aaron–Cook, Christopher
570	Clarke, Lemuel–Clarke, William Case	634	Cook, Daniel–Cook, Elisha
571	Clarkson, Constantine–Claxton, Rosannah	635	Cook, Elizabeth–Cook, Jacob
572	Clay, Benjamin–Clays, Peter	636	Cook, James–Cook, John
573	Clayton, Augustine–Clearwaters, Benjamin	637	Cook, Johnson–Cook, Lucy
574	Cleary, William–Cleaveland, William	638	Cook, Marimon–Cook, Paul
575	Cleavenger, Isaiah–Clemens, John	639	Cook, Peter–Cook, Solomon
576	Clement, Christopher–Clements, William	640	Cook, Stephen–Cook, Warren
577	Clemm, William–Clevedence, John	641	Cook, William–Cook, Zachariah
578	Cleveland, Absalom–Cleveland, William	642	Cooke, Arthur–Cooledge, Silas
579	Clevenger, Eden–Clifton, William	643	Cooley, Aaron–Cooley, William
580	Clinckenbeard, John–Clinton, William	644	Coolidge, Daniel–Coombs, William
581	Clizbe, Joseph–Clother, Jesse	645	Coomer, John–Coop, Horatio
582	Cloud, D. Forest–Clough, Jonathan	646	Cooper, Abel–Cooper, David
583	Clough, Joseph–Cluff, Samuel	647	Cooper, Eiles–Cooper, James
584	Clum, Adam–Cluxton, Samuel	648	Cooper, John–Cooper, Moses
585	Coakley, Robert–Cobann, Joseph	649	Cooper, Obediah–Cooper, William
586	Cobb, Abel–Cobb, Isaiah	650	Coosard, Valentine–Copeland, William
587	Cobb, Jacob–Cobb, Salmon	651	Copelin, Jonathan–Coplin, William
588	Cobb, Samuel–Cobler, Frederick	652	Copp, Aaron–Corbett, Samuel
589	Coborn, James–Coburn, Zebediah	653	Corbin, Anderson–Corbitt, Thomas
590	Cochran, Benjamin–Cochran, William	654	Cordell, John–Corey, William
591	Cochrane, Abner–Cockley, John	655	Coriell, Elisha–Corn, William
592	Cockran, Blaney–Cody, Samuel	656	Cornagey, William–Cornell, William

Roll	Description
657	Cornenelison, John–Cornwell, William
658	Corothers, Thomas–Corun, William
659	Corvin, John–Cory, William
660	Coryell, David–Cotterill, Thomas
661	Cottle, Elizabeth–Cotton, William
662	Cottrell, Asa–Couch, William
663	Couger, Zenos–Courson, Timothy
664	Court, John–Covart, Isaac
665	Covel, David–Coverly, Thomas
666	Covert, Burgun–Covill, Samuel
667	Covington, John–Cowdry, William
668	Cowell, Isaac–Cowherd, Jonathan
669	Cowin, William–Cownover, Garret
670	Cox, Andrew–Cox, James
671	Cox, Javan–Cox, Phinehas
672	Cox, Reeves–Coxe, Bartlett
673	Coy, Christopher–Cozzens, Richard
674	Crabb, Abijah–Craford, James
675	Craft, Aaron–Crago, Robert
676	Craig, Abijah–Craig, John
677	Craig, Matthew–Craigee, William
678	Craighead, Robert–Craley, Hugh
679	Cram, Benjamin–Crammer, Henry
680	Crampton, Jonathan–Crandal, Sylvester
681	Crandall, Abner–Crandol, Ammariah
682	Crane, Aaron–Crane, James
683	Crane, John–Crane, Mayfield
684	Crane, Nathaniel–Crane, Zebulon
685	Crank, Peleg–Crary, Nathan
686	Crass, Abraham–Crawford, Jacob
687	Crawford, James–Crawford, John
688	Crawford, Joseph–Crawford, William
689	Crawley, Charles–Creepman, John
690	Creery, William–Crews, Redman
691	Crider, David–Criswell, Samuel
692	Critchet, Benjamin–Croce, Philip
693	Crocker, Ansel–Crocker, Zebulon
694	Crockett, Alexander–Crofut, Seth
695	Croghan, William–Cronts, Michael
696	Crook, Andrew–Cropper, John
697	Crosby, Alpheus–Crosby, Obed
698	Crosby, Samuel–Crosman, Thomas
699	Cross, Abijah–Cross, Moses
700	Cross, Nathan–Cross, Zachariah
701	Crossan, John–Croswell, John
702	Crouch, Christopher–Crow, William
703	Crowder, John–Crowell, Thomas
704	Crower, Rudolph–Cruize, Walter
705	Crum, Adam–Crumpton, James
706	Crunk, John–Crysel, Jeremiah
707	Cucksey, William–Cully, Charles
708	Culp, John–Cumberford, James
709	Cuming, John–Cummings, John
710	Cummings, Jonathan–Cummins, William
711	Cump, Henry–Cunningham, James
712	Cunningham, Jeremiah–Cunningham, Peter
713	Cunningham, Richard–Cunningham, William
714	Cupp, Leonard–Currier, David
715	Currier, Ebenezer–Currier, Willis
716	Currill, Nicholas–Curry, William
717	Curtice, David–Curtis, David
718	Curtis, Ebenezer–Curtis, Joel
719	Curtis, John–Curtis, Robert
720	Curtis, Russel–Curtis, Zarah

Roll	Description
721	Curtiss, Agur–Curtiss, William
722	Curtner, Anthony–Cushing, William
723	Cushman, Amos–Cushman, Jonah
724	Cushman, Jonathan–Cushman, Zebedee
725	Cusick, Christopher–Cutler, Isaac
726	Cutler, John–Cutter, William
727	Cutting, Aaron–Cyrus, Exeter
728	Daball, Benjamin–Dagger, Peter
729	Dagget, Jacob–Daggett, William
730	Daghl, John–Daily, William
731	Daimwood, Boston–Daley, Silas
732	Daliba, George–Daly, John
733	Dam, Edward–Damons, Gamaliel
734	Dampeer, Daniel–Danfield, John
735	Danford, Joseph–Danforth, William
736	Daniel, Andrew–Daniel, William
737	Danielly, Daniel–Daniels, John
738	Daniels, Jonathan–Daniels, Thomas
739	Danielson, Altamont–D'Antignac, John
740	Darbe, Asa–Darlin, David
741	Darling, Aaron–Darling, Zelek
742	Darlington, John–Darrow, Zaccheus
743	Darsey, Joel–Daulton, Moses
744	Davenport, Abner–Davenport, James
745	Davenport, Joel–Davenport, William
746	Daverson, Josiah–Davidson, Giles
747	Davidson, Hezekiah–Davidson, Josiah
748	Davidson, Paul–Davies, William
749	Davis, Aaron–Davis, Asa
750	Davis, Benaijah–Davis, Cyrus
751	Davis, Daniel–Davis, Dudley
752	Davis, Ebenezer–Davis, Ezra
753	Davis, Forrest–Davis, Hugh
754	Davis, Ichabod–Davis, Jacob
755	Davis, James
756	Davis, Jesse–Davis, John (N.H.)
757	Davis, John (N.J.)–Davis, John (S.C.)
758	Davis, John (Va.)–Davis, Jonathan
759	Davis, Joseph
760	Davis, Joshua–Davis, Kitteridge
761	Davis, Lathrop–Davis, Moses
762	Davis, Nancy–Davis, Phinehas
763	Davis, Reuben–Davis, Sampson
764	Davis, Samuel
765	Davis, Sanford–Davis, Surry
766	Davis, Thomas
767	Davis, Thompson–Davis, William(Md.)
768	Davis, William(Mass.)–Davis, William(N.C.)
769	Davis, William(Pa.)–Davis, Zebulon
770	Davise, John–Davol, William
771	Daw, Benjamin–Dawson, William
772	Day, Aaron–Day, Isaac
773	Day, James–Day, Justin
774	Day, Levi–Day, Zebina
775	Dayhoff, George–Dazey, Thomas
776	Deacon, Aaron–Deamer, Philip
777	Dean, Aaron–Dean, Ephraim
778	Dean, Gideon–Dean, Josiah
779	Dean, Lemuel–Dean, Robert
780	Dean, Samuel–Dean, Zimey
781	Deane, Ashbel–Dearborn, Simon
782	Dearing, Henry–Decilva, William
783	Deck, Henry–Decker, Jacob
784	Decker, James–Decker, William

Roll	Description	Roll	Description
785	Deckirtt, John–Deen, Thomas	849	Drake, Abial–Drake, Isaac
786	Deer, Martin–Deforrest, David	850	Drake, Jacob–Drake, Moses
787	Defrance, John–Dehart, Winant	851	Drake, Nicholas–Drake, William
788	Dehaven, Edward–Delaney, Martin	852	Dralle, John–Dressner, John
789	Delano, Aaron–Delano, Thomas	853	Drew, Andrew–Drew, William
790	Delanoy, Ellen–Delleber, John	854	Drewry, John–Drought, Richard
791	Dellinger, Christian–Demery, Thomas	855	Drown, Caleb–Drum, Robert
792	Deming, Alpheus–Deming, Zebulon	856	Drumbar, Henry–Dryden, Artemas
793	Demint, Jarret–Dempsey, Timothy	857	Duba, John–Dudderow, John
794	Denbo, Cornelius–Denison, Gilbert	858	Dudley, Ambrose–Dudly, Samuel
795	Denison, Henry–Denning, William	859	Duduit, William–Dugger, William
796	Dennis, Adonijah–Dennis, William	860	Duggins, William–Dull, William
797	Dennison, Amos–Denny, William	861	Dum, Peter–Dunbar, George
798	Denoon, John–Denwood, Levin	862	Dunbar, Jacob–Dunber, Ebenezer
799	Deo, Elias–Depuy, Moses	863	Duncan, Alexander–Duncan, Jesse
800	Dequise, Charles–Desbrow, Justus	864	Duncan, John–Dungan, Thomas
801	Desearn, Frederick–Deveaux, Peter	865	Dunham, Abishai–Dunham, Jacob
802	Deveney, Daniel–Devlin, James	866	Dunham, James–Dunham, William
803	Devoe, Anthony–Dewett, George	867	Dunikin, Daniel–Dunlap, William
804	Dewey, Abijah–Dewey, Timothy	868	Dunlavy, Francis–Dunn, John
805	Dewing, Elijah–Dewitt, Moses	869	Dunn, Joseph–Dunn, William
806	Dewitt, Nancy–Dews, William	870	Dunnavant, William–Dunovan, Hannah
807	Dexter, Abigail–Dexter, William	871	Dunphey, James–Dunworth, George
808	Dey, Daniel–Dibol, Moses	872	Dupar, John–Durand, William
809	Dibrell, Anthony–Dickens, William	873	Durant, Allen–Durfey, Joseph
810	Dickenson, Edward–Dickeson, Isham	874	Durgey, Moses–Durham, William
811	Dickey, Adam–Dickey, William	875	Durkee, Asahel–Durkee, William
812	Dickin, Joseph–Dickinson, Joel	876	Durnell, John–Duston, Zacheus
813	Dickinson, John–Dickinson, William	877	Dutail, John–Dutton, William
814	Dickison, Isaac–Dickson, William	878	Duttroe, Jacob–Dwight, Timothy
815	Dicsen, Thomas–Diggs, William	879	Dwinel, Aaron–Dycus, Edward
816	Dike, Adin–Dilks, Samuel	880	Dye, George–Dyer, Esek
817	Dill, Archibald–Dilleber, John	881	Dyer, Francis–Dyer, Robert
818	Dillen, Benjamin–Diman, David	882	Dyer, Samuel–Dyson, Thomas
819	Dimick, Benjamin–Dimond, Reuben	883	Eabs, Emanuel–Ealy, John
820	Dinah, James–Disbrow, Simon	884	Eames, Charles–Earick, Henry
821	Disharoon, John–Dix, William	885	Earl, Cornelius–Earll, Watson
822	Dixon, Alexander–Dixon, Wynne	886	Earls, Cornelius–Easor, Aaron
823	Dixson, John–Dobbs, Nathaniel	887	East, Isham–Eastman, Eli
824	Dobel, John–Dockum, William	888	Eastman, Henry–Eastman, Zachariah
825	Dod, Daniel–Dodds, Zachariah	889	Easton, Ahimaaz–Eatinger, Jacob
826	Dodge, Abner–Dodge, John	890	Eaton, Abiathar–Eaton, Ezra
827	Dodge, Levi–Dodge, William	891	Eaton, Hannah–Eaton, Moses
828	Dodson, Caleb–Dolby, William	892	Eaton, Nathan–Eatton, Joseph
829	Dole, Amos–Dolley, John	893	Eavans, Wiggin–Ector, Samuel
830	Dollif, Richard–Dond, Richard	894	Eddings, William–Eddy, John
831	Done, Richard–Donnolly, John	895	Eddy, Joshua–Eddy, William
832	Donoho, James–Dopson, Jessey	896	Edegh, Jacob–Edgar, Thomas
833	Doran, Abraham–Dormire, Anna	897	Edgarton, Edward–Edgerton, Roger
834	Dorn, Abraham–Dorville, John	898	Edgman, William–Edmond, William
835	Dosher, Peter–Dotter, Samuel	899	Edmonds, Andrew–Edmundson, William
836	Dotty, Moses–Doty, Jerathmeel	900	Edney, Robert–Edson, Thomas
837	Doty, John–Doty, Zebulon	901	Edward, David–Edwards, Evan
838	Douberman, Henry–Douge, Peter	902	Edwards, Fletcher–Edwards, John
839	Dougherty, Andrew–Dougherty, William	903	Edwards, Johnathan–Edwards, Peter
840	Doughten, William–Douglas, Thomas	904	Edwards, Reuben–Edwards, William
841	Douglass, Alexander–Douglass, Phinehas	905	Edy, Samuel–Eggert, John
842	Douglass, Randall–Dovin, John	906	Egglesone, Asa–Egolff, Henry
843	Dow, Alexander–Dow, Zebulon	907	Ehle, Anthony–Eittinger, Jacob
844	Dowberman, Henry–Dowers, Jacob	908	Ekeheart, Frederick–Eldred, Samuel
845	Dowlan, George–Downie, Alexander	909	Eldredg, Robert–Eldrige, Hannah
846	Downing, Daniel–Downing, Stephen	910	Eley, William–Elkins, William
847	Downman, Rawleigh–Dowrey, Joe	911	Ella, David–Ellinwood, Benjamin
848	Dows, Eleazer–Dozier, Richard	912	Elliot, Archibald–Elliot, William

Roll	Description	Roll	Description
913	Elliott, Abraham–Elliott, Robert	977	Finney, Bethuel–Fisemire, John
914	Elliott, Samuel–Elliott, Zachariah	978	Fish, Aaron–Fish, Thomas
915	Ellis, Aaron–Ellis, Freeman	979	Fishback, Jacob–Fisher, Frederick
916	Ellis, Gamaliel–Ellis, Lyman	980	Fisher, George–Fisher, John
917	Ellis, Marvel–Ellis, William	981	Fisher, Joseph–Fishley, George
918	Ellison, Charles–Ellworth, William	982	Fisk, Abijah–Fiske, Squire
919	Ellwell, John–Elmes, Eliphalet	983	Fislar, John–Fitch, William
920	Elmore, Daniel–Elsworth, William	984	Fitchett, Joshua–Fitzgerrald, Joseph
921	Elter, John–Elwood, Thomas	985	Fitzgibbons, James–Flagg, William
922	Ely, Abner–Ely, William	986	Flake, George–Flanders, Stephen
923	Elzey, William–Emerson, John	987	Flanigan, Henry–Flek, Peter
924	Emerson, Jonathan–Emerson, William	988	Fleming, Allison–Flemming, Robert
925	Emert, Frederick–Emery, Joshua	989	Flenniken, David–Fletcher, Luke
926	Emery, Levi–Emmerson, William	990	Fletcher, Mary–Flinner, Henry
927	Emmert, Frederick–Emons, Phineas	991	Flint, Aaron–Flint, Zacheus
928	Emory, Gideon–Engler, Leonard	992	Flippen, Joseph–Flowers, William
929	Englis, Andrew–Englisher, John	993	Floyd, Abraham–Foat, Isaac
930	Engly, Timothy–Enos, Roger	994	Fobes, Daniel–Foght, John
931	Ensign, Daniel–Eply, John	995	Fogle, George–Folsom, Thomas
932	Epperly, George–Erskine, John	996	Folts, Conrad–Fooshee, John
933	Ervin, Charles–Erwin, William	997	Foot, Abraham–Foote, Stephen
934	Eschleman, Abraham–Essop, Samuel	998	Fopless, John–Forbs, James
935	Estabrook, John–Estes, Thomas	999	Forburk, Alexander–Ford, Benjamin
936	Estey, Moses–Etter, John	1000	Ford, Caleb–Ford, Joseph
937	Ettick, George–Eustis, William	1001	Ford, Joshua–Ford, William
938	Evans, Abel–Evans, David	1002	Fordham, Nathan–Ferguson, John
939	Evans, Edward–Evans, Jesse	1003	Forgy, Hugh–Forrester, Stephen
940	Evans, John–Evans, Moses	1004	Forrey, Jacob–Fortner, Ezekiel
941	Evans, Nancy–Evans, Thomas	1005	Fortune, Gardiner–Fossett, Robert
942	Evans, Walter–Evelt, Daniel	1006	Foster, Abel–Foster, Ezra
943	Evens, Abiathar–Everett, William	1007	Foster, Faith–Foster, John
944	Everhard, Frederick–Everitt, Thomas	1008	Foster, Jonathan–Foster, Rufus
945	Everly, George–Everts, Stephen	1009	Foster, Samuel–Foster, William
946	Every, Thomas–Ewers, Rufus	1010	Foulk, John–Fowler, Isaac
947	Ewing, Alexander–Ezell, Timothy	1011	Fowler, Jacob–Fowls, Samuel
948	Fackenthall, Michael–Fairbank, William	1012	Fox, Aaron–Fox, Israel
949	Fairbanks, Abel–Fairchild, Stephen	1013	Fox, Jabez–Fox, Nathaniel
950	Faire, Jonathan–Falkner, Robert	1014	Fox, Patrick–Foye, Moses
951	Fall, Aaron–Fanshar, James	1015	Fradenburgh, John–Francis, Micajah
952	Fant, George–Fariss, William	1016	Francis, Robert–Frankfort, Henry
953	Farley, Benjamin–Farmer, William	1017	Franklin, Abel–Franklyn, Edward
954	Farnam, Benjamin–Farnsler, Henry	1018	Franks, David–Frazar, James
955	Farnsworth, Amos–Farnworth, Ebenezer	1019	Frazee, Jonas–Frazier, William
956	Farquher, James–Farrare, Emanuel	1020	Fream, William–Freelove, David
957	Farrell, Isaac–Farris, William	1021	Freeman, Aaron–Freeman, Doss
958	Farrow, Abraham–Faughey, William	1022	Freeman, Edmund–Freeman, Joel
959	Faulconer, James–Fawver, Henry	1023	Freeman, John–Freeman, Rufus
960	Faxon, Allen–Fay, William	1024	Freeman, Salisbury–Freligh, Valentine
961	Fayerweather, Samuel–Feith, John	1025	French, Aaron–French, Jacob
962	Felch, Jabez–Felmott, Dorus	1026	French, James–French, Nathaniel
963	Felps, Thomas–Fenly, Uz	1027	French, Nehemiah–French, Zenas
964	Fenn, Benjamin–Fenstermacher, John	1028	Freneau, Philip–Frink, Willard
965	Fent, Matthew–Fergus, John	1029	Frisbee, Jonah–Fronebarger, John
966	Ferguson, Abraham–Fergusson, William	1030	Frost, Aaron–Frost, Zephaniah
967	Ferier, Charles–Ferrioll, Alexander	1031	Frothingham, Benjamin–Frye, Theophilus
968	Ferris, Coenradt–Ferver, Henry	1032	Fryer, Charles–Fullam, Oliver
969	Fesemire, John–Fidler, John	1033	Fuller, Aaron–Fuller, Ebenezer
970	Fiealds, John–Field, Joshua	1034	Fuller, Edward–Fuller, Job
971	Field, Lemuel–Fields, William	1035	Fuller, John–Fuller, Meshack
972	Fiendley, John–Figla, Peter	1036	Fuller, Nathan–Fuller, Witt
973	File, Samuel–Filmore, Henry	1037	Fullerton, Arunah–Fuqua, Joseph
974	Finch, Abigail–Finch, William	1038	Furbeck, John–Fysel, William
975	Fincher, James–Finks, Mark	1039	Gabbard, Jacob–Gafford, Joseph
976	Finlay, Robert–Finnell, Charles	1040	Gage, Aaron–Gage, Zenas

Roll	Description	Roll	Description
1041	Gager, Samuel–Galbreath, William	1105	Graham, Amos–Graham, John
1042	Gale, Abraham–Gale, Samuel	1106	Graham, Joseph–Graims, Adam
1043	Gall, George–Gallup, William	1107	Grainger, Zaccheus–Granniss, Enos
1044	Gallusha, Daniel–Gammage, William	1108	Grant, Aaron–Grant, Jesse
1045	Gammar, Joseph–Gantt, Erasmus	1109	Grant, John–Grant, William
1046	Gapen, Stephen–Gardner, Cornelius	1110	Grantham, Henry–Graves, Boston
1047	Gardner, David–Gardner, John	1111	Graves, Chauncey–Graves, Julius
1048	Gardner, Jonathan–Gardner, William	1112	Graves, Levi–Grawbargar, Henry
1049	Garee, Christopher–Garlin, John	1113	Gray, Aaron–Gray, Frederick
1050	Garlinghouse, Benjamin–Garnsey, Samuel	1114	Gray, Gabriel–Gray, Joel
1051	Garrabrants, Garabrant–Garrisham, James	1115	Gray, John–Gray, Presley
1052	Garrison, Aaron–Garrisson, John	1116	Gray, Richard–Gray, Willis
1053	Garrit, John–Gary, Thomas	1117	Graybill, Philip–Green, Benjamin
1054	Gasaway, Thomas–Gatchell, Zachariah	1118	Green, Beriah–Green, Francis
1055	Gates, Adam–Gates, Luther	1119	Green, Gabriel–Green, Joel
1056	Gates, Marvin–Gates, Zebulon	1120	Green, John–Green, Jonathan
1057	Gatewood, Dudley–Gaw, Chambers	1121	Green, Joseph–Green, Peleg
1058	Gay, Allen–Gay, Zerobabel	1122	Green, Peter–Green, Stephen
1059	Gaylard, Levi–Geddins, John	1123	Green, Thomas–Green, Zeeb
1060	Gee, David–Geery, John	1124	Greenawalt, John–Greene, Zachariah
1061	Geesler, John–Geohegan, Anthony	1125	Greenelsh, Edward–Greenslit, John
1062	George, Amos–Georgia, Simon	1126	Greentree, Benjamin–Greggs, Robert
1063	Gephart, John–Giard, Gabriel	1127	Gregory, Abram–Gregory, Joseph
1064	Gibb, William–Gibbs, James	1128	Gregory, Joshua–Gregory, William
1065	Gibbs, John–Gibbs, Zenas	1129	Greinder, Martin–Grider, Valentine
1066	Giberson, James–Gibson, Joel	1130	Gridley, Asahel–Grier, Thomas
1067	Gibson, John–Gibson, William	1131	Grifen, Thomas–Griffin, Joseph
1068	Giddeman, John–Gilam, Robert	1132	Griffin, Joshua–Griffing, Stephen
1069	Gilbert, Allen–Gilbert, Jonathan	1133	Griffis, Abner–Griffith, Jeremiah
1070	Gilbert, Joseph–Gilbirt, James	1134	Griffith, John–Griffy, John
1071	Gilbreath, Thomas–Gilkie, Samuel	1135	Griger, Cato–Grimes, William
1072	Gill, Amos–Gill, William	1136	Grimke, John–Grist, Jacob
1073	Gillam, Ezekiel–Gillespy, William	1137	Griswold, Aaron–Griswold, Francis
1074	Gillet, Adna–Gillette, Benoni	1138	Griswold, George–Griswold, Zenas
1075	Gilley, Francis–Gillum, William	1139	Grite, William–Groscost, Jacob
1076	Gilman, Andrew–Gilman, William	1140	Grose, Philip–Grouse, George
1077	Gilmor, Thomas–Gilmour, James	1141	Grout, Abel–Grove, Windle
1078	Gilpatrick, Joseph–Giroux, Jean	1142	Grovener, Polly–Grownhart, John
1079	Gish, Sany–Glanton, John	1143	Grub, Darius–Guernsey, Southmayd
1080	Glasco, Caleb–Glazebrook, Julius	1144	Guess, Benjamin–Guilder, Daniel
1081	Glazer, Aaron–Gleezen, Caleb	1145	Guile, Abraham–Gully, John
1082	Glen, Andrew–Gloucester, James	1146	Gum, Shepherd–Gunnison, Josiah
1083	Glover, Alexander–Glover, William	1147	Gunsalus, Daniel–Gurney, Zachariah
1084	Gloyd, Asa–Goddy, Bartholomew	1148	Gushee, Elijah–Guttry, Nathaniel
1085	Godfrey, Ard–Goewey, Garet	1149	Guy, James–Gwynn, John
1086	Goff, Abel–Goffe, Samuel	1150	Haas, Christian–Hackworth, William
1087	Goffigan, Laban–Goldthwait, Timothy	1151	Hadar, William–Haffernan, Hugh
1088	Goldy, John–Goodall, Silas	1152	Hagadorn, Jacob–Hager, Stephen
1089	Goodcourage, John–Goodhard, David	1153	Hagerman, Barnet–Haigler, Jacob
1090	Goodhue, Joseph–Goodown, Jacob	1154	Hail, Garshom–Hains, Simeon
1091	Goodrich, Abel–Goodrich, Simeon	1155	Hair, Daniel–Haldridge, Jehiel
1092	Goodrich, Solomon–Goodwill, John	1156	Hale, Aaron–Hales, Isaiah
1093	Goodwin, Aaron–Goodwin, Julius	1157	Haley, Ambrose–Halkuston, Robert
1094	Goodwin, Lemuel–Goodwyn, William	1158	Hall, Aaron–Hall, Benoni
1095	Goody, Lambert–Goosely, James	1159	Hall, Caleb–Hall, Ebenezer
1096	Gordan, Bernard–Gordon, Jesse	1160	Hall, Edward–Hall, Hudson
1097	Gordon, John–Gordon, Zebulon	1161	Hall, Ignatius–Hall, Job
1098	Gore, Avery–Gorsline, Samuel	1162	Hall, John
1099	Gorton, Benjamin–Goss, William	1163	Hall, Jonathan–Hall, Lyman
1100	Gossard, Rufus–Gough, John	1164	Hall, Martha–Hall, Robert
1101	Gould, Abraham–Gould, Jonathan	1165	Hall, Samuel–Hall, Titus
1102	Gould, Joseph–Gould, William	1166	Hall, Wildman–Hall, Zachariah
1103	Gouldman, Francis–Graaf, John	1167	Halladay, Eli–Hally, Timothy
1104	Grace, Aaron–Gragg, William	1168	Halsey, Abraham–Ham, William

Roll	Description	Roll	Description
1169	Hamar, James–Hamill, Robert	1233	Hayes, Aaron–Hayes, Levi
1170	Hamilton, Abner–Hamilton, Hosea	1234	Hayes, Nathaniel–Hayne, Henry
1171	Hamilton, James–Hamilton, Joseph	1235	Haynes, Aaron–Hayns, Joseph
1172	Hamilton, Joshua–Hamilton, William	1236	Hays, Aaron–Hayse, John
1173	Hamiston, Jared–Hamlin, William	1237	Hayslet, Thomas–Hayward, Ziba
1174	Hamlinton, Daniel–Hammon, Thomas	1238	Haywood, Benjamin–Hazeltine, William
1175	Hammond, Abijah–Hammond, Obadiah	1239	Hazelton, Abraham–Hazzard, William
1176	Hammond, Paul–Hammons, Joseph	1240	Head, Britin–Headly, Carey
1177	Hamner, Henry–Hancks, Abraham	1241	Headman, William–Healy, William
1178	Hancock, Austin–Hancox, Edward	1242	Heape, Archibald–Hearsey, Zadok
1179	Hand, Aaron–Handly, Samuel	1243	Heart, Frederick–Heath, Josiah
1180	Handy, Benjamin–Handy, William	1244	Heath, Peleg–Heath, Zebadiah
1181	Haner, William–Hankinson, Joseph	1245	Heathcock, James–Hebron, William
1182	Hanks, Abner–Hannah, John	1246	Heck, Youst–Hedger, William
1183	Hannaman, William–Hanscome, Jeremiah	1247	Hedges, Benjamin–Hegin, Edward
1184	Hansdon, Allen–Haptonstall, Abraham	1248	Heidler, Joshua–Helme, William
1185	Haraden, John–Hardee, William	1249	Helmer, Adam–Hembree, Drewry
1186	Harden, James–Hardin, William	1250	Hemenway, David–Hendershot, John
1187	Harding, Abiel–Harding, William	1251	Henderson, Alexander–Henderson, John
1188	Hardison, Benjamin–Hardy, William	1252	Henderson, Jonathan–Henderson, Zoath
1189	Hardyear, Elijah–Hariman, Jacob	1253	Hendley, William–Hendrixen, Isaac
1190	Haring, Abraham–Harlon, Jonathan	1254	Hendron, William–Hennussey, William
1191	Harlow, Ansel–Harlow, William	1255	Henry, Adam–Henry, John
1192	Harman, Charles–Harmon, William	1256	Henry, Joseph–Henry, Wills
1193	Harmony, Nicholas–Harper, John	1257	Hensel, George–Henze, Frederick
1194	Harper, Joseph–Harpoole, Henry	1258	Hepburn, Peter–Herington, Benjamin
1195	Harps, Manon–Harringer, William	1259	Herman, Frederick–Herrendeen, Thomas
1196	Harrington, Abiel–Harrington, Jonathan	1260	Herrick, Abel–Herrick, Zebulon
1197	Harrington, Joshua–Harriott, Samuel	1261	Herriden, Elizabeth–Hermann, John
1198	Harris, Abiel–Harris, Ezekiel	1262	Herron, Allan–Hesser, Frederick
1199	Harris, Fanny–Harris, Jesse	1263	Hester, Abraham–Hewes, William
1200	Harris, John	1264	Hewet, Gideon–Hewit, William
1201	Harris, Jonathan–Harris, Overton	1265	Hewitt, Bartimeus–Hezelton, Joseph
1202	Harris, Paul–Harris, Walter	1266	Hiatt, Asa–Hicklin, Jonathan
1203	Harris, William–Harris, Winans	1267	Hickman, Adam–Hickmon, Theophilus
1204	Harrison, Aaron–Harrison, Job	1268	Hickock, Ichabod–Hicks, James
1205	Harrison, John–Harrison, Robert	1269	Hicks, Jesse–Hicks, Zechariah
1206	Harrison, Sarah–Harsin, Garret	1270	Hicock, David–Higginbotham, William
1207	Hart, Aaron–Hart, Hosea	1271	Higgins, Ananias–Higgins, William
1208	Hart, Ithurel–Hart, Nicholas	1272	Higgs, Henry–Hiland, Amasa
1209	Hart, Oliver–Hart, Zachariah	1273	Hilbert, John–Hiliard, Joseph
1210	Hartchell, John–Hartsfield, John	1274	Hill, Aaron–Hill, Daniel
1211	Hartshorn, Aaron–Hartwell, Thomas	1275	Hill, David–Hill, Israel
1212	Hartwick, Barent–Harvey, Jonathan	1276	Hill, Jacob–Hill, John
1213	Harvey, Joseph–Harvey, Zadock	1277	Hill, Jonas–Hill, Primus
1214	Harvick, Jacob–Harwood, Thomas	1278	Hill, Reuben–Hill, Stephen
1215	Hasbrouck, Benjamin–Haskell, Job	1279	Hill, Stukley–Hill, Zimri
1216	Haskell, John–Haskill, Nathaniel	1280	Hillan, James–Hillock, Robert
1217	Haskin, Abraham–Hastin, William	1281	Hills, Asahel–Hills, Zimry
1218	Hastings, Abijah–Hastings, Zacheus	1282	Hillsinger, Elias–Hilton, Joseph
1219	Hasty, Archibald–Hatch, Ede	1283	Hilton, Morral–Hincher, Josiah
1220	Hatch, Eliakim–Hatch, Moses	1284	Hinckley, Abner–Hindman, James
1221	Hatch, Nathan–Hatch, Zachariah	1285	Hinds, Abijah–Hines, William
1222	Hatcher, Benjamin–Hatfield, Richard	1286	Hinesman, Henry–Hinkson, Samuel
1223	Hathaway, Abial–Hathaway, Timothy	1287	Hinman, Benjamin–Hinton, Lewis
1224	Hathcock, Holiday–Haupt, Philip	1288	Hiott, Joseph–Hitch, Gillis
1225	Hause, Leonard–Havens, William	1289	Hitchcock, Aaron–Hitchcock, Lemuel
1226	Havey, Daniel–Hawkey, Henry	1290	Hitchcock, Levi–Hitchman, Salisbury
1227	Hawkins, Abraham–Hawkins, John	1291	Hite, Abraham–Hixt, William
1228	Hawkins, Joseph–Hawkins, Zopher	1292	Hoadley, Culpeper–Hoasman, Poal
1229	Hawkinsbury, John–Hawley, James	1293	Hoback, Philip–Hobbs, William
1230	Hawley, Joseph–Hawwawas, Nicholas	1294	Hobby, Hezekiah–Hodgdon, Samuel
1231	Hay, Abram–Hayden, Ezra	1295	Hodge, Abraham–Hodgeman, Thomas
1232	Hayden, Jacob–Haydon, Peleg	1296	Hodges, Abednego–Hodges, Zebulon

Roll	Description	Roll	Description
1297	Hodggets, Emanuel–Hodgman, Zacheus	1361	Hughes, Richard–Huitt, John
1298	Hodsdon, Benjamin–Hoffman, William	1362	Hukell, Daniel–Hulit, John
1299	Hoffmire, Samuel–Hogeboom, Richard	1363	Hull, Abner–Hull, Israel
1300	Hogekeys, Samuel–Hoisington, Vespasian	1364	Hull, James–Hull, Zephaniah
1301	Hoit, Benjamin–Holbert, Aaron	1365	Hullderman, John–Humphlet, Thomas
1302	Holbrook, Abel–Holbrook, Jesse	1366	Humphrees, Samuel–Humphrey, William
1303	Holbrook, John–Holburton, William	1367	Humphreys, Alexander–Humphries, Robert
1304	Holcomb, Abel–Holcomb, Obed	1368	Humphry, Abraham–Hungerman, Nicholas
1305	Holcomb, Peter–Holden, Job	1369	Hunkins, John–Hunt, Davis
1306	Holden, John–Holden, Timothy	1370	Hunt, Ebenezer–Hunt, Jacob
1307	Holder, Daniel–Hollanbeck, Ruth	1371	Hunt, James–Hunt, Julius
1308	Holland, Charles–Holland, William	1372	Hunt, Laban–Hunt, Samuel
1309	Hollaway, Thomas–Holliday, William	1373	Hunt, Sarah–Hunt, Zebulon
1310	Hollidayoke, Daniel–Hollis, William	1374	Hunter, Alexander–Hunter, John
1311	Hollister, Asa–Hollowell, Miles	1375	Hunter, Jonathan–Hunting, Moses
1312	Holly, Abraham–Holman, Thomas	1376	Huntingdon, John–Huntington, Ziba
1313	Holmes, Abijah–Holmes, Isaac	1377	Huntley, Abner–Huntoon, Thomas
1314	Holmes, Jabez–Holmes, Lazarus	1378	Huntress, Jonathan–Hurd, Zadok
1315	Holmes, Lemuel–Holmes, Simeon	1379	Hurdell, Lawrence–Hurleroy, John
1316	Holmes, Stephen–Holston, William	1380	Hurley, Arthur–Husbands, William
1317	Holt, Abel–Holt, John	1381	Huse, Isaac–Hutch, John
1318	Holt, Jonathan–Holt, William	1382	Hutchens, Charles–Hutchings, William
1319	Holten, Jonathan–Honson, Aurt	1383	Hutchins, Amasa–Hutchins, Zadoc
1320	Hood, Aaron–Hood, William	1384	Hutchinson, Abijah–Hutchinson, William
1321	Hoof, James–Hooker, John	1385	Hutchison, Cornelius–Hutto, Henry
1322	Hooker, Martin–Hooper, Robert	1386	Hutton, Christopher–Hyatt, William
1323	Hooper, Sarah–Hopewell, John	1387	Hyde, Agur–Hyde, John
1324	Hopkins, Archibald–Hopkins, Jesse	1388	Hyde, Jonathan–Hyslop, Levin
1325	Hopkins, John–Hopkins, Zaphas	1389	Iams, John–Ilsley, Isaiah
1326	Hopkinson, Caleb–Horless, Philip	1390	Imeson, John–Ingell, Zadock
1327	Horn, Aaron–Horn, William	1391	Ingersol, George–Ingols, Amos
1328	Hornbaker, Philip–Horsley, Samuel	1392	Ingraham, Amos–Inlow, Potter
1329	Horsom, Benjamin–Horton, Isaac	1393	Inman, Aaron–Irons, John
1330	Horton, James–Horton, Zephaniah	1394	Irvin, Andrew–Irwin, Thomas
1331	Hortwick, Barnabas–Hoskins, Zipporah	1395	Isaacs, Isaac–Ittig, Jacob
1332	Hoskinson, Basil–Hosum, Jonathan	1396	Ivens, Solomon–Izeley, Philip
1333	Hotchkis, Thebus–Hotchkiss, Trueman	1397	Jabine, John–Jackson, Benjamin
1334	Hotman, George–Houghtalin, James	1398	Jackson, Caleb–Jackson, Henry
1335	Houghton, Aaron–Hougton, Ebenezer	1399	Jackson, Isaac–Jackson, Jonathan
1336	Houk, Michael–House, William	1400	Jackson, Joseph–Jackson, Pomp
1337	Householder, Jacob–Houston, John	1401	Jackson, Reuben–Jackson, William
1338	Houston, Peter–Hovey, Zaccheus	1402	Jackway, Daniel–Jacobs, Joseph
1339	How, Aaron–How, Timothy	1403	Jacobs, Lemuel–Jamerson, Robert
1340	Howard, Aaron–Howard, Edward	1404	James, Aaron–James, Jonathan
1341	Howard, Elisha–Howard, Job	1405	James, Joseph–James, William
1342	Howard, John–Howard, Ruth	1406	Jameson, Adam–Janson, Johannes
1343	Howard, Samuel–Howdershell, Lawrence	1407	Japson, William–Jarvins, Daniel
1344	Howe, Abner–Howe, Joel	1408	Jarvis, Bill–Jeffers, William
1345	Howe, John–Howe, Zadok	1409	Jefferson, Justinian–Jenison, William
1346	Howel, Charles–Howell, Philip	1410	Jenkins, Aaron–Jenkins, John
1347	Howell, Reuben–Howey, George	1411	Jenkins, Joseph–Jenkins, Zaccheus
1348	Howland, Abraham–Hoyles, John	1412	Jenkinson, William–Jennings, Esbon
1349	Hoyt, Abraham–Hoyt, Jonathan	1413	Jennings, George–Jennings, William
1350	Hoyt, Joseph–Hoyt, William	1414	Jennison, Moses–Jett, William
1351	Hubard, Richard–Hubbard, Joel	1415	Jewel, Ephraim–Jewell, William
1352	Hubbard, John–Hubbard, William	1416	Jewett, Alpheus–Jewitt, John
1353	Hubbart, John–Hubbell, William	1417	Jigney, John–Johns, Zachariah
1354	Hubbert, Anthony–Hubpert, Casper	1418	Johnson, Abel–Johnson, Benedict
1355	Hucans, Abiah–Hudnut, Richard	1419	Johnson, Benjamin–Johnson, Daniel
1356	Hudson, Abraham–Hudson, James	1420	Johnson, David–Johnson, Elijah
1357	Hudson, John–Hudson, William	1421	Johnson, Eliphalet–Johnson, Hugh
1358	Hudspeth, Carter–Huff, Stephen	1422	Johnson, Ichabod–Johnson, Jacob
1359	Huffman, Christian–Hughe, George	1423	Johnson, James–Johnson, Job
1360	Hughes, Absolom–Hughes, Peter	1424	Johnson, John–Johnson, John (N.J.)

Roll	Description	Roll	Description
1425	Johnson, John (N.Y.)–Johnson, Jonathan	1489	King, Joseph–King, Rozina
1426	Johnson, Joseph–Johnson, Luther	1490	King, Sabrit–King, Zebulon
1427	Johnson, Mary–Johnson, Phinehas	1491	Kinglay, Savil–Kingsbury, Tilley
1428	Johnson, Reuben–Johnson, Samuel	1492	Kingsley, Aaron–Kinnard, Joseph
1429	Johnson, Seth–Johnson, Thomas	1493	Kinnaston, David–Kinny, Samuel
1430	Johnson, Timothy–Johnson, William (N.H.)	1494	Kinsaul, John–Kinyon, William
1431	Johnson, William (N.J.)–Johnson, Zopher	1495	Kip, James–Kirkham, Samuel
1432	Johnston, Andrew–Johnston, James	1496	Kirkland, Gideon–Kirtland, Nathan
1433	Johnston, John–Johnston, Michael	1497	Kisby, Richard–Kittle, Joseph
1434	Johnston, Nathaniel–Johnston, Witter	1498	Kittredge, Francis–Klyne, Gabriel
1435	Johnstone, George–Jonce, Henry	1499	Knap, Charles–Knapp, Joel
1436	Jones, Aaron–Jones, Britain	1500	Knapp, John–Knapp, William
1437	Jones, Cadwallader–Jones, Diodate	1501	Knecht, Jacob–Kniffing, Amos
1438	Jones, Eaton–Jones, Gabriel	1502	Knight, Abraham–Knight, John
1439	Jones, George–Jones, Jacob	1503	Knight, Jonathan–Knight, Zachariah
1440	Jones, James–Jones, Joel	1504	Knighten, Thomas–Knowles, William
1441	Jones, John	1505	Knowlton, Abraham–Knowlton, Thomas
1442	Jones, Jonathan–Jones, Matthew	1506	Knows, John–Knox, William
1443	Jones, Michael–Jones, Reuben	1507	Koch, Adam–Kosciuszko, Thaddeus
1444	Jones, Richard–Jones, Samuel	1508	Kouchenour, Jacob–Krom, Simeon
1445	Jones, Sarah–Jones, Taverner	1509	Kronkhite, David–Kyzer, Frederick
1446	Jones, Thomas	1510	Laar, Jacob–Lacky, Andrew
1447	Jones, Tim–Jones, William (N.H.)	1511	Lacorn, John–Lady, Philip
1448	Jones, William (N.J.)–Jones, Zimri	1512	Lafar, Joseph–LaJenness, Prudent
1449	Jongst, Peter–Jordan, John	1513	Lake, Asa–Lakin, Winslow
1450	Jordan, Josiah–Jordon, William	1514	Lallen, Michael–Lamb, William
1451	Jose, John–Jourden, Edmund	1515	Lambart, Samuel–Lamkin, Sampson
1452	Joy, Abiathar–Juckett, Elijah	1516	Lamley, Philip–Lamson, Thomas
1453	Judd, Abia–Judd, William	1517	Lamunyon, Philip–Landerkin, Daniel
1454	Judkins, Benjamin–Jumpt, William	1518	Landers, Aqrilla–Lands, Lewis
1455	June, Abraham–Justus, Moses	1519	Lane, Abial–Lane, Hezekiah
1456	Kachlein, Peter–Kaup, Peter	1520	Lane, Isaac–Lane, Joseph
1457	Kausler, John–Keele, Richard	1521	Lane, Joshua–Lane, William
1458	Keeler, Aaron–Keeler, Uriah	1522	Laneey, Thomas–Langham, Joshua
1459	Keeley, Joseph–Keenon, Nicholas	1523	Langlee, Thomas–Lannum, Joseph
1460	Keep, Jabez–Keister, Peter	1524	Lanphear, Shubael–Laquir, John
1461	Keith, Alexander–Keith, William	1525	Lara, James–Larkcom, Paul
1462	Keizer, Lewis–Keller, Simon	1526	Larken, John–Larner, Robert
1463	Kelley, Charles–Kelley, William	1527	LaRochelle, Michael–Larymore, Thomas
1464	Kellicut, Thomas–Kellogg, Joseph	1528	Lasambert, Antoine–Latham, William
1465	Kellogg, Josiah–Kellum, Reuben	1529	Lathers, Christian–LaTurrett, Daniel
1466	Kelly, Abraham–Kelly, Jonathan	1530	Lauaray, Isaac–Lavoke, Augustus
1467	Kelly, Joseph–Kelly, William	1531	Law, Barton–Lawrence, James
1468	Kelp, Andrew–Keltz, Nicholas	1532	Lawrence, John–Lawrentz, Wendel
1469	Kemble, Hazadiah–Kench, Thomas	1533	Lawrey, Giles–Lawson, William
1470	Kendal, Clayton–Kendle, William	1534	Lawton, Benjamin–Layman, William
1471	Kendrick, Abel–Kenneday, Thomas	1535	Layne, Anthony–Lea, Owen
1472	Kennedy, Andrew–Kennedy, William	1536	Leach, Abner–Leach, Zemus
1473	Kennelly, John–Kensyl, Frederick	1537	Leadbetter, Increase–Leary, William
1474	Kent, Abel–Kent, Phineas	1538	Leas, John–Leavesley, Thomas
1475	Kent, Richard–Kerby, William	1539	Leavett, Edward–Leavitt, William
1476	Kercheval, John–Kersche, George	1540	Leay, William–Ledyard, Robert
1477	Kersey, Edward–Kever, James	1542	Lee, Abial–Lee, Israel
1478	Key, Bingham–Keys, William	1542	Lee, James–Lee, Owen
1479	Keysacker, George–Kickeland, Heinrich	1543	Lee, Parker–Lee, Zebulon
1480	Kidd, Alexander–Kilander, Philip	1544	Leech, Archibald–Leeton, Benjamin
1481	Kilbern, Henry–Killam, Phinehas	1545	Leface, John–Legue, Edmund
1482	Killebrew, Kinchan–Kilty, William	1546	Leha, John–Leitz, Henry
1483	Kimbal, Abraham–Kimball, Joseph	1547	Leland, David–Lemon, William
1484	Kimball, Joshua–Kimbrell, Thomas	1548	Lemond, William–Lentz, Henry
1485	Kimmer, Nicholas–Kiney, James	1549	Leonard, Adam–Leonard, James
1486	King, Aaron–King, David	1550	Leonard, John–Leonardson, John
1487	King, Ebenezer–King, Isaac	1551	Leper, Jacob–Lesson, George
1488	King, Jacob–King, Jonathan	1552	Lester, Alexander–Letts, John

Roll	Description	Roll	Description
1553	Leucaw, Peter–Lewin, Thomas	1617	Makemson, John–Mallen, William
1554	Lewis, Aaron–Lewis, Beriah	1618	Malleroy, Nathaniel–Mallory, William
1555	Lewis, Caleb–Lewis, Francis	1619	Mallow, George–Maltsar, Benjamin
1556	Lewis, George–Lewis, Joel	1620	Man, Aaron–Mandeville, Yelles
1557	Lewis, John–Lewis, Lockhard	1621	Mandigo, Jeremiah–Manly, Nathan
1558	Lewis, Marsh–Lewis, Samuel	1622	Mann, Abel–Mann, Jesse
1559	Lewis, Sarah–Lewis, Willis	1623	Mann, John–Mann, William
1560	Lewter, Hardy–Libby, Harvey	1624	Mannan, John–Manning, Luther
1561	Libby, Isaac–Lidy, Simon	1625	Manning, Nathaniel–Mansell, Joseph
1562	Lierly, Zachariah–Likes, John	1626	Mansfield, Charles–Mansfield, William
1563	Lilburn, Andrew–Linch, William	1627	Manship, Henry–Maphet, Robert
1564	Lincoln, Abiathar–Lincoln, Jerome	1628	Maple, Benjamin–Marble, Thomas
1565	Lincoln, John–Lincoln, Thomas	1629	Marbury, Joseph–Mardis, William
1566	Lind, John–Lindsey, Robert	1630	Marean, Samuel–Markley, Catharine
1567	Lindsey, Samuel–Lining, Charles	1631	Marks, Abisha–Marselus, John
1568	Link, Adam–Linsly, Solomon	1632	Marsh, Aaron–Marsh, Jonathan
1569	Lint, Isaac–Lippitt, Thomas	1633	Marsh, Joseph–Marsh, Zebulon
1570	Lipscomb, Ambrose–Lithgow, Arthur	1634	Marshal, Benjamin–Marshall, James
1571	Litle, Alexander–Little, William	1635	Marshall, Jenepher–Marshall, William
1572	Littlebridge, Thomas–Litzinger, Henry	1636	Marshammer, Sebastian–Marther, Abner
1573	Livasay, George–Livingston, William	1637	Martin, Aaron–Martin, Cornelius
1574	Lloyd, Bateman–Lochridge, John	1638	Martin, Daniel–Martin, Hugh
1575	Lock, Ayres–Lockart, Aaron	1639	Martin, Ichabod–Martin, Job
1576	Locke, Eben–Locks, Moses	1640	Martin, John–Martin, Joseph
1577	Lockwood, Betsey–Lockwood, William	1641	Martin, Joshua–Martin, Peter
1578	Locus, Valentine–Login, Joseph	1642	Martin, Philip–Martin, Stephen
1579	Logsdon, Edward–London, Eliel	1643	Martin, Thomas–Martin, Zachariah
1580	Long, Adam–Long, Jonathan	1644	Martindale, Ebenezer–Mashler, Adam
1581	Long, Joseph–Long, William	1645	Mason, Aaron–Mason, George
1582	Longby, James–Loofbourrow, David	1646	Mason, Hannah–Mason, Michael
1583	Look, Cheney–Loomis, Jacob	1647	Mason, Moses–Mason, William
1584	Loomis, Jerome–Lorance, William	1648	Massay, John–Massy, Jacob
1585	Lord, Aaron–Lord, Jeremiah	1649	Mast, Jacob–Matheny, William
1586	Lord, John–Lord, William	1650	Mather, Abner–Matheson, Daniel
1587	Lorden, George–Losley, James	1651	Mathew, Isaac–Mathews, John
1588	Lot, Jeremiah–Loucks, William	1652	Mathews, Joseph–Mathewson, William
1589	Loud, Benjamin–Loux, Hendrick	1653	Mathias, James–Matthay, Frederick
1590	Love, Charles–Love, William	1654	Matthew, Frederick–Matthews, William
1591	Lovegrove, Hampton–Loveland, Trueman	1655	Matthewson, Elisha–Maury, William
1592	Loveless, David–Lovett, Samuel	1656	Maus, Matthew–Maxson, Stephen
1593	Lovewell, Nehemiah–Low, Jonathan	1657	Maxwell, Adam–Maxwell, William
1594	Low, Lawrence–Lowe, William	1658	May, Abram–May, William
1595	Lowell, Barnard–Lowrance, Jacob	1659	Maybee, David–Maynadier, Henry
1596	Lowrey, James–Lucado, Isaac	1660	Maynard, Abel–Maynard, Zebediah
1597	Lucas, Abijah–Lucas, Randolph	1661	Mayner, Henry–McAdow, John
1598	Lucas, Samuel–Luches, Henry	1662	McAfee, Mathew–McBrayer, Hugh
1599	Luck, John–Lufberry, Abraham	1663	McBride, Alexander–McCalla, Thomas
1600	Luffkin, Jacob–Lumereaux, Joseph	1664	McCalley, Hugh–McCarroll, John
1601	Lumis, Oliver–Lunter, Peter	1665	McCarter, Charles–McCarty, Thomas
1602	Lupardus, William–Lutes, Henry	1666	McCary, Richard–McChristy, Michael
1603	Luther, Aaron–Luther, Wheaton	1667	McClain, Abijah–McClease, Cornelius
1604	Luts, John–Lyles, Thomas	1668	McCleland, Daniel–McClunie, Michael
1605	Lyman, Asa–Lynam, Andrew	1669	McClure, Alexander–McColm, Samuel
1606	Lynch, David–Lynott, Thomas	1670	McComas, Aaron–McCord, William
1607	Lyon, Abraham–Lyon, John	1671	McCorkel, James–McCown, Alexander
1608	Lyon, Jonas–Lyon, William	1672	McCoy, Alexander–McCoy, William
1609	Lyons, Barnabas–Lyttle, Thomas	1673	McCracken, Gilbert–McCrum, William
1610	Maabe, John–Machrell, James	1674	McCubbin, James–McCulluck, Robert
1611	Mack, Abner–Mackintire, Rufus	1675	McCullum, James–McDade, William
1612	Mackintosh, Peter–Macumber, John	1676	McDanal, John–McDole, John
1613	Maddan, Michael–Madon, Joseph	1677	McDonald, Alexander–McDonald, William
1614	Maeck, Frederick–Magruder, Norman	1678	McDonel, Robert–McDowle, Thomas
1615	Maguira, Peter–Maillett, Baptiste	1679	McDuff, Daniel–McEntee, Barney
1616	Main, Amos–Majory, John	1680	McEntire, Daniel–McFaren, William

Roll	Description
1681	McFarland, Andrew–McFarling, John
1682	McFarran, Samuel–McGeary, Neal
1683	McGee, Charles–McGhee, William
1684	McGhoggan, Alexander–McGrigger, James
1685	McGuier, Luke–McHatton, William
1686	McHenry, Charles–McIntee, Barney
1687	McIntier, William–McIntyre, William
1688	McIsaacks, Isaac–McKee, William
1689	McKeel, Thomas–McKent, James
1690	McKenzie, Alexander–McKinley, William
1691	McKinney, Andrew–McKinstry, John
1692	McKinzey, James–McLachlan, Colin
1693	McLaen, Alexander–McLaughlin, William
1694	McLaurine, James–McLucas, John
1695	McLuer, James–McManners, William
1696	McMannis, Charles–McMickin, Robert
1697	McMillan, Daniel–McMullin, John
1698	McMurdy, John–McNeely, William
1699	McNees, James–McPheeters, John
1700	McPheran, Andrew–McRoberts, John
1701	McShane, Robert–McWright, Matthew
1702	Meach, Elijah–Mead, Jasper
1703	Mead, Jeremiah–Meade, William
1704	Meadearis, John–Meanly, John
1705	Means, George–Medcalf, John
1706	Meddack, Emanuel–Meek, Samuel
1707	Meeker, Caleb–Meier, John
1708	Meigs, Abel–Mellon, William
1709	Mellott, Benjamin–Meltz, Frederick
1710	Melven, George–Mercy, John
1711	Meredeth, David–Merow, David
1712	Merrel, Samuel–Merrifield, Robert
1713	Merril, Aaron–Merrill, Jesse
1714	Merrill, John–Merrils, Samuel
1715	Merriman, Asaph–Merritt, William
1716	Merriwether, David–Meryman, William
1717	Meser, William–Messler, Simon
1718	Metcalf, Benjamin–Metcalfe, Samuel
1719	Meteer, William–Middlesworth, John
1720	Middleton, Basil–Mileham, William
1721	Miles, Benajah–Miles, William
1722	Miley, Jacob–Millener, Alexander
1723	Miller, Aaron–Miller, Cyrus
1724	Miller, Daniel–Miller, Fredrick
1725	Miller, Gavin–Miller, Isaac
1726	Miller, Jacob–Miller, Johannes
1727	Miller, John (Conn.)–Miller, John (R.I.)
1728	Miller, John (S.C.)–Miller, Lewis
1729	Miller, Ludwick–Miller, Noah
1730	Miller, Paul–Miller, Samuel
1731	Miller, Sarah–Miller, Zephaniah
1732	Millerd, Abiather–Milligan, Moses
1733	Millign, Josep–Milloway, Isaac
1734	Mills, Aaron–Mills, James
1735	Mills, Jedediah–Mills, Philip
1736	Mills, Reuben–Mills, Zebulon
1737	Millsaps, Thomas–Minear, David
1738	Miner, Aaron–Miner, William
1739	Mines, Peter–Minor, William
1740	Minott, Jonathan–Mitchel, William
1741	Mitchell, Aaron–Mitchell, Hiram
1742	Mitchell, Ichabod–Mitchell, John
1743	Mitchell, Joseph–Mitchell, Rotheas
1744	Mitchell, Samuel–Mitchell, Zephaniah

Roll	Description
1745	Mitchellor, Jacob–Mizner, Henry
1746	Moast, John–Moltrup, Moses
1747	Momie, Jacob–Monroe, James
1748	Monroe, Jonn–Montfort, Peter
1749	Montgomery, Alexander–Montgomery, William
1750	Month, Ambrose–Moody, John
1751	Moody, Joseph–Moony, William
1752	Moor, Benjamin–Moor, William
1753	Moore, Abigail–Moore, David
1754	Moore, Ebenezer–Moore, Isaac
1755	Moore, Jacob–Moore, Joel
1756	Moore, John
1757	Moore, Jonathan–Moore, Nicholas
1758	Moore, Obadiah–Moore, Sampson
1759	Moore, Samuel–Moore, Thomas
1760	Moore, Timothy–Moore, Zedekiah
1761	Moorehead, Charles–Morehead, William
1762	Morehouse, Aaron–Morewise, Jacob
1763	Morey, Benjamin–Morford, Stephen
1764	Morgan, Abel–Morgan, Evan
1765	Morgan, George–Morgan, John
1766	Morgan, Jonas–Morgan, Reuben
1767	Morgan, Rhoda–Morgan, Zackquil
1768	Morgert, Peter–Morrell, William
1769	Morril, Judah–Morrill, William
1770	Morris, Abel–Morris, Jacob
1771	Morris, James–Morris, Micajah
1772	Morris, Nathaniel–Morris, Zephaniah
1773	Morrison, Abraham–Morrison, Moses
1774	Morrison, Patrick–Morrow, William
1775	Morrs, William–Morse, Elijah
1776	Morse, Eliphalet–Morse, Josiah
1777	Morse, Levi–Morse, William
1778	Morseman, Oliver–Morton, William
1779	Morvies, Daniel–Moser, William
1780	Moses, Abraham–Mosier, William
1781	Mosley, Hezekiah–Moss, Zeally
1782	Mosser, George–Moulthrop, Reuben
1783	Moulton, Bartholomew–Moulton, William
1784	Moultrie, William–Mowlan, Richard
1785	Mowrey, Reuben–Mozley, James
1786	Muchemore, James–Mullener, Moses
1787	Mullens, John–Mullins, William
1788	Mulloy, Hugh–Mundy, William
1789	Munford, James–Munnerlyn, Loftus
1790	Munro, Edward–Munrow, Samuel
1791	Munsel, Benjamin–Munson, Wilmot
1792	Murcer, James–Muret, Charles
1793	Murfree, George–Murphy, George
1794	Murphy, Henry–Murphy, William
1795	Murrah, Joshua–Murray, John
1796	Murray, Mark–Murry, Thomas
1797	Mursh, Robert–Myat, John
1798	Myer, Abraham–Myers, Henry
1799	Myers, Jacob–Mytinger, Jacob
1800	Nabb, Joseph–Narramore, John
1801	Nash, Abner–Nash, William
1802	Nason, Benjamin–Neagus, Benjamin
1803	Neal, Andrew–Neale, James
1804	Nealey, Andrew–Neely, Samuel
1805	Neer, Charles–Nelms, Charles
1806	Nelson, Abraham–Nelson, John
1807	Nelson, Joseph–Nelson, William
1808	Nephew, Mathias–Nettleton, William

Roll	Description	Roll	Description
1809	Neu, Peter–New, William	1873	Parker, John–Parker, Jotham
1810	Newall, Calvin–Newcomer, Peter	1874	Parker, Kader–Parker, Samuel
1811	Newel, Deborah–Newelle, Thomas	1875	Parker, Silas–Parker, Wyman
1812	Newens, Nehemiah–Newlun, William	1876	Parkers, George–Parkman, Thomas
1813	Newman, Abner–Newmann, Philip	1877	Parks, Aaron–Parks, William
1814	Newnam, Joshua–Newton, Hannah	1878	Parley, James–Parmor, Charles
1815	Newton, Henry–Niblet, William	1879	Parnell, Benjamin–Parrish, Thomas
1816	Niccols, William–Nichols, David	1880	Parrit, Silas–Parsley, Thomas
1817	Nichols, Ebenezer–Nichols, John	1881	Parson, George–Parsons, Jonathan
1818	Nichols, Jonas–Nichols, Philip	1882	Parsons, Joseph–Parsons, William
1819	Nichols, Reuben–Nichols, Zepaniah	1883	Partee, Edmund–Pastley, John
1820	Nicholson, Boling–Nickerson, Uriah	1884	Patch, Ephraim–Patchon, Woolcot
1821	Nickins, James–Niles, William	1885	Pate, Matthew–Pattee, Richard
1822	Nillson, Robert–Noakes, George	1886	Patten, Asa–Pattengell, Jacob
1823	Nobel, Tahan–Nobel, William	1887	Patterson, Adam–Patterson, Samuel
1824	Nobles, Azer–Nolom, John	1888	Patterson, Sherman–Pattison, William
1825	Nolte, John–Norman, William	1889	Patton, Alexander–Patton, William
1826	Norris, Abner–Norris, Ziba	1890	Pattrick, Ebenezer–Paul, William
1827	Norstrant, Johannes–Northgate, Abraham	1891	Paulding, John–Paylor, William
1828	Northrop, Abijah–Northwear, George	1892	Payn, Ebenezer–Payne, William
1829	Norton, Aaron–Norton, Jared	1893	Paynter, Nathaniel–Peabody, Thomas
1830	Norton, John–Norton, Zerah	1894	Peace, John–Peaney, Simon
1831	Norvel, Enos–Nourse, William	1895	Pearce, Abraham–Pearce, William
1832	Nowe, Lewis–Noys, Eliphalet	1896	Pearcy, James–Pearson, John
1833	Nuckolls, Richard–Nurss, Timothy	1897	Pearson, Jonathan–Peary, Winthrop
1834	Nute, John–Nuttle, Charles	1898	Pease, Abner–Pease, Zechariah
1835	Nye, Abigail–Nye, William	1899	Peasely, Mary–Peck, David
1836	Oadham, George–Oatley, Joseph	1900	Peck, Ebenezer–Peck, Johnathan
1837	O'Bannon, Andrew–O'Conner, Thomas	1901	Peck, Joseph–Peck, William
1838	Odall, John–Odum, Seybert	1902	Peckam, Braddock–Peedrick, Benjamin
1839	O'Farrell, Dennis–O'Gullion, John	1903	Peek, Abel–Peiffer, John
1840	O'Hara, Francis–Oldham, Richard	1904	Peirce, Abel–Peirce, Zebulon
1841	Oldis, Robert–Olis, Boston	1905	Peirson, Abraham–Pelts, James
1842	Olive, John–Oliver, Jonathan	1906	Pember, Eli–Pendleton, Zebulon
1843	Oliver, Nicholas–Olliver, William	1907	Pendock, Rufus–Pennetent, John
1844	Olmstead, Ashbel–Olvie, Lorant	1908	Penney, Abraham–Perady, Emanuel
1845	Omack, Thomas–O'Niel, George	1909	Peran, Henry–Perkinpine, Elizabeth
1846	Onion, David–Ore, Jacob	1910	Perkins, Aaron–Perkins, Ezekiel
1847	Orear, Daniel–O'Rouke, James	1911	Perkins, Francis–Perkins, Joshua
1848	Orr, Alexander–Orwig, Henry	1912	Perkins, Leonard–Perkins, Zophar
1849	Osbon, John–Osborn, Josiah	1913	Perkinson, Ezekiel–Perrow, Daniel
1850	Osborn, Levi–Osbourne, Thomas	1914	Perry, Abel–Perry, Job
1851	Osburn, Aaron–Osterhout, Isaac	1915	Perry, John–Perry, Sylvanus
1852	Osterman, Christian–Otis, Richard	1916	Perry, Thomas–Peterman, Jacob
1853	Ott, Adam–Outwater, Daniel	1917	Peters, Absalom–Peters, William
1854	Ovaitt, William–Ovutt, William	1918	Peterson, Abraham–Peterson, Turner
1855	Owan, Thomas–Owen, Philip	1919	Petigru, William–Pettibone, Stephen
1856	Owen, Samuel–Ozmund, Abraham	1920	Petticrew, John–Petts, Jonathan
1857	Pace, Jesse–Packard, Shepard	1921	Petty, Abiel–Phelon, Peter
1858	Packer, Eldredge–Pagan, David	1922	Phelps, Aaron–Phelps, Elijah
1859	Page, Abel–Page, Joss	1923	Phelps, Eliphalet–Phelps, Judah
1860	Page, Leme–Paige, Timothy	1924	Phelps, Lancelot–Phelps, William
1861	Pain, Charles–Paine, Zebediah	1925	Phexix, Matthew–Philippie, Christopher
1862	Painter, Deliverance–Palmatier, Isaac	1926	Philips, Abraham–Phillippi, Abraham
1863	Palmer, Aaron–Palmer, Ezekiel	1927	Phillips, Aaron–Phillips, Israel
1864	Palmer, Fones–Palmer, Joel	1928	Phillips, Jacob–Phillips, John
1865	Palmer, John–Palmer, Noah	1929	Phillips, Jonathan–Phillips, Samuel
1866	Palmer, Ozias–Palmer, Zuer	1930	Phillips, Sarah–Phillips, Zebedee
1867	Palmerton, John–Parchment, Peter	1931	Phillis, Jacob–Pickard, Thomas
1868	Pardee, Aaron–Paris, William	1932	Pickens, Andrew–Pier, Solomon
1869	Parish, Charles–Parke, Zebulon	1933	Pierce, Abel–Pierce, John
1870	Parker, Aaron–Parker, Benjamin	1934	Pierce, Jonas–Pierce, Zebulon
1871	Parker, Cader–Parker, Ezra	1935	Pierceall, Richard–Pigsley, Welcome
1872	Parker, Francis–Parker, Jesse	1936	Pike, Aaron–Pike, Zebulon

Roll	Description	Roll	Description
1937	Pikins, William–Pinckney, William	2001	Rankin, Andrew–Rankins, Robert
1938	Pindar, James–Pintard, John	2002	Ranlet, Jonathan–Ransone, Thomas
1939	Pinto, Solomon–Pitchford, Daniel	2003	Ranstead, James–Rathfon, Jacob
1940	Pitkin, John–Pitts, Thomas	2004	Ratliff, Nathan–Raxford, Joseph
1941	Pittsley, Benjamin–Plank, John	2005	Ray, Andrea–Ray, Jesse
1942	Plant, Eli–Platz, George	2006	Ray, John–Ray, Zaccheus
1943	Pleasant, William–Plumbe, William	2007	Raybold, Jacob–Raymond, Moses
1944	Plumer, Isaac–Plympton, Zeba	2008	Raymond, Naphtali–Reab, Eorge
1945	Poage, William–Polland, Samuel	2009	Read, Abijah–Read, Jacob
1946	Pollard, Absolem–Pollard, William	2010	Read, James–Reade, Amos
1947	Polleresky, John–Pomroy, Simeon	2011	Readen, William–Reany, Joseph
1948	Pond, Adam–Poobles, Thomas	2012	Rear, Martin–Redder, Nicholas
1949	Pool, Abijah–Pool, Joshua	2013	Reddick, William–Reece, John
1950	Pool, Oliver–Pootman, Arent	2014	Reed, Aaron–Reed, Frederick
1951	Pope, Adam–Pope, William	2015	Reed, Garret–Reed, Joel
1952	Popham, Benjamin–Porter, Billy	2016	Reed, John–Reed, Joshua
1953	Porter, Charles–Porter, Isaac	2017	Reed, Josiah–Reed, Samuel
1954	Porter, James–Porter, Nicholas	2018	Reed, Sarah–Reed, Zadock
1955	Porter, Ockelo–Porter, William	2019	Reeder, Andrew–Reesor, Philip
1956	Porterfield, Charles–Poss, Nicholas	2020	Reeve, Elisha–Reeves, William
1957	Post, Abraham–Pottage, Jabez	2021	Reewark, James–Reigel, Michael
1958	Potter, Aaron–Potter, Gilbert	2022	Reilay, John–Remer, Lewis
1959	Potter, Holliman–Potter, Lyman	2023	Remick, Elkanah–Remmington, Anthony
1960	Potter, Mariam–Potter, Zebedee	2024	Remsen, Anne–Requa, Joseph
1961	Potterf, Casper–Powe, William	2025	Resseguie, Alexander–Reymond, Issac
1962	Powel, Britain–Powell, John	2026	Reynold, James–Reynolds, Grindall
1963	Powell, Jonathan–Powelson, Henry	2027	Reynolds, Hamilton–Reynolds, Joseph
1964	Power, Benjamin–Powers, Jonathan	2028	Reynolds, Justus–Reynolds, Zachariah
1965	Powers, Joseph–Prather, Thomas	2029	Reynow, Simeon–Rhoden, Thomas
1966	Pratt, Aaron–Pratt, Elam	2030	Rhodes, Alexander–Riblett, Peter
1967	Pratt, Elias–Pratt, Jonathan	2031	Rice, Abel–Rice, David
1968	Pratt, Joseph–Pratt, Seth	2032	Rice, Eber–Rice, Jesse
1969	Pratt, Silas–Pratt, Zimri	2033	Rice, John–Rice, Nathaniel
1970	Praul, Edward–Presby, Richard	2034	Rice, Naum–Rice, William
1971	Prescot, Benjamin–Presson, Lemuel	2035	Rich, Amos–Richard, Silas
1972	Preston, Abner–Preston, Zera	2036	Richards, Abel–Richards, Joel
1973	Prestwood, Jonathan–Pribble, Thomas	2037	Richards, John–Richards, William
1974	Price, Abner–Price, Mathew	2038	Richardson, Abel–Richardson, Enoch
1975	Price, Nathaniel–Price, Williamson	2039	Richardson, Ezekiel–Richardson, John
1976	Prichard, Asahel–Prier, William	2040	Richardson, Jonas–Richardson, Samuel
1977	Priest, Abel–Priest, William	2041	Richardson, Sanford–Richie, William
1978	Priestley, John–Pringle, Joseph	2042	Richman, Abiathar–Richmond, Zebulon
1979	Printrop, Joseph–Probasco, Gerrit	2043	Richter, Nathaniel–Rickert, Marcus
1980	Procter, Josiah–Proctor, William	2044	Rickets, Edward–Rideout, William
1981	Proffit, William–Prouty, Stephen	2045	Rider, Adam–Rider, Timothy
1982	Provance, Joseph–Pryor, William	2046	Ridgeway, Isaac–Rigdon, James
1983	Pucket, William–Pullen, William	2047	Riggs, Eleazer–Riggs, Zenas
1984	Pulley, William–Puntenney, George	2048	Right, Bazzell–Rily, Christopher
1985	Purbeck, Aaron–Purinton, Joseph	2049	Rimee, Conrad–Rion, Thomas
1986	Purkett, Henry–Puterbaugh, Joseph	2050	Ripley, Abraham–Ripley, William
1987	Putman, Aaron–Putnam, William	2051	Rippeto, William–Rittenhouse, Jacob
1988	Putney, Asa–Pytts, Jonathan	2052	Ritter, Adam–Roach, William
1989	Quackenboss, Abraham–Quarrell, James	2053	Roads, Anna–Robbe, Samuel
1990	Quarrier, Alexander–Quick, Samuel	2054	Robbens, Miller–Robbins, Jonathan
1991	Quickel, Adam–Quimby, Zachariah	2055	Robbins, Joseph–Robbins, Zachariah
1992	Quin, Francis–Quy, Libbeus	2056	Robecheau, James–Roberts, Ephraim
1993	Rabenstine, Dewalt–Ragland, John	2057	Roberts, Esek–Roberts, Joel
1994	Ragsdale, Baxter–Ralls, Kenaz	2058	Roberts, John–Roberts, Joseph
1995	Ralph, Charles–Ramser, Christopher	2059	Roberts, Joshua–Roberts, Rufus
1996	Ramsey, Alexander–Ramsey, William	2060	Roberts, Samuel–Roberts, Ziba
1997	Ramson, Jacob–Rand, Zachariah	2061	Robertson, Abraham–Robertson, John
1998	Randal, Amos–Randall, James	2062	Robertson, Joseph–Robertson, Zachariah
1999	Randall, Jedediah–Randall, Ziba	2063	Robeson, Daniel–Robins, William
2000	Rande, Isham–Rankhorn, Joseph	2064	Robinson, Abel–Robinson, Eber

Roll	Description	Roll	Description
2065	Robinson, Edmond–Robinson, Joel	2129	Sayre, David–Scantling, William
2066	Robinson, John–Robinson, Jonathan	2130	Scarborough, Elisha–Schellinger, Abraham
2067	Robinson, Joseph–Robinson, Prince	2131	Schenck, Chrineyonce–Schoff, Jacob
2068	Robinson, Reuben–Robinson, Zophar	2132	Schofield, David–Schreeder, John
2069	Robison, Benjamin–Rock, William	2133	Schrimshear, John–Scobey, James
2070	Rockafellar, Peter–Rodes, Peter	2134	Scoffield, Seely–Scoonmaker, Daniel
2071	Rodgers, Abraham–Rodgers, William	2135	Scott, Abel–Scott, Drury
2072	Rodman, Mingo–Roff, Samuel	2136	Scott, Ebenezer–Scott, Joel
2073	Rogers, Aaron–Rogers, Ebenezer	2137	Scott, John–Scott, Jonathan
2074	Rogers, Edward–Rogers, Jeremiah	2138	Scott, Joseph–Scott, Samuel
2075	Rogers, John–Rogers, Josiah	2139	Scott, Severn–Scott, Zerah
2076	Rogers, Kinsey–Rogers, Robert	2140	Scouten, Jacob–Scranton, Torey
2077	Rogers, Samuel–Rogers, Zephaniah	2141	Scriber, Peter–Scudder, William
2078	Rogerson, John–Rollings, Thomas	2142	Scull, Mourning–Sealy, Samuel
2079	Rollins, Aaron–Ronemous, Philip	2143	Seaman, Andrew–Search, Lot
2080	Roney, George–Roosa, Peter	2144	Searcy, Asa–Searls, Samuel
2081	Root, Aaron–Root, Joseph	2145	Sears, Allen–Sears, Willard
2082	Root, Joshua–Roots, Michael	2146	Sease, Michael–Seayres, Thomas
2083	Roper, David–Roscrow, Henry	2147	Seber, Henry–Seekell, Abiathar
2084	Rose, Abner–Rose, John	2148	Seele, John–Seelye, Seth
2085	Rose, Jonathan–Rose, Winthrop	2149	Seemore, Burges–Seldon, Asa
2086	Roseberry, John–Ross, George	2150	Seley, Abraham–Sellick, Peter
2087	Ross, Horatio–Ross, Joseph	2151	Sellman, Jonathan–Servoss, John
2088	Ross, Lemuel–Ross, Zephaniah	2152	Sessions, Abijah–Sevy, Isaac
2089	Rossell, Elias–Roughfcorn, Simon	2153	Sewal, Daniel–Sewell, William
2090	Roun, Thomas–Rousse, Oliver	2154	Sexton, Aaron–Seymour, Stephen
2091	Routon, James–Rowdon, George	2155	Seymour, Thomas–Shadwick, Levi
2092	Rowe, Andrew–Rowe, Zebulon	2156	Shaeffer, Henry–Shaffer, Thomas
2093	Rowel, Philander–Rowlandson, Reuben	2157	Shaffner, George–Sharlock, Ichabod
2094	Rowlee, Samuel–Roxford, Denison	2158	Sharp, Adam–Sharpe, William
2095	Roy, Beverly–Rucastle, John	2159	Sharpless, Robert–Shavers, Shadrach
2096	Rucker, Angus–Rudtolfh, Johan	2160	Shaw, Abiather–Shaw, David
2097	Rudy, Jacob–Ruggles, York	2161	Shaw, Eliab–Shaw, John
2098	Ruick, Owen–Rundleman, Martin	2162	Shaw, Jonathan–Shaw, Robert
2099	Rundler, Nathaniel–Runyon, Samuel	2163	Shaw, Samuel–Shaw, Zachariah
2100	Rupert, Adam–Russ, Nathan	2164	Shawke, Jacob–Shearin, Lewis
2101	Russel, Absalom–Russell, Cornelius	2165	Shearman, Abiel–Shed, Lemuel
2102	Russell, Daniel–Russell, Jeffrey	2166	Sheehane, Thomas–Shelcut, Ezekiel
2103	Russell, John–Russell, Phillip	2167	Shelden, Ephraim–Sheldon, William
2104	Russell, Reuben–Russell, William	2168	Sheley, Jacob–Shenefelt, Nicholas
2105	Russey, James–Rutherford, William	2169	Shepard, Abigail–Shepard, William
2106	Rutland, Abednego–Ryant, Joseph	2170	Shepardson, Nathan–Shepherd, William
2107	Rybecker, John–Ryon, Susannah	2171	Shepherdson, David–Sherlock, Edward
2108	Saben, Israel–Sacrey, James	2172	Sherman, Abiel–Sherman, Peter
2109	Saddler, Christopher–Sager, John	2173	Sherman, Reuben–Sherwin, John
2110	Sailor, Peter–Salier, Zaccheus	2174	Sherwood, Abel–Sherwood, Zachariah
2111	Salisbury, Anthony–Salsbury, William	2175	Sheshing, John–Shim, John
2112	Salter, Francis–Sampley, Jesse	2176	Shindel, Peter–Shippey, William
2113	Sampson, Aaron–Sampson, Zephaniah	2177	Shires, Nicholas–Shoefelt, Christopher
2114	Sams, Edmund–Sanborn, Benjamin	2178	Shoemaker, Abraham–Shoptaw, John
2115	Sanborn, David–Sandeford, Samuel	2179	Shor, Gabriel–Shouler, John
2116	Sanders, Augustus–Sanders, Mary	2180	Shoun, John–Shuck, Philip
2117	Sanders, Nathaniel–Sanders, Zachariah	2181	Shufeldt, Christopher–Shumway, Stephen
2118	Sanderson, Amaziah–Saner, Michael	2182	Shuntz, Christian–Sias, John
2119	Sanford, Archibald–Sanford, Zacheus	2183	Sibbliss, Thomas–Sidore, Isaac
2120	Sanger, Daniel–Sargeant, William	2184	Sidway, James–Sillcocks, Valentine
2121	Sargent, Amos–Sarjeant, Elijah	2185	Sillery, John–Simmers, John
2122	Sarle, Thomas–Sauls, Henry	2186	Simmins, Henry–Simmons, Joel
2123	Saunders, Abel–Saunders, William	2187	Simmons, John–Simms, William
2124	Saunderson, David–Savedge, Hartwell	2188	Simon, Cummy–Simons, William
2125	Savell, George–Sawtell, Solomon	2189	Simonson, Christopher–Simpson, Jeremiah
2126	Sawyer, Abel–Sawyer, Joatham	2190	Simpson, John–Simpson, Zebadiah
2127	Sawyer, John–Sawyers, William	2191	Simrall, Alexander–Sinclear, Samuel
2128	Sax, Andrew–Saylor, Michael	2192	Sine, Peter–Siscow, Nicholas

Roll	Description	Roll	Description
2193	Sisim, Peter–Skain, Nicholas	2257	Spencer, Reuben–Spenser, Moses
2194	Skeel, Amos–Skillman, Thomas	2258	Spera, William–Spicer, William
2195	Skimmer, John–Skinner, Jesse	2259	Spickard, George–Spofford, Samuel
2196	Skinner, John–Skinner, Zenas	2260	Spohn, Philip–Spradling, John
2197	Skipper, James–Slasson, Deliverance	2261	Sprage, Elkanah–Spraker, John
2198	Slate, James–Slauterback, Michael	2262	Sprigg, Leven–Springum, John
2199	Slaven, Dennis–Slitor, James	2263	Sproat, Thomas–Spyres, Richard
2200	Sloan, Bryant–Slone, William	2264	Squares, Calvin–Squyres, Thomas
2201	Slonecker, John–Slyter, Nicholas	2265	Srope, Christopher–Stadleman, John
2202	Smack, Christian–Smallwood, William	2266	Stafford, Andrew–Stafford, William
2203	Smart, Caleb–Smiley, William	2267	Stag, Isaac–Stanard, William
2204	Smith, Aaron–Smith, Albertson	2268	Stanbery, Recompence–Staniford, Jeremiah
2205	Smith, Alexander–Smith, Augustine	2269	Stanley, Adin–Stannard, Seth
2206	Smith, Aury–Smith, Benjamin	2270	Stanphill, James–Stanwood, William
2207	Smith, Benoni–Smith, Comfort	2271	Stapel, Mark–Staples, William
2208	Smith, Conrad–Smith, Daniel	2272	Stapleton, Thomas–Starke, William
2209	Smith, David–Smith, Duncan	2273	Starker, Michael–Starns, William
2210	Smith, Eben–Smith, Eleazer	2274	Starr, David–Stearman, William
2211	Smith, Eli–Smith, Elnathan	2275	Stearnes, Joseph–Stearns, William
2212	Smith, Elwiley–Smith, Frederick	2276	Stebbens, Lewis–Steedman, Edward
2213	Smith, Gabriel–Smith, Griffith	2277	Steel, Archibald–Steel, William
2214	Smith, Hannah–Smith, Hugh	2278	Steele, Ashbell–Steelman, Zephaniah
2215	Smith, Ira–Smith, Israel	2279	Steen, Edward–Stent, Othniel
2216	Smith, Ithamar–Smith, Jairus	2280	Stephens, Balam–Stephens, William
2217	Smith, James–Smith, Jasiel	2281	Stephenson, Abiathar–Sterrit, Stewart
2218	Smith, Jedediah–Smith, Joel	2282	Sterry, Cyprian–Steurt, Edward
2219	Smith, John–Smith, John (Hazen's Regiment)	2283	Stevens, Aaron–Stevens, Daniel
2220	Smith, John (Md.)—Smith, John (N.J.)	2284	Stevens, David–Stevens, James
2221	Smith, John (N.Y.)–Smith, John (Pa., Va.)	2285	Stevens, Jeduthan–Stevens, Judah
2222	Smith, John (R.I.)–Smith, John	2286	Stevens, Lemuel–Stevens, Safford
2223	Smith, Johnson–Smith, Jonathan	2287	Stevens, Samuel–Stevens, Zachariah
2224	Smith, Joseph–Smith, Joseph	2288	Stevenson, Alexander–Steves, Jeremiah
2225	Smith, Joshua–Smith, Levi	2289	Steward, Albert–Stewart, Christopher
2226	Smith, Lewis–Smith, Moses	2290	Stewart, Daniel–Stewart, Jesse
2227	Smith, Nahum–Smith, Noah	2291	Stewart, John–Stewart, Paul
2228	Smith, Obadiah–Smith, Peter	2292	Stewart, Ralph–Stewart, William
2229	Smith, Phebe–Smith, Reynard	2293	Steymets, Jasper–Stigefuse, John
2230	Smith, Richard–Smith, Roswell	2294	Stiles, Aaron–Stiles, Silas
2231	Smith, Samuel–Smith, Samuel	2295	Still, Ebenezer–Stilwill, James
2232	Smith, Sarah–Smith, Solomon	2296	Stimmel, Isaac–Stinson, William
2233	Smith, Sparrow–Smith, Theophilus	2297	Stipe, Frederick–Stober, Valentine
2234	Smith, Thomas–Smith, Thomas	2298	Stoch, Victor–Stocum, Reuben
2235	Smith, Timothy–Smith, William (Md., Mass.)	2299	Stodard, Melzar–Stodder, Samuel
2236	Smith, William (Mass.)–Smith, William (Pa.)	2300	Stoel, Asa–Stolts, Jacob
2237	Smith, William (R.I.)–Smith, Zephaniah	2301	Stone, Abel–Stone, Ezekiel
2238	Smither, William–Snagg, Henry	2302	Stone, George–Stone, Jonathan
2239	Snail, Christopher–Snelbaker, George	2303	Stone, Joseph–Stone, Samuel
2240	Snell, Abraham–Snell, Thaddeus	2304	Stone, Seth–Stone, Windsor
2241	Snellbaker, George–Snook, Philip	2305	Stonebarger, Lewis–Stopplebeen, Jacob
2242	Snow, Aaron–Snow, Joseph	2306	Storer, Dorothy–Storum, Charles
2243	Snow, Joshua–Snowden, Jonathan	2307	Story, Andrew–Story, William
2244	Snyder, Abraham–Snyder, William	2308	Stotes, John–Stouseberger, John
2245	Sockman, Henry–Sommerville, William	2309	Stout, Abraham–Stout, William
2246	Son, Anthony–Souder, Christopher	2310	Stoutenburgh, Andrew–Stowell, Samuel
2247	Soul, Amasa–Southern, William	2311	Stowers, John–Straley, Andrew
2248	Southgate, Elijah–Soward, William	2312	Strang, Gilbert–Straughan, James
2249	Sowder, Christopher–Spainhour, Michael	2313	Strause, Detrick–Streve, Paul
2250	Spalding, Aaron–Spalding, Wright	2314	Stribling, Clayton–Stron, Richard
2251	Spanbergh, Jacob–Spatz, Michael	2315	Strong, Alexander–Strong, William
2252	Spaulding, Asahel–Spaulding, William	2316	Strongman, William–Stryker, Simon
2253	Speagle, Samuel–Speary, Lemuel	2317	Stuart, Alexander–Studwell, Henry
2254	Specht, Adam–Spence, Nathan	2318	Stufflebean, John–Sturgeon, Robert
2255	Spencer, Aaron–Spencer, Israel	2319	Sturges, Aquila–Sturtvant, Lemuel
2256	Spencer, Jabez–Spencer, Peter	2320	Stutson, Levi–Sullings, John

Roll	Description	Roll	Description
2321	Sullivan, Barnabas–Sullivant, Owen	2385	Thum, Peter–Thurston, Thomas
2322	Sulser, William–Summersett, Thomas	2386	Thweatt, Thomas–Tibo, Michael
2323	Sumner, Clement–Suthard, Isaac	2387	Tice, Elias–Tiers, Margaret
2324	Sutherland, Alexander–Suttle, Edward	2388	Tiff, Major–Tift, Solomon
2325	Sutton, Abraham–Sutton, Zebulon	2389	Tignor, Isaac–Tilley, Samuel
2326	Suydam, Cornelius–Swallow, Andrew	2390	Tillien, Henry–Tilson, Timothy
2327	Swan, Adin–Swany, Timothy	2391	Tilton, Abigail–Timson, Robert
2328	Swart, Adam–Swartzwalder, Peter	2392	Tinan, Joseph–Tinor, Joshua
2329	Swasey, Richard–Sweeny, Owen	2393	Tinsley, Cornelius–Tison, James
2330	Sweet, Benaiah–Sweet, William	2394	Titchenor, Joseph–Toby, Joseph
2331	Sweeten, Benjamin–Swetland, Luke	2395	Tod, Thadeus–Todd, Yale
2332	Swett, Allen–Swift, William	2396	Todhunter, Joseph–Tomer, Christopher
2333	Swindel, John–Syfritt, Andrew	2397	Tomkies, Charles–Tomm, Henry
2334	Sykes, Ashbel–Sytez, George	2398	Tompkins, Amos–Tompkins, William
2335	Tabb, Augustin–Tackles, Alexander	2399	Tompson, William–Tooly, James
2336	Taff, George–Taft, William	2400	Toombs, Emanuel–Torrens, Samuel
2337	Tager, Jacob–Talbut, Ebenezer	2401	Torrey, Asa–Torry, Timothy
2338	Talcott, Aaron–Tallman, William	2402	Toser, Jared–Towberman, Henry
2339	Tallow, Thomas–Tannehill, Josiah	2403	Tower, Abraham–Towles, Oliver
2340	Tanner, Abraham–Tanney, Zopher	2404	Town, Daniel–Towns, Joseph
2341	Tapervine, John–Tarpening, Lawrence	2405	Townsen, John–Townshend, Robert
2342	Tarr, Abraham–Tasker, Richard	2406	Townsley, Dan–Trabue, John
2343	Tate, David–Tay, Nathaniel	2407	Tracey, John–Tracy, William
2344	Taylar, Elias–Taylor, Christopher	2408	Trader, Arthur–Trasee, William
2345	Taylor, Daniel–Taylor, Elijah	2409	Trask, Benjamin–Trask, Thomas
2346	Taylor, Eliphalet–Taylor, Isaac	2410	Traver, Adam–Treacle, William
2347	Taylor, Jacob–Taylor, Joel	2411	Treadway, Alpheus–Tredwell, Cato
2348	Taylor, John–Taylor, John (Vt.)	2412	Tree, John–Treuttle, Jonathan
2349	Taylor, John (Va.)–Taylor, Jude	2313	Trevett, Benjamin–Trion, Charity
2350	Taylor, Laroy–Taylor, Othniel	2414	Trip, Everitt–Trotter, William
2351	Taylor, Paul–Taylor, Russel	2415	Troup, Robert–Trowbridge, William
2352	Taylor, Samuel–Taylor, Stephen	2416	Trowell, James–True, Zebulon
2353	Taylor, Tertius–Taylor, Zalmon	2417	Trueman, Alexander–Trux, John
2354	Tayntor, Jedediah–Tedrick, Michael	2418	Try, Jacob–Tuck, Thomas
2355	Teed, John–Tellotson, Nathan	2419	Tucker, Abel–Tucker, Isaac
2356	Temple, Anna–Tench, William	2420	Tucker, James–Tucker, Lemuel
2357	Ten Eick, Andrew–Terhune, John	2421	Tucker, Morris–Tuckerman, Abraham
2358	Terms, Peter–Terrill, Stephen	2422	Tuder, John–Tullerton, Benjamin
2359	Terry, Asaph–Terry, Zeno	2423	Tullis, Aaron–Turnee, Henry
2360	Terrybury, John–Tewgood, Jonathan	2424	Turner, Aaron–Turner, George
2361	Thacher, Benjamin–Thaosagwat, Hanjoost	2425	Turner, Henry–Turner, Josiah
2362	Tharp, Abel–Thaxton, William	2426	Turner, Laban–Turner, Seth
2363	Thayar, William–Thayer, Henry	2427	Turner, Simeon–Turner, Zebedee
2364	Thayer, Isaac–Thayer, Rufus	2428	Turney, Aaron–Tuthill, William
2365	Thayer, Samuel–Thayer, Zebah	2429	Tutle, Samuel–Tuttle, Isaiah
2366	Theames, Jonathan–Thom, Mary	2430	Tuttle, James–Tuttle, William
2367	Thomas, Aaron–Thomas, David	2431	Tutwiler, John–Tye, William
2368	Thomas, Edmund–Thomas, Holmes	2432	Tylar, John–Tyler, Jonathan
2369	Thomas, Ichabod–Thomas, Jesse	2433	Tyler, Joseph–Tzor, Gabriel
2370	Thomas, John–Thomas, Joseph	2434	Udell, William–Underwood, William
2371	Thomas, Joshua–Thomas, Samuel	2435	Unger, Lawrence–Upshaw, Thomas
2372	Thomas, Seth–Thomlinson, Jabez	2436	Upson, Asa–Urton, Peter
2373	Thompson, Aaron–Thompson, Burwell	2437	Uselton, George–Utzman, Jacob
2374	Thompson, Caleb–Thompson, Hugh	2438	Vacher, John–Vamilia, Benjamin
2375	Thompson, Isaac–Thompson, Joel	2439	Vanacka, George–Vanasdall, Cornelius
2376	Thompson, John–Thompson, John	2440	Van Atta, John–Van Buskirk, Richard
2377	Thompson, Jonathan–Thompson, Richard	2441	Van Camp, Cornelius–Vandaman, Frederick
2378	Thompson, Robert–Thompson, Theodore	2442	Van De Bogart, Joseph–Vanderburgh, John
2379	Thompson, Thomas–Thompson, Timothy	2443	Van Der Cook, Henry–Vanderwerkin, Martiness
2380	Thompson, William–Thompson, Zebulon	2444	Van Deusen, Abraham–Vandventer, James
2381	Thoms, Samuel–Thorn, Thomas	2445	Van Dyck, Cornelius–Vanfliet, Carick
2382	Thornbury, Francis–Thorowgood, Lemuel	2446	Vanfossen, Jacob–Van Hoosen, Garret
2383	Thorp, Amos–Thorp, Thomas	2447	Van Horn, Abraham–Van Ingen, Joseph
2384	Thrall, Jesse–Thruston, Robert	2448	Vankauren, Hazael–Van Netter, Samuel

Roll	Description
2449	Van Ney, Vincent–Vanpool, Jacob
2450	Van Rensselaer, Elsie–Vansyckle, Cornelius
2451	Van Tassel, Abraham–Van Volkenburgh, Bartholomew
2452	Van Voorhase, William–Van Wart, William
2453	Van Wickle, Evert–Vanzile, Harmonus
2454	Vargison, Elijah–Vastfall, Abraham
2455	Vaughan, Abram–Vaughn, William
2456	Vawler, William–Venus, Michael
2457	Verano, Peter–Verony, Joseph
2458	Verrian, John–Vibbird, David
2459	Vicall, Adam–Vigal, Adam
2460	Villas, Noah–Vinson, William
2461	Vinton, Abiathar–Von Steuben, Frederick
2462	Voorhees, Abraham–Vorys, Isaiah
2463	Vosberg, Peter–Vought, Henry
2464	Vowles, Charles–Vyer, John
2465	Waalradt, Isaac–Wade, George
2466	Wade, Henry–Wade, William
2467	Wadham, Abigail–Wagg, Rhoda
2468	Waggener, Andrew–Wagster, William
2469	Wahr, Frederick–Wak-ar-an-thar-aus, James
2470	Wakefield, Abel–Wakly, John
2471	Walace, Christian–Waldren, John
2472	Waldrepe, James–Waliser, Christian
2473	Walker, Aaron–Walker, Ezekiel
2474	Walker, Francis–Walker, Joanna
2475	Walker, John–Walker, Moses
2476	Walker, Nathan–Walker, Simons
2477	Walker, Solomon–Walkup, Samuel
2478	Wall, Arthur–Wall, William
2479	Wallace, Aaron–Wallace, John
2480	Wallace, Joseph–Wallace, William
2481	Wallar, William–Wallinback, John
2482	Walling, Carhart–Walliser, Michael
2483	Wallradt, Henry–Waltamyer, David
2484	Waltar, John–Walters, Solomon
2485	Walthall, Henry–Walton, William
2486	Walts, Conrad–Warble, Henry
2487	Ward, Aaron–Ward, Elnathan
2488	Ward, George–Ward, John
2489	Ward, Jonas–Ward, Samuel
2490	Ward, Simon–Ward, Zebediah
2491	Wardell, Robert–Wardwell, William
2492	Ware, Amos–Wares, Elias
2493	Warfield, Aaron–Warneck, Frederick
2494	Warner, Amasa–Warner, Israel
2495	Warner, Jabez–Warner, Nathaniel
2496	Warner, Nicholas–Warral, Benjamin
2497	Warren, Aaron–Warren, Hugh
2498	Warren, Jabez–Warren, Neverson
2499	Warren, Oliver–Warren, Zenas
2500	Warrener, Aaron–Washam, Charles
2501	Washbourne, Alden–Washburn, William
2502	Washer, Elias–Waterhouse, William
2503	Waterman, Abram–Waterman, Zenas
2504	Waterous, Benjamin–Watford, William
2505	Watkins, Abner–Watkins, Zachariah
2506	Watlington, John–Watson, Guy
2507	Watson, Jack–Watson, Levin
2508	Watson, Major–Watson, Winthrop
2509	Watt, James–Watts, William
2510	Waufle, John–Wayt, William
2511	Weaden, Peleg–Weatherstine, John

Roll	Description
2512	Weaver, Abiel–Weaver, John
2513	Weaver, Joseph–Weavor, Jacob
2514	Webb, Abner–Webb, Isaac
2515	Webb, James–Webb, Jonathan
2516	Webb, Joseph–Webb, William
2517	Webber, Benjamin–Weber, Peter
2518	Webster, Aaron–Webster, John
2519	Webster, Joseph–Webster, Zephaniah
2520	Wechter, Anthony–Weed, Jesse
2521	Weed, John–Weedon, Peleg
2522	Weekes, James–Weeks, William
2523	Weemer, Charles–Welburn, William
2524	Welch, Amos–Welch, John
2525	Welch, Jonas–Welchons, William
2526	Weld, Benjamin–Welles, Noah
2527	Welling, John–Wellons, Charles
2528	Wells, Abner–Wells, Gideon
2529	Wells, Hannah–Wells, Oliver
2530	Wells, Paul–Wells, Zachariah
2531	Welman, Jacob–Wentling, George
2532	Wentworth, Alpheus–Wentworth, William
2533	Wentz, John–Wesson, Mabel
2534	West, Aaron–West, Hezekiah
2535	West, Ichabod–West, Littleton
2536	West, Moses–West, Willoughby
2537	Westbrook, Aaron–Westcott, Wright
2538	Westerdall, Francis–Westmoreland, Jesse
2539	Weston, Abner–Weston, Zachariah
2540	Westray, Daniel–Weysor, Henry
2541	Whalan, Richard–Whatley, William
2542	Wheadon, Abraham–Wheeland, Michael
2543	Wheeler, Aaron–Wheeler, Isaiah
2544	Wheeler, Jacob–Wheeler, Plomer
2545	Wheeler, Prosper–Wheeler, Zenas
2546	Wheeley, John–Whelan, Richard
2547	Whelchel, Davis–Whipley, Amos
2548	Whippel, Robert–Whipple, Zebulon
2549	Whippy, John–Whitcher, Chace
2550	Whitcom, John–Whitcraft, William
2551	White, Abel–White, Charles
2552	White, Christopher–White, Elias
2553	White, Elijah–White, Israel
2554	White, Jacob–White, Joel
2555	White, John–White, John
2556	White, Jonathan–White, Moses
2557	White, Nancy–White, Royal
2558	White, Samuel–White, Stephen
2559	White, Tarpley–White, Vincent
2560	White, William–White, Zachariah
2561	Whitecar, Joseph–Whitehouse, Thomas
2562	Whitehurst, Anthony–Whitin, Samuel
2563	Whiting, Aaron–Whiting, William
2564	Whitington, Faddy–Whitlow, Thomas
2565	Whitman, Abiel–Whitman, Woolery
2566	Whitmarsh, Ebenezer–Whitmyer, Philip
2567	Whitney, Abner–Whitney, John
2568	Whitney, Jonas–Whitney, Zebulun
2569	Whiton, Abijah–Whitting, Samuel
2570	Whittington, Cornelius–Wickes, Zophar
2571	Wicket, Obadiah–Wiett, Edward
2572	Wiggin, Andrew–Wigginton, John
2573	Wigglesworth, Edward–Wilbanks, William
2574	Wilbar, Isaac–Wilcklow, Jacob
2575	Wilcox, Abner–Wilcox, William

Roll	Description
2576	Wilcoxen, Daniel–Wilde, Richard
2577	Wilder, Aaron–Wilder, Willis
2578	Wildes, Benjamin–Wiley, William
2579	Wilfong, David–Wilkie, Augustus
2580	Wilkin, James–Wilkins, William
2581	Wilkinson, Abel–Wilkinson, Young
2582	Wilkison, Aaron–Willard, William
2583	Willbanks, Richard–Willcutt, Thomas
2584	Wille, Benjamin–William, Tall
2585	Williams, Abel–Williams, Benjamin
2586	Williams, Bennett–Williams, Davenport
2587	Williams, David–Williams, Ezekiel
2588	Williams, Francis–Williams, Isaiah
2589	Williams, Jabez–Williams, Joel
2590	Williams, John–Williams, John (not Revolutionary War, Ky. Mil., Gen. Harmar's War, 1790)
2591	Williams, John (Pa.)–Williams, Jonathan
2592	Williams, Joseph–Williams, Moses
2593	Williams, Nathan–Williams, Robert
2594	Williams, Robinson–Williams, Thaddeus
2595	Williams, Thomas–Williams, Wilke
2596	Williams, William–Williams, Zebedee
2597	Williamson, Alexander–Williamson, Joseph
2598	Williamson, Littleton–Willington, Thomas
2599	Willis, Abisha–Willis, Joseph
2600	Willis, Lewis–Willoughby, Edlyne
2601	Wills, Conrad–Willsie, William
2602	Willson, Alexander–Willson, William
2603	Willy, John–Wilsie, Jacob
2604	Wilson, Aaron–Wilson, Charles
2605	Wilson, Daniel–Wilson, Israel
2606	Wilson, Jacob–Wilson, Joab
2607	Wilson, John–Wilson, John
2608	Wilson, Jonathan–Wilson, Nathaniel
2609	Wilson, Nehemiah–Wilson, Samuel
2610	Wilson, Stafford–Wilson, Warren
2611	Wilson, William–Wilson, Zachariah
2612	Wilt, Jacob–Winchell, John
2613	Winchester, Amariah–Winchester, William
2614	Winchip, Joel–Winfrey, Philip
2615	Wing, Aaron–Winmer, Jacob
2616	Winn, Elisha–Winship, Richard
2617	Winslow, Abraham–Winsor, William
2618	Winstead, Francis–Wirtz, William
2619	Wiscarver, George–Wissenbagh, Henry
2620	Wisswell, Israel–Witham, Thomas
2621	Withee, Uzziel–Withrow, Samuel
2622	Witman, Abraham–Wizer, Michael
2623	Woelper, David–Wolever, Phillip
2624	Wolf, Adam–Wonicutt, Richard
2625	Wood, Aaron–Wood, Charles
2626	Wood, Clement–Wood, Gideon
2627	Wood, Henry–Wood, Joel
2628	Wood, John–Wood, Joseph
2629	Wood, Joshua–Wood, Robertson
2630	Wood, Sampson–Wood, Thomas
2631	Wood, Thurston–Wood, Zephaniah
2632	Woodall, Charles–Woodburn, Moses
2633	Woodbury, Anna–Woodbury, William
2634	Woodcock, Bartholomew–Woodland, Rhode
2635	Woodman, Abner–Woodrow, Simeon
2636	Woodruf, Baldwin–Woodrum, Stephen
2637	Woods, Abel–Woods, William
2638	Woodside, Archibald–Woodsum, Samuel

Roll	Description
2639	Woodward, Aaron–Woodward, John
2640	Woodward, Jonathan–Woodwell, Lydia
2641	Woodworth, Abel–Woodworth, Ziba
2642	Woody, Benjamin–Woollard, John
2643	Woolley, Asa–Wooton, Silas
2644	Worcester, Eldad–Works, James
2645	Wordley, Polley–Worster, William
2646	Wort, John–Wriggins, Thomas
2647	Wright, Aaron–Wright, Cyprion
2648	Wright, Daniel–Wright, George
2649	Wright, Hannah–Wright, Joel
2650	Wright, John–Wright, Joseph
2651	Wright, Joshua–Wright, Roxavene
2652	Wright, Samuel–Wright, William
2653	Wrightington, George–Wyckoff, Samuel
2654	Wyer, George–Wyly, James
2655	Wyman, Asa–Wysor, Henry
2656	Yacobi, Pfillib–Yarbrough, Nathan
2657	Yard, Daniel–Yeasting, Peter
2658	Yeates, Benjamin–Yeomans, Samuel
2659	Yerks, Aaron–Yoress, John
2660	York, Aaron–York, William
2661	Yorkshire, Thomas–Young, Benjamin
2662	Young, Caleb–Young, Guy
2663	Young, Henry–Young, Johannis
2664	Young, John–Young, Joseph
2665	Young, Levi–Young, Ruth
2666	Young, Samuel–Young, Zebulon
2667	Youngblood, Jacob–Yurkse, John
2668	Zachary, William–Ziegler, George
2669	Zielie, Martinis–Zweier, John
2670	Miscellaneous Records

U.S. Revolutionary War Bounty Land Warrants Used in the U.S. Military District of Ohio and Related Papers (Acts of 1788, 1803, and 1806). M829. 16 rolls. DP.

This microfilm publication reproduces U.S. Revolutionary War bounty land warrants dated 1789–1833 and related papers dated as late as 1880. The warrants were issued under acts of July 9, 1788 (Journals of the Continental Congress); March 3, 1803 (2 Stat. 236); and April 15, 1806 (2 Stat. 378).

Roll	Description
1	Index to the Register of Army Land Warrants Register of Army Land Warrants per Acts of 1796 and 1799 Index to Revolutionary War Military Bounty Land Warrants Issued Under the Acts of 1803 and 1806 Register of Military Land Warrants Presented at the Treasury for Locating and Patenting, 1804–35
2	Warrants Issued Under Act of 1788: 1– 6999
3	7000– 7499
4	7500– 7999
5	8000– 8599
6	8600– 9299
7	9300–10099
8	10100–10899
9	10900–11699
10	11700–12599
11	12600–13399
12	13400–14220

Roll	Description
13	Warrants Issued Under Act of 1803
	1– 272
	Warrants Issued Under Act of 1806
	273– 299
14	300– 699
15	700– 1099
16	1100– 2119
	Warrants Issued Under Acts of 1835, 1842, 1848
	1299, 2314, 2340,
	2346, 2359, 2418,
	2436, 2442, 2453,
	2455, 2458, 2462,
	2467, 2468, 2470,
	2471, 2475, 2479

Additional Pension Records

The following publications reproduce records relating to pension claims. Most Revolutionary War pension records were microfilmed with the bounty land warrant applications on M804 and M805, described in the previous section. The publications are arranged chronologically; some date spans and coverage overlap.

Virginia Half Pay and Other Related Revolutionary War Pension Application Files. M910. 18 rolls. DP.

This microfilm publication reproduces pension application files based on military and naval service in the Revolutionary War. A few records, or copies of records, are dated as early as 1778, but most of the documents in the files are dated between 1830 and 1875. A large number of them pertain to half-pay pensions of Virginia soldiers and sailors. Generally for each soldier or sailor there is an envelope that contains applications for pensions based on his service.

In May 1779 the General Assembly of Virginia authorized the payment of half pay for life to the State's military and naval officers, including chaplains, physicians, surgeons, and surgeons' mates, who served until the end of the war in State units within the State's borders or in the Continental Army. Eventually, the Federal Government assumed financial responsibility for these pensions. Many of the records were borrowed by the Third Auditor from the Bureau of Pensions, and there is a great deal of correspondence in the files between the Commissioner of Pensions and the Third Auditor concerning the claims and the transfer of records.

A typical file may contain approximately 50 documents. The pension files are arranged in two series, one relating to soldiers and one relating to sailors, and thereunder alphabetically by surname of soldier or sailor. Both of the series contain files relating to Virginia half-pay claims, and the series of soldiers' files also contains pension applications under other Revolutionary War and later acts. A few of the files pertain to veterans of the Mexican, Indian, and Civil Wars. A few pension files in the naval series also relate to marines.

Roll	Description
Pensions Relating to Soldiers:	
1	Adams–Berry
2	Bishop–Browning
3	Calvitt–Crump
4	Dabney–Doty
5	Edinburgh–Fox
6	Galt–Gunsaulis
7	Hamestreet–Jones
8	Keller–Ludington
9	Madden–Muzzy
10	Nash–Quirk
11	Ravenscroft–Russey
12	Sacrey–Straley
13	Tabb–Vowles
14	Walls–Yeates
Pensions Relating to Sailors:	
15	Applewhaite–Crew
16	De Kay–Humphlett
17	James–Pasteur
18	Reynolds–Woneycott

War of 1812 Bounty Land Warrants and Pensions

War of 1812 Military Bounty Land Warrants, 1815–1858. M848. 14 rolls. DP.

This microfilm publication reproduces 105 bound volumes containing two series of military bounty land warrants issued between 1815 and 1858 to veterans of the War of 1812, and 4 volumes of indexes to the warrants.

The first series of warrants resulted from acts passed December 24, 1811 (2 Stat. 669), January 11, 1812 (2 Stat. 672), and May 6, 1812 (2 Stat. 729), in which Congress provided that noncommissioned officers and soldiers serving for 5 years (unless discharged sooner), or their heirs, would be entitled to 160 acres of land from the public domain in partial compensation for military service. A total of 6 million acres of land were to be surveyed and reserved for this purpose, 2 million acres in each of the Territories of Michigan, Illinois, and Louisiana (present-day Arkansas).

The second series resulted from an act of December 10, 1814 (3 Stat. 147), by which Congress doubled the acreage offered to soldiers enlisting after that date. Warrants issued under this act were called double bounty warrants.

The warrants contain the following information: (1) the name of the veteran, (2) his rank on discharge from military service, (3) his company, regiment, and branch of service, (4) the date the warrant was issued, and (5) usually the date the land was located and the page on which the location is recorded in Abstracts of Military Bounty Land Warrant Locations.

They are arranged according to warrant number and are in chronological order. For warrants appearing in this microfilm publication, issue dates of the first series (Act of 1812, 160 acres) extend from August 19, 1815, to June 2, 1858, and for the second series (Act of 1814, 320 acres) from August 23, 1815, to April 1, 1839.

Four indexes, applying to both series, have been included on roll 1.

Roll	Description	Warrant Numbers
1	Indexes for Acts of 1812, 1814, 1842	
Act of 1812:		
	1–6	1–1726

Roll	Description	Warrant Numbers
2	7–14	1727–4010
3	15–22	4011–6314
4	23–30	6315–8618
5	31–38	8619–10918
6	39–46	10919–13220
7	47–54	13221–15524
8	55–62	15525–17826
9	63–70	17827–20120
10	71–78	20121–22382
11	79–83	22383–23870
	Unnumbered (3 vols.)	23871–24770
12	Unnumbered (7 vols.)	24771–26870
13	Unnumbered (8 vols.)	26871–28085

Act of 1814:

14	1–3	1–855
	Unnumbered (1 vol.)	856–1076

Index to War of 1812 Pension Application Files. M313. 102 rolls. DP.

This microfilm publication reproduces the faces of the envelopes containing War of 1812 pension applications arranged alphabetically by name of veteran. The files in this War of 1812 series relate to claims based on service rendered between 1812 and 1815. All pensions granted to veterans of the War of 1812 and their surviving dependents before 1871 were based exclusively on service-connected disability or death.

The amount of information shown on the envelopes varies considerably. Each shows the name of a veteran, the name of his widow if she applied, the pension claim or file number or numbers, and some indication either of the type of service or of the organization in which the veteran served. Many of the envelopes also give certain personal identifying data about the veteran and/or his widow. Information in the upper right-hand corner of some of the envelopes relates to applications for bounty land. A file, however, may contain bounty land applications even though there is no such indication on the face of the envelope.

There are cross-reference cards for names that appear in the records under more than one spelling.

Roll	Description
1	A–Alld
2	Alle–And
3	Ane–Aus
4	Aut–Bak
5	Bal–Baro
6	Barr–Bear
7	Beas–Ben
8	Ber–Blai
9	Blak–Bop
10	Bor–Brai
11	Brak–Broo
12	Bros–Broz
13	Bru–Burm
14	Burn–By
15	C–Carl
16	Carm–Cast
17	Casw–Che
18	Chi–Cla
19	Cle–Cold
20	Cole–Conl
21	Conn–Corm
22	Corn–Crav
23	Craw–Cum
24	Cun–Dau
25	Dav–Daz
26	De
27	Di–Dot
28	Dou–Dunh
29	Dunk–Edr
30	Eds–Ep
31	Er–Fa
32	Fe–Fla
33	Fle–Fou
34	Fow–Full
35	Fulm–Ga
36	Ge–Gi
37	Gl–Go
38	Gra–Gree
39	Greg–Gy
40	H–Hame
41	Hami–Harm
42	Harn–Has
43	Hat–Hed
44	Hee–Hib
45	Hic–Hiz
46	Hoa–Hon
47	Hoo–Howe
48	Howk–Huns
49	Hunt–I
50	J–Jod
51	Joh–Jol
52	Jon–Ju
53	K–Ke
54	Ki–Kna
55	Kne–Land
56	Lane–Led
57	Lee–Lez
58	Li–Lon
59	Loo–Ly
60	M–McC
61	McD–McK
62	McL–Mann
63	Mano–Mas
64	Mat–Merr
65	Mers–Mill
66	Milm–Moon
67	Moor–Morr
68	Mors–Mu
69	My–Ne
70	Ni–Ny
71	O
72	P–Pas
73	Pat–Pen
74	Pep–Pic
75	Pid–Por
76	Pos–Pr
77	Pu–Ra
78	Re–Rice
79	Rich–Robb
80	Robe–Rol
81	Rom–Ry
82	S–Sci
83	Sco–Shar
84	Shas–Shy
85	Si–Smil

Roll	Description
86	Smit–Smith, R.
87	Smith, S.–Spe
88	Spi–Step
89	Ster–Sto
90	Str–Sy
91	T–Thi
92	Tho–Tim
93	Tin–Turb
94	Turc–Vanr
95	Vans–Walk
96	Wall–Wats
97	Watt–Wes
98	Wet–Wie
99	Wig–Willi
100	Willk–Won
101	Woo–Wr
102	Wu–Z

Indexes to Pensions Including Civil War and Later Service

Old War Index to Pension Files, 1815–1926. T316. 7 rolls. 16mm.

This microfilm publication reproduces a card index to the "Old Wars" series of pension files, 1815–1926. These files relate chiefly to claims based on death or disability incurred in service in the Regular Army, Navy, or Marine Corps between the end of the Revolutionary War in 1783 and the outbreak of the Civil War in 1861.

Each card shows the name of a veteran; the name and class of dependent, if any; the service unit; the application, file, and certificate number; and the State from which the claim was filed.

Roll	Description
1	Aaron, Wm.–Brinson, Zebulon
2	Briscoe, Wm.–Duncan, Alexander
3	Duncan, Daniel C.–Herrin, Lemuel
4	Herring, Charles–McDonnell, James
5	McDonnell, John–Porter, Thomas J.
6	Porter, W.C.B.S.–Sullivan, Dennis
7	Sullivan, Eugene–Zeuinge, Anton

General Index to Pension Files, 1861–1934. T288. 544 rolls. 16mm.

This microfilm publication reproduces a general index to pension files, 1861–1934. The pension applications to which this index applies relate chiefly to Army, Navy, and Marine Corps service performed between 1861 and 1916. Most of the records relate to Civil War service; some relate to earlier service by Civil War veterans; others relate to service in the Spanish-American War, the Philippine Insurrection, the Boxer Rebellion, and the Regular Establishment. There are no records of service in Confederate forces. Confederate pensions were granted by Southern States after the war, and the files are State, not Federal, records. For more information, contact the Museum of the Confederacy, 1201 East Clay Street, Richmond, Va. 23219.

Each card in the general index gives a veteran's name, rank, unit, and term of service; names of dependent(s); the filing date; the application number; the certificate number; and the State from which the claim was filed. The darker cards relate to naval service.

Roll	Description
1	Aab–Ackerman, Garrett
2	Ackerman, George–Adams, Lige
3	Adams, Lincoln–Ah, Her Saw
4	Ah, Qua Rah–Aldrich, Walter
5	Aldrich, Warren–Allen, Clarence
6	Allen, Clarence–Allen, William
7	Allen, William–Americas, Edward
8	Ames, Alge–Anderson, James
9	Anderson, Jas.–Andrews, Dan
10	Andrews, Daniel–Appenfelder, Frederick
11	Appenfelder, Frederick–Armstrong, James
12	Armstrong, James–Arthurs, Abraham
13	Arthur, Robert–Atkinson, Felix
14	Atkinson, Francis–Axe, Lorenzo
15	Axe, Peter–Bacon, Lester
16	Bacon, Levi–Bailey, Samuel
17	Bailey, Samuel O.–Baker, Jacob
18	Baker, Jacob–Baldwin, Julius
19	Baldwin, Justin R.–Bangert, Geo.
20	Bangert, Henry–Barentzen, Lauritz
21	Barepole, Charley–Barnes, James
22	Barnes, James–Barre, Lucius
23	Barre, Onesime–Bartlett, Charles F.
24	Bartlett, Charles G.–Batchelor, Geo.
25	Batchelor, Henry–Baumgardner, Christian
26	Baumgardner, Daniel–Beamen, James
27	Beamenderfer, John H.–Bechtol, George
28	Bechtol, Henry–Beekman, Arthur
29	Beekman, Chancey–Bell, James R.
30	Bell, James R.–Benford, John H.
31	Benford, Joseph–Benning, John
32	Benning, Charles–Bernard, Dennis
33	Bernard, Dennis–Bettman, Alfred
34	Bettman, Gotleib–Biggs, Elijah
35	Biggs, Elisha–Birk, Gottfield
36	Birk, Jacob–Black, John W.
37	Black, John W.–Blair, John W.
38	Blair, Jonas–Blase, Wm. F.
39	Blasedell, Joseph–Bluit, Anthony
40	Bluitt, Lyman–Bogue, Silas
41	Bogue, Stephen–Boner, Peter
42	Boner, Peter–Boreman, Jacob
43	Boreman, Thomas–Boulson, Kenneth
44	Boult, Frank–Bowles, Daniel
45	Bowles, Daniel–Boyo, Wm. H.
46	Boyd, Wm. H.–Bradford, James
47	Bradford, James–Braisted, Wm.
48	Braisure, Amos–Branum, Charles
49	Branum, Charles–Brennan, Jeremiah
50	Brennan, Jeremiah–Brewer, Katie
51	Brewer, Lafayette–Brileya, Peter
52	Brilhart, Hiram–Brockway, Stephen
53	Brockway, Stephen–Brophy, Wm.
54	Brophy, Wm.–Brown, Dennis
55	Brown, Dennis–Brown, James B.
56	Brown, James B.–Brown, Oscar
57	Brown, Oscar–Browne, Byron
58	Browne, Charles–Brussard, Eugen
59	Brusse, Henry–Buck, Haven
60	Buck, Harvey–Bull, James R.
61	Bull, Jefferson–Burd, Wm.
62	Burd, Wm.–Burke, Thomas

Roll	Description
63	Burke, Thomas–Burns, Hiram
64	Burns, Hiram–Burt, Lucius
65	Burt, Luther–Butcher, Jesse
66	Butcher, John–Buzan, Wm.
67	Buzan, Wm.–Cager, Robert
68	Cagg, Andrew–Callahan, John
69	Callahan, John–Campbell, Geo.
70	Campbell, Geo. S.–Canfield, Lewis
71	Canfield, Lewis–Carkhuff, John
72	Carkhuff, Samuel–Carpenter, Harry
73	Carpenter, Harry–Carroll, James
74	Carroll, James–Carter, Lewis
75	Carter, Lewis–Case, Henry O.
76	Case, Henry W.–Castle, Wm. D.
77	Castle, Wm.–Chadwick, Adel
78	Chadwick, Albert–Chance, Wm. T.
79	Chance, Wm. W.–Chappel, Robert
80	Chappel, Robert C.–Cheney, Isaiah
81	Cheney, Ithamar–Chrisman, Lorenzo
82	Chrisman, Luke–Clammer, Jacob
83	Clamor, Engracio–Clark, Hiland
84	Clark, Hinman H.–Clark, Vincent B.
85	Clark, Vincent E.–Cleveland, Albert B.
86	Cleaveland, Albert H.–Cline, Wm.
87	Cline, Wm.–Cobb, Oliver
88	Cobb, Oliver–Coggin, Wm. T.
89	Coggins, Anthony–Cole, Robert H.
90	Cole, Robert M.–Collins, Berta
91	Collins, Bertrand–Colton, Edward
92	Colton, Edward H.–Conger, Alex.
93	Conger, Anson–Connolly, Bart
94	Connolly, Bernard–Cook, Christopher
95	Cook, Christopher–Cooley, Nathan L.
96	Cooley, Nathan M.–Cooper, Wyley
97	Cooper, Youle–Cornelius, Gust.
98	Cornelius, Hardin–Cotter, Michael
99	Cotter, Michael–Cowan, Theodore
100	Cowan, Theodore–Coyle, James J.
101	Coyle, James J.–Crandall, James R.
102	Crandall, James S.–Crays, Andrew
103	Crays, David–Crockett, Francis M.
104	Crockett, Francis T.–Crosser, Adam
105	Crosser, Harrison–Crumrine, Bishop
106	Crumrine, Boyd–Cummins, Oliver
107	Cummins, Orange S.–Curry, Michael
108	Curry, Michael–Dabney, Clark
109	Dabney, Cornelius–Danforth, Clarence
110	Danforth, Clarence–Daniels, Isaiah
111	Daniels, J. S.–Davenport, Alfred
112	Davenport, Alfred–Davis, Decon
113	Davis, Dewey–Davis, John P.
114	Davis, John P.–Davison, Isaiah
115	Davison, Jacob–Dean, Charles B.
116	Dean, Charles B.–Decook, Henry
117	Decook, Peter–Delap, Joseph
118	Delap, Joseph–Dennewitz, Conrad
119	Denney, Abram–Deschler, Maurice
120	Deschler, Valentine–Dewitt, Geo. W.
121	Dewitt, Geo. W.–Dickson, Benjamin
122	Dickson, Benjamin–Dillon, John F.
123	Dillon, John F.–Dixon, Joseph C.
124	Dixon, John–Dohn, Adam
125	Dohn, Andrew–Donnely, William
126	Donnely, William–Doss, Charles
127	Doss, Charles W.–Dow, Francis R.
128	Dow, Frank–Doyle, Cornelius
129	Doyle, James–Doyle, Jacob
130	Doyle, James–Drinkwater, Alpheus
131	Drinkwater, Charles–Duff, James W.
132	Duff, James W.–Duncan, Joseph
133	Duncan, Joseph–Dunn, Thomas
134	Dunn, Thomas B.–Dutton, Edward
135	Dutton, Edward–Earl, Robert R.
136	Earl, Robert W.–Eberling, Wm.
137	Eberly, Albert M.–Edmonds, John
138	Edmonds, John A.–Eggers, Emil
139	Eggers, Peter–Eliott, Halbert
140	Eliott, James–Ellis, John B.
141	Ellis, John C.–Emerson, James P.
142	Emerson, James R.–Engstrom, John
143	Engstrom, John–Erb, George
144	Erb, Harvey–Estover, George
145	Estrada, Antonio–Evans, Wm. T.
146	Evans, Wm. T.–Failing, Charles
147	Failing, Cornelius–Farmer, Thompson
148	Farmer, Traais–Faunce, George
149	Faunce, Martin–Fennen, Henry
150	Fenner, Albert C.–Fesler, Benjamin
151	Fesler, Cassius A.–Filey, Wm. H.
152	Filley, Wm. H.–Fish, Thomas S.
153	Fish, Thomas J.–Fitch, John A.
154	Fitch, John A.–Flanders, Samuel
155	Flanders, Samuel B.–Flew, William
156	Flewallen, Alfred–Foglesang, Eli W.
157	Foglesang, Nathaniel–Ford, John B.
158	Ford, John–Foster, Aaron
159	Foster, Aaron–Fowler, Olin N.
160	Fowler, Oliver–Francisco, Juan
161	Francisco, Levi–Frech, Henry
162	Frech, Hubert–French, John
163	French, John–Frost, Benjamin
164	Frost, Benjamin–Fuller, John W.
165	Fuller, John W.–Furneisen, H.
166	Furneld, George–Callagher, Jas. H.
167	Gallagher, James H.–Garcelon, W.
168	Garch, Joseph–Garnier, John
169	Garnier, Joseph–Gaston, James
170	Gaston, James W.–Gee, Charles R.
171	Gee, Christopher C.–Gehris, Wilson
172	Gehrike, Albert–German, Linsey
173	German, Littleton–Gibson, James L.
174	Gibson, James M.–Gilbert, John B.
175	Gilbert, John C.–Gilliam, Peter
176	Gilliam, Primus–Givier, Edwin
177	Givier, George–Glidden, Arno
178	Glidden, Augustus–Golden, Andrew
179	Golden, Andrew–Goodrich, Bertrand
180	Goodrich, Bethuel–Gorham, William
181	Gorham, Wm. E.–Gowman, Wm.
182	Gowner, Lewis–Grane, Herman
183	Grane, Mikal O.–Gray, Edward
184	Gray, Edward–Green, David L.
185	Green, David M.–Greenberger, B.
186	Greenburgh, Samuel–Gresh, Henry
187	Gresh, Samuel–Griggs, Albert P.
188	Griggs, Alexander–Gross, Daniel
189	Gross, Daniel–Guest, John W.
190	Guest, Joseph–Gutline, Ethru F.

Roll	Description
191	Gutling, Wm.–Haffner, W.
192	Hafford, B.–Halbert, Silas
193	Halbert, Smith–Hall, Ivory
194	Hall, Ivory A.–Halliman, Thomas
195	Halliman, Wm.–Hamilton, Robert
196	Hamilton, Robert–Hanchett, John
197	Hanchett, Joseph–Hannefin, J.
198	Hanneford, Wm.–Hardin, Robert
199	Hardin, Ruburtus–Harmer, Alfred
200	Harmer, Amos–Harrington, Michael
201	Harrington, Michael B.–Harris, Stephen
202	Harris, Stephen–Hart, Jacob
203	Hart, Jacob–Harvey, Adam
204	Harvey, Albert–Hatch, David G.
205	Hatch, David O.–Haw, William
206	Haw, William–Hayes, Charles W.
207	Hayes, Charles W.–Hazel, Jack
208	Hazel, James H.–Heck, Theodore
209	Hechinger, Clifford–Heiple, Henry
210	Heiple, Henry F.–Henderson, Charles
211	Henderson, Charles–Hennessy, Michael
212	Hennessey, Michael–Hepler, Andrew
213	Hepler, Clarence–Hershey, Isaac
214	Hershey, Isaac–Hibbard, Harris
215	Hibbard, Harry–Higgins, Jason
216	Higgins, Jasper–Hill, Henry H.
217	Hill, Henry H.–Hiltman, Abraham
218	Hiltman, John–Hirschfeld, Emanuel
219	Hirschfeld, Ernest–Hockman, Wm. W.
220	Hockman, Wm. W.–Hoffman, Werner L.
221	Hoffman, Wesley R.–Holder, Edward
222	Holder, Eleano–Holly, Daniel
223	Holly, Daniel W.–Holverson, Frank
224	Holverson, Halver–Hopes, J. Solomon
225	Hopes, Thomas W.–Horney, Joseph
226	Horney, Joseph M.–Houghton, Geo. W.
227	Houghton, Geo. W.–Howard, John
228	Howard, John–Howland, Herbert V.
229	Howland, Herman–Hudon, Louis
230	Hudon, Ombro–Hughes, George
231	Hughes, Geo. W.–Humbell, John
232	Humber, Carroll–Hunt, William
233	Hunt, William–Hurd, Thomas W.
234	Hurd, Thomas–Hutchinson, Mathias
235	Hutchinson, Mayheir–Imfeld, Ferd.
236	Imfeld, Franz–Irvine, Robert W.
237	Irvine, Samuel–Jackson, Charles F.
238	Jackson, Charles F.–Jackson, Wm. A.
239	Jackson, William A.–James, William
240	James, W.–Jauslin, Joseph
241	Jauss, Christian–Jenkins, John
242	Jenkins, John–Jewett, Charles A.
243	Jewett, Charles A.–Johnson, Chris
244	Johnson, Chris–Johnson, James
245	Johnson, James–Johnson, Ogden
246	Johnson, Okey M.–Johnson, Wm. P.
247	Johnson, Wm. Q.–Jones, Chesley
248	Jones, Chesley–Jones, James W.
249	Jones, James. W.–Jones, Smith
250	Jones, Smith E.–Jordan Wm. O.
251	Jordan, William P.–Kaf Fes Sah
252	Kaffey, Martin–Kauble, Benjamin
253	Kauble, Benjamin F.–Keeley, John
254	Keeley, John–Kell, Nathaniel

Roll	Description
255	Kell, Noah–Kellum, Daniel F.
256	Kellum, Edward M.–Kelter, Daniel
257	Keltner, Dion B.–Kennedy, Richard
258	Kennedy, Richard–Kerney, Timothy
259	Kerney, Whit–Keys, Southey
260	Keys, Stephen W.–Kimball, Chas.
261	Kimball, Chas. C.–King, Harry
262	King, Harry–Kinley, Jacob
263	Kinley, James–Kurkendall, Rich.
264	Kirkendall, Robert–Kleinhans, M.
265	Kleinhays, Wm.–Knapp, Zero
266	Knappe, Adolph–Knowlton, Daniel
267	Knowlton, Daniel–Kooner, Thos.
268	Koones, Albert–Kriege, William
269	Kriegel, Emil F.–Kurtz, John
270	Kurtz, John–LaGraff, John B.
271	LaGraff, Michael–LaMont, John
272	Lamont, John–Lane, John M.
273	Lane, John M.–Lapay, Pedro
274	Lape, Aamon–Lathbury, John
275	Lathe, Abner P.–Lawrence, Edward
276	Lawrence, Edward–Leach, James
277	Leach, James M.–Lee, Dwight, M.
278	Lee, Earl–Leger, William
279	Legere, Andrew–Lennon, Edward
280	Lennon, Francis–Levan, Obediah
281	Leven, Oscar–Lewis, Joseph
282	Lewis, Joseph–Lewis, Wm. I.
283	Lewis, Wm. J.–Lincoln, Thomas
284	Lincoln, Thomas A.–Linson, Lyman
285	Linson, Theo.–Livermore, Ben.
286	Livermore, Ben. W.–Loftus, Martin
287	Loftus, Martin V.–Long, Wm. H.
288	Long, William, J.–Loucks, Peter
289	Loucks, Peter B.–Lowe, Wm.
290	Lowe, Wm.–Ludwig, John
291	Ludwig, John–Lyle, Wm. W.
292	Lyles, Alexander–Lythe, Wm. C.
293	Lytle, Aaron W.–McCabe, Francis
294	McCabe, Francis–McCartney, Wm.
295	McCartney, Wm.–McClintick, H.
296	McClintick, Henry C.–McComb, John
297	McComb, John–McCormic, Touson
298	McCormic, H.–McCume, P.
299	McCume, Philip–McDonald, John
300	McDonald, John W.–McFadden, Alex.
301	McFadden, Alex.–McGinnis, Edward J.
302	McGinnis, Edward J.–McGuire, John
303	McGuire, John–McKain, James
304	McKain, James–McKibbin, James
305	McKibben, James F.–McLaughlin, James B.
306	McLaughlin, James B.–McMican, Joseph
307	McMichael, Abraham–McNeil, George
308	McNeil, George–McTigue, Michael
309	McTigue, Patrick–Maglalang, Julian
310	Maglalang, Marce–Malarkey, Dennis
311	Malarkey, James–Mangan, John
312	Mangan, John–Manuel, Marcelin
313	Manuel, Mark–Marlin, Wm. T.
314	Marline, Aaron A.–Marshall, Thomas
315	Marshall, Thomas–Martin, John
316	Martin, John–Mary, Matthew
317	Marx, Michael–Mathers, John D.
318	Mathers, John F.–Mattoon, Charles

Roll	Description
319	Mattoon, Charles H.–Mayer, George
320	Mayer, George–Mechling, Amos
321	Mechling, Augustus A.–Melcoon, Samuel
322	Meloon, Samuel S.–Merithew, Wm. H.
323	Meritt, Allen–Metcalf, James
324	Metcalf, James–Mickleborough, F.
325	Mickleby, Theo. A.–Miller, Anthony M.
326	Miller, Anthony W.–Miller, Henry L.
327	Miller, Henry M.–Miller, Marvin
328	Miller, May E.–Millington, Thos.
329	Millington, Wm.–Minnis, Charles
330	Minnis, Charles M.–Mitchell, Thos.
331	Mitchell, Thomas–Monaghan, Thomas
332	Monaghan, Thomas–Moody, Jesse G.
333	Moody, John–Moore, Henry H.
334	Moore, Henry W.–Moore, Wm. H.
335	Moore, Wm. H.–Moran, James
336	Moran, James J.–Morgan, Samuel
337	Morgan, Samuel B.–Morris, Samuel P.
338	Morris, Samuel P.–Morinmer, Mabel
339	Mortimer, Marcellus–Moulton, Frank
340	Moulton, Frank P.–Mullane, Wm. H.
341	Mullaney, Anthony–Munson, Fred
342	Munson, Fred–Murphy, Thomas
343	Murphy, Thomas–Myers, Geo. A.
344	Myers, Geo. B.–Nash, Charles A.
345	Nash, Charles A.–Neff, John M.
346	Neff, John S.–Nesbitt, Wm. E.
347	Nesbitt, Wm. E.–Newman, Lazarus
348	Newman, Leon–Nichols, Wilber
349	Nichols, Wilbur–Noble, Geo. W.
350	Noble, Geo. W.–Norris, Isaac
351	Norris, Isaac–Nuckles, Wm. H.
352	Nuckolls, Asa H.–O'Brien, John
353	O'Brien, John–O'Donnell, Daniel
354	O'Donnell, Daniel–Olds, Isaac
355	Olds, Isaac–O'Neal, John T.
356	O'Neal, John T.–Orr, William
357	Orr, William–Otly, James L.
358	Otman, Sylvester–Owens, Thomas
359	Owens, Thomas–Painter, Jacob
360	Painter, Jacob–Pama, Erasmo
361	Pamanyag, Vincente–Parker, Jacob W.
362	Parker, James–Parrett, Joseph
363	Parrett, Dawson A.–Patterson, Alonzo
364	Patterson, Alonzo F.–Paulter, John
365	Paulus, Abraham–Peary, John
366	Peary, John C.–Pence, Francis W.
367	Pence, Franklin–Perkins, Isa
368	Perkins, Isaac–Perry, Thos. H.
369	Perry, Thomas H.–Pettegreew, Wm.
370	Pettengail, Clark–Philipsen, Herman
371	Philipsen, One V.H.–Pick, Earle
372	Pick, Ernest–Pigott, John
373	Pigott, John–Pixley, John S.
374	Pixley, John W.–Plunket, Wm.
375	Plunkett, Abraham–Pool, Thomas
376	Pool, Thomas–Post, Joseph
377	Post, Joseph–Powell, Thomas
378	Powell, Thomas–Prentice, Geo. W.
379	Prentice, Geo. W.–Price, Timothy
380	Price, Timothy–Pruett, Daniel
381	Pruett, Daniel B.–Putnam, John J.
382	Putnam, John L.–Quino, Flavio
383	Quino, Marcelino–Rambo, William
384	Rambo, William–Rannie, Alexander
385	Rannie, Geo. A.–Ray, John G.
386	Ray, John E.–Records, Thos. S.
387	Records, Thompson, L.–Reed, John A.
388	Reed, John A.–Reeves, Thomas F.
389	Reeves, Thos G.–Reissig, Adolph
390	Reissig, John–Reynolds, Edmund
391	Reynolds, Edwin–Rhone, Dandridge
392	Rhone, Daniel L.–Richards, John
393	Richards, John O.–Richmond, Wm. R.
394	Richmond Wm. S.–Rigby, Wm. H.
395	Rigby, Wm. H.–Rinier, Peter
396	Rinier, Samuel–Rizer, William
397	Rizer, Wm.–Roberts, Geo. F.
398	Roberts, Geo. F.–Robilliard, John
399	Robin, Alfred–Robinson, Robert A.
400	Robinson, Robt.–Robinson, Wm. F.
401	Robinson, Wm. G.–Roe, Charles
402	Roe, Charles–Rogge, Charles H.
403	Rogge, Diedrich–Root, John E.
404	Root, John E.–Ross, George
405	Ross, George–Roush, George
406	Roush, George A.–Rubin, Arcadio
407	Rubio, Charles–Rupley, Henry
408	Rupley, Henry C.–Russum, J.
409	Russum, John W.–Sabin, Charles C.
410	Sabin, Frederick–Sames, Pearl
411	Sames, William J.–Sandquist, Gustave
412	Sandra, Francis H.–Saunders, John R.
413	Saunders, John R.–Savage, Isom
414	Savage, Jacob–Schaefer, Nicholas
415	Schafer, Nicholas–Schlaich, Henry
416	Schlaich, John–Schnelzer, Francis
417	Schnemilch, Wm.–Schuler, Wm. H.
418	Schuler, Wm. W.–Scott, Charles H.
419	Scott, Charles H.–Scoville, Thomas
420	Scoville, Wallace–Sedelbauer, John L.
421	Sedello, Pablo–Sells, David L.
422	Sells, David M.–Shade, Geo. W.
423	Shade, Harry–Shannon, William J.
424	Shannon, Wm. J.–Shaw, Prince
425	Shaw, Rodney K.–Sheldon, Shepard L.
426	Sheldon, Shepard–Sherman, Chas. A.
427	Sherman, Charles A.–Shinkle, Erastus
428	Shinkle, Eugen M.–Short, John H.
429	Short, John J.–Shuttlesworth, Wm. R.
430	Shuttleton, John–Sim, Archibald
431	Sim, Archie–Simpson, James W.
432	Simpson, James W.–Siver, Robert
433	Siver, Robert–Slaughter, Wm. R.
434	Slaughter, Wm. K.–Smathers, Reuben
435	Smathers, Robert F.–Smith, Chas. G.
436	Smith, Chas. G.–Smith, George
437	Smith, George–Smith, Jacob
438	Smith, Jacob–Smith, John H.
439	Smith, John H.–Smith, John J.
440	Smith, John L.–Smith, Oscar C.
441	Smith, Oscar–Smith, Varde
442	Smith, Varius Q.–Snakle, Peter
443	Snaman Geo. W.–Snyder, James K.
444	Snyder, James L.–Soules, Francis
445	Soules, Benjamin–Speakman, Charles
446	Speakman, Charles Y.–Spickler, Benjamin

Roll	Description
447	Spickler, Chas.–Spurgeon, Jeremiah
448	Spurgeon, Jeremiah–Stanbrough, Joseph B.
449	Stanbrough, Levi–Starling, Abraham
450	Starlin, Adam–Steerman, Charles
451	Steers, Abraham–Sterling, John B.
452	Sterling, John C.–Stevenson, Wm.
453	Stevenson, Wm.–Stickle, Wm. H.
454	Stickle, Wm. H.–Stoddard, Hez.
455	Stoddard, John A.–Stork, Wm.
456	Stork, William–Strauch, Thomas
457	Strauch, Wm.–Stryhn, Louis
458	Stryke, Chas.–Sullivan, Edward
459	Sullivan, Edward–Surkant, Louis
460	Surd, Albert–Swartwood, Almond
461	Swartwood, Alonzo–Swink, Fred
462	Swink, Fred–Tallmadge, Mose
463	Tallmadge, Nenell–Taylor, Chas. E.
464	Taylor, Charles F.–Taylor, George S.
465	Taylor, George T.–Taylor, Septimus
466	Taylor, Seth B.–Temple, Palmer C.
467	Temple, Park E.–Tharp, Washington
468	Tharp, Wilber A.–Thomas, George
469	Thomas, George–Thomas, William
470	Thomas, Wm.–Thompson, Henry R.
471	Thompson, Henry R.–Thompson, Thos.
472	Thompson, Thomas–Thost, Julius
473	Thostenson, Ole–Tilford, Lewis
474	Tilford, Nicholas–Tittsworth, James
475	Tittsworth, John C.–Tompkins, Addison
476	Tompkins, Albert–Towle, Elisha
477	Towle, Ethelbert–Trask, James H.
478	Trask, James H.–Triplett, James H.
479	Triplett, James H.–Truman, Geo. W.
480	Truman, Geo. W.–Tullar, John F.
481	Tullar, John M.–Turner, Leander
482	Turner, Leander–Tyas, Jonathan
483	Tyas, Richard–Underwood, Alonzo
484	Underwood, Ambrose–Valentine, Levi
485	Valentine, Levi–Vandermark, Abram
486	Vandermark, Abram–VanMarter, John
487	VanMarter, Joseph–VanZant, Henry
488	VanZant, Henry P.–Vermillion, Marcus
489	Vermillion, Martin–Visscher, Geo.
490	Visscher, Henry–Vreeland, Benjamin
491	Vreeland, Charles–Wagner, Jasper
492	Wagner, Jeremiah–Waldron, Isaac
493	Waldron, James–Walker, Lyman
494	Walker, Lyman–Wallace, Jos.
495	Wallace, Joseph–Walter, Andrew A.
496	Walter, Andrew F.–Wandross, Mingo
497	Wands, Alburtus–Wardell, George J.
498	Wardell, Henry–Warren, Alonzo
499	Warren, Alonzo S.–Washington, Geo.
500	Washington, Geo.–Watkins, John B.
501	Watkins, John C.–Watt, Levi
502	Watt, Levi–Weaver, Geo. K.
503	Weaver, George–Weber, Adolph
504	Weber, Adolph–Weeks, David
505	Weidenhamer, Chas. H.–Welch, John
506	Welch, John–Wells, James W.
507	Wells, James–Wentzel, Samuel
508	Wentzel, Simon–West, Prima
509	West, Ralph M.–Whalen, James B.
510	Whalen, James E.–Wheelock, DeForest

Roll	Description
511	Wheelock, Edgar L.–White, Charles
512	White, Charles L.–White, Jordan
513	White, Joseph–Whitehead, William K.
514	Whitehead, Wm. W.–Whitlock, Henry L.
515	Whitlock, Hiran E.–Whitten, Geo. W.
516	Whitten, Gilman–Wiesman, Berhard
517	Wiesman, Ferdinand–Wilcoxen, Anthony
518	Wilcoxen, Charles–Wilkerson, Gus
519	Weeks, David–Willan, Thomas
520	Willan, Charles B.–Williams, Daniel
521	Williams, Daniel–Williams, Jacob
522	Williams, Jacob–Williams, Manuel
523	Williams, Mansfield–Williams, Wm. H.
524	Williams, Wm. H.–Willoughby, Wm. A.
525	Willoughby, Wm. A.–Wilson, George
526	Wilson, Geo. A.–Wilson, Joseph
527	Wilson, Joseph–Wilson, Wm. S.
528	Wilson, Wm. S.–Winkley, Edson S.
529	Winkley, Frank H.–Wise, Edward M.
530	Wise, Edward W.–Wixson, Mengo
531	Wixson, Robert–Wolverton, Isaac
532	Wolverton, Jacob–Wood, James
533	Wood, James–Woodcock, Alexander
534	Woodcock, Almon–Woods, Patrick F.
535	Woods, Patrick H.–Wootton, Burton
536	Wootton, Daniel H.–Wright, Alexander
537	Wright, Alexander B.–Wright, Louis
538	Wright, Louis H.–Wyatt, Frederick
539	Wyatt, Garland M.–Yates, Asa
540	Yates, Aubyn Arthur–York, Dan C.
541	York, Daniel–Young, David I.
542	Young, David J.–Young, Rutledge E.
543	Young, Salathiel–Zellman, John
544	Zellman, Wm.–Zytkoskie, Edmund

Index to Mexican War Pension Files, 1887–1926. T317. 14 rolls. 16mm.

This microfilm publication reproduces an alphabetical index to Mexican War pension files, 1887–1926. These pension files are based on service performed in 1846–48. An entry in this index shows the name of a veteran; the name and class of dependent, if any; service data; the application number; and, for an approved claim, the pension certificate number and the State from which the claim was made.

Roll	Description
1	Aaron–Anderson, Aucley
2	Anderson, Charles–Brooks, James H.
3	Brooks, James M.–Cooley, Edward
4	Cooley, Horace K.–Elmore, Stephen
5	Elmore, Thomas–Griffith, Wm. A.
6	Griffith, Wm. D.–Howard, Joshua
7	Howard, Josiah–Lazenby, Robert
8	Lea, Adolphe–Memorank, F.
9	Menard, Alfred B.–Ott, Wm. H.
10	Otten, Heinrich–Robeson, Robert
11	Robey, Thomas–Smith, John
12	Smith, John–Usher, John P.
13	Ussey, Wm. J.–Wright, J. P.
14	Wright, John T.–Zexick, Wm.

Index to Indian Wars Pension Files, 1892–1926. T318. 12 rolls. 16mm.

This microfilm publication reproduces a card index to pension files relating to service in the Indian campaigns between 1817 and 1898. An entry in this index shows the name of a veteran; the name and class of dependent, if any; service data; the application number; and, for an approved claim, the pension certificate number and the State from which the claim was made.

For pension application files concerning men who were disabled or killed in Indian wars and in whose behalf no service claims were made, see the records in the "Old Wars" series. For pension applications relating to persons who served in Indian campaigns during the War of 1812, Mexican War, or Civil War, see the pension indexes relating to claims based on service in those wars.

Roll	Description
1	Aagard, Andrew J.–Bent, Wm.
2	Bentall, Maurice–Chalmers, James
3	Chalmers, Tom Green–Dingins, Mose
4	Dingler, John T.–Gerhardt, John
5	Gerhardt, Karl–Hines, Squire
6	Hines, Wiley–Kirk, Charles
7	Kirk, Frederick–McDonald, Samuel T.
8	McDonald, Sidney B.–Na-Te-Cli
9	Nat-O-E–Ready, George
10	Regan, Daniel–Smith, John
11	Smith, Aaron–Truckey, Nicholas
12	True, Judson E.–Zweig, Louis

Organization Index to Pension Files of Veterans Who Served Between 1861 and 1900. T289. 765 rolls. 16mm.

The index cards reproduced on this microfilm publication refer to pension applications of veterans who served in the U.S. Army between 1861 and 1917. The majority of the records pertain to Civil War veterans, but they also include veterans of the Spanish-American War, the Philippine Insurrection, Indian wars, and World War I.

The information provided here is virtually the same as that in the *General Index to Pension Files, 1861–1934,* T288. Unlike the alphabetical *General Index,* however, this index groups the applicants according to the units in which they served. The cards are arranged alphabetically by State, thereunder by arm of service (infantry, cavalry, artillery), thereunder numerically by regiment, and thereunder alphabetically by veteran's surname.

Each card gives the soldier's name, rank, unit, and terms of service; names of relationships of any dependents; the application number; the certificate number; and the State from which the claim was filed.

A list of abbreviations used in the roll listings follows:

Abbreviation	Full name
Art.	Artillery
Bn.	Batallion
Brig.	Brigade
Btry.	Battery
C.A.C.	Coast Artillery Corps
Cav.	Cavalry
Engs.	Engineers
Engs. & Mech.	Engineers & Mechanics
Enroll.	Enrolled
F & S	Field and Staff
Gds.	Guards
Gen. Serv.	General Service

Abbreviation	Full name
H. Art.	Heavy Artillery
H.G.	Home Guard
Hosp.	Hospital
Ind. Terr.	Indian Territory
Indep.	Independent
Inf.	Infantry
L. Art.	Light Artillery
Mech.	Mechanic
Med.	Medical
Mil.	Militia
Mtd.	Mounted
Phil.	Philippine
Prov.	Provisional
Q.M.	Quartermaster
Q.M.D.	Quartermaster Department
Regt.	Regiment
Res.	Reserve(s)
SAW	Spanish-American War
Squad.	Squadron
SS	Sharp Shooters
Unassign.	Unassigned
Unatt.	Unattached
U.S.A.	U.S. Army
Vet.	Veterans
V.R.C.	Veterans Reserve Corps
Vols.	Volunteers

Roll	Co., Regiment	Name
Alabama:		
1	Unassign., 1 Ala. Col'd Inf.–Co. C, 29 Ala. Inf.	
Alabama–Arkansas:		
2	Unassign., 1 Ala. Inf. (SAW)–Co. A, 1 Ark. Inf.	
Arkansas:		
3	Co. B, 1 Ark. Inf.–Co. A, 1 Ark. Cav.	
4	Co. B, 1 Ark. Cav.–Co. K, 3 Ark. Cav.	
5	Co. L, 3 Ark. Cav.–Co. L, 2 Ark. Inf. (SAW)	
Arkansas–California:		
6	Co. M, 2 Ark. Inf. (SAW)–Co. E, 6 Calif. Inf.	
California:		
7	Co. F, 6 Calif. Inf.–Co. L, 2 Calif. Cav.	
8	Co. M, 2 Calif. Cav.–Co. E, 8 Calif. Inf. (SAW)	
California–Colorado:		
9	Co. F, 8 Calif. Inf. (SAW)–Co. K, 1 Colo. Cav.	
Colorado:		
10	Co. L, 1 Colo. Cav.–Btry. A, 1 Colo. Lt. Art. (SAW)	
Connecticut:		
11	F & S, 1 Conn. Inf.–Co. C, 6 Conn. Inf.	
12	Co. D, 6 Conn. Inf.–Co. B, 9 Conn. Inf.	
13	Co. C, 9 Conn. Inf.–Co. A, 12 Conn. Inf.	
14	Co. B, 12 Conn. Inf.–F & S, 15 Conn. Inf.	
15	Co. A, 15 Conn. Inf.–Co. C, 18 Conn. Inf.	

Roll	Co., Regiment	Name
16	Co. D, 18 Conn. Inf.–	
	Co. C, 22 Conn. Inf.	
17	Co. D, 22 Conn. Inf.–	
	Co. C, 27 Conn. Inf.	
18	Co. D, 27 Conn. Inf.–	Conn. Cav.
	Co. B, 1 Conn. H. Art.	
19	Co. C, 1 Conn. H. Art.–	
	Co. M, 2 Conn. H. Art.	

Connecticut–North Dakota:

20	Indep. Btry., 1 Conn. Lt. Art.–	
	Co. I, 1 N. Dak. Inf. (SAW)	

North Dakota–Delaware:

21	Co. M, 1 N. Dak. Inf. (SAW)–	
	Co. F, 3 Del. Inf.	

Delaware:

22	Co. G, 3 Del. Inf.–	
	Co. C, 1 Del. Cav.	

Delaware–District of Columbia:

23	Co. D, 1 Del. Cav.–	
	Co. A, 2 Bn., D.C. Inf.	

District of Columbia:

24	Co. B, 2 Bn., D.C. Inf.–	
	Co. M, 1 D.C. Inf.	

Florida–Georgia:

25	F & S, 1 Fla. Cav.–	
	2 Ga. Inf. (SAW)	

Georgia–Illinois:

26	Co. A, 2 Ga. Inf. (SAW)–	Murphy
	Co. C, 7 Ill. Inf.	

Illinois:

27	Co. D, 7 Ill. Inf.–	
	Co. A, 9 Ill. Inf.	
28	Co. B, 9 Ill. Inf.–	
	Co. I, 10 Ill. Inf.	
29	Co. K, 10 Ill. Inf.–	
	Co. F, 12 Ill. Inf.	
30	Co. G, 12 Ill. Inf.–	
	Co. A, Vet. Bn., 14/15 Ill. Inf.	
31	Co. B, Vet. Bn., 14/15 Ill. Inf.–	
	Co. I, 16 Ill. Inf.	
32	Co. K, 16 Ill. Inf.–	
	Co. F, 19 Ill. Inf.	
33	Co. G, 19 Ill. Inf.–	
	Co. H, 22 Ill. Inf.	
34	Co. I, 22 Ill. Inf.–	
	Co. I, 25 Ill. Inf.	
35	Co. K, 25 Ill. Inf.–	
	Co. I, 28 Ill. Inf.	Likes
36	Co. I, 28 Ill. Inf.–	McCoy
	Co. A, 31 Ill. Inf.	
37	Co. B, 31 Ill. Inf.–	
	Co. G, 33 Ill. Inf.	
38	Co. H, 33 Ill. Inf.–	
	Co. E, 36 Ill. Inf.	
39	Co. F, 36 Ill. Inf.–	
	Co. F, 39 Ill. Inf.	
40	Co. G, 39 Ill. Inf.–	
	Co. H, 42 Ill. Inf.	
41	Co. I, 42 Ill. Inf.–	
	Co. D, 45 Ill. Inf.	
42	Co. E, 45 Ill. Inf.–	
	Co. F, 47 Ill. Inf.	
43	Co. G, 47 Ill. Inf.–	
	Co. A, 50 Ill. Inf.	
44	Co. B, 50 Ill. Inf.–	

Roll	Co., Regiment	Name
	F & S, 53 Ill. Inf.	
45	Co. A, 53 Ill. Inf.–	
	Co. K, 56 Ill. Mech. Fusilers	
46	F & S, 56 Ill. Inf.–	
	Co. H, 58 Ill. Inf.	
47	Co. I, 58 Ill. Inf.–	
	Co. F, 61 Ill. Inf.	
48	Co. G, 61 Ill. Inf.–	
	Co. G, 64 Ill. Inf.	
49	Co. H, 64 Ill. Inf.–	
	Co. F, 67 Ill. Inf.	
50	Co. G, 67 Ill. Inf.–	
	Co. B, 72 Ill. Inf.	
51	Co. C, 72 Ill. Inf.–	
	Co. K, 75 Ill. Inf.	
52	F & S, 76 Ill. Inf.–	
	Co. A, 79 Ill. Inf.	
53	Co. B, 79 Ill. Inf.–	
	— , 83 Ill. Inf.	
54	Co. A, 83 Ill. Inf.–	
	Co. H, 86 Ill. Inf.	
55	Co. I, 86 Ill. Inf.–	
	Co. B, 91 Ill. Inf.	
56	Co. C, 91 Ill. Inf.–	
	Co. G, 94 Ill. Inf.	
57	Co. H, 94 Ill. Inf.–	
	Co. B, 98 Ill. Inf.	
58	Co. C, 98 Ill. Inf.–	
	Co. H, 101 Ill. Inf.	
59	Co. I, 101 Ill. Inf.–	
	Co. H, 105 Ill. Inf.	
60	Co. I, 105 Ill. Inf.–	
	Co. B, 110 Ill. Inf.	
61	Co. C, 110 Ill. Inf.–	
	Co. K, 113 Ill. Inf.	
62	F & S, 114 Ill. Inf.–	
	Co. B, 118 Ill. Inf.	
63	Co. C, 118 Ill. Inf.–	
	Co. I, 122 Ill. Inf.	
64	Co. K, 122 Ill. Inf.–	
	Co. G, 126 Ill. Inf.	
65	Co. H, 126 Ill. Inf.–	
	Co. B, 131 Ill. Inf.	
66	Co. C, 131 Ill. Inf.–	
	Co. H, 135 Ill. Inf.	
67	Co. I, 135 Ill. Inf.–	
	Co. D, 140 Ill. Inf.	
68	Co. E, 140 Ill. Inf.–	
	Co. H, 144 Ill. Inf.	
69	Co. I, 144 Ill. Inf.–	
	Co. I, 148 Ill. Inf.	
70	Co. K, 148 Ill. Inf.–	
	Co. C, 153 Ill. Inf.	
71	Co. D, 153 Ill. Inf.–	
	Misc. Ill. Vols.	
72	F & S, 1 Ill. Cav.–	
	Co. B, 3 Ill. Cav.	
73	Co. C, 3 Ill. Cav.–	
	Co. A, 5 Ill. Cav.	
74	Co. B, 5 Ill. Cav.–	
	Co. B, 7 Ill. Cav.	
75	Co. C, 7 Ill. Cav.–	
	Co. M, 8 Ill. Cav.	
76	F & S, 9 Ill. Cav.–	
	Co. L, 10 Ill. Cav.	Lynch
77	Co. L, 10 Ill. Cav.–	McGee
	Co. G, 12 Ill. Cav.	
78	Co. H, 12 Ill. Cav.–	

Roll	Co., Regiment	Name
	Co. A, 15 Ill. Cav.	
79	Co. B, 15 Ill. Cav.–	
	F & S, 1 Ill. Lt. Art.	
80	Co. A, 1 Ill. Lt. Art.–	
	Co. D, 2 Ill. Lt. Art.	
81	Co. E, 2 Ill. Lt. Art.–	
	Co. I, 1 Ill. Inf. (SAW)	
82	Co. K, 1 Ill. Inf. (SAW)–	
	Co. G, 4 Ill. Inf. (SAW)	
83	Co. H, 4 Ill. Inf. (SAW)–	
	Co. H, 7 Ill. Inf. (SAW)	
84	Co. I, 7 Ill. Inf. (SAW)–	
	Co. K, 1 Ill. Cav. (SAW)	

Illinois–Indiana:

Roll	Co., Regiment	Name
85	Co. L, 1 Ill. Cav. (SAW)–	
	Co. A, 8 Ind. Inf.	

Indiana:

Roll	Co., Regiment	Name
86	Co. B, 8 Ind. Inf.–	
	Co. A, 10 Ind. Inf.	
87	Co. B, 10 Ind. Inf.–	
	F & S, 12 Ind. Inf.	
88	Co. A, 12 Ind. Inf.–	
	Co. K, 13 Ind. Inf.	
89	F & S, 14 Ind. Inf.–	
	F & S, 17 Ind. Inf.	
90	Co. A, 17 Ind. Inf.–	
	F & S, 20 Ind. Inf.	
91	Co. A, 20 Ind. Inf.–	
	Co. C, 22 Ind. Inf.	
92	Co. D, 22 Ind. Inf.–	
	Co. F, 24 Ind. Inf.	
93	Co. G, 24 Ind. Inf.–	
	F & S, 27 Ind. Inf.	
94	Co. A, 27 Ind. Inf.–	
	Co. G, 30 Ind. Inf.	
95	Co. H, 30 Ind. Inf.–	
	Co. C, 33 Ind. Inf.	
96	Co. D, 33 Ind. Inf.–	
	Co. H, 35 Ind. Inf.	
97	Co. I, 35 Ind. Inf.–	
	Co. H, 38 Ind. Inf.	
98	Co. I, 38 Ind. Inf.–	
	Co. F, 42 Ind. Inf.	
99	Co. G, 42 Ind. Inf.–	
	Co. H, 44 Ind. Inf.	
100	Co. I, 44 Ind. Inf.–	
	Co. I, 48 Ind. Inf.	
101	Co. K, 48 Ind. Inf.–	
	Co. G, 51 Ind. Inf.	
102	Co. H, 51 Ind. Inf.–	
	Co. K, 53 Ind. Inf.	
103	F & S, 54 Ind. Inf.–	
	Co. K, 57 Ind. Inf.	
104	F & S, 58 Ind. Inf.–	
	Co. D, 60 Inf. Ind.	
105	Co. E, 60 Ind. Inf.–	
	Co. A, 67 Ind. Inf.	
106	Co. B, 67 Ind. Inf.–	
	Co. F, 70 Ind. Inf.	
107	Co. G, 70 Ind. Inf.–	
	Co. C, 74 Ind. Inf.	
108	Co. D, 74 Ind. Inf.–	
	Co. D, 80 Ind. Inf.	
109	Co. E, 80 Ind. Inf.–	
	Co. D, 84 Ind. Inf.	
110	Co. E, 84 Ind. Inf.–	
	Co. A, 88 Ind. Inf.	

Roll	Co., Regiment	Name
111	Co. B, 88 Ind. Inf.–	
	Co. E, 93 Ind. Inf.	
112	Co. F, 93 Ind. Inf.–	
	Co. D, 101 Ind. Inf.	
113	Co. E, 101 Ind. Inf.–	
	Co. D, 118 Ind. Inf.	
114	Co. E, 118 Ind. Inf.–	
	Co. A, 128 Ind. Inf.	
115	Co. B, 128 Ind. Inf.–	
	Co. A, 133 Ind. Inf.	
116	Co. B, 133 Ind. Inf.–	
	Co. A, 137 Ind. Inf.	
117	Co. B, 137 Ind. Inf.–	
	F & S, 142 Ind. Inf.	
118	Co. A, 142 Ind. Inf.–	
	Co. A, 146 Ind. Inf.	
119	Co. B, 146 Ind. Inf.–	
	Co. I, 149 Ind. Inf.	
120	Co. K, 149 Ind. Inf.–	
	Co. G, 153 Ind. Inf.	
121	Co. H, 153 Ind. Inf.–	
	F & S & Band, 158 Ind. Inf. (SAW)	
122	Co. A, 158 Ind. Inf. (SAW)–	
	Co. M, 160 Ind. Inf. (SAW)	
123	F & S, 161 Ind. Inf. (SAW)–	
	Co. C, 1 Ind. Cav.	
124	Co. D, 1 Ind. Cav.–	
	Unassign. and F & S, 4 Ind. Cav.	
125	Co. A, 4 Ind. Cav.–	
	Co. H, 6 Ind. Cav.	
126	Co. I, 6 Ind. Cav.–	
	Co. F, 9 Ind. Cav.	
127	Co. G, 9 Ind. Cav.–	
	Co. K, 12 Ind. Cav.	
128	Co. L, 12 Ind. Cav.–	
	Btry. 1 Indep. Btry. Ind. Lt. Art.	
129	Indep. Btry.(2) Ind. Lt. Art.–	
	Indep. Btry., 20 Ind. Lt. Art. (Ind. Ter.)	
130	Indep. Btry., 21 Ind. Lt. Art.–	
	Co. M, 3 Ind. H.G. Inf.	

Indiana–Iowa:

Roll	Co., Regiment	Name
131	F & S, 4 Ind. T.H.G. Inf.–	
	Co. K, 3 Iowa Inf.	

Iowa:

Roll	Co., Regiment	Name
132	F & S, 4 Iowa Inf.–	
	Co. B, 7 Iowa Inf.	
133	Co. C, 7 Iowa Inf.–	
	F & S, 10 Iowa Inf.	
134	Co. A, 10 Iowa Inf.–	
	Co. K, 12 Iowa Inf.	
135	Unassign. and F & S, 13 Iowa Inf.–	
	Co. C, 15 Iowa Inf.	
136	Co. D, 15 Iowa Inf.–	
	Co. C, 18 Iowa Inf.	
137	Co. D, 18 Iowa Inf.–	
	Co. K, 21 Iowa Inf.	
138	F & S, 22 Iowa Inf.–	
	Co. F, 25 Iowa Inf.	
139	Co. G, 25 Iowa Inf.–	
	Unassign. and F & S, 29 Iowa Inf.	
140	Co. A, 29 Iowa Inf.–	
	Co. C, 32 Iowa Inf.	
141	Co. D, 32 Iowa Inf.–	
	Co. I, 34 Iowa Inf.	
142	Co. K, 34 Iowa Inf.–	
	Co. E, 38 Iowa Inf.	

Roll	Co., Regiment	Name
143	Co. F, 38 Iowa Inf.– Co. C, 45 Iowa Inf.	
144	Co. D, 45 Iowa Inf.– Co. M, 49 Iowa Inf. (SAW)	
145	Unassign. and F & S, 50 Iowa Inf. (SAW)– Co. L, 52 Iowa Inf. (SAW)	
146	Co. M, 52 Iowa Inf. (SAW)– Co. H, 2 Iowa Cav.	
147	Co. I, 2 Iowa Cav.– Co. H, 4 Iowa Cav.	
148	Co. I, 4 Iowa Cav.– Co. C, 7 Iowa Cav.	
149	Co. D, 7 Iowa Cav.– Indep. Btry., 2 Iowa Lt. Art.	

Iowa–Kansas:

Roll	Co., Regiment	Name
150	Indep. Btry., 3 Iowa Lt. Art.– Co. K, 3 Kans. Inf.	

Kansas:

Roll	Co., Regiment	Name
151	Co. L, 3 Kans. Inf. & Cav.– Co. B, 7 Kans. Cav.	
152	Co. C, 7 Kans. Cav.– Co. A, 10 Kans. Inf.	
153	Co. B, 10 Kans. Inf.– Co. A, 13 Kans. Inf.	
154	Co. B, 13 Kans. Inf.– Co. I, 16 Kans. Cav.	
155	Co. K, 16 Kans. Cav.– Co. I, 21 Kans. Inf. (SAW)	
156	Co. K, 21 Kans. Inf. (SAW)– Indep. Btry., 2 Kans. Lt. Art.	Longacre

Kansas–Kentucky:

Roll	Co., Regiment	Name
157	Indep. Btry., 2 Kans. Lt. Art.– Co. E, 3 Ky. Inf.	McKinzey

Kentucky:

Roll	Co., Regiment	Name
158	Co. F, 3 Ky. Inf.– Co. E, 6 Ky. Inf.	
159	Co. F, 6 Ky. Inf.– Co. D, 9 Ky. Inf.	
160	Co. E, 9 Ky. Inf.– Co. F, 12 Ky. Inf.	
161	Co. G, 12 Ky. Inf.– Co. D, 15 Ky. Inf.	
162	Co. E, 15 Ky. Inf.– Co. C, 18 Ky. Inf.	
163	Co. D, 18 Ky. Inf.– Co. K, 21 Ky. Inf.	
164	Unassign. and F & S, 22 Ky. Inf.– F & S, 26 Ky. Inf.	
165	Co. A, 26 Ky. Inf.– Co. A, 32 Ky. Inf.	
166	Co. B, 32 Ky. Inf.– Co. B, 39 Ky. Inf.	
167	Co. C, 39 Ky. Inf.– Co. K, 45 Ky. Inf.	
168	Unassign. Misc., 46 Ky. Inf.– Co. H, 52 Ky. Mtd. Inf.	Lucas
169	Co. I, 52 Ky. Mtd. Inf.– Co. A, Halls Gap Bn., Capitol Gds. Ky. Inf.	
170	Co. B, Halls Gap Bn., Capitol Gds. Ky. Inf.– Co. H, 1 Ky. Cav.	Luttrell
171	Co. H, 1 Ky. Cav.– Co. L, 4 Ky. Cav.	McClanahan
172	F & S, 5 Ky. Cav.– Co. I, 7 Ky. Cav.	

Roll	Co., Regiment	Name
173	Co. K, 7 Ky. Cav.– Co. K, 10 Ky. Cav.	
174	Co. L, 10 Ky. Cav.– Co. K, 13 Ky. Cav.	
175	Co. L, 13 Ky. Cav.– Co. K, 17 Ky. Cav.	
176	Co. L, 17 Ky. Cav.– Co. A, 3 Ky. Inf. (SAW)	

Kentucky–Louisiana:

Roll	Co., Regiment	Name
177	Co. B, 3 Ky. Inf. (SAW)– Co. B, 2 La. Inf.	

Louisiana:

Roll	Co., Regiment	Name
178	Co. C, 2 La. Inf.– Co. K, 4 La. Corps d'Afrique Inf.	
179	Co. A, 5 La. Corps d'Afrique Inf.– Co. I, 11 La. Corps d'Afrique Inf.	
180	Co. K, 11 La. Corps d'Afrique Inf.– Co. F, 1 La. Corps d'Afrique Engs.	
181	Co. G, 1 La. Corps d'Afrique Engs.– Co. K, 1 La. Inf. (SAW)	

Louisiana–Maine:

Roll	Co., Regiment	Name
182	Co. L, 1 La. Inf. (SAW)– Co. E, 3 Maine Inf.	

Maine:

Roll	Co., Regiment	Name
183	Co. F, 3 Maine Inf.– Co. K, 6 Maine Inf.	
184	Unassign. and F & S, 7 Maine Inf.– Co. E, 9 Maine Inf.	
185	Co. F, 9 Maine Inf.– Co. B, 12 Maine Inf.	
186	Co. C, 12 Maine Inf.– Co. G, 14 Maine Inf.	
187	Co. H, 14 Maine Inf.– Co. B, 17 Maine Inf.	
188	Co. C, 17 Maine Inf.– Co. C, 20 Maine Inf.	
189	Co. D, 20 Maine Inf.– Co. C, 24 Maine Inf.	
190	Co. D, 24 Maine Inf.– Unassign. and F & S, 29 Maine Inf.	
191	Co. A, 29 Maine Inf.– Co. H & Unassign., 31 Maine Inf.	
192	Co. I, 31 Maine Inf.– Unassign. And F & S, 1 Maine Cav.	
193	Co. A, 1 Maine Cav.– Co. L, 1 Maine Cav.	Ludden
194	Co. L, 1 Maine Cav.– Co. G, 1 Maine H. Art.	McAllister
195	Co. H, 1 Maine H. Art.– Co. F, 1 Maine Inf. (SAW)	

Maine–Maryland:

Roll	Co., Regiment	Name
196	Co. G, 1 Maine Inf. (SAW)– Co. F, 2 Md. Inf.	

Maryland:

Roll	Co., Regiment	Name
197	Co. G, 2 Md. Inf.– Co. H, 5 Md. Inf.	
198	Co. I, 5 Md. Inf.– Co. K, 9 Md. Inf.	Roach
199	Unassign. and F & S, 10 Md. Inf.– Co. I, 13 Md. Inf.	
200	Co. K, 13 Md. Inf.– Co. C, 2 Md. Inf., Potomac Home Brig.	
201	Co. D, 2 Md. Inf., Potomac Home Brig.– Co. C, 1 Md. Cav.	
202	Co. D, 1 Md. Cav.–	

Roll	Co., Regiment	Name
	Co. A, Purnell Legion, Md. Cav.	

Maryland–Massachusetts:

Roll	Co., Regiment	Name
203	Co. B, Purnell Legion, Md. Cav.– F & S, 1 Mass. Inf.	

Massachusetts:

Roll	Co., Regiment	Name
204	Co. A, 1 Mass. Inf.– Co. D, 3 Mass. Inf.	
205	Co. E, 3 Mass. Inf.– Co. A, 5 Mass. Inf.	
206	Co. B, 5 Mass. Inf.– Co. E, 7 Mass. Inf.	
207	Co. F, 7 Mass. Inf.– Co. K, 9 Mass. Inf.	
208	Unassign. and F & S, 10 Mass. Inf.– Co. G, 12 Mass. Inf.	
209	Co. H, 12 Mass. Inf.– Co. A, 16 Mass. Inf.	
210	Co. B, 16 Mass. Inf.– Co. D, 18 Mass. Inf.	
211	Co. E, 18 Mass. Inf.– Co. I, 20 Mass. Inf.	
212	Co. K, 20 Mass. Inf.– Co. G, 23 Mass. Inf.	
213	Co. H, 23 Mass. Inf.– Co. A, 26 Mass. Inf.	
214	Co. B, 26 Mass. Inf.– Co. G, 28 Mass. Inf.	
215	Co. H, 28 Mass. Inf.– Co. E, 31 Mass. Inf.	
216	Co. F, 31 Mass. Inf.– Co. I, 33 Mass. Inf.	
217	Co. K, 33 Mass. Inf.– Co. F, 36 Mass. Inf.	
218	Co. G, 36 Mass. Inf.– Co. D, 39 Mass. Inf.	
219	Co. E, 39 Mass. Inf.– Co. G, 42 Mass. Inf.	
220	Co. H, 42 Mass. Inf.– Co. D, 46 Mass. Inf.	
221	Co. E, 46 Mass. Inf.– Co. C, 50 Mass. Inf.	
222	Co. D, 50 Mass. Inf.– Unassign. and F & S, 54 Mass. Inf.	
223	Co. A, 54 Mass. Inf.– Co. B, 57 Mass. Inf.	
224	Co. C, 57 Mass. Inf.– Co. E, 59 Mass. Inf.	
225	Co. F, 59 Mass. Inf.– Unattached, 25 Unatt. Co. Mass. Inf.	
226	Unattached, 26 Unatt. Co. Mass. Inf.– Co. L, 2 Mass. Cav.	Swank
227	Unassign. and F & S, 3 Mass. Cav.– Co. F, 5 Mass. Cav.	
228	Co. G, 5 Mass. Cav.– Co. F, 2 Mass. H. Art.	
229	Co. G, 2 Mass. H. Art.– Co. I, 4 Mass. H. Art.	
230	Co. K, 4 Mass. H. Art.– Indep. Btry., 13 Mass. Lt. Art.	
231	Indep. Btry., 14 Mass. Lt. Art.– Co. A, 8 Mass. Inf. (SAW)	

Massachusetts–Michigan:

Roll	Co., Regiment	Name
232	Co. B, 8 Mass. Inf. (SAW)– Co. I, 1 Mich. Inf.	

Michigan:

Roll	Co., Regiment	Name
233	Co. K, 1 Mich. Inf.– Co. A, 4 Mich. Inf.	

Roll	Co., Regiment	Name
234	Co. B, 4 Mich. Inf.– Co. H, 6 Mich. Inf.	
235	Co. I, 6 Mich. Inf.– Co. G, 9 Mich. Inf.	
236	Co. H, 9 Mich. Inf.– Co. C, 12 Mich. Inf.	
237	Co. D, 12 Mich. Inf.– Co. E, 14 Mich. Inf.	
238	Co. F, 14 Mich. Inf.– Co. G, 17 Mich. Inf.	
239	Co. H, 17 Mich. Inf.– Co. C, 21 Mich. Inf.	
240	Co. D, 21 Mich. Inf.– Co. A, 24 Mich. Inf.	
241	Co. B, 24 Mich. Inf.– Co. K, 27 Mich. Inf.	
242	Unassign. and F & S, 28 Mich. Inf.– Co. L, 31 Mich. Inf. (SAW)	
243	Co. M, 31 Mich. Inf. (SAW)– Co. G, 35 Mich. Inf. (SAW)	
244	Co. H, 35 Mich. Inf. (SAW)– Co. G, 1 Mich. Engs. & Mech.	
245	Co. H, 1 Mich. Engs. & Mech.– F & S, 2 Mich. Cav.	
246	Co. A, 2 Mich. Cav.– Co. C, 4 Mich. Cav.	
247	Co. D, 4 Mich. Cav.– Co. B, 7 Mich. Cav.	
248	Co. C, 7 Mich. Cav.– Co. C, 9 Mich. Cav.	
249	Co. D, 9 Mich. Cav.– Co. B, 1 Mich. Lt. Art. and U.S. Lancers, Mich. Cav.	

Michigan–Minnesota:

Roll	Co., Regiment	Name
250	Co. C, 1 Mich. Lt. Art.– Co. A, 1 Minn. Inf.	Lyons

Minnesota:

Roll	Co., Regiment	Name
251	Co. A, 1 Minn. Inf.– Co. I, 3 Minn. Inf.	McCulloch
252	Co. K, 3 Minn. Inf.– Co. B, 7 Minn. Inf.	
253	Co. C, 7 Minn. Inf.– Co. F, 11 Minn. Inf.	
254	Co. G, 11 Minn. Inf.– Co. I, 14 Minn. Inf. (SAW)	
255	Co. K, 14 Minn. Inf. (SAW)– Co. E, Hatch's Bn., Minn. Cav.	

Minnesota–Mississippi:

Roll	Co., Regiment	Name
256	Co. F, Hatch's Bn., Minn. Cav.– Co. D, 6 Miss. Inf.	

Mississippi:

Roll	Co., Regiment	Name
257	Co. E, 6 Miss. Inf.– Co. E, 3 Miss. Inf. (SAW)	

Mississippi–Missouri:

Roll	Co., Regiment	Name
258	Co. F, 3 Miss. Inf. (SAW)– Co. D, 4 Mo. Inf.	

Missouri:

Roll	Co., Regiment	Name
259	Co. E, 4 Mo. Inf.– Co. C, 9 Mo. Inf.	
260	Co. D, 9 Mo. Inf.– Co. A, 14 Mo. Inf.	
261	Co. B, 14 Mo. Inf.– Co. E, 21 Mo. Inf.	
262	Co. F, 21 Mo. Inf.– Co. E, 25 Mo. Inf.	Fletcher
263	Co. E, 25 Mo. Inf.– Co. B, 31 Mo. Inf.	Guyer

Roll	Co., Regiment	Name
264	Co. C, 31 Mo. Inf.– Cos. intermingled, 37 Mo. Inf.	
265	Cos. intermingled, 38 Mo. Inf.– Co. I, 43 Mo. Inf.	Collins
266	Co. K, 43 Mo. Inf.– Co. E, 48 Mo. Inf.	
267	Co. F, 48 Mo. Inf.– Co. E, 2 Mo. Col'd. Inf.	
268	Co. F, 2 Mo. Col'd Inf.– Co. C, 5 Prov. Enroll. Mo. Militia	
269	Co. D, 5 Prov. Enroll. Mo. Militia– Co. I, 9 Prov. Enroll. Mo. Militia	
270	Cos. intermingled, 10 Enroll. Mo. Militia– Co. C, 44 Enroll. Mo. Militia	
271	Co. D, 44 Enroll. Mo. Militia– Co. B, 69 Enroll. Mo. Militia	
272	Co. C, 69 Enroll. Mo. Militia– Co. K, Mo. Engs. of the West	
273	Co. L, Mo. Engs. of the West– Co. F, Cass County Mo. H.G. Cav.	
274	Co. G, Cass County Mo. H.G. Cav.– Mayo's Prov. Enroll. Mo. Militia	
275	Co. Mercer, Bn. Mo. Militia Inf.– Co. D, Webster County Mo. H.G.	
276	Westerberg's Indep. Co., Mo. Militia Cav.– Co. I, 1 U.S. Res. Corps, Mo. Inf.	
277	Co. K, 1 U.S. Res. Corps, Mo. Inf.– Co. F, 1 Bn. U.S. Res. Corps, Mo. Inf.	
278	F & S, 1 Mo. State Militia Inf.– Co. C, 1 Mo. Cav.	
279	Co. D, 1 Mo. Cav.– Co. F, 3 Mo. Cav.	
280	Co. G, 3 Mo. Cav.– Co. D, 6 Mo. Cav.	
281	Co. E, 6 Mo. Cav.– Co. C, 10 Mo. Cav.	
282	Co. D, 10 Mo. Cav.– Co. F, 13 Mo. Cav.	
283	Co. G, 13 Mo. Cav.– Co. I, 2 Bn. Mo. Militia Cav.	Murphey
284	Cos. intermingled, 10 Bn. Mo. Militia Cav.– Co. C, 3 Mo. State Militia Cav.	Orendor
285	Co. C, 3 Mo. State Militia Cav.– Co. I, 5 Mo. State Militia Cav.	Payton
286	Co. K, 5 Mo. State Militia Cav.– Co. H, 8 Mo. State Militia Cav.	
287	Co. I, 8 Mo. State Militia Cav.– Co. C, 11 Mo. State Militia Cav.	Loeffler
288	Co. C, 11 Mo. State Militia Cav.– Co. L, 1 Mo. Lt. Art.	McCallister
289	Co. M, 1 Mo. Lt. Art.– Co. G, 1 Mo. Inf. (SAW)	
290	Co. H, 1 Mo. Inf. (SAW)– Co. G, 5 Mo. Inf. (SAW)	

Missouri–Nebraska:
291	Co. H, 5 Mo. Inf. (SAW)– Co. I, 1 Neb. Cav.	

Nebraska:
292	Co. K, 1 Neb. Cav.– F & S and Unassign., 3 Neb. Inf. (SAW)	

Nebraska–New Hampshire:
293	Co. A, 3 Neb. Inf. (SAW)– Co. B, 3 New Hamp. Inf.	

New Hampshire:
Roll	Co., Regiment	Name
294	Co. B, 3 New Hamp. Inf.– Co. F & S, 6 New Hamp. Inf.	
295	Co. A, 6 New Hamp. Inf.– Co. C, 9 New Hamp. Inf.	
296	Co. D, 9 New Hamp. Inf.– Co. B, 13 New Hamp. Inf.	
297	Co. C, 13 New Hamp. Inf.– Co. E, 18 New Hamp. Inf.	
298	Co. F, 18 New Hamp. Inf.– Co. I, 1 New Hamp. H. Art.	

New Hampshire–New Jersey:
299	Co. K, 1 New Hamp. H. Art.– Co. D, 2 N.J. Inf.	

New Jersey:
300	Co. E, 2 N.J. Inf.– Co. K, 4 N.J. Inf.	
301	F & S, 5 N.J. Inf.– Co. B, 8 N.J. Inf.	
302	Co. C, 8 N.J. Inf.– Co. K, 10 N.J. Inf.	
303	F & S, 11 N.J. Inf.– Co. G, 13 N.J. Inf.	
304	Co. H, 13 N.J. Inf.– Co. I, 22 N.J. Inf.	
305	Co. K, 22 N.J. Inf.– Co. F, 27 N.J. Inf.	
306	Co. G, 27 N.J. Inf.– Co. C, 33 N.J. Inf.	
307	Co. D, 33 N.J. Inf.– Co. K, 38 N.J. Inf.	
308	F & S, 39 N.J. Inf.– Co. E, 2 N.J. Cav.	
309	Co. F, 2 N.J. Cav.– Co. G, 1 N.J. Inf. (SAW)	

New Jersey–New Mexico:
310	Co. H, 1 N.J. Inf. (SAW)– Co. E, 1 New Mex. Inf.	

New Mexico:
311	Co. F, 1 New Mex. Inf.– Vigil's New Mex. Cav.	

New Mexico–New York:
312	Simpson's Indep. Mtd. Spies & Scouts, New Mex.– Co. A, 5 N.Y. Inf.	Loud

New York:
313	Co. A, 5 N.Y. Inf.– Co. B, 8 N.Y. Inf.	McAuliffe
314	Co. C, 8 N.Y. Inf.– Co. C, 11 N.Y. Inf.	
315	Co. D, 11 N.Y. Inf.– Co. B, 16 N.Y. Inf.	
316	Co. C, 16 N.Y. Inf.– Co. G, 20 N.Y. Inf.	
317	Co. H, 20 N.Y. Inf.– Co. D, 25 N.Y. Inf.	
318	Co. E, 25 N.Y. Inf.– Co. D, 29 N.Y. Inf.	
319	Co. E, 29 N.Y. Inf.– Co. G, 34 N.Y. Inf.	
320	Co. H, 34 N.Y. Inf.– Co. C, 39 N.Y. Inf.	
321	Co. D, 39 N.Y. Inf.– F & S, 42 N.Y. Inf.	
322	Co. A, 42 N.Y. Inf.– Co. I, 45 N.Y. Inf.	

Roll	Co., Regiment	Name
323	Co. K, 45 N.Y. Inf.–	
	Co. A, 49 N.Y. Inf.	
324	Co. B, 49 N.Y. Inf.–	
	Co. C, 54 N.Y. Inf.	
325	Co. D, 54 N.Y. Inf.–	
	Co. E, 58 N.Y. Inf.	
326	Co. F, 58 N.Y. Inf.–	
	Co. C, 109 N.Y. Inf.	Worrick

Entire 59 N.Y. Inf., also Co. G, 106 N.Y. Inf. (beginning with McNanny). See roll 340.

Roll	Co., Regiment	Name
327	Unassign. and F & S, 60 N.Y. Inf.–	
	Co. F, 63 N.Y. Inf.	
328	Co. G, 63 N.Y. Inf.–	
	Co. D, 67 N.Y. Inf.	
329	Co. E, 67 N.Y. Inf.–	
	Co. G, 70 N.Y. Inf.	
330	Co. H, 70 N.Y. Inf.–	
	Co. B, 75 N.Y. Inf.	
331	Co. C, 75 N.Y. Inf.–	
	Co. A, 78 N.Y. Inf.	
332	Co. B, 78 N.Y. Inf.–	
	Co. H, 81 N.Y. Inf.	
333	Co. I, 81 N.Y. Inf.–	
	Co. E, 85 N.Y. Inf.	
334	Co. F, 85 N.Y. Inf.–	
	Co. B, 90 N.Y. Inf.	
335	Co. C, 90 N.Y. Inf.–	
	Co. I, 92 N.Y. Inf.	
336	Co. K, 92 N.Y. Inf.–	
	Co. I, 95 N.Y. Inf.	
337	Co. K, 95 N.Y. Inf.–	
	Co. F, 98 N.Y. Inf.	
338	Co. G, 98 N.Y. Inf.–	
	Co. B, 102 N.Y. Inf.	
339	Co. C, 102 N.Y. Inf.–	
	Co. G, 106 N.Y. Inf.	Lyman (see roll 326)
340	Co. G, 106 N.Y. Inf.–	Mead (see roll 326)
	Co. C, 109 N.Y. Inf.	
341	Co. D, 109 N.Y. Inf.–	
	Co. F, 112 N.Y. Inf.	
342	Co. G, 112 N.Y. Inf.–	
	Co. A, 117 N.Y. Inf.	
343	Co. B, 117 N.Y. Inf.–	
	Co. I, 120 N.Y. Inf.	
344	Co. K, 120 N.Y. Inf.–	
	Co. C, 124 N.Y. Inf.	
345	Co. D, 124 N.Y. Inf.–	
	Co. C, 128 N.Y. Inf.	Lyden
346	Co. C, 128 N.Y. Inf.–	
	Co. E, 134 N.Y. Inf.	McKown
347	Co. F, 134 N.Y. Inf.–	
	Co. C, 140 N.Y. Inf.	
348	Co. D, 140 N.Y. Inf.–	
	Co. I, 143 N.Y. Inf.	
349	Co. K, 143 N.Y. Inf.–	
	Co. F, 147 N.Y. Inf.	
350	Co. G, 147 N.Y. Inf.–	
	Co. D, 151 N.Y. Inf.	
351	Co. E, 151 N.Y. Inf.–	
	Co. H, 154 N.Y. Inf.	
352	Co. I, 154 N.Y. Inf.–	
	Co. B, 160 N.Y. Inf.	
353	Co. C, 160 N.Y. Inf.–	
	Co. I, 162 N.Y. Inf.	
354	Co. K, 162 N.Y. Inf.–	

Roll	Co., Regiment	Name
	Co. I, 173 N.Y. Inf.	
355	Co. K, 173 N.Y. Inf.–	
	Co. C, 182 N.Y. Inf.	
356	Co. D, 182 N.Y. Inf.–	
	Co. D, 188 N.Y. Inf.	
357	Co. E, 188 N.Y. Inf.–	
	Co. D, 7 N.Y. Mil. Inf.	
358	Co. E, 7 N.Y. Mil. Inf.–	
	Co. H, 20 N.Y. Mil. Inf.	
359	Co. I, 20 N.Y. Mil. Inf.–	
	Co. B, 69 N.Y. Mil. Inf.	
360	Co. C, 69 N.Y. Mil. Inf.–	
	Co. E, 1 N.Y. Engs.	
361	Co. F, 1 N.Y. Engs.–	
	Co. A, 50 N.Y. Engs.	
362	Co. B, 50 N.Y. Engs.–	
	Co. B, 1 N.Y. Mtd. Rifles	
363	Co. C, 1 N.Y. Mtd. Rifles–	
	Co. M, 1 N.Y. Cav.	
364	Unassign. and F & S, 2 N.Y. Cav.–	
	Co. L, 3 N.Y. Cav.	Libeau
365	Co. L, 3 N.Y. Cav.–	McCarthy
	Co. B, 7 N.Y. Cav.	
366	Co. C, 7 N.Y. Cav.–	
	Co. C, 9 N.Y. Cav.	
367	Co. D, 9 N.Y. Cav.–	
	Co. H, 11 N.Y. Cav.	
368	Co. I, 11 N.Y. Cav.–	
	Co. G, 15 N.Y. Cav.	
369	Co. H, 15 N.Y. Cav.–	
	Co. C, 20 N.Y. Cav.	
370	Co. D, 20 N.Y. Cav.–	
	Co. B, 24 N.Y. Cav.	
371	Co. C, 24 N.Y. Cav.–	
	Co. A, 2 N.Y. Vet. Cav.	
372	Co. B, 2 N.Y. Vet. Cav.–	
	Co. E, 3 N.Y. Prov. Cav.	
373	Co. F, 3 N.Y. Prov. Cav.–	
	Co. L, 1 N.Y. Lt. Art.	
374	Co. M, 1 N.Y. Lt. Art.–	
	Co. B, 3 N.Y. Lt. Art.	
375	Co. C, 3 N.Y. Lt. Art.–	
	Co. E, 4 N.Y. H. Art.	
376	Co. F, 4 N.Y. H. Art.–	
	Co. L, 5 N.Y. H. Art.	
377	Co. M, 5 N.Y. H. Art.–	
	Co. A, 7 N.Y. H. Art.	
378	Co. B, 7 N.Y. H. Art.–	
	Co. A, 9 N.Y. H. Art.	
379	Co. B, 9 N.Y. H. Art.–	
	Co. C, 10 N.Y. H. Art.	
380	Co. D, 10 N.Y. H. Art.–	
	Co. B, 14 N.Y. H. Art.	
381	Co. C, 14 N.Y. H. Art.–	
	Co. B, 16 N.Y. H. Art.	
382	Co. C, 16 N.Y. H. Art.–	
	6 Indep. Btry., N.Y. Lt. Art.	
383	7 Indep. Btry., N.Y. Lt. Art.–	
	30 Indep. Btry., N.Y. Lt. Art.	
384	31 Indep. Btry., N.Y. Lt. Art.–	
	Co. C, 8 N.Y. Inf. (SAW)	
385	Co. D, 8 N.Y. Inf. (SAW)–	
	Co. F, 22 N.Y. Inf. (SAW)	
386	Co. G, 22 N.Y. Inf. (SAW)–	
	Co. I, 71 N.Y. Inf. (SAW)	

Roll	Co., Regiment	Name
	New York–North Carolina:	
387	Co. K, 77 N.Y. Inf. (SAW)–	
	Co. E, 1 N.C. Inf.	
	North Carolina:	
388	Co. F, 1 N.C. Inf.–	
	Misc. Vols.–N.C., Unknown Service,	
	Unassign. recruits, Citizens Vol.,	
	some SAW	
	North Carolina–Ohio:	
389	F & S, 1 N.C. Inf. (SAW)–	
	Co. F, 1 Ohio Inf.	
	Ohio:	
390	Co. G, 1 Ohio Inf.–	
	Co. F, 4 Ohio Inf.	
391	4 Ohio Inf.–	
	Co. E, 7 Ohio Inf.	
392	Co. F, 7 Ohio Inf.–	
	Co. A, 11 Ohio Inf.	
393	Co. B, 11 Ohio Inf.–	
	Co. A, 12 Ohio Inf.	
394	Co. B, 12 Ohio Inf.–	
	Co. F, 14 Ohio Inf.	
395	Co. G, 14 Ohio Inf.–	
	Co. I, 16 Ohio Inf.	
396	Co. K, 16 Ohio Inf.–	
	Co. H, 18 Ohio Inf.	
397	Co. I, 18 Ohio Inf.–	
	Co. H, 20 Ohio Inf.	
398	Co. I, 20 Ohio Inf.–	
	Co. C, 23 Ohio Inf.	
399	Co. D, 23 Ohio Inf.–	
	Co. C, 26 Ohio Inf.	
400	Co. D, 26 Ohio Inf.–	
	Co. F, 29 Ohio Inf.	
401	Co. G, 29 Ohio Inf.–	
	Co. C, 32 Ohio Inf.	
402	Co. D, 32 Ohio Inf.–	
	Co. E, 35 Ohio Inf.	
403	Co. F, 35 Ohio Inf.–	
	Co. E, 38 Ohio Inf.	
404	Co. F, 38 Ohio Inf.–	
	Co. G, 41 Ohio Inf.	
405	Co. H, 41 Ohio Inf.–	
	Co. I, 44 Ohio Inf.	Titus
406	Co. K, 44 Ohio Inf.–	
	Co. C, 48 Ohio Inf.	
407	Co. D, 48 Ohio Inf.–	
	Co. B, 49 Ohio Inf.	
408	Co. C, 49 Ohio Inf.–	
	Co. B, 52 Ohio Inf.	
409	Co. C, 52 Ohio Inf.–	
	Co. I, 55 Ohio Inf.	Love
410	Co. I, 55 Ohio Inf.–	
	Co. F, 59 Ohio Inf.	McConnell
411	Co. G, 59 Ohio Inf.–	
	Co. G, 62 Ohio Inf.	
412	Co. H, 62 Ohio Inf.–	
	Co. I, 65 Ohio Inf.	
413	Co. K, 65 Ohio Inf.–	
	Unassign. and F & S, 69 Ohio Inf.	
414	Co. A, 69 Ohio Inf.–	
	Co. I, 72 Ohio Inf.	
415	Co. K, 72 Ohio Inf.–	
	Co. D, 76 Ohio Inf.	
416	Co. E, 76 Ohio Inf.–	
	Co. F, 79 Ohio Inf.	
417	Co. G, 79 Ohio Inf.–	

Roll	Co., Regiment	Name
	Co. I, 82 Ohio Inf.	
418	Co. K, 82 Ohio Inf.–	
	Co. E, 86 Ohio Inf.	
419	Co. F, 86 Ohio Inf.–	
	Co. G, 89 Ohio Inf.	
420	Co. H, 89 Ohio Inf.–	
	Co. H, 91 Ohio Inf.	
421	Co. I, 91 Ohio Inf.–	
	Co. D, 92 Ohio Inf.	
422	Co. E, 92 Ohio Inf.–	
	Co. D, 96 Ohio Inf.	
423	Co. E, 96 Ohio Inf.–	*
	Co. G, 100 Ohio Inf.	
	Co. D of the 99 Ohio Inf. follows Co. H.	
424	Co. H, 100 Ohio Inf.–	
	Co. I, 104 Ohio Inf.	
425	Co. K, 104 Ohio Inf.–	
	Co. E, 110 Ohio Inf.	
426	Co. F, 110 Ohio Inf.–	
	Unassign. and F & S, 115 Ohio Inf.	Sharer
427	Co. A, 115 Ohio Inf.–	
	Co. I, 120 Ohio Inf.	
428	Co. K, 120 Ohio Inf.–	
	Unassign. and F & S, 125 Ohio Inf.	
429	Co. A, 125 Ohio Inf.–	
	Co. I, 129 Ohio Inf.	
430	Co. I, 129 Ohio Inf.–	
	Co. I, 134 Ohio Inf.	
431	Co. K, 134 Ohio Inf.–	
	Co. F, 140 Ohio Inf.	
432	Co. G, 140 Ohio Inf.–	
	Co. E, 145 Ohio Inf.	
433	Co. F, 145 Ohio Inf.–	
	Co. D, 150 Ohio Inf.	
434	Co. E, 150 Ohio Inf.–	
	Co. F, 155 Ohio Inf.	
435	Co. G, 155 Ohio Inf.–	
	Co. E, 161 Ohio Inf.	
436	Co. F, 161 Ohio Inf.–	
	Unassign. and F & S, 167 Ohio Inf.	
437	Co. A, 167 Ohio Inf.–	
	Co. B, 172 Ohio Inf.	
438	Co. C, 172 Ohio Inf.–	
	Co. H, 176 Ohio Inf.	
439	Co. I, 176 Ohio Inf.–	
	Co. F, 181 Ohio Inf.	
440	Co. G, 181 Ohio Inf.–	
	Co. G, 185 Ohio Inf.	
441	Co. H, 185 Ohio Inf.–	
	Co. A, 191 Ohio Inf.	
442	Co. B, 191 Ohio Inf.–	
	Co. G, 195 Ohio Inf.	
443	Co. H, 195 Ohio Inf.–	
	Misc. & Unknown, Various Ohio Cos.	Lyons
444	Misc. & Unknown, Various Ohio	McCaslin
	Cos.–	
	Co. A, 3 Ohio Cav.	
445	Co. B, 3 Ohio Cav.–	
	Co. E, 5 Ohio Cav.	
446	Co. F, 5 Ohio Cav.–	
	Co. C, 8 Ohio Cav.	
447	Co. D, 8 Ohio Cav.–	
	Co. B, 11 Ohio Cav.	
448	Co. C, 11 Ohio Cav.–	
	—, 3 Indep. Ohio Cav.	
449	—, 4 Indep. Ohio Cav.–	
	Co. L, 2 Ohio H. Art.	
450	Co. M, 2 Ohio H. Art.–	

Roll	Co., Regiment	Name
	—, 5 Indep. Btry., Ohio Lt. Art.	
451	—, 6 Indep. Btry., Ohio Lt. Art.– Co. C, 1 Ohio Inf. (SAW)	
452	Co. D, 1 Ohio Inf. (SAW)– Co. H, 4 Ohio Inf. (SAW)	
453	Co. I, 4 Ohio Inf. (SAW)– Co. C, 8 Ohio Inf. (SAW)	

Ohio–Oregon:

Roll	Co., Regiment	Name
454	Co. D, 8 Ohio Inf. (SAW)– Misc., Various Oregon Cos. (including some Indian wars)	

Oregon–Pennsylvania:

Roll	Co., Regiment	Name
455	Unassign. and F & S, 1 Oregon Inf.– Co. K, 2 Pa. Inf.	

Pennsylvania:

Roll	Co., Regiment	Name
456	F & S, 3 Pa. Inf.– Co. A, 11 Pa. Inf.	
457	Co. B, 11 Pa. Inf.– Co. C, 17 Pa. Inf.	
458	Co. D, 17 Pa. Inf.– Co. H, 24 Pa. Inf.	
459	Co. I, 24 Pa. Inf.– Co. N, 28 Pa. Inf.	
460	Co. O, 28 Pa. Inf.– Co. G, 32 Pa. Inf.	
461	Co. H, 32 Pa. Inf.– Co. D, 35 Pa. Inf.	
462	Co. E, 35 Pa. Inf.– Co. I, 39 Pa. Inf.	
463	Co. K, 39 Pa. Inf.– Co. H, 45 Pa. Inf.	
464	Co. I, 45 Pa. Inf.– Co. F, 48 Pa. Inf.	
465	Co. G, 48 Pa. Inf.– Co. B, 51 Pa. Inf.	
466	Co. C, 51 Pa. Inf.– Co. I, 53 Pa. Inf.	
467	Co. K, 53 Pa. Inf.– Co. F, 56 Pa. Inf.	
468	Co. G, 56 Pa. Inf.– Co. D, 61 Pa. Inf.	
469	Co. E, 61 Pa. Inf.– Co. B, 67 Pa. Inf.	
470	Co. C, 67 Pa. Inf.– Co. A, 72 Pa. Inf.	
471	Co. B, 72 Pa. Inf.– Co. K, 76 Pa. Inf.	
472	Co. H, 76 Pa. Inf.– Co. C, 78 Pa. Inf.	
473	Co. D, 78 Pa. Inf.– Co. B, 82 Pa. Inf.	
474	Co. C, 82 Pa. Inf.– Co. G, 84 Pa. Inf.	
475	Co. H, 84 Pa. Inf.– Co. A, 87 Pa. Inf.	
476	Co. B, 87 Pa. Inf.– Co. C, 91 Pa. Inf.	
477	Co. D, 91 Pa. Inf.– Co. L, 95 Pa. Inf.	
478	Co. F, 96 Pa. Inf.– Co. I, 98 Pa. Inf.	
479	Co. K, 98 Pa. Inf.– Co. B, 101 Pa. Inf.	
480	Co. C, 101 Pa. Inf.– Co. G, 103 Pa. Inf.	
481	Co. H, 103 Pa. Inf.– Co. F, 106 Pa. Inf.	

Roll	Co., Regiment	Name
482	Co. G, 106 Pa. Inf.– Co. E, 111 Pa. Inf.	
483	Co. F, 111 Pa. Inf.– Co. E, 119 Pa. Inf.	
484	Co. F, 119 Pa. Inf.– Co. F, 125 Pa. Inf.	Lewis
485	Co. F, 125 Pa. Inf.– Co. C, 130 Pa. Inf.	McClure
486	Co. D, 130 Pa. Inf.– Co. I, 134 Pa. Inf.	Folks
487	Co. I, 134 Pa. Inf.– Co. H, 139 Pa. Inf.	Hague
488	Co. I, 139 Pa. Inf.– Co. I, 143 Pa. Inf.	
489	Co. K, 143 Pa. Inf.– Co. K, 148 Pa. Inf.	
490	Unassign. and F & S, 149 Pa. Inf.– F & S, 155 Pa. Inf.	
491	Co. A, 155 Pa. Inf.– Co. D, 167 Pa. Inf.	
492	Co. E, 167 Pa. Inf.– Co. H, 173 Pa. Inf.	
493	Co. I, 173 Pa. Inf.– Co. B, 183 Pa. Inf.	
494	Co. C, 183 Pa. Inf.– Co. I, 188 Pa. Inf.	
495	Co. K, 188 Pa. Inf.– Co. B, 193 Pa. Inf.	
496	Co. C, 193 Pa. Inf.– Co. H, 197 Pa. Inf.	
497	Co. I, 197 Pa. Inf.– Co. I, 201 Pa. Inf.	
498	Co. K, 201 Pa. Inf.– Unassign. and F & S, 207 Pa. Inf.	
499	Co. A, 207 Pa. Inf.– Co. G, 211 Pa. Inf.	
500	Co. H, 211 Pa. Inf.– Co. C, 29 Pa. Mil. Inf.	Lowe
501	Varied, not in order, 29 Pa. Mil. Inf.– Varied, not in order, 54 Pa. Mil. Inf.	McCarter Lyon
502	Varied, not in order, 54 Pa. Mil. Inf.– Varied, not in order, Erie Pa. Inf.	McAteer Lytle
503	Varied, not in order, Erie Pa. Inf.– Misc., Pa. Cav.	McClelland Manns
504	Varied, not in order, Mason's Bn., Pa. Mil.– Co. K, 2 Pa. Cav. *There is 1 Inf.: Mason's Bn., Pa. Mil.	
505	Co. L, 2 Pa. Cav.– Unassign. and F & S, 5 Pa. Cav.	
506	Co. A, 5 Pa. Cav.– Co. M, 6 Pa. Cav.	
507	Co. B, 7 Pa. Cav.– Co. B, 9 Pa. Cav.	
508	Co. C, 9 Pa. Cav.– Co. H, 12 Pa. Cav.	
509	Co. I, 12 Pa. Cav.– Co. A, 15 Pa. Cav.	
510	Co. B, 15 Pa. Cav.– Co. A, 17 Pa. Cav.	
511	Co. B, 17 Pa. Cav.– Co. A, 20 Pa. Cav.	
512	Co. B, 20 Pa. Cav.– Co. B, 22 Pa. Cav.	
513	Co. C, 22 Pa. Cav.– Co. A, 3 Pa. Prov. Cav.	
514	Co. B, 3 Pa. Prov. Cav.– Co. D, 2 Pa. H. Art.	Lynch

Roll	Co., Regiment	Name
515	Co. D, 2 Pa. H. Art.–	McCartney
	Co. D, 3 Pa. H. Art.	
516	Co. E, 3 Pa. H. Art.–	
	Co. B, 6 Pa. H. Art.	
517	Co. C, 6 Pa. H. Art.–	
	Co. D, Indep. Btry., Pa. Lt. Art.	Fry
518	Co. D, Indep. Btry., Pa. Lt. Art.–	Gable
	Co. H, Indep. Btry., Pa. Lt. Art.	
519	Co. I, Indep. Btry., Pa. Lt. Art.–	
	Co. L, 4 Pa. Inf. (SAW)	
520	Co. M, 4 Pa. Inf. (SAW)–	
	Co. G, 9 Pa. Inf. (SAW)	
521	Co. H, 9 Pa. Inf. (SAW)–	
	Co. A, 16 Pa. Inf. (SAW)	

Pennsylvania–Rhode Island:

522	Co. B, 16 Pa. Inf. (SAW)–	
	Co. F, 2 R.I. Inf.	

Rhode Island:

523	Co. G, 2 R.I. Inf.–	
	Co. A, 11 R.I. Inf.	
524	Co. B, 11 R.I. Inf.–	
	Co. A, 1 R.I. Lt. Art.	
525	Co. B, 1 R.I. Lt. Art.–	
	F & S, 1 R.I. Inf. (SAW)	

Rhode Island–South Carolina:

526	Co. A, 1 R.I. Inf. (SAW)–	
	Co. L, 1 S.C. Inf. (SAW)	

South Carolina–Tennessee:

527	Co. M, 1 S.C. Inf. (SAW)–	
	Co. D, 3 Tenn. Inf.	

Tennessee:

528	Co. E, 3 Tenn. Inf.–	
	Co. A, 8 Tenn. Inf.	
529	Co. B, 8 Tenn. Inf.–	
	Co. A, 2 Tenn. Mtd. Inf.	
530	Co. B, 2 Tenn. Mtd. Inf.–	
	Co. F, 7 Tenn. Mtd. Inf.	
531	Co. G, 7 Tenn. Mtd. Inf.–	
	Co. G, 3 Tenn. Cav.	
532	Co. H, 3 Tenn. Cav.–	
	Co. C, 5 Tenn. Cav.	
533	Co. D, 5 Tenn. Cav.–	
	Co. E, 8 Tenn. Cav.	
534	Co. F, 8 Tenn. Cav.–	
	Co. C, 11 Tenn. Cav.	
535	Co. D, 11 Tenn. Cav.–	
	Co. E, 1 Tenn. H. Art.	
536	Co. F, 1 Tenn. H. Art.–	
	Co. H, 2 Tenn. Inf. (SAW)	

Tennessee–Texas:

537	Co. I, 2 Tenn. Inf. (SAW)–	
	Co. H, 1 Tex. Cav.	

Texas:

538	Co. I, 1 Tex. Cav.–	
	Co. M, 1 Tex. Inf. (SAW)	
539	F & S, 2 Tex. Inf. (SAW)–	
	Co. K, 1 Tex. Cav. (SAW)	

Texas–U.S. Cavalry:

540	Co. L, 1 Tex. Cav. (SAW)–	
	Co. B, 4 U.S.C. Inf.	

U.S. Cavalry:

541	Co. C, 4 U.S.C. inf.–	
	Co. G, 7 U.S.C. Inf.	
542	Co. H, 7 U.S.C. Inf.–	
	Co. K, 10 U.S.C. Inf.	
543	F & S, 11 U.S.C. Inf.–	

Roll	Co., Regiment	Name
	Co. I, 13 U.S.C. Inf.	
544	Co. K, 13 U.S.C. Inf.–	
	Co. I, 16 U.S.C. Inf.	
545	Co. K, 16 U.S.C. Inf.–	
	Co. A, 20 U.S.C. Inf.	Freeman
546	Co. A, 20 U.S.C. Inf.–	Gurnett
	Co. G, 23 U.S.C. Inf.	
547	Co. H, 23 U.S.C. Inf.–	
	Co. D, 25 U.S.C. Inf.	
548	Co. E, 25 U.S.C. Inf.–	
	Co. A, 29 U.S.C. Inf.	
549	Co. B, 29 U.S.C. Inf.–	
	Co. A, 33 U.S.C. Inf.	
550	Co. B, 33 U.S.C. Inf.–	
	Co. F, 36 U.S.C. Inf.	
551	Co. G, 36 U.S.C. Inf.–	
	Co. A, 40 U.S.C. Inf.	
552	Co. B, 40 U.S.C. Inf.–	
	Co. G, 44 U.S.C. Inf.	
553	Co. H, 44 U.S.C. Inf.–	
	Co. I, 48 U.S.C. Inf.	
554	Co. K, 48 U.S.C. Inf.–	
	Co. H, 52 U.S.C. Inf.	
555	Co. I, 52 U.S.C. Inf.–	
	Co. H, 56 U.S.C. Inf.	
556	Co. I, 56 U.S.C. Inf.–	
	Co. E, 60 U.S.C. Inf.	
557	Co. F, 60 U.S.C. Inf.–	
	Co. D, 64 U.S.C. Inf.	
558	Co. E, 64 U.S.C. Inf.–	
	Co. E, 68 U.S.C. Inf.	
559	Co. F, 68 U.S.C. Inf.–	
	Co. H, 74 U.S.C. Inf.	
560	Co. I, 74 U.S.C. Inf.–	
	Co. D, 79 U.S.C. Inf.	
561	Co. E, 79 U.S.C. Inf.–	
	Co. B, 81 U.S.C. Inf.	
562	Co. C, 81 U.S.C. Inf.–	
	Co. H, 84 U.S.C. Inf.	
563	Co. I, 84 U.S.C. Inf.–	
	Co. I, 92 U.S.C. Inf.	
564	Co. K, 92 U.S.C. Inf.–	
	Co. A, 100 U.S.C. Inf.	
565	Co. B, 100 U.S.C. Inf.–	
	Co. C, 104 U.S.C. Inf.	
566	Co. D, 104 U.S.C. Inf.–	
	Co. A, 110 U.S.C. Inf.	
567	Co. B, 110 U.S.C. Inf.–	
	Co. E, 114 U.S.C. Inf.	
568	Co. F, 114 U.S.C. Inf.–	
	Co. G, 118 U.S.C. Inf.	
569	Co. H, 118 U.S.C. Inf.–	
	Co. I, 123 U.S.C. Inf.	
570	Co. K, 123 U.S.C. Inf.–	
	Co. C, 135 U.S.C. Inf.	

U.S. Cavalry–U.S. Colored Troops:

571	Co. D, 135 U.S.C. Inf.–	
	Unknown, U.S.C.T.	Byles
572	Unknown, U.S.C.T.–	Cabney
	Co. G, 3 U.S.C. Cav.	
573	Co. H, 3 U.S.C. Cav.–	
	Co. C, 1 U.S.C. H. Art.	
574	Co. D, 1 U.S.C. H. Art.–	
	Co. B, 4 U.S.C. H. Art.	
575	Co. C, 4 U.S.C. H. Art.–	
	Co. K, 5 U.S.C. H. Art.	
576	Co. L, 5 U.S.C. H. Art.–	
	Co. F, 8 U.S.C. H. Art.	

Roll	Co., Regiment	Name
577	Co. G, 8 U.S.C. H. Art.– Co. L, 11 U.S.C. H. Art.	
578	Co. M, 11 U.S.C. H. Art.– Co. F, 14 U.S.C. H. Art.	

U.S. Colored Troops–Utah:

Roll	Co., Regiment	Name
579	Co. G, 14 U.S.C. H. Art.– Misc. Utah Mil. Cav.(some Inf., some Indian wars)	Jensen

Utah–Vermont:

Roll	Co., Regiment	Name
580	Misc. Utah Mil. Cav.(some Indian Wars; 1 Utah Home Gds. Inf.)– Co. A, 3 Vt. Inf.	Jeppesen

Vermont:

Roll	Co., Regiment	Name
581	Co. B, 3 Vt. Inf.– Co. F, 5 Vt. Inf.	
582	Co. G, 5 Vt. Inf.– Co. C, 8 Vt. Inf.	
583	Co. D, 8 Vt. Inf.– Co. A, 11 Vt. Inf.	
584	Co. B, 11 Vt. Inf.– Co. B, 15 Vt. Inf.	
585	Co. C, 15 Vt. Inf.– Co. G, 1 Vt. Cav.	
586	Co. H, 1 Vt. Cav.– —, 3 Indep. Btry., Vt. Lt. Art.	

Vermont–Veterans Reserve Corps:

Roll	Co., Regiment	Name
587	F & S, 1 Vt. Inf. (SAW)– Co. C, 4 V.R.C.	

Veterans Reserve Corps:

Roll	Co., Regiment	Name
588	Co. D, 4 V.R.C.– Co. E, 8 V.R.C.	
589	Co. F, 8 V.R.C.– Co. A, 12 V.R.C.	
590	Co. B, 12 V.R.C.– Co. I, 15 V.R.C.	
591	Co. K, 15 V.R.C.– Co. H, 19 V.R.C.	
592	Co. I, 19 V.R.C.– Co. I, 23 V.R.C.	
593	Co. K, 23 V.R.C.– Co. 18, 2 Btry. V.R.C.	
594	Co. 19, 2 Btry. V.R.C.– Co. 64, 2 Bn. V.R.C.	
595	Co. 65, 2 Bn. V.R.C.– Co. 115, 2 Bn. V.R.C.	
596	Co. 116, 2 Bn. V.R.C.– Co. 163, 2 Bn. V.R.C.	

Veterans Reserve Corps–Virginia:

Roll	Co., Regiment	Name
597	Co. 164, 2 Bn. V.R.C.– Co. B, 2 Va. Inf. (SAW)	Rison

Virginia–Washington Territory:

Roll	Co., Regiment	Name
598	Co. B, 2 Va. Inf. (SAW)– F & S, 1 Wash. Ter. Inf.	Robertson

Washington Territory–West Virginia:

Roll	Co., Regiment	Name
599	Co. A, 1 Wash. Ter. Inf.– Co. H, 2 W. Va. Inf.	McGinley

West Virginia:

Roll	Co., Regiment	Name
600	Co. H, 2 W. Va. Inf.– Co. A, 6 W. Va. Inf.	McNally
601	Co. B, 6 W. Va. Inf.– Co. F, 7 W. Va. Inf.	
602	Co. F, 7 W. Va. Inf.– Co. A, 11 W. Va. Inf.	Lewellan Lightner Lyon
603	Co. A, 11 W. Va. Inf.–	Kelley

Roll	Co., Regiment	Name
	Co. E, 14 W. Va. Inf.	Haught, E.
604	Co. E, 14 W. Va. Inf.– Co. D, 2 W. Va. Vet. Inf.	Haught
605	Co. E, 2 W. Va. Vet. Inf.– Co. E, 2 W. Va. Cav.	B Pine
606	Co. E, 2 W. Va. Cav.– Co. K, 5 W. Va. Cav.	Porter Brown
607	Co. K, 5 W. Va. Cav.– —, Indep. Btry. D, W. Va. Lt. Art.	Broy Smith

West Virginia–Wisconsin:

Roll	Co., Regiment	Name
608	—, Indep. Btry. D, W. Va. Lt. Art.– Co. F, 1 Wis. Inf.	Snider Lovell
609	Co. F, 1 Wis. Inf.– Co. K, 3 Wis. Inf.	McCabe Corbett
610	Co. K, 3 Wis. Inf.– Co. H, 6 Wis. Inf.	Cossentine Hall
611	Co. H, 6 Wis. Inf.– Co. G, 9 Wis. Inf.	Harlocker Dilges
612	Co. G, 9 Wis. Inf.– Co. H, 12 Wis. Inf.	Eberhardt Tabor
613	Co. H, 12 Wis. Inf.–	Tabor, R. Dicken
	Co. K, 15 Wis. Inf.	
614	Co. K, 15 Wis. Inf.– Co. C, 18 Wis. Inf.	Ellefson Evans
615	Co. E, 18 Wis. Inf.– Unassign. and F & S, 22 Wis. Inf.	A Blood
616	Unassign. and F & S, 22 Wis. Inf.– Co. H, 25 Wis. Inf.	Bloodgood Betts
617	Co. H, 25 Wis. Inf.– Co. H, 29 Wis. Inf.	Brauner W
618	Co. I, 29 Wis. Inf.– Co. E, 33 Wis. Inf.	A Roark
619	Co. E, 33 Wis. Inf.– F & S, 38 Wis. Inf.	Robinson W
620	Co. A, 38 Wis. Inf.– Co. F, 43 Wis. Inf.	
621	Co. G, 43 Wis. Inf.– Co. E, 48 Wis. Inf.	A Lippert
622	Co. E, 48 Wis. Inf.– F & S, 1 Wis. Cav.	Maresch Fox
623	Unassign. and F & S, 1 Wis. Cav.– Co. A, 3 Wis. Cav.	Goodrich Jordan
624	Co. A, 3 Wis. Cav.– Co. A, 1 Wis. H. Art.	Keyes Z
625	Co. B, 1 Wis. H. Art.– —, 13 Indep. Btry., Wis. Lt. Art.	A Jones
626	—, 13 Indep. Btry., Wis. Lt. Art.– Co. H, 4 Wis. Inf. (SAW)	Kappelman Z

Wisconsin–U.S. Infantry:

Roll	Co., Regiment	Name
627	Co. I, 4 Wis. Inf. (SAW)– Co. E, 1 U.S. Inf.	

U.S. Infantry:

Roll	Co., Regiment	Name
628	Co. F, 1 U.S. Inf.– Co. A, 2 U.S. Inf.	Boroughs
629	Co. A, 2 U.S. Inf.– Co. G, 2 U.S. Inf.	Bottorff Evins
630	Co. G, 2 U.S. Inf.– Co. A, 3 U.S. Inf.	Falkor Krois
631	Co. A, 3 U.S. Inf.– Co. H, 3 U.S. Inf.	Lafayette Swint
632	Co. H, 3 U.S. Inf.– Co. D, 4 U.S. Inf.	Talley Gunset
633	Co. D, 4 U.S. Inf.– Co. M, 4 U.S. Inf.	Habedank Y
634	F & S, 5 U.S. Inf.–	A

Roll	Co., Regiment	Name
	Co. F, 5 U.S. Inf.	Cuskes
635	Co. F, 5 U.S. Inf.–	Daniels
	Unassign. and F & S, 6 U.S. Inf.	Myers
636	Unassign. and F & S, 6 U.S. Inf.–	Neal
	Co. H, 6 U.S. Inf.	Descole
637	Co. H, 6 U.S. Inf.–	Devine
	Co. B, 7 U.S. Inf.	Z
638	Co. C, 7 U.S. Inf.–	
	Co. I, 7 U.S. Inf.	
639	Co. K, 7 U.S. Inf.–	A
	Co. D, 8 U.S. Inf.	Kelly
640	Co. D, 8 U.S. Inf.–	Kelly, T.
	Co. L, 8 U.S. Inf.	Barker
641	Co. L, 8 U.S. Inf.–	Gus Barker
	Co. F, 9 U.S. Inf.	Collins
642	Co. F, 9 U.S. Inf.–	Wm. B. Collins
	Co. A, 10 U.S. Inf.	Moss
643	Co. A, 10 U.S. Inf.–	Mullin
	Co. H, 10 U.S. Inf.	Z
644	Co. I, 10 U.S. Inf.	Abel / Gow
	Co. I, 10 U.S. Inf.	Z
645	Co. K, 10 U.S. Inf.–	
	Co. C, 1 Bn., 11 U.S. Inf.	
646	Co. C, 11 U.S. Inf.–	Yeatman
	Co. K, 11 U.S. Inf.	Monroe
647	Co. K, 11 U.S. Inf.–	Moore
	Co. D, 2 Bn., 12 U.S. Inf.	Houck
648	Co. D, 1 Bn., 12 U.S. Inf.–	Phillip Houck
	Co. L, 12 U.S. Inf.–	McGehee
649	Co. L, 12 U.S. Inf.–	McGeraty
	Co. E, 13 U.S. Inf.	Pruitt
650	Co. E, 13 U.S. Inf.–	Purcell
	Supply and F & S, 14 U.S. Inf.	Swindall
651	Unassign. and F & S, Det. 14 U.S. Inf.–	Tate
	Co. F, 14 U.S. Inf.	Curtis
652	Co. F, 14 U.S. Inf.–	Fallon
	—, Cas. Det. 15 U.S. Inf.	Pettit
653	—, Cas. Det. 15 U.S. Inf.–	Petty
	Co. F, 1 Bn., 15 U.S. Inf.	Renzer
654	Co. F, 1 Bn., 15 U.S. Inf.–	Revis
	Co. A, 16 U.S. Inf.	Peyton
655	Co. A, 2 Bn., 16 U.S. Inf.–	Phatt
	Co. G, 1 Bn., 16 U.S. Inf.	Whalen
656	Co. G, 16 U.S. Inf.–	Wild
	Co. B, 17 U.S. Inf.	Z
657	Co. C, 17 U.S. Inf.–	A
	Co. K, 17 U.S. Inf.	Fuller
658	Co. K, 17 U.S. Inf.–	Gallagher
	Unassign., 18 U.S. Inf.	Sweet
659	Cas. Det., Unassign. and F & S, 18 U.S. Inf.–	Tarman
	Co. E, 18 U.S. Inf.	Simmons
660	Co. E, 18 U.S. Inf.–	Smith
	Co. L, 18 U.S. Inf.	Landas
661	Co. L, 18 U.S. Inf.–	Lavy
	Co. E, 19 U.S. Inf.	Byrne
662	Co. E, 19 U.S. Inf.–	Cahn
	Co. M, 19 U.S. Inf.	Z
663	F & S, 20 U.S. Inf.–	A
	Co. E, 20 U.S. Inf.	Findley
664	Co. E, 20 U.S. Inf.–	Fisher
	Co. B, 21 U.S. Inf.	Curley
665	Co. B, 21 U.S. Inf.–	Dakin
	Co. I, 21 U.S. Inf.	Guise
666	Co. I, 21 U.S. Inf.–	Gunselus
	Co. E, 22 U.S. Inf.	Morton
667	Co. E, 22 U.S. Inf.–	Mulcahy
	Co. A, 23 U.S. Inf.	Vale
668	Co. A, 23 U.S. Inf.–	Vance
	Co. I, 23 U.S. Inf.	Henison
669	Co. I, 23 U.S. Inf.–	Henry
	Co. B, 24 U.S. Inf.	Elliot
670	Co. B, 24 U.S. Inf.–	Ellis
	Co. K, 24 U.S. Inf.	Kyler
671	Co. K, 24 U.S. Inf.–	Larkins
	Co. G, 25 U.S. Inf.	Myles
672	Co. G, 25 U.S. Inf.–	Nelson
	Co. H, 26 U.S. Inf.	Rutherford
673	Co. H, 26 U.S. Inf.–	Sanders
	Co. L, 27 U.S. Inf.	Martinez
674	Co. L, 27 U.S. Inf.–	Maukkin
	Co. B, 29 U.S. Inf.	Benge
675	Co. B, 29 U.S. Inf.–	Bartley
	Co. E, 30 U.S. Inf.	Curran
676	Co. E, 30 U.S. Inf.–	Daily
	Co. H, 33 U.S. Inf.	Johnson
677	Co. H, 33 U.S. Inf.–	Jones
	Co. D, 40 U.S. Inf.	Thomas
678	Co. D, 40 U.S. Inf.–	Toney
	Various, 54 U.S. Inf.	Z
679	Various, 55 U.S. Inf.–	A
	Unassign. and F & S, 5 U.S. Vol. Inf.	Wanless
680	Co. A, 5 U.S. Vol. Inf.–	Adams
	Co. H, 6 U.S. Vet. Vol. Inf.	Ludwig
681	Co. H, 6 U.S. Vet. Vol. Inf.–	M
	Co. M, 3 U.S. Vol. Inf. (SAW)	Y
682	F & S, 4 U.S. Vol. Inf. (SAW)–	B
	Co. C, 9 U.S. Vol. Inf. (SAW)	T
683	Co. D, 9 U.S. Vol. Inf. (SAW)–	A
	Co. I, 28 U.S. Vol. Inf. (SAW)	Christy
684	Co. I, 28 U.S. Vol. Inf. (SAW)–	Clark
	Co. D, 32 U.S. Vol. Inf. (SAW)	Sommers
685	Co. D, 32 U.S. Vol. Inf. (SAW)–	Spangler
	Co. K, 35 U.S. Vol. Inf. (SAW)	Reed
686	Co. K, 35 U.S. Vol. Inf. (SAW)–	Riley
	Co. L, 39 U.S. Vol. Inf. (SAW)	Jordan
687	Co. L, 39 U.S. Vol. Inf. (SAW)–	Kantola
	Co. G, 43 U.S. Vol. Inf. (SAW)	Blake
688	Co. G, 43 U.S. Vol. Inf. (SAW)–	Boston
	Co. B, 47 U.S. Vol. Inf. (SAW)	Englert
689	Co. B, 47 U.S. Vol. Inf. (SAW)–	Evans
	Various, Puerto Rican U.S. Vol. Inf. (SAW)	Chacon

U.S. Infantry–U.S. Cavalry:

Roll	Co., Regiment	Name
690	Various, Puerto Rican U.S. Vol. Inf. (SAW)–	Charron
	Co. E, 1 U.S. Cav.	Bond

U.S. Cavalry:

Roll	Co., Regiment	Name
691	Co. E, 1 U.S. Cav.–	William Bond
	Co. L, 1 U.S. Cav.	Ullman
692	Co. L, 1 U.S. Cav.–	Van Houton
	Co. F, 2 U.S. Cav.	Jackson
693	Co. F, 2 U.S. Cav.–	James
	Cas. Det., Unassign. and F & S, 3 U.S. Cav.	Shadoan
694	Cas. Det., Unassign. and F & S, 3 U.S. Cav.–	Shank
	Co. F, 3 U.S. Cav.	McGovern

Roll	Co., Regiment	Name	Roll	Co., Regiment	Name
695	Co. F, 3 U.S. Cav.–	McGowan	725	Co. 4, U.S. C.A.C.–	Saylor
	Co. A, 4 U.S. Cav.	Isham		Co. 15, U.S. C.A.C.	Grant
696	Co. A, 4 U.S. Cav.–	Jacobson	726	Co. 15, U.S. C.A.C.–	Robert
	Co. H, 4 U.S. Cav.	Stewart			Grant
697	Co. H, 4 U.S. Cav.–	Struad		Co. 36, U.S. C.A.C.	McCarthy
	Co. C, 5 U.S. Cav.	Cerrita	727	Co. 36, U.S. C.A.C.–	McHargue
698	Co. C, 5 U.S. Cav.–	Chandler		Co. 59, U.S. C.A.C.	Hammond
	Co. D, 5 U.S. Cav.	Proffitt	728	Co. 59, U.S. C.A.C.–	Edward
699	Co. D, 5 U.S. Cav.–	Quinlan			Hammond
	Co. M, 5 U.S. Cav.	Barton		Co. 78, U.S. C.A.C.	Yettaw
700	Co. M, 5 U.S. Cav.–	Bushon	729	Co. 79, U.S. C.A.C.–	A
	Co. E, 6 U.S. Cav.	Thomas		Co. 106, U.S. C.A.C.	Joseph
701	Co. E, 6 U.S. Cav.–	Otha			Conrad
		Thomas	730	Co. 106, U.S. C.A.C.–	Cormier
	Co. L, 6 U.S. Cav.	Jamison		Co. 144, U.S. C.A.C.	Yung
702	Co. L, 6 U.S. Cav.–	Janis	731	Co. 145, U.S. C.A.C.–	A
	Co. G, 7 U.S. Cav.	Dunlap		8 Band, U.S. C.A.C.	Stretz
703	Co. G, 7 U.S. Cav.–	Dunn	732	8 Band, U.S. C.A.C.–	Summers
	Co. C, 8 U.S. Cav.	King		Brig. Band, U.S. Vols.	Hamilton
704	Co. C, 8 U.S. Cav.–	Kingrey	733	Brig. Band, U.S. Vols.–	Harkinson
	Unassign., Cas. Det., 9 U.S. Cav.	Brew		Co. A, 1 Bn., U.S. Engs.	Lyons
705	F & S, Unassign., & Cas. Det., 9 U.S. Cav.–	Brinson	734	Co. A, 1 Bn., U.S. Engs.–	McCarthy
				Co. K, 3 Bn., U.S. Engs.	Pope
	Co. I, 9 U.S. Cav.	Duncan	735	Co. K, 3 Bn., U.S. Engs.–	Prow
706	Co. I, 9 U.S. Cav.–	Danker		Various, 16 U.S. Engs.	Stark
	Co. F, 10 U.S. Cav.	Johnson, M.	736	Co. A, 16 U.S. Engs.–	Streeter
				Co. M, 3 U.S. Vol. Engs.	Z
707	Co. F, 10 U.S. Cav.–	Johnson, W.	737	(Presidents of the U.S.)	
				Commander in Chief, U.S.A.–	Adams
	Co. K, 11 U.S. Cav.	Z		Gen. Serv. U.S.A., Misc. groups & Unassign.	Churchill
708	Co. L, 11 U.S. Cav.–	A			
	Co. C, 14 U.S. Cav.	Westivell	738	Gen. Serv. U.S.A.–	Charles Churchill
709	Co. C, 14 U.S. Cav.–	Wiggins			
	Co. C, 1 U.S. Vol. Cav.	Hill		Gen. Serv. U.S.A., Serv. U.S. Cav.	Howard
			739	Gen. Serv. U.S.A. & Misc.–	Frank Howard
U.S. Cavalry–U.S. Artillery:					
710	Co. C, 1 U.S. Vol. Cav.–	Howland		Unassign. U.S.A., Gen. Serv. U.S.A. & Misc.	Pickerell
	Co. A, 1 U.S. Art.	Dalton	740	Gen. Serv. U.S.A.–	Pickering
U.S. Artillery:				2 Regt., Gen. Serv. U.S. Engs., Gen. Serv. U.S.A.	Power
711	Co. A, 1 U.S. Art.–	Eaker	741	2 Regt., Gen. Serv. U.S.A.–	James Power
	Co. H, 1 U.S. Art.	Mangan			
712	Co. H, 1 U.S. Art.–	Manhns		Hosp. Corps, U.S.A., Med. Dept. U.S.A.	Beckner
	Co. H, 1 U.S. Art.	Young	742	Hosp. Corps, U.S.A., Med. Dept. U.S.A.–	Beckton
713	Co. I, 1 U.S. Art.–	A			
	Co. C, 2 U.S. Art.	Boyson		Hosp. Corps, U.S.A.	Hairrold
714	Co. C, 2 U.S. Art.–	Bozi	743	Hosp. Corps, U.S.A.–	Hake
	Co. K, 2 U.S. Art.	Knapp		Hosp. Corps, U.S.A.	Newman
715	Co. K, 3 U.S. Art.–	Murphy	744	Hosp. Corps, U.S.A.–	William Newman
	Co. C, 3 U.S. Field Art.	Painter			
716	Co. C, 3 U.S. Art.–	Rivinius		Hosp. Corps, U.S.A.	White
	Co. L, 3 U.S. Art.	Mahoney	745	Hosp. Corps, U.S.A.–	White
717	Co. L, 3 U.S. Art.–	March		Med. Dept., U.S. Vols.	Cutler
	Co. F, 4 U.S. Art.	Barrick	746	Med. Dept., U.S. Vols.–	Dailey
718	Co. F, 4 U.S. Art.–	Callahan		Med. Dept., U.S.A. (nurses)	Kauffman
	Co. A, 5 U.S. Art.	Z	747	Med. Dept., U.S. Vols. (nurses)–	Keane
719	Co. B, 5 U.S. Art.–	Abbott		Unknown U.S. Vols.	Nichols
	Co. I, 5 U.S. Art.	Kurtz	748	Unknown U.S. Vols.–	Harns
720	Co. I, 5 U.S. Art.–	Lacey			Nickels
	Co. L, 6 U.S. Art.	Guy		Miss. Gunboat Flotilla, U.S. Vols.	Josiah
Miscellaneous Units:			749	West. Gunboat Flotilla, M.M.B., U.S. Vols. Inf.,	
721	Co. L, 6 U.S. Art.–	Hajek		Miss. Gunboat Flotilla, U.S. Vols.–	Keating
	Various Cos., 11 U.S. Field Art.	Rumore		Ord. Dept. U.S.A.	Zalanf
722	Various Cos., 11 U.S. Field Art.–	Rupp	750	Fin. Dept. U.S.A., Paymaster U.S. Vols.–	A
	Various Cos., 81 U.S. Field Art.	Yuhasy			
723	Co. A, 82 U.S. Field Art.–	Allen		2 Md. U.S. Vols.	Fitch
	—, 15 Btry., U.S. Field Art.	Ziegler			
724	—, 16 Btry., U.S. Field Art.–	A			
	Co. 4, U.S. C.A.C.	Savage			

Roll	Co., Regiment	Name
751	Q.M. Corps U.S.A.-	Fite
	Q.M. Corps U.S.A.	Tarter
752	Q.M. Corps U.S.A.	Tasker
	Q.M.D. U.S. Vols.	Rose
753	2 Q.M.D. U.S. Vols.-	Rosenauer
	Ret. U.S.A. (Indian Wars)	Bennett
754	Ret. U.S.A.-	Frank
		Buinett
	Ind. Scouts, U.S.A.	Black
755	Ind. Scouts, U.S.A.-	Black
		Hills
	Various Phil. Scouts, U.S.A.	Antonio
756	26 Phil. Scouts, U.S.A.-	Fausto
		Antonio
	20 Phil. Scouts, U.S.A.	Basilio
		Loquiao
757	38 & 39 Phil. Scouts, U.S.A.-	Lora
	B Squad. Phil. Cav. U.S. Vols.	Navarro
758	Co. B, Squad., Phil. Cav. U.S. Vols.-	Otis
	Co. E, Signal Corps, U.S.A.	Fikes
759	Signal Corps, U.S.A.-	Findling
	Various Tank Corps, U.S.A.	Clark
760	Tank Corps, U.S.A.-	Clark
	Various Units from different states, border	
	defense—WWI	McBride
761	Var. WWI Units, border defense (Nat. Guard, U.S. Inf.)-	James
		McBride
	Misc. WWI units (Guards, U.S. Inf, etc.)	Bobsien
762	Misc. WWI Units (Inf, U.S. Engs., Field Art.)-	Bocateat
	Misc. WWI units (Guards, U.S. Inf., U.S. Engs., etc.)	Hendry
763	Misc. WWI units (U.S. Inf., U.S. Engs., Guards, etc.)-	Hengesbach
	Misc. WWI units (U.S. Inf., U.S. Engs., Field Art., Guards, etc.)	Maclay
764	Misc. WWI units (U.S. Inf., Guards, Field Art., etc.)-	Mares
	Misc. WWI units (U.S. Inf., U.S. Engs., Guards, Field Art.)	Szurminki
765	Misc. WWI units (U.S. Inf., U.S. Engs., etc.)-	Tabaka
	Misc. WWI units (U.S. Inf., U.S. Field Art., U.S. Engs., etc.)	Zanker

Veterans Administration Pension Payment Cards, 1907–1933. M850. 2,539 rolls. DP.

This microfilm publication reproduces Pension Office award cards that record payments to pensioners on the rolls, 1907–33, except World War I pensioners. The cards are arranged alphabetically by surname of pensioner. Cards for Indian names are arranged alphabetically and filmed under the pertinent letter of the alphabet before cards for other names beginning with that letter.

Roll	Description
1	A–Abbott, Gustavus A.
2	Abbott, H. Emory–Abeita, J. Jesus
3	Abel, Abigail–Ablitz, Pauline
4	Abner, Ellen–Acison, Mattie
5	Ackard, Elizabeth A.–Ackiss, Laucinda
6	Acklam, Benjamin–Adamowich, Andrew
7	Adams, A.–Adams, Christopher H.
8	Adams, Clara–Adams, Freeman D.
9	Adams, Gabriel–Adams, Joel M.
10	Adams, John–Adams, Lyman W.
11	Adams, McGray C.–Adams, Prudy
12	Adams, Rachel–Adams, Zylpha
13	Adamsky, Eliza–Adkins, Joshus K.
14	Adkins, Kinchen–Agey, Vernie
15	Agg, Sarah J.–Aikey, Zachariah
16	Aikin, Almira C.–Akey, Winfield S.
17	Akie, Henry–Alberts, Sarah J.
18	Albertsen, Andreas–Alcoke, William W.
19	Alcorn, Agnes–Aldrich, Eugene S.
20	Aldrich, Fanny–Alexander, Austin A.
21	Alexander, Barnard–Alexander, Kezia E.
22	Alexander, Laura A.–Alexander, Zachariah T.
23	Alexandry, Nicolos–Allbee, Sarah J.
24	Allbert, Delana–Allen, Byron M.
25	Allen, Calista E.–Allen, Elydia A.
26	Allen, Emaline–Allen, Huldah M.
27	Allen, I. Clifton–Allen, King P.
28	Allen, L. Scott–Allen, May F.
29	Allen, Mehitable–Allen, Syrous B.
30	Allen, Tabitha–Alleyne, Samuel
31	Allfie, John A.–Allison, Willinoth
32	Alliss, Albert–Alsover, Mary M.
33	Alspach, Amanda–Alumbaugh, Winifred B.
34	Alvarado, Jose G.–Amery, Mary G.
35	Ames, Aaron S.–Amlung, Hedwig
36	Ammack, Emily–Anderseck, Lorenz
37	Andersen, Albert–Anderson, Celista
38	Anderson, Chaney–Anderson, Frederieke
39	Anderson, Gabriel–Anderson, Jetty M.
40	Anderson, Joanna–Anderson, Lynn B.
41	Anderson, M. Louise–Anderson, Owen
42	Anderson, Page–Anderson, Virginia M.
43	Anderson, Walker–Andretsch, Arthur M.
44	Andrew, Abbie S.–Andrews, Gustavus
45	Andrews, Hamilton–Andrews, Ruth
46	Andrews, Sally–Angevine, William F.
47	Angie, Lugie J.–Anslyn, Minnie
48	Anson, Abraham H.–Antoszak, John
49	Antram, Elvira T.–Appleford, Willington
50	Applegarth, Adda J.–Arbor, Cynthia
51	Arbuckel, William C.–Ardric, Thomas
52	Areay, George V.–Armfield, Warren Ormthede
53	Armiger, Caroline M.–Armstrong, Frederick
54	Armstrong, Gabriela–Armstrong, Preston W.
55	Armstrong, Rachel–Arnoe, Joseph
56	Arnold, Aaron–Arnold, Joel
57	Arnold, John–Arnold, William T.
58	Arnoldi, August–Artist, Thomas W.
59	Artley, Anne E.–Ashard, William H.
60	Ashba, Daniel–Ashkittle, Nancy J.
61	Ashlan, Michael–Askey, William
62	Askie, Elsie–Athey, Wesley B.
63	Athington, Andrew J.–Atkinson, Lydia
64	Atkinson, Maggie–Atwood, Freeman
65	Atwood, George–Augur, Sarah L.
66	Augus, Jennie–Austill, George L.
67	Austin, Aaron–Austin, Isom
68	Austin, Jabez L.–Autes, William
69	Auth, Apollonia–Avery, William W.

Roll	Description	Roll	Description
70	Aves, Frederick–Ayers, Ezra M.	134	Beatson, John–Beaulieu, William
71	Ayers, Florence E.–Azor, Addison	135	Beauman, Mary–Bechtolt, William
72	B–Babcock, Dwight	136	Beck, Abbie–Beck, Sylvester J.
73	Babcock, Eben G.–Baccus, Seymore	137	Beck, Theodore–Beckert, Mary A.
74	Bach, Adam–Bacome, William	138	Becket, Ending–Beckwith, Isaac O.
75	Bacon, Abel–Badershall, Amanda E.	139	Beckwith, James–Bee, William
76	Badgeley, Anna R.–Baggs, William	140	Beebe, Abagail–Beecroft, Robert H.
77	Bagley, Aaron, Jr.–Bailey, Avaline	141	Beed, Adelia M.–Beernink, Henry
78	Bailey, Bancroft A.–Bailey, Guy G.	142	Beers, Abbey J.–Begun, Christian
79	Bailey, H. Louisa–Bailey, Lymus	143	Beha, Catharine–Beiswenger, Charles
80	Bailey, Mahala–Bailey, Turner S.	144	Beitel, Alonzo F.–Belknapp, Seba
81	Bailey, Uriah L.–Bair, William W.	145	Bell, Ada–Bell, Guy
82	Baird, Abigail–Bakenhus, Herman	146	Bell, Hagen–Bell, Martha S.
83	Baker, Aaron–Baker, Cyrus G.	147	Bell, Mary–Bell, Zilpha
84	Baker, D. Amelia–Baker, Freeling H.	148	Bellah, Sarah C.–Belrose, William
85	Baker, Gardner L.–Baker, Jesse P.	149	Belsar, Frank–Bemus, William
86	Baker, Job–Baker, Lyman M.	150	Ben, Ellen–Benecke, Louis
87	Baker, M. Ella–Baker, Norvel H.	151	Benedetto, Charles P.–Benites, Manuel A.
88	Baker, Obadiah–Baker, Virgil A.	152	Benjamin, Abram–Bennethum, William
89	Baker, Wallace W.–Balch, William W.	153	Bennett, A. P.–Bennett, Ezra W.
90	Baldt, Paulina–Baldwin, Lyvina J.	154	Bennett, F. Oscar–Bennett, Julius
91	Baldwin, Mabel E.–Balkow, Louis	155	Bennett, Kate–Bennett, Ruvina
92	Ball, Aaron–Ball, Porter	156	Bennett, Salem–Bensman, Caroline D.
93	Ball, Rachel–Ballard, Winfield S.	157	Benso, Elizabeth–Benter, Daniel M.
94	Ballarman, Anna–Balston, Oscar F.	158	Bentfield, Elisabeth–Benton, Willis H.
95	Balt, Julius E.–Banforth, Christina	159	Bentram, Margaret–Bergeon, John C.
96	Bang, Anna–Banks, Moses R.	160	Berger, Amanda–Berkwater, Cyntha Jane
97	Banks, Nancy–Baquie, Mary E.	161	Berlage, Catharina–Berrweekes, John W.
98	Bar, Allen–Barber, Julius C.	162	Berry, Aaron–Berry, Katie
99	Barber, Kate–Barcly, John M.	163	Berry, Laura–Berstler, Samuel C.
100	Barcock, Emily–Bargen, Henry V.	164	Bert, Anna M.–Bessy, Wellington
101	Barger, Abel J.–Barker, Gustavus	165	Best, Adam J.–Bettridge, Thomas
102	Barker, Hamilton–Barkis, Laura J.	166	Betts, Aaron C.–Beves, Michael
103	Barkley, Abraham–Barmour, Jasper	167	Bevier, Charles–Bichulaitis, Frank A.
104	Barn, Henry–Barnes, Brigham	168	Bick, Augusta–Bickum, Jacob W.
105	Barnes, Caleb A.–Barnes, Iva J.	169	Bidaman, Caroline T.–Bienz, Phillip
106	Barnes, J. W.–Barnes, Priscilla	170	Bier, Barbara–Bigford, Thomas J.
107	Barnes, R. Lovinia–Barnett, Ivy G.	171	Bigg, Lillie–Bilezikjian, Missak
108	Barnett, Jacob L.–Barneycastle, Lydia E.	172	Bilfor, Mary–Billingsly, Rebecca I.
109	Barnfield, Alonzo Harvey–Barnum, Willis P.	173	Billington, Adelia–Bingey, Joseph
110	Barnwell, David–Barrere, Nelson	174	Bingham, A. Maria–Birchett, Mark H.
111	Barret, Allen–Barrett, Myron H.	175	Birchfield, Andris J.–Birdlow, Manuel
112	Barrett, Nancy S.–Barrow, William M.	176	Birdsall, Abram H.–Bisby, Rosena
113	Barrowcliff, Cyreno E.–Barry, Winnifred	177	Bisch, Anthony–Bishop, Ivay J.
114	Bars, Nancy K.–Bartke, John S.	178	Bishop, Jabez Adams–Bishopp, Weller
115	Bartl, Francis–Bartlett, Lydia S.	179	Bisig, Appolonia–Bitzer, Thomas J.
116	Bartlett, M. Lettie–Barton, Bert	180	Bivans, Barbary A.–Black, Ezra W.
117	Barton, Caleb A.–Barton, Willis H.	181	Black, Fannie A.–Black, Ruth J.
118	Bartoo, Eddie E.–Basquin, Susan M.	182	Black, Sabra–Blackburne, George
119	Bass, Adaline C.–Bassuener, Henry	183	Blackden, Goff M.–Blackstrom, Philip G.
120	Bast, Amanda–Bater, William	184	Blackwater, Thomas–Blains, Edward
121	Bates, Abbie–Bates, Lydia C.	185	Blair, Aaron L.–Blaire, Hilarion I.
122	Bates, Major–Batson, William H.	186	Blais, Edgar E.–Blake, Lydia M.
123	Batt, Amanda–Bauduy, Sadie C.	187	Blake, Madison–Blaker, William W.
124	Bauer, Abraham–Baughner, Christian	188	Blakes, Ellen–Blanchard, Lydia A.
125	Baugness, Richard J.–Bawor, Karl	189	Blanchard, Mahala–Blankenhorn, William
126	Bax, Adam–Bay, Winslow	190	Blankenship, Alonzo–Blazure, Henry C.
127	Baya, Avena–Bazzoni, Carolina	191	Blea, Abeline–Bleything, William H.
128	Bea, Kathrina–Beacox, Anna	192	Blibom, William–Blizzard, William D.
129	Beade, Rebecca–Bealin, William	193	Blo, Alexander–Bloodworth, William R.
130	Beall, Alavan–Beams, Samuel	194	Bloom, Abraham T.–Blonvet, Marion E.
131	Bean, Aaron–Beanston, Rosetta	195	Blow, Amanda M.–Blunton, John E.
132	Bear, Abner–Beardow, Mary L.	196	Blurton, Augustus–Boaz, Thomas H.
133	Bearshear, Ellen S.–Beaton, William M.	197	Bob, Jim–Bodge, William H.

Roll	Description	Roll	Description
198	Bodi, Julie–Bofman, John W.	262	Brown, Ann–Brown, Castanus
199	Boga, William–Boggy, David	263	Brown, Catharine–Brown, Cyrus
200	Bogia, Alphonsia W.–Bohyer, Rodney	264	Brown, Daisy–Brown, Eliza W.
201	Boice, Abigail E.–Bolerjack, Thomas C.	265	Brown, Elizabeth–Brown, Ezra H.
202	Boles, Alben H.–Bollje, Margareth	266	Brown, F. Ella–Brown, George T.
203	Bollman, Andrew J.–Bomboy, Thomas T.	267	Brown, George W.–Brown, Henry W.
204	Bomen, Felonise–Bondy, Mariah	268	Brown, Henson–Brown, James O.
205	Bone, Alfred E.–Bonnemort, Elijah	269	Brown, James P.–Brown, John Cook
206	Bonner, Abe–Booher, William H.	270	Brown, John D.–Brown, Justus N.
207	Book, Benjamin F.–Boopher, Jonas	271	Brown, Kate–Brown, Lyman W.
208	Boor, Elijah–Booth, Wilson	272	Brown, Maclista–Brown, Mary
209	Boothby, Adney D.–Bordy, Albert	273	Brown, Mary A.–Brown, Mettie E.
210	Borecky, Anna–Borstman, Robert H.	274	Brown, Miander B.–Brown, Quincy A.
211	Bort, Alfred–Bostick, William F.	275	Brown, R. Carrie–Brown, Sania
212	Bostler, Conrad–Botimer, William	276	Brown, Sara K.–Brown, Sylvina A.
213	Botkin, Adeline–Boughner, William T.	277	Brown, Tabitha J.–Brown, William C. A.
214	Boughten, Orin E.–Bousum, William H.	278	Brown, William D.–Browne, William R.
215	Bout, George W.–Bowell, Samantha L.	279	Brownell, Abram–Brownlow, Rebecca
216	Bowen, A. Adelia–Bowen, Myron	280	Brownmiller, Charles–Bruce, Minnie B.
217	Bowen, Nancy–Bowermaster, Sophia E.	281	Bruce, Nancy E.–Brumlow, Albert S. J.
218	Bowers, Abbie–Bowers, Wright	282	Brumm, Charles–Brunkhorst, Sophie
219	Bowersmith, Isaac–Bowlin, William H.	283	Brunn, Adeline E.–Brunzek, John F.
220	Bowling, Ada B.–Bowman, Justice H.	284	Bry, Daniel–Bryant, Cyrus W.
221	Bowman, Kate–Bowzer, William	285	Bryant, DeCosta–Bryant, Rufus O.
222	Box, Annie E.–Boyd, Frederick W.	286	Bryant, Sallie G.–Buchanan, Eunice
223	Boyd, Gabriella–Boyd, Sylvester W.	287	Buchanan, Fannie H.–Bucjnam, Sarah S.
224	Boyd, Tamar–Boyer, Kate	288	Buck, Aaron M.–Buck, Sylvester
225	Boyer, Laanna–Boyle, Julia A.	289	Buck, Tamar–Buckley, Julia A.
226	Boyle, Laura J.–Bozzell, Catharine	290	Buckley, Kathryn P.–Bucy, Zachariah
227	Braam, Fannie–Bracy, William W.	291	Buda, Curtis B.–Bueman, Charles
228	Brada, Elizabeth–Bradford, Kate	292	Buffaloe, Aldora–Bukowski, Stephen F.
229	Bradford, Landon–Bradley, Ishmael E.	293	Bulach, John G.–Bullfrog, Nancy
230	Bradley, Jacob–Bradley, Wilhelmine	294	Bullick, Anna–Bummersbach, Peter
231	Bradman, Christopher W.–Brady, Frederick A.	295	Bump, Aaron P.–Bunion, Thomas
232	Brady, Garvin S.–Brager, Marit	296	Bunker, Abbie A.–Buntz, Herman
233	Bragg, Aaron S.–Brallier, Susie M.	297	Bunworth, Mary–Burch, Zebulon W.
234	Bram, Anthony–Brandel, Margareth	298	Burcham, Abijah–Burdge, Mary
235	Brandemant, Smith–Branham, William	299	Burdic, Cevila F.–Burgener, John H.
236	Branian, Henry–Brant, William W.	300	Burger, Abbie–Burgess, Lydia L.
237	Brantas, Henry–Bratzman, Nahum	301	Burgess, Maggie L.–Buris, Mary E.
238	Brau, Frederick–Brayshair, Walter	302	Burk, Aaron H.–Burke, Isabelle
239	Brayton, Alice E.–Breech, William	303	Burke, Jack–Burkes, Nelson
240	Breed, Albert T.–Brelsford, William H.	304	Burket, Aaron–Burkolder, John F.
241	Brem, Anna–Brennen, William	305	Burks, Addaline–Burmood, Peter
242	Brenner, Adam F.–Brewen, William H.	306	Burn, Annie–Burnette, Nettie C.
243	Brewer, A. Ursula–Brewer, Zion	307	Burney, Arnetter–Burns, Augusta
244	Brewerton, Julia F.–Brickey, William	308	Burns, Barbara–Burns, Justus
245	Brickhill, Ellen–Bridgewater, Theresa	309	Burns, Kate–Burns, Zurilda J.
246	Bridgforth, Jackson–Briggs, Freemen D.	310	Burnsed, Julia A.–Burrell, Willis
247	Briggs, Garrett W.–Briggs, Zeal E.	311	Burrer, Lucinda–Burroughs, Wilson
248	Brigham, Abbie J.–Brilnart, William W.	312	Burrow, Ames D.–Burt, Fred E.
249	Brill, Albert A.–Brink, William T.	313	Burt, General Cato–Burton, Frederick N.
250	Brinker, A. Elizabeth–Briskey, Charles	314	Burton, Gale W.–Burton, Zedrick J. H.
251	Brisland, James–Brittnacker, Nicholas	315	Burtop, Sarah C.–Bush, Eurotus H.
252	Britto, Charlotte–Broands, Elizabeth	316	Bush, Fanny C.–Bushey, William G.
253	Brobeck, Anna M.–Brockus, William K.	317	Bushfield, Frederica–Busz, Simon
254	Brockway, Abby A.–Brollyer, Mary M.	318	Butah, Magdalena–Butler, Edwin V.
255	Bromagen, Howard–Brookey, Mary E.	319	Butler, Elbridge–Butler, Lyman P.
256	Brookfield, Benjamin C.–Brooks, Ezra S.	320	Butler, M. Eva–Butler, Winston
257	Brooks, Fannie–Brooks, Lysander	321	Butman, Amy A.–Butterworth, William H.
258	Brooks, McDonald–Brookshire, Zarilda H.	322	Buttery, Elisha–Buvinger, William H.
259	Broom, Adam–Brotts, Henry	323	Buxbaum, Julius–Byern, Margaritha
260	Brotz, Robert–Browley, James	324	Byers, Abraham–Byrd, Horace W.
261	Browman, Martin–Brown, Anice	325	Byrd, James–Byxbee, Theodore

Roll	Description
326	C–Cady, George W.
327	Cady, Hannah W.–Cahow, Sarah A.
328	Cail, Carrie C.–Cakerice, Anna M.
329	Caladisa, Carolina–Caldwell, Myra L.
330	Caldwell, Nancy–Calhoun, Zipporah
331	Calice, Emile–Callagy, John
332	Callahan, Carrie A.–Callies, Gustav E.
333	Calligan, Clark E.–Camby, William
334	Camden, Andrew J.–Camn, Curtis H.
335	Camp, David–Campbell, Bryant D.
336	Campbell, Calfurnia L.–Campbell, Ezra N.
337	Campbell, Fannie–Campbell, Jay
338	Campbell, Jefferson–Campbell, Marquis D.
339	Campbell, Martha–Campbell, Ruth T.
340	Campbell, Sadie A.–Campbell, Zeb C.
341	Campdoras, Eliza M.–Canfield, Lydia
342	Canfield, M. Melissa–Canon, Sarah J.
343	Canright, Eugene–Capito, Louise E.
344	Caple, Charity–Cardey, Nancy
345	Cardiff, Christopher–Carez, Francis F.
346	Carfrey, Anna M.–Carlile, William S.
347	Carlin, Alfred J.–Carlysle, Rebecca J.
348	Carmac, Bacus–Carmouche, Prevat
349	Carn, Abram–Carnline, Tabitha
350	Carnman, Elizabeth–Carpenter, Elvira
351	Carpenter, Emanuel–Carpenter, Marion M.
352	Carpenter, Marjorie A.–Carqueville, Belle
353	Carr, Aaron S.–Carr, Jesse
354	Carr, Joab–Carr, Yarmouth
355	Carradine, James–Carroll, Dixon
356	Carroll, Edith E.–Carroll, Susanna
357	Carroll, Theodore–Carson, Lydia J.
358	Carson, Maggie–Carter, Cyrus L.
359	Carter, Dafney–Carter, Jasper N.
360	Carter, Jean V.–Carter, Myrah B.
361	Carter, Nancy–Carter, Zery
362	Carteret, Bertha–Carvey, Edwin B.
363	Carvill, Henry W.–Case, Dwight C.
364	Case, Edgar S.–Case, Zenas L.
365	Casebeer, Alexander–Casford, Hortense M.
366	Cash, Ada–Cass, William S.
367	Cassabaum, Mary E.–Cassriel, Henry H.
368	Cast, Almarinda–Castner, Theodore
369	Casto, Adaline–Catey, Winfield S.
370	Cath, Selenia–Caukins, Amanda
371	Caul, Albert R.–Cavy, William H.
372	Caw, George F.–Cezar, Garnet G.
373	Chabbott, George–Chaffey, Letilia
374	Chaffin, Abbie C.–Chamberlain, Isidore F.
375	Chamberlain, Jacob–Chamberlin, William N.
376	Chambers, Aaron Culver–Chambers, Ruth
377	Chambers, Salmon M.–Chance, William W.
378	Chancellor, Alfred W.–Chandler, Norman T.
379	Chandler, Obediah G.–Chapin, Birch
380	Chapin, Caroline–Chapman, Celia E.
381	Chapman, Charles–Chapman, Kisiah
382	Chapman, Laura A.–Chapman, Wright W.
383	Chapoton, Anthony–Charlson, Sophia
384	Charlton, Alec–Chase, Frederick W.
385	Chase, Gardner M.–Chase, Sylvester T.
386	Chase, T. Abel–Chedisler, Mary R.
387	Cheek, Adline–Chennowerth, John W.
388	Chenot, Henry L.–Chessmore, David A.
389	Chestain, Mary–Chilcutt, Milton L.

Roll	Description
390	Child, Abbie S.–Childs, Phebe B.
391	Childs, Rachel E.–Chitty, William J.
392	Chitwood, Aaron–Christhilf, Henry B.
393	Christia, George R.–Christner, Christian
394	Christofel, Frederick–Chupp, Jacob
395	Church, Abby E.–Church, Zeno G.
396	Churchell, Amos–Cipperly, Mercy
397	Cirbus, Charles–Clancy, Zachariah R.
398	Clandaniel, Mary E.–Clarius, Andrew
399	Clark, A. Johnson–Clark, Byron T.
400	Clark, C. B.–Clark, Egbert B.
401	Clark, Elbert B.–Clark, Freeman M.
402	Clark, Gabriel–Clark, Henry W.
403	Clark, Hepsie, S.–Clark, Johanna C.
404	Clark, John–Clark, Lewis W.
405	Clark, Lillian H.–Clark, Mary C.
406	Clark, Mary E.–Clark, Priscilla B.
407	Clark, Rachel–Clark, Sylvia A.
408	Clark, T. Elwood–Clark, Zilpha M.
409	Clarke, Abial P.–Clarridge, Sarah J.
410	Clarry, Elmira–Claxton, William P.
411	Clay, Aaron–Clayson, Robert H.
412	Clayter, Susan–Cleavland, Rachel
413	Cleborne, Jane E.–Clement, William W.
414	Clements, Albert–Clery, Mary
415	Cless, Daniel–Cleye, Martin
416	Cliborne, John F. G.–Clindinin, Stillman
417	Cline, Abbie E.–Cline, Wyatt
418	Clinebell, William L.–Clore, Nancy J.
419	Clos, Jacob–Cloughly, Mary A.
420	Cloukey, Joseph C.–Cluster, Martha E.
421	Clutch, George H.–Coatney, William T.
422	Coats, Aaron–Cobb, Ruth H.
423	Cobb, S. Augusta–Coby, May J.
424	Coca, Antonio–Cochran, Zylpha A.
425	Cochrane, Albert–Codyer, Peter
426	Coe, Abigail M.–Coffie, Susie
427	Coffield, Alfred H.–Cogan, Thomas
428	Cogburn, Henry P.–Cokley, Jeremiah
429	Colabine, Annie E.–Colby, Wilson S.
430	Colchen, Julia C.–Cole, Edwin W.
431	Cole, Eleanor D.–Cole, Jonathan L.
432	Cole, Joseph–Cole, Sarah U.
433	Cole, Scott–Coleman, Eveline
434	Coleman, Fannie–Coleman, Susie T.
435	Coleman, Thaddeus–Colleps, Mary
436	Coller, Amehia–Collini, Alonzo L.
437	Collins, Aaron–Collins, Ezra J.
438	Collins, Fannie–Collins, Julius
439	Collins, Kate–Collins, Rutha M.
440	Collins, Sadie–Colopy, Theresa M.
441	Colp, Charles–Colvyhouse, Callie M.
442	Colwat, Joseph–Comely, Frederick
443	Comer, Abigail–Compty, Henry
444	Comrey, Andrew–Conaway, William W.
445	Conboy, Bridget–Conforth, Mary C.
446	Congar, Abigail M.–Conklin, Ivan V.
447	Conklin, Jacob V.–Conley, Zachariah
448	Conliff, Ernestine–Connell, Zachariah D.
449	Connellee, Jane E.–Conner, Lyman
450	Conner, Maggee–Connor, Dennis
451	Connor, Edgar M.–Conquest, Sarah
452	Conrad, Abigal–Conry, Patrick
453	Consadine, Catherine–Conway, Lucy A.

Roll	Description
454	Conway, Malissa–Cook, Byron H.
455	Cook, Calvin E.–Cook, Ezra A.
456	Cook, Fannie–Cook, Jesse M.
457	Cook, Joanna–Cook, Marvin J.
458	Cook, Mary–Cook, Sarah T.
459	Cook, Sebastian–Cooke, Winfield S.
460	Cooken, Charles F.–Cooley, Zara
461	Coolican, Bridget–Coon, Zachary T.
462	Coonan, Bridget T.–Cooper, Byron T.
463	Cooper, Cadwallader R.–Cooper, Izora
464	Cooper, Jack H.–Cooper, Maryette
465	Cooper, Mason–Cooper, Zona
466	Cooperider, Caroline M.–Copeland, Roxana
467	Copeland, Samuel–Coquillette, Mary J.
468	Cora, William T.–Corbyn, Phila Ann
469	Corcellious, Louis–Corettsca, Mary
470	Corey, Achsah L.–Cormier, William
471	Corn, Abram–Corney, Robert
472	Cornfield, James–Corres, Gandencia
473	Corrick, Charles J.–Corwine, William A.
474	Cory, Aaron–Cossum, Henry
475	Cost, Anna F. D.–Cottey, William R.
476	Cotti, Warren–Cottrill, Thomas J.
477	Cotts, Pauline–Coultas, Ruth
478	Coulter, Abraham–Courtis, William C.
479	Courtland, Charles C.–Covault, Sarah E.
480	Cove, Elizabeth–Coveyou, Michael
481	Covil, Abner–Cowdry, William F.
482	Cowe, James–Cowwick, Martha Frances
483	Cox, Aaron–Cox, Gusta S.
484	Cox, Hannah–Cox, Mary W.
485	Cox, Massey–Coxwell, Martha E.
486	Coy, Abby M.–Cozzins, Samuel G. W.
487	Crab, Eliza–Crafts, William G.
488	Cragon, Bridget–Craig, Lyman
489	Craig, Mahala–Craite, George
490	Craker, Amanda M.–Cramton, Nathaniel A.
491	Cranage, John G.–Crane, Dominick
492	Crane, E. Mary–Crankshaw, Sarah E.
493	Cranmer, Alfred S.–Cravin, Walter C.
494	Craw, Ambrose W.–Crawford, Huldah E.
495	Crawford, Ida–Crawford, Myrtle
496	Crawford, Nancy–Crazy, Thunder
497	Crea, Clara A.–Crehore, William M.
498	Creider, Simon S.–Crezelous, Jacob
499	Cribb, George R.–Crismore, Marietta
500	Crisp, Amanda J.–Criteser, Thomas
501	Crith, Frank–Croco, Susannah
502	Croddy, Charles–Cronchett, Frances
503	Crone, Arabella–Crookham, Matthew E.
504	Crooks, Abbie S.–Crosby, William W.
505	Crose, Amrilla–Cross, Israel P.
506	Cross, J. Wesley–Crosslin, Jennie
507	Crossman, Aaron J.–Croupe, Sarah E.
508	Crouse, Albert Y.–Crowdus, Louisa
509	Crowe, Alexander F.–Crowmeans, Thursa A.
510	Crown, Annie L.–Crumb, William P.
511	Crumbacher, Nancy J.–Csech, Ludwig
512	Cuaron, Jesus–Culkin, Bridget
513	Cull, Ann–Culley, William C.
514	Cullifer, Martha–Cummings, Bryant
515	Cummings, Caroline–Cummings, Zerilda
516	Cummins, Abraham–Cunningham, Augustus
517	Cunningham, Bainbridge L.–Cunningham, Julia E.

Roll	Description
518	Cunningham, Kate–Cuppy, Thomas W.
519	Curas, Clayanna–Curran, Lydia J.
520	Curran, Manus J.–Currier, William H. B.
521	Currigan, Edward W.–Curtin, William P.
522	Curtis, Abbeygail–Curtis, Ivy
523	Curtis, Jackson–Curtis, Zenas B.
524	Curtise, Charity–Cushway, Maud M.
525	Cusic, Albert L.–Cutler, Lydia Ann
526	Cutler, Maggie E.–Czyzewski, Julius
527	D–Dahlke, Dorothea Sophia
528	Dahlman, Beata–Daily, William T.
529	Dain, Alonzo M.–Daley, Wived
530	Dalfers, Louise G.–Dalwick, George F.
531	Daly, Alice–Damps, August
532	Damrell, Joseph–Danhiser, Maria E.
533	Danico, Augustus H.–Daniels, Isabella
534	Daniels, Jacinth A.–Danmarkel, Gabriel
535	Dann, Addie T.–Darkus, Lydia Ann
536	Darland, Amanda–Darphy, George J.
537	Darr, Adam–Dasy, Elam
538	Datarman, Margaret–Dautry, Nancy
539	Davage, Mary F.–Davey, William W.
540	David, Adaline–Davidson, Juliette L.
541	Davidson, Kate W.–Davion, Alexander
542	Davis, A. Judson–Davis, Azubah F.
543	Davis, Barbara–Davis, Cyrus W.
544	Davis, Dabner–Davis, Ellis C.
545	Davis, Elmina–Davis, George Y.
546	Davis, Georgiana–Davis, Jabez P.
547	Davis, Jacie J.–Davis, Johanna
548	Davis, John–Davis, Jonathan S.
549	Davis, Joseph–Davis, Lysena
550	Davis, M.–Davis, Mary H.
551	Davis, Mary J.–Davis, Owen W.
552	Davis, P. Matilda–Davis, Sarah B.
553	Davis, Sarah C.–Davis, Tyrenia
554	Davis, Ulysses S.–Davis, Zylpha A.
555	Davison, Abbie E.–Dawsey, William L.
556	Dawson, Aaron J.–Daxon, Margaret
557	Day, Aaron C.–Day, Israel, Jr.
558	Day, Jacob–Day, Winifred
559	Dayan, Harvey H.–Deamude, Daniel C.
560	Dean, Abbie B.–Dean, Lydia M.
561	Dean, Mack F.–Dearborne, Theresa
562	de Archibeque, Louisa Chavez–DeBaum, William S.
563	Debbie, Simon P.–Deckelnick, Otto
564	Decker, Aaron–Decker, Ruth R.
565	Decker, Samuel–Deems, William
566	Deen, Annie E.–DeFuyter, Peter
567	de Galis, Teresita Alarid–DeHays, Sarah B.
568	Deheck, Susanna–Delamotte, Peter
569	Delan, Irene B.–Delayfountain, George W.
570	Delb, Iphraine–Delony, Owen T.
571	de Lopes, Aniceta R.–Dement, Solomon
572	Demer, Scott–Demozzi, Lena
573	Dempcy, Hattie A.–Denious, Oliver
574	Denis, Catherine–Dennington, William M.
575	Dennis, Aaron–Dennis, Willis
576	Dennison, Abby J.–Denstadt, John
577	Dent, Addison–DePry, Daniel T.
578	Depu, Elizabeth–Derp, Frank
579	Derr, Adam K.–Deshong, Robert
580	DeSilva, Dwight M.–Detzel, George
581	Deubach, Elise–Devettere, Margaret J.

Roll	Description	Roll	Description
582	de Vickers, Amelia V.–DeVoe, William W.	646	Duval, Adolph–Dwyer, Susan F.
583	Devoge, Theophilus–Dewester, Jacob	647	Dwyer, Theophilus V.–Dyer, Gracia E.
584	Dewey, Addison–Dewitz, William	648	Dyer, Haeney A.–Dzozdzynski, Michael F.
585	DeWolf, Abbie M.–Dials, William F.	649	E–Ealy, William A.
586	Diamant, Harry–Dickelman, Mary H.	650	Eaman, Eleanora V.–Earls, William H.
587	Dicken, Abner–Dicket, Mary A.	651	Early, A. Nelson–East, William T.
588	Dickey, Aaron F.–Dickinson, Lydia A.	652	Eastabrooks, Ella F.–Eastman, Sydney
589	Dickinson, M. Nelson–Dicky, Henry H.	653	Eastman, Theodore–Eaton, Frederika
590	Dicus, Alice B.–Diepold, Leonard	654	Eaton, Garrit F.–Eavory, John C.
591	Dier, Angeline–diFrancesco, Fiumara Maria	655	Eayre, George S.–Eberwine, Mary
592	Digan, Eliza–Dillane, James	656	Ebey, Daniel–Eckensberger, Amanda J.
593	Dillard, Amanda–Dillmore, Michael	657	Ecker, Aaron–Ecuacion, Juan
594	Dillon, Aaron–Diltz, William T.	658	Edaburn, Dorcas B.–Edes, Warren S.
595	Dilwood, Thomas, Jr.–Diniwoodie, Rufus	659	Edgar, Alexander–Edinston, Noble
596	Dink, John E.–Dismukes, William	660	Edison, Curt–Edmundson, William N.
597	Disney, Abbiegail–Divver, Mary J.	661	Edner, Albina–Edwards, Cyrus L.
598	Dix, Addie E.–Dixon, Lyman	662	Edwards, Daniel–Edwards, Jasper
599	Dixon, Mahala S.–Doane, Wilson	663	Edwards, Jemima–Edwards Moses D.
600	Dobay, George S.–Dobyns, Mary J.	664	Edwards, Nancy–Edworthy, John W.
601	Dochart, George C.–Dodez, Helen	665	Edy, Benjamin F.–Eggimann, Lavina
602	Dodge, Aaron B.–Dodge, Zachariah	666	Egglan, Charles H.–Ehrgott, Louisa
603	Dodgen, Mariah–Doherty, William W.	667	Ehrhardt, August–Eifler, Esther A.
604	Dohl, George–Doll, William H.	668	Eigabroadt, Fred T.–Ekdahl, Charles
605	Dollahite, Martha J.–Donahower, Jeremiah C.	669	Ekel, John–Eldert, John B.
606	Donahue, Adaline H.–Dondt, Kat	670	Eldred, Abbie J.–Elhardt, Josephine
607	Done, Elizabeth–Donnells, Nancy A.	671	Eli, George W.–Ellhuff, Philip
608	Donnelly, Abbin B.–Donoughe, James A.	672	Ellibee, Erastus–Elliott, Ezra F.
609	Donovan, Albert D.–Dooling, William	673	Elliott, Fannie–Elliott, Martin V. B.
610	Doolittle, Abbie J.–Dorley, Joseph	674	Elliott, Mary–Elliott, Zimri
611	Dormady, Esther–Dorsett, William T.	675	Ellis, A. Inghram–Ellis, Isadora
612	Dorsey, Aimee–Dotson, Millie	676	Ellis, J. Wallace–Ellis, Prudence E.
613	Dotson, Nancy E.–Dougher, James J.	677	Ellis, Quincy A.–Ellison, Wright T.
614	Dougherity, William–Dougherty, Young	678	Elliston, Andrew J.–Elmstedt, John N.
615	Doughman, Eliza J.–Douglass, Byron J.	679	Elolff, Fritz–Elwell, Zeno P.
616	Douglass, Campbell–Douglass, Zenith	680	Elwin, James–Embury, William
617	Douings, Sarah A.–Dowbiggin, Mary E.	681	Emch, Anna E.–Emerton, William W.
618	Dowd, Alexander–Downer, William V.	682	Emery, Aaron R.–Emlott, Marcus L.
619	Downes, Amasa–Downing, Lysander	683	Emmack, Charles H.–Emswiler, Samuel
620	Downing, Mahlon F.–Doxzene, Daniel M.	684	Enard, Ludivin–Enghouser, Edward
621	Doy, Alfred E.–Dozier, Zachary T.	685	Engl, Theresa–Engley, James R.
622	Draa, James–Drake, Julia M.	686	Englis, Daniel–Ennolds, Rebecca
623	Drake, Kate–Drappo, Albert	687	Eno, Byron E.–Enzewiler, Maria J.
624	Drash, Catharine–Dressor, Nancy A.	688	Eoff, Alfred–Erhart, Theresia
625	Dreulard, Mary E.–Drips, Henry W.	689	Erich, Eliza L.–Ertz, Nicholas
626	Driscall, Elizabeth–Drozeski, Arthur F.	690	Ervans, Maria–Esip, Francis
627	Drube, William–Druyor, Nicholas	691	Eskan, Amalia–Estas, John
628	Dry, Adam–Duckery, John	692	Este, David–Esworthy, Thomas T.
629	Duckett, Albert–Dudy, David H.	693	Etaouck, John–Euwer, Sayers B.
630	Due, Eliza–Duffus, William	694	Eva, Henry–Evans, Elzy J.
631	Duffy, Ann–Dugan, Michael F.	695	Evans, Emaline–Evans, Johanna
632	Dugan, Nancy–Dukette, Charles W.	696	Evans, John–Evans, Myrtie B.
633	Dula, Elbert S. J.–Dunbach, David	697	Evans, Nancy–Evans, Zophar
634	Dunbar, Aaron–Duncan, Frederick T.	698	Evanshine, Edwin–Everfield, Kiah
635	Duncan, Gabriel–Duncan, Verbal	699	Everham, Benjamin S.–Evertz, Frederick
636	Duncan, Walker–Dunham, Lydia M.	700	Every, Addison–Ewing, Isabelle
637	Dunham, Margaret–Dunlap, Israel	701	Ewing, Jacob W.–Ezzell, John T.
638	Dunlap, Jacob B.–Dunn, Cynthia	702	F–Fahn, Hermann
639	Dunn, David–Dunn, Lyman H.	703	Fahr, Agnes E.–Fairburn, William
640	Dunn, Maggie–Dunne, William F.	704	Fairchild, Abraham–Faldston, William
641	Dunnegan, Alfred J.–Duodik, Augustus	705	Falen, John–Famulener, Jonathan
642	Dupar, Eliza G.–Durey, John T.	706	Fancey, Frank–Farkick, John
643	Durf, Frederick–Durkin, William J.	707	Farl, James M.–Farmer, Frederick
644	Durlacher, Hannah–Dussman, Robert	708	Farmer, George–Farnley, Mary Ann
645	Dust, Ernst C.–Duty, William	709	Farns, Bridget–Farrand, Zoeth S.

Roll	Description
710	Farrar, Abel–Farrelly, Thomas
711	Farren, Alexander–Fasquelle, Martha
712	Fass, David N.–Faulknor, Samuel R. W.
713	Faulks, Eliza–Faxton, Samantha E.
714	Fay, Aaron–Feazel, William H.
715	Feback, Gustus H.–Feigly, Henry
716	Feik, Ernest–Fellmann, Hermann
717	Fellon, Catherine–Femuels, Tumes
718	Fence, John–Fentiman, Nancy J.
719	Fenton, Abraham–Ferguson, Cyrus E.
720	Ferguson, Danford–Ferguson, Norman C.
721	Ferguson, Olga–Ferreira, Mary A.
722	Ferrel, Caroline–Ferriter, Luke
723	Ferron, Elizabeth A.–Fetty, William Lloyd
724	Fetz, Charles–Fichler, Mary E.
725	Fiel, Augustus–Fielding, Uriah
726	Fields, Aaron–Fierman, Christine
727	Fiero, Abraham–Filkins, William H.
728	Fill, Harriet E.–Finch, William W.
729	Fincham, Angeline–Finks, Thomas M.
730	Finlan, Mary–Finnegan, William J.
731	Finnell, Annie–Firth, William
732	Fiscel, Lizzie–Fish, Lyman C.
733	Fish, Maggie–Fisher, Celestia M.
734	Fisher, Chalystia–Fisher, Hattie R.
735	Fisher, Helen L.–Fisher, Lyman H.
736	Fisher, Maggie–Fisher, Tobias
737	Fisher, Ulyssa E.–Fister, Ranslo
738	Fitch, Abbie S.–Fitzgeorge, James Theus
739	Fitzgerald, Albert A.–Fitzgerrell, James J.
740	Fitzgibben, John–Fivey, Magda
741	Fix, Abraham M.–Flancher, Frank A.
742	Flander, Josiah C.–Fleanor, Virginia C.
743	Flechsig, August–Fleming, Eveline
744	Fleming, Fatima–Flemmings, George W.
745	Flenagin, Maranda H.–Fletcher, Julia M.
746	Fletcher, Kate A.–Flimesta, Joseph
747	Flin, Annie–Flomerfelt, Nancy Jane
748	Flood, Abba R.–Flowerree, Armie E.
749	Flowers, Aaron M.–Fluhrer, William
750	Fluke, Annie W.–Fockler, Simon
751	Foddert, Charles–Foldson, William
752	Folensbee, Charity V.–Folks, Thomas
753	Foll, Anna M.–Fones, Nancy
754	Fong, Otto F.–Foran, William
755	Forbach, Anna–Forcum, Mamie E.
756	Ford, Aaron E.–Ford, Ivan S.
757	Ford, Jabez–Ford, Ruthia
758	Ford, Sallie–Foreman, Zachariah
759	Foren, Ellen–Forrer, Mathias
760	Forress, John H.–Forsythe, William T.
761	Fort, Absalom D.–Fosnough, James N.
762	Foss, Ada Z.–Foster, Christie
763	Foster, Cinderella–Foster, Issachar
764	Foster, Jackson–Foster, Mary D.
765	Foster, Mary E.–Foster, Zorel
766	Fostman, William–Foust, Susan N.
767	Fout, Zelinda–Fowler, Iza May
768	Fowler, J. L.–Fowzer, Ellen J.
769	Fox, Aaron–Fox, Izettar
770	Fox, Jackson–Fox, Priscilla
771	Fox, Rachel–Frakes, William A.
772	Frala, William W.–Francis, Gilbert E.
773	Francis, Hannah–Franikh, Nancy
774	Frank, Abby J.–Frankfurther, Sara
775	Frankhouser, Henry–Frankman, John
776	Franks, Adam–Fraszer, Daniel
777	Frater, James S.–Frazier, Giles
778	Frazier, Hannah–Fredendall, James
779	Frederic, Martin W.–Freece, Nancy A.
780	Freed, Aaron–Freeman, Dwight
781	Freeman, Edford–Freeman, Moses D.
782	Freeman, Nancy–Fremont, Sally B. A.
783	French, Aaron A.–French, Justin E.
784	French, Kate–Fresquis, Esquipula
785	Fretios, Antonio–Frictsch, Michael
786	Friday, Elizabeth–Friery, Ann
787	Fries, Adam–Friton, Julius
788	Frits, Valentine–Frolkey, Magdalena
789	From, Elizabeth–Froster, Charles
790	Frothingham, Amanda M.–Fry, Justine
791	Fry, Kisiah–Frysinger, Margaret A.
792	Fuarey, Charles H.–Fullenwider, William H.
793	Fuller, Abbie–Fuller, Hyman V.
794	Fuller, Ichabod C.–Fuller, Russell
795	Fuller, Sallie–Fulte, Carl
796	Fulton, Abigail–Funiaock, Mary
797	Funk, Abraham–Furkin, James A.
798	Furl, Jonas–Fyson, Harriet
799	G–Gaddy, Nancy M.
800	Gade, August–Gagle, John H.
801	Gagne, Albert–Gaitz, John
802	Gajeway, Etta–Gallagan, Mary J.
803	Gallager, Charles–Gallahue, Warren C.
804	Gallamore, Jacob G.–Galloway, William K.
805	Gallt, Rachel A.–Gambold, Mary E.
806	Gambrall, Elizabeth–Ganoung, William H.
807	Gans, Adam–Garcin, Robert E. L.
808	Gard, Abraham L.–Gardner, Dora E.
809	Gardner, Earl S.–Gardner, Lewis R.
810	Gardner, Lillian A.–Gardoux, Philomene
811	Gare, John J.–Garlow, William E.
812	Garma, Martina–Garnsey, Hannah
813	Garr, Georg A.–Garrett, Noah
814	Garrett, Oliver Perry–Garrison, Julia A.
815	Garrison, Kate E.–Gartner, Sophia
816	Garton, Andrew–Garzee, Henry E.
817	Gasahl, Andrew–Gastmeyer, Christian
818	Gastoe, Adam–Gates, Israel
819	Gates, Jacob–Gatzman, Augusta W.
820	Gau, Anna C.–Gavville, Xavier
821	Gaw, Albert–Gazzam, Margaret I.
822	Geabhart, Eliza A.–Gee, William R.
823	Geedey, John C.–Geegley, Warren S.
824	Geil, Catharine–Genrow, Ruth
825	Gens, William–George, Frederick W.
826	George, George–Geothe, John
827	Gepford, Jeremiah–Gerlt, Theresia
828	Germain, Adelle–Gerz, Joseph
829	Gesche, Johanna–Getz, Elizabeth J.
830	Geyer, Ella L.–Gibbony, Mary
831	Gibbs, Abbie E.–Gibbs, Zebulon
832	Gibbud, Duncan D.–Gibson, Guy W.
833	Gibson, H. Amelia–Gibson, Moses W.
834	Gibson, Nancy–Gidow, Eliza
835	Giebe, Charles–Gift, William R.
836	Gigandet, Joseph–Gilbert, Jessie
837	Gilbert, Joel–Gilboyne, Michael

Roll	Description	Roll	Description
838	Gilbreath, Barbara A.–Giles, Willis S.	902	Griss, Abbie–Grodzki, Maximilian
839	Gilfeather, Sophia–Gill, Prentiss	903	Groebe, Ernst–Grorud, Hans
840	Gill, Rachel J.–Gillespie, Israel	904	Gros, Harriet B.–Gross, Zeno Burtus
841	Gillespie, James–Gillhespy, Thomas	905	Grossardt, William–Grove, William S.
842	Gilliam, Addine–Gillno, Ezra	906	Grovefield, Charles G.–Grovier, Christiana
843	Gillo, Peter–Gilmore, Isaac R.	907	Grow, Abigail A.–Grugett, Roy E.
844	Gilmore, Jacob B.–Gilzer, Frederick C.	908	Gruhl, Elizabeth–Guenthner, Magdalena
845	Giman, George–Girling, Martha	909	Guepe, Magdalena–Guiley, Jacob H.
846	Girmus, Gottlieb–Glackin, Mary A.	910	Guilfoil, Ellen–Guly, John
847	Glad, Eugene–Glaspy, Robert M.	911	Gum, Abby J.–Gunnulson, Laura P.
848	Glass, Abram–Glazner, Sion B.	912	Guno, Rhoda Ann–Gussman, Marie
849	Gleadall, Sarah A. A.–Glenert, August	913	Gust, Elizabeth–Gutshall, Sarah J.
850	Glenn, Abraham B.–Glinny, Patrick	914	Gutt, Dorothea–Gyves, Michael
851	Glisan, Dora F.–Glysson, Hannah E.	915	H–Haby, Leopold
852	Gmehlin, August–Godding, Rebecca A.	916	Hacey, James A.–Hackney, William P.
853	Gode, Jane L.–Goemmel, George	917	Hackson, Catherine–Hadly, Charles F.
854	Goen, Ellen–Goforth, William M.	918	Hadnett, William–Hagans, William H.
855	Gogan, Bridget–Goldenstedt, Sophia	919	Hagar, Abbie L.–Hagerson, Mary
856	Golder, Abraham H.–Golzenleuchter, Rosina	920	Hagert, Louise–Hagyard, George P.
857	Gomah, George–Good, Winchester	921	Haha, Frances L.–Haimovitz, Abraham
858	Goodacre, Alice L.–Goodger, Lovenie M.	922	Hain, Adam–Haines, Susana
859	Goodhand, Charlotte–Goodmunsen, Eli	923	Haines, Theodore B.–Haldorsen, Raquel
860	Goodner, Alice E.–Goodrich, Williston W.	924	Hale, Abbie E.–Hale, Ruth C.
861	Goodrick, Anna A.–Goodwin, Ivory L.	925	Hale, Sallie C.–Halkyard, James
862	Goodwin, Jacob–Gordak, Lucy M.	926	Hall, A. Dutton–Hall, Cyrus B.
863	Gordan, Samuel W.–Gordon, Jesse C.	927	Hall, Dalzena–Hall, Frona M.
864	Gordon, Johanna–Gordy, William F.	928	Hall, Galley–Hall, Jacob I.
865	Gore, Agnes S.–Gormong, Emanuel	929	Hall, James–Hall, Killis
866	Gornall, Henry–Gosper, Waitie E.	930	Hall, Lafayette–Hall, Mayme
867	Goss, Aaron–Gotta, Emma J.	931	Hall, Melissa–Hall, Sarah W.
868	Gottbrecht, Adolph–Gould, Israel	932	Hall, Savannah M.–Hall, Zilpha K.
869	Gould, J. Harold–Gouze, Marie E.	933	Hallacher, George S.–Halliwill, Sarah A.
870	Govan, Frank–Grabowsky, Viktorya	934	Hallman, Anna B.–Halsy, Margaret
871	Grace, Alexander–Graff, William H.	935	Halt, Joseph M.–Hamata, Kangei
872	Graffam, Albert–Graham, Ezra C.	936	Hambacher, Lucy–Hamill, William S.
873	Graham, Fannie L.–Graham, Lyman M.	937	Hamilton, Aaron–Hamilton, Isaiah
874	Graham, Maggie E.–Grahem, Rebecca J.	938	Hamilton, Jacob–Hamilton, Myntie L.
875	Grahlman, Henry–Granstrom, Charles	939	Hamilton, Nancy–Hamler, Viola E.
876	Grant, A. Belle–Grant, Myra F.	940	Hamlet, Albert T.–Hamment, Mary
877	Grant, Nahum B.–Grauweller, John	941	Hammer, Adam–Hammond, Ezekiel A.
878	Grav, Johanna C.–Graves, Lydia F.	942	Hammond, Fannie–Hammons, William H.
879	Graves, Maggie E.–Gray, Bushrod	943	Hammontree, Alexander–Hamstreet, David W.
880	Gray, Caleb–Gray, Israel J.	944	Han, Lidy L.–Hancox, Jennie H.
881	Gray, Jacob–Gray, Moses	945	Hand, Agnes H.–Handyside, Reuben
882	Gray, Nancy–Gray, Zebulon	946	Hane, Adam–Hankart, Gustave
883	Grayam, Mary E.–Greemore, James	947	Hanke, Julius–Hanlyen, Henrietta
884	Green, Aaron–Green, Duty	948	Hanmer, Adam–Hannahs, William
885	Green, Easter–Green, Gustavus C.	949	Hannaka, Ellen C.–Hansdatter, Gertrude Marie
886	Green, Hadley William–Green, John K.	950	Hanse, George A.–Hanson, Hulvor E.
887	Green, John L.–Green, Mary D.	951	Hanson, Ida F.–Harazin, John
888	Green, Mary E.–Green, Sarah D.	952	Harb, Jacob–Hardeman, William
889	Green, Sarah E.–Greenclay, Siegfried	953	Harden, Abbie S.–Hardin, Lucy C.
890	Greene, Addie E.–Greene, Wilson T.	954	Hardin, Maggie R.–Hardman, William H.
891	Greenebaum, Samuel–Greentree, Mary	955	Hardnack, Anna M.–Hardzog, Henry
892	Greenup, Bascom N.–Greeves, Victor J.	956	Hare, Adam I.–Harjo, Millie
893	Grefe, August H.–Gregory, Isabelle	957	Hark, Eliza A.–Harland, Willard P.
894	Gregory, Jacob W.–Grems, William H.	958	Harle, James H.–Harmany, Webster S.
895	Grenade, Silas J.–Grierson, William F.	959	Harmas, Almira–Harmuth, Friedrich S.
896	Gries, Elizabeth–Griffin, Isom	960	Harn, Alfred M.–Harper, Ellsworth
897	Griffin, J. Ellen–Griffing, Nellie M.	961	Harper, Emarilla–Harpster, William P.
898	Griffinham, Augustus–Griffith, Newton S.	962	Harquet, Susan–Harrington, Cyrus E.
899	Griffith, Oliver–Grigwire, Peter	963	Harrington, Daniel–Harrirell, Minerva A.
900	Griley, Joseph F.–Grimley, William	964	Harris, A. Edward–Harris, Dorothy E.
901	Grimm, Adaline–Grisot, Caroline	965	Harris, Early–Harris, Hulda C.

Roll	Description	Roll	Description
966	Harris, Ida–Harris, Loyd G.	1030	Hessel, Catharine–Hettsheimer, Andrew
967	Harris, Lucien A.–Harris, Ritty	1031	Hetu, Jean–Hewitt, Ezekiel G.
968	Harris, Robert–Harrisberger, Pauline	1032	Hewitt, Fanny A.–Hezlett, Mary
969	Harrison, Abner–Harrison, Jordan C.	1033	Hiam, Charles–Hickethier, Charles
970	Harrison, Joseph–Harriss, William B.	1034	Hickey, Aaron J.–Hickman, Zachariah
971	Harritt, Flora E.–Harston, Mary J.	1035	Hickney, William A.–Hicks, Jasper N.
972	Hart, Aaron–Hart, Hugh S.	1036	Hicks, Jemima–Hicks, Zachary T.
973	Hart, Ida L.–Hart, Owen B.	1037	Hicksenhizer, Sue–Higgins, Edwin P.
974	Hart, Parkason W.–Hartew, John H.	1038	Higgins, Elijah–Higgins, William W.
975	Hartfelter, Florence–Hartmaier, Marie E.	1039	Higginson, Annis L.–Hilckman, Karl
976	Hartman, A. Elizabeth–Hartmann, William	1040	Hild, Adam–Hilkirt, Lou
977	Hartmaster, Adelhied–Harty, William C.	1041	Hill, Aaron–Hill, Drusilla E.
978	Hartz, Adam–Harvey, John F. D.	1042	Hill, Eady–Hill, Hezekiah
979	Harvey, John J.–Harwood, Lyman C.	1043	Hill, Hiram–Hill, Lizzina
980	Harwood, Maggie–Haskill, Sherman R.	1044	Hill, Locena–Hill, Riley
981	Haskin, Albert M.–Hassey, Robert	1045	Hill, Robert–Hill, Zubia L.
982	Hassfurther, Eva–Haswell, William S.	1046	Hillabold, Lyman S.–Hillkirk, Isaac
983	Hatany, James–Hatchman, Norman	1047	Hillman, Alexander H.–Hilsz, Elizabeth
984	Hate, Charles–Hathaway, Isabelle T.	1048	Hilt, Agnes–Himes, William S.
985	Hathaway, James–Hatzler, Philippine	1049	Himighaefer, Charles–Hindy, John
986	Hau, Amalia–Haury, Wilhelmina	1050	Hine, Agnes–Hineys, Margaret
987	Haus, Amelia D.–Havenstrite, James H.	1051	Hinfey, Maria–Hinshilwood, Thomas J.
988	Haver, Albert A.–Hawke, Wesley I.	1052	Hinske, Auguste–Hirst, William H.
989	Hawken, Anna J.–Hawkins, Jasper S.	1053	Hirt, Adam–Hitchcox, Theodore
990	Hawkins, Jemima S.–Hawkins, Zalmon S., Jr.	1054	Hitchell, William–Hlvsa, Wenzel
991	Hawks, Abraham S.–Hawsman, Louisa	1055	Hoadley, Amanda E.–Hoban, Patrick
992	Hawthorn, Adelia B.–Hayden, Jesse G.	1056	Hobard, Emma V.–Hobron, John D.
993	Hayden, Joanna T.–Hayes, Hurlburt C.	1057	Hobson, Adelina–Hodgdon, Westbury G.
994	Hayes, Ida J.–Hayes, Zilphia	1058	Hodge, Albert D.–Hodges, Kezia
995	Hayford, Abbie–Haynes, Louretta C.	1059	Hodges, Laura A.–Hodum, John M.
996	Haynes, Leander–Hayes, Jasper F.	1060	Hoe, Lizzie–Hoffert, Rebecca
997	Hays, Jennett–Hayward, Cyrus W.	1061	Hoffhaus, Clarence P.–Hoffman, John F.
998	Hayward, Daniel L.–Hazeltine, William B.	1062	Hoffman, John H.–Hoffmüller, Hulda
999	Hazelton, Aaron–Hazzard, William H.	1063	Hoffnagle, Henry–Hogan, Winfred
1000	Hea, Harper H.–Healde, John	1064	Hogancamp, Catharine–Hohmeyer, William F.
1001	Heale, George–Heaston, William C.	1065	Hohn, Andrew–Holby, Sarah E.
1002	Heasty, Alexander M.–Heath, Zachariah	1066	Holcher, Anna M.–Holden, Lydia N.
1003	Heathcock, Joseph–Hechtman, Augusta	1067	Holden, Magalene–Holiday, William H.
1004	Heck, Abraham–Hector, William	1068	Holifield, Charles L.–Holland, Zelpha J.
1005	Hed, James–Hedtke, Fred E.	1069	Hollander, Barbara–Holliday, William W.
1006	Heeb, Catharine–Hefty, Thomas	1070	Hollidge, Harry H.–Hollis, William H.
1007	Heg, Cornelia–Heilweck, Jacob B.	1071	Hollister, Abraham O.–Hollwarth, William
1008	Heim, Adam–Heiry, Katharine B.	1072	Holly, Ada J.–Holmes, Charles W.
1009	Heis, Charles–Heljeson, Ellick	1073	Holmes, Chauncey–Holmes, Julius J.
1010	Helk, Maggie–Helmcke, Max G. C.	1074	Holmes, Kate–Holmes, Zachariah H.
1011	Helme, Abby F.–Helvy, William M.	1075	Holmesly, Sarah M.–Holt, Lyman
1012	Helwagen, Anna–Hempy, William I.	1076	Holt, Maggie J.–Holtzworth, Rebecca W.
1013	Hemrick, Anthony–Henderson, Dorcas	1077	Holubar, Joseph–Honeter, George
1014	Henderson, Edward–Henderson, Lyman H.	1078	Honey, Allen–Hood, Winfield S.
1015	Henderson, Mabel–Henderson, Winnie	1079	Hoodacheck, Anna–Hoopengarner, Nicholas
1016	Hendeny, David–Hendrickson, Isabella G.	1080	Hooper, Abbie F.–Hoover, Correnna F.
1017	Hendrickson, Jacob–Henizer, Nicholas	1081	Hoover, Daniel–Hoovler, Mary E.
1018	Henk, Conrad–Hennighausen, Louis P.	1082	Hopcraft, Giorge F.–Hopkins, Isora
1019	Hennin, Thomas C.–Henry, Dudley G.	1083	Hopkins, J. Ray–Hopkirk, William H.
1020	Henry, Edgar–Henry, Lydia M. P.	1084	Hopler, Alfred–Horcher, Samuel
1021	Henry, M. Jennie–Hense, William	1085	Hord, Alexander–Horn, William S.
1022	Hensel, Adaline–Hensyl, Sarah E.	1086	Hornaday, Armatha–Horneyer, Herman
1023	Hente, Friedrich–Herbetz, Magdalena	1087	Horni, Elizabeth–Horton, Cyrenus F.
1024	Herbig, Caroline–Herman, William W.	1088	Horton, Daniel B.–Horzesky, Frank J.
1025	Hermonce, Agnes L.–Herrguth, Carl R.	1089	Hosack, Alfred–Hospodsky, Henry F.
1026	Herrian, Erna–Herring, William P.	1090	Hoss, Adelia–Hottle, Martha
1027	Herrington, Aaron–Hersey, William S.	1091	Hottman, Charles–Houghn, George
1028	Hersh, Alice–Hespenheid, Henry	1092	Houghtailing, Abram M.–Housberger, Edwin H.
1029	Hess, Aaron–Hesse, Sarah J.	1093	House, Abbie E.–Houser, Dillen

Roll	Description	Roll	Description
1094	Houser, Edgar–Housworth, Valentine	1158	Jangraw, Basiles–Jarow, Henry L.
1095	Hout, John J.–Howard, Byron W.	1159	Jarra, Thomas–Jax, Mary M.
1096	Howard, Cammie–Howard, Israel J.	1160	Jay, Aaron–Jeffers, William M.
1097	Howard, Jackson–Howard, Myron E.	1161	Jefferson, Adam–Jeklin, Friederika
1098	Howard, Nancy–Howard, Zirelda	1162	Jelf, Armstead–Jenkins, Edwin W.
1099	Howardson, James–Howe, Lyston, D.	1163	Jenkins, Elcie–Jenkins, Martin
1100	Howe, Maggie A.–Howell, Franklin R.	1164	Jenkins, Mary–Jenkyns, William H.
1101	Howell, Garrett–Howells, Winifred	1165	Jenna, Mary H.–Jennings, John W.
1102	Howen, Katharina–Howry, Nancy	1166	Jennings, Jonathan–Jepson, William H.
1103	Hows, Amanda–Hoyt, Gideon	1167	Jerald, Maranda–Jetmore, Rebecca
1104	Hoyt, Hannah A.–Hubbard, Fredrick B.	1168	Jett, Albert N.–Jewett, Lydia L.
1105	Hubbard, George–Hubbartt, Pallace	1169	Jewett, Mahala A.–Joerns, Nicholaus
1106	Hubbell, Albert–Huberty, Peter	1170	Joffray, Margaret–Johns, Wyatt R.
1107	Hubig, Henry–Hudson, Drucilla A.	1171	Johnsen, Bertha–Johnson, Angieline
1108	Hudson, E. Herbert–Hudson, Zeadric B.	1172	Johnson, Ann–Johnson, Carter
1109	Hudsonpillar, Apseda A.–Huff, Swan B.	1173	Johnson, Casandra L.–Johnson, Cyrus N.
1110	Huff, Taylor–Huffmann, Omer E.	1174	Johnson, D. Ozias–Johnson, Elizur G.
1111	Huffmaster, Johanna–Hughes, Ceolak	1175	Johnson, Ella–Johnson, Fritz
1112	Hughes, Charity C.–Hughes, Jesse M.	1176	Johnson, G. Stewart–Johnson, Haze
1113	Hughes, Job–Hughes, Owen	1177	Johnson, Hector O.–Johnson, Jake
1114	Hughes, Patrick–Hughs, Young S.	1178	Johnson, James–Johnson, Johanna M.
1115	Hughson, Anna M.–Hull, Bishop A.	1179	Johnson, John–Johnson, Jordan
1116	Hull, Calista–Hull, Zilpha A.	1180	Johnson, Joseph–Johnson, Lowsenie
1117	Hullan, Margaret–Humelsine, Mary F.	1181	Johnson, Lubie–Johnson, Martinia L.
1118	Humer, Gertrude E.–Humphrey, Frederick R.	1182	Johnson, Mary–Johnson, Mitchell B.
1119	Humphrey, George–Humprey, Otis M.	1183	Johnson, Mollie–Johnson, Rezin L.
1120	Humpton, Agnes–Hunt, Cephas B.	1184	Johnson, Rhoda–Johnson, Sarah Emma
1121	Hunt, Chalkley B.–Hunt, Josie M.	1185	Johnson, Sarah F.–Johnson, Voltaire W.
1122	Hunt, Judson–Hunten, Joseph	1186	Johnson, W. Bird–Johnson, William M. C.
1123	Hunter, Aaron–Hunter, Julius	1187	Johnson, William N.–Johnston, Hyrcanus
1124	Hunter, Kate–Hunter, Winney	1188	Johnston, Ibbia A.–Johnston, Ruth Jane
1125	Hunterman, John–Huonker, Louis	1189	Johnston, Sabrah Almeda–Jondro, Peter
1126	Hupbach, Charles–Hurlburt, William	1190	Jones, A. Parker–Jones, Anthony
1127	Hurlbut, Adelaide–Hurson, James S.	1191	Jones, Arabell–Jones, Christopher T.
1128	Hurst, Aaron–Husfield, William G.	1192	Jones, Cinderella–Jones, Eliza W.
1129	Hush, Aaron–Huston, Katharine C.	1193	Jones, Elizabeth–Jones, Freeman S.
1130	Huston, Lelitia–Hutchins, Zannie	1194	Jones, G. Emma–Jones, Hezekiah
1131	Hutchinson, Abbie S.–Hutchinson, Zilpha E.	1195	Jones, Hilliard–Jones, Jasper N.
1132	Hutchison, Alexander–Hutto, Mary J.	1196	Jones, Jeanette–Jones, Jordan
1133	Hutton, Abia–Hyatt, Myron	1197	Jones, Joseph–Jones, Lyman R.
1134	Hyatt, N. Secor–Hydorn, Sanford	1198	Jones, M. Evelyn–Jones, Mary A.
1135	Hye, Agnes–Hyzer, William W.	1199	Jones, Mary B.–Jones, Nancy E.
1136	I–Ilhardt, Mary E.	1200	Jones, Nancy H.–Jones, Rina
1137	Iliff, Alpheus–Ingels, William B.	1201	Jones, Robert–Jones, Sherman A.
1138	Ingemorson, Stone–Ingoman, William D.	1202	Jones, Siddy–Jones, Wiley E.
1139	Ingraham, A. Sylvester–Ingwood, Nellie	1203	Jones, William–Joray, Peter
1140	Inhelder, Ulrich–Iredell, Virginia E.	1204	Jordan, Abbie–Jordan, Jonathan
1141	Irelan, Andrew–Irsch, Mary	1205	Jordan, Joseph–Jordan, Talman
1142	Irven, Lavina–Irwin, George W.	1206	Jordt, Hans–Joy, Isaac
1143	Irwin, James–Isaat, Samuel	1207	Joy, James–Juddy, John A.
1144	Isabel, Mahaly–Isphording, William	1208	Judell, Bonifaz–Jump, William K.
1145	Israel, Ada J.–Izzard, Margaret J.	1209	Jumper, Amanda F.–Juvinall, Margaret J.
1146	J–Jackson, Andrew S.	1210	K–Kairo, Michael
1147	Jackson, Angeline–Jackson, Elvis B.	1211	Kaiser, Amalie–Kamus, Anna G.
1148	Jackson, Emaline–Jackson, James A.	1212	Kanable, Almira A.–Kanouse, Thomas
1149	Jackson, James B.–Jackson, Manning H.	1213	Kans, Wilhelmine–Karpus, John
1150	Jackson, Maranda–Jackson, Ruth E.	1214	Karr, Aaron L.–Kaucher, Seno
1151	Jackson, Sabelia–Jackson, Zuleima B.	1215	Kauf, Charles–Kawood, Jerry
1152	Jackstock, Cora M.–Jacobs, John D.	1216	Kay, Allie G.–Kearnes, Samuel J.
1153	Jacobs, John F.–Jacobson, William	1217	Kearney, Abigail A.–Kebo, Alice
1154	Jacobus, Abraham–Jamerson, Mary A.	1218	Kech, Minna–Keeks, John H.
1155	James, Abraham–James, Juliaett	1219	Keel, Abraham W.–Keen, William W.
1156	James, Kate–James, Zachariah D.	1220	Keena, William–Keersted, William T.
1157	Jameson, Abbie J.–Janezeck, John J.	1221	Kees, Aaron–Keilly, Elizabeth C.

Roll	Description
1222	Keilman, Conrad–Keith, Wilson R.
1223	Keithler, John–Keller, Ezekiel T.
1224	Keller, Ferdinand–Kellette, John W.
1225	Kelley, Aaron W.–Kelley, Jacob W.
1226	Kelley, James–Kelley, Norman
1227	Kelley, Oliver M.–Kellogg, Eveleen L.
1228	Kellogg, Fannie S.–Kelly, Burr
1229	Kelly, Caleb J. McNutly–Kelly, Jasper N.
1230	Kelly, Jean B.–Kelly, Maurice
1231	Kelly, Merritt P.–Kelly, Thersa A.
1232	Kelm, Elise W.–Kelzer, Eva
1233	Kem, Augusten–Kempher, Sarah E.
1234	Kempin, Leopold A.–Kenderdine, Thaddeus S.
1235	Kendig, Alice M.–Kenneaster, Charles W.
1236	Kenneda, Thomas–Kennedy, Isabelle
1237	Kennedy, Jacob–Kennedy, Moses B.
1238	Kennedy, Nancy–Kenney, Bridget
1239	Kenney, Caroline S.–Kenstler, Frank
1240	Kent, Aaron L.–Kenworthy, William R.
1241	Keny, William–Keppy, Lydia M.
1242	Ker, Almira S.–Kernon, James
1243	Kerns, Aaron–Kerr, Spencer G.
1244	Kerr, Stephen B.–Kessler, Daniel W.
1245	Kessler, Edmund–Ketzner, Elizabeth
1246	Keubel, Henry–Keyse, Thomas
1247	Keyser, Abram–Kidde, Louise
1248	Kidder, Adelbert–Kiepler, Helena
1249	Kier, Adella M.–Kilcummins, Luke
1250	Kildare, Ellen A.–Killitz, Martha A.
1251	Killman, Andrew P.–Kimball, Ivory G.
1252	Kimball, Jacob S.–Kimble, Julia A.
1253	Kimble, Laura I.–Kinberger, Mary Louisa
1254	Kincade, Alice–Kineyea, Adeline
1255	King, A. Ella–King, Edwin R.
1256	King, Elbertha B.–King, Hennitta E.
1257	King, Henry–King, Lizzie S.
1258	King, Loda B.–King, Priscilla
1259	King, R. Susan–King, Zoa
1260	Kingan, Martha–Kingwill, Mary R.
1261	Kinhachi, Torniya–Kinnett, William E.
1262	Kinney, Aaron–Kinny, William G.
1263	Kinross, Andrew W.–Kinzy, Warren
1264	Kio, Eugene–Kirby, William S.
1265	Kirch, Catharina–Kirk, Zachary T.
1266	Kirkbride, Adelia J.–Kirkpatrick, Lucy J.
1267	Kirkpatrick, Madison B.–Kiser, William W.
1268	Kish, Christopher–Kitchner, Henry
1269	Kite, Abraham–Kjellesvig, Turine
1270	Klaar, Caroline–Klein, William
1271	Kleinan, Anna–Kline, John W.
1272	Kline, Jonas–Klinzing, Wilhelmina
1273	Klipfel, Anthony–Knapp, Cyrus W.
1274	Knapp, David–Knapton, Robert
1275	Knard, John L.–Knezel, Annie M.
1276	Knibb, Charles M.–Knight, Isabella
1277	Knight, Jabez–Knights, William W.
1278	Knilaus, Eleanor F.–Knostman, Orville C.
1279	Knote, Daniel–Knowlson, John
1280	Knowlton, Aaron–Knoy, Godfrey
1281	Knuchal, Arnold J.–Kocker, George
1282	Koderhandt, Theresa–Kogler, Jacob
1283	Kohane, Margaret–Komst, Elisabeth
1284	Konantz, Charles Frank–Kopseng, Martha J.
1285	Koral, William J.–Kraetzer, Julius F.
1286	Kraff, Herman–Kraszynski, Maurice
1287	Krater, Catharine–Krehmeyer, Mary
1288	Kreibaum, Mina–Kreyser, William
1289	Kribble, David A.–Kromrei, Emil Friedrich
1290	Kron, Catherine–Krupp, Ludamina
1291	Krus, Bernard T.–Kuhmann, Elisabetha
1292	Kuhn, Abraham–Kunitz, Maria A.
1293	Kunk, Anton B.–Kurzydloska, Agnes Z.
1294	Kus, William–Kyte, Sarah A.
1295	L–Lacey, William F. M.
1296	Lachall, James–Lacy, Zachariah
1297	Ladam, Adelia–Lafewell, Alfred
1298	Laffam, Annie E.–Lahmon, Mariah
1299	Lahna, Frank–Lajoy, Thomas
1300	Lake, Aaron J.–Lalumendier, Theophile
1301	Lam, Cordelia–Lamb, Ruth A.
1302	Lamb, Sallie–Lambert, Ruth E.
1303	Lambert, Sabina–Lamory, Ellsworth E.
1304	Lamos, Carrie B.–Lamy, Theodore
1305	Lanagan, Ann–Landenwich, Anthony Hamon
1306	Lander, Albert–Landon, Cymantha
1307	Landon, Daniel–Lane, Drusilla L.
1308	Lane, E. Clarkson–Lane, Marcus M.
1309	Lane, Margaret–Lanfred, Amalia
1310	Lang, Aaron–Langenschwadt, Hedwig
1311	Langer, Augusta–Langtree, Jennie
1312	Langwell, Cathrine–Lanphierd, Wilbur T.
1313	Lans, Mary E.–Lapman, Edward A.
1314	Lapoint, Adelia–Largy, Catharine
1315	Larick, Amanda E.–Larney, Patrick
1316	Laro, Nellie–Lartz, Carl
1317	Larue, Abraham–Lasswell, Willis T.
1318	Last, August–Latlip, Gott
1319	Latner, Pinkus–Lauersdorf, Maria
1320	Lauf, Christine–Lauthers, Eliza J.
1321	Lautner, Paul O.–Law, William T.
1322	Lawajeck, Margaret–Lawrence, Centre H.
1323	Lawrence, Charity–Lawrence, Lyman
1324	Lawrence, Mark–Lawshe, Huldie E.
1325	Lawsin, Norman–Lawson, Zadoc
1326	Lawther, Hutter–Laymore, Sarah M.
1327	Layne, A. L.–Leach, Eunice A.
1328	Leach, Florence A.–Leake, Walter A.
1329	Leakey, Amos C.–Leasure, William M.
1330	Leatch, Jan E.–Lebkucher, Frank I.
1331	Leblanc, Alphonse–Ledyard, William B.
1332	Lee, Aaron–Lee, Furman D.
1333	Lee, Gardner W.–Lee, King David
1334	Lee, Lafayette–Lee, Ruth Ann
1335	Lee, Sabina E.–Leedy, William C.
1336	Leef, Robert M.–LeFevre, William R.
1337	Leff, Caroline–Leguire, William R.
1338	Leh, Albert W.–Leicy, Edward
1339	Leidberg, John L.–Leisure, William S.
1340	Leitch, Ada C.–Lemly, William H.
1341	Lemm, Hattie–Lengr, John
1342	Lenham, Leverich G.–Lenzen, Anna Maria
1343	Leo, Alice F.–Leonard, Lyman B.
1344	Leonard, Maggie–Lequire, James C.
1345	Lerat, Leonie–Lessor, Mary Adelia
1346	Lester, Abner–Letzner, Frank H.
1347	Leu, Anna M.–Levyson, Bernhart
1348	Lew, Burt E.–Lewis, Byron F.
1349	Lewis, C. Frances–Lewis, Elzona

Roll	Description
1350	Lewis, Emaline–Lewis, Israel T.
1351	Lewis, J. Woodruff–Lewis, Kitty S.
1352	Lewis, Lafayette–Lewis, Mary Jane E.
1353	Lewis, Mary K.–Lewis, Sanford G.
1354	Lewis, Sarah–Lewis, William S.
1355	Lewis, William T.–Libby, Woodbury S.
1356	Libe, Amanda–Liermann, Mary
1357	Lies, Estrella–Lighty, William L.
1358	Ligier, Joseph–Lilly, Wilson S.
1359	Lima, Julia E.–Lincoln, Zuleeka S.
1360	Lind, Albert M.–Lindrob, Maria
1361	Lindsay, Abigail–Lindsey, Zachary T.
1362	Lindskog, Charles V.–Linington, Theodore
1363	Link, Adaliza–Linstruth, Henry B.
1364	Lint, Conrad–Liptrap, Angeline
1365	Lisbon, Margaret–Litson, Louisa M.
1366	Litt, Caroline–Little, Kate
1367	Little, Laura–Littlehales, William
1368	Littlejohn, Abraham–Livery, Jane
1369	Livesay, Andrew J.–Llewelyn, Samuel
1370	Lloyd, Aaron–Lobsinger, Ellen A.
1371	Locey, Frances E.–Lockey, Josephine E.
1372	Lockhard, Elizabeth Ann–Lockwood, Munson M.
1373	Lockwood, Nancy A.–Loftus, Winifred F.
1374	Logel, David W.–Logo, Josephine
1375	Logsden, Anthony–Lompe, Marie
1376	Lonabaugh, Joseph R.–Long, Doran H.
1377	Long, E. Frances–Long, Jesse
1378	Long, Joanna–Long, Morton
1379	Long, Nide–Long, Zoe A. F.
1380	Longa, Archie B.–Longyear, William D.
1381	Lonie, Edward–Loomis, Winfield S.
1382	Loonen, Patrick–Lord, Benjamin L.
1383	Lord, Caius C.–Lorge, Jean B.
1384	Lorick, Dinah–Lotspike, Ellen A.
1385	Lott, Abragal–Loufman, James
1386	Lougan, Emma J.–Louzader, Terriza
1387	Lov, Christof–Love, William S.
1388	Loveall, Alexander–Lovell, Lydia P.
1389	Lovell, M. Anna–Low, William S.
1390	Lowance, Peter–Lowe, Willis C.
1391	Loweberg, Johan W. A.–Lowpossy, Margaret E.
1392	Lowrance, Bertie–Loyall, Jesse
1393	Loyd, Adam–Lucas, Israel
1394	Lucas, Jackson–Lucey, Timothy
1395	Lüch, Heinrich–Ludvikson, Gabriel
1396	Ludway, Thomas R.–Lukemires, John F.
1397	Luken, Caroline–Lundy, Willits
1398	Luney, Robert–Luskuski, Nikolai
1399	Luss, Dorothea–Lutz, Friedericke
1400	Lutz, George–Lyles, Wiot E.
1401	Lyman, A. Sidney–Lynch, Grace R.
1402	Lynch, Hannah–Lynch, William W.
1403	Lynd, Andrew–Lyon, Isaac S.
1404	Lyon, Jacob–Lyons, Julius A.
1405	Lyons, Kate–Lyzott, Charles F.
1406	McAbee, Ann–McAllister, Kate F.
1407	McAllister, Lester S.–McAtere, William
1408	McAulay, Bridget–McBride, Julia T.
1409	McBride, Kate I.–McCabe, Winfield S.
1410	McCachran, Ann–McCall, William W.
1411	McCalla, Addie–McCann, Josie F.
1412	McCann, Lelia–McCarthy, Cornelius
1413	McCarthy, Daniel–McCartt, Millie A.

Roll	Description
1414	McCarty, Addie E.–McCasky, Louisa W.
1415	McCasland, Almedia C. A.–McClaid, Lucetta
1416	McClain, Aaron–McClay, Zachariah T.
1417	McClead, Alfred C.–McClelland, Winna J.
1418	McClellen, George–McCloy, Samuel M.
1419	McClucass, Annette I.–McClure, Susie
1420	McClure, Theodore A.–McColum, Carrie E.
1421	McComas, Burnett–McConnell, Dyer B.
1422	McConnell, Edgar–McCoppin, William T. S.
1423	McCord, Abby L.–McCormick, Isaiah H.
1424	McCormick, Jacob–McCown, William L.
1425	McCoy, Aaron–McCoy, Myrtle
1426	McCoy, Nancy–McCraw, William
1427	McCray, Addison–McCrystal, William J. P.
1428	McCuaig, Alexander–McCullough, Moses
1429	McCullough, Nancy–McCurtin, Nathaniel
1430	McCusker, Alice A.–McDaniel, Susan J.
1431	McDaniel, Tama–McDoll, Peter
1432	McDonagh, Catherine–McDonald, Isaiah H.
1433	McDonald, Jack–McDonald, Priscilla T.
1434	McDonald, R. Elvina–McDonough, William I.
1435	McDorman, Amanda J.–McDowell, Zachariah W.
1436	McDuell, Elise–McElroy, William T.
1437	McElvain, Aidlia C.–McFadzen, William
1438	McFail, Augustus–McFarland, Zadoc
1439	McFarlane, Alexander–McGaw, Sarah F.
1440	McEachy, Edward C.–McGiffin, William
1441	McGilbra, Amy–McGinnis, Lydia A.
1442	McGinnis, Margaret–McGourty, Mary E.
1443	McGoven, John–McGranor, Mary A.
1444	McGrath, Abbie–McGregory, Mary Abby
1445	McGrellis, Elizabeth–McGuire, James A.
1446	McGuire, James B.–McHatton, William, Jr.
1447	McHendrie, Eliza J.–McInroy, Otis O.
1448	McIntee, John–McIntosh, Zerilda
1449	McInturf, Daniel–McKavitt, Mary
1450	McKay, Aaron–McKee, Evaline
1451	McKee, Fannie A.–McKeever, William P.
1452	McKegg, Isaac–McKenty, Daniel
1453	McKenzie, Alexander–McKiddy, William C.
1454	McKie, Charles W.–McKinney, Ellen
1455	McKinney, Emeline–McKinny, Perry
1456	McKinsey, Alfred T.–McKrill, Rebecca
1457	McKuan, John–McLauchlin, Samuel S.
1458	McLaughlan, Daniel–McLaughlin, Moses H.
1459	McLaughlin, Nancy A.–McLeister, John
1460	McLeland, Carrie–McMahn, John
1461	McMahon, Abbie F.–McManon, John
1462	McManus, Amelia J.–McMillan, Duncan J.
1463	McMillan, Edgar D.–McMillon, William M.
1464	McMindes, Augusta–McMurray, Zerilda A.
1465	McMurren, Alexander–McNamara, Lucy
1466	McNamara, Margaret–McNeece, William H.
1467	McNeal, Effie–McNew, Zedakiah
1468	McNichol, Elizabeth–McPeters, Mary J.
1469	McPhail, Alexander–McPyke, Margaret
1470	McQuade, Ann–McRell, Joseph
1471	McReynolds, Amos H.–McVay, William H. H.
1472	McVea, David M.–McZimmerman, Michael
1473	M–Macey, William
1474	Macfadden, Emma B.–Mackall, Verlinda
1475	Mackay, Anabel B.–MacMurray, Henrietta V. A.
1476	Macnab, James–Maddex, William T.
1477	Maddic, Andrewener–Madison, William J.

Roll	Description
1478	Madla, Damian–Magher, William
1479	Magie, Ambrose H.–Magwood, Robert
1480	Mahady, Annie M.–Mahnken, Mary A.
1481	Mahogany, Ellen E.–Maimbourg, Rebecca B.
1482	Main, Abiah B.–Majors, Wilson E.
1483	Maka, Samuel–Mallay, Jules
1484	Mallegol, Pierre–Malnburg, John
1485	Malo, Elizabeth–Malony, William N.
1486	Maloon, Frances E.–Mancourt, S. Matilda
1487	Mand, Fred B.–Manjarres, Carlos
1488	Mank, Jacob F.–Mann, Isabella A.
1489	Mann, Jacob–Manning, Eva E.
1490	Manning, Fannie–Manser, Mary A. H.
1491	Mansfield, Addie A.–Manzischke, Reinhard
1492	Maog, Tranquilino–Marcey, Orrin J.
1493	March, Aaron–Margut, Florence A.
1494	Marhefka, Charles J.–Markit, William H.
1495	Markla, Jacob–Markworth, Henrietta R.
1496	Marlan, John T.–Marqwadt, Fred W.
1497	Marr, Agnes–Marsh, Eliza M.
1498	Marsh, Elizabeth–Marsha, David
1499	Marshal, John–Marshall, Israel
1500	Marshall, Jackson–Marshall, Ruth Ann
1501	Marshall, Sabra–Martels, Charles V.
1502	Marten, Benjamin T.–Martin, Celia F.
1503	Martin, Chana–Martin, Ezra H.
1504	Martin, Fannie–Martin, Israel
1505	Martin, J. Adolph–Martin, John W.
1506	Martin, Johny–Martin, Martina A.
1507	Martin, Mary–Martin, Prudence Z.
1508	Martin, Rachael–Martin, Vituly C.
1509	Martin, W. Ben–Martsolf, Minnie
1510	Martter, Elizabeth–Masner, Michael
1511	Mason, Aaron M.–Mason, Jiney J.
1512	Mason, Joanna–Mason, Sylvester
1513	Mason, Tabitha–Massy, Peter
1514	Mast, Anna B.–Matevia, Amelia
1515	Matha, John H.–Mathews, Dyer R.
1516	Mathews, Ebenezer–Mathews, Zalmon T.
1517	Mathewson, Abigail L.–Matsom, William T.
1518	Matt, Alexander–Matthews, Frederick E.
1519	Matthews, Garrett–Mattice, William G.
1520	Mattick, Mary E.–Mauff, Rosalie
1521	Maug, Philippma H.–Mavity, Wesley A. J.
1522	Maw, Ah–Maxwell, Burr
1523	Maxwell, C. Blanche–Maxworthe, John
1524	May, Ada–May, Sylvester S.
1525	May, Theodore–Mayewski, Mary
1526	Mayfield, Abram–Mayntzer, Joseph
1527	Mayo, Abbie M. W.–Mead, Dwight
1528	Mead, Edgar–Meades, James
1529	Meadler, John W.–Meany, Morris B.
1530	Mear, Clinton E.–Medlar, Zachariah
1531	Medlen, Charity–Meek, William W.
1532	Meeker, Abraham–Megguier, Mary J.
1533	Mehaffey, Catharine–Mekula, Charles M.
1534	Melampy, Patrick–Meloy, William W.
1535	Melratle, Anna B.–Mendelssohn, James R.
1536	Mendenhall, Absalom–Menzner, Josephine
1537	Meo, Donato–Merdoff, George S.
1538	Mere, Basile–Merow, Mary F.
1539	Merrall, Michael H.–Merrill, Eulissa
1540	Merrill, Ferdinand W.–Merriss, William W.
1541	Merrit, Daniel H.–Merssman, Isaac
1542	Mertel, Malinda–Messenheimer, William I.
1543	Messer, Alexander–Metcalf, Julia A.
1544	Metcalf, Kate–Metzer, Pauline
1545	Metzgar, Abby W.–Meyer, Cynthia
1546	Meyer, Daniel–Meyero, Mary
1547	Meyers, Abraham–Michael, Minnie D.
1548	Michael, Nancy A.–Micue, Mary R.
1549	Miday, Eugene J.–Miexsell, Peter
1550	Mifferd, George–Miles, Docia E.
1551	Miles, Eda A.–Miles, Zephaniah
1552	Milet, Ellen–Millenkamp, Frederick
1553	Miller, A. Howard–Miller, Annette Lundy
1554	Miller, Annie–Miller, Charles A.
1555	Miller, Charles B.–Miller, Dwight E.
1556	Miller, Easter J.–Miller, Emory A.
1557	Miller, Engel D.–Miller, George T.
1558	Miller, George W.–Miller, Henry Witmer
1559	Miller, Herbert–Miller, James F.
1560	Miller, James G.–Miller, John E. L.
1561	Miller, John F.–Miller, Julius W.
1562	Miller, Keiyiah–Miller, Lyman W.
1563	Miller, McCoy–Miller, Mary
1564	Miller, Mary A.–Miller, Mittie Ann
1565	Miller, Mollie–Miller, Rhode
1566	Miller, Richard–Miller, Sherwood
1567	Miller, Sibba–Miller, William
1568	Miller, William A.–Millhuff, Francis
1569	Millian, Nannie A.–Millross, Albert J.
1570	Mills, Aaron–Mills, Jeremiah
1571	Mills, Jesse–Mills, Zilpha J.
1572	Millsack, Frederick G.–Mindman, Mathias
1573	Minear, Adam–Minick, William T.
1574	Minier, Aaron–Minott, Wilbur V.
1575	Mins, Francis–Mitchek, Frank J.
1576	Mitchel, Catharine–Mitchell, Elvira
1577	Mitchell, Emaline–Mitchell, Jesse E.
1578	Mitchell, Joanna L. H.–Mitchell, Myron
1579	Mitchell, Nancy–Mitchell, Zephy
1580	Mitchelson, Arthur E.–Moatz, John
1581	Mobberly, John W.–Moeves, Edward
1582	Mofet, Harriet–Mohr, William H.
1583	Mohrbacher, Adam–Monagle, Emma
1584	Monahan, Alice–Monrean, Maud
1585	Monreau, Joseph–Monroe, Zurial
1586	Monrok, Frances–Montgomery, Grace P.
1587	Montgomery, Hadie–Montgomery, Sarah A.
1588	Montgomery, Sarah B.–Moody, Frederick A.
1589	Moody, G. Garrett–Moon, Jane
1590	Moon, Jehu–Moonshower, Jacob
1591	Moor, Anderson S.–Moore, Byron W.
1592	Moore, Caleb–Moore, Eliza P.
1593	Moore, Elizabeth–Moore, Guy S.
1594	Moore, H. Miles–Moore, James W. V.
1595	Moore, Jane–Moore, Justus G.
1596	Moore, Kate–Moore, Mary
1597	Moore, Mary A.–Moore, Purlina J.
1598	Moore, Quintillie–Moore, Sylvester P.
1599	Moore, T. Mark–Moore, Zovalda
1600	Moored, Elvina J.–Moran, Miles J.
1601	Moran, Nancy E.–Morehouse, Kingsley C.
1602	Morehouse, Lenard–Morgado, Pedro Jose
1603	Morgan, Aaron–Morgan, Evin
1604	Morgan, Fannie E.–Morgan, Julius B.
1605	Morgan, Kate R.–Morgan, Ryan

Roll	Description
1606	Morgan, S. Minerva–Moritz, William H.
1607	Mork, Jacob–Morring, Eliza A.
1608	Morris, Aaron–Morris, Furman
1609	Morris, Gabriel T.–Morris, Lyman T.
1610	Morris, Madison H.–Morris, Syrena
1611	Morris, Tabitha E.–Morrison, Hugh
1612	Morrison, Ida A.–Morrison, Zachariah T.
1613	Morrisroe, Margaret–Morry, Jahn
1614	Mors, Selah–Morse, Lysander C.
1615	Morse, Mabelia–Morton, Bridget
1616	Morton, Caroline–Mory, Henry C.
1617	Mosak–Mosey, Marion
1618	Mosgeller, Christina–Mosquera, Gelacia
1619	Moss, A. Seaborn–Motes, Nancy
1620	Mothell, Dee–Moulson, Ephraim
1621	Moulter, William C.–Mountz, William A.
1622	Mourer, Amos–Moxter, Henry
1623	Moy, Emily–Muckridge, Carrie A.
1624	Mudd, Almont R.–Mukes, Susan
1625	Muladore, John C.–Mullaly, Richard
1626	Mullan, Amelia C.–Mullenweg, William H.
1627	Müller, Adolph–Mullikin, William T.
1628	Mullin, Adelaide L.–Mulyern, Frank
1629	Muma, Benjamin F.–Munford, William H.
1630	Munganest, Maria–Munsinger, George
1631	Munson, Abbie–Mure, Sarah
1632	Murfey, Rachel A.–Murphy, Edwin
1633	Murphy, Ela A.–Murphy, John
1634	Murphy, John A.–Murphy, Mitchell
1635	Murphy, Monterville–Murphy, Zora Z.
1636	Murr, David S.–Murray, Jesse C.
1637	Murray, John–Murray, Russel B.
1638	Murray, Sallie S.–Mury, Henry
1639	Musbach, Jacob F.–Musty, John C.
1640	Muta, Edward–Myers, Catherine P.
1641	Myers, Celestine–Myers, Hattie
1642	Myers, Heber–Myers, Louisiana
1643	Myers, Lucinda–Myers, Savilla A.
1644	Myers, Selena–Mytton, Ellen
1645	N–Naile, William H.
1646	Nailer, Daniel B.–Naser, Fred
1647	Nash, Aaron–Nason, William K.
1648	Nass, Edward–Nazworthy, John W.
1649	Neabrey, John–Neander, Catharina M. S.
1650	Near, Alfred J.–Neeld, Verena M.
1651	Neele, John H.–Neftel, Knight
1652	Negangard, Mary L.–Neisz, John K.
1654	Neithammer, Henry C.–Nelson, Emma V. B.
1655	Nelson, Ener–Nelson, Martin
1655	Nelson, Mary–Neltopski, John W.
1656	Nemand, Jennie H.–Netzly, Jacob
1657	Neu, Aloysius–Nevyus, Louisa S.
1658	New, Abner A.–Newcome, Mitchell
1659	Newcomer, Abner–Newhart, Sarah P.
1660	Newhaus, Phillip–Newman, Isaiah E.
1661	Newman, Jacob–Newsum, William
1662	Newth, Francis–Nexsen, George W.
1663	Ney, Adam–Nicholoy, Susan
1664	Nichols, Aaron S.–Nichols, George G.
1665	Nichols, George H.–Nichols, Marion L.
1666	Nichols, Martha–Nichols, Wyatt
1667	Nicholson, A. Laurie–Nickelson, William G.
1668	Nickem, Lucinda E.–Nicoson, William L.
1669	Nida, John R.–Nihuff, Elizabeth J.

Roll	Description
1670	Nikel, Nanette–Nisewanner, Thomas H.
1671	Nish, Adelia–Nobinger, Mary
1672	Noble, Albert D.–Nobles, William L. F.
1673	Noblet, Anthony–Nokes, William H.
1674	Nolan, Adia–Nollsh, Frederick
1675	Nolop, Daniel–Norling, Anna M.
1676	Norman, Abigail–Norris, Ezra
1677	Norris, Fannie–Norris, Zoe D.
1678	Norrish, Carrie J.–Northroup, John, Jr.
1679	Northrup, Abby–Norton, Gould G.
1680	Norton, Hannah J.–Norton, Zina
1681	Nortoni, Hannah T.–Nowitney, Joseph
1682	Nowlan, Alexina–Nugui, Perfecta
1683	Nuhfer, Andrew–Nuthmann, Charles Theodore
1684	Nutt, Abigal–Nytko, John H.
1685	O–Oatts, Mary E.
1686	Obainor, Julia–O'Brien, Cornelius J.
1687	O'Brien, Daniel–O'Brien, Phillip
1688	O'Brien, Rebecca–O'Connell, William W.
1689	O'Conner, Ada F.–Oddy, Sarah
1690	Ode, Albertine E.–Odoms, Mary
1691	O'Donahoe, Margaret–Oetzel, William
1692	O'Fallon, William–Ogin, Henry
1692	Ogle, Albert–O'Harrow, Robert E.
1694	Ohaver, Anna L.–Olcott, Roy
1695	Old, Amas–Olehy, William J.
1696	Oleman, Bediance–Oliver, Cyrus
1697	Oliver, Daniel M.–Olivier, Raphael
1698	Olk, Bridget–Olsmith, Frank
1699	Olson, Abelona–Ondrizek, John
1700	O'Neail, Joseph–O'Neil, William J.
1701	O'Neill, Abby–Opocensky, Frank W.
1702	Opp, Dorthulia J.–Orey, William
1703	Orfe, Barbara–Orput, Rezin
1704	Orr, Ada M.–Orswell, Mary A.
1705	Ort, Adam–Osborn, Ezra J.
1706	Osborn, Fanny–Osborn, Winfield S.
1707	Osborne, Abraham–Osinski, Casimir
1708	Oskey, Rebecca J.–Osts, John
1709	O'Sullivan, Anne–Ott, William S.
1710	Ottarson, Asa C.–Ouzts, John E.
1711	Ovaitt, Anna–Overstreet, Willis G.
1712	Overt, Charles–Owen, Mary R.
1713	Owen, Matilda O.–Owens, Lewis S.
1714	Owens, Lodemia C.–Ozwill, George W.
1715	P–Packer, William O.
1716	Packet, Milley–Page, Catherine
1717	Page, Charles–Page, Ottilia
1718	Page, Parker–Paine, Rufus H.
1719	Paine, Samuel–Palmby, Robert
1720	Palmer, Aaron–Palmer, Guinnie E.
1721	Palmer, Hallie–Palmer, Martin Dwight
1722	Palmer, Mary–Palmore, Stephen
1723	Palmquist, Johanna–Parcels, Walter H.
1724	Parcher, Anna–Parisotti, Sarah C.
1725	Park, Abraham–Parker, Azor A.
1726	Parker, Barbara–Parker, Frederick J.
1727	Parker, Gad C.–Parker, John P. E.
1728	Parker, John R.–Parker, Myrtilla C.
1729	Parker, N. Addison–Parker, William
1730	Parker, William A.–Parkman, William H.
1731	Parks, Aaron–Parkyn, John W.
1732	Parlaman, Lizzie B.–Parres, Lucy J.
1733	Parret, Eva A.–Parslow, Sarah A.

Roll	Description	Roll	Description
1734	Parsohn, Frank–Parsons, Rufus D.	1798	Poor, Abbie G.–Poper, Nancy A.
1735	Parsons, S. DeWitt–Pascual, Valentina	1799	Popham, Annie E.–Porter, Elvira M.
1736	Pasetsk, Ila–Paton, William	1800	Porter, Emanuel–Porter, Lydia S.
1737	Paton, William W.–Patterf, Emma	1801	Porter, M. Louisa–Porter, Zeley W.
1738	Patterson, Aaron–Patterson, Isaiah M.	1802	Porterfield, Alice M. M.–Post, Zilpha
1739	Patterson, Jacob–Patterson, Myrtle M.	1803	Postal, Esther A.–Potter, Friederike
1740	Patterson, Nancy–Pattleton, Richard	1804	Potter, George–Potter, Viola E.
1741	Patton, Abraham–Patton, Worthie H.	1805	Potter, Wallace–Poundstone, John W.
1742	Pattorff, Lucinda J.–Paulding, William R.	1806	Pousland, Mary I.–Powell, Jincy
1743	Paule, Eugene–Paxton, Wilson N.	1807	Powell, Joanna–Powelson, William A.
1744	Pay, Alexander–Payne, Lyman	1808	Power, Abner–Powers, Katherine
1745	Payne, M. Elizabeth–Pazia, Simon	1809	Powers, Lafayette–Präfke, Franz
1746	Pea, Andrew–Peaks, Thomas J.	1810	Prag, Jane A.–Pratt, Egbert D.
1747	Peal, Allen S.–Pearsall, William	1811	Pratt, Elbridge J.–Pratt, Ruth G.
1748	Pearse, Celia M.–Peary, Sarah M.	1812	Pratt, Salem–Prenot, Ernestine
1749	Pease, Abner J.–Pecinovsky, Joseph W.	1813	Prentice, Adlaid–Prestmon, Mary
1750	Peck, Aaron–Peck, Ruthven O.	1814	Preston, Aaron–Preston, Zephaniah 2d
1751	Peck, Sabrina–Peedon, William H.	1815	Prestwich, Thomas–Price, Evelyn C.
1752	Peehl, Anna–Peipher, Michael	1816	Price, Fannie–Price, Lydia B.
1753	Peirce, Abbie L.–Peltier, William C.	1817	Price, Mack–Price, Zachariah
1754	Pelton, Adalaide L.–Pendexter, Rose W.	1818	Pricer, Alexander–Prifold, George
1755	Pendill, Hiram K.–Penn Wiseman	1819	Prigge, Louise–Prinzler, Oscar J. K.
1756	Pennea, Cornelius–Pennsyl, Philip H.	1820	Prior, Alameda–Probus, Ezekiel
1757	Penny, Abraham–Peppell, Laura	1821	Procasky, Elizabeth–Prospert, Mary A.
1758	Pepper, Albert–Perkinpine, Joseph F.	1822	Pross, Ann–Prudot, Augusta
1759	Perkins, Aaron–Perkins, Izora L.	1823	Prue, Annie–Puckett, William Y.
1760	Perkins, J. Herbert–Perky, Mary E.	1824	Pudenz, Simon–Pulk, David M.
1761	Perl, Agatha–Perry, Burton R.	1825	Pull, George H.–Purcell, Kate
1762	Perry, Caleb H.–Perry, Juliaette	1826	Purcell, Lawrence–Purnsley, Sallie
1763	Perry, Kate–Perry, Zilpha E.	1827	Purper, Isabella–Putnam, Israel P.
1764	Perryman, Absalom–Peternee, Kestro	1828	Putnam, Jacob–Pyzer, Fanny A.
1765	Peters, Aaron–Peters, Myron H.	1829	Qua, Ada M.–Query, Mathias
1766	Peters, Nancy A.–Peterson, Gustavus	1830	Quesenberry, Drucilla–Quigley, Winfield S.
1767	Peterson, Hall–Petersson, Johan P.	1831	Quilan, Joseph–Quinn, Isaac M.
1768	Petery, Frances–Pettingill, William H.	1832	Quinn, Jacob–Qwüttschreiber, Barbara
1769	Pettis, Aletha A.–Pevy, John H.	1833	R–Raddish, William G.
1770	Pew, Alfred–Pfitzinger, John	1834	Radebach, Hiland R.–Raftis, John
1771	Pflager, August–Phelps, Dyer	1835	Ragain, Edward B.–Rainburg, Henry J.
1772	Phelps, Earl–Phelps, Zachariah R.	1836	Raine, Charles A., Jr.–Ralphsnider, Eliza C.
1773	Phemister, Andrew J.–Phillippi, William	1837	Ralstian, William–Ramsby, Wellington
1774	Phillipps, Charles V.–Phillips, Elzwic S.	1838	Ramsdell, Abbie J.–Ramseyer, Joseph
1775	Phillips, Emaline E.–Phillips, Jessie E.	1839	Ramshaw, Peter–Randall, Gondelia
1776	Phillips, Joanna H.–Phillips, Myra J.	1840	Randall, H. Monroe–Randle, Zilla M.
1777	Phillips, Nancy–Phillips, Zebulon S.	1841	Randleman, Elizabeth–Ranke, William
1778	Phillipsen, Anton–Piburn, Thomas B.	1842	Ranken, David M.–Ranslow, George P.
1779	Picard, Annie M.–Pickert, Martin	1843	Ransom, Agnes–Raquitt, Mary
1780	Picket, Albert–Pierce, Austris A.	1844	Rarden, Aaron–Ratfield, Carrie M.
1781	Pierce, Barbara E.–Pierce, Joel C.	1845	Rath, Albert–Rau, William
1782	Pierce, John–Pierce, Square William	1846	Raub, Abram A.–Raxroth, Eva Christina
1783	Pierce, Stella A.–Pierucci, Mary R.	1847	Ray, Abel T., Jr.–Ray, Rufus
1784	Pies, Christina–Piklowski, Frank M.	1848	Ray, Sabina B.–Raymond, Horace H.
1785	Piland, Anderson H.–Pinfield, James	1849	Raymond, Isaac E.–Rea, Wilmina
1786	Ping, Caroline–Piotti, Frank	1850	Reace, Emeline–Reagor, Emily
1787	Pipe, Amelia–Pistorius, Frederick	1851	Reahard, Frances F.–Reauveau, William J. F.
1788	Pitcairn, Charles W.–Pittroff, Katharina	1852	Reavely, Bridget L.–Rector, Willis
1789	Pitts, Akin–Placot, John	1853	Red, Greenberry–Redhouse, William Henry
1790	Pladwell, George H.–Platt, Myrtilla J.	1854	Redic, Melinda–Reecers, Sarah
1791	Platt, Nancy L.–Ployhart, Mary	1855	Reed, Aaron A.–Reed, Dwight A.
1792	Plubel, George–Plumtree, Lydia M.	1856	Reed, E. Antoinette–Reed, Isom
1793	Plunges, Peter–Pohner, Michael	1857	Reed, J. Eugene–Reed, Lyman C.
1794	Poiles, Moses L.–Polkey, Margaret	1858	Reed, M. Gertrude–Reed, Ruth E.
1795	Poll, Annie L.–Pollye, Sarah	1859	Reed, S. Amanda–Reede, William M.
1796	Polm, John H.–Ponsler, George	1860	Reedenbach, Mary–Rees, Moses
1797	Pontbriant, Walter J.–Pooley, Willie Holmes	1861	Rees, Naomi E.–Reess, Elizabeth S.

Roll	Description
1862	Reester, Elizabeth M.–Reezer, William
1863	Refe, Charles W.–Reichburg, Augusta C.
1864	Reiche, Carl H.–Reid, William W.
1865	Reidabaugh, Luther C.–Reily, William H. H.
1866	Reim, Anna–Reisert, Theresa A.
1867	Reish, David–Remis, Robert
1868	Remler, August–Rennert, John C.
1869	Rennheeck, Ernst–Rerig, Catharine J.
1870	Resa, Barnhard–Revord, John
1871	Rew, Amelia–Reynolds, Cyrus M.
1872	Reynolds, Daniel–Reynolds, Ivins D.
1873	Reynolds, Jackson W.–Reynolds, Myron
1874	Reynolds, Nancy–Reynolds, Zelma L.
1875	Reynoldson, Robert–Rhoades, Zada
1876	Rhoads, Andrew J.–Rhodes, Isaiah
1877	Rhodes, Jacob–Ricco, Annie
1878	Rice, A. Mellen–Rice, Greenville
1879	Rice, Hannah–Rice, Martin W.
1880	Rice, Mary–Rice, Zeniee M.
1881	Ricedorff, Fannie E.–Richards, Austin
1882	Richards, Barbara–Richards, Jonathan
1883	Richards, Joseph–Richards, Zimri
1884	Richardson, A. Maynard–Richardson, Frisky N.
1885	Richardson, Gedney K.–Richardson, Lyne S.
1886	Richardson, M. Nettie–Richardson, Zilpha
1887	Richart, Anna–Richmond, Horace C.
1888	Richmond, Ida–Rickenberg, Elizabeth A.
1889	Ricker, Abbie A.–Rickrode, Susan
1890	Ricks, Alfred–Rideout, William H. H.
1891	Rider, Abigail–Ridlon, William
1892	Ridner, Adam–Riexinger, William
1893	Rife, Amanda S.–Riggles, Richard
1894	Riggs, Abbie–Rikeman, James A.
1895	Riland, Amanda–Riley, Jesse
1896	Riley, John–Riley, Zachariah 2d
1897	Riliea, George–Ringe, Susannah
1898	Ringeisen, Katharine–Ripley, Plesant H.
1899	Ripley, Rachel D.–Rissmiller, Susanna L.
1900	Rist, Albert–Rittenour, William A.
1901	Ritter, Aaron–Rivert, Edward
1902	Rives, Amelia N.–Roadruck, Ella C.
1903	Roads, Abbie C.–Robberts, Sarah
1904	Robbin, Frederick–Robbins, Louise A.
1905	Robbins, Lucina E.–Roberson, Wyatt
1906	Robert, Adelina T.–Roberts, Emmett G.
1907	Roberts, Enoch–Roberts, John H.
1908	Roberts, John J.–Roberts, Owen D.
1909	Roberts, Patience A.–Robertshaw, Nancy J.
1910	Robertson, Aaron D.–Robertson, Lydia M.
1911	Robertson, M. Lou–Robins, Zachariah H.
1912	Robinson, A. Jennette W.–Robinson, Cyrus W.
1913	Robinson, Daisy A.–Robinson, Griffith M.
1914	Robinson, Halliet D.–Robinson, John L.
1915	Robinson, John M.–Robinson, Mary H.
1916	Robinson, Mary J.–Robinson, Sylvia S.
1917	Robinson, Tarrent P.–Robison, Zenetta
1918	Robitaille, Joseph–Rockaway, William
1919	Rocke, Jacob–Roddan, Thomas H.
1920	Rodde, Elise–Rodgers, Isabella
1921	Rodgers, Jackson J.–Rody, William
1922	Roe, Agnes P.–Roganski, Frank J.
1923	Roger, Elliott–Rogers, Elsie D.
1924	Rogers, Emerson–Rogers, John A.
1925	Rogers, John B.–Rogers, Mozelle H.

Roll	Description
1926	Rogers, Nancy–Rogers, Zilpha S.
1927	Rogerson, Ann–Rolfson, Lewis
1928	Rolin, Jeremiah–Rolwine, Peter
1929	Rom, Ely–Ronzone, Mary
1930	Rooch, August–Roosevelt, James H.
1931	Root, A. Maria–Roques, James K.
1932	Rorabacher, Claude–Rose, Gustave
1933	Rose, Hannah–Rose, Zibia H.
1934	Roseau, Anne–Rosezelle, Eliza J.
1935	Rosha, Fannie E.–Ross, Guy Austin
1936	Ross, Hamilton M.–Ross, Martin H.
1937	Ross, Mary–Rosse, John R.
1938	Rosseau, Helen–Roth, Louise M.
1939	Roth, Magdalena–Roum, Sarah
1940	Rounce, Ann Eliza–Rousey, Jordan
1941	Roush, Absalom–Rowdybush, Charley R.
1942	Rowe, Abigail–Rowe, Zachariah P.
1943	Rowekamp, James W.–Rowlette, James
1944	Rowley, A. Stewart–Roycroft, Annie M.
1945	Roydhouse, Henry–Ruby, William F.
1946	Ruch, Albert F.–Rudnick, Morris
1947	Rudoff, Elizabeth–Rufus, Robert
1948	Rugaard, Viggo–Rumbout, Kate
1949	Rume, John–Runtschke, Ernst
1950	Runyan, Aaron–Ruschpler, Alphons
1951	Rusco, Anson J.–Russeau, George
1952	Russel, Augusta F.–Russell, Ezra R.
1953	Russell, Fannie–Russell, Junius T.
1954	Russell, Kate–Russell, Sylvester W.
1955	Russell, Theodore–Ruthardt, George
1956	Ruther, Christiana–Ryals, Venus
1957	Ryan, Abby–Ryan, Jonathan
1958	Ryan, Joseph–Ryason, William H.
1959	Rybacki, Theodore–Rzezniacki, Joseph V.
1960	St. Abbe, Gustavus A. F.–St. Vrain, Charles
1961	S–Sadorus, Phebe J.
1962	Saeber, Lizzie–Sailsbury, Marietta
1963	Saims, James G.–Sallyards, William
1964	Salmans, Levi C.–Samms, William P.
1965	Samo, Sophia–Samstag, William
1966	Samuel, Alfred A.–Sandeowe
1967	Sander, Adolphus–Sanders, Jesse W.
1968	Sanders, Joel–Sanders, Ziba
1969	Sandersfeld, John–Sandstrum, Honora
1970	Sandt, Aaron–Sanges, Martha T.
1971	Sangle, Henrietta–Sargen, Myers
1972	Sargent, Abbie Y.–Sarwash, Elizabeth
1973	Sasely, Adam–Saults, John M.
1974	Saum, Augustus B.–Sauzenbacher, Maria
1975	Savacool, Charles–Savoy, Minnie M.
1976	Sawatzky, Maria–Sawyer, Kathrine L.
1977	Sawyer, Lavina–Sayford, Samuel M.
1978	Saygers, Elizabeth–Scamyhorn, Oliver
1979	Scanadoah, David–Schadt, Mary C.
1980	Schaeber, Albert F.–Schaitel, Elisabeth
1981	Schakel, Christian W.–Scheble, Rebecca
1982	Schechter, Charles W.–Schenzle, Anthony
1983	Scheock, Charlotte–Schikan, Philip B.
1984	Schilb, Frederick–Schleith, Sadie
1985	Schlekan, Wilhelmena–Schmidmayr, Ida
1986	Schmidt, Acenath–Schmidt, William O.
1987	Schmidtborn, Frederick–Schneickert, Louisa
1988	Schneid, Charles F.–Schneyer, Mary M.
1989	Schnicke, Barbara–Schoknett, Catharine

Roll	Description
1990	Scholan, George–Schoos, Anni
1991	Schopbach, Rosina B.–Schreihart, Peter
1992	Schrein, Frieda–Schroll, Susan
1993	Schrom, Maria–Schulties, Christian
1994	Schults, George H.–Schumpf, John Conrad
1995	Schunall, Daniel–Schwanzel, John
1996	Schwar, Amelia B.–Schwemler, Wilhelmina
1997	Schwenck, Louisa–Scoskie, Paul T.
1998	Scot, Sara D. S.–Scott, Dwight R.
1999	Scott, E. McLean B.–Scott, Hyrum C.
2000	Scott, Ida D.–Scott, Kitty
2001	Scott, L. Charlotte–Scott, Norman H.
2002	Scott, Oliver–Scott, Westley S.
2003	Scott, Wilber C.–Scribner, William H.
2004	Scriggins, Clara–Seacrist, Sylvester W.
2005	Seadle, Barbary A.–Searer, Kate
2006	Seares, Thomas M.–Sears, Zachariah T.
2007	Searson, Edward–Sebury, Catherine
2008	Secater, Leanzo J.–Seeck, Peter
2009	Seed, Andrew J.–Seery, Thomas
2010	Sees, Abraham S.–Seids, Adam
2011	Seif, Johanna R.–Selby, William Z.
2012	Selcer, Henry–Sellinger, Mary C.
2013	Sellman, Alexander–Sensor, Sarah J.
2014	Sent, Martin–Setser, Paten
2015	Settell, Helen L.–Sewatick, Minnie
2016	Sewel, Elizabeth–Seymour, Frederick W.
2017	Seymour, George–Shady, Raymond C.
2018	Shaefer, Albert C.–Shaffer, Cynthia L.
2019	Shaffer, Daniel–Shaffer, Zillottie A.
2020	Shaffery, Margaret–Shanely, Lydia A.
2021	Shaneor, George W.–Shannessy, Thomas
2022	Shannon, Aaron–Sharitt, Frank
2023	Shark, Annie–Sharp, Lyman
2024	Sharp, Madison R.–Shastid, Lydia
2025	Shatlain, Louis–Shavor, Harry H.
2026	Shaw, Aaron–Shaw, Greenbury R.
2027	Shaw, Hannah–Shaw, Mary W.
2028	Shaw, Mathew–Shaw-wah-ne-pe-nass, John
2029	Shay, Abram–Sheane, Andrew
2030	Shear, Abram–Sheedy, Mary
2031	Sheehan, Adelaide W.–Sheetz, William H.
2032	Shefbuch, Conrad–Sheldon, Lydia M.
2033	Sheldon, Mercia–Shellor, John
2034	Shelly, Adaline–Sheopkee, Augusta
2035	Shepard, A. Warner–Shepherd, Ezra H.
2036	Shepherd, Fannie–Shepperd, William
2037	Shepperle, John–Sherman, Brown W.
2038	Sherman, Calista H.–Sherman, Myron
2039	Sherman, N. Albert–Sherwin, William F.
2040	Sherwood, Aaron–Shickling, Mary
2041	Shidaker, John A.–Shiesley, Henry
2042	Shifely, Leah–Shinliver, Milly J.
2043	Shinn, Adeline–Shipman, Zenes
2044	Shipner, Caroline F.–Shitz, Isabella
2045	Shive, Alfred–Shodl, Frederick
2046	Shoe, Alfred–Shoey, Thomas
2047	Shofer, John–Shordon, Martha A.
2048	Shore, Albert–Short, Zebulon
2049	Shortall, Ann–Showard, Charles H.
2050	Showell, Henry–Shrom, William P.
2051	Shronce, Mary E.–Shuley, Mary
2052	Shulka, Anton–Shulze, William H.
2053	Shumake, Henry W.–Shurtz, William W.

Roll	Description
2054	Shuss, Susannah–Sickels, William E.
2055	Sickenberger, Adam–Sieckmann, Marie Elise
2056	Sied, Barbara–Siglinger, Mary
2057	Sigman, Alexander–Silmser, Charles M.
2058	Silsbe, Elias W.–Simler, Sarah W.
2059	Simm, James–Simmons, Isham C.
2060	Simmons, J. Victoria–Simmons, Victorine
2061	Simmons, Walker–Simonds, Isabella R.
2062	Simonds, James F.–Simplot, Mary J.
2063	Simpsen, William–Simpson, Jones
2064	Simpson, Jordan–Simpson, Zurelli J.
2065	Simrell, Alexander–Sinclair, Lydia C.
2066	Sinclair, Malcolm–Sininger, Rebecca
2067	Sink, Agnes–Siscoe, Samuel
2068	Sise, Martin L.–Sivard, Mary C.
2069	Sive, George H.–Skeines, Mary J.
2070	Skelcher, Henry–Skinnard, Edward
2071	Skinner, Aaron–Skinner, Zophar
2072	Skinnin, Harriet F.–Slaten, Nancy A.
2073	Slater, Abba G.–Slaughterbeck, William C.
2074	Slauson, Amanda M.–Slims, Josephine
2075	Slinde, Nels M.–Sloas, John
2076	Sloat, Adelia–Slusser, William J.
2077	Sluter, Henry D.–Small, Susannah
2078	Small, Thomas–Smaroo, Christian
2079	Smashey, Ruth T.–Smisor, Margaret E.
2080	Smith, A. Eliza–Smith, Algie J.
2081	Smith, Alia–Smith, Ann B.
2082	Smith, Ann C.–Smith, Azuba L.
2083	Smith, B. Catherine–Smith, Cary H.
2084	Smith, Casander–Smith, Charles H.
2085	Smith, Charles I.–Smith, Cyrus W.
2086	Smith, D. Franklin, Jr.–Smith, Dyantha E.
2087	Smith, E. Emily–Smith, Eliza S.
2088	Smith, Elizabeth–Smith, Elnora
2089	Smith, Elon–Smith, Fannie C. W.
2090	Smith, Fannie E.–Smith, Fulton J.
2091	Smith, G. Franklin–Smith, George V.
2092	Smith, George W.–Smith, Harriette
2093	Smith, Harris B.–Smith, Henry L.
2094	Smith, Henry M.–Smith, Ives
2095	Smith, J. August–Smith, James G. M.
2096	Smith, James H.–Smith, Jeptha W.
2097	Smith, Jere–Smith, John B. F.
2098	Smith, John C.–Smith, John V. D.
2099	Smith, John W.–Smith, Josie W.
2100	Smith, Judah E.–Smith, Lewis W.
2101	Smith, Libbie–Smith, Lyman L.
2102	Smith, McCall–Smith, Martha C.
2103	Smith, Martha E.–Smith, Mary Ann
2104	Smith, Mary B.–Smith, Mary N.
2105	Smith, Mary O.–Smith, Nannie L.
2106	Smith, Naomi J.–Smith, Persis M.
2107	Smith, Peter–Smith, Ritta Ann
2108	Smith, Robert–Smith, Samuel H. W.
2109	Smith, Samuel J.–Smith, Sarah Louisa
2110	Smith, Sarah M.–Smith, Sylvia A.
2111	Smith, T. Garland–Smith, Whitson
2112	Smith, Wilber F.–Smith, William G.
2113	Smith, William H.–Smith, Zilpha A.
2114	Smitha, Alexander W.–Smyser, William H.
2115	Smyth, Abner C.–Snell, Huldah
2116	Snell, Ida M.–Snidow, James W.
2117	Sniff, Adaline–Snow, Byron D.

Roll	Description
2118	Snow, Caroline–Snydam, Hester E.
2119	Snyder, Aaron–Snyder, Ezra
2120	Snyder, Fannie A.–Snyder, Julius
2121	Snyder, Kate–Snyder, Sylvia
2122	Snyder, Tabitha J.–Solly, William M.
2123	Solmar, Jacob–Sommerville, William W.
2124	Son, George–Sory, John
2125	Sosa, Miguel–South, Zedekiah
2126	Southall, Addison–Sovinsky, William F.
2127	Sowarby, Julia A.–Spake, Manurvia J.
2128	Spalckhaver, Anna–Sparhawk, Sarah J.
2129	Sparka, Adam–Spatzer, Francis
2130	Spaude, Louis–Speany, Sarah A.
2131	Spear, Abby S.–Speedy, William W.
2132	Speece, Catherine–Spelts, Perry F.
2133	Spenard, Alice–Spencer, Elmina P.
2134	Spencer, Emanuel G.–Spencer, Mary E. R.
2135	Spencer, Mary F.–Sperrow, Mary A.
2136	Sperry, Adaline–Spigner, William H.
2137	Spika, Rosa–Splittstosser, Augusta E.
2138	Spoehr, Ernst–Spragins, Henry
2139	Sprague, Abby–Sprague, Zerelda J.
2140	Sprain, Mary A.–Springer, Lulu E.
2141	Springer, Margaret–Spung, David
2142	Spur, Sarah A.–Squyres, Wilson B.
2143	Srack, Samuel B.–Stady, Christian
2144	Staebler, Mary R.–Staggs, William R.
2145	Stagley, David E.–Staley, Zachary T.
2146	Stalford, Emma J.–Stamps, William R.
2147	Stanaback, James–Stankowsky, Joseph
2148	Stanley, Abram B.–Stanly, Matthew B.
2149	Stanmire, Mary J.–Stantz, Michael
2150	Stanup, David–Starita, Mattero
2151	Stark, Abraham H.–Starks, William T.
2152	Starkweather, Alice J.–Starry, William F.
2153	Start, Anna C.–Stayton, William H. H.
2154	Steabold, Christopher–Steaward, Steaven
2155	Stebbens, Edgar B.–Steel, Willis
2156	Steele, Aaron–Steele, Zottu C.
2157	Steeley, Jackson–Stegtmeyer, Charles
2158	Stehfest, Margaret–Steines, Johanna
2159	Steinfeld, Edwin B.–Steph, George
2160	Stephan, Andreas–Stephens, Lytle A.
2161	Stephens, Mahala A.–Stephenson, Julia A.
2162	Stephenson, Lansing R.–Stermer, William
2163	Stern, Adolph–Stevener, John
2164	Stevens, A. Elma–Stevens, Frisby
2165	Stevens, Garrett–Stevens, Marcus
2166	Stevens, Margaret–Stevens, Zittilla
2167	Stevenson, Aaron–Stevenson, Zelia
2168	Steventon, Albert–Stewart, Brule A.
2169	Stewart, Caleb–Stewart, Guy
2170	Stewart, H. Truesdel–Stewart, Julius H.
2171	Stewart, Karene A.–Stewart, Queen
2172	Stewart, R. Amanda–Stewart, Zenobia E.
2173	Stewartson, Benjamin–Stietzer, August
2174	Stifal, Elizabeth E.–Stilley, William
2175	Stillgess, Isaac–Stimson, Zipporah
2176	Stinaff, Ellen–Stinson, William
2177	Stinwith, George–Stockart, Mary K.
2178	Stockbarger, David–Stockum, Ella
2179	Stockweather, George–Stokem, Jennie M.
2180	Stoker, Adaline–Stonbreaker, Joseph H.
2181	Stone, Abbie A.–Stone, Guy A.
2182	Stone, Hannah–Stone, Moses W.
2183	Stone, Nancy–Stonemetz, Wilhelmina C.
2184	Stoner, Aaron E.–Stores, Wilhelmina
2185	Storey, Ann Maria–Story, Ziba
2186	Storz, Emilie–Stout, Isabella F.
2187	Stout, Jackson–Stovin, Anthony T.
2188	Stow, Abindia L.–Strahorn, William L.
2189	Straib, Anna D.–Strassweg, Reinhard
2190	Strate, Abram–Straup, Isaac W.
2191	Straus, Annie–Street, William W.
2192	Streeter, Addison E.–Strickland, Zack
2193	Strickle, Melissa L.–Strodtman, William G.
2194	Stroebe, Friderike–Stronk, Kate
2195	Stroop, Emma L.–Stroyick, John G.
2196	Strub, Mary–Stuart, Louise M.
2197	Stuart, M. Ellen–Stucy, Frederick
2198	Studabaker, Clem A.–Stummets, David
2199	Stump, Adam–Sturgess, William N.
2200	Sturgill, Alonzo–Styler, Solomon
2201	Styles, Alice H.–Sullins, Sarah
2202	Sullivan, Aaron–Sullivan, Isabella D.
2203	Sullivan, James–Sullivan, Mercy A.
2204	Sullivan, Michael–Summerfield, William J.
2205	Summerhayes, Martha W.–Summy, William H.
2206	Sumner, Aaron B.–Suprenant, Thomas
2207	Sur, Achilles H.–Sutliffe, Edgar C.
2208	Sutman, John M.–Sutton, Kimsey
2209	Sutton, Laura B.–Swaim, William F.
2210	Swain, Abraham–Swan, Moses
2211	Swan, Nancy–Swarthout, William H.
2212	Swartley, Catharine–Swearer, Rachel J.
2213	Swearingen, Abraham T.–Sweeny, William J.
2214	Sweeper, Binah–Sweeting, William R.
2215	Sweetland, Abijah W.–Swift, Cyrenius H.
2216	Swift, Daniel D.–Swingle, William M.
2217	Swingler, Eliza–Swortwood, William O.
2218	Swosinski, Stanislaw–Szymanski, Stanaslaus
2219	T–Taft, Cornelius A.
2220	Taft, Daniel E.–Talbert, Missouri C.
2221	Talbert, Nathan–Talliaferro, Anne C.
2222	Tallmadge, Addie C.–Tannehill, Zachariah L.
2223	Tanner, Abel–Tapy, Mary
2224	Tara, Paul–Tatch, Frederick
2225	Tate, Adolphus H.–Tayhan, John
2226	Tayler, Frank C.–Taylor, Cathrine
2227	Taylor, Cecilia C.–Taylor, Elizabeth W.
2228	Taylor, Ella–Taylor, Gladys M.
2229	Taylor, Grace–Taylor, James K. P.
2230	Taylor, James L.–Taylor, Jones A.
2231	Taylor, Josefa–Taylor, Marvin O.
2232	Taylor, Mary–Taylor, Ozyal B.
2233	Taylor, Page J.–Taylor, Sylvia
2234	Taylor, T. Clara–Taylor, Zachary F.
2235	Tayman, George H.–Tedrow, William C.
2236	Tee, John J.–Telless, Charles
2237	Tellier, Eli–Tenly, Mary J.
2238	Tennant, Adaline–Terrell, Willis R.
2239	Terrett, Annie D.–Tervilleger, Frederick
2240	Terwiliger, Catharine–Teytand, August P.
2241	Thaalson, Thomas H.–Thaxton, Parham
2242	Thayer, Abel H.–Thery, Seraphim T.
2243	Thesen, Anna C.–Thomans, Algot
2244	Thomas, A. Delia–Thomas, Cyrus K.
2245	Thomas, Daniel–Thomas, Freeman A.

Roll	Description
2246	Thomas, Gabriel–Thomas, Jasper N.
2247	Thomas, Jeff–Thomas, Lloyd
2248	Thomas, Lonie–Thomas, Moses S.
2249	Thomas, Nancy–Thomas, Synthia
2250	Thomas, T. Snowden–Thompkins, William
2251	Thompson, Aaron E.–Thompson, Byron W.
2252	Thompson, Caleb J.–Thompson, Eliza Jane
2253	Thompson, Elizabeth–Thompson, Guy E.
2254	Thompson, Hadda–Thompson, James W.
2255	Thompson, Jane–Thompson, Joseph W.
2256	Thompson, Josephine–Thompson, Martin Van Buren
2257	Thompson, Mary–Thompson, Puss
2258	Thompson, Rachel–Thompson, Sylvester V.
2259	Thompson, Tabitha A.–Thompson, Zilpha M.
2260	Thoms, Ada L.–Thornbrugh, Margaret A.
2261	Thornburg, Adeline–Thornton, Lyman
2262	Thornton, Maggie J.–Thoussen, Susan B.
2263	Thraen, Frederich–Thurber, William L.
2264	Thurecht, William–Tibbens, Jackson
2265	Tibbet, Henry–Ticknor, William A.
2266	Tidabeck, Annie–Tifton, Ermine
2267	Tigar, Frank H.–Tillyer, James W.
2268	Tilman, Adah M.–Timmony, Mary E.
2269	Timms, Arthur–Tinkham, William P.
2270	Tinkle, Andrew J.–Tirey, William T.
2271	Tirre, Frederick W.–Titus, Isadore S.
2272	Titus, Jacob–Tock, Orson W.
2273	Tod, Elizabeth–Todd, William W.
2274	Todden, Lucinda–Tolliver, Reuben
2275	Tollman, Edward A.–Tomphson, Elijah H.
2276	Tompkins, Aaron B.–Tonto, Jack
2277	Tooden, Sophia–Toquet, Benjamin H.
2278	Toran, George–Totzell, Valentine
2279	Touché, Bertha Ann–Towling, Jeremiah
2280	Town, Adelbert L.–Townsend, Frederick P.
2281	Townsend, General–Tozier, Wilber S.
2282	Trab, George–Trafzer, Elizabeth
2283	Traganza, Annie–Traux, John
2284	Travaille, Melle–Treadway, Winfield S.
2285	Treadwell, Abram–Trempler, Gottlieb
2286	Trenaman, Margaret–Trickler, Rebecca J.
2287	Tridel, Bridget Agnes–Tripney, Thomas
2288	Tripp, Adaline–Tromter, Harry
2289	Tron, Henry F.–Trout, William S.
2290	Trouth, John–Truatt, Nathan A.
2291	Traux, Adelia A.–Truex, William
2292	Trufant, Arba H.–Trunels, Maria L.
2293	Trunick, Casandra–Tuck, William S.
2294	Tucker, Aaron–Tucker, Jesse F.
2295	Tucker, Joe L.–Tucker, Zeek
2296	Tuckerman, Adelia White–Tuney, Frank C.
2297	Tung, George S.–Turnell, Edwin N.
2298	Turner, Aaron–Turner, Ezra T.
2299	Turner, Fannie D.–Turner, Justina
2300	Turner, Kate M.–Turner, Susannah
2301	Turner, Tabitha–Tuther, Emma S.
2302	Tuthill, Adelaide–Tuttle, Sylvia
2303	Tuttle, Thaddeus J.–Twyman, William H.
2304	Tyack, Josiah H.–Tyler, Myra S.
2305	Tyler, Nancy A.–Tzschoppe, Julius
2306	Uart, Mary A.–Ulp, Mary E.
2307	Ulrey, Augusta M.–Underhill, William P.
2308	Underkoffer, Isaac–Unsold, Rachel
2309	Unspaw, Benjamin F.–Upton, Wisdom W.

Roll	Description
2310	Urack, Max H.–Uzzell, William F.
2311	Vacanti, Louis–Valery, Jerome
2312	Valiant, Anna E.–Van Atter, Elisabeth
2313	Van Auken, Abram–Vancaster, Maria Therese
2314	Vance, A. Frank–Vandawarker, Edward
2315	Vande, Abiel–Vanderripe, George A.
2316	Vanders, Frank J.–Vandover, Nancy J.
2317	Van Drake, Theresa–Van Fleet, William
2318	Van Gaasbeek, Edith E.–Van Horner, Frank
2319	Van Horson, Louis K.–Van Moos, Mary K. E.
2320	Vann, Clora–Van Orsdoll, Mary J.
2321	Vanosdale, Emily–Van Scyoc, Shannon S.
2322	Vansel, William N.–Van Valzah, Hannah E.
2323	Van Vechten, Henry C.–Vanyea, George
2324	Van Zandt, Abram–Vary, John B.
2325	Vasbinder, Augusta C.–Vaughn, Isaac
2326	Vaughn, Jalana D.–Vedernjak, Alois
2327	Vedrines, James J.–Vermule, Simeon D.
2328	Vernal, Georgiette–Viars, Thomas C.
2329	Vibart, Augustus–Vifquain, Caroline
2330	Vigdor, Jacob–Vincum, Richard
2331	Vine, Amanda J.–Vlk, Barbara
2332	Voak, Lorin D.–Vokins, Thomas J.
2333	Voland, William–Voog, Betsey G.
2334	Voorese, Peggy–Voskul, Bernard
2335	Vosler, Christian–Vyse, Thomas A., Jr.
2336	W–Wade, Isaac S.
2337	Wade, Jacob B.–Wady, William I.
2338	Waechly, Sibilla–Wagman, Katharina
2339	Wagner, Adam–Wagner, Jared
2340	Wagner, Jennette–Wagner, William N.
2341	Wagnitz, Katie E.–Waist, Henry S.
2342	Wait, Abner C.–Wakefield, Joseph F.
2343	Wakefield, Katherine–Waldner, Jonas
2344	Waldo, Albert M.–Walkenhorst, William F.
2345	Walker, Aaron–Walker, Duncan S.
2346	Walker, E. Louisa–Walker, Israel L.
2347	Walker, Jack–Walker, Lyman S.
2348	Walker, Madison M.–Walker, Ruth Margaret
2349	Walker, Sadie A.–Walker, Zudie
2350	Walkey, Sarah J.–Wallace, Dora A.
2351	Wallace, Edward–Wallace, Lymus
2352	Wallace, M. Elizabeth–Wallace, Zachariah
2353	Wallack, Ellen E.–Wallize, Israel
2354	Wallk, Harry–Walsh, Isabel
2355	Walsh, James–Walter, Ezekiel C.
2356	Walter, Francis–Walters, Dennis
2357	Walters, E. Evelyn–Walterspiel, Joseph
2358	Walthall, Ann–Walton, Zimri W.
2359	Waltrick, Joseph H.–Wanmer, Ellen
2360	Wann, Amanda L.–Ward, Cyrus J.
2361	Ward, Dallas–Ward, Job A.
2362	Ward, Johanna C.–Ward, Myron
2363	Ward, Naaman–Ward, Zophar W.
2364	Wardall, Abbie M.–Wares, Martin
2365	Warf, Legrand B.–Warner, Byron
2366	Warner, Caleb L.–Warner, Jeston R.
2367	Warner, Joel F.–Warner, Zophar
2368	Warnes, Helen M.–Warren, Huron
2369	Warren, Ichabod S.–Warren, Zenas
2370	Warrenburg, David P.–Washburn, Etta M.
2371	Washburn, Fannie–Washington, General George
2372	Washington, George–Wason, William
2373	Wass, Amanda E.–Waterous, Henry

Roll	Description
2374	Waters, Aaron–Watke, Mena
2375	Watkins, Charles W.–Watkinson, William
2376	Watland, Jacob–Watson, Frederick R.
2377	Watson, George–Watson, Martin
2378	Watson, Mary–Watstein, Anna
2379	Watt, Albert–Watts, Luranda
2380	Watts, Malinda–Way, William S., Jr.
2381	Waybill, Amos A.–Weatherman, William M.
2382	Weathers, Addison F.–Weaver, Henry H.
2383	Weaver, Henry J.–Weaver, Sarepta J.
2384	Weaver, Silas A.–Webb, Isabella M.
2385	Webb, J. Henry–Webb, Wilson H.
2386	Webber, Abbie H.–Weber, Isadora
2387	Weber, Jacob–Webster, Eunice A.
2388	Webster, Fannie E.–Webster, Winfield S.
2389	Wechselberger, Agnes–Weehunt, Robert K.
2390	Week, John A.–Weeks, William W.
2391	Weeman, Ebenezer F.–Weidner, William H.
2392	Weier, Annie–Weinhold, William S.
2393	Weinick, Mary–Weisrock, Anton
2394	Weiss, Abram–Welch, Eveline
2395	Welch, F. Louise–Welch, Rowland J.
2396	Welch, Sallie B.–Welker, William F.
2397	Welkley, John–Wellpott, Katharine
2398	Wells, A. Judson–Wells, Freeman E.
2399	Wells, G. Wiley–Wells, Lyman
2400	Wells, McDonald–Wells, Zachary T.
2401	Wellshaus, Jane–Weltner, Lloyd M.
2402	Welton, Agnes–Wening, George
2403	Wenk, Carl L. E.–Wentzsell, Maria
2404	Wenz, Andrew–Wertner, Jacob
2405	Werts, Abraham–Wesson, William
2406	West, A. Y.–West, Isabelle F.
2407	West, Jacob–West, Ruth
2408	West, Sabilla–Westcott, Zado K.
2409	Westeiude, Hubregt Vant–Westlake, William H.
2410	Westland, Emily–Wethered, Henry
2411	Wetherel, Edwin–Weykman, Peter
2412	Weyl, Charles–Whartnaby, Samuel R.
2413	Wharton, Addie A.–Wheelen, William A.
2414	Wheeler, Abbie F.–Wheeler, Friend P.
2415	Wheeler, George–Wheeler, Martha M.
2416	Wheeler, Mary–Wheeller, John W.
2417	Wheelock, Addie A.–Whipp, William G.
2418	Whipper, Samuel P.–Whitaker, Eva
2419	Whitaker, Fanny C.–Whitcroft, Isaac
2420	White, Aaron–White, Cena
2421	White, Chainey–White, Elvira B.
2422	White, Emanuel–White, Helena Adelia
2423	White, Henderson–White, John B.
2424	White, John C.–White, Lysander H.
2425	White, M. Alcie–White, Myron P.
2426	White, Nancy–White, Sarah W.
2427	White, Sedgwick–White, Zimri
2428	Whiteacre, Rebecca H.–Whiteknact, John N.
2429	Whitelam, George–Whithurst, Vinton
2430	Whiting, Abigail M.–Whitlow, William
2431	Whitman, Adam–Whitner, Valentine
2432	Whitney, Abbie D. T.–Whitney, Myron W.
2433	Whitney, Nancy–Whittelsey, William E.
2434	Whittemore, Abbie E.–Whittymore, Dillard
2435	Whitus, Isabel A.–Wickey, Oliver
2436	Wickham, Albert R.–Widvey, Theodore J.
2437	Wieand, Andrew J.–Wifvat, John A.
2438	Wigal, Amanda–Wigton, William H.
2439	Wihley, Henry–Wilcomb, Mary J.
2440	Wilcox, A. Tryphena–Wilcox, Lyman
2441	Wilcox, Madalena M.–Wildenthaler, Maria Ann
2442	Wilder, Abbie L.–Wilett, William
2443	Wiley, A. William–Wiley, Zachary T.
2444	Wilfang, John–Wilkes, William J.
2445	Wilkeson, Ellen A.–Wilkins, Worden J.
2446	Wilkinson, Abner–Wilky, Magdalena
2447	Will, Aaron–Willes, Mary E.
2448	Willet, Adaline–Willi, William G.
2449	William, Charles–Williams, Azel
2450	Williams, B. Frank–Williams, Czarina A.
2451	Williams, Dabney–Williams, Elvira R.
2452	Williams, Emaline–Williams, George R.
2453	Williams, George S.–Williams, Hutton
2454	Williams, Ibbie M.–Williams, Jim
2455	Williams, Joan–Williams, Jordan G.
2456	Williams, Joseph–Williams, Lyman A.
2457	Williams, McCarty–Williams, Mary D.
2458	Williams, Mary E.–Williams, Pauline C.
2459	Williams, Peggy–Williams, Sanford N.
2460	Williams, Sarah–Williams, Sexton R.
2461	Williams, Thomas I.–Williams, Zurretta A.
2462	Williams-Foote, Ambrose C. G.–Williamson, Norris
2463	Williamson, Obed–Willis, Israel D.
2464	Willis, Jack–Williston, William C.
2465	Willits, Alonzo D.–Willsie, Myron
2466	Willson, Abel P.–Wilsmann, Joseph H.
2467	Wilson, Aaron–Wilson, Byron F.
2468	Wilson, Caleb B.–Wilson, Dwight O.
2469	Wilson, Earl H.–Wilson, Fuller
2470	Wilson, G. Maria–Wilson, Hyrum
2471	Wilson, Ibbie M. C.–Wilson, Johanna T.
2472	Wilson, John–Wilson, Joseph W. F.
2473	Wilson, Josephine–Wilson, Marshall L.
2474	Wilson, Martha–Wilson, Myrtle
2475	Wilson, Nancy–Wilson, Samuel D.
2476	Wilson, Samuel E.–Wilson, Tyler A.
2477	Wilson, Ulric W.–Wilson, Zulima H.
2478	Wilsoncroft, Joel S.–Wimans, Wright
2479	Winant, Charles–Windmueller, George W.
2480	Windnes, Tobine A.–Wing, Eva
2481	Wing, Frances L.–Winklepleck, Seth
2482	Winkler, Adam–Winrow, Louisa
2483	Wins, Joshua–Wintemute, Mary
2484	Winter, Abby I.–Winters, Myron L.
2485	Winters, Nancy–Wisdom, William T.
2486	Wise, Aaron C.–Wise, Zelma E.
2487	Wiseburn, John L.–Wiszneauckas, George
2488	Witaker, Rachel–Withus, Margret
2489	Witker, Fredrick E.–Witzmann, Robert
2490	Wivel, Levi–Wolever, Zenas
2491	Wolf, Aaron–Wolf, Lydia J.
2492	Wolf, Magdalina–Wolfe, Lydia A.
2493	Wolfe, Mahala J.–Woliver, Peter
2494	Wolke, Christina–Woobey, William
2495	Wood, Aaron–Wood, Dwight
2496	Wood, Edgar–Wood, Haynes
2497	Wood, Helen–Wood, Kittie P.
2498	Wood, LaFayette–Wood, Otto
2499	Wood, Paris E.–Wood, Ziba S.
2500	Woodal, Sarah–Woodcock, Sylvanus D.
2501	Woodcock, Theodore–Woodmansee, Martha

Roll	Description
2502	Woodmansee, Nathan–Woodrum, William T.
2503	Woods, Aaron–Woods, Julietta
2504	Woods, Kate S.–Woodville, Roderick M.
2505	Woodward, Aaron–Woodward, Zopher C.
2506	Woodwell, James S.–Woolfork, Joseph
2507	Woolheater, Helen–Woozley, William
2508	Woratzeck, Josephine–Workwell, John
2509	Worl, Annie M.–Worswick, William H.
2510	Wort, Barney B.–Wozencraft, Anna E.
2511	Wraalstad, John Olson–Wright, Byron A.
2512	Wright, C. Ella–Wright, Ezra S.
2513	Wright, Fannie–Wright, Jasper N.
2514	Wright, Jefferson–Wright, Marvin B.
2515	Wright, Mary–Wright, Rutha A.
2516	Wright, S. Augusta–Writht, Zeness R.
2517	Wrighter, Guilford M.–Wyatt, Hiram C.
2518	Wyatt, Inez E.–Wyly, Fannie
2519	Wymack, Nancy–Wyzard, Elmyra
2520	Xander, Allen–Yarington, William A.
2521	Yark, Emily H.–Yazle, William R. W.
2522	Ybanes, Eugene–Yelvington, Harvey D.
2523	Yemans, Nancy–Yockey, Sarah M.
2524	Yocom, Amanda–York, Esther
2525	York, Fanny D.–Youndt, Simon E.
2526	Young, Aaron–Young, Cyrus S.
2527	Young, Daniel–Young, George G.
2528	Young, George H.–Young, Jay G.
2529	Young, Jean MacLeod–Young, Loywell
2530	Young, Lua J.–Young, Myron D.
2531	Young, Nancy–Young, Stillman
2532	Young, Susan–Younges, Edward
2533	Youngham, Caroline–Yuma, Charley
2534	Zabe, Sarah–Zeggle, Henry
2535	Zeh, David–Zenz, Wilhelmina
2536	Zepeda, Jesus–Zilz, Friederika
2537	Ziman, Magdalene–Zimmerman, Martin V.
2538	Zimmerman, Mary–Zoll, William
2539	Zollars, Catharine–Zynn, George W.

Selected Pension Application Files Relating to the Mormon Battalion. T1196. 21 rolls.

This microfilm publication reproduces Mexican War pension files for members of the Mormon Battalion. The files are arranged in alphabetical order by name of veteran. A complete list of the names is reproduced at the beginning of each roll. The Mormon Battalion is described in more detail on page 42.

Roll	Description
1	Abott, Joshua–Babcock, Lorenzo
2	Badham, Samuel–Bates, Joseph
3	Bean, George–Borrowman, John
4	Boyd, George–Brown, Jesse S.
5	Brown, John–Callahan, Thomas
6	Calvert, John–Colton, Philander
7	Coons, William–Dutcher, Thomas P.
8	Dykes, George–Hancock, Charles
9	Hancock, George–Hendricks, William
10	Hendrickson, James–Hullett, Schuyler
11	Hunsacker, Abraham–Kelley, Nicholas
12	Kelly, William–Martin, Edward
13	Martin, Jesse–Morris, Thomas
14	Moss, David–Park, William
15	Pearson, Ephriam–Richardson, Thomas
16	Richmond, Benjamin–Shupe, James

Roll	Description
17	Simmons, William–Standage, Henry
18	Stoddard, Rufus–Taggart, George
19	Tanner, Myron–Tyler, Daniel
20	Wade, Moses–Wilkin, David
21	Willes, Ira J.–Zabriskie, Jerome

Ledgers of Payments, 1818–1872, to U.S. Pensioners Under Acts of 1818 Through 1858, From Records of the Third Auditor of the Treasury. T718. 23 rolls.

This microfilm publication reproduces Treasury Department pension payment volumes that record semiannual payments for 1818 to 1871. The entries are arranged by the act of Congress under which payment was made and thereunder by name of pension agency. The pensioners' names appear in rough alphabetical order by initial letter of surname. Each volume contains a record of payments made for a specific period. Succeeding payments are in the next volume. Each entry shows the name of the pensioner, the name of the veteran (if different), the name of the pension agency through which payment was made, and the quarter and year of the last payment to the pensioner. When an heir or a legal representative claimed an unpaid balance due the pensioner at the time of death, the date of death of the pensioner is given and the date of the final payment made to the family or heirs.

Roll	Description
Revolutionary War pensioners:	
1	1818–32
2	1818–32
3	1820–42
4	1833–48
5	1833–49
6	1831–48
7	1831–48
8	1831–48
9	1849–64
10	1831–50
Invalid pensioners:	
11	1843–56
12	1855–67
13	1855–66
Revolutionary War pensioners:	
14	1848–68
Widow pensions:	
15	1831–43
16	1843–62
17	1836–48
18	1835–50
19	1848–62
20	1848–62
21	1862–72
22	1853–72
23	1858–72

Other Records Relating to Veterans' Claims (Record Groups 29, 94, and 407)

Special Schedules of the Eleventh Census (1890) Enumerating Union Veterans and Widows of Union Veterans of the Civil War. M123. 118 rolls.

An act of March 1, 1889, provided that the Superintendent of Census in taking the Eleventh Census should "cause to be taken on a special schedule of inquiry, according to such form as he may prescribe, the names, organizations, and length of service of those who had served in the Army, Navy, or Marine Corps of the United States in the war of the rebellion, and who are survivors at the time of said inquiry, and the widows of soldiers, sailors, or marines."

Each entry shows the following information: the name of the veteran (or if he did not survive, the names of both the widow and her deceased husband); the veteran's rank, company, regiment, or vessel; date of enlistment, date of discharge, and length of service in years, months, and days; post office and address of each person listed; disability incurred by the veteran; and remarks necessary for a complete statement of his term of service.

Practically all of the schedules for the States of Alabama through Kansas and approximately half of those for Kentucky appear to have been destroyed, possibly by fire, before the transfer of the remaining schedules to the National Archives in 1943. In a few cases, names of Confederate veterans were recorded inadvertently.

The schedules are arranged alphabetically by State or Territory, thereunder by county, and thereunder by minor subdivision.

Roll	Description
	Kentucky:
1	Boone, Bourbon, Bracken, Campbell, Clark, Fayette, Franklin, Gallatin, Grant, Harrison, Jessamine, Kenton, Owen, Pendleton, Scott, and Woodford Counties
2	Bath, Boyd, Carter, Elliott, Fleming, Floyd, Greenup, Johnson, Lawrence, Lewis, Magoffin, Martin, Mason, Menifee, Montgomery, Morgan, Nicholas, Pike, Powell, Robertson, Rowan, and Wolfe Counties
3	Adair, Bell, Boyle, Breathitt, Casey, Clay, Clinton, Cumberland, Estill, Garrard, Harlan, Jackson, Knott, Knox, Laurel, Lee, Leslie, Letcher, Lincoln, Madison, Owsley, Perry, Pulaski, Rockcastle, Russell, Wayne, and Whitley Counties and certain Federal, State, and local institutions throughout Kentucky
	Louisiana:
4	Orleans, Bienville, Bossier, Caddo, De Soto, Grant, Natchitoches, Rapides, Sabine, Vernon, Webster, and Winn Parishes
5	Ascension, Avoyelles, Caldwell, Catahoula, Claiborne, Concordia, East Baton Rouge, East Carroll, East Feliciana, Franklin, Jackson, Jefferson, Lafourche, Lincoln, Livingston, Madison, Morehouse, Ouachita, Plaquemines, Pointe Coupee, Richland, St. Bernard, St. Charles, St. Helena, St. James, St. John the Baptist, St. Landry, St. Martin, St. Mary, St. Tammany, Tangipahoa, Tensas, Terrebonne,

Roll	Description
	Union, Vermilion, West Baton Rouge, West Carroll, West Feliciana, Acadia, Assumption, Calcasieu, Cameron, Iberia, Iberville, and Lafayette Parishes
	Maine:
6	Androscoggin, Cumberland, Franklin, Kennebec, Oxford, Sagadahoc, Somerset, and York Counties
7	Aroostook, Hancock, Knox, Lincoln, Penobscot, Piscataquis, Waldo, and Washington Counties
	Maryland:
8	Baltimore City and Baltimore County
9	Caroline, Cecil, Dorchester, Harford, Kent, Queen Annes, Somerset, Talbot, Wicomico, and Worcester Counties
10	Allegany, Anne Arundel, Calvert, Carroll, Charles, Frederick, Garrett, Howard, Montgomery, Prince Georges, St. Marys, and Washington Counties
	Massachusetts:
11	Hampshire, Norfolk, and Plymouth Counties
12	Middlesex County
13	Barnstable, Berkshire, Bristol, Dukes, Franklin, and Nantucket Counties
14	Hampden County
15	Essex County
16	Suffolk County
	Michigan:
17	Branch, Calhoun, Hillsdale, Jackson, Lenawee, Monroe, Washtenaw, and Wayne Counties
18	Genesee, Huron, Lapeer, Macomb, Oakland, Saginaw, St. Clair, Sanilac, and Tuscola Counties
19	Clinton, Eaton, Gratiot, Ingham, Ionia, Isabella, Livingston, Mecosta, Midland, Montcalm, and Shiawassee Counties
20	Allegan, Barry, Berrien, Cass, Kalamazoo, Kent, Muskegon, Newaygo, Oceana, Ottawa, St. Joseph, and Van Buren Counties
21	Alcona, Alger, Alpena, Antrim, Arenac, Baraga, Bay, Benzie, Charlevoix, Cheboygan, Chippewa, Clare, Crawford, Delta, Emmet, Gladwin, Gogebic, Grand Traverse, Houghton, Iosco, Iron, Isle Royale, Kalkaska, Keweenaw, Lake, Leelanau, Luce, Mackinac, Manistee, Manitou, Marquette, Mason, Menominee, Missaukee, Montgomery, Ogemaw, Ontonagon, Osceola, Oscoda, Otsego, Presque Isle, Roscommon, Schoolcraft, and Wexford Counties
	Minnesota:
22	Blue Earth, Brown, Cottonwood, Dodge, Fairbault, Fillmore, Freeborn, Houston, Jackson, Lac qui Parle, Lincoln, Lyon, Martin, Mower, Murray, Nicollet, Nobles, Olmsted, Pipestone, Redwood, Rock, Steele, Waseca, Watonwan, Winona, and Yellow Medicine Counties and certain Federal, State, local, and private institutions
23	Big Stone, Carver, Chippewa, Dakota, Goodhue, Hennepin, Kandiyohi, Le Sueur, McLeod, Meeker, Renville, Rice, Scott, Sibley, Swift, Wabasha, and Wright Counties
24	Aitkin, Anoka, Benton, Carlton, Cass, Chisago, Cook, Crow Wing, Isanti, Itasca, Kanabec, Lake, Mille Lacs, Morrison, Pine, Ramsey, St. Louis, Sherburne, and Washington Counties

Roll	Description
25	Becker, Beltrami, Clay, Douglas, Grant, Hubbard, Kittson, Marshall, Norman, Otter Tail, Polk, Pope, Stearns, Stevens, Todd, Traverse, Wadena, and Wilkin Counties

Mississippi:

Roll	Description
26	Entire State

Missouri:

Roll	Description
27	Jefferson, St. Charles, and St. Louis Counties and certain Federal, State, local, and private institutions
28	Bollinger, Butler, Cape Girardeau, Carter, Dunklin, Iron, Madison, Mississippi, New Madrid, Oregon, Pemiscot, Perry, Reynolds, Ripley, St. Francois, St. Genevieve, Scott, Shannon, Stoddard, Washington, and Wayne Counties
29	Audrain, Boone, Callaway, Camden, Cole, Crawford, Dent, Franklin, Gasconade, Lincoln, Maries, Miller, Montgomery, Osage, Phelps, Pike, Pulaski, and Warren Counties
30	Barry, Christian, Dade, Dallas, Douglas, Greene, Howell, Jasper, Laclede, Lawrence, McDonald, Newton, Ozark, Polk, Stone, Taney, Texas, Webster, and Wright Counties
31	Adair, Chariton, Clark, Howard, Knox, Lewis, Linn, Macon, Marion, Monroe, Putnam, Ralls, Randolph, Schuyler, Scotland, Shelby, and Sullivan Counties
32	Barton, Bates, Benton, Cass, Cedar, Cooper, Henry, Hickory, Johnson, Lafayette, Moniteau, Morgan, Pettis, St. Clair, Saline, and Vernon Counties
33	Andrew, Atchison, Caldwell, Carroll, Clinton, Grundy, Harrison, Holt, Livingston, Mercer, Nodaway, Ray, and Worth Counties
34	Buchanan, Clay, Jackson, and Platte Counties

Montana:

Roll	Description
35	Entire State

Nebraska:

Roll	Description
36	Adams, Butler, Chase, Clay, Dundy, Fillmore, Franklin, Frontier, Furnas, Gosper, Hamilton, Harlan, Hayes, Hitchcock, Jefferson, Kearney, Nuckolls, Phelps, Polk, Red Willow, Saline, Seward, Thayer, Webster, and York Counties
37	Antelope, Arthur, Banner, Blaine, Boone, Box Butte, Brown, Buffalo, Burt, Cedar, Cherry, Cheyenne, Colfax, Cuming, Custer, Dakota, Dawes, Dawson, Deuel, Dixon, Dodge, Garfield, Grant, Greeley, Hall, Holt, Hooker, Howard, Keith, Keya Paha, Kimball, Knox, Lincoln, Logan, Loup, McPherson, Madison, Merrick, Nance, Perkins, Pierce, Platte, Rock, Scotts Bluff, Sheridan, Sherman, Sioux, Stanton, Thomas, Thurston, Valley, Washington, Wayne, and Wheeler Counties
38	Cass, Douglas, Gage, Johnson, Lancaster, Nemaha, Otoe, Pawnee, Richardson, Sarpy, and Saunders Counties

Nevada:

Roll	Description
39	Entire State

New Hampshire:

Roll	Description
40	Entire State

New Jersey:

Roll	Description
41	Bergen, Essex, Morris, Passaic, Sussex, and Warren Counties
42	Hudson, Hunterdon, Mercer, Middlesex, Somerset, and Union Counties

Roll	Description
43	Atlantic, Burlington, Camden, Cape May, Cumberland, Gloucester, Monmouth, Ocean, and Salem Counties

New Mexico:

Roll	Description
44	Entire Territory

New York:

Roll	Description
45	New York County (in part)
46	New York County (in part)
47	Kings, Queens, Richmond, and Suffolk Counties
48	Columbia, Dutchess, Putnam, and Westchester Counties
49	Delaware, Orange, Rockland, Sullivan, and Ulster Counties
50	Albany, Greene, Otsego, Rensselaer, and Schoharie Counties
51	Fulton, Hamilton, Herkimer, Montgomery, Saratoga, Schenectady, Warren, and Washington Counties
52	Clinton, Essex, Franklin, Jefferson, Lewis, and St. Lawrence Counties
53	Cayuga, Madison, Oneida, Onondaga, and Oswego Counties
54	Allegany, Broome, Chemung, Chenango, Cortland, Schuyler, Steuben, Tioga, and Tompkins Counties
55	Genesee, Livingston, Monroe, Ontario, Orleans, Seneca, Wayne, Wyoming, and Yates Counties
56	Cattaraugus, Chautauqua, Erie, and Niagara Counties
57	Certain Federal, State, local, and private institutions throughout New York State

North Carolina:

Roll	Description
58	Entire State

North Dakota:

Roll	Description
59	Entire State

Ohio:

Roll	Description
60	Allen, Crawford, Defiance, Fulton, Henry, and Paulding Counties
61	Putnam, Sandusky, Seneca, Van Wert, Williams, and Wyandot Counties
62	Hancock, Lucas, Ottawa, and Wood Counties
63	Auglaize, Champaign, Clark, Drake, Greene, and Hardin Counties
64	Logan, Mercer, Miami, Montgomery, Preble, and Shelby Counties
65	Butler, Clermont, Clinton, and Warren Counties
66	Hamilton County
67	Adams, Brown, and Gallia Counties
68	Highland, Hocking, Jackson, Lawrence, Pike, Ross, Scioto, and Vinton Counties
69	Delaware, Fairfield, Fayette, and Franklin Counties
70	Knox, Licking, Madison, Marion, Morrow, Perry, Pickaway, and Union Counties
71	Ashland and Cuyahoga Counties
72	Erie, Holmes, Huron, Lorain, Medina, Richland, and Wayne Counties
73	Athens, Belmont, Coshocton, Guernsey, Harrison, Meigs, Monroe, Morgan, Muskingum, Noble, and Washington Counties
74	Ashtabula, Carroll, Columbiana, Geauga, Jefferson, Lake, Mahoning, Portage, Stark, Summit, Trumbull, and Tuscarawas Counties
75	Federal, State, local, and private institutions throughout Ohio

Roll	Description
	Oklahoma and Indian Territories:
76	Entire Territory
	Oregon:
77	Entire State
	Pennsylvania:
78	Philadelphia County (in part)
79	Philadelphia County (in part)
80	Philadelphia County (in part)
81	Chester, Delaware, Lancaster, and York Counties
82	Berks, Bucks, Lehigh, Montgomery, and Northampton Counties
83	Columbia, Dauphin, Lebanon, Montour, Northumberland, and Schuylkill Counties
84	Carbon, Lackawanna, Luzerne, Monroe, Pike, Susquehanna, Wayne, and Wyoming Counties
85	Bradford, Cameron, Center, Clearfield, Clinton, Elk, Lycoming, McKean, Potter, Sullivan, and Tioga Counties
86	Adams, Bedford, Blair, Cumberland, Franklin, Fulton, Huntingdon, Juniata, Mifflin, Perry, Snyder, and Union Counties
87	Armstrong, Cambria, Clarion, Indiana, Jefferson, and Westmoreland Counties
88	Allegheny County
89	Butler, Crawford, Erie, Forest, Lawrence, Mercer, Venango, and Warren Counties
90	Beaver, Fayette, and Greene Counties
91	Somerset and Washington Counties and certain Federal, State, local, and private institutions throughout Pennsylvania
	Rhode Island:
92	Entire State
	South Carolina:
93	Entire State
	South Dakota:
94	Entire State
	Tennessee:
95	Anderson, Blount, Campbell, Carter, Claiborne, Cocke, Grainger, Greene, Hamblen, Hancock, Hawkins, Jefferson, Johnson, Knox, Loudon, Morgan, Roane, Scott, Sevier, Sullivan, Unicoi, Union, and Washington Counties
96	Bledsoe, Bradley, Cannon, Clay, Cumberland, DeKalb, Fentress, Grundy, Hamilton, Jackson, James, McMinn, Macon, Marion, Meigs, Monroe, Overton, Pickett, Polk, Putnam, Rhea, Sequatchie, Smith, Van Buren, Warren, and White Counties
97	Bedford, Cheatham, Coffee, Davidson, Franklin, Giles, Lincoln, Marshall, Maury, Moore, Robertson, Rutherford, Sumner, Trousdale, Williamson, and Wilson Counties
98	Benton, Carroll, Chester, Crockett, Decatur, Dickson, Dyer, Fayette, Gibson, Hardin, Hardeman, Haywood, Henry, Henderson, Hickman, Houston, Humphreys, Lake, Lauderdale, Lawrence, Lewis, Madison, McNairy, Montgomery, Obion, Perry, Shelby, Stewart, Tipton, Wayne, and Weakley Counties
	Texas:
99	Anderson, Angelina, Bowie, Camp, Cass, Chambers, Cherokee, Delta, Fannin, Franklin, Galveston, Gregg, Harris, Harrison, Henderson, Hopkins, Houston, Hunt, Jefferson, Lamar, Liberty, Marion, Montgomery, Morris, Nacogdoches, Newton, Orange, Panola, Polk, Rains, Red River, Rusk, Sabine, San Jacinto, Shelby, Smith, Titus, Trinity, Tyler, Upshur, Van Zandt, Walker, and Wood Counties
100	Collin, Cooke, Dallas, Denton, Ellis, Grayson, Hill, Johnson, Kaufman, McLennan, Navarro, Rockwall, and Tarrant Counties
101	Austin, Bexar, Brazoria, Brazos, Burleson, Calhoun, Caldwell, Cameron, Colorado, Comal, DeWitt, Dimmit, Duval, Falls, Fayette, Fort Bend, Frio, Freestone, Goliad, Gonzales, Grimes, Guadalupe, Hays, Hidalgo, Jackson, Karnes, Kinney, La Salle, Lavaca, Lee, Leon, Live Oak, Limestone, Madison, Matagorda, Maverick, Medina, Milam, Nueces, Robertson, San Patricio, Starr, Travis, Uvalde, Victoria, Waller, Washington, Webb, Wilson, Wharton, Zapata, and Zavala Counties
102	Archer, Armstrong, Bandera, Baylor, Bell, Blanco, Bosque, Brewster, Briscoe, Brown, Buchel, Burnet, Callahan, Carson, Childress, Clay, Coleman, Collingsworth, Comanche, Coryell, Cottle, Dallam, Deaf Smith, Dickens, Donley, Eastland, Ector, Edwards, El Paso, Erath, Fisher, Foley, Gillespie, Gray, Hale, Hall, Hamilton, Hardeman, Hartley, Haskell, Hemphill, Hood, Harvard, Jack, Jeff Davis, Jones, Kendell, Kent, Kerr, Kimble, King, Knox, Lampasas, Lipscomb, Llano, McCulloch, Martin, Mason, Menard, Midland, Mills, Mitchell, Montague, Nolan, Ochiltree, Oldham, Palo Pinto, Parker, Pecos, Potter, Randall, Reeves, Roberts, Runnels, San Saba, Scurry, Shackelford, Sherman, Somervell, Stephens, Stonewall, Sutton, Swisher, Taylor, Throckmorton, Tom Green, Val Verde, Wheeler, Wichita, Wilbarger, Williamson, Wise, and Young Counties
	Utah:
103	Entire State
	United States Vessels and Navy Yards:
104	
	Vermont:
105	Entire State
	Virginia:
106	Accomack, Charles City, Elizabeth City, Essex, Gloucester, Greensville, Isle of Wight, James City, King and Queen, King William, Lancaster, Mathews, Middlesex, Nansemond, New Kent, Norfolk, Northampton, Northumberland, Prince George, Princess Anne, Richmond, Southampton, Surry, Sussex, Warwick, Westmoreland, York, Amelia, Appomattox, Brunswick, Buckingham, Charlotte, Chesterfield, Cumberland, Dinwiddie, Fluvanna, Goochland, Halifax, Henrico, Lunenburg, Mecklenburg, Nottoway, Powhatan, Prince Edward, Alexandria, Caroline, Clarke, Culpeper, Fairfax, Fauquier, Frederick, Hanover, King George, Loudoun, Louisa, Madison, Orange, Page, Prince William, Rappahannock, Rockingham, Shenandoah, Spotsylvania, Stafford, and Warren Counties
107	Albemarle, Alleghany, Amherst, Augusta, Bath, Bedford, Botetourt, Campbell, Franklin, Henry, Highland, Nelson, Patrick, Pittsylvania, Rockbridge, Buchanan, Carroll, Craig, Dickenson, Floyd, Grayson, Lee, Montgomery, Pulaski, Roanoke, Russell, Scott, Smyth,

Roll	Description
	Tazewell, Washington, Wise, and Wythe Counties, Hampton Normal and Agricultural Institute, and two Federal institutions in Elizabeth City County

Washington:

Roll	Description
108	Entire State

West Virginia:

Roll	Description
109	Barbour, Berkeley, Brooke, Calhoun, Doddridge, Gilmer, Grant, Hampshire, Hancock, Hardy, Harrison, Jefferson, Lewis, Marion, Marshall, Mineral, Monongalia, Morgan, Ohio, Pendleton, Pleasants, Preston, Randolph, Ritchie, Taylor, Tucker, Tyler, Upshur, Wetzel, Wirt, and Wood Counties
110	Boone, Braxton, Cabell, Clay, Fayette, Greenbrier, Jackson, Kanawha, Lincoln, Logan, McDowell, Mason, Mercer, Monroe, Nicholas, Pocahontas, Putnam, Raleigh, Roane, Summers, Wayne, Webster, and Wyoming Counties

Wisconsin:

Roll	Description
111	Milwaukee and Walworth Counties
112	Dodge, Jefferson, Kenosha, Ozaukee, Racine, Washington, and Waukesha Counties
113	Crawford, Dane, Grant, Green, Iowa, Juneau, Lafayette, Richland, Rock, Sauk, and Vernon Counties
114	Adams, Brown, Calumet, Columbia, Door, Fond du Lac, Green Lake, Kewaunee, Manitowoc, Marquette, Outagamie, Sheboygan, Waushara, and Winnebago Counties
115	Ashland, Clark, Florence, Forest, Langlade, Lincoln, Marathon, Marinette, Oconto, Oneida, Portage, Price, Shawano, Taylor, Waupaca, and Wood Counties
116	Barron, Bayfield, Buffalo, Burnett, Chippewa, Douglas, Dunn, Eau Claire, Jackson, La Crosse, Monroe, Pepin, Pierce, Polk, St. Croix, Sawyer, Trempealeau, and Washburn Counties

Wyoming:

Roll	Description
117	Entire State

Washington, D. C., and miscellaneous:

Roll	Description
118	Entire District

Index to General Correspondence of the Record and Pension Office, 1889–1920. M686. 385 rolls. 16mm. DP.

This microfilm publication reproduces a card index to general correspondence of the Record and Pension Office, 1889–1904.

Most of the microfilmed index cards refer to names of soldiers. Each card gives, in addition to the name of the soldier, the organization in which he served, the name of the person or office who made the inquiry, the subject of the inquiry, and the file number. Other cards refer to names of volunteer organizational units and of States; some subjects are also included. The records to which these indexes refer are not available on microfilm.

Roll	Description
1	A–Ac
2	Ad–Add
3	Ade–Alb
4	Alc–Alk
5	All–Allf
6	Allg–Am
7	An–Andi

Roll	Description
8	Andl–Aq
9	Ar–Arm
10	Arn–Ash
11	Ask–Aul
12	Aum–Az
13	B–Bah
14	Bai
15	Bak–Balc
16	Bald–Bani
17	Bank–Bark
18	Barl–Barn
19	Baro–Bars
20	Bart–Batd
21	Bate–Baz
22	Bea–Beb
23	Bec–Beg
24	Beh–Bell
25	Belm–Benn
26	Beno–Berr
27	Bers–Bif
28	Big–Bir
29	Bis–Blae
30	Blag–Blaz
31	Ble–Boa
32	Bob–Boll
33	Bolm–Boo
34	Bop–Boui
35	Bouk–Bowl
36	Bowm–Boyn
37	Boys–Brah
38	Brai–Braz
39	Bre
40	Bri–Bris
41	Brit–Bron
42	Broo–Browl
43	Brown, A.–Brown, G.
44	Brown, H.–Brown, M.
45	Brown, N.–Brows
46	Brox–Brya
47	Bryc–Bue
48	Buf–Burc
49	Burd–Burk
50	Burl–Burn
51	Buro–Buse
52	Bush–Butm
53	Butn–By
54	C–Cald
55	Cale–Camo
56	Camp–Camu
57	Can–Care
58	Carg–Carp
59	Carr–Cars
60	Cart–Case
61	Casg–Caz
62	Ce–Cham
63	Chan–Chap
64	Char–Chet
65	Cheu–Chun
66	Chur–Clari
67	Clark–Clark, J.
68	Clark, K.–Clay
69	Cle–Clin
70	Clip–Coc
71	Cod–Cold

Roll	Description	Roll	Description
72	Cole–Colk	136	Gill–Gind
73	Coll–Colm	137	Gine–Glu
74	Coln–Comp	138	Gly–Gooc
75	Comn–Conm	139	Good–Gord
76	Conn–Conr	140	Gore–Grag
77	Cons–Cook	141	Grah–Grav
78	Cool–Cooy	142	Graw–Green, H.
79	Cop–Corm	143	Green, I.–Greg
80	Corn–Cot	144	Greh–Grim
81	Cou–Cow	145	Grin–Gud
82	Cox–Crak	146	Gue–Gy
83	Cral–Craz	147	H–Haim
84	Cre–Crof	148	Hain–Hall, G.
85	Crog–Crov	149	Hall, H.–Hamb
86	Crow–Cul	150	Hamd–Hamm
87	Cum–Curr	151	Hamn–Hanr
88	Curs–Cz	152	Hans–Hard
89	D–Damo	153	Hare–Harrio
90	Damp–Darl	154	Harris
91	Darm–Davin	155	Harrit–Hart
92	Davis–Davis, I.	156	Harv–Hath
93	Davis, J.–Davit	157	Hati–Hax
94	Davl–Dea	158	Hay–Hazi
95	Deb–Dei	159	Hazl–Hee
96	Dej–Denm	160	Hef–Henc
97	Denn–Desd	161	Hend–Heno
98	Dese–Dich	162	Henr–Herm
99	Dick–Dier	163	Hern–Hia
100	Dies–Disc	164	Hib–Hik
101	Dise–Doll	165	Hil–Hill
102	Dolm–Dorn	166	Hilp–Hl
103	Doro–Doug	167	Ho–Hoga
104	Doul–Drak	168	Hogc–Holl
105	Dral–Dud	169	Holm–Hood
106	Due–Dune	170	Hooe–Horn
107	Dunf–Durd	171	Horo–Hour
108	Dure–Dz	172	Hous–Howd
109	E–Eckl	173	Howe–Hubb
110	Eckm–Ega	174	Hube–Hugg
111	Egb–Ellio	175	Hugh–Hump
112	Ellis–Emic	176	Humr–Hurk
113	Emig–Epp	177	Hurl–Hy
114	Epr–Evans, F.	178	I–Ink
115	Evans, G.–Ez	179	Inl–Iz
116	F–Farm	180	J–Jack
117	Farn–Faz	181	Jacc–Jee
118	Fe–Fern	182	Jef–Jewa
119	Fero–Finh	183	Jewe–Johnson, F.
120	Fini–Fish	184	Johnson, G.–Johnson, L.
121	Fisk–Flan	185	Johnson, M.–Johu
122	Flar–Flo	186	Joi–Jones, I.
123	Flu–Forc	187	Jones, J.–Jones, W.
124	Ford–Fort	188	Jones, Y.–Jy
125	Forw–Fow	189	K–Keas
126	Fox–Fran	190	Keat–Kelk
127	Frap–Frem	191	Kell
128	Fren–Fru	192	Kelm–Kenn
129	Fry–Fy	193	Keno–Ket
130	G–Gall	194	Keu–Kinb
131	Galm–Gard	195	Kinc–King
132	Gare–Gat	196	Kini–Kirk
133	Gau–Geop	197	Kirl–Knal
134	Geor–Gibb	198	Knap–Kob
135	Gibe–Gilk	199	Koc–Krea

Roll	Description
200	Kreb–Ky
201	L–Lamb
202	Lamd–Lanf
203	Lang–Lart
204	Laru–Lawr
205	Laws–Lecl
206	Leco–Lehm
207	Lehn–Lets
208	Lett–Lewi
209	Lewl–Line
210	Ling–Llov
211	Lloy–Lone
212	Long–Los
213	Lot–Lowm
214	Lown–Luss
215	Lust–Ly
216	M–Mahn
217	Maho–Mal
218	Mam–Marg
219	Mari–Mars
220	Mart
221	Maru–Math
222	Mati–Max
223	May–McBo
224	McBr–McCi
225	McCl–McCor
226	McCos–McDi
227	McDo–McE
228	McF–McGn
229	McGo–McIl
230	McIn–McKe
231	McKi–McLa
232	McLe–McNa
233	McNe–Meac
234	Mead–Meeh
235	Meek–Merp
236	Merr–Mich
237	Mici–Miller, C.
238	Miller, D.–Miller, M.
239	Miller, N.–Milz
240	Mim–Miss
241	Mist–Molk
242	Moll–Moon
243	Moore
244	Moorh–Morp
245	Morr
246	Mors–Mous
247	Mout–Munl
248	Munn–Murp
249	Murr–Myen
250	Myer–My
251	N–Nebo
252	Nebr–Nels
253	Nelt–Newl
254	Newm–Nice
255	Nich–Niv
256	Nix–Nors
257	Nort–Ny
258	O–Odem
259	Oden–Ok
260	Ol–Oq
261	Or–Oste
262	Osth–Oz
263	P–Pan

Roll	Description
264	Pap–Park
265	Parl–Pats
266	Patt–Paym
267	Payn–Peci
268	Peck–Penm
269	Penn–Peo
270	Pep–Peta
271	Pete–Pheg
272	Phel–Pich
273	Pick–Pine
274	Ping–Pl
275	Po–Pors
276	Port–Pot
277	Pou–Pra
278	Pre–Prim
279	Prin–Pt
280	Pu–Py
281	Q
282	R–Ram
283	Ran–Rat
284	Rau–Reck
285	Reco–Reec
286	Reed–Reep
287	Rees–Rem
288	Ren–Reyn
289	Reys–Rice
290	Rich
291	Rick–Rile
292	Rili–Robb
293	Robe
294	Robi–Roch
295	Rock–Roge
296	Rogg–Rose
297	Rosh–Rov
298	Row–Ruk
299	Rul–Russ
300	Rust–Ry
301	S–Sanc
302	Sand–Sat
303	Sau–Sche
304	Schi–Schu
305	Schv–Scou
306	Scov–Sef
307	Seg–Sew
308	Sex–Shan
309	Shao–Shed
310	Shee–Shep
311	Sher–Ship
312	Shir–Shuk
313	Shul–Sil
314	Sim–Sinc
315	Sind–Slas
316	Slat–Smin
317	Smit–Smith, D.
318	Smith, E.–Smith, H.
319	Smith, I.–Smith, J.
320	Smith, K.–Smith, S.
321	Smith, T.–Snei
322	Snel–Soli
323	Soll–Spar
324	Spat–Spil
325	Spin–Stae
326	Staf–Stap
327	Star–Stea

Roll	Description	Roll	Description
328	Steb–Steu	357	Wald–Walk
329	Stev	358	Wall–Walte
330	Stew–Stie	359	Walth–Ward
331	Stif–Stol	360	Ware–Washe
332	Stom–Stoy	361	Washi–Watr
333	St. P–Stro	362	Wats–Weau
334	Stru–Sul	363	Weav–Wed
335	Sum–Swap	364	Wee–Wello
336	Swar–Sz	365	Wells–Wen
337	T–Tayh	366	Weo–Wet
338	Tayl–Taylor, R.	367	Wev–Whis
339	Taylor, S.–Ten	368	Whit–White, J.
340	Tep–Thol	369	White, K.–Whitm
341	Thom–Thomo	370	Whitn–Wilb
342	Thomp–Thompson, P.	371	Wilc–Wilk
343	Thompson, R.–Tib	372	Will–Williams, G.
344	Tic–Tl	373	Williams, H.–Williams, R.
345	To–Tos	374	Williams, S.–Wilq
346	Tot–Trat	375	Wils–Wilson, J.
347	Trau–Tro	376	Wilson, K.–Winf
348	Tru–Turner, E.	377	Wing–Wism
349	Turner, F.–Ty	378	Wisn–Woob
350	U	379	Wood–Wood, W.
351	V–Vande	380	Wood, Z.–Woos
352	Vandi–Vans	381	Woot–Wright, I.
353	Vant–Verm	382	Wright, J.–Wy
354	Vern–Vit	383	X–Young, C.
355	Viv–Vy	384	Young, D.–Yu
356	W–Walc	385	Z

Miscellaneous Records Relating to Military Service

Additional Revolutionary War Records (Record Groups 39, 53, 92, 93, 94, 107, and 217)

Personnel Returns of the 6th Massachusetts Battalion, 1779–1780, and Returns and Accounts of Military Stores for the 8th and 9th Massachusetts Regiments, 1779–1782. M913. 1 roll. DP.

The personnel returns of the 6th Massachusetts Battalion, kept by Lt. Samuel Frost, which consist of one volume, contain weekly and monthly returns, inspection returns, field returns, descriptive returns, and lists of officers and men. The battalion, also referred to as a regiment, was commanded by Col. Thomas Nixon. The returns provide the number and rank of officers and noncommissioned officers and the number of "rank and file" present for duty, the number needed to fill vacancies, and alterations since the previous return. The alterations column enumerates the men who had died or deserted or who had been discharged, transferred, taken prisoner, reduced in rank, or promoted. Notations on many returns give the names of officers and men absent, the length and reason for their absence, and their location. Descriptive returns give the soldier's name, age, stature, complexion, color of hair and eyes, occupation, place of birth, and last place of residence.

The volume also contains a list of field officers and a list of captains in the Massachusetts line and descriptive lists of men in the regiment's Light Infantry Company and 5th Company (Capt. John Holden's Company). The descriptive lists provide information similar to that found on the descriptive returns mentioned above. There is also an account of the regiment's arms and equipment for the period January–June 1780 that was made by Lt. Nathan Holbrook, the regimental quartermaster. Returns, lists, and accounts that pertain to Captain Holden's Company, January–July 1780, are included at the end of the volume. Generally, the returns and other records are arranged chronologically.

The second volume, the returns and accounts of military stores for the 8th and 9th Massachusetts Regiments, November 1779–December 1782, complete this roll. Quartermaster Joshua Clapp made the returns in this volume for the 9th Massachusetts Regiment until January 1781, when a reorganization placed many of the officers and men of this regiment in the 8th Massachusetts Regiment.

The volume also contains an inspection return of the 9th Massachusetts Regiment made in December 1780.

Returns are arranged generally in chronological order and thereunder by company. Accounts are arranged by company and thereunder chronologically.

Central Treasury Records of the Continental and Confederation Governments Relating to Military Affairs, 1775–1789. M1015. 7 rolls. DP.

This microfilm publication reproduces fiscal records of the central treasury of the Continental and Confederation Governments, 1775–89, relating to military activities. The records consist of journals of expenditures relating to the armies; accounting records kept in Albany, N.Y.; records relating to purchases of military supplies and stores, July 1, 1779–October 27, 1783; several volumes relating to officers' accounts, including George Washington's account books of 1775–83; certificates of indebtedness issued to foreign officers; registers of certificates of indebtedness issued to soldiers by Paymaster General John Pierce; and ledgers of Revolutionary War pension payments made in Pennsylvania, 1785–1804.

This microfilm publication also reproduces records created during the periods when the Board of Treasury, the Superintendent of Finance, and the Board of War were operating, and records of officers' accounts created during the Revolution. Some of the records were used by the Federal Government in the settlement of Revolutionary War accounts or claims. Because of their fragmentary character, it was not feasible to arrange the records by military unit. Wherever possible, however, the records were arranged by the functions they represent. Numbered blank pages have not been filmed.

The journals of expenditures (roll 1 and part of roll 2) are records of the Pay Office and payments made by various paymasters in Philadelphia, New York, and in the field. The journal and the ledger of sundry accounts, maintained by the Commissioners of Accounts at Albany, December 2, 1776–May 16, 1780 (roll 2), contain entries for military expenditures in New York State and Canada, including pay of troops; purchases of arms, provisions, and clothing; recruiting expenses; prize money paid for vessels seized on St. Lawrence River; and expenditures for prisoners of war. The ledger contains accounts in the names of Deputy Adjutant General John Trumbull, Deputy Paymaster General Jonathan Trumbull, Jr., Quartermaster General Morgan Lewis, and many other officers in the Northern Army.

The journal and ledger of military accounts (roll 3) show amounts credited to military officers and civilians responsible for the functions of the Commissary General of Purchases in the States. The cashbook and clothing account ledger (also on roll 3) and the account books of the various officers (roll 4) appear to have been used after the war in the settlement of officers' accounts, including those of George Washington.

The contents of the registers of certificates of indebtedness (in 5 volumes, with a gap between the 4th and 5th) issued to soldiers for deferred payment by Paymaster General John Pierce (roll 6) are arranged numerically by certificate number. The Daughters of the American Revolution (DAR) prepared an index to Pierce's register and published it in their *17th Annual Report* (roll 5). The certificates of indebtedness issued to foreign officers (also on roll 5) were issued in 1784 to replace earlier certificates that had depreciated in value. Information concerning their redemption and the Dutch loan of 1792 is found in *National Loans of the United States From July 4, 1776 to June 30, 1880,* by Rafael A. Bayley (Washington, 1882), pp. 26, 107.

The ledgers of pension payments (roll 7) may have been submitted as evidence in a claim of the State of Pennsylvania for payment when the Pension Act of July 4, 1836, was being debated in the Congress.

Roll	Description	Date
1	Journal of Expenditures Relating to the Armies of the Continental and Confederation Governments	June 25, 1776–May 15, 1784
2	Journals and Ledger of Expenditures Relating to the Armies of the Continental and Confederation Governments, Albany, N.Y.	Dec. 2, 1776–May 24, 1786
3	Records Relating to Supplies and Stores	July 1, 1779–Oct. 27, 1783
4	Records Relating to Officers' Accounts	1775–88
5	Certificates of Indebtedness Issued to Foreign Officers and Related Documents	1784–1828
	DAR Index to Pierce's Register	1915
6	Registers of Certificates of Indebtedness Issued to Soldiers of the Continental Army by John Pierce, Paymaster General Volumes 1–4b	July 11, 1783–Mar. 2, 1786
7	Ledgers of Pension Payments to Revolutionary War Invalids, Widows, and Orphans of Pennsylvania Ledgers 1–4	1785–1804

Special Index to Numbered Records in the War Department Collection of Revolutionary War Records, 1775–1783. M847. 39 rolls. DP.

This microfilm publication reproduces an alphabetically arranged card index, called the Special Index, to names of persons that appear in three series containing numbered record books and numbered unbound documents relating to the Revolutionary War period. Most of the records were created between 1775 and 1783, but some are later. The indexed, numbered records pertain mainly to military operations, service of individuals, procurement and distribution of supplies, and pay and settlement of accounts of officers and men.

Although the War Department Collection of Revolutionary War Records consists of many series of related records, only three of them are indexed in whole or in part by the Special Index.

One series is a file of miscellaneous numbered records, referred to collectively as the Manuscript File. As the Record and Pension Office compiled military service records for Revolutionary War soldiers, it placed the muster rolls and related personnel records in a file arranged by military organization. Unbound records that were not abstracted—including letters, pay receipts, enlistment papers, supply returns, commissions, and orders—were numbered and placed in the Manuscript File, which contains about 35,500 items indexed by the Special Index. The records are microfilmed on M859.

The second series consists of the photographic copies made by the War Department in 1914 and 1915 of State records from Massachusetts, North Carolina, and Virginia. The records that were photographed were primarily correspondence and reports of State boards of war, Governors, and military officers; minutes of boards; prize vessel accounts; rolls and returns; court records; and receipts for money and supplies. The photographic copies of State records have not been microfilmed.

The third series is composed of 199 record books that were numbered and bound by the War Department. About a third of the volumes in this series are orderly books. The remainder consists chiefly of lists of officers and men of various military organizations; volumes containing commissions, oaths of allegiance, and oaths of office; receipt books, account books, letter books, and other records of the activities of the Quartermaster General's Department and of the Commissary General of Military Stores Department; and records of pay and settlement of accounts of the Paymaster General's Department. Volume 163 contains only the names of British soldiers. The numbered record books are microfilmed on M853.

The Special Index indexes all or some of the names in the three series of records. The entries refer mainly to names of U.S. military personnel, Government officials, and private persons, and some U.S. naval personnel, French and German officers, and British prisoners of war. A complete index card for a U.S. officer or enlisted man shows his given name and surname, the name of the State and organization in which he served, his rank, the number of the book or unbound record in which his name appears, the page number if necessary, and information describing the record. A complete index card for a civilian shows occupation instead of rank and State or place of residence instead of organization. Many index cards, however, lack items of information, depending on the completeness of the indexed record. Some cards contain only a surname and a number. In a few instances, the carbon copy of a War Department answer to an inquiry about a person named in the Special Index has been filed with the index card. A single index card may list many numbered records in which the name of a person appears. For some people, several index cards were required to list all the numbered records containing their names.

A significant and frequent departure from strict alphabetical arrangement of cards in the Special Index occurs in most cases of surnames that are pronounced similarly but spelled differently. Cards for such names are generally filed together under the most common spelling of the surname and arranged thereunder by given name. Thus index cards for persons named "Kain" are filed with those for persons named "Cain," and cards for persons named "Rodgers" are filed under "Rogers." Cross-reference cards direct searchers to the proper index locations.

Index cards for persons with surnames such as St. Clair and St. John are filed in the "St." section of the index. "Mac" may be filed as "Mc" and vice versa. In such cases, cross-reference cards direct the researcher to the proper index location. Index cards for persons identified in records by only their given names are filed under the given names. A few cards for illegible or incomplete names are filed under "Miscellaneous" at the end of the Special Index.

Roll	Description
1	A
2	B–Bem
3	Ben–Bram
4	Bran–By
5	C–Ci
6	Cl–Con
7	Coo–Cy
8	D–Dh
9	Di–Dy
10	E
11	F–Fl
12	Fo–Fy
13	G–Gn
14	Go–Gy
15	H–Ha
16	He–Hop
17	Hor–Hy
18	I–J
19	K
20	L–Le
21	Li–Ly
22	M–Maz
23	McA–McW
24	Me–Mi
25	Mo–My
26	N–O
27	P–Pf
28	Ph–Q
29	R–Ri
30	Ro–Ry
31	S–Sh
32	Si–Sr
33	St–Sy
34	T–Th
35	Ti–Tz
36	U–V
37	W–We
38	Wh–Wl
39	Wo–Z
	Miscellaneous

Miscellaneous Numbered Records (The Manuscript File) in the War Department Collection of Revolutionary War Records, 1775–1790's. M859. 125 rolls. DP.

This microfilm publication reproduces about 35,500 miscellaneous numbered records (the Manuscript File), originals and copies, pertaining to Revolutionary War military operations, service of individuals, pay and settlement of accounts, and supplies. Most of the original records date from 1775 to the early 1790s, but some were created in the 19th century, generally in connection with settling accounts and granting pensions to former servicemen and their heirs. The name index to these records is microfilmed on M847.

The Manuscript File mainly concerns services performed by individual military officers and enlisted men, the settlement of their pay and other accounts, the operations of several large staff departments of the Continental Army responsible for supplying and paying troops, and military operations. The records primarily include pay accounts of officers and enlisted men; accounts of supplies received and delivered; assignments of pay; certificates of nonindebtedness; commissions; correspondence between military officers about military operations; correspondence between heads of Continental Army staff departments and subordinates, other military officers, civil officers, and private citizens about supplies, transportation, pay, and settlement of accounts; enlistment papers; letters of administration; military orders; oaths of allegiance and of office; pay orders and orders for the delivery of supplies; powers of attorney; receipts for supplies, pay, and other sums of money; resignations; returns of supplies and personnel; and statements of service performed by individuals. There are usually hundreds of each of these kinds of records.

The records also include abstracts of payrolls; abstracts of records of issuance of supplies; pay accounts of civilians; books showing receipt and delivery of supplies; contracts for supplies; personal letters sent and received by Army staff officers; court-martial proceedings; military discharges; estimates of needed supplies; final settlement certificates; inspection reports; inventories and invoices of supplies; lists of supplies, military organizations, and pensioners; minutes of councils of war; muster rolls and payrolls; pension certificates; petitions to State legislatures; recommendations concerning the discharge of officers; registers of certificates issued in settlement of accounts; and resolutions of State legislatures and the Continental Congress concerning military matters.

The descriptive pamphlet to M859 includes three appendices: an outline of the arrangement of the Manuscript File, a list of the principal kinds of records in the Manuscript File, and a chronological list of sources of records in the Manuscript File.

Roll	Description
1	1–369
2	369½–770
3	771–1080
4	1081–1267
5	1268–1593
6	1594–1907
7	1908–2234
8	2235–2460
9	2461–3018
10	3019–3397

Roll	Description
11	3398–3889
12	3890–4096
13	4097–4455
14	4456–4749
15	4750–5088
16	5089–5359
17	5360–5660
18	5661–5960
19	5961–6261
20	6262–6542
21	6543–6860
22	6861–7279
23	7280–7466
24	7467–7859
25	7860–8092
26	8093–8393
27	8394–8712
28	8713–8950
29	8951–9424
30	9425–9669
31	9670–9957
32	9958–10296
33	10297–10605
34	10606–11047
35	11048–11375
36	11376–11712
37	11713–12086
38	12087–12439
39	12440–12774
40	12775–13176
41	13177–13569
42	13570–13866
43	13867–14369
44	14370–14392 (with gaps)
45	14393–14576
46	14577–14775
47	14776–15198
48	15199–15549
49	15550–15700
50	15701–15976
51	15977–16486
52	16487–16865
53	16866–17132
54	17133–17471
55	17472–17694
56	17695–17940
57	17941–18256
58	18257–18456
59	18457–18746
60	18747–18976
61	18977–19397
62	19398–19760
63	19761–20155
64	20156–20420
65	20421–20542
66	20543–20718
67	20719–20941
68	20942–21059
69	21060–21154
70	21155–21266
71	21267–21393
72	21394–21806
73	21807–21829

Roll	Description
74	21830–21962
75	21963–22063
76	22064–22237
77	22238–22538
78	22539–22740
79	22741–23070
80	23071–23359
81	23360–23661
82	23662–23949
83	23950–24243
84	24244–24541
85	24542–24837
86	24838–25137
87	25138–25435
88	25436–25715
89	25716–26032
90	26033–26329
91	26330–26610
92	26611–26916
93	26917–27306
94	27307–27602
95	27603–27931
96	27932–28286
97	28287–28610
98	28611–28636
99	28637–28834
100	28835–29090
101	29091–29371
102	29372–29564
103	29565–29802
104	29803–30074
105	30075–30462
106	30463–30631
107	30632–30745
108	30746–30849
109	30850–31123
110	31124–31469
111	31470–31755
112	31863–32248
113	32249–32646
114	32647–32761
115	32762–33201
116	33202–33529
117	33530–33809
118	33810–34127
119	34128–34390
120	34391–34543
121	34544–34850
122	34851–35192
123	35193–35317
124	35318–35501
125	49984–49999
	50202–50208
	Unnumbered Records

Numbered Record Books Concerning Military Operations and Service, Pay and Settlement of Accounts, and Supplies in the War Department Collection of Revolutionary War Records. M853. 41 rolls. DP.

This microfilm publication reproduces 199 numbered record books, with related separate indexes and one unnumbered record book, concerning Revolutionary War military operations and service, pay and settlement of accounts, and supplies. Most of the numbered record books were created from 1775 to 1783, but some were begun or continued in the early postwar years; a few are copies made after 1800 of earlier records. The name index to these records is microfilmed on M847.

The records are arranged in four categories: (1) comprehensive indexes, (2) records of military operations and service, (3) records of pay and settlement of accounts, and (4) supply records. In each category records have been further arranged by subject matter, kind of record, or author or office of origin, as dictated by the nature of the records. The descriptive pamphlet for the publication summarizes the number and overall character of the records and provides additional information that may aid in using or understanding them. In the roll list below, an asterisk before a volume number indicates that a separate index to the volume exists and has been filmed before the volume on the same roll.

Roll	Volume	Description	Date
Comprehensive indexes:			
1		Catalog and subject index of numbered record books; index to oaths of allegiance and fidelity, oaths of office, commissions, and resignations (unnumbered indexes)	
Records of military operations and service:			
2	12, 196, 195, 193, *13, 14, 194, *15, 197	Orderly books	June 23, 1775–Dec. 10, 1778
3	*16, 17, 18, 19, 20, *21, 22	Orderly books	May 23, 1777–Mar. 25, 1780
4	*23, *24, 25, *26, 27, *28, 29	Orderly books	Apr. 18, 1778–Aug. 4, 1779
5	*32, *30, *31, *33, *34	Orderly books	Feb. 20, 1779–Mar. 22, 1780
6	*35, *36, 37, 38, 39, *40, *41, *42	Orderly books	Feb. 21,–Sept. 20, 1780
7	*43, *46, *45, *47, *48	Orderly books	Aug. 9, 1780–June 14, 1781
8	*49, *50, 51, *52, *53, *54	Orderly books	Jan. 15–Nov. 2, 1781
9	*55, *56, *57, *58, *59, *60	Orderly books	Aug. 22, 1781–Aug. 9, 1782
10	*61, *62, *63, 64, *65, 66	Orderly books	May 7–Nov. 14, 1782
11	*67, *68, *69, *70, 71, 72, *73, *74, *75, 76	Orderly books	Sept. 8, 1782–Sept. 27, 1783
12	165, 166, 167, 168	Oaths of allegiance and fidelity and oaths of office	1778–1781
13	169	Commissions and resignations	1775–80
14	1, 3, 8	Lists of Connecticut, Massachusetts, and Rhode Island troops	1776–83
15	2, 4, 5, unnumbered volume, 7	Lists of Delaware, New Jersey, New York, and Pennsylvania troops	1775–83
16	6, 9, 10, 11	Lists of North Carolina and South Carolina troops and of officers and men of Continental organizations raised from more than one State	1775–83
17	174, *156, 153, 163, 154, 162, 161, 158	Miscellaneous records of military operations and service	1775–83, 1785–1813
Records of pay and settlement of accounts:			
18	134	Letters sent by John Pierce	Apr. 19, 1786–May 14, 1788
19	136, 135, 138, 137	Letters sent and received by Joseph Howell	Aug. 13, 1784–Jan. 20, 1789, Jan. 2–Dec. 30, 1794
20	147, 147½, 145, 146	Receipt books of John Pierce, John White, George Reid, and Joseph Howell	July 1783–Aug. 1790
21	171, 172, 173, 157	Records of pay and settlement of accounts pertaining to Pennsylvania officers and men	Jan. 1777–June 1778, Sept. 21, 1818, and Feb. 27, 1830
22	99, 159, 175, 176, 139, 140	Records of pay and settlement of accounts pertaining to Virginia, New York, and Georgia officers and men and to members of the Hospital Department for the Southern Army	1775–1856
23	178, 136½, 142	Records of pay and settlement of accounts pertaining mainly to Maryland and North Carolina officers and men	1775–85, 1788
24	143, 170, 185, 189, 188, 141, 101	Records of pay and settlement of accounts pertaining to officers and men of various States, including Connecticut, Massachusetts, and New Hampshire, and to the Quartermaster General's Department	1775–84, 1786–90
Supply records:			
25	126, 123, 124, 125	Letters sent by Timothy Pickering, Quartermaster General	Aug. 5, 1780–May 10, 1781

Roll	Volume	Description	Date
26	89, 127, 82, 83	Register of letters received by Timothy Pickering	May–Aug. 1781
		Letters sent by Timothy Pickering	May 10, 1781– May 9, 1782
27	84, 85, *90, 86	Letters sent by Timothy Pickering, Quartermaster General	Jan. 4, 1782– June 21, 1783
28	87, 88	Letters sent by Timothy Pickering, Quartermaster General	Jan. 8, 1783– July 9, 1787
29	*148, *103	Estimates and returns of supplies, funds, and personnel, Quartermaster General's Department and Commissary General of Military Stores Department	1780–93
30	108, 107, 102, 160, 109	Records of Capt. Charles Russell, Assistant Deputy Quartermaster, Virginia	Feb, 1781–July 5, 1782
31	183, 190, 95, 97, 187, 191, 192	Records of disbursement, Quartermaster General's Department	Aug. 1780– Mar. 1784
32	98, 164, 149, 180, 181, 177, 179, 186, 182, 184	Miscellaneous records of receipts, disbursements, accounts, returns, issuances, and activities, Quartermaster General's Department	1776–90
33	*111, *110, *92, *93	Letters sent by Samuel Hodgdon, Richard Frothingham, and Benjamin Flower	July 19, 1778– May 24, 1784
34	78, 77, 81, *105, 79, 106, 80, 104	Receipt books of Samuel Hodgdon	Oct. 1778–Nov. 1789
35	*152, *155, *117, 114	Records of accounts, receipts, and disbursements associated with Samuel Hodgdon	1777–98
36	144, 100, *96	Records of accounts, receipts, and disbursements associated with Samuel Hodgdon	1778–92
37	*133, *94	Records of military stores received and delivered at Philadelphia	Mar. 1780–July 1783
38	*122, 132	Records of military stores received and delivered at Philadelphia	Mar. 1781– Sept. 1784
39	*129, 130, 131, 151	Records of military stores received and delivered at various places	Feb. 15, 1777– Aug. 8, 1783
40	*118, 119, 120, 128, 91, 113, 116, 150, 115	Miscellaneous records of military stores received and delivered, receipts, returns, pay orders and accounts, Commissary General of Military Stores Department	1776–85
41	112, 121	Records of issuance and receipt of provisions	1776–83, 1786

Correspondence of the War Department Relating to Indian Affairs, Military Pensions, and Fortifications, 1791–1797. M1062. 1 roll. DP.

This microfilm publication reproduces a volume that contains copies of War Department correspondence concerning Indian affairs, Revolutionary War invalid pensions, and military fortifications. This volume generally consists of (1) correspondence of the Secretary of War submitted to the Congress in 1792 and 1794 to inform them concerning relations between the United States and various tribes in different parts of the country, (2) reports made by the Secretary of War to the Congress, 1794–96, and (3) miscellaneous documents pertaining to military fortifications, pay, and regulations.

The overall arrangement is roughly chronological. Pagination (the numbers usually found at the top center of the pages) is somewhat irregular, with some gaps and duplication in the numbering sequence. In some cases, the pages have no numbers. Blank pages have not been reproduced. The descriptive pamphlet describes the specific contents of the "War Office Letter Book."

Letters, Orders for Pay, Accounts, Receipts, and Other Supply Records Concerning Weapons and Military Stores, 1776–1801. M927. 1 roll. DP.

This microfilm publication reproduces a volume that contains: orders for pay of the Commissary General of Military Stores Department, Oct. 2, 1780–June 2, 1781, and letters sent by the Superintendent of Military Stores, July 26, 1799–Aug. 19, 1801; a ledger of military stores for the main army in the field, 1780–83; a ledger of military stores received and delivered, Mar. 1780–May 1795; a receipt book of Samuel Hodgdon, Assistant Commissary General and Commissary General of Military Stores, June 9–Nov. 15, 1781; and 15 miscellaneous unbound record items that relate to procurement, production, issuing, and control of arms, munitions, and related military stores.

Other Records Relating to Confederates (Record Groups 45 and 109)

Records Relating to Confederate Naval and Marine Personnel. M260. 7 rolls. 16mm. DP.

This microfilm publication reproduces records relating to individuals serving in the Confederate Navy and Marine Corps. These records are in three series: (1)

compiled hospital and prison records of naval and marine personnel, (2) reference cards and papers relating to naval personnel, and (3) reference cards and papers relating to marine personnel.

The first series, arranged alphabetically by surname of sailor or marine, consists of cards containing abstracts of entries relating to the individual in Union and Confederate hospital registers, prescription books, and Union prison and parole rolls. It also includes original papers, primarily from prison records, relating to individuals.

The second and third series consists of reference cards and the originals of any papers relating solely to a particular sailor or marine, arranged alphabetically by surname. The reference cards indicate the rank of the sailor or marine and contain references to vessel papers, payrolls, muster rolls, and volumes in the War Department Collection of Confederate Records.

Some of the original documents relating to a particular individual were at some time removed from the second and third series. In some instances, however, the envelopes—which show the serviceman's name and rank—were retained in the files.

Roll	Description
Hospital and prison records of naval and marine personnel:	
1	A–E
2	F–L
3	M–R
4	S–Z
Reference cards and papers relating to naval personnel:	
5	A–G
6	H–P
7	Q–Z
Reference cards and papers relating to marine personnel:	
8	A–Z

Selected Records of the War Department Relating to Confederate Prisoners of War, 1861–1865. M598. 145 rolls. DP.

This microfilm publication reproduces 427 bound volumes of records relating to Confederate prisoners of war confined by Federal authorities, 1861–65, with two of the volumes extending to 1866.

The volumes consist mainly of registers and lists. There is a vast duplication of names of prisoners and information relating to them throughout the volumes. There are discrepancies in the spelling of names, information regarding military organizations, dates of capture, and other data. The volumes have no standard overall arrangement. Some volumes have page or folio numbers, but many pages are unnumbered. A few volumes contain name indexes. In the alphabetically arranged volumes there are no names under "X"; "I," and "J," and "U" and "V" are sometimes combined; "Mc" is generally combined with "M"; and some letters are missing.

Various numbers indicating several prior numbering schemes appear in the volumes. In general, the significance of the numbers is obscure. For these reasons, and to prevent confusion in the citation of volume numbers, the volumes have been renumbered by the National Archives in a continuous series from 1 to 427.

The various series of bound volumes have been arranged in two main sections: records relating to Confederate prisoners of war and to political prisoners without regard to specific prison or place of confinement, and records of individual military prisons or stations. The records under the second heading have been further arranged by the name of the particular prison or station to which the records pertain. A third section contains a few records of several prisons. Not all of the records relating to Confederate prisoners of war are reproduced here.

Records of Individual Prisons or Stations

The volumes are arranged alphabetically by the name of the military prison or other place of confinement. For each prison or station there are generally three main types of records: registers compiled by the Office of the Commissary General of Prisoners, general registers, and auxiliary registers. Registers for a particular prison seldom give a complete listing of all prisoners who were confined. For some prisons there are no Commissary General registers, and for others there are no general registers. For some places of confinement other than military prisons neither type of register has been found.

The general registers are the basic record of arrivals, confinements, and dispositions of prisoners. The auxiliary registers consist of registers of prisoners confined, registers of deaths, lists of prisoners, ledgers, correspondence, morning reports, and various other records.

In many of the Commissary General registers, the entries are arranged alphabetically. The arrangement of entries in both general and auxiliary registers is usually alphabetical by initial letter of the prisoner's surname or chronological. There are name indexes in most of the ledgers and letterbooks and in a few of the other volumes. Many volumes contain lists of contents that refer to letters of the alphabet and to page numbers. Some of the registers continue from volume to volume, while others are complete within a volume. In some registers, the entries for names of prisoners are numbered either within each letter of the alphabet or consecutively for the entire volume. In a few groups of registers the numbers continue under each letter of the alphabet from one volume to another. Some registers have two separate lists under each letter of the alphabet, one for officers and another for other prisoners. Many registers and other volumes include records of civilian and Federal prisoners with those of Confederate prisoners, and a few volumes contain only names of Federal prisoners. Several volumes contain information relating only to paroled prisoners.

Roll	Volume	Description	Date
Records relating to all prisoners:			
1	1	Register of prisoners, compiled by the Office of the Commissary General of prisoners	1863–65
2	2	"	"
3	3	"	"
4	4	"	"
5	5	Register of deaths of prisoners, compiled by the Office of the Commissary General of Prisoners	1862–65
6	6	"	"
7	7–9	Registers of prisoners' applications for	1863–65

Roll	Volume	Description	Date
		release and decisions, compiled by the Office of the Commissary General of Prisoners	
8	10–13	Registers relating to the release of prisoners, compiled by the Office of the Commissary General of Prisoners	1861–65
9	14–16	Registers relating to prisoners' possessions, miscellaneous reports, and correspondence of the Office of the Commissary General of Prisoners	1862–66
10	17–18	Registers of deaths of prisoners, compiled by the Surgeon General's Office	1862–65
11	19–20	"	"
12	21	"	"

Records relating to individual prisons or stations:
Alton, Ill., military prison:

Roll	Volume	Description	Date
13	22–26	Letters sent and received and general registers of prisoners	1862–65
14	27–28	Registers of prisoners, compiled by the Office of the Commissary General of Prisoners	1861–65
15	29–30	Registers of prisoners	1862–65
16	31–35	Registers and lists of prisoners	1862–65
17	36–37	Morning reports of prisoners	Apr.–Dec. 1862
18	38	"	Jan. 1863–Mar. 1864
19	39–40	Morning reports of prisoners and attendants in the military prison hospital	June 1864–July 1865
20	41–47	Reports, registers, and miscellaneous records relating to prisoners	1862–65

Bowling Green, Va., provost marshal's office:

Roll	Volume	Description	Date
21	48	Register of prisoners	May 1865–Nov. 1866

Camp Butler, Ill., military prison:

Roll	Volume	Description	Date
	49–52	Registers and descriptive list of prisoners	1862–63

Camp Chase, Ohio, military prison:

Roll	Volume	Description	Date
22	53	Register of prisoners, compiled by the Office of the Commissary General of Prisoners	1863–65
23	54	"	1863–65

Roll	Volume	Description	Date
24	55–57	Registers of prisoners	1862–63
25	58–60	Descriptive lists of prisoners	1862–63
26	61–65	Lists of prisoners paroled, released, transferred, escaped, and deceased	1862–65
27	66–68	Registers of deaths and burials	1863–65
28	69–72	Registers, lists, and reports of prisoners	1861–63, 1865
29	73–83	Roll call books	1861–63
30	84	Ledger of prisoners' accounts	1862–63
31	85	"	1864–65
32	86	Journal of prisoners' accounts	Nov. 1864–June 1865
33	87–88	Stubs of prisoners' receipts	Aug. 1863–Jan. 1865
34	89–91	"	Sept. 1864–Jan. 1865
35	92–95	"	Jan.–June 1865
36	96–98	Registers relating to prisoners' articles and money received and unidentified name index	1862–65

Cincinnati, Ohio:

Roll	Volume	Description	Date
37	99–102	Registers of prisoners	1862–64

Fort Columbus, N.Y.:

Roll	Volume	Description	Date
	103	Register of prisoners	Mar.–Sept. 1862

Department of the Cumberland, Nashville, Tenn.:

Roll	Volume	Description	Date
38	104	Register of prisoners	1862–63
39	105–106	"	1863–65

Fort Delaware, Del., military prison:

Roll	Volume	Description	Date
40	107	General register of prisoners	1863
41	108–109	"	1863–65
42	110	Register of prisoners, compiled by the Office of the Commissary General of Prisoners	1863–64
43	111–112	"	1864–65
44	113–116	Registers of prisoners	1863–64
45	117–151	Registers of prisoners in prison division Nos. 1–6, 8–12, 15–20, and 22–39	1863–65
46	152–160	Registers of prisoners from Confederate State organizations in various prison divisions	1864–65
47	161–168	Registers of prisoner patients in the hospital, registers of deaths, and morning reports of prisoners	1862–65
48	169–172	Ledgers of prisoners' accounts	July 1863–July 1864
49	173–175	"	July 1864–Jan. 1865
50	176–178	"	Nov. 1864–July 1865

Roll	Volume	Description	Date
51	179–183	Registers of prisoners' accounts	1862–65
52	184–187	Registers of articles and currency received for prisoners and receipts for money sent by the Adams Express Co.	1864–65

Camp Douglas, Ill., military prison:

Roll	Volume	Description	Date
53	188	General register of prisoners	Aug. 1863–Dec. 1864
54	189	Register of prisoners, compiled by the Office of the Commissary General of Prisoners	1862–63
55	190–191	"	1863–65
56	192–194	Register of prisoners	1862
57	195–196	Registers of prisoners	1862–64
58	197–201	Registers of prisoners confined, sentenced, exchanged, released, and deceased	1862–65
59	202–205	Morning reports of prisoners	1862, 1864–65
60	206–207	Statistical reports of prisoners and account of checks and packages received for prisoners	1864–65
61	208–209	Ledgers of prisoners' accounts	1862–63
62	210	Ledger of prisoners' accounts and name index	1863–64
63	211–212	"	1864
64	213–217	Ledger of prisoners' accounts and miscellaneous records	1862, 1864–65

Elmira, N.Y., military prison:

Roll	Volume	Description	Date
65	218–220	General registers of prisoners	1862–65
66	221	Register of prisoners, compiled by the Office of the Commissary General of Prisoners	1864–65
67	222–224	Registers of prisoners confined and deceased	1864–65
68	225–226	Morning reports of prisoners	July 1864–July 1865
69	227–229	Registers of receipt and disposition of money and articles of prisoners	1864–65
70	230–231	Ledgers of prisoners' accounts	July–Dec. 1864
71	232–235	Ledger of prisoners' accounts, blotter to ledgers, and check stubs for the First National Bank of Elmira	1864–65

Gratiot and Myrtle Streets prisons, St. Louis, Mo.:

Roll	Volume	Description	Date
72	236–239	Registers of prisoners, compiled by the Office of the Commissary General of Prisoners, and descriptive list of prisoners	1862–65

Department of the Gulf:

Roll	Volume	Description	Date
73	240–243	Registers of prisoners paroled at Gainesville, Ala.	May 1865
74	244–245	Registers of prisoners paroled in Louisiana	June–July 1865
75	246–249	Registers of prisoners paroled in Louisiana and Texas	June–July 1865
76	250–254	Registers of prisoners paroled in Mississippi and Alabama	May 1865
77	255–258	"	May–July 1865
78	259–264	"	May 1865

Hart Island, N.Y., prison camp:

Roll	Volume	Description	Date
79	265–268	Registers and miscellaneous records relating to prisoners	1864–65

Hilton Head, S.C., prison camp:

Roll	Volume	Description	Date
	269	Receipts for letters containing money addressed to prisoners	Nov. 1864–Apr. 1865

Johnson's Island, Ohio, military prison:

Roll	Volume	Description	Date
80	270–271	Letters sent relating to prisoners and general register of prisoners	1862–64
81	272–273	Register of prisoners	1862–65
82	274–276	Registers of prisoners confined, transferred, released, and deceased	1862–65
83	277–280	Miscellaneous records relating to prisoners	1865

Knoxville, Tenn., military prison:

Roll	Volume	Description	Date
84	281–283	Registers of prisoners	1863–65

Fort Lafayette, N.Y., military prison:

Roll	Volume	Description	Date
85	284–286	General register of prisoners and accounts of money and effects of prisoners	1861–65
86	287–288	Accounts of money and effects of prisoners	1864

Little Rock, Ark., military prison:

Roll	Volume	Description	Date
87	289–291	Registers of prisoners	1863–65

Louisville, Ky., military prison:

Roll	Volume	Description	Date
88	292–293	General registers of prisoners	1862–64
89	294	"	Apr. 1863–Jan. 1864
90	295	"	Dec. 1863–Jan. 1865

Roll	Volume	Description	Date
91	296	"	Jan. 1864–Jan. 1865
92	297	General register of prisoners and rolls of Confederate deserters received	1863–65
93	298	Register of prisoners, compiled by the Office of the Commissary General of Prisoners	1863–64
94	299	"	1863–65
95	300–304	Register of prisoners, compiled by the Office of the Commissary General of Prisoners; registers of political prisoners; and hospital register	1863–65

Fort McHenry, Md., military prison:

Roll	Volume	Description	Date
96	305–310	Registers of prisoners and ledger of prisoners' accounts	1861–65

McLean Barracks, Cincinnati, Ohio:

Roll	Volume	Description	Date
97	311–317	Registers of prisoners and order books	1863–65

Memphis, Tenn., military prison:

Roll	Volume	Description	Date
98	318–321	Registers and descriptive list of prisoners	1863–65

Department of the Missouri:

Roll	Volume	Description	Date
	322	Register of prisoners	Mar.–Apr. 1862

Camp Morton, Ind., military prison:

Roll	Volume	Description	Date
99	323–324	Letters sent	Dec. 1863–Sept. 1865
100	325	General register of prisoners	July 1863–July 1865
101	326–327	Registers of prisoners, compiled by the Office of the Commissary General of Prisoners	1863–65
102	328–331	Lists of prisoners, register of deaths, and morning reports of prisoners	1862–65
103	332–334	Ledgers of prisoners' accounts and cash books	1864–65

New Orleans, La.:

Roll	Volume	Description	Date
104	335	Letters sent	Aug.–Dec. 1864
105	336–337	"	Dec. 1864–July 1865
106	338–343	Registers of prisoners and hospital register	1863–65

Newport News, Va., military prison:

Roll	Volume	Description	Date
107	344–345	Register of prisoners and ledger of prisoners' accounts	1865
108	346–347	Ledger of prisoners' accounts and petty cash account book	May–July 1865

Department of the Ohio:

Roll	Volume	Description	Date
109	348	Register of prisoners in the custody of provost marshals	1864–65

Old Capitol Prison, Washington, D.C.:

Roll	Volume	Description	Date
110	349–351	Registers of prisoners, compiled by the Office of the Commissary General of Prisoners, and register of passes issued to visitors	1863–65

Point Lookout, Md., military prison:

Roll	Volume	Description	Date
111	352	Letters sent	Feb. 1864–Mar. 1865
112	353	"	Nov. 1864–Sept. 1865
113	354–355	General registers of prisoners	1863–65
114	356	"	1863–65
115	357	"	1863–65
116	358	Register of prisoners	1863–65
117	359	"	1863–65
118	360	"	1865
119	361–362	"	1863–65
120	363	Register of prisoners transferred from Point Lookout	Sept. 1863–May 1865
121	364–365	Registers of prisoners transferred from Hammond General Hospital and of dispositions of prisoners	1863–65
122	366	Register of dispositions of prisoners	1863–65
123	367–368	"	1863–65
124	369–373	Registers of prisoners exchanged, paroled, and released, and of prisoners taking oaths of allegiance and list of prisoners released for employment on public works	1864–65
125	374–375	Register and lists of prisoners enlisting in the United States Service and of valuables and money belonging to prisoners and list of prisoners transferred to Hammond General Hospital	1863–65
126	376–378	Lists of money and property of prisoners	1864–65
127	379–385	Registers of letters and packages received for and delivered to prisoners and of prisoners' money	1863–65
128	386	Ledger of prisoners' accounts and name index	Mar. 1864–June 1865

Roll	Volume	Description	Date
129	387–390	List of letters received containing money and registers of clothing issued to prison divisions	1864–65

Richmond, Va.:

130	391–392	Register of oaths of allegiance and lists relating to paroled prisoners	1865

Rock Island Barracks, Ill., military prison:

131	393–394	Registers of prisoners	1862–65
132	395–397	Register of deaths and miscellaneous records	1863–65
133	398–399	Ledger of prisoners' accounts and name index	1863–65
134	400–402	Ledger of prisoners' accounts, name index, and journal of accounts with prisoners	1863–65
135	403–405	Journals of accounts with prisoners and blotter book	1864–65

Ship Island, Miss.:

136	406–408	Register of prisoners and miscellaneous records	1864–65

Fort Warren, Mass., military prison:

137	409–413	Letters sent and registers of prisoners	1861–66
138	414–415	List of prisoners received and ledgers of prisoners' accounts	1861–64
139	416–417	Cash books	1863–65

Division of West Mississippi:

140	418–419	Registers of paroled prisoners	1865
141	420	"	1865
142	421–422	"	1865

District of West Tennessee, provost marshal's office:

143	423	Register of paroled prisoners	1865

Other prisons:

144	424	Register of prisoners at Fort Delaware, Del., Fort Lafayette, N.Y., and Fort McHenry, Md.	1863–64
145	425–427	Registers of prisoners at various military prisons	1861–65

Register of Confederate Soldiers, Sailors, and Citizens Who Died in Federal Prisons and Military Hospitals in the North, 1861–1865. M918. 1 roll. DP.

This microfilm publication reproduces a 665-page register of Confederate soldiers, sailors, and citizens who died in Federal prisons and military hospitals in the North, 1861–65. The register was compiled in 1912 in the Office of the Commissioner for Marking the Graves of Confederate Dead.

The burial lists are generally arranged alphabetically by name of prison camp or other location where the deaths occurred. The table of contents at the beginning of the volume is similarly arranged, although a few cemetery names are also listed; appropriate page numbers are cited in each instance.

Entries on the individual burial lists are arranged alphabetically by name of deceased and generally give the name, rank, company, regiment, date of death, and number and location of grave for each individual interred.

Records of the Virginia Forces, 1861. M998. 7 rolls. DP.

This microfilm publication reproduces records of the armies designated as the "Virginia Forces," which were mobilized by the State of Virginia at the outset of the Civil War. Records of both the Richmond Command Headquarters and the subordinate Division of State Forces In and Around Richmond are included. The records consist of 14 volumes and some unbound documents. The volumes include letters and endorsements sent, registers of letters and telegrams received, general and special orders, and morning reports of troops around Richmond. The unbound documents consist primarily of letters and telegrams received.

The bound volumes were classified, according to a crude approximation of provenance, into groups called "chapters," and the volumes numbered serially within each chapter. These numbers are in parentheses in the rolls.

The descriptive pamphlet includes a select list of field commanders and their command locations.

Roll	Description	Dates
	Records of Command Headquarters:	
1	Letters sent (VIII, 234)	Apr. 24–Nov. 4, 1861
	Endorsements sent (VIII, 236)	May 8–Dec. 3, 1861
	Registers of letters and telegrams received:	
	Name index to register 1	Apr. 13–Nov. 14 and
	Volume 1 (VIII, 233)	Apr. 18–July 16, 1861
	Name index to register 2	July 16–Nov. 30, 1861
	Volume 2 (VIII, 233)	
	Registered letters and telegrams received:	
2	1–83	Apr. 13–Nov. 14, 1861
	84–550	Apr. 18–May 13, 1861
3	551–1,100	May 13–29, 1861
4	1,101–1,650	May 29–June 26, 1861
5	1,651–2,090	June 26–July 16, 1861
6	2,091–2,650	July 16–Oct. 2, 1861
7	2,651–2,835	Oct. 2–Nov. 30, 1861
	Unregistered letters received	Apr. 29–Sept. 2, 1861
	General orders (VIII, 237)	Apr. 23–Nov. 5, 1861

Roll	Description	Dates
7 (cont.)	Special orders (VIII, 240)	Apr. 26–Oct. 28, 1861

Registers of appointments:

	Description	Dates
	Volume 1 (I, 125)	Apr.–July 1861
	Volume 2 (I, 126)	Apr.–Nov. 1861
	Unbound lists of appointments	Apr.–Sept. 1861
	Miscellaneous records	Apr.–Sept. 1861

Records of the Division of State Forces in and around Richmond:

	Description	Dates
	Letters sent (VIII, 235)	May 1–31, June 17–July 27, and Sept. 12–Oct. 9, 1861
	Orders and special orders (VIII, 239)	Apr. 27–Oct. 18, 1861
	Letters and orders received (VIII, 238)	Apr. 26–Nov. 5, 1861
	Consolidated morning reports (VIII, 241)	May 1–Nov. 5, 1861

Confederate States Army Casualties: Lists and Narrative Reports, 1861–1865. M836. 7 rolls. DP.

This microfilm publication reproduces part of the unbound lists and narrative reports of casualties submitted to the Confederate War Department by units of the Confederate States Army, 1861–65.

The records are generally nominal lists of casualties that were not published in the *Official Records* as a matter of policy, statistical lists from which abstracts were compiled and published, and narrative reports that were not published for such reasons as the relative unimportance of the reporting unit.

The lists and reports reproduced in this publication contain some errors. For example, the spelling of the name of an individual on a list or report does not always agree with the spelling on muster rolls and payrolls. This kind of error may have occured when lists were prepared without access to the rolls or other reliable headquarters personnel records.

Roll	Description
1	

Alabama:

Fort Morgan, Aug. 5, 1864
　Various organizations

Arkansas:

Boston Mountains, Nov. 28, 1862
　MacDonald's Missouri Cavalry
Brownsville, Aug. 24–Sept. 6, 1863
　Marmaduke's Brigade
　Shelby's Brigade
Elkhorn Tavern, Mar. 6–8, 1862
　3d (Greer's) Texas Cavalry
　2d Brigade, Missouri Volunteer Corps
　3d Brigade, Missouri State Guard
　4th Regiment, 3d Division, Missouri State Guard
　3d, 6th, and 8th Divisions, Missouri State Guard
Helena, July 4, 1863
　Marmaduke's Division

Roll	Description

　Parsons' Brigade, Missouri State Guard
　3d Brigade, Price's Division, Arkansas Infantry
Jenkins' Ferry, Apr. 30, 1864
　1st Brigade, Parsons' Division, Army of Arkansas
　2d Brigade, Missouri Infantry, Army of Arkansas
Little Rock, Aug. 25–Sept. 14, 1863
　Newton's Cavalry Brigade
　Shelby's Brigade
Marks' Mill, Apr. 25, 1864
　4th (Gordon's) Arkansas Cavalry
　Shelby's Brigade
Prairie Grove, Dec. 7, 1862
　West's Arkansas Battery
　1st (Crump's) Texas Partisan Cavalry
　MacDonald's Cavalry Brigade, 4th Division, Trans-Mississippi Army
West Point, Aug. 14, 1863
　Shelby's Brigade

Florida:

Olustee (Ocean Pond), Feb. 20, 1864
　Dyke's Florida Light Artillery
　1st (Colquitt's) Brigade
　2d (Harrison's) Brigade
Santa Rosa Island, Oct. 9, 1861
　Consolidated list

Georgia:

Allatoona, Oct. 1864
　Sears' Brigade
Atlanta Campaign, May–Sept. 1864
　12th (Armistead's) Mississippi Cavalry
　2d, 4th, 5th, and 9th Kentucky Mounted Infantry (Dalton and vicinity)
　9th Kentucky Mounted Infantry (Jonesboro)
　50th Alabama Infantry
　1st Louisiana (Strawbridge's) Infantry
　1st Missouri (Cockrell's) Brigade
　Cantey's Brigade
　Featherston's Brigade
　Lewis' Brigade
　Manigault's Brigade
　Pillow's Brigade
　Scott's Brigade
　Walthall's Brigade
Chickamauga, Sept. 19–20, 1863
　Calvert's Arkansas Battery
　Eufaula Light Artillery
　Darden's Co., Mississippi Light Artillery (Jefferson Artillery)
　58th Alabama Infantry
　19th and 24th Arkansas Infantry
　4th Georgia Battalion (Caswell's Sharpshooters)
　37th and 47th Georgia Infantry
　9th Kentucky Infantry
　8th Tennessee Infantry
　15th and 37th (Tyler's) Tennessee Infantry
　20th Tennessee Infantry
　Brown's Brigade
　Clayton's Brigade
　Stewart's Division
　Casualties in the Left Wing (Longstreet's)
Dalton, Feb. 1864
　Hotchkiss Artillery Battalion
　Company B, Hawkins' Battalion of Sharpshooters
　Pettus' Brigade
　Reynolds' Brigade

Roll	Description
1 (cont.)	Fort McAllister, Feb. 1, 1863
	Consolidated report
	Whitemarsh Island, Apr. 16, 1862
	13th Georgia Infantry
	Miscellaneous, Oct. 1863
	Report of the Chief Surgeon, Stewart's
	Division

Kentucky:

Logan's (Webb's) Cross-Roads, Jan. 19–20, 1862
  29th Tennessee Infantry
Middle Creek, Jan. 10, 1862
  1st Kentucky Mounted Rifles
  5th Kentucky Infantry
  29th Virginia Infantry
Munfordville, Sept. 14, 1862
  Alabama State (Garrity's) Artillery
  7th and 9th Mississippi Infantry
  9th Battalion, Mississippi Sharpshooters
  10th and 29th Mississippi Infantry
  2d Brigade, Reserve Division, Right Wing,
    Army of Mississippi
Perryville, Oct. 8, 1862
  17th and 44th Tennessee Infantry
  1st Division, Right Wing, Army of Mississippi
Richmond, Aug. 30, 1862
  1st and 2d Brigades, 4th Division, Army of
    Kentucky
Camp Wild Cat, Oct. 21, 1861
  17th Tennessee Infantry

2

Louisiana:

Baton Rouge, Aug. 5, 1862
  4th Alabama Battalion
  35th Alabama Infantry and 3d, 6th, and 7th
    Kentucky Infantry
  5th Kentucky Infantry
  4th Louisiana Infantry, Boyd's Louisiana
    Battalion, and the Confederate (Semmes')
    Light Battery
  30th Louisiana Infantry
  1st Division
  List of wounded in the hands of the enemy
Bayou Fourche, Sept. 10, 1863
  Marmaduke's Brigade
Bayou Teche, Apr. 12–13, 1863
  Confederate States (Barnes') Light Battery
Calcasieu Pass, May 6–10, 1864
  Command of Col. Wm. H. Griffin
Fort De Russy, May 4, 1863
  Consolidated report
Donaldsonville, June 28, 1863
  1st and 2d Texas Cavalry Brigades
Forts Jackson and St. Philip, Apr. 18–28, 1862
  Consolidated report
Milliken's Bend, June 7, 1863
  McCulloch's Brigade
Pleasant Hill, Apr. 9, 1864
  11th Missouri Infantry
Port Hudson
  Picket Engagements, Mar. 1863
  Report of Maj. Gen. Franklin Gardner, May
    and June 1863

Maryland:

Antietam (Sharpsburg), Sept. 16–17, 1862
  Rockbridge Artillery (Poague's Co.)
  13th South Carolina Infantry
  23d (Durham's) South Carolina Infantry
  27th Virginia Infantry
  Hampton Legion

Roll	Description
	South Mountain (Boonsborough), Sept. 14, 1862
	23d (Durham's) South Carolina Infantry
	Williamsport, July 6, 1863
	54th North Carolina Infantry
	58th Virginia Infantry
	Early's Division

Mississippi:

Baker's Creek, May 16, 1863
  Featherston's Brigade
  Tilghman's Brigade
Blackland, June 7, 1862
  Report of Col. John F. Lay, Confederate
    States Cavalry
Coffeeville, Dec. 5, 1862
  9th Arkansas Infantry, 8th Kentucky Infantry,
    and 14th, 23d, and 26th Mississippi Infantry
Corinth (includes Hatchie Bridge, Tenn.), Oct.
  3–5, 1862
  Louisiana Washington Artillery Battalion
    (Pritchard's Co.)
  McNally's Battery
  1st Battalion, Arkansas Cavalry (Stirman's
    Sharpshooters)
  3d Arkansas Cavalry
  6th and 9th Texas Cavalry
  42d Alabama Infantry
  35th Mississippi Infantry
  2d Texas Infantry
  1st, 3d, and 4th Brigades, 1st Division, Army
    of the West
  Boone's Arkansas Regiment
  Lyles' Arkansas Regiment
  Cabell's Brigade
  Phifer's Brigade
Farmington, May 9, 1862
  11th, 16th, and 18th Louisiana Infantry
  36th Mississippi Infantry
  Anderson's Brigade
  Fagan's Brigade
  Consolidated Report, Army of the West
Franklin, Jan. 2, 1865
  Griffin's Brigade of Cavalry
Grand Gulf, Mar. 31, 1863
  Bowen's Command
Harrisburg, July 14–15, 1864
  2d Division, Forrest's Cavalry
Iuka, Sept. 19, 1862
  14th Arkansas Infantry
  17th (Griffith's) Arkansas Infantry
  Hebert's Brigade
Jackson, May 14, 1863
  46th Georgia Infantry
  14th Mississippi Infantry
  24th South Carolina Infantry
  Breckinridge's Division
Meridian Expedition, Feb. 3–Mar. 6, 1864
  Forrest's Cavalry
  Company of Scouts
Raymond, May 12, 1863
  1st (Colm's) Battalion, Tennessee Infantry
  3d (Walker's) Tennessee Infantry
  10th, 30th, and 50th Tennessee Infantry
  7th Texas Infantry
Tishomingo Creek, June 10, 1864
  Forrest's Cavalry Command
Vicksburg, May 18–July 27, 1862
  31st Alabama Infantry
Vicksburg, Dec. 20, 1862–Jan. 3, 1863
  1st Brigade, 1st Division, E. K. Smith's Army

Roll	Description

2 (cont.)
S. D. Lee's Command
Stevens' Command
Vicksburg, Jan. 20–July 4, 1863
   23d Louisiana Artillery (22d Louisiana
      Infantry)
   46th Alabama Infantry
   Hebert's Brigade
   Moore's Brigade
   Shoup's Brigade
   Vaughn's Brigade
More Than One Location in Mississippi, May
   and June 1863
   46th Alabama Infantry

3

Missouri:
Cape Girardeau, Apr. 26, 1863
   Jeffer's Missouri Cavalry
Carthage, July 5, 1861
   Consolidated report
Hartville, Jan. 11, 1863
   MacDonald's Missouri Cavalry
   Shelby's Cavalry Brigade
Lexington, Sept. 13–20, 1861
   1st Infantry, 4th Division, Missouri State
      Guard
   1st Battalion, Platte County, Missouri State
      Guard
   2d, 4th, and 6th Divisions, Missouri State
      Guard
Missouri (Marmaduke's) Expedition, Dec. 31,
   1862–Jan. 25, 1863
   MacDonald's Regiment, Missouri Cavalry
Missouri (Price's) Expedition, Aug. 29–Dec. 2,
   1864
   Shelby's Brigade
Newtonia, Sept. 30, 1862
   Howell's Artillery Co.
   1st Regiment, Texas Partisan Cavalry (22d
      Texas Cavalry)
   Alexander's Regiment, Hawpe's Regiment, and
      Stevens' Regiment, Texas Cavalry
   1st Choctaw Regiment
   1st Choctaw and Chickasaw Regiment
   Bryan's Battalion of Cherokees
   Cooper's Division
   Hawpe's Regiment
   Shelby's Brigade
Wilson's Creek, Aug. 10, 1861
   1st State Cavalry (Arkansas)
   2d Arkansas Cavalry
   2d Arkansas Mounted Rifles
   1st Battalion Cavalry, 3d Division, Missouri
      State Guard
   1st Regiment Cavalry, 4th Division, Missouri
      State Guard
   3d (Gratiot's) Arkansas Infantry
   5th Arkansas State Infantry
   3d (Hebert's) Louisiana Infantry
   1st Regiment, 3d Division, Missouri State
      Guard
   2d Brigade, 2d Division, Missouri State Guard
   3d, 4th, 6th, and 8th Divisions, Missouri State
      Guard
   South Kansas and Texas Regiment
   McBride's Command

New Mexico:
Scouting Report, Sept. 1861
   Report of Capt. Bethel Coopwood

North Carolina:

Roll	Description

Fort Fisher, Dec. 7–27, 1864
   Consolidated report
Goldsborough Bridge, Dec. 17, 1862
   Stark's Artillery (2d Regiment, North Carolina
      Artillery, Battery B); 10th North Carolina
      Infantry and Company F; 40th North
      Carolina Infantry
Kinston, Dec. 14, 1862
   Mallett's North Carolina Battalion
New Berne, Mar. 14, 1862
   37th North Carolina Infantry
White Hall, Dec. 16, 1862
   Robertson's Brigade

Pennsylvania:
Gettysburg, July 1–3, 1863
   Fraser's (Georgia) Battery, Light Artillery
      (Pulaski Artillery)
   Green's Co., Louisiana Guard Battery, North
      Carolina Artillery
   5th, 6th, 21st (Kirkland's), 54th, and 57th
      North Carolina Infantry
   33d Virginia Infantry
   Archer's Brigade
   Early's Division
   Gordon's Brigade
   Hays' Brigade
   Longstreet's Corps
   Smith's Brigade
   Stonewall Brigade
   Lists of officers under fire, killed, wounded,
      and missing:
      Daniel's Brigade
      Doles' Brigade
      Iverson's Brigade
      Ramseur's Brigade
      Rodes' Brigade

South Carolina:
Fort Beauregard, Nov. 7, 1861
   Beaufort Volunteer South Carolina Artillery
Campaign of the Carolinas, Jan. 1–Apr. 26, 1865
   4th Kentucky Mounted Infantry
James and John's Islands, May 29, 1862–July 10,
   1864
   1st Battalion, South Carolina Cavalry, and
      Rutledge Mounted Riflemen at Pocotaligo
      and James Island, May 29, 1862
   1st South Carolina Cavalry, June 8–9, 1862
   25th South Carolina Infantry (Eutaw
      Regiment), June 16, 1862
   Colquitt's Brigade, July 16, 1863
   1st Georgia Infantry, Aug. 12–19, 1863
   Battery Cheves and Fort Johnson
      Engagements, Sept. 15, 1863
   Report of the following units, July 1–10, 1864:
      Inglis Light Artillery
      Louisiana Washington Light Artillery
      Marion Light Artillery
      4th Georgia Cavalry
      1st Georgia Infantry (Regulars)
      32d and 47th Georgia Infantry, Bonard's
       Battalion
   Tabular statement of casualties (includes
      Sullivan's Island), Sept. 1863
Legare's Point, June 3, 1862
   Charleston (Gaillard's) Battalion, South
      Carolina Infantry (Beauregard Light
      Infantry), Pee Dee Rifles, and Evans Guard
Legareville (Legare's Point), Dec. 12, 1863
   Report of engagement with federal gunboats
      (Charles', Smith's, and Webb's Batteries)

Roll	Description
3 (cont.)	Morris Island, July–Sept. 1863
	3d South Carolina Artillery (Company D, 1st South Carolina Infantry, Regulars)
	15th (Lucas') Battalion, South Carolina Heavy Artillery
	Artillery and Infantry Commands July 1863
	Various Organizations at Battery Wagner July 18–Sept. 6, 1863
	Pocotaligo, Oct. 22, 1862
	Beaufort Volunteer South Carolina Artillery
	Lamkins' and Nelson's Companies, Virginia Light Artillery
	1st Battalion, South Carolina Cavalry
	Rutledge's Co., Cavalry Militia (Charleston Light Dragoons)
	Company B, 1st Battalion, South Carolina Sharp Shooters
	7th South Carolina Infantry Battalion
	Company I, 11th South Carolina Infantry (9th Volunteers)
	Walker's Brigade
	Port Royal Ferry, Jan. 1, 1862
	12th and 14th South Carolina Infantry
	Secessionville, June 16, 1862
	4th Louisiana Battalion
	1st (Lamar's) South Carolina Artillery (2d South Carolina Artillery)
	1st South Carolina (Charleston) Battalion, Infantry
	24th South Carolina Infantry
	25th South Carolina Infantry (Eutaw Regiment)
	South Carolina Battalion, Infantry (Pee Dee Legion)
	Engagement at Secessionville
	Sullivan's Island, Sept. 8, 1863
	3d South Carolina Artillery (1st South Carolina Infantry, Regulars)
	Fort Sumter, Aug. 1863–Sept. 16, 1864
	Reports of bombardments
	Battery Wagner, Apr. 7, 1863
	Accidental explosion of ammunition chest
	Fort Walker, Nov. 7, 1861
	Companies F and H, 9th South Carolina Infantry
	15th South Carolina Infantry
4	
	Tennessee:
	Beech Grove, June 26, 1863
	Johnson's Brigade
	Brentwood, Mar. 25, 1863
	1st Division, 1st (Forrest's) Cavalry Corps
	Chattanooga, Aug. 27, 1863
	8th Mississippi Infantry
	Chattanooga, Dec. 26, 1863
	Engagement at Chattanooga and Ringgold Gap, Ga.
	Franklin, Nov. 30, 1864
	29th Alabama Infantry
	French's Division
	Loring's Division
	Sears' Brigade (list of officers and men who reached the main line of the enemy's works)
	Sears' Brigade (list of officers killed, wounded, and missing)
	Consolidated list of casualties
	Hartsville, Dec. 7, 1862
	Morgan's Command
	Forts Henry and Donelson, Feb. 3–16, 1862

Roll	Description
	14th and 20th, Mississippi Infantry
	26th and 41st Tennessee Infantry
	Wharton's Cavalry
	List of officers and enlisted men surrendered at Fort Henry, Feb. 6, 1862
	Hoover's Gap, June 24–26, 1863
	Bates' Brigade
	Knoxville, June 20, 1863
	Consolidated report
	Knoxville, Nov. and Dec. 1863
	Report of siege
	Lewisburg Pike, Apr. 4, 1863
	1st Division, 1st (Forrest's) Cavalry Corps
	Liberty Gap, June 24–27, 1863
	Liddell's Brigade
	Lookout Mountain, Nov. 24, 1863
	42d Alabama Infantry
	16th, 32d, and 45th Tennessee Infantry
	Jenkins' Brigade
	Moore's Brigade
	Pettus' Brigade
	Walthall's Brigade
	Expedition into Morgan and Scott Counties (Montgomery), Mar. 28, 1862
	1st Tennessee Cavalry and 3d Tennessee Infantry (Provisional Army)
	Nashville, Dec. 15–16, 1864
	29th Alabama Infantry
	Shiloh, Apr. 6–7, 1862
	Bains' Co., Vaiden Alabama Artillery
	1st Battalion, Alabama Cavalry
	1st Mississippi Cavalry
	Holloway's Co., Alabama Cavalry (General Bragg's Bodyguard)
	The Mississippi and Alabama Battalion of Cavalry
	22d Alabama Infantry
	5th Kentucky Infantry (list of men who returned from battle without their arms)
	4th and 13th Tennessee Infantry
	2d Confederate Regiment
	Consolidated list of Tennessee regiments: 2d, 4th (Provisional Army), and 23d, 24th, 27th, 44th, and 55th Infantry
	I, II, and III Corps, Army of Mississippi
	Consolidated report: I, II, III, and Reserve Corps, Army of Mississippi
	Reserve Corps
	Consolidated report
	Stone's River (Murfreesboro), Dec. 31, 1862–Jan. 3, 1863
	Barret's Missouri Artillery
	Eufaula Light Artillery
	Semple's Battery, Alabama Light Artillery
	5th Georgia Cavalry
	41st Alabama Infantry
	2d Battalion, Georgia Sharpshooters
	8th and 36th Mississippi Infantry
	Hawkins' Battalion, Mississippi Sharpshooters
	11th Tennessee Infantry
	1st–4th Brigades, 1st Division, Polk's Corps, Army of Tennessee
	Adams' Brigade
	Chalmers' Brigade
	Cleburne's Brigade
	Deas' Brigade
	Jackson's Brigade
	McCown's Division
	Pillow's Brigade
	Preston's Brigade

Roll	Description
4 (cont.)	Walthall's Brigade
	Thompson's Station, Mar. 5, 1863
	1st (Van Dorn's) Cavalry Corps
	Forrest's Campaign of 1864
	Consolidated list, Forrest's Cavalry Command (incomplete)

Texas:

Engagement with Federal Screw Propeller *Montgomery,* Apr. 4, 1862
   13th (Bates') Texas Infantry
Las Rucias, June 25, 1864
   Consolidated list
Nueces River, Aug. 10, 1862
   Consolidated list
Operations against Indians from Fort Inge, Oct. 17, 1861
   Report of W. Barrett, Sergeant, Confederate States Cavalry

5

Virginia:

Aldie, June 17, 1863
   3d Virginia Cavalry
Bailey's Cross-Roads (Upton's Hill), Aug. 27, 1861
   Consolidated report
Ball's Bluff (includes vicinity of Leesburg), Oct. 21–22, 1861
   13th, 17th, and 18th Mississippi Infantry
   8th Virginia Infantry
   Consolidated report
Beverly Ford, Aug. 23, 1862
   Louisiana Washington Artillery Battalion (3d Co.)
Beverly Ford, June 9, 1863
   Stewart's Command
Blackburn's Ford, July 18, 1861
   Louisiana Washington Artillery Battalion
   Consolidated list
Blackwater River, Dec. 8–12, 1862
   Report of skirmish
Brandy Station, June 9, 1863
   12th Virginia Cavalry
   35th Virginia Cavalry Battalion
   Lee's Cavalry Brigade
   Hampton's Brigade
Bristoe Campaign, Oct. 9–22, 1863
   Gordon's Cavalry Brigade
   Lee's Cavalry Brigade
   5th, 12th, 20th, and 23d North Carolina Infantry
   Anderson's Division
   Walker's Brigade
   III Corps
Bull Run (Manassas), July 21, 1861
   Louisiana Washington Artillery Battalion
   30th Virginia Cavalry (2d Virginia Cavalry)
   Terry's Cavalry Corps
   17th and 18th Mississippi Infantry
   8th South Carolina Infantry
   8th, 17th, and 49th Virginia Infantry
   Stonewall Brigade
   I and II Corps (list of officers killed, wounded, and missing)
Bull Run (Manassas), Aug. 30, 1862
   1st Maryland Battery
   Lee's Battalion, Virginia Light Artillery
   Louisiana Washington Artillery Battalion
   Staunton Virginia Artillery
   Stuart Horse Artillery Battalion

Roll	Description

13th, 26th, 31st, 38th, 60th, and 61st Georgia Infantry
1st South Carolina Rifles
13th South Carolina Infantry
4th Texas Infantry
2d, 7th, 13th, 24th, 25th, 31st, 33d, 44th, 49th, and 52d Virginia Infantry
Early's Brigade
Hays' Brigade
Jackson Division
Jenkins' Brigade
Trimble's Brigade
Winder's Brigade
Cedar Creek, Oct. 19, 1864
   23d North Carolina Infantry
Cedar Mountain (Ripley's Station), Aug. 9, 1862
   27th Virginia Infantry
Cedar Run, Aug. 9, 1862
   2d and 4th Virginia Infantry
   Jackson's Division, Army of the Valley
   Trimble's Brigade
Chancellorsville, May 1–3, 1863
   3d, 5th, 6th, 12th, and 26th Alabama Infantry
   4th, 6th, 19th, 21st, 27th, 28th, and 44th Georgia Infantry
   5th, 12th, 20th, and 23d North Carolina Infantry
   1st Tennessee Infantry (Provisional Army)
   10th Virginia Infantry
   Perry's Brigade (includes Spotsylvania and Fredericksburg)
   Posey's Brigade (includes Spotsylvania)
   Thomas' Division
   Wright's Brigade
   Lists of officers under fire, killed, wounded, and missing:
      Doles' Brigade
      Hill's Division
      Iverson's Brigade
      Ramseur's Brigade
Cross Keys, June 8, 1862
   List of officers killed and wounded
Drewry's Bluff, May 12–16, 1864
   Lightfoot's Battalion of Light Artillery
Fair Oaks (Seven Pines), May 31–June 1, 1862
   53d Virginia Infantry
Fredericksburg, Dec. 11–15, 1862
   Alexander's Battalion of Artillery
   Alleghany Rough Artillery (Carpenter's Co.)
   Louisiana Washington Artillery Battalion (1st Co.)
   8th Florida Infantry
   13th, 26th, 31st, 38th, 60th, and 61st Georgia Infantry
   1st Louisiana Brigade
   2d, 4th, and 5th Virginia Infantry
   Anderson's Division
   Early's Brigade
   Hood's Division
   Lawton's Brigade
   McLaws' Division
   Pickett's Division
   Ransom's Division
   Trimble's Brigade

| **6** | Fredericksburg, May 3–4, 1863 |

   Company A, Garnett's Battalion, Light Artillery
   Andrews' Battalion of Artillery
   Louisiana Washington Artillery Battalion (1st Co.)
   10th Alabama Infantry

Roll	Description
6 (cont.)	1st Battalion, North Carolina Sharpshooters

1st Battalion, North Carolina Sharpshooters
6th, 21st, 54th, and 57th North Carolina
Infantry
Early's Division
Gordon's Brigade
Hays' Brigade
Smith's Brigade
Giles Courthouse, May 10, 1862
1st Brigade, Army of New River
James River, Aug. 5, 1863
French's Co., Virginia Light Artillery
Report of engagement with Federal
gunboats
James River, May 1864
Louisiana Washington Artillery Battalion (3d
Co.)
Louisiana Washington Artillery Battalion (4th
Co.)
Jonesville, Jan. 3, 1864
64th Virginia Mounted Infantry (64th Virginia
Cavalry)
Kelly's Ford, Mar. 17, 1863
Lee's Cavalry Brigade
Kelly's Store, Jan. 30, 1863
Pryor's Brigade
King's School-House, June 25, 1862
53d Virginia Infantry
Wright's Brigade
Manassas Gap, July 23, 1863
Wright's Brigade
McDowell, May 8, 1862
52d Virginia Infantry
3d Brigade, Army of the Valley
Consolidated report
Medical Director's report
Mine Run (includes Payne's Farm and Locust
Grove), Nov. 26–Dec. 2, 1863
3d Alabama Infantry
2d, 32d, and 43d North Carolina Infantry
21st, 25th, 42d, 44th, 48th, and 50th Virginia
Infantry
Daniel's Brigade
Ewell's Corps
Hays' Brigade
Hoke's Brigade
Pegram's Brigade
Stafford's Brigade
Stonewall Brigade
New Bridge, May 23–24, 1862
5th Louisiana Infantry
New Market, May 15, 1864
Report of cadets from Virginia Military
Institute
Orange Courthouse, Aug. 2, 1862
7th (Jones') Virginia Cavalry
Petersburg, May 5–16, 1864
Louisiana Washington Artillery Battalion (1st
Co.)
Petersburg, Nov. 5, 1864
Holcomb's Legion
Port Republic, June 8–9, 1862
Alleghany Rough Artillery (Carpenter's Co.)
Rockbridge Artillery (Poague's Co.)
2d, 4th, and 27th Virginia Infantry
Ewell's Division
Taylor's Brigade
Rappahannock Station, Aug. 23, 1862
Louisiana Washington Artillery Battalion
Salem Church, May 3, 1863
8th, 9th, 11th, and 14th Alabama Infantry

Seven Days' Campaign, June 25–July 1, 1862
Crenshaw's Virginia Battery
Graham's Co., Virginia Light Artillery
(Rockbridge Artillery)
Purcell Battery, Cayce's Co., Virginia Light
Artillery (Purcell Artillery)
Wooding's Battery, Price's Co., Virginia Light
Artillery (Danville Artillery)
Cavalry Brigade, Army of Northern Virginia
1st Georgia Infantry (Regulars)
2d, 7th, 8th, 9th, 11th, 15th, 16th, 17th, 18th,
20th, and 24th Georgia Infantry
Cobb's Georgia Legion
2d Louisiana Infantry
1st Maryland Infantry (Maryland Line)
3d, 15th, and 23d North Carolina Infantry
2d South Carolina Rifles (Infantry)
3d (Nance's) South Carolina Infantry
4th (Mattison's) South Carolina Battalion
5th, 6th, and 13th South Carolina Infantry
1st, 4th, and 5th Texas Infantry
2d and 4th Virginia Infantry
5th Battalion, Virginia Volunteers
5th, 9th, 10th, 14th, 23d, 27th, 33d, 37th, 38th,
53d, and 57th Virginia Infantry
3d Brigade, Huger's Division
3d Brigade, 4th Brigade, 5th Brigade, and 6th
Brigade, Longstreet's Division
Hampton Legion
Kemper's Brigade
Law's Brigade
Palmetto Sharpshooters
Texas Brigade
Lists of officers killed and wounded:
Elzey's Brigade
Seymour's Brigade (8th Brigade, Ewell's
Division)
Trimble's Brigade

| 7 | Shenandoah Valley, June 8–9, 1862 |

Shenandoah Valley, June 8–9, 1862
4th Virginia Infantry
Swift Creek, May 9, 1864
Johnson's Brigade
White Oak Swamp Bridge (Darbytown), June
30, 1862
Pickett's Brigade
Williamsburg, May 5, 1862
9th Alabama Infantry
2d Florida Infantry
2d Mississippi Battalion
19th Mississippi Infantry
23d North Carolina Infantry
24th and 38th Virginia Infantry
Jenkins' Brigade
Winchester, Mar. 23, 1862
Rockbridge Artillery Consolidated report
Rockbridge Artillery (Waters' Co.)
1st Virginia Battalion
2d, 4th, 5th, 21st, 23d, 37th, 27th, and 42d
Virginia Infantry
Winchester, May 25, 1862
Alleghany Rough Artillery (Carpenter's Co.)
Rockbridge Artillery (Poague's Co.)
2d, 5th, 10th, 23d, 27th, 33d, 37th, 42d, and
48th Virginia Infantry
Ewell's Division
Stonewall Brigade
Taylor's Brigade
Trimble's Brigade
Winchester, June 15, 1863
15th Louisiana Infantry
57th North Carolina Infantry

Roll	Description
7 (cont.)	Early's Division
	Gordon's Brigade
	Hays' Brigade
	Smith's Brigade
	Yorktown, Apr. 16, 1862
	15th North Carolina Infantry
	Miscellaneous, 1862–65
	Cobb's Legion, June 26–July 10, 1862
	Ewell's Division, Aug. 22–Sept. 20, 1862
	Brown's Battery, Chesapeake, Virginia, 1862
	Artillery, at Bristoe Station, Manassas, and Fredericksburg
	6th Virginia Cavalry, July 1863
	12th Virginia Cavalry, June 17–July 20, 1863
	Lee's Cavalry Brigade, Oct. 11–22, 1863
	Campaigns of 1864:
	4th and 44th Alabama Infantry
	7th, 8th, 9th, 11th, and 59th Georgia Infantry
	Benning's Brigade
	Bratton's Brigade
	Stevens' Command, Mar. 1, 1864
	Kilpatrick's Raid Against Richmond
	23d North Carolina Infantry at Winchester, Fisher's Hill, and near New Market, 1864
	48th Alabama Infantry, May–Oct. 1864
	15th Alabama Infantry, May 1864–Mar. 1865

West Virginia:

Camp Alleghany, Dec. 13, 1861
    Johnson's Command
Carrick's Ford, July 13, 1861
    23d Virginia Infantry
Droop Mountain, Nov. 6, 1863
    Jenkins' Cavalry Brigade
Greenbrier River, Oct. 3, 1861
    3d Arkansas Infantry
    Consolidated list
Greenland Gap, Apr. 25, 1863
    7th Virginia Cavalry
    Jones' Command
Harper's Ferry, Oct. 16, 1861
    Consolidated report
Kanawha Valley, Sept. 6–16, 1862
    Report of Medical Director, Department of Southwestern Virginia
White Sulphur Springs, Aug. 26–27, 1863
    Chapman's Virginia Light Artillery (Monroe Battery)
    22d Virginia Infantry
    23d Battalion, Virginia Volunteers
    26th (Edgar's) Virginia Battalion
    45th Virginia Infantry

More Than One State:

13th Mississippi Infantry, Oct. 1861
    Edwards Ferry, Va., and Kephart, Md.
17th South Carolina Infantry, Aug.–Sept. 1862
    Maryland and Virginia
22d South Carolina Infantry, Aug.–Sept. 1862
    Rappahannock Station, Va., South Mountain, Md., and near Sharpsburg, Md.
4th Brigade, Jackson's Division, Aug.–Sept. 1862
    Manassas, Va., and Sharpsburg, Md.
23d South Carolina Infantry, Aug.–Sept. 1862
    Manassas, Va., Boonsborough and Sharpsburg, Md.
Early's Division, June and July 1863
    Winchester, Va., and Gettysburg campaign, Pa.
Smith's Brigade, May–July, 1863

Roll	Description
	Gettysburg campaign, Pa.
	7th Virginia Cavalry, June 17–July 12, 1863
	From time it crossed the Rapidan until it recrossed the Potomac
	1st (Dobbins') Arkansas Cavalry, Aug. and Sept. 1863
	Bayou Meto, Ark., and Bayou Fourche, Ark.–La.
	1st Military District of South Carolina, Georgia, and Florida, July–Sept. 1863
	Consolidated report
	Chalmers' Raid Into Mississippi and Tennessee, Oct. 1863
	3d Mississippi State Cavalry
	2d Missouri Cavalry
	14th (West) Tennessee Cavalry
	Battle of Collierville, Tenn.
	Pleasant Hill, La., and Jenkins' Ferry, Ark., Apr. 1864
	10th and 16th Missouri Infantry
	Forrest's Raid Into Mississippi and Tennessee, Aug. 1864
	1st Brigade, 1st Division
	Taliaferro's Brigade
	From the time General Lee took command at Gordonsville until the Army left the Valley

Indian Territory:

Cabin Creek, Sept. 19, 1864
    Gano's Brigade
Chustenahlah, Dec. 26, 1861
    6th (Stone's) Texas Cavalry
Old Fort Wayne, Oct. 22, 1862
    Howell's Artillery Co.
    1st Cherokee Regiment
    2d Creek Regiment with elements of 1st Cherokee Regiment
Round Mountain and Chuhtotahlasah (Bird's Creek), Nov. 19, 1861
    Consolidated report

Records Relating to United States Military Academy Cadets and United States Naval Academy Midshipmen (Record Groups 94 and 405)

United States Military Academy Cadet Application Papers, 1805–1866. M688. 242 rolls. DP.

This microfilm publication reproduces application papers of cadets for appointment to the U.S. Military Academy, 1805–66. The unbound papers include letters from applicants requesting appointment, letters of recommendation, notifications from the War Department if the candidate was appointed, and letters of acceptance from the candidates.

Most of the application papers in this microfilm publication are arranged by year and thereunder numerically by file number. The file designation for an applicant consists of the year in which the application was received and the number assigned to the file. Letters of application that for one reason or another were not numbered have been filed by the National Archives as unnumbered letters at the end of the year of the application and thereunder alphabetically by the name of the candidate.

The National Archives has not located application papers for 1811. In 1810 and 1812 Secretary of War William Eustis assigned the officers and cadets to other duties and fewer cadets were enrolled at the academy.

Reproduced on the first roll of this microfilm publication is a name index to the letters of application. The index is arranged alphabetically by initial letter of the surname of the applicant, thereunder by initial vowel sound of the surname, and thereunder chronologically by the date of the application. The index shows the name of the applicant, the year of the application, the State from which the candidate applied, and the file number of the application papers. Entries for which correspondence has been found have been marked by the National Archives staff with an asterisk.

In some instances the name of the candidate has been spelled incorrectly in the index. The National Archives has not attempted to correct such errors. For a few entries, the file number for the correspondence has been omitted; where this has occurred the National Archives has added the number to the index in brackets.

Not all names of applicants were entered in the index by the War Department clerks. In those instances where names have been omitted, the National Archives has prepared supplemental index entries that are filmed in the appropriate places.

Roll	Description	Date
1	Name Index	
2	Application Papers	
	1–5	1805
	1–8	1806
	1–8	1807
	1–10	1808
	1–3	1809
	1–2	1810
	1	1812
	Unnumbered	1812
	Unnumbered	1813
3	1–108	1814
	Unnumbered	1814
4	1–89	1815
	Unnumbered	1815
5	1–96	1816
	Unnumbered	1816
6	1–108	1817
	Unnumbered	1817
7	1–59	1818
8	60–129	1818
9	130–198	1818
10	1–69	1819
11	70–129	1819
12	130–204	1819
	Unnumbered	1819
13	1–59	1820
14	60–129	1820
15	130–190	1820
16	191–254	1820
17	1–79	1821
18	80–145	1821
19	1–29	1822
20	30–59 ½	1822
21	60–99 ½	1822
22	100–157	1822

Roll	Description	Date
23	1–59	1823
24	60–112	1823
25	113–179	1823
26	180–249	1823
27	250–319	1823
28	1–69	1824
29	70–119	1824
30	120–149	1824
31	150–201	1824
32	202–256	1824
33	257–318	1824
34	319–364	1824
35	365–421	1824
36	1–44	1825
37	45–124	1825
38	125–189	1825
39	190–230	1825
40	231–286	1825
	Unnumbered	1825
41	1–58	1826
42	59–106	1826
43	107–157	1826
44	158–189	1826
45	190–225	1826
46	226–255	1826
	Unnumbered	1826
47	1–45	1827
48	46–96	1827
49	97–134½	1827
50	135–175	1827
51	176–213	1827
52	1–49	1828
53	50–94	1828
54	95–133	1828
55	134–176	1828
56	177–234	1828
57	1–30	1829
58	31–71	1829
59	72–112	1829
60	113–162	1829
61	163–197	1829
62	198–226	1829
63	227–245	1829
64	246–274	1829
65	275–293	1829
66	1–35	1830
67	36–67	1830
68	68–115	1830
69	116–151	1830
70	152–204	1830
71	205–226	1830
72	227–248	1830
73	249–269	1830
74	1–35	1831
75	36–79	1831
76	80–118	1831
77	119–153	1831
78	154–191	1831
79	192–210	1831
80	1–32	1832
81	33–66	1832
82	67–104	1832
83	105–149	1832
84	150–191	1832
85	192–234	1832

Roll	Description	Date		Roll	Description	Date
86	235–271	1832		147	122–169	1843
87	1–38	1833		148	170–222	1843
88	39–78	1833		149	223–288	1843
89	79–118	1833		150	289–331	1843
90	119–162	1833			Unnumbered	1843
91	163–211	1833		151	1–74	1844
92	1–38	1834		152	75–136	1844
93	39–77	1834		153	137–222	1844
94	78–132	1834		154	223–275	1844
95	133–170	1834		155	3–79	1845
96	171–209	1834		156	80–130	1845
97	210–252	1834		157	131–198	1845
	Unnumbered	1834		158	199–259	1845
98	1–44	1835		159	260–310	1845
99	45–101	1835		160	1–71	1846
100	102–149	1835		161	72–138	1846
101	150–196	1835		162	139–210	1846
	Unnumbered	1835		163	211–281	1846
102	1–57	1836		164	282–325	1846
103	58–106	1836		165	1–83	1847
104	107–159	1836		166	84–160	1847
105	160–208	1836		167	161–235	1847
106	209–250	1836		168	236–302	1847
	Unnumbered	1836		169	303–335	1847
107	1–44	1837		170	1–79	1848
108	45–94	1837		171	80–160	1848
109	95–143	1837		172	161–214	1848
110	144–183	1837		173	215–278	1848
111	184–225	1837		174	279–330	1848
112	226–275	1837		175	2–77	1849
113	276–315	1837		176	78–165	1849
114	1–56	1838		177	166–240	1849
115	57–101	1838		178	241–348	1849
116	102–157	1838		179	349–414	1849
117	158–207	1838		180	1–77	1850
118	208–245	1838		181	78–161	1850
119	246–262	1838		182	162–260	1850
120	1–65	1839		183	261–345	1850
121	66–115	1839		184	1–75	1851
122	116–170	1839		185	76–162	1851
123	171–203	1839		186	163–243	1851
124	1–48	1840		187	244–294	1851
125	49–105	1840			Unnumbered	1851
126	106–165	1840		188	1–78	1852
127	166–215	1840		189	79–153	1852
128	216–268	1840		190	154–230	1852
129	269–309	1840		191	231–329	1852
130	310–360	1840		192	1–88	1853
131	1–73	1841		193	89–226	1853
132	74–105	1841		194	227–329	1853
133	106–154	1841			Unnumbered	1853
134	155–212	1841		195	1–86	1854
135	213–261	1841		196	87–204	1854
136	262–318	1841		197	205–273	1854
137	319–361	1841		198	1–91	1855
	Unnumbered	1841		199	92–169	1855
138	1–61	1842		200	170–239	1855
139	62–133	1842		201	1–101	1856
140	134–201	1842		202	102–235	1856
141	202–262	1842		203	236–353	1856
142	263–302	1842		204	1–100	1857
143	303–348	1842		205	101–207	1857
144	349–384	1842		206	208–299	1857
145	1–58	1843		207	300–385	1857
146	59–121	1843		208	1–75	1858

Roll	Description	Date
209	76–150	1858
210	151–271	1858
211	272–351	1858
212	1–115	1859
213	116–224	1859
214	225–316	1859
215	1–92	1860
216	93–170	1860
217	1–135	1861
218	136–294	1861
219	295–381	1861
220	382–492	1861
221	493–641	1861
222	642–752	1861
223	753–851	1861
224	852–973	1861
225	1–114	1862
226	115–228	1862
227	229–345	1862
228	1–100	1863
229	101–200	1863
230	201–313	1863
231	314–400	1863
232	401–480	1863
233	1–101	1864
234	102–235	1864
235	236–339	1864
236	340–428	1864
237	1–139	1865
238	140–255	1865
239	256–360	1865
240	361–434	1865
241	1–120	1866
242	121–200	1866

United States Naval Academy Registers of Delinquencies, 1846–1850 and 1853–1882, and Academic and Conduct Records of Cadets, 1881–1908. M991. 45 rolls. DP.

This microfilm publication reproduces 55 bound volumes of registers of delinquencies, also referred to as "conduct rolls" or "conduct rolls of cadets," 1846–50 and 1853–82, and 36 bound volumes containing the academic and conduct records of cadets, 1881–1908. Various terms were assigned during the last period to these volumes of academic and conduct records, including "record and conduct roll," "cadet and conduct record," "record of naval cadets," and "conduct record."

Variations in the spelling of names of cadets and midshipmen are common among these records. Variants were checked against the *Navy Register*, and have been mentioned in the roll notes.

Registers of Delinquencies

The register covering 1846–50 is arranged by type of offense, thereunder by academic year, and thereunder by date of offense. The pages of the register are divided into various categories of offense or delinquency. The dates the offenses were committed, the names of the offenders, and occasional remarks describing details of the delinquencies and the punishments received are entered under each category. No registers for academic years 1851–53 have been located.

The registers covering October 1853–June 1855 and October 1867–May 1882 are arranged by academic year and thereunder alphabetically by initial letter of surname of midshipman or cadet. The registers for October 1855–May 1867 are arranged by academic year, thereunder generally by class, and thereunder alphabetically by initial letter of surname of midshipman or cadet. Beginning in academic year 1871–72, the conduct records of cadet-engineers were entered in the registers of delinquencies or conduct rolls following the records of cadet-midshipmen.

In all of the registers of delinquencies for October 1853–May 1882, the name of each midshipman or cadet appears at the top of the page on which his record begins, and in most registers after 1870 class ranks one through four are also entered. Under the cadet's name, the register pages are divided into columns in which are entered the date and description of each delinquency, the name of the reporting officer, the number of demerits received or the manner in which the delinquency was disposed of, and remarks indicating the plea of the midshipmen or cadet. After the adoption during academic year 1862–63 of a plan for removing demerits, the registers usually indicate the number removed each month. Resignations, revocations of appointments, detachments, dismissals, desertions, and deaths are noted in the registers, and some volumes include conduct reports on midshipmen or cadets on summer practice cruises.

An appropriate reference usually indicates the continuance of the conduct record of a midshipman or cadet on another page of the same volume or in a new volume. (Sometimes "liber" and "folio" are used rather than "volume" and "page.") When it was necessary to continue records in more than the two volumes begun in the opening month of the academic year, supplementary volumes were sometimes used. These supplementary volumes are described on the roll notes.

During 1859–68 most of the fourth-class midshipmen were quartered on board one of the three naval vessels assigned to the Academy as schoolships—the U.S.S. *Plymouth, Constitution,* and *Santee.* The registers of delinquencies that were kept on board these vessels are identified in the roll list by the name of the schoolship in parentheses.

Academic and Conduct Records of Cadets

The academic and conduct record of a cadet was begun at the time of his admission to the Academy and was continued in the same volume until the completion of his 4 years of study or until his withdrawal from the Academy. Exceptions to this are the academic and conduct records in volumes 1 and 2. Volume 1 contains the records for the first- and second-class years of cadets admitted in 1879, and volume 2 contains the records for the first-, second-, and third-class years of cadets admitted in 1880. The conduct records of second- and third-class cadets for academic year 1881–82 are duplicated in volumes 392–394 of the registers of delinquencies. After 1881, if a cadet was expelled and later readmitted to the Academy, or if he remained at the Academy but was turned back to a lower class, a new record was begun for him.

The academic and conduct records of cadets are, in general, arranged by date of admission (entrance examinations were usually held in the spring and fall) and thereunder alphabetically by initial letter of surname of cadet. In the earlier volumes, the academic and conduct records of cadet-engineers were entered after those of cadet-midshipmen. Other variations in arrangement are explained in the pertinent roll notes.

An entry for each cadet in the academic and conduct records contains his name, date of admission, the name of the appointing official, his place and date of birth, the city or town of the cadet's residence at the time of appointment, his previous education (public or private), his religious denomination, and the name, address, and occupation of his parent or guardian. In the earlier volumes the cadet signed the record to attest to the accuracy of this information, but this procedure was discontinued with the class admitted in 1889. The academic and conduct records contain the same kind of information about conduct found in the old registers of delinquencies, in addition to weekly and monthly course grades, examination grades, and annual and semiannual examination results.

Roll	Volumes	Academic Years
Registers of Delinquencies, 1846–50, 1853–82:		
1	346	1846–50
	347	1853–55
	348	1855–56
	349	1856–57
2	350	1857–58
	351	1858–59
	352 (*Plymouth*)	1859–60
	353	"
3	354	1860–61
	355 (*Constitution*)	"
	356 (*Santee*)	1861–62
	357 (*Santee* and *Constitution*)	1861–63
4	358	1862–63
	359 (*Santee*)	"
	360 (*Constitution*)	1863–64
	361 (*Santee*)	"
5	363	"
	362 (*Santee*)	1864–65
	364 (*Constitution*)	"
6	365	"
	366 (*Santee*)	1865–66
	367 (*Constitution*)	"
	368	"
7	369 (*Constitution*)	1866–67
	370	"
	371 (*Constitution*)	1867–68
8	372	"
	373 (*Constitution*)	1868–69
9	374	1869–70
	375	1870–71
10	376	1871–72
	377	1872–73
11	378	1873–74
12	379	1874–75
	380	"
	397	"
	399	"
13	381	1875–76
	382	"
	400	"
14	383	1876–77
	401	"
15	384	1877–78
	385	"
	402	"
16	386	1878–79
	387	"
17	388	1879–80
	389	"
18	390	1880–81

Roll	Volumes	Academic Years
	n.n.	"
	391	"
19	392	1881–82
	393	"
	394	"
Academic and conduct records of cadets, 1881–1908:		
20	1	1881–82
	2	1881–84
21	4 (Pts. 1–3)	1881–85
	3	1882–86
22	5 (Pts. 1–3)	1883–87
	6	"
23	7	1884–88
24	8	1885–89
25	9	1886–90
26	10	1887–91
27	11	1888–92
28	12	1889–93
29	13	1890–94
30	14	1891–95
31	15	1892–96
32	16	1893–97
33	17	1894–98
34	18	1895–99
35	19	1896–1900
36	20	1897–1901
37	21	1898–1902
38	22	1899–1903
39	23	1900–1904
40	24	1901–5
41	25	1902–6
42	26 (Pts. 1–3)	1903–7
43	27	"
	28	"
44	29	1904–8
45	30	1904–8

Selected Records Relating to Black Servicemen (Record Groups 94, 107, and 153)

The Negro in the Military Service of the United States, 1639–1886. M858. 5 rolls. DP.

This microfilm publication reproduces compiled records published by the Colored Troops Division of the Adjutant General's Office (AGO). This compilation, "The Negro in the Military Service of the United States: A Compilation of Official Records, State Papers, Historical Extracts, etc., Relating to his Military Status and Service, from the date of his introduction into the British North American Colonies," consists principally of documents copied from published and unpublished primary sources. In addition, there are a few original documents and extracts from secondary sources that cover periods of history for which primary sources were not readily available. The volumes are part of the Records of the Adjutant General's Office, 1780's–1917, Record Group 94.

The records in the compilation are arranged into chapters corresponding roughly to 9 periods, and thereunder into sections by subject. Those sections concerned with military employment and civil status are further divided between Confederate States and United States. The contents are discussed in more detail beginning on page 4 of the descriptive pamphlet. Within each section the documents are arranged chronologically. Some editing of the documents, varying in amount from volume to volume, was done, indicating that the work was being prepared for the press and that mistakes had been made by the copyists. On the last page of the compilation there is a heading "Statistical Tables" and a note stating that the tables were too bulky to be placed with the copies of the records to be bound. Despite extensive searches these statistical tables have not been located.

Roll	Description	Dates
1	Colonial Period	
	War of the Revolution	1774–83
	War of 1812	1812–15
	War of the Rebellion	1861–62
	Census Report	
	Fugitive Slaves, Contraband of War, Laborers, etc.	
	Military Employment	
	Events, Battle Reports	
2	War of the Rebellion	1863
	Military Employment	
	Correspondence Relative to Civil Status, Labor, etc.	
	Events, Battle Reports, etc.	
3	War of the Rebellion	1864
	Military Employment	
	Correspondence Relative to Civil Status, Labor, etc.	
	Events, Battle Reports, etc.	
4	War of the Rebellion and the Reconstruction Period	1865–67, with some documents of later dates
	Military Employment	
	Correspondence Relative to Civil Status, Labor, etc.	
	Events, Battle Reports, etc.	
5	Treatment and Exchange of Prisoners of War	1866–86
	Regular Army	

Selected Documents Relating to Blacks Nominated for Appointment to the United States Military Academy During the 19th Century, 1870–1887. M1002. 21 rolls. DP.

This microfilm publication reproduces documents relating to 27 blacks nominated for appointment to the U.S. Military Academy from 1870 to 1887, apparently the only blacks nominated during the 19th century. The documents include nomination and appointment papers, correspondence, reports of examinations, consolidated weekly reports of class grades and conduct rolls, orders, and court-martial case files. No documents have been filmed that relate to the military careers of nominees following their graduation from the Academy.

Of the 27 black nominees, 21 were from Southern States. Eleven were nominated by black Members of the U.S. House of Representatives from Florida, Louisiana, North Carolina, and South Carolina. Five of the 11 were nominated by Representative Robert Smalls of South Carolina. The names of the nominees, the dates of their nominations, the Representatives who nominated them, and the congressional districts and States from which they were nominated are listed in the descriptive pamphlet.

Roll	Description	Dates
1	Charles Sumner Wilson	
	Henry Alonzo Napier	
	Michael Howard	
	James Webster Smith	
2	James Elias Rector	
	Thomas Van Rensslear Gibbs	
	Henry Ossian Flipper	
	John Washington Williams	
	William Henry Jarvis, Jr.	
	William Henry White	
	Whitefield McKinlay	
	William Narcese Werles	
3	Johnson Chestnut Whittaker	
	Correspondence, Reports, Orders	
	Proceedings, Findings, and Sentence of the General Court-Martial of Cadet John B. McDonald	Feb. 8, 1877
4	Index to Proceedings and Proceedings of the Court of Inquiry in the Case of Cadet Whittaker	Apr. 9–17, 1880
5	Proceedings of the Court of Inquiry in the Case of Cadet Whittaker	Apr. 19–22, 1880
6	Proceedings of the Court of Inquiry in the Case of Cadet Whittaker	Apr. 23–May 15, 1880
7	Proceedings, Report of Facts, Conclusion, and Opinion of the Court of Inquiry in the Case of Cadet Whittaker	May 17, 18, 28, and 29, 1880
8	Letter of Transmittal, Index to Proceedings, and Proceedings of the General Court-Martial of Cadet Whittaker	Jan. 20–Feb. 11, 1881
9	Proceedings of the General Court-Martial of Cadet Whittaker	Feb. 14–25, 1881
10	"	Feb. 28–Mar. 14, 1881
11	"	Mar. 15–22, 1881
12	"	Mar. 23–30, 1881
13	"	Mar. 31–Apr. 8, 1881
14	"	Apr. 9–22, 1881
15	"	Apr. 23–May 3, 1881
16	"	May 4–12, 1881
17	"	May 13–June 2, 1881
18	"	June 3–10, 1881
	Prosecution Exhibits	Feb. 3–June 10, 1881
19	Defense and Unidentified Exhibits	Mar. 15–May 17, 1881
	Correspondence, Newspaper Clippings, and Other Documents Accompanying	1880–86

Roll	Description	Dates
	the Proceedings of the General Court-Martial of Cadet Whittaker	
20	Correspondence Accompanying the Proceedings of the General Court- Martial of Cadet Whittaker	1881–1903
21	Joseph Thomas Dubuclet	
	John Augustus Simkins	
	Charles Augustus Minnie	
	Lemuel W. Livingston	
	John Hanks Alexander	
	Daniel Cato Sugg	
	Robert Shaw Wilkinson	
	Charles Young	
	Julius Linoble Mitchell	
	William Trent Andrews	
	John S. Outlaw	
	William Achilles Hare	
	Henry Wilson Holloway	
	Eli W. Henderson	

Documents Relating to the Military and Naval Service of Blacks Awarded the Congressional Medal of Honor from the Civil War to the Spanish-American War. M929. 4 rolls. DP.

On December 21, 1861, President Lincoln approved the congressional bill establishing the Navy Medal of Honor to be given to noncommissioned officers and enlisted men of the Navy and Marine Corps for "extraordinary bravery." A joint resolution of Congress that authorized the preparation of 2,000 Medals of Honor to be presented to noncommissioned officers and privates of the Army and the Volunteer Forces for "gallantry in action" and other "soldier-like qualities" was approved by President Lincoln on July 12, 1862.

The first Congressional Medal of Honor awarded to a black enlisted man of the U.S. Navy was announced in General Order 32, Navy Department, April 16, 1864. Not until April 6, 1865, were black privates and noncommissioned officers of the U.S. Colored Troops awarded the Congressional Medal of Honor.

The documents reproduced here consist mostly of copies of letters sent, letters received, and reports. Issuances and a small number of court-martial case files and log entries are also included. The ranks and ratings shown respectively for the Army noncommissioned officers and privates and Navy enlisted men are those held by the men at the time the medals were awarded.

The documents microfilmed for the Navy Medal of Honor winners, including parts of ships' logs, relate only to the acts of bravery for which they were cited and to the award of the medals. The documents reproduced for the Army Medal of Honor winners, however, often provide other information relating to their military service. A few documents, less than 75 years old and relating to two Army Medal of Honor winners, have not been filmed because they contain medical information, the disclosure of which would constitute an invasion of personal privacy. The documents that have not been filmed are identified in roll notes that appear at the beginning of roll 3.

Documents relating to Seminole-Negro Indian scouts who served with the U.S. Army during the Indian campaigns of the 1870s and were awarded the Congressional Medal of Honor have been included. These scouts were the descendents of blacks who married Seminole Indians in Florida and migrated to Mexico in the 1830s. In 1870 the Seminole-Negro Indians began crossing the Mexican border into Texas, settling in the areas around Fort Clark and Fort Duncan.

Roll	Description
Civil War—U.S. Colored Troops:	
1	Pvt. William H. Barnes
	1st Sgt. Powhatan Beaty
	1st Sgt. James H. Bronson
	Sgt. William H. Carney
	Sgt. Decatur Dorsey
	Sgt. Maj. Christian A. Fleetwood
	Pvt. James Gardiner
	Sgt. James H. Harris
	Sgt. Maj. Thomas R. Hawkins
	Sgt. Alfred B. Hilton
	Sgt. Maj. Milton M. Holland
	Cpl. Miles James
	1st Sgt. Alexander Kelly
	1st Sgt. Robert A. Pinn
	1st Sgt. Edward Ratcliff
	Pvt. Charles Veal
Indian Campaigns—U.S. Regular Army:	
2	Sgt. Thomas Boyne
	Sgt. Benjamin Brown
	Sgt. John Denny
	Pvt. Pompey Factor
	Cpl. Clinton Greaves
	Sgt. Henry Johnson
	Sgt. George Jordan
	Cpl. Isaiah Mays
	Sgt. William McBryar
	Pvt. Adam Paine
	Trumpeter Isaac Payne
	Sgt. Thomas Shaw
	Sgt. Emanuel Stance
	Pvt. Augustus Walley
	Sgt. John Ward
	1st Sgt. Moses Williams
	Cpl. William O. Wilson
	Sgt. Brent Woods
Spanish-American War—U.S. Regular Army:	
3	Sgt. Maj. Edward L. Baker, Jr.
	Pvt. Dennis Bell
	Pvt. Fitz Lee
	Pvt. William H. Thompkins
	Pvt. George H. Wanton
Civil War—U.S. Navy:	
4	Landsman Aaron Anderson
	Landsman Robert Blake
	Landsman William H. Brown
	Landsman Wilson Brown
	Landsman John Lawson
	Engineer's Cook James Mifflin
	Seaman Joachim Pease
Interim Period (1865–98)—U.S. Navy:	
	Ship's Cook Daniel Atkins
	Ordinary Seaman John Davis
	Seaman John Johnson
	Cooper William Johnson
	Seaman Joseph B. Noil
	Seaman John Smith
	Ordinary Seaman Robert A. Sweeney
Spanish-American War—U.S. Navy:	
	Fireman 1st Class, Robert Penn

Index to Publication Numbers

ORDER BLANKS CORRECTLY FILLED IN HELP TO SPEED
PROCESSING OF YOUR ORDER

Microfilm publication numbers (preceded by an "M" or "T") are
assigned to each microfilm publication. Please enter microfilm publication number and roll number in the proper
column. As we accept orders for individual rolls as well as
for complete microfilm publications, we must know which
rolls you wish to purchase.

The microfilm pricing policy is described on page ix of this catalog.

Sample of Correctly Completed Form

M, T, or A NUMBER	ROLL NUMBER	PRICE
T624	1138	$20
T1270	89	$20

Additional order forms are available
upon request.

MICROFILM ORDER *(Prices subject to change)*		MICRO. PUB. NUMBER	ROLL NUMBER	PRICE
TO	Cashier (NAJ)–Military Service National Archives Trust Fund Board Washington, DC 20408			
Please send me the microfilm listed in this order. Enclosed is ☐ CHECK ☐ MONEY ORDER for $ _____ or charge my ☐ VISA ☐ MASTER CHARGE				
ACCOUNT NUMBER EXPIRATION DATE				
SIGNATURE				
FROM	Name			
	Address (Number and street)			
	City, State and ZIP Code		**TOTAL PRICE**	

NATIONAL ARCHIVES TRUST FUND BOARD

NATF Form 36 (8-79)

Due to increased printing and postage costs, the National Archives Trust Fund Board is charging individuals $5.00 for this catalog. This catalog is not produced at taxpayer expense and the $5.00 will be used to defray costs so that we can publish more microfilm subject-area catalogs. Catalogs will continue to be issued free of charge to libraries, genealogical societies, and other organizations.

$5.00 Credit

Clip and enclose this coupon
for **$5.00** toward the purchase of
one or more rolls of Military
Service microfilm.

(Offer applies only to individual
purchasers, not organizations)

This coupon may not be duplicated

	TOTAL PRICE